Emerson in His Journals

EMERSON
in His Journals

Selected and Edited by
JOEL PORTE

THE BELKNAP PRESS OF
Harvard University Press
Cambridge, Massachusetts
London, England
1982

Copyright © 1982 by the President and Fellows of Harvard College

The Journals and Miscellaneous Notebooks of Ralph Waldo Emerson:
Copyright © 1960, 1961, 1963, 1964, 1965, 1969, 1970, 1971, 1973, 1975, 1977, 1978, 1982 by the President and Fellows of Harvard College

Library of Congress Cataloging in Publication Data

Emerson, Ralph Waldo, 1803–1882.
   Emerson in his journals.

   Selected from the Journals and miscellaneous notebooks.
   Includes index.
   1. Emerson, Ralph Waldo, 1803–1882—Diaries.
2. Authors, American—19th century—Biography.   I. Porte,
Joel.   II. Title.
PS1631.A33   1982   814'.3   81-20255
ISBN 0-674-24861-9   AACR2

Preface

WHEN EMILY DICKINSON was twenty-one years old she wrote her brother Austin requesting shocking details from his experience as a teacher in Boston's North End. "I like to get such *facts* to set down in my *journal*," she explained facetiously, "also anything else that's *startling* which you may chance to know—I don't think deaths or murders can ever come amiss in a young woman's journal." From our vantage point, Dickinson's little joke in 1851 takes on added meaning, for we know that her own "journal," then scarcely launched, would take the form of gnomic verses filled with startling facts, including deaths and murders, far more affecting than the usual run of sentiment and sensation to be found elsewhere. She would devote her private writing career to recording her inmost being and thereby exemplify a signal aspect of the reticent New England mind. "Introspection," Henry James notes, "thanks to the want of other entertainment, played almost the part of a social resource." Appropriately, "Says I to myself" would serve as the motto of Henry Thoreau's journal. And Emerson, in an essay published seven years before Emily Dickinson wrote her letter to Austin, suggested with perhaps only slight hyperbole the intensely intimate significance of these private scriptures for the spiritual isolatoes of his time and place: "Each young and ardent person writes a diary, in which, when the hours of prayer and penitence arrive, he inscribes his soul. The pages thus written are to him burning and fragrant; he reads them on his knees by midnight and by the morning star; he wets them with his tears; they are sacred; too good for the world, and hardly yet to be shown to the dearest friend." Though some may balk at imagining Ralph Waldo Emerson in the fervent posture described here, he too attempted to inscribe his soul in pages reserved for his eyes alone.

For over fifty years—in Hollis Hall at Harvard, in hotel rooms at home and abroad, in ships at sea and railway cars, in his study in Concord—he filled a motley assortment of more than two hundred ledgers, notebooks, and diaries with what has come to be known collectively as his "journal." Readers familiar only with Emerson the Guru—a seldom-smiling public man of indeterminate antiquity—may find it a little hard to believe that this distant figure, descendant of generations of Puritan divines, was capable of unburdening himself privately with the unflinching candor of a Montaigne and the passion of a Rousseau or a Byron. Beginning with his troubled adolescence, Emerson's development was marked by sharp crises of thought, emotion, and identity, and by much inner and outer conflict. Throughout it all, in an age, as he said, when "the mind had become aware of itself," he continued to anatomize his consciousness and experience in these pages with scrupulous honesty.

I have placed the word journal in quotation marks because Emerson's compilation is in no sense a typical record of daily events. His own conception of what he was engaged in was fluid, and the definitions he offers of his journal are as varied as its contents. The earliest booklets (Emerson's "Wide Worlds"), with their dedications—to the imagination, to the future, to eloquence, to America—begin as self-conscious dissertations on set topics, though they quickly take on the character of a diary with their confessions and "childish sentiment." Emerson also used many of these pages as a commonplace book where he could record his discoveries of the best that had been thought and said by others, "all those words & sentences that in all your reading have been to you like the blast of trumpet." By means of elaborate indexes, he drew on this rich fund of reading when he came to prepare his lectures and essays, as he did also with his own thoughts, for Emerson sometimes conceived of his book as a "Savings Bank" where he could deposit his daily "fractions" and hope to see them grow into "integers." In even the smallest fragment of his jottings he tried to draw on all his experience. "One word of this sentence," he notes, "I learned in Boston, one in Cambridge, one in Europe." He defined his journal additionally as "a book of constants" in which he could build up for himself an enduring compendium of literary and scientific wisdom. "Man paints himself out with secular patience," he observes, meaning that the record of his thoughts must be made with an eye to the centuries and not just to the passing days.

But Emerson by no means neglected the quotidian in this lifelong autobiographical project. He understood that he could not capitalize on his experience without cataloguing even the most insignificant event or mood. His intent was to set everything down. "If it be agreed," he writes, "that I am always to express my thought, what forbids me to tell the company that a flea bites me or that my occasions call me behind the house?" He goes on to say here (in October 1832) that a visit to the outhouse will, on reflection, probably seem less significant than other, higher matters. But two years later he would ask, "what is there of the divine in a barber's shop or a privy?" and respond, "Much. All." Later still he would record Henry Thoreau's observation "that God was in the jakes" and conclude that Spinoza had little to teach such a precocious metaphysician. The transcendent integer that Emerson thus constructed from such trivial fractions was clearly not predictable from the start, but the frankness and inclusiveness of his journal allowed for surprises of this sort. It is interesting to note that similar speculations are not to be found in Emerson's regular published writings.

A large portion of Emerson's journals was first made available by his son and grandson in a series of volumes published between 1909 and 1914, and these were in turn the source for Bliss Perry's popular selection, *The Heart of Emerson's Journals*, in 1926. As the editors of the new Harvard edition have pointed out, "In the first printing of the journals we lost much of Emerson. The Montaigne in him was unduly overshadowed by the Plotinus, the brooding doubter by the cosmic optimist, the private man in his freedom and infinitude by the public man in the confining garments of 'the gentleman.'" According to the Victorian canons of pre–World War I America, Emerson in his journals first appeared considerably regularized and cleaned up. Whatever was deemed too personal or unseemly was excised, many entries were printed only in part for the same reason, and a good deal of material was suppressed altogether. Emerson was presented mainly as a wisdom-writer and cultural commentator in line with his son's preference for the detached reflection and the genial overview. Largely missing from this presentation were the sharp edges and dark corners of Emerson's private jottings. He was not often allowed to be angry, frightened, silly, puzzled, shocked, sarcastic, or satiric. And he was almost never permitted to exhibit an interest in such things as sex or the functions of the body. As a result, when Emerson wondered if there was anything divine in base things, he was given leave to talk of a barbershop or a load of bricks, but not of a privy. His observation that he had "organs" and delighted in pleasure but feared that "this pleasure is the bait of a trap" went unprinted, as did his curious admission, in 1851, that he preferred the "engendering of snails" to the sentimental disguising of sexuality in religious enthusiasm. It is not surprising, then, that Hemingway scorned Emerson (along with "Hawthorne, Whittier, and Company") for being overly fastidious and avoiding "the words that people always have used in speech, the words that survive in language." On the evidence available to him, Hemingway could see only that these representatives of the American literary establishment had "nice, dry, clean minds" but no bodies. "This," he insists, "is all very dull."

An eviscerated and bowdlerized Emerson might indeed seem dull, but we are no longer constrained to keep him muffled under the deadening weight of Victorian editorial standards. In 1833 Emerson doubted that any man renders "written account to himself of himself" and wondered if the time would come when he would "be able without a blush & without harm to utter to the world [his] inmost thought." One hundred years after Emerson's death, readers of the journal in its original form can reconstruct his remarkable life in a way not possible before and explore the issues raised by Henry James in 1888: "the question of [Emerson's] inner reserves and skepticisms, his secret ennuis and ironies." Though Emerson himself sometimes believed that "the last chamber, the last closet," of any man's life is never opened, that "there is always a residuum unknown, unanalysable," he nevertheless provided the materials for such an analysis as few other writers have done and thus came close to writing the book that Poe said could never be written, *My Heart Laid Bare.* In Emerson's hands, however, it is not the blazing self-confession that Poe longed for, but a more subtle and difficult achievement—the steady and candid recording of thoughts and feelings and fantasies without inhibition or reservation. This was his way of satisfying Rousseau's desire, which he applauded, to entertain and utter the unvarnished truth about a human life. We must be privileged not only to experience, along with our diarist, the Transcendental sublime but also to "know the worst," as Emerson says, "and tread the floors of hell."

As he was reading Rousseau's *Confessions* in 1847, Emerson

reminded himself "that it is not the events in one's life, but in the
faculty of selecting & reporting them, that the interest lies." It is
the Emersonian angle of vision that gives his journal entries their
special flavor and value, and I have titled this volume *Emerson in
His Journals* so as to draw attention to that unique presence. In
making my selections from the more than three million words of
the now indispensable Harvard edition of Emerson's *Journals
and Miscellaneous Notebooks,* I have been biased in favor of material that serves to bring Emerson most vividly to life. Naturally
those passages that tell us something about Emerson personally
had a strong claim to be included—entries that cast light on his
doubts, dreams, fears, aspirations, quirks, social and intimate relations, and the like. He was a great human character, not simply
a dispenser of timeless wisdom in Yankee accents, and that is the
Emerson who deserves to stand forth in these pages. This book is
not intended as a chrestomathy of choice passages for the student
of nineteenth-century American literature; nor is it designed for
scholars concerned with the detailed development of Emerson's
thought; still less is it offered as a monument to an American
Worthy. I have placed my emphasis on the *diary* aspect of Emerson's journals, since it is the Transcendental and philosophical
Emerson who has been set in marble and thereby distanced from
us. But I have not turned away from serious reflection in favor
only of anecdote and personal revelation. Emerson appears here
in all his moods and modes. There is, however, as even Bliss
Perry was willing to admit, "some over-writing of spiritual experience" in the full journal, and it is no longer necessary to sustain
Emerson's reputation on the jet stream of high-minded abstraction. One of my aims has been to illustrate Emerson's peculiar
strengths as an observer and writer—his keen eye for truth or
folly, his penetrating wit, his verbal agility, his quotable apo-
thegms. But I have not only leaned toward polished sentences and
paragraphs such as one finds in the orations and essays. Emerson's words are often more powerful in homespun than in the
elegant garb of the public man of letters. His journals are valuable
precisely for the glimpses they afford of his restless mind groping
toward its formulations.

The text presented here is essentially that of *The Journals
and Miscellaneous Notebooks* minus the elaborate scholarly apparatus that was needed to reproduce the manuscript pages in

type but that tends to impede the general reader. I have left Emerson's erratic spelling untouched and have emended his punctuation only occasionally for the sake of clarity or to correct an obvious slip of the pen. Some paragraphing has been added, especially in cases where Emerson's intention is uncertain. I have not followed now outmoded practices that add nothing to the sense or rhythm of Emerson's sentences (such as commas before and after dashes or before and within parentheses). Emerson's own usage in this regard was not consistent, and he himself often omits the redundant punctuation. Ellipses within or at the end of sentences are indicated in the usual way, and a space between entries under the same date marks either the omission of intervening material or a change of subject. I have adopted a uniform mode of dating entries in place of Emerson's haphazard practice, though I should add that a great many of the entries cannot be dated with precision, even when they occur between dates supplied by Emerson himself; he often added material later on or skipped around chronologically. Lacking any sure indication, I have sometimes used my intuition or made an educated guess. I have also rearranged the order of entries that are clearly or probably misplaced. Words in brackets represent my own interpolations, and footnotes are my own unless marked [RWE] for Emerson's notes or [*JMN*] for annotations borrowed from the full Harvard edition. In general, my policy has been to prefer parsimony to an abundance of notation, since the sixteen volumes of *Journals and Miscellaneous Notebooks* are available to readers who wish more information on Emerson's allusions.

Emerson once endorsed Goethe's practice of publishing his book "without preface" and letting it "lie unexplained." I have already violated that injunction in order to give the reader of this volume some sense of the history of Emerson's journals and their place in his life's work as a writer. But I could not ignore the first piece of advice he gives in the same 1836 journal entry: "Stick by yourself." Though I have been guided by the rather loose principles of selection enunciated above, I have not hesitated to make choices on the basis of my own tastes and interests. Especially in those cases where I have carved out a portion of a longer entry or ventured to piece together the *disjecta membra* of seemingly random or disparate jottings, I have had to depend on my own sense of what—to use Oliver Wendell Holmes's phrase—is Emersonially Emersonian. I am well aware, in view of the enormous wealth and variety of Emerson's journals, that other choices could have been made just as reasonably: *quot doctores tot lectiones.* But as I have proceeded I have kept in mind Ben Jonson's words on Shakespeare: "He was, indeed, honest, and of an open and free nature; had an excellent phantasy, brave notions, and gentle expressions, wherein he flowed with that facility, that sometime it was necessary he should be stopped." I hope I have never stopped Emerson from uttering the best he had to say. In any case, readers intrigued by the microcosm presented here will find further delights awaiting them in the full body of his work.

J. P.

Contents

Illustrations

Chronology

1803	May 25, Election Day, Emerson is born in Boston, the fourth child of William and Ruth Haskins Emerson.
1811	William Emerson dies on May 12, age forty-two.
1812–1817	Attends Boston Public Latin School.
1817–1821	At Harvard College.
1821–1825	Teaching in Boston at his brother William's school for girls.
1825	February, admitted to Harvard Divinity School; studies interrupted by eye trouble; teaching in Chelmsford.
1826	Teaching in Roxbury and Cambridge; approbated to preach on October 10; lung trouble; November, voyages south.
1827	Returns to Cambridge in June; meets Ellen Tucker in December.
1828	Brother Edward becomes deranged; Emerson engaged to Ellen on December 17.
1829	Ordained junior pastor of Boston's Second Church; marries Ellen on September 30.
1831	Ellen dies on February 8, age nineteen.
1832	Increasing ill health; decides he can no longer serve communion, resigns pastorate; sails for Europe on December 25.
1833–34	Travels in Italy, France, and Great Britain; meets Carlyle; begins career as lecturer with talks on "natural history"; continues to preach; receives first half of the Tucker inheritance in the spring; October, Edward dies.
1835	Lectures in Boston on biography; buys home in Concord on August 15; marries Lydia Jackson in September.
1836	Completes lecture series on English literature; brother Charles dies in May; Margaret Fuller visits in July; *Nature* published anonymously in Boston in September; Waldo born, October 30; winter, lectures on the philosophy of history.
1837	Receives final portion of Tucker estate in July; August, Thoreau graduates from Harvard, where Emerson delivers "The American Scholar"; fall-winter, lectures on human culture.
1838	April, writes President Van Buren about Cherokees; July 15, delivers address at Harvard Divinity School; July 24, Dart-

mouth Oration ("Literary Ethics"); winter, lectures on human life.

1839   Preaches last sermon in January; Ellen born, February 24; winter, lectures on "The Present Age."

1840   July, first issue of Transcendental journal, *The Dial.*

1841   First series of *Essays* published in March; spring, Thoreau joins household; November 22, Edith born; winter, lectures on "The Times."

1842   January 27, Waldo dies; Emerson succeeds Fuller as editor of *The Dial.*

1844   Edward born on July 10; April, last issue of *The Dial;* October, *Essays, Second Series* published.

1845   July 4, Thoreau moves to Walden Pond; winter, lectures on "Representative Men."

1846   December, *Poems* published.

1847–48 Second trip to Europe, October–July.

1849   Lectures on "Mind and Manners in the Nineteenth Century"; *Nature; Addresses, and Lectures* published.

1850   January, *Representative Men* published; July, Margaret Fuller Ossoli drowns off Fire Island.

1851   Excoriates Webster for supporting the Fugitive Slave Law; winter, lectures on "The Conduct of Life."

1853   Ruth Haskins Emerson dies.

1854   Lectures on "Topics of Modern Times" in Philadelphia; heavy lecture schedule throughout the country.

1855   Antislavery lectures in Boston, New York, and Philadelphia; sends letter to Whitman praising *Leaves of Grass,* July 21.

1856   August, *English Traits* published.

1860   December, *The Conduct of Life* published.

1862   Lectures on "American Civilization" in Washington and meets President Lincoln; Thoreau dies on May 6.

1863   Aunt Mary Moody Emerson dies in May.

1864   Emerson attends Hawthorne's funeral on May 23.

1865   April, Lincoln assassinated.

1866   Lectures in the west; receives Doctor of Laws degree from Harvard.

1867   *May-Day and Other Pieces* published in April; named Overseer of Harvard College; delivers second Phi Beta Kappa address ("The Progress of Culture").

1870   Writes preface to *Plutarch's Morals;* publishes *Society and Solitude;* lectures at Harvard on "Natural History of Intellect."

1871   April–May, travels to California by train.

1872   Speaks at Howard University; house burns on July 24; October, sets out for Europe and Egypt with Ellen.

1873   May, returns from trip; summer, begins new term as Harvard Overseer.

1874   December, *Parnassus* published.

1875   December, *Letters and Social Aims* published, edited by James Elliot Cabot.

1882   April 27, Emerson dies of pneumonia in Concord; Whitman visits his grave and observes: "A just man, poised on himself, all-loving, all-inclosing, and sane and clear as the sun."

Emerson in His Journals

Prospects

1820-1824

WE FIRST MEET Emerson in his journals in the middle of his junior year at Harvard, when he was not yet seventeen. Having recently decided to call himself Waldo (mainly because there were so many Ralphs in his family), Emerson seems to have come to a new sense of his nascent identity; this may account for his decision to begin a journal, entitled "The Wide World," as both a "receptacle of ... old ideas" and a "record of new thoughts." The title suggests a self-consciously grandiose intent and may indicate that Waldo was trying to import into his pages some of the urbanity of a Dr. Johnson ("Let observation with extensive view,/Survey mankind, from China to Peru"). The young scholar was already well steeped in eighteenth-century British literature—from Swift and Addison and Steele to Fielding, Johnson, and Burke—and their influence was marked on both his style and his ideas. "They have censured vice with wit and recommended virtuous principles in moral strains so artfully," he notes, "that they could not displease."

Yet there was a newer literature from old England finding its way into the eager hands of Harvard students, and Emerson puzzled over its implications. In a college theme book presumably kept in his sophomore year, the young (and sometimes priggish) moralist "thirsted to abuse the poetical character of Mr Wordsworth" and wondered whether the vaunted originality and genius of the Romantic school justified their abandoning "the good old-fashioned march of Milton or Pope & Dryden." Much as Emily Dickinson sixty years later would ambivalently proclaim that Hawthorne "appalls–entices," Waldo ventured cautiously

I

into the strange seas of Byronic self-reliance and observed—with how much unconscious approval and identification we can only guess—that "the proud feelings of independence which distinguish him seem to have imparted the wish not to be governed by the opinions & customs of others."

For the young Emerson, pride and self-doubt unquestionably weighed in equal measure. The Emerson family, well established in New England since Puritan times and distinguished for a long line of divines, mingled in Waldo's blood with the prosperous mercantile Haskins family on his mother's side. But the premature death of his father in 1811 had left the family destitute and dependent on charity. Though Waldo could be proud of his respectable ancestry, his prospects in 1820 were not bright. As the President's freshman (or orderly) at Harvard, he had learned to respond quickly to the tap of Mr. Kirkland's foot. During vacations he was obliged to teach at his uncle's school in Waltham in order to meet expenses, and in his junior year he waited on table at the student commons. Prestigious and costly clubs such as the Porcellian and the Hasty Pudding were out of the question for him. Nor did he manage to stand out in his scholastic performance. Though an avid reader and a budding litterateur, he considered himself dreamy and lazy—"often idle, vagrant, stupid, & hollow," as he noted in October 1820. "This is somewhat appalling & if I do not discipline myself with diligent care I shall suffer severely from remorse & the sense of inferiority hereafter." Although the gravity of this self-appraisal is clearly qualified by self-mockery (note the "somewhat"), Emerson here begins the endless process of soul searching that constitutes one of the principal interests of his journal. There is no better example, in these early years, of Emerson's extraordinary ability to set his life down on paper than the journal entry of April 18, 1824, in which—preparing to enter his majority—he unsparingly examines what he is, what he has been, and what he may reasonably expect to become. Though Emerson describes himself as the "dupe of hope," he was at least not self-deceived.

In view of the fact that his father, grandfather, and great-grandfather were all ministers, his decision to devote himself to divinity had to be influenced by the opinions and customs of others. What his own heart dictated was clearly a life in literature, but that scarcely represented a well-defined or potentially remu-

nerative career in the America of the 1820s. If one were indepen-
dently wealthy, like James Fenimore Cooper, or inured to poverty, like Edgar Allan Poe, such a choice would be possible. But
the young Emerson's sense of obligation—to his self-sacrificing
mother and to his family's traditions and well-being—was strong.
The church would have to serve as his platform for eloquence,
and sermons would, temporarily at least, take the place of songs
and sonnets. Most immediately, however, Emerson's decision to
become a clergyman promised to extricate him from the horrible
alternative of schoolteaching—"the hot, steaming, stove-ed,
stinking, dirty, a 'b'-spelling school room"—which in fact
claimed much of his time and energy during the five years after
his graduation from Harvard in 1821.

As he prepared to begin his studies at the Harvard Divinity
School in February 1825, Waldo Emerson was both professionally hopeful and personally relieved. "I turn now to my lamp &
my tomes," he notes in the journal, suggesting perhaps that what
really attracted him was not so much the study of religion as the
chance to pursue his career as Man Thinking. Though he did not
know yet where they would lead, Waldo was determined to pursue his speculations with confidence, to worry less about the harvest than the sowing. "There is no thought which is not seed as
well as fruit," he observes, in a voice that begins to sound like the
true Emerson. "It spawns like fish."

Jan. 25, 1820
THE WIDE WORLD   NO. 1
Mixing with the thousand pursuits & passions & objects of the world
as personified by Imagination is profitable & entertaining. These pages
are intended at this their commencement to contain a record of new
thoughts (when they occur); for a receptacle of all the old ideas that
partial but peculiar peepings at antiquity can furnish or furbish; for tab-
let to save the wear & tear of weak Memory & in short for all the various
purposes & utility real or imaginary which are usually comprehended
under that comprehensive title *Common Place book*.

Jan. 26, 1820
I do hereby nominate & appoint "Imagination" the generalissimo &
chief marshal of all the luckless raggamuffin Ideas which may be collected & imprisoned hereafter in these pages.

The first journal page

Jan.? 1820

It is a singular fact that we cannot present to the imagination a longer space than just so much of the world as is bounded by the visible horizon; so that even in this stretching of thought to comprehend the broad path lengthening itself & widening to recieve the rolling Universe stern necessity bounds us to a little extent of a few miles only. But what matters it? We can talk & write & think it out.

Aug. 8? 1820

There is a strange face in the Freshman class whom I should like to know very much. He has a great deal of character in his features & should be a fast friend or a bitter enemy. His name is Gay.* I shall endeavour to become acquainted with him & wish if possible that I might be able to recall at a future period the singular sensations which his presence produced at this.

Aug. 21, 1820

In the Harvard College Athenaeum I enjoyed a very pleasant hour reading the life of Marlborough in the Quarterly Review. I was a little troubled there by vexatious trains of thought; but once found myself stopping entirely from my reading & occupied in throwing guesses into futurity while I was asking myself if, when ten or a dozen years hence, I am gone far on the bitter perplexing roads of life, when I shall then recollect these moments now thought so miserable shall I not fervently wish the possibility of their return & to find myself again thrown awkwardly on the tilted chair in the Atheneum study with my book in my hand; the snuffers & lamps & shelves around; & Motte coughing over his newspaper near me & ready myself to saunter out into gaiety & Commons when that variously-meaning *bell* shall lift up his *tongue*.

Oct. 15, 1820

Different mortals improve resources of happiness which are entirely different. This I find more apparent in the familiar instances obvious at college recitations. My more fortunate neighbours exult in the display of mathematical study, while I after feeling the humiliating sense of dependance & inferiority which like the goading soul-sickening sense of extreme poverty, palsies effort, esteem myself abundantly compensated, if with my pen, I can marshal whole catalogues of nouns & verbs, to express to the life the imbecility I felt.

Oct. 24, 1820

Exhibition night. This tumultuous day is done. The character of its thought-weather is always extremely singular. Fuller than any other day of great thoughts—& poets' dreams, of hope & joy & pride & then closed with merriment & wine evincing or eliciting gay fraternal feeling enough, but brutalized & defiled with excess of physical enjoyment; leaving the mind distracted & unfit for pursuits of soberness.

---

*The name is crossed out. For information about Martin Gay, see *JMN* 1.22.

I begin to believe in the Indian doctrine of eye-fascination. The cold
blue eye of ———— has so intimately connected him with my thoughts &
visions that a dozen times a day & as often by night I find myself wholly
wrapped up in conjectures of his character & inclinations. We have had
already two or three long profound stares at each other. Be it wise or
weak or superstitious I must know him.

Oct. 25, 1820

I find myself often idle, vagrant, stupid, & hollow. This is somewhat
appalling & if I do not discipline myself with diligent care I shall suffer
severely from remorse & the sense of inferiority hereafter. All around
me are industrious & will be great, I am indolent & shall be insignificant. Avert it heaven! avert it virtue! I need excitement.

Nov. 1, 1820

I wish I might be so witched with study, so enamoured of glory for a
little time, that it were possible to forget self & professions & tasks & the
dismal crowd of ordinary circumstances in a still & rapid & comprehensive course of improvement. How immensely would a scholar enlarge
his power could he abstract himself wholly, body & mind from the din-
ning throng of casual recollections that summon him away, from his
useful toil to endless, thankless, reveries; informing him for instance, for
a whole rueful half hour of what he has done, is doing, & will do today,
all which he knew at six o'clock in the morning & is condemned to learn
anew twenty times in the course of the day. Perhaps this ugly disorder is
peculiar to myself & I must envy that man's uninterrupted progress,
who is not obliged by his oath to nature to answer this idle call. If this is
to continue it will weaken the grasp with which I would cling—with
which every young man would cling, to "visions of glory." My talents
(according to the judgement of friends or to the whispered suggestions of
vanity) are popular, are fitted to enable me to claim a place in the inclinations & sympathy of men. But if I would excel & outshine the circle of
my peers those talents must be put to the utmost stretch of exertion,
must be taught the confidence of their own power; and lassitude & these
desultory habits of thinking with their melancholy pleasure must be
grappled with & conquered. These soliloquies are certainly sweeter
than Chemistry!

Nov. 18, 1820

I shall subjoin some recipes for the cure of the horrible void which
ruins ever & anon the mind's peace, & is otherwise called Unhappiness.

1. Take Scott's Novels & read carefully the mottoes of the chapters;
or if you prefer reading a novel itself take the Bride of Lammermoor.

Emerson's sketch of his room at Harvard (Hollis 15)

2. Sometimes (seldom) the finest parts of Cowper's Task will answer the purpose. I refer to the home-scenes.

3. For the same reason that I would take Scott's Mottoes I would also take an old tragedy such as Ben Jonson's, Otway's, Congreve's, in short, any thing of that kind which leads as far as possible from the usual trains of thought.

4. Make recipes to add to this list.

Dec. 15, 1820

I claim & clasp a moment's respite from this irksome school to saunter in the feilds of my own wayward thought. The afternoon was gloomy & preparing to snow—dull, ugly weather. But when I came out from the hot, steaming, stove-ed, stinking, dirty, a "b"-spelling school room I almost soared & mounted the atmosphere at breathing the free magnificent air, the noble breath of life. It was a delightful exhilaration; but it soon passed off.

Jan. 9, 1821

How frequently I am led to consider the distinguished advantages which this generation enjoy above our fathers. Have heard today another consecrated display of genius—of the insinuating & overwhelming effect of eloquent manners & style when made sacred & impregnable by the subject which they are to enforce. Mr Everett's sermon before the Howard Benevolent Society. He told a very affecting anecdote. "I have known a woman in this town go out to work with her own hands to pay for the wooden coffin which was to enclose the dust of her only child. I prayed with her when there was none to stand by her but he who was to bear that dust to the tomb."

There was a vast congregation, but while he spoke, as silent as death. Unluckily, in the pauses, however they shook the house with their hideous convulsions; for when he raised his handkerchief to his face after a pause in the sermon it seemed almost a concerted signal for the Old South to cough.

Let those now cough who never coughed before
And those who always cough cough now the more.

Well, I am sorry to have learned that my friend is dissolute. or rather the anecdote which I accidentally heard
of him shews him more like his neighbours
than I should wish him to be. But I shall
have to throw him up, after all, as a cheat
of fancy. Before I ever saw him, I wished my
friend to be different from any individual
I had seen. I invested him with a solemn cast
of mind, full of poetic feeling, & an idolater of
friendship, & possessing a vein of rich sober thought;
When I saw ....
....
complete character which fancy had formed and
though entirely .... was pleased
to observe the notice which ....
.... for a year I have entertained towards him
the .... & I should be sorry to lose him
altogether before we have ever exchanged above a
dozen words.

NB   By the way this book is of an infer-
our character & contains so much doubtful matter
that I believe I shall have to burn the
second number of the Wide World immediately
upon its completion.

The entry of April 1, 1821

March 25, 1821   Sabbath
      I am sick—if I should die what would become of me? We forget
ourselves & our destinies in health, & the chief use of temporary sickness is to remind us of these concerns. I must improve my time better. I
must prepare myself for the great profession I have purposed to undertake. I am to give my soul to God & withdraw from sin & the world the

idle or vicious time & thoughts I have sacrificed to them; & let me consider this as a resolution by which I pledge myself to act in all variety of circumstances & to which I must recur often in times of carelessness and temptation—to measure my conduct by the rule of conscience.

April 1, 1821

Well, I am sorry to have learned that my friend is dissolute; or rather the anecdote which I accidentally heard of him shews him more like his neighbours than I should wish him to be. I shall have to throw him up, after all, as a cheat of fancy. Before I ever saw him, I wished my *friend* to be different from any individual I had seen. I invested him with a solemn cast of mind, full of poetic feeling, & an idolater of friendship, & possessing a vein of rich sober thought. When I saw ———'s pale but expressive face & large eye, I instantly invested him with the complete character which fancy had formed and though entirely unacquainted with him was pleased to observe the notice which he appeared to take of me. For a year I have entertained towards him the same feelings & should be sorry to lose him altogether before we have ever exchanged above a dozen words.*

NB   By the way this book is of an inferiour character & contains so much doubtful matter that I believe I shall have to burn the second number of the Wide World immediately upon its completion.

May 2, 1821

I am more puzzled than ever with ———'s conduct. He came out to meet me yesterday and I observing him, just before we met turned another corner and most strangely avoided him. This morning I went out to meet him in a different direction and stopped to speak with a lounger in order to be directly in ———'s way, but turned into the first gate and went towards Stoughton. All this baby play persists without any apparent design, and as soberly as if both were intent on some tremendous affair.† With a most serious expectation of burning this book I am committing to it more of what I may by and by think childish sentiment than I should care to venture on vagabond sheets which Somebody else may light upon. (Mr Somebody, will it please your impertinence to be conscience-struck!)

Aug. 8, 1821

I have been reading Montesquieu's Lettres Persanes. It is a book which answered a very good purpose, if, as I suppose, it was written be-

---

*Most of this and the preceding sentence is crossed out.
† The entry to this point is crossed out and some words are obscured.

fore modern Essayists (Rambler Spectator &c) were in vogue; for the letters are short unconnected essays on all sorts of subjects. One object of the book is to satirize passing events, characters, fashions of Paris. It is no recommendation of the book that he has placed among the first letters in the book, as a lure and attracting point, a sensual one from the seraglio. There is no attempt to preserve any peculiarities of character, though a variety of persons are engaged in the correspondence. Of the *style* I am no judge but the book abounds with brilliant and touching thoughts.

Aug. 12? 1821

Mr Wordsworth is a poet whom we read with caution in whom the eye always is afraid lest it should meet with something offensive at every turn. It subtracts vastly from the pleasure of poetry if you read with this evil timidity. It is like faltering upon a mountain for fear of a precipice. In the midst of an eloquent strain of sentiment or description your admiration is brought up with a noted vulgarism or glaring false taste. . . .

Although the theory does not run counter to our own theory of poetry or to any sound views of the art yet experience has not shewn any final decisive success to follow the experiment. On the contrary Mr Southey, Mr Coleridge, & Mr Wordsworth have gained less honour than ridicule by their poetry not because it wanted genius but it wanted nature. The affectation of simplicity was but too apparent; the poetry was too puerile for the taste of their northern countrymen. And the experiment yet remains to be tried.

Oct. 21, 1821

It is the misfortune of America that her sudden maturity of national condition was accompanied with the knowledge of good and *evil* which would better belong to an older country. We have recieved our drama line for line and precept for precept from England and in so doing have inherited a stained and rotten web of corruptions in which a few geniuses have condescended to weave their golden threads but whose whole tissue is consistent in nothing but pollution. But in this country public feeling is much more pure and on this encouragement we build all our hope of reform and improvement. In England they are hardened by long unquestioned custom to survey with indifference this odious spectacle. Indeed I know not what of malignant crime, of dark enormity, or wide-spread wickedness would startle the public mind there. I am proud and thankful when I contrast this with the uncontaminated innocence of my own country and it is this comparative purity joined to the energy of a youthful people still free from the complicated difficulties of an old government which constitutes the distinction and promise of this nation.

Jan. 12, 1822

After a considerable interval I am still willing to think that these commonplace books are very useful and harmless things—at least sufficiently so, to warrant another trial. Besides every one writes differently when he composes for the eyes of others, and when his pen scampers away over mote and rut for the solitary edification of its lord and master.

Jan. 12? 1822

The History of Religion involves circumstances of remarkable interest and it is almost all that we are able to trace in the passage of the remote ages of the world. It is a beautiful picture and just as it should be that in the character of Noah, of Abraham, and the early denizens of the world we trace no feature which does not belong peculiarly to their religion;—it was their life. It was natural that when the Mountains were just swelling upward under the hand of the Creator, when his bow was just built and painted in the sky, when the stone-tables were yet unbroken by Moses which now lie mouldering in fragments upon Sinai—that Men should walk with God. As we come downward and leave the immediate precincts of the tabernacle although we become sensible of the progressive departure from the truth yet each superstition retains the inherent beauty of the first form, disguised and defaced in some degree, by ill adjusted and needless apparel. Indeed the only records by which the early ages of any nation are remembered is their religion. We know nothing of the first empires which grasped the sceptre of the earth in Egypt, Assyria, or Persia, but their modes of worship. And this fact forcibly suggests the idea that the only true and legitimate vehicle of immortality, the only bond of connection which can traverse the long duration which separates the ends of the world and unite the first people to the knowledge and sympathy of the last people, is religion.

Feb. 26, 1822

I have not much cause, I sometimes think, to wish my Alma Mater well, personally; I was not often highly flattered by success, and was every day mortified by my own ill fate or ill conduct. Still, when I went today to the ground where I had had the brightest thoughts of my little life and filled up the little measure of my knowledge and had felt sentimental for a time, and poetical for a time, and had seen many fine faces, and traversed many fine walks, and enjoyed much pleasant, learned, or friendly society—I felt a crowd of pleasant thoughts—as I went posting about from place to place, and room to chapel.

Feb. 28, 1822

Few of my pages have been filled so little to my own satisfaction as these—and why?—because the air has been so fine, and my visits so pleasant, and myself so full of pleasant social feelings—for a day or two past that the mind has not possessed sufficiently the cold frigid tone which is indispensable to become so *oracular* as it hath been of late.

March 2, 1822

It is manifest from a little reflection how little improvement is made in a separate *unsocial* state even supposing for a moment that the race could be reared and educated in solitudes. Indeed, every thing upon this topic is so plain and obvious, that it is hardly pardonable to state our views. Man was as evidently intended for society, as the eye for vision, or the ear to hear.

May 1, 1822

The peace of Europe of right belongs to the perfection of its *police.* There is no such mixture of disagreeable truth, in the quiet of our own nation. The entire internal repose of this country owes nothing to vigorous restriction or armed law. The spirit of the people is peace, & the sword at its side is for ornament rather than use. I will not believe that it is ignorance to esteem my birthright in America as a preferable gift to the honours of any other nation that breathes upon Earth. The Genius of Britain treads with fear upon an unsound & perilous footing, burning beneath with flame to an unknown extent. And America has inherited the free step & unconstrained attitude which her parent hath lost by age.

Dum a dum, now, but the book *does* grow better.

May 7, 1822

Tuesday Evg. Amid my diseases & aches & qualms I will write to see if my brains are gone. For a day or two past we have had a wind precisely *annual;* which I discover by *this,* that I have a return of the identical thoughts & temperament which I had a year ago. But this Sun shines upon & these ill winds blow over—a changed person in condition, in hope. I was then delighted with my recent honours, traversing my chamber (Hollis 9) flushed & proud of a poet's fancies, & the day when they were to be exhibited; pleased with ambitious prospects & Careless because ignorant of the future. But now I'm a hopeless Schoolmaster just entering upon years of trade to which no distinct limit is placed; toiling through this miserable employment even without the poor satisfaction of discharging it well, for the good suspect me, & the geese dislike me. Then again look at this: there was pride in being a collegian, & a poet, & somewhat romantic in my queer acquaintance with Gay;* and poverty presented nothing mortifying in the meeting of two young men whom their common relation & character as scholars equalised. But when one becomes a droning schoolmaster, and the other is advancing his footing in good company & fashionable friends, the cast of countenance on meeting is somewhat altered. Hope, it is true, still hangs out, though at further distance, her gay banners; but I have found her a cheat once, twice, many times, and shall I trust the deceiver again? And what am I the better for two, four, six years delay? Nine months are gone, and except some rags of Wideworlds, half a dozen general notions &c I am precisely the same World's humble servant that left the University in August. Good people will tell me that it is a Judgement & lesson for my character, to make me fitter for the office whereto I aspire; but if I come out a dispirited, mature, broken hearted miscreant—how will Man or myself be bettered? Now I have not thought all this time that I was complaining at Fate although I suppose it amounts to the same; these are the suggestions only of a disappointed spirit brooding over the fall of castles in the air. My fate is enviable contrasted with that of others; I have only to blame myself who had no right to build them. Waldo E.

May 12, 1822
 I have a nasty appetite which I will not gratify.†

May 13, 1822
 In twelve days I shall be nineteen years old; which I count a miserable thing. Has any other educated person lived so many years and lost so many days? I do not say acquired so little for by an ease of thought & certain looseness of mind I have perhaps been the subject of as many ideas as many of mine age. But mine approaching maturity is attended with a goading sense of emptiness & wasted capacity; with the conviction that vanity has been content to admire the little circle of natural accomplishments, and has travelled again & again the narrow round, instead of adding sedulously the gems of knowledge to their number. Too tired and too indolent to travel up the mountain path which leads to good learning, to wisdom & to fame, I must be satisfied with beholding

---

*The name is crossed out.

†The sentence is crossed out.

with an envious eye the laborious journey & final success of my fellows, remaining stationary myself, until my inferiors & juniors have reached & outgone me. And how long is this to last? How long shall I hold the little acclivity which four or six years ago I flattered myself was enviable, but which has become contemptible now? It is a child's place & if I hold it longer I may quite as well resume the bauble & rattle, grow old with a baby's red jocky on my grey head & a picturebook in my hand, instead of Plato and Newton. Well, and I am he who nourished brilliant visions of future grandeur which may well appear presumptuous & foolish now. My infant imagination was idolatrous of glory, & thought itself no mean pretender to the honours of those who stood highest in the community, and dared even to contend for fame with those who are hallowed by time & the approbation of ages. It was a little merit to concieve such animating hopes, and afforded some poor prospect of the possibility of their fulfilment. This hope was fed & fanned by the occasional lofty communications which were vouchsafed to me with the Muses' Heaven and which have at intervals made me the organ of remarkable sentiments & feelings which were far above my ordinary train. And with this lingering earnest of better hope (I refer to this fine exhilaration which now & then quickens my clay) shall I resign every aspiration to belong to that family of giant minds which live on earth many ages & rule the world when their bones are slumbering, no matter, whether under a pyramid or a primrose? No I will yet a little while entertain the Angel.

Look next from the history of my intellect to the history of my heart. A blank, my lord. I have not the kind affections of a pigeon. Ungenerous & selfish, cautious & cold, I yet wish to be romantic. Have not sufficient feeling to speak a natural hearty welcome to a friend or stranger and yet send abroad wishes & fancies of a friendship with a man I never knew. There is not in the whole wide Universe of God (my relations to Himself I do not understand) one being to whom I am attached with warm & entire devotion—not a being to whom I have joined fate for weal or wo, not one whose interests I have nearly & dearly at heart; and this I say at the most susceptible age of man.

Perhaps at the distance of a score of years, if I then inhabit this world, or still more, if I do not, these will appear frightful confessions; they may or may not; it is a true picture of a barren & desolate soul.

May 14, 1822

My body weighs 144 pounds.—In a fortnight I intend, Deo volente, to make a journey on foot. A month hence I will answer the question whether the pleasure was only in the *hope*.

May 24, 1822

How noble a masterpiece is the tragedy of Hamlet! It can only be spoken of & described by superlatives. There is a deep & subtle wit, with an infinite variety, and every line is golden.

June 9, 1822

Upon a mountain-solitude a man instantly feels a sensible exaltation and a better claim to his rights in the universe. He who wanders in the woods percieves how natural it was to pagan imagination to find gods in every deep grove & by each fountain head. Nature seems to him not to be silent but to be eager & striving to break out into music. Each tree, flower, and stone, he invests with life & character; and it is impossible that the wind which breathes so expressive a sound amid the leaves— should mean nothing.

June 10, 1822

I think it is pretty well known that more is gained to a man's business by one half hour's conversation with his friend, than by very many letters; for, face to face, each can distinctly state his own views; and each chief objection is started & answered; and, moreover, a more definite notion of one's sentiments & intentions, with regard to the matter, are gathered from his look and tones, than it is possible to gain from paper. It is therefore a hint borrowed from Nature, when a lesson of morals is conveyed to an audience in the engaging form of a dialogue, instead of the silence of a book, or the cold soliloquy of an orator. When this didactic dialogue is improved by the addition of pathetic or romantic circumstances and in the place of indifferent speakers, we are presented with the characters of great & good men, of heroes and demigods, thus adding to the sentiments expressed the vast weight of virtuous life & character—the wit of the invention is doubled. Lastly a general moral is drawn from an event, where all the parts of the piece are made to tend & terminate; this is what is called the distribution of poetical justice, and is nothing but an inevitable inference of some great moral truth, which the mind readily makes, upon the turn of affairs. For greater delight, we add music, painting, & poetry, well aware that the splendour of embellishment will fix the eye, after the mind grows weary. These are the advantages comprehended in the dramatic art. Truths otherwise impertinent are told with admirable effect in this little epitome of life; and every philosophic Christian must be loth to lose to religion, an instrument of such tried powers.

June 20? 1822

There is certainly something deeply interesting in the history of one who invades the coast of an unknown continent and first breaks the silence which hath reigned there since the creation. As he goes alone to the wilderness and sets his axe to the root of the forest and we reflect that this stroke which echoes through the wood begins a dominion which shall never end till this green and silent woodland shall groan beneath the feet of countless multitudes and shall exchange the solitary warble of a bird for the noise of nations, the outcry of human passion, and the groan of human misery. Under these views the settler ceases to be an ordinary adventurer, providing for himself and his son, or his friend—but becomes the representative of human nature, the father of the Country, and, in a great measure, the Arbiter of its future destinies.

July 11, 1822

I dedicate my book to the Spirit of America.* I dedicate it to that living soul, which *doth* exist somewhere beyond the Fancy, to whom the Divinity hath assigned the care of this bright corner of the Universe. I bring my little offering, in this month, which covers the continent with matchless beauty, to the shrine, which distant generations shall load with sacrifice, and distant ages shall admire afar off. With a spark of prophetic devotion, I hasten to hail the Genius, who yet counts the tardy years of childhood, but who is increasing unawares in the twilight, and swelling into strength, until the hour, when he shall break the cloud, to shew his colossal youth, and cover the firmament with the shadow of his wings.

July 11, 1822   Evening

It is a slow patriotism which forgets to love till all the world have set the example. If the nations of Europe can find anything to idolize in their ruinous & enslaved institutions, we are content, though we are astonished at their satisfaction. But let them not ignorantly mock at the pride of an American, as if it were misplaced or unfounded, when that freeman is giving an imperfect expression to his sense of his condition. He rejoices in the birthright of a country where the freedom of opinion & action is so perfect that every man enjoys exactly that consideration to which he is entitled, and each mind, as in the bosom of a family, institutes & settles a comparison of its powers with those of its fellow, & quietly takes that stand which nature intended for it. He points to his native land as the only one where freedom has not degenerated to licentiousness; in whose well ordered districts education & intelligence dwell

---

*Emerson had just begun the seventh of his "Wide World" journals.

with good morals; whose rich estates peacefully descend from sire to son, without the shadow of an interference from private violence or public tyranny; whose offices of trust and seats of science are filled by minds of republican strength & elegant accomplishments. Xenophon and Thucydides would have thought it a theme, better worthy of their powers, than Persia or Greece; and her Revolution would furnish Plutarch with a list of heroes. If the Constitution of the United States outlives a century, it will be matter of deep congratulation to the human race; for the Utopian dreams which visionaries have pursued and sages exploded, will find their beautiful theories rivalled & outdone by the reality, which it has pleased God to bestow upon United America.

Oct. 1822

When I was a lad—said the bearded islander—we had commonly a kind of vast musical apparatus in the Pacific islands which must appear as fabulous to you as it proved fatal to us. On the banks of the rivers there were abundance of Siphar Trees which consist of vast trunks perforated by a multitude of natural tubes without having any external verdure. When the roots of these were connected with the waters of the river the water was instantly sucked up by some of the tubes and discharged again by others and when properly echoed the operation attended by the most beautiful musical sounds in the world. My countrymen built their churches to the Great Zoa upon the margin of the water and enclosed a suitable number of these trees, hoping to entertain the ears of the god with this sweet harmony. Finding however by experience that the more water the pipes drew the more rich and various were the sounds of the Organ, they constructed a very large temple with high walls of clay and stone to make the echoes very complete, and enclosed a hundred Siphars. When the edifice was complete six thousand people assembled to hear the long expected song. After they had waited a long time and the waters of the river were beginning to rise, the Instrument suddenly began to emit the finest notes imaginable. Through some of the broader pipes the water rushed with the voice of thunder, and through others with the sweetness of one of your lutes. In a short time the effect of the music was such that it seemed to have made all the hearers mad. They laughed and wept alternately and began to dance and such was their delight that they did not percieve the disaster which had befallen their Organ. Owing to the unusual swell of the River and to some unaccountable irregularity in the ducts the pipes began to discharge their contents within the chapel. In a short time the evil became but too apparent, for the water rose in spouts from the top of the larger ducts and fell upon the multitudes within. Meantime the Music swelled louder and louder, and every note was more ravishing than the last. The inconvenience of the falling water which drenched them, was entirely forgotten until finally the whole host of pipes discharged every one a volume of water upon the charmed congregation. The faster poured the water the sweeter grew the music and the floor being covered with the torrent the people began to float upon it with intolerable extacies. Finally the whole Multitude swam about in this deluge holding up their heads with open mouths and ears as if to swallow the melody whereby they swallowed much water. Many hundreds were immediately drowned and the enormous pipes as they emptied the river swelled their harmony to such perfection that the ear could no longer bear it and they who escaped the drowning died of the exquisite music. Thenceforward there was no more use of the Siphar trees in the Pacific islands.

Nov. 2, 1822

I believe we fight against phantoms when we laboriously contend for the surpassing power of God. It is that attribute, the proofs of which are most gross and undeniable, in the view of every being to whom that Power has communicated the organs of sense. Does the man wake who doubts it? Hath he an eye and an ear, touch and smell? I recommend to him to turn his face to the East and see the sun; to look at the light, what it is? to climb the everlasting hills; to go where Deep calleth unto Deep and find the fountains of the sea; to open his ears to the thunder, and his eye to the fire of the cloud; and if his fastidious soul find amid these, instances rather of decay & weakness than of power, why I will bid this over-proud worm estimate the force which is here required in these ordinary phenomena; I will bid him make trial of his stength and compare it if he durst with Omnipotence. Put forth now thine arm and arrest the fierce comet in his journey to the sun. Like Joshua bid the sun stand still in Gideon & the Moon in the valley of Ajalon. Pluck out a world from yon wilderness of stars, and extinguish its light forever. In vain. They all move serenely on, looking down from their immeasurable height with pity upon the insolent reptile. Let the hand that sustains the Universe for a moment be withdrawn—wilt thou put thy shoulder to the Centre and support the falling worlds? No they stand and move by higher forces which thy little will is not able to hinder or supply; no, not to conceive. Creep into thy grave, for the Universe hath no need of thee; Omnipotence is planted for its preservation.

Nov. 4, 1822

I have come to the close of the sheets which I dedicated to the Genius of America, and notice that I have devoted nothing in my book to any peculiar topics which concern my country. But is not every effort that her sons make to advance the intellectual interests of the world, and every new thought which is struck out from the mines of religion & morality—a forward step in the path of her greatness? Peace be with her progressing greatness—and prosperity crown her giant minds. A victory is achieved today for one,* whose name perchance is written highest in the volume of futurity.

Nov. 8–14, 1822

I believe that nobody now regards the maxim 'that all men are born equal,' as any thing more than a convenient hypothesis or an extravagant declamation. For the reverse is true—that all men are born unequal in personal powers and in those essential circumstances, of time, parentage, country, fortune. The least knowledge of the natural history of man adds another important particular to these; namely, what class of men he belongs to—European, Moor, Tartar, African? Because Nature has plainly assigned different degrees of intellect to these different races, and the barriers between are insurmountable.

This inequality is an indication of the design of Providence that some should lead, and some should serve. For when an effect invariably takes place from causes which Heaven established, we surely say with safety, that Providence designed that result.

Throughout Society there is therefore not only the direct and acknowledged relation of king & subject, master & servant, but a secret dependence quite as universal, of one man upon another, which sways habits, opinions, conduct. This prevails to an infinite extent and however humbling the analogy, it is nevertheless true, that the same pleasure and confidence which the dog and horse feel when they rely upon the superior intelligence of man is felt by the lower parts of our own species with reference to the higher.

Now with these concessions the question comes to this: whether this known and admitted assumption of power by one part of mankind over the other, can ever be pushed to the extent of total possession, and that, without the will of the slave?

It can hardly be said that the whole difference of *the will*, divides the *natural* servitude of which we have spoken from the forced servitude of 'Slavery.' For it is not voluntary, on my part, that I am born a subject; contrariwise, if my opinion had been consulted, it is ten to one I should have been the Great Mogul. The circumstances in which every man finds himself he owes to fortune and not to himself. And those men who happen to be born in the lowest caste in India, suffer much more perhaps than the kidnapped African with no other difference in their lot

---

*Webster was chosen representative to Congress by a majority of 1078 votes this morning. [RWE]

than this, that God made the one wretched and man, the other. Except that there is a dignity in suffering from the ordinances of Supreme power, which is not at all common to the other class—one lot is as little enviable as the other.

When all this is admitted, the question may still remain entirely independent and untouched—apart from the consideration of slavery as agreeable or contradictory to the analogies of nature—whether any individual has a right to deprive any other individual of freedom without his consent; or whether he may continue to withold the freedom which another hath taken away?

Upon the first question 'whether one man may forcibly take away the freedom of another,' the weakness and incapacity of Africans would seem to have no bearing; though it may affect the second. Still it may be advanced that the beasts of the field are all evidently subjected to the dominion of man, and, with the single restriction of the laws of humanity, are left entirely at his will. And why are they, and how do we acquire this declaration of heaven? Manifestly from a view of the perfect adaptation of these animals to the necessities of man and of the advantage which many of them find in leaving the forest for the barnyard. If they had *reason*, their strength would be so far superior to ours, that, besides our inability to use them, it would be inconsistent with nature. So that these three circumstances are the foundation of our dominion; viz. their want of reason; their adaptation to our wants; and their own advantage (when domesticated). But these three circumstances may very well apply to the condition of the Blacks and it may be hard to tell exactly where the difference lies. Is it in *Reason?* If we speak in general of the two classes Man and Beast, we say that they are separated by the distinction of Reason, and the want of it; and the line of this distinction is very broad. But if we abandon this generalization, and compare the classes of one with the classes of the other we shall find our boundary line growing narrower and narrower and individuals of one species approaching individuals of the other, until the limits become finally lost in the mingling of the classes.

It can hardly be true I think that the difference lies in the attribute of Reason; I saw ten, twenty, a hundred large lipped, lowbrowed black men in the streets who, except in the mere matter of language, did not exceed the sagacity of the elephant. Now is it true that these were created superior to this wise animal, and designed to controul it? And in comparison with the highest orders of men, the Africans will stand so low as to make the difference which subsists between themselves & the sagacious beasts inconsiderable. It follows from this, that this is a distinction which cannot be much insisted on.

And if not this, what is the preeminence? Is it in the upright form, and countenance raised to heaven—fitted for command? But in this re-spect also the African fails. The Monkey resembles Man, and the Afri-can degenerates to a likeness of the beast. And here likewise I apprehend we shall find as much difference between the head of Plato & the head of the lowest African, as between this last and the highest species of Ape.

If therefore the distinction between the beasts and the Africans is found neither in Reason nor in figure i.e. neither in mind or body—where then is the ground of that distinction? is it not rather a mere name & prejudice and are not they an upper order of inferior animals?

Moreover if we pursue a revolting subject to its greatest lengths we should find that in all those three circumstances which are the founda-tions of our dominion over the beasts, very much may be said to apply them to the African species; even in the last, viz. the advantage which they derive from our care; for the slaveholders violently assert, that their slaves are happier than the freedmen of their class; and the slaves refuse oftentimes the offer of their freedom. Nor is this owing merely to the barbarity which has placed them out of the power of attaining a compe-tence by themselves. For it is true that many a slave under the warm roof of a humane master with easy labours and regular subsistence enjoys more happiness than his naked brethren parched with thirst on a burning sand or endangered in the crying wilderness of their native land.

This is all that is offered *in behalf* of slavery; we shall next attempt to knock down the hydra.

Nov. 14? 1822

To establish by whatever specious argumentation the perfect expe-diency of the worst institution on earth is *prima facie* an assault upon Reason and Common sense. No ingenious sophistry can ever reconcile the unperverted mind to the pardon of *Slavery;* nothing but tremendous familiarity, and the bias of private *interest.* Under the influence of better arguments than can be offered in support of Slavery, we should sustain our tranquillity by the confidence that no surrender of our opinion is ever demanded and that we are only required to discover the lurking fallacy which the disputant acknowledges to exist. It is an old dispute which is not now and never will be totally at rest, whether the human mind be or be not a free agent. And the assertor of either side must be scandalized by the bare naming of the theory that man may impose ser-vitude on his brother. For if he is himself free, and it offends the attrib-utes of God to have him otherwise, it is manifestly a bold stroke of impi-ety to wrest the same liberty from his fellow. And if he is not free, then this inhuman barbarity ascends to derive its origin from the author of all necessity.

A creature who is bound by his hopes of salvation to imitate the benevolence of better beings, and to do all the kindness in his power, fastens manacles on his fellow with an ill grace.

A creature who holds a little lease of life upon the arbitrary tenure of God's good pleasure improves his moment strangely by abusing God's best works, his own peers.

Nov. 29, 1822

The ardour of my college friendship for Gay* is nearly extinct, and it is with difficulty that I can now recall those sensations of vivid pleasure which his presence was wont to waken spontaneously, for a period of more than two years. To be so agreeably excited by the features of an individual personally unknown to me, and for so long a time, was surely a curious incident in the history of so cold a being, and well worth a second thought. At the very beginning of our singular acquaintance, I noticed the circumstance in my Wideworld, with an expression of curiosity with regard to the effect which time would have upon those feelings. To this day, our glance at meeting, is not that of indifferent persons, and were he not so thoroughly buried in his martial cares, I might still entertain the hope of departed hours. Probably the abatement of my solitary enthusiasm is owing to the discouraging reports which I have gathered of his pursuits and character, so entirely inconsistent with the indications of his face. But it were much better that our connexion should stop, and pass off, as it now will, than to have had it formed, and then broken by the late discovery of insurmountable barriers to friendship. From the first, I preferred to preserve the terms which kept alive so much sentiment rather than a more familiar intercourse which I feared would end in indifference.

Pish

Dec. 21, 1822

There is everything in America's favour, to one who puts faith in those proverbial prophecies of the Westward progress of the Car of Empire. Though there may be no more barbarians left to overrun Europe & extinguish forever the memory of its greatness yet its rotten states like Spain may come to their decline by the festering & inveteracy of the faults of government. Aloof from the contagion during the long progress of their decline America hath ample interval to lay deep & solid foundations for the greatness of the New World. And along the shores of the South Continent, to which the dregs & corruption of European society

---

*The name is crossed out.

"There is a strange face in the Freshman class whom I should
like to know very much."

had been unfortunately transplanted, the fierceness of the present conflict for independence will, no doubt, act as a powerful remedy to the
disease, by stirring up the slumbering spirits of those indolent zones to a
consciousness of their power & destiny. Here then, new Romes are
growing, & the Genius of man is brooding over the wide boundaries of
infant empires, where yet is to be drunk the intoxicating draughts of
honour & renown; here are to be played over again the bloody games of
human ambition, bigotry, & revenge and the stupendous Drama of the
passions to be repeated. Other Cleopatras shall seduce, Alexanders fight,
and Caesars die. The pillars of social strength which we occupy ourselves in founding thus firmly to endure to future ages as the monuments of the wisdom of this, are to be shaken on their foundations with
convulsions proportioned to their adamantine strength. The time is
come, the hour is struck; already the actors in this immense & tremendous scene have begun to assemble. The doors of life in our mountain-
land are opened, and the vast swarm of population is crowding in, bearing in their hands the burden of Sorrow & Sin, of glory & science,
which are to be mingled in their future fates. In the events & interests of
these empires, the old tales of history & the fortunes of departed nations
shall be thoroughly forgotten & the name of Rome or Britain fall seldom
on the ear.

In that event, when the glory of Plato of Greece, of Cicero of Rome,
& of Shakspeare of England shall have died, who are they that are to
write their names where all time shall read them, & their words be the
oracle of millions? Let those who would pluck the lot of Immortality
from Fate's Urn, look well to the future prospects of America.

Jan.? Feb.? 1823

The history of America since the Revolution is meagre because it has been all that time under better government, better circumstances of religious, moral, political, commercial prosperity than any nation ever was before. History will continually grow less interesting as the world grows better. Professor Playfair of Edinburgh, the greatest or one of the greatest men of his time, died without a biography for there was no incident in the life of a great & good man worth recording. Nelson & Buonaparte, men of abilities without principle, found four or five biographers apiece.

The true epochs of history should be those successive triumphs which age after age the communities of men have achieved, such as the Reformation, the Revival of letters, the progressive Abolition of the Slave-trade.

March 6, 1823

My brother Edward asks me Whether I have a right to make use of animals? I answer "Yes," and shall attempt to give my reasons. A poor native of Lapland found himself in mid winter destitute of food, of clothing and light, and without even a bow to defend himself from the beasts. In this perplexity he met with a reindeer which he killed & conveyed to his hut. He now found himself supplied with oil to light his lamp, with a warm covering for his body & with wholesome & strengthening food, and with bowstrings withal, whereby he could again procure a similar supply. Does any mind question the innocence of this starving wretch in thus giving life & comfort to a desolate family in that polar corner of the world? Now there is a whole *nation* of men precisely in this condition, all reduced to the alternative of killing the beasts, or perishing themselves. Let the tender hearted advocate of the brute creation go there, & choose whether he will make the beasts *his* food, or be himself, *theirs.*

Just such a picture may be made of the Arabian & his camel; and of the Northern Islanders & their Whales; in all these instances, the positive law of Necessity asserts our right. But the use of the sheep for clothing, the ox, the horse, & the ass, for beasts of burden is parallel to these, and their necessity though less seen is equally strong. "Increase & Multiply" said the Creator to Man; and caused all the brute creation to pass before him & recieve their names in token of subjection. The use of these enables man to *increase & multiply* a thousand fold more rapidly, than would be practicable if he abstained from their use. Their universal application to our purposes & especially that remarkable adaptation that is observed in many instances of the Animal to the wants of the country in which he is found constitute the grand Argument on this side. (Besides Camel, Whale &c, that were mentioned, I believe the Mule, surest footed animal which walks, is found in the mountains to transverse whose precipices man wants his steady step.)

But it will be said they have rights.

March 10, 1823

Ascetic mortification and an unintermitting livelong martyrdom of all the sensual appetites although far more innocent than the contrary extreme is nevertheless unwise because it fails of its intended effect. Hermits who believed that by this merciless crucifixion of the lusts of the body they should succeed in giving to the winds the rags & tatters of a corrupt nature, and elevate & purge the soul in exact proportion to the sufferings of the flesh, have been disappointed in their hopes; at least if they have succeeded in decieving themselves, they have grievously disappointed the world. The age ceased but a few centuries since when the cells upon the mountains of Palestine, the dreary caverns of Lybyan desart echoed day & night for hundreds of years to the remorseless lash & half suppressed groan of those mad tormentors of themselves. In their own age, Fame told far and wide the story of their self devotion and men came out in processions from the cities & the fields to find these Christian Stoics & ascertain the success of that bold experiment which they had made upon their nature. They looked to see their earthly parts faded, and the spirit waxed brighter & brighter, and breaking out from the clayey tenement, in effulgent manifestations of celestial love. They looked to find in those who had forsworn the seductions of the world & come out with disdain from the active contamination, the Sodom & Gomorrah of human society for the avowed purpose of conversing with God & Christ & his saints—some ray of fervid & burning benevolence, some extraordinary force of mind to speak or of hand to work, *good;* or in their dwelling, some footstep of their etherial visitants. But these golden dreams of a rapid amelioration of the world to issue from the prayers & penances that stormed heaven from these solitudes, vanished away. The solitary man was as other men are. His sufferings had soured his temper, or inflamed his pride; the current of thought had been checked & frozen. His powers & dispositions were diverted from useful ends & were barren & selfish. Instead of the blessed plant which they thought had sprung for the healing of the nations, was a dry & withered branch; it was sundered from its root, producing neither blossoms, nor leaves, nor fruits, 'twas fit only for the fire.

March 18, 1823

After two moons I shall have fulfilled twenty years. Amid the fleeting generations of the human race and in the abyss of years I lift my solitary voice unheeded & unknown & complain unto inexorable Time.

'Stop, Destroyer, Overwhelmer, stop one brief moment this uncontrollable career. Ravisher of the creation, suffer me a little space, that I may
pluck some spoils, as I pass onward, to be the fruits & monuments of the
scenes, through which I have travelled.'—Fool! you implore the deaf
torrent to relax the speed of its cataract.

It is often alleged with a great mass of instances to support the assertion, that the spirit of philosophy & a liberal mind is at discord with the
principles of religion, so far at least as to imply that hoary error that religion is a prejudice which statesmen cherish in the vulgar as a wholesome terror. Those whom Genius or Education have rescued from the
common ignorance have openly discarded the humble creeds of men and
vaunted their liberty. They have mounted, it is pretended, to some loft-
ier prospect of man's dependance or independence upon God & have
discovered that human beings foolishly trouble themselves by their
shallow & slavish fear of some great Power in the Universe who notices
& remembers their actions. For these clearer-sighted intellects have
darted their glance into the secrets of the other world & have satisfied
themselves, either that there is no Divinity at all, beyond the vain names
& fantastic superstitions of men, or else, if there *be*—a sphered & potent
Dweller in the Abyss, he is incurious and indifferent to the petty
changes of the world. In this confidence therefore, these bold speculators cast off the fetters of opinion & those apprehensions which so cleave
to our poor nature & are willing to survey at ease the gorgeous spectacle
of the Universe, the fabric of society, & the closet of the Mind; and to
make themselves proud of this birthright of thoughts . . . This perilous
recklessness, I find with regret in many of the intellectual Guides of
these latter times engendered in some, no doubt, by the too faithful
copying of the others from whom they had themselves recieved the first
impulse, and arising in them from feelings of superiority & spiritual
pride. Hume, Gibbon, Robertson, Franklin, certain Scotch geniuses of
the present day, & the profligate Byron have expressed more or less explicitly their dissent from the popular faith. Composing in themselves a
brilliant constellation of minds variously & richly endowed they have
taken out its welcome influence from the cause of good will to men & set
it in the opposite scale. Like the star seen in the Apocalypse they have
cast a malign light upon the earth, turning the sweet waters to bitter &c.
. . . I believe nothing is more ungrounded than the assertion, that, scep-
ticism is, in any manner, the natural fruit of a superior understanding.
The legitimate fruits of a master spirit are a dearer love to virtue, and an
ardent & thrilling desire to burst the bonds of the flesh & begin a per-
fecter existence. In those moments which every wise man counts the
best of his life—who hath not been smitten, with a burning curiosity,

to rend asunder the veil of mortality, & gaze, with pious violence, upon the unutterable glories beyond? The names which I mentioned as apostate, weigh nothing against the greater names of Bacon, Milton, Newton, & the like, whose hearts cleaved to the divine revelations as the pledge of their resurrection to eternity.

March 23, 1823

A man is made great by a concentration of motive. Bacon might have lived & died a courtier, disgraced & forgotten, but for a fixed resolution at eighteen years old—to reform Science. Milton should have slumbered but for that inspiration to write an epic; Luther, but for his obstinate hatred of Papacy; Newton, but for his perseverance, thro' all obstacles, to identify the fall of his apple & of the moon; (Shakespeare is an outlaw from all systems and would be great in despite of all.) So of inferior men; Peter the Hermit sent men to die in Crusades; Modern Mr Lancaster, a stupid man, fills the world with his schools; only from a concentrated attention to one design. Human power is here of indefinite extent; no one can prescribe the bound beyond which human exertions cannot go with effect. But *times* must be observed, and in great things a man always acts with more effect when the evil is far gone, than when it is nascent. Thus if Luther had preached one or two centuries earlier it might have been vain. . . .

I have rambled far away from my original thought, still there is a loose unity which binds these reflections together and which leads me back to the dubious theme—myself. One youth among the multitudes of mankind, one grain of sand on the seashore, unknown in the midst of my contemporaries, I am hastening to put on the manly robe. From childhood the names of the great have ever resounded in my ear. And it is impossible that I should be indifferent to the rank which I must take in the innumerable assembly of men, or that I should shut my eyes upon the huge interval which separates me from the minds which I am wont to venerate. Every young man is prone to be misled by the suggestions of his own ill founded ambition which he mistakes for the promptings of a secret Genius, and thence dreams of an unrivalled greatness. More intercourse with the world and closer acquaintance with his own faults wipes out from his fancy every trace of this majestic dream. Time, who is the rough master of the feast, comes to this concieted & highly-placed guest, and saith, 'Friend come down to this lower seat, for thy neighbour is worthier than thou.' Nevertheless it is not Time nor Fate nor the World that is half so much his foe as the demon Indolence within him. A man's enemies are those of his own household. Men sometimes carelessly & sometimes profanely cast off the blame of their insignificance in society, upon God their maker, or upon Circumstance, the god (as they

term him) of this world. It is a skilful masquerade which they have
vamped up to tickle the sense & to lull them to repose. They thus contrive to lay quietly an oppressive burden upon the Atlantean shoulders
of fate. But if a man shall diligently consider what it is which most forcibly impedes the natural greatness of his mind, he will assuredly find
that slothful sensual indulgence is the real unbroken barrier, and that
when he has overleaped this, God has set no bounds to his progress. The
maxim is true to an indefinite extent—"Faber quisque fortunae suae."*
We boast of our free agency. What is this but to say God has put into
our hands the elements of our character, the iron & the brass, the silver
& the gold, to choose & to fashion them as we will. But we are afraid of
the toil, we bury them in a napkin instead of moulding them into rich &
enduring vessels.

This view is by far the most animating to exertion. It speaks life &
courage to the soul. Mistrust no more your ability, the rivalry of others,
or the final event. Make speed to plan, to execute, to fulfil; forfeit not one
moment more in the dalliance of sloth; for the work is vast, the time is
short, and Opportunity is a headlong thing which tarries for no man's
necessities. . . . *Make Haste.*

April 8, 1823
Powerful & concentrated motive, it was remarked above, is necessary to a man, who would be great. And young men whose hearts burn
with the desire of distinction may complain perhaps that the paths in
which a man may be usefully illustrious, are always taken up and that
they have fallen in too late an age to be benefactors of mankind. Truly I
wish it were so. I wish that human grandeur had gone so high—if the
thing were possible—that it had exhausted all the stores from which the
mighty pile was supplied—and that there remained no ignorance to
teach, no errors to correct, no sin to purge. But alas! The wildest dreams
of poetry have uttered no such thing. There *is* a huge & disproportionate abundance of *evil* on earth. Indeed the good that is here, is but a little
island of light, amidst the unbounded ocean. . . . Let the young American withdraw his eyes from all but his own country, and try if he can
find employment there, considerable enough to task the vigorous intellect he brings. I am of opinion that the most extraordinary powers that
ever were given to a human being would lose themselves in this vast
sphere. Separated from the contamination which infects all other civilized lands this country has always boasted a great comparative purity.
At the same time, from obvious causes, it has leaped at once from infancy to manhood; has covered & is covering millions of square miles

---

*"Every man is the architect of his own fortune." [*JMN*]

with a hardy & enterprizing population. The free institutions which
prevail here & here alone have attracted to this country the eyes of the
world. In this age the despots of Europe are engaged in the common
cause of tightening the bonds of monarchy about the thriving liberties &
laws of men and the unprivileged orders, the bulk of human society
gasping for breath beneath their chains, and darting impatient glances
towards the free constitution of other countries. To America, therefore,
monarchs look with apprehension & the people with hope. But the vast
rapidity with which the desarts & forests of the interior of this country
are peopled have led patriots to fear lest the nation grow *too fast* for its
virtue & its peace. In the raw multitudes who lead the front of emigration men of respectability in mind & morals are rarely found—it is well
known. The pioneers are commonly the offscouring of civilized society
who have been led to embark in these enterprizes by the consciousness
of ruined fortunes or ruined character or perchance a desire for that
greater license which belongs to a new & unsettled community. These
men & their descendants compose the western frontier population of the
United States and are rapidly expanding themselves. At this day, the
axe is laid to the root of the forest; the Indian is driven from his hut &
the bison from the plains; in the bosom of mountains where white men
never trod, already the voice of nations begins to be heard—haply heard
in ominous & evil accents. Good men desire, & the great Cause of
human nature demands that this abundant & overflowing richness
wherewith God has blessed this country be not misapplied & made a
curse of; that this new storehouse of nations shall never pour out upon
the world an accursed tribe of barbarous robbers. Now the danger is
very great that the Machine of Government acting upon this territory at
so great distance will wax feeble or meet with resistance and that the
Oracles of Moral law and Intellectual wisdom in the midst of an ignorant & licentious people will speak faintly & indistinctly. Human foresight can set no bounds to the ill consequences of such a calamity if it is
not reasonably averted. And, on the contrary, if the senates that shall
meet hereafter in those wilds shall be made to speak a voice of wisdom &
virtue, the reformation of the world would be to be expected from
America. How to effect the check proposed is an object of momentous
importance. And in view of an object of such magnitude, I know not
who he is that can complain that motive is lacking in this latter age,
whereby men should become great.

June 11, 1823 Epilogue
    When Memory rakes up her treasures, her ingots of thought, I fear
she will seldom recur to the Muse's tenth son; and yet it should have
been able to gather & condense something from the wealth of fancy

which Nature supplies in the beautiful summer. I have played the Enthusiast with my book in the greenwood, the huntsman with my gun; have sat upon rocks, & mused o'er flood & fell, have indulged the richest indolence of a Poet & am therefore a creditor to Nature for some brilliant & unusual inspiration. But the Goddess is slow of payment—or has forgotten an old bantling. If she was partial once, she is morose now; for Familiarity (if awful Nature will permit me to use so bold a word) breeds disgust; & Vinegar is the son of Wine; peradventure I may yet be admitted to the contemplation of her inner magnificence, & her favour may find me, no shrine indeed, but some snug niche, in the temple of Time. 'Tut,' says Fortune—'and if you fail, it shall never be from lack of vanity.'

WALK TO THE CONNECTICUTT

Aug. 22, 1823   Friday Noon, Warren's Hotel, Framingham
After a delightful walk of 20 miles I reached this inn before Noon, and in the near recollection of my promenade through Roxbury, Newton, Needham, Natick, do recommend the same, particularly as far as the Lower Falls in Newton, to my friends who are fond of fine scenery.

To this stage of mine errantry no adventure has befallen me; no, not the meeting with a mouse. I both thought & talked a little with myself on the way, and gathered up & watered such sprigs of poetry as I feared had wilted in my memory. I thought how History has a twofold effect, viz intellectual pleasure & moral pain. And in the midst of a beautiful country I thought how monotonous & uniform is Nature; but I found now as ever that maugre all the flights of the sacred Muse, the profane solicitudes of the flesh, elevated the Tavern to a high rank among my pleasures.

Worcester, Evening 8 o'clock
I reached Worcester ½ an hour ago having walked 40 miles without difficulty. Every time I traverse a turnpike I find it harder to concieve how they are supported; I met but 3 or four travellers between Roxbury & W. The scenery all the way was fine, and the turnpike, a road of inflexible principle, swerving neither to the right hand nor the left, stretched on before me, always in sight. A traveller who has nothing particular to think about is apt to make a very lively personification of his Road & so make the better companion of it. The Kraken, thought I, or the Sea-Worm, is *three English* miles long; but this *land-worm* of mine is some forty, & those of the hugest.

Saturday, Rice's Hotel, Brookfield

After passing through Leicester, Spencer & North Brookfield I am comfortably seated in South B. 60 miles from home. In Leicester, I met with Stephen Elliot in the Bar room of the inn, on his way, it appeared, to Stafford Springs. He guessed with me a few minutes concerning the design & use of a huge white building opposite the house & could not decide whether it were Courthouse or whether it were Church. But the stageman called, & he went on his way. The building I found to be an Academy containing ordinarily 80 students—boys & girls. "Not so many girls now," added the bar-keeper, "because there is no female instructer, & they like a woman to teach them the higher things." Ye stars! thought I, if the Metropolis get this notion, the Mogul* & I must lack bread. At Spencer I sympathized with a Coachman who complained, that, 'ride as far or as fast as he would, the milestones were all alike, & told the same number.' Mr Stevens of N. Brookfield is an innholder after my heart—corpulent & comfortable, honest to a cent, with high opinions of the clergy. And yet he told me there was a mournful rise of schisms since he was a boy—Unitarians & Universalists—which, he said, he believed were all one, and he never heard their names till lately. I asked him the cause of all this frightful heterodoxy? The old Serpent, he said, was at work decieving men. He could not but think people *behaved* about as well now as their fathers did; but then Mr Bisby (the Universalist minister of B.) is a cunning fox. & by & bye he & his hosts will show what & how bad they really are. My good landlord's philanthropic conclusion was, that there was a monitor within and if we minded that, no matter how we speculated.

Aug. 24, 1823 Sunday Evg.

I rested this Sabbath day on the banks of the Quebog. Mr Stone, a worthy Calvinist, who had been already recommended to my respect, by the hearty praises of my last-named landlord, preached all day, and reminded me forcibly of one of my idols, Dr. N. of Portland. My lord Bacon, my trusty counsellor all the week, has six or seven choice essays for holy time. The aforesaid lord knew passing well what was in man, woman, & child, what was in books, & what in palaces. This possessor of transcendant intellect was a mean slave to courts and a conniver at bribery. And now perchance if mental distinctions give place to moral ones at the end of life—now this intellectual giant who has been the instructor of the world and must continue to be a teacher of mankind till the end of time—has been forced to relinquish his preeminence and in

---

*His brother William, like Emerson a schoolteacher. [*JMN*]

another world to crawl in the dust at the feet of those to whom his mounting spirit was once a sacred guide. One instant succeeding dissolution will perhaps satisfy us, that there is no inconsistency in this. Till then I should be loth to ascribe any thing less than celestial state to the Prince of philosophers.

Belchertown, Clapp's Hotel, Monday Afternoon

After noticing the name of M. Rice upon the Hatstore, upon the Blacksmith's shop, & upon the Inn of S. Brookfield, I made inquiries of my landlord, and learned that this omni-trader was he himself, who, moreover, owned two lines of stages! This morning, Phoebus and I set out together upon our respective journies; and I believe we shall finish them together, since this village is ten miles from Amherst. The morning walk was delightful; and the Sun amused himself & me by making rainbows on the thick mist which darkened the country. After passing through W. Brookfield I breakfasted among some right worshipful waggoners at the pleasant town of Western, and then passed through a part of Palmer (I believe) & Ware to this place. I count that road pleasant & that air good, which forces me to smile from mere animal pleasure, albeit I may be a smiling man; so I am free to commend the road from Cutler's Tavern in Western, as far as Babcock's in *Ware*, to any youthful traveller, who walks upon a cloudless August Morning. Let me not forget to record here, the benevolent landlady of Ware who offered me her liquors & crackers upon the precarious credit of my return, rather than exchange my bills.

Monday Evg., Bartlett's, Amherst

My worthy landlord wishes blessings to the Amherst Institution, which, saith he, howbeit it may have had a muddy foundation, yet the Lord hath blessed.

Aug. 28? 1823

Tuesday Morning I engaged Mr Bartlett to bring me to Mrs Shepard's and I think the worthy man returned with some complacent recollections of the instructions & remarks he had dropped on the way for the stranger's edification. Our wagon ride was somewhat uneasy from below but its ups & downs were amply compensated by the richness & grandeur visible above & around. Hampshire County rides in wagons. In this pleasant land I found a house-full of friends, a noble house—very good friends. In the afternoon I went to the College. The infant college is an Infant Hercules. Never was so much striving, outstretching, & advancing in a literary cause as is exhibited here. The students all feel a personal responsibility in the support & defence of their young Alma

Mater against all antagonists, and as long as this battle abroad shall continue, the Government, unlike all other Governments, will not be compelled to fight with its students within. The opposition of other towns & counties produces moreover a correspondent friendship & kindness from the people in Amherst, and there is a daily exhibition of affectionate feeling between the inhabitants & the scholars, which is the more pleasant as it is so uncommon. They attended the Declamation & Commencement with the interest which parents usually shew at the exhibitions of schools where their own children are engaged. I believe the affair was first moved, about three years ago, by the Trustees of the Academy. When the corner stone of the South College was laid, the Institution did not own a dollar. A cartload of stones was brought by a farmer in Pelham, to begin the foundation; and now they have two large brick edifices, a President's house, & considerable funds. Dr Moore has left them six or seven thousand dollars. A poor one-legged man died last week in Pelham, who was not known to have any property, & left them 4000 dollars to be appropriated to the building of a Chapel, over whose door is to be inscribed his name, Adams Johnson. Wm Phillips gave a thousand & Wm Eustis a hundred dollars and great expectations are entertained from some rich men, friends to the Seminary who will die without children.

They have wisely systematized this spirit of opposition which they have found so lucrative, & the students are all divided into thriving opposition societies which gather libraries, laboratories, mineral cabinets, &c, with an indefatigable spirit, which nothing but rivalry could inspire. Upon this impulse, they write, speak, & study in a sort of fury, which, I think, promises a harvest of attainments. The Commencement was plainly that of a young college, but had strength and eloquence mixed with the apparent 'vestigia ruris.' And the scholar who gained the prize for declamation the evening before, would have a first prize at any Cambridge competition. The College is supposed to be worth net 85000 dollars.

After spending three days very pleasantly at Mrs Shepard's, among orators, botanists, mineralogists, & above all, Ministers, I set off on Friday Morning with Thos Greenough & another little cousin in a chaise to visit Mount Holyoke. How high the hill may be, I know not; for, different accounts make it 8, 12, & 16 hundred feet from the river. The prospect repays the ascent and although the day was hot & hazy so as to preclude a distant prospect, yet all the broad meadows in the immediate vicinity of the mountain through which the Connecticutt winds, make a beautiful picture seldom rivalled. After adding our names in the books to the long list of strangers whom curiosity has attracted to this hill we descended in safety without encountering rattlesnake or viper that have given so bad fame to the place. We were informed that about 40 people ascend the mountain every fair day during the summer. After passing through Hadley meadows, I took leave of my companions at Northampton bridge, and crossed for the first time the far famed Yankee river.

From the Hotel in Northampton I visited Mr. Theodore Strong, where I have been spending a couple of days of great pleasure. His five beautiful daughters & son make one of the finest families I ever saw. In the afternoon, I went on horse back (oh Hercules!) with Allen Strong to Round Hill, the beautiful site of the Gymnasium, & to Shepherd's Factory about 4 miles from the centre of the town. Saturday Morning we went in a chaise in pursuit of a lead mine said to lie about five miles off which we found after great & indefatigable search. We tied our horse & descended, by direction, into a somewhat steep glen at the bottom of which we found the covered entrance of a little canal about 5 ft. wide. Into this artificial cavern we fired a gun to call out the miner from within. The report was long & loudly echoed & after a weary interval we discerned a boat with lamps lighted in its sides issuing from this dreary abode. We welcomed the Miner to the light of the Sun and leaving our hats without, & binding our heads we lay down in the boat and were immediately introduced to a cave varying in height from 4 to 6 & 8 feet, hollowed in a pretty soft sandstone through which the water continually drops. When we lost the light of the entrance & saw only this gloomy passage by the light of lamps it required no effort of imagination to believe we were leaving the world, & our smutty ferryman was a true Charon. After sailing a few hundred feet the vault grew higher & wider overhead & there was a considerable trickling of water on our left; this was the ventilator of the mine & reaches up to the surface of the earth. We continued to advance in this manner for 900 feet & then got out of the boat & walked on planks a little way to the end of this excavation. Here we expected to find the lead vein, & the operations of the subterranean man, but were sadly disappointed. He had been digging through this stone for 12 years, & has not yet discovered any lead at all. Indications of lead at the surface led some Boston gentleman to set this man at work in the expectation that after cutting his dark canal for 1000 feet, he would reach the vein, & the canal would then draw off the water which prevented them from digging from above. As yet, he has found no lead but, as he gravely observed 'has reached some *excellent granite.*' In this part of the work he has 40 dollars for every foot he advances and it occupies him ten days to earn this. He has advanced 975 feet & spends his days, winter & summer, alone in this damp & silent tomb. He says the place is excellent for meditation, & that he sees no goblins. Many visiters come to his dark residence, & pay him a shilling apiece for the sight. A young man, he said, came the day before us, who after going in a little way was taken with terrors & said he felt faint, & returned. Said Miner is a brawny personage & discreet withal; has a wife, & lives near the hole. All his excavations are performed by successive blastings.

In the afternoon I set out on my way to Greenfield intending to pass the Sabbath with George Ripley. Mr Strong insisted on carrying me to Hatfield, & thence I passed chiefly on foot through Whately & Deerfield over sands & pinebarrens, & across Green River to Greenfield, and did not arrive there till after ten o'clock & found both taverns shut up. I should have staid in Deerfield if Mr S. had not ridiculed the idea of getting to Greenfield that night. In the morning I called at Mr Ripley's, & was sorely disappointed to learn that his son was at Cambridge. The family were exceedingly hospitable, and I listened with no great pleasure to a sermon from Rev. Mr Perkins of Amherst in the morng & in the afternoon rode over to the other parish with Mr R. to hear Rev Lincoln Ripley. After service Mr L. R returned with us, and in the evening we heard another sermon from Mr Perkins which pleased me abundantly better than his matins. He is a loudvoiced scripture-read divine, & his compositions have the elements of a potent eloquence, but he lacks taste. By the light of the Evening star, I walked with my reverend uncle, a man who well sustains the character of an aged missionary. It is a new thing to him, he said, to *correspond* with his wife, and he attends the mail regularly every Monday morng. to send or recieve a letter.

After a dreamless night, & a most hospitable entertainment I parted from Greenfield & through an unusually fine country, crossed the Connecticut (shrunk to a rivulet in this place somewhere in Montagu). My solitary way grew somewhat more dreary, as I drew nearer Wendell and the only relief to hot sandy roads & a barren monotonous region was one fine forest with many straight clean pinetrees upwards of a hundred feet high 'fit for the mast of some great Admiral.' All that day was a thoughtless heavy pilgrimage and Fortune deemed that such a crowded week of pleasure demanded a reaction of pain. At night I was quartered in the meanest caravansera which has contained my person since the tour began. Traveller! weary & jaded, who regardest the repose of thine earthly tenement; Traveller, hungry & athirst whose heart warms to the hope of animal gratification; Traveller of seven or seventy years beware, beware, I beseech you of Mr Haven's Inn in New Salem. Already he is laying a snare for your kindness or credulity in fencing in a mineral spring for your infirmities. Beware—

From Mr Haven's garret bed I sallied forth Tuesday morng towards Hubbardston, but my cramped limbs made little speed. After dining in Hubbardston I walked seven miles farther to Princeton designing to ascend Wachusett with my tall cousin Thomas Greenough if I should find him there, & then set out for home in the next day's stage. But when morning came, & the stage was brought, and the mountain was a mile & a half away—I learned again an old lesson, that, the beldam Disappointment sits at Hope's door. I jumped into the stage & rode away, Wachusett untrod. At Sterling I learned that Oliver Blood studies physic in Worcester; at Bolton I saw Nat Wood on his way to Amherst N. H. to study law, his pedagogical career being terminated—O fortunate nimium!*

Close cooped in a stage coach with a score of happy dusty rustics the pilgrim continued his ride to Waltham, and alighting there, spent an agreeable evening at Rev. Mr Ripley's. Home he came from thence the next morning, right glad to sit down once more in a quiet wellfed family—at Canterbury.

Sept. 1823   Canterbury

I have often found cause to complain that my thoughts have an ebb & flow. Whether any laws fix them & what the laws are I cannot ascertain. I have quoted a thousand times the memory of Milton & tried to bind my thinking season to one part of the year or to one sort of weather; to the sweet influence of the Pleiades, or to the summer reign of Lyra. The worst is, that the ebb is certain, long & frequent, while the flow comes transiently & seldom. Once when *vanity* was full fed, it sufficed to keep me at work & to produce some creditable scraps; but alas! it has long been dying of a galloping starvation & the Muse, I fear me, will die too. The dreams of my childhood are all fading away & giving place to some very sober & very disgusting views of a quiet mediocrity of talents & condition—nor does it appear to me that any application of which I am capable, any efforts, any sacrifices could at this moment restore any reasonableness to the familiar expectations of my earlier youth.

Oct. 1823

I heard Dr Channing deliver a discourse upon Revelation as standing in comparison with Nature. I have heard no sermon approaching in excellence to this, since the Dudleian Lecture. The language was a transparent medium, conveying with the utmost distinctness, the pictures in his mind, to the minds of the hearers. He considered God's word to be the only expounder of his works, & that Nature had always been found insufficient to teach men the great doctrines which Revelation inculcated. Astronomy had in one or two ways an unhappy tendency. An universe of matter in which Deity would display his power & greatness must be of infinite extent & complicate relations and of course too vast

---

*"O you lucky dog!" Emerson was still an unwilling schoolteacher.

to be measured by the eye & understanding of man. Hence errors. Astron. reveals to us infinite number of worlds like our own accommodated for the residence of such beings as we of gross matter. But to kindle our piety & urge our faith, we do not want such a world as this but a purer, a world of morals & of spirits. La Place has written in the mountain album of Switzerland his avowal of Atheism. Newton had a better master than Suns & Stars. He learned of heaven ere he philosophized. & after travelling through mazes of the universe he returned to bow his laurelled head at the feet of Jesus of Nazareth. Dr C. regarded Revelation as much a part of the order of things as any other event. It would have been wise to have made an abstract of the Discourse immediately.

Oct.? 1823

I would to God that none of the good purposes of his children upon earth failed of their accomplishment; that every humane design; every heart bleeding for the sorrows of men; every liberal feeling which would pardon their faults or relieve their woes—might go on to the fine ultimate issues which it contemplated. The melancholy truth is that there are ten thousand abortive to one successful accomplishment. Who does not know, who has not felt that unnumbered good purposes spring up in the clean & strong soil of the youthful breast, until Sloth gives a relaxing fatness to the ground, which kills the growth. I call every man to witness whatever be his lot, be he the minion of fortune or the child of sorrow, Pagan or Christian, bond or free, that if he be sinful his hands have not always ministered to his designs, that virtue is not a name unknown to his ears or overlooked in his thoughts. No there is an impulse to do good continually urging us, an eternal illumination upon virtuous deeds that attracts the beholder. His heart applauds; it is his hands that fail. It strikes my mind as a beautiful & adorable truth that the good spirit who made all things is daily working in this lower sphere by presenting to ten thousand thousand minds images & occasions of goodness, striving as he can, without infringing their freedom to bind them to the right interest, inviting them with benignant importunity to thought & duty, & imparting a bias which if obeyed will make the heart burn with gratitude. The more we magnify this benevolence the more depraved & besotted is man's negligence or frowardness. He averts his sullen eye from all the riches to which his nature made him heir.

Nov.? 1823

A French philosopher said We may now anticipate the time when the whole world will all be united under the same laws, the same religion, & *the same system of weights & measures.*

* * *

"Where are you going Mr. Whitefield?" said Dr. Chauncy. "I'm going to Boston, sir."—"I'm very sorry for it," said Dr C. "So is the Devil" replied the eloquent preacher.*

Dec. 1823

There is danger of a *poetical* religion from the tendencies of the age. There is a celebrated passage in the prose works of the great Christian bard, which is precious to the admirers of Milton. I refer to the II Book of Reason of Church Government, &c. There is probably no young man who could read that eloquent chapter, without feeling his heart warm to the love of virtue & greatness & without making fervent resolutions that his age should be made better, because he had lived. Yet these resolutions, unless diligently nourished by prayer & expanded into action by intense study will be presently lost in the host of worldly cares. But they leave one fruit, that may be poisonous; they leave a self complacency arising from having thought so nobly for a moment, which leads the self deciever to believe himself better than other men.

Dec. 21, 1823

Who is he that shall controul me? Why may not I act & speak & write & think with entire freedom? What am I to the Universe, or, the Universe, what is it to me? Who hath forged the chains of Wrong & Right, of Opinion & Custom? And must I wear them? Is Society my anointed King? Or is there any mightier community or any man or more than man, whose slave I am? I am solitary in the vast society of beings; I consort with no species; I indulge no sympathies. I see the world, human, brute & inanimate nature; I am in the midst of them, but not *of* them; I hear the song of the storm—the Winds & warring Elements sweep by me—but they mix not with my being. I see cities & nations & witness passions—the roar of their laughter—but I partake it not;—the yell of their grief—it touches no chord in me; their fellowships & fashions, lusts & virtues, the words & deeds they call glory & shame—I disclaim them all. I say to the Universe, Mighty one! thou art not my mother; Return to chaos, if thou wilt, I shall still exist. I live. If I owe my being, it is to a destiny greater than thine. Star by Star, world by world, system by system shall be crushed—but I shall live.

---

*Emerson's implicit approval of the great eighteenth-century evangelical preacher George Whitefield seems to have personal significance, since the rationalist Charles Chauncy, who opposed Whitefield, was pastor of Boston's First Church, where Emerson's father succeeded him in 1799. William Emerson admired Chauncy and named his youngest son after him.

Dec. 1823

The tendencies of literature in different ages observable. In France & England has sometimes run strongly towards drama, as in the rude Mysteries; in England in the last Century was historical—Hume, Gibbon, Robertson. In this day runs to Periodical writing, to newspaper, magazine, encyclopedia, & review. Causes & uses. Newspapers not known in Greece or Rome; (the first was published in England, in Elizabeth's time, 1538) their help & harm pretty evenly balanced. Inasmuch as it is good the peasant in his humble cot should be acquainted with his government, the actions, interests, characters of his rulers & distinguished fellow citizens; that he should have a rational & exciting amusement; that he should not be liable to be misled by rumours, parents of national evils—in so much, a newspaper is good. In a nation large as the United States, without prints, to what unruly extravagance false reports about men & events would grow before they could be corrected, is easily concieved. For a report cannot be *denied;* but a *printed* rumour can. But as vehicles of slander & virulent party spirit they are fatally convenient. Dr Channing thought them eminently useful in enlarging the sphere of human sympathy; confederating us with distant Greece, enabling a nation to unite in one feeling & hence in one effort.—But Crusades without prints excited intenser sympathy. This example will go in favour of newspapers, for, as was said above, they were, for want of rapidly circulating information, ignorant, foolish, uncorrected excitements. Newspapers are the proper literature of America, which affects to be so practical & unromantic a land.

Jan. 1824

Few bodies or parties have served the world so well as the Puritans. From their irreverent zeal came most of the improvements of the British Constitution. It was they who settled N. America. Bradford & Winthrop & Standish, Mathers & Jonathan Edwards, Otis, Hawley, Hancock, Adams, Franklin, & whatever else of vigorous sense, or practical genius, this country shews, are the issue of Puritan stock. The community of language with England has doubtless deprived us of that original characteristic literary growth that has ever accompanied, I apprehend, the first bursting of a nation from the bud. Our era of exploits & civilization is ripe enow. And, had it not been dissipated by the unfortunate rage for periodical productions, our literature should have been born & grown ere now to a Greek or Roman stature. Franklin is such a fruit as might be expected from such a tree. Edwards, perhaps more so.

Jan. 5, 1824

"A friend should bear a friend's infirmities." This does not chime perfectly with my fancies. Friends should not have infirmities; that is, discordant infirmities; Friendship will melt like snow if there be anything likely to disgust, between parties. I may be the friend of a passionate man perhaps but not of an illhumoured one & bear his ill humour nor of a proser, & bear his long stories; nor of a plebeian, & tolerate his vulgarities. Hearts must be of a mould to match. I have heard of instances indeed where contrary inclinations have agreed well, the projections of one character happening to adjust themselves, as it seemed to the cavities of the other. But I believe this was a companionship & no nearer love. For there must be no hollowness or artifice in the sympathy that would be permanent. As there necessarily must be where one cannot relish or concieve the pleasures of the other.

Jan. 10? 1824

Aristocracy is a good sign. Aristocracy has been the hue & cry in every community where there has been anything good, any society worth associating with, since men met in cities. It must be every where. 'Twere the greatest calamity to have it abolished. It went nearest to its death in the French Revolution, of all time. And if, tonight, an earthquake should sink every patrician house in the city, tomorrow there would be as distinct an aristocracy as now. The only change would be that the second sort would have become first but they would be as unmingling, as much separated from the lower class as ever the rich men of today were from them. No man would consent to live in society if he was obliged to admit every body to his house that chose to come. Robinson Crusoe's island would be better than a city if men were obliged to mix together indiscriminately heads & points with all the world. Envy is the tax which all distinction must pay.

Jan.? 1824

It is excellent advice both in writing & in action to avoid a too great elevation at first. Let one's beginnings be temperate & unpretending & the more elevated parts will rise from these with a just & full effect. We were not made to breath oxygen or to talk poetry, or to be always wise.

Men in this age do not produce new works but admire old ones; Are content to leave the fresh pastures awhile, & to chew the cud of thought in the shade.

Does *Marriage* produce good-Order in Society or the desire & necessity of good order give rise to marriage. Yea or Nay?

Feb. 1824

"La nature," says Pascal, "confond les pyrrhoniens et la raison confond les dogmatistes." & Sir J. Mackintosh calls the sentence the sub-
limest of human composition. It is fortunate & happy but a sublimity
not difficult to gain, as it did not occur to Pascal when he first revolved
the subject, but is the last generalization at which he arrives. And it is
easier to build up one subject into a cone with a broad base of examples
narrowing up into a formula expressing a general truth, than to detach
subtle facts from subjects partially known.

'Please to praise me,' is the ill disguised request of almost all literary
men. All men are cheered by applause & vexed by censure.

Feb. 17, 1824

Pliny's uncle had a slave read while he eat. In the progress of Watt &
Perkin's philosophy the day may come when the scholar shall be provided with a Reading Steam Engine; when he shall say Presto—& it
shall discourse eloquent history—& Stop Sesame & it shall hush to let
him think. He shall put in a pin, & hear poetry; & two pins, & hear a
song. That age will discover Laputa.

Asia, Africa, Europe, old, leprous & wicked, have run round the goal
of centuries till we* are tired and they are ready to drop. But now a
strong man has entered the race & is outstripping them all. Strong Man!
youth & glory are with thee. As thou wouldst prosper forget not the
hope of mankind. Trample not upon thy competitors though unworthy.
Europe is thy father—bear him on thy Atlantean shoulders. Asia, thy
grandsire, regenerate him. Africa, their ancient abused bondman. Give
him his freedom.

Noah was not dinned to death with Aristotle & Bacon & Greece &
Rome. The patriarchs were never puzzled with libraries of names &
dates, with First ages & dark ages; & Revivals & upper empires & lower
empires; with the balance of power & the balance of trade; with fighting
chronologies & dagger-drawing creeds. Life is wasted in the necessary
preparation of finding which is the true way, & we die just as we
enter it.

Feb. 20, 1824

None that can understand Milton's Comus can read it without
warming to the holy emotions it panegyrizes. I would freely give all I

---

* '*We*' means beings better than we. [RWE]

Sketches from the college journals

ever hoped to be, even when my airblown hopes were brilliant & glorious—not as now, to have given down that sweet strain to posterity to do
good in a golden way—to bewitch young hearts by eloquent verses to
the love of goodness, to bias manhood & edify gray hairs. Would not a
man die to do such an office to mankind? The service that such books as
this & the "Prelaty" & Bunyan &c render, is not appreciable but is im-

mense. These books go up & down the world on the errand of charity & where sin & sorrow have been, where malignity festers & ignorance thickens, pour their balm of Gilead, & cleanse the foul humours & purify the channels of life.

Feb. 1824

The theological notions of a Chinese are anomalous I trust in besotted perversity. The godhead that infests his thoughts is a certain cleverness & skill that implies no merit in the divinity but of which the yellow man may avail himself as he would of the swiftness of a horse or the fecundity of the earth. So he prays to his God for an event; if his prayer be answered he puts a copper or two on his shrine; if not, he curses & kicks him; the day, it may be, is not distant when the huge & sluggard wave of oriental population shall be stirred & purified by the conflict of counter currents, when the Resurrection of the East shall cast off the incubus that has so long ridden its torpid mind.

Metaphysicians are mortified to find how entirely the whole materials of understanding are derived from sense. No man is understood who speculates on mind or character until he borrows the specific imagery of Sense. A mourner will try in vain to explain the extent of his bereavement better than to say a *chasm* is opened in society. I fear the progress of Metaphysical philosophy may be found to consist in nothing else than the progressive introduction of apposite metaphors.

Feb.–March 1824

How do you do sir? Very well sir. You have a keen air among your rocks & hills. Yes sir. I never saw a country which more delighted me. A man might travel many hundred miles & not find so fine woodland as abound in this neighbourhood. But the good people who live in them do not esteem them. It is people born in town who are intoxicated with being in the country. It certainly is a good deal like being drunk, the feelings of a cit in the hills. In Cambridge there is some wild land called Sweet Auburn upwards of a mile from the Colleges & yet the students will go in bands over a flat sandy road & in summer evenings the woods are full of them. They are so happy they do not know what to do. They will scatter far & wide too among some insignificant whortleberry bushes, pricked with thorns & stung by musquetoes for hours for the sake of picking a pint of berries; occasionally chewing a bug of indescribable bad relish. You count it nothing more to go among green bushes than on the roads, but those who have been educated in dusty streets enjoy as much from sauntering here as you would in the Orange

groves & Cinnamon gardens of the East Indies. They say there is a tune
which is forbidden to be played in the European Armies because it
makes the Swiss desert since it reminds them so forcibly of their hills at
home. I have heard many *Swiss tunes* played in college. Balancing between getting & not getting a hard lesson, a breath of fragrant air from
the fields coming in at the window would serve as a Swiss tune & make
me *desert* to the glens from which it came. Nor is that vagabond inclination wholly gone yet. And many a sultry afternoon last summer I left
my Latin & my English to go with my gun & see the rabbits & squirrels
& robins in the woods. Good bye, Sir. Stop a moment. I have heard a
clergyman of Maine say that in his Parish are the Penobscot Indians &
that when any one of them in summer has been absent for some weeks a
hunting he comes back among them a different person & altogether unlike any of the rest, with an eagle's eye, a wild look, & commanding carriage & gesture; but after a few weeks it wears off again into the indolent
drone like apathy which all exhibit. Good day Sir.

I notice that Words are as much governed by Fashion as dress, both
in written & spoken style. A negro said of another today 'That's a *curious genius.*'

March 1824
Our forefathers believed that in the East was a great empire whose
simple political institutions had a recorded antiquity at least triple the
fabled period of any other; that this nation augmented its territory with
its age, incorporating all it took by the inherent virtues of its policy; that
by reason of its perfect adaptation to human wants the paternal yoke of
the government embraced the densest population in the world; that this
population had for ages enjoyed all the great inventions that had recently been imparted to Europe as the Compass, the Press, & Gunpowder, that it was possessed of science unknown in Europe & that the peas-
ants of this sunny land lived in greater luxury than the priveleged orders
in the Western nations. This plausible tale is true in the particular but
false on the whole. The Celestial Empire—hang the Celestial Empire! I
hate Pekin. I will not drink of the waters of the Yellow Sea. Exorciso *tea,*
celestissime, even *tea*. One is apt to mix up an idea of the productions of
a nation in our opinion of the producers, & Tea the insignificant sop of
an herb, wholly a luxury in the West, the frivolous employment of millions in the making & tens of millions in the drinking is a fit representative of China. It is useful to know the state of man in circumstances
widely dissimilar. It is a help to an inference concerning our progress.
'Tis like getting two angles to compute a third. But I hate China. 'Tis a
tawdry vase. Out upon China. Words! Words.

March 1824

Shall I embroil my short life with a vain desire of perpetuating its memory when I am dead & gone in this dirty planet? I complain daily of my world, that it is false, disappointing, imperfect, & uncomfortable; & reason would that I should get thro' it as silently & hastily as I can & especially avoiding to tie any hopes or fears to it. I make it my best boast that I am the citizen of a far country far removed from the low influences of earth & sea, of time & change; that my highly destined nature spurns its present abode & aspires after a mode of existence & a fellowship of beings which shall eclipse & efface the gaudy glory of this. When my body shall be in the clods my triumphant soul, glad of any deliverance, will think no more of it or its habitation. Am I then to give my days & nights to a gnawing solicitude to get me a reputation, a fame, forsooth among these worm-eaten, worm-eating creatures of clay, these boys of the universe, these infants of immortality as they all must be while they live on earth?

April 18, 1824

I am beginning my professional studies. In a month I shall be *legally* a man. And I deliberately dedicate my time, my talents, & my hopes to the Church. Man is an animal that looks before & after; and I should be loth to reflect at a remote period that I took so solemn a step in my existence without some careful examination of my past & present life. Since I cannot alter I would not repent the resolution I have made & this page must be witness to the latest year of my life whether I have good grounds to warrant my determination.

I cannot dissemble that my abilities are below my ambition. And I find that I judged by a false criterion when I measured my powers by my ability to understand & to criticise the intellectual character of another. For men graduate their respect not by the secret wealth but by the outward use; not by the power to understand, but by the power to act. I have or had a strong imagination & consequently a keen relish for the beauties of poetry. The exercise which the practice of composition gives to this faculty is the cause of my immoderate fondness for writing, which has swelled these pages to a voluminous extent. My reasoning faculty is proportionately weak, nor can I ever hope to write a Butler's Analogy or an Essay of Hume. Nor is it strange that with this confession I should choose theology, which is from everlasting to everlasting 'debateable Ground.' For, the highest species of reasoning upon divine subjects is rather the fruit of a sort of moral imagination, than of the 'Reasoning Machines' such as Locke & Clarke & David Hume. Dr Channing's Dudleian Lecture is the model of what I mean, and the faculty which produced this is akin to the higher flights of the fancy. I may

add that the preaching most in vogue at the present day depends chiefly
on imagination for its success, and asks those accomplishments which I
believe are most within my grasp. I have set down little which can gratify my vanity, and I must further say that every comparison of myself
with my mates that six or seven, perhaps sixteen or seventeen, years
have made has convinced me that there exists a signal defect of character
which neutralizes in great part the just influence my talents ought to
have. Whether that defect be in the *address*, in the fault of good forms,
which Queen Isabella said were like perpetual letters commendatory, or
deeper seated in an absence of common *sympathies*, or even in a levity of
the understanding, I cannot tell. But its bitter fruits are a sore uneasiness
in the company of most men & women, a frigid fear of offending & jealousy of disrespect, an inability to lead & an unwillingness to follow the
current conversation, which contrive to make me second with all those
among whom chiefly I wish to be first.

Hence my bearing in the world is the direct opposite of that good
humoured independence & self esteem which should mark the gentleman. Be it here remembered that there is a decent pride which is conspicuous in the perfect model of a Christian man. I am unfortunate also,
as was Rienzi, in a propensity to laugh or rather snicker. I am ill at ease
therefore among men. I criticize with hardness; I lavishly applaud; I
weakly argue; and I wonder with a foolish face of praise.

Now the profession of Law demands a good deal of personal address,
an impregnable confidence in one's own powers, upon all occasions expected & unexpected, & a logical mode of thinking & speaking—which I
do not possess, & may not reasonably hope to obtain. Medicine also
makes large demands on the practitioner for a seducing Mannerism.
And I have no taste for the pestle & mortar, for Bell on the bones or
Hunter or Celsus.

But in Divinity I hope to thrive. I inherit from my sire a formality of
manner & speech, but I derive from him or his patriotic parent a passionate love for the strains of eloquence. I burn after the 'aliquid im-
mensum infinitumque'* which Cicero desired. What we ardently love
we learn to imitate. My understanding venerates & my heart loves that
Cause which is dear to God & man—the laws of Morals, the Revelations
which sanction, & the blood of martyrs & triumphant suffering of the
saints which seal them. In my better hours, I am the believer (if not the
dupe) of brilliant promises, and can respect myself as the possessor of
those powers which command the reason & passions of the multitude.
The office of a clergyman is twofold; public preaching & private influence. Entire success in the first is the lot of few, but this I am en-

---

*"Something great and immeasurable." [*JMN*]

couraged to expect. If however the individual himself lack that moral worth which is to secure the last, his studies upon the first are idly spent. The most prodigious genius, a seraph's eloquence will shamefully defeat its own end, if it has not first won the heart of the defender to the cause he defends, but the coolest reason cannot censure my choice when I oblige myself *professionally* to a life which all wise men freely & advisedly adopt. I put no great restraint on myself & can therefore claim little merit in a manner of life which chimes with inclination & habit. But I would learn to love Virtue for her own sake, I would have my pen so guided as was Milton's when a deep & enthusiastic love of goodness & of God dictated the Comus to the bard, or that prose rhapsody in the 3rd Book of Prelaty. I would sacrifice inclination to the interest of mind & soul. I would remember that "Spare Fast oft with Gods doth diet," that Justinian devoted but one out of twenty four hours to sleep & this week (for instance) I will remember to curtail my dinner & supper sensibly & rise from table each day with an appetite; & so see if* it be fact that I can understand more clearly.

I have mentioned a defect of character; perhaps it is not one, but many. Every wise man aims at an entire conquest of himself. We applaud as possessed of extraordinary good sense, one who never makes the slightest mistake in speech or action; one in whom not only every important step of life, but every passage of conversation, every duty of the day, even every movement of every muscle—hands, feet, & tongue, are measured & dictated by deliberate reason. I am not assuredly that excellent creature. A score of words & deeds issue from me daily, of which I am not the master. They are begotten of weakness & born of shame. I cannot assume the elevation I ought—but lose the influence I should exert among those of meaner or younger understanding, for want of sufficient *bottom* in my nature, for want of that confidence of manner which springs from an erect mind which is without fear & without reproach. In my frequent humiliation, even before women & children I am compelled to remember the poor boy who cried, "I told you, Father, they would find me out." Even those feelings which are counted noble & generous, take in me the taint of frailty. For my strong propensity to friendship, instead of working out its manly ends, degenerates to a fondness for particular casts of feature perchance not unlike the doting of old King James. Stateliness & silence hang very like Mokannah's suspicious silver veil, only concealing what is best not shewn. What is called a warm heart, I have not.

The stern accuser Conscience cries that the Catalogue of Confessions is not yet full. I am a lover of indolence, & of the belly. And the

---

*N.B. Till Tuesday Evg next. [RWE]

good have a right to ask the Neophyte who wears this garment of scarlet sin, why he comes where all are apparelled in white? Dares he hope that some patches of pure & generous feeling, some bright fragments of lofty thought, it may be of divine poesy shall charm the eye away from all the particoloured shades of his Character? And when he is clothed in the vestments of the priest, & has inscribed on his forehead 'Holiness to the Lord', & wears on his breast the breastplate of the tribes, then can the Ethiopian change his skin & the unclean be pure? Or how shall I strenuously enforce on men the duties & habits to which I am a stranger? Physician, heal thyself. I need not go far for an answer to so natural a question. I am young in my everlasting existence. I already discern the deep dye of elementary errors, which threaten to colour its infinity of duration. And I judge that if I devote my nights & days *in form*, to the service of God & the War against Sin—I shall soon be prepared to do the same *in substance*.

I cannot accurately estimate my chances of success, in my profession, & in life. Were it just to judge the future from the past, they would be very low. In my case I think it is not. I have never expected success in my present employment. My scholars are carefully instructed, my money is faithfully earned, but the instructor is little wiser. & the duties were never congenial with my disposition. Thus far the dupe of hope I have trudged on with my bundle at my back, and my eye fixed on the distant hill where my burden would fall. It may be I shall write *dupe* a long time to come & the end of life shall intervene betwixt me & the release. My trust is that my profession shall be my regeneration of mind, manners, inward & outward estate; or rather my starting point, for I have hoped to put on eloquence as a robe, and by goodness and zeal and the awfulness of virtue to press & prevail over the false judgments, the rebel passions & corrupt habits of men. We blame the past, we magnify & gild the future and are not wiser for the multitude of days. Spin on, Ye of the adamantine spindle, spin on, my fragile thread.

April–May 1824

There is a dreaminess about my mode of life (which may be a depravity), which loosens the tenacity of what should be most tenacious—this my grasp on heaven & earth. I am the servant more than the master of my fates. They seem to lead me into many a slough where I do no better than despond. And as to the life I lead & the Works & the days, I should blush to recite the unprofitable account. But prophets & philosophers assure me that I am immortal and sometimes my own imagination goes into a fever with its hopes & conceptions. Tell me, my soul, if this be true; if these indolent days & frivolous nights, these insignificant accomplishments, this handful of thought, this pittance of vir-

tues are to form my trust & claim on an existence as imperishable as my
Maker's.

July 8, 1824

In the succession of ages, the times must always assume & utter a
decided tone some time, before its spirit can be embodied in a proportioned system of education which shall be faithful to public sentiment.
It was perhaps a late generalization to speak of the spirit of an age but it
escapes the imputation of paradox. For men are so close in their connexions & press so hard on each other that it is improbable a strong sentiment, or a marked character should anywhere arise without sending its
strong contagion to an indefinite extent. Sympathy's "electric chain
wherewith we are darkly bound" is true to its office of transmitting
common excitements of whatever sort. Man of every hue & race is sensitive to the lot of man & though the drops be severed a moment from
the mass of waters they always rejoice to reunite in a perfect union.

July 18, 1824

When this country is censured for its foolhardy ambition to take a
stand in its green years among old & proud nations it is no reproach &
no disqualification to be told But you have no literature. It is admitted
we have none. But we have what is better. We have a government and a
national spirit that is better than poems or histories & these have a premature ripeness that is incompatible with the rapid production of the
latter. We should take shame to ourselves as sluggish & Boeotian if it
were righteously said that we had done nothing for ourselves neither in
learning nor arts nor government nor political economy. But we see &
feel that in the space of two generations this nation has taken such a start
as already to outstrip the bold freedom of modern speculation which ordinarily (universally, but for this case) is considerably in advance of
practice. No man calls Mr Hume an old fashioned & short sighted politician yet many pages of his history have lost their credit already by the
practical confutation of their principles. 'Tis no disgrace to tell Newton
he is no poet nor America even.

July–Aug. 1824

Apart from the vast mess of transitory volumes which occasional
politics or a thousand ephemeral magnalia elicit, books for the most part
record the progress of science or exhibit only successive forms of taste in
Poetry, letters & fiction. But there is another sort of book which appears
now & then in the world once in two or three Centuries perhaps and
which soon or late gets a foothold in popular esteem. I allude to those
books which collect & embody the wisdom of their times & so mark the

stages of human improvement. Such are the Proverbs of Solomon, the Essays of Montaigne, & eminently the Essays of Bacon. Such also (though in my judgment in far less degree) is the proper merit of Mr. Pope's judicious poems, the Moral Essays & Essay on Man which without originality seize upon all the popular speculations floating among sensible men & give them in a compact & graceful form to the following age. I should like to add another volume to this valuable work. I am not so foolhardy as to write Sequel to Bacon on my title page, and there are some reasons that induce me to suppose that the undertaking of this enterprise does not imply any censurable arrogance. Although it is perhaps a generalization which the mind but tardily makes to speak of the character of a *Nation* or *Age*, it is yet a manner of thinking which has a foundation in fact. There is frequently, perhaps invariably, a spirit & tone of thought according to which a multitude's habits of feeling may be guided without any one reaching all its results or viewing more than a few subjects in that light.

Why has my motley diary no jokes? Because it is a soliloquy & every man is grave alone.

Oct.? 1824

I have ever been noted for my fondness for children & children are always fond of me. Nature has so vigilantly provided for the care of children in the affections of parents that at a certain season of life these irrepressible feelings break forth in bachelors also & secure a thousand endearments for the child that comes in their way.

A Reluctant Priest
1825–1832

I T MAY BE a measure of the divided spirit Emerson brought to his divinity studies that, about a month after commencing them, he suffered eye trouble sufficiently serious to interrupt his work. Emerson's own description of his problem—he speaks of his eyes as "refusing to read"—suggests a psychosomatic origin or component to the complaint; and indeed the whole period between Emerson's enrolling in divinity school and his being approbated to preach in October 1826 is marked by persistent difficulty with his health.

It seems particularly significant that the onset of lung disease that drove Emerson south in quest of renewed vigor occurred at the time he was attempting to make his mark by preaching from the pulpit of Boston's First Church—the pulpit his father had occupied. This incident casts an interesting light retrospectively on a journal entry from January 1825, in which he notes that though he was educated to prize "pedigree" it was his own humor to despise it. His father's sister Mary, he goes on, frequently recited "the virtues of her & mine ancestors. They have been clergymen for many generations & the piety of all & the eloquence of many is yet praised in the Churches. But the dead sleep in their moonless night; my business is with the living." That Waldo was chafing under the weight of his ministerial ancestry seems clear enough; and it is equally clear that docilely following in his father's footsteps was a source of considerable conflict.

The journals of these years are filled with questioning of the Christian tradition and the role of the priest; over and over again

51

we see the young Emerson struggling, not very successfully, to accommodate his new vision to the prisms supplied by the past. As a result, his strong condemnation of his own profession on January 10, 1832, hardly comes as a surprise: "It is the best part of the man, I sometimes think, that revolts most against his being the minister." That best part was the one that refused to conform to the expectations and practices handed down from father to son: "The difficulty is that we do not make a world of our own but fall into institutions already made & have to accomodate ourselves to them."

Emerson's journey to Charleston and St. Augustine between November 1826 and April 1827 not only improved his health but also strengthened him in his professional and spiritual crisis. Voyaging from Florida to South Carolina, he shared a cabin with Achille Murat, the urbane and brilliant nephew of Napoleon, and found himself drawn to this ardent truth seeker who was also "a consistent Atheist." Emerson was undoubtedly surprised to discover that he loved and honored "this intrepid doubter" who was still noble and virtuous despite his rejection of all religious tradition, and his stirring journal entry of April 17, 1827, seems to owe much to his realization that a man without belief or adherence to a creed could nevertheless be good and true. Emerson was moved, accordingly, to celebrate the mind's "own glory" and choose "greatness of soul" over conventional achievement. He felt a new life quickening within and a new career expanding before him. "Strange thoughts start up like angels in my way & beckon me onward."

Whatever the nature of these strange thoughts, Emerson in fact continued upon his return home to study and preach and worry about his health. But an angel of sorts was indeed about to cross his path and change his life. In December 1827 Waldo preached in Concord, New Hampshire, and met the lovely, intelligent, and delicate heiress who was to become his first wife on September 30, 1829. The seventeen-year-old Ellen Louisa Tucker was sensitive and devout, and her religious intensity must have been sharpened by her awareness that she was dying of tuberculosis. Emerson's anxiety over his own health and prospects was now naturally transferred to Ellen, and when she died in February 1831 he effectively buried with her his commitment to continuing as a Unitarian minister. Ellen's death, in fact, would make it possible for Emerson to contemplate leaving the pulpit, since her portion of the Tucker inheritance would eventually come to him and allow him to eke out a living as a lecturer and writer.

Though the first half of Ellen's money would not be his until the spring of 1834, Emerson instituted legal proceedings shortly after her death and straightaway felt compelled to ask what objects he was pursuing "with undivided aim." He wondered whether or not he was truly fixed "by principles" and secure in the stakes he had planted. He was fearful that his sect—indeed, every sect—was suspicious of the "whole of truth" and devoted to stifling "the flame of holy love which young & heroic minds are nourishing"; he worried too that the priest was necessarily forced to become a divided man, feeling one thing in private but saying something else in public. Obviously disgusted with the requirement that he act always like a saint, he rejected the notion that any man should "try to angel it thro' the world."

Although Emerson's formal break with Boston's Second Church (where he had become junior pastor in January 1829) would occur over the issue of his refusing to serve the Eucharist, it is thus clear that he had been a reluctant priest for a good while. He had come to realize that his true ministry could take place only outside the church. "The profession is antiquated," he noted in June 1832. "In an altered age, we worship in the dead forms of our forefathers." Emerson was even willing to entertain the notion that a "Socratic paganism" might be preferable to "an effete superannuated Christianity." All that remained for this conscientious apostate was to imitate Luther and stand his ground. Accordingly, he resigned his pastorate in September 1832 and, aware that he needed a moratorium for his ailing body and troubled emotions, he looked toward Europe. On Christmas day, secure in his principles but vague in his aims, he set sail for the consolations and wisdom of the Old World.

Jan. 4, 1825
I have closed my school. I have begun a new year. I have begun my studies. And this day a moment of indolence engendered in me phantasms & feelings that struggled to find vent in rhyme. I thought of the

passage of my years, of their even & eventless tenor and of the crisis which is but a little way before when a month will determine the dark or bright dye they must assume forever. I turn now to my lamp & my tomes. I have nothing to do with society. My unpleasing boyhood is past, my youth wanes into the age of man and what is the unsuppressed glee, the cheering games, the golden hair & shining eyes of youth unto me? I withdraw myself from their spell. A solemn voice commands me to retire. And if in those scenes my blood & brow have been cold, if my tongue has stammered where fashion & gaiety were voluble & I have had no grace amid the influences of beauty & the festivities of Grandeur I shall not hastily conclude my soul ignobly born & its horoscope fully cast. I will not yet believe that because it has lain so tranquil, great argument could not make it stir. I will not believe because I cannot unite dignity, as many can to Folly that I am not born to fill the eye of great expectation, to speak when the people listens nor to cast my mite into the great treasury of morals & intellect. I will not quite despair nor quench my flambeau in the dust of Easy live & quiet die.

Jan. 1825

It is my own humor to despise pedigree. I was educated to prize it. The kind Aunt whose cares instructed my youth (& whom may God reward) told me oft the virtues of her & mine ancestors. They have been clergymen for many generations & the piety of all & the eloquence of many is yet praised in the Churches. But the dead sleep in their moonless night; my business is with the living.

Feb. 8, 1825

It is the evening of February eighth, which was never renowned that I know. But be that as it may 'tis the last evening I spend in Canterbury. I go to my College Chamber tomorrow a little changed for better or worse since I left it in 1821. I have learned a few more names & dates, additional facility of expression, the gage of my own ignorance, its sounding places, & bottomless depths. I have inverted my inquiries two or three times on myself, and have learned what a sinner & a saint I am. My cardinal vice of intellectual dissipation—sinful strolling from book to book, from care to idleness, is my cardinal vice still; is a malady that belongs to the Chapter of Incurables. I have written two or three hundred pages that will be of use to me. I have earned two or three thousand dollars which have paid my debts & obligated my neighbours so that I thank Heaven I can say none of my house is the worse for me. In short, I have grown older and have seen something of the vanity & something of the value of existence, have seen what shallow things men are & how independent of external circumstances may be the states of mind called good & ill.

Feb. 1825

Today I went to Quincy to see its Patriarch. The old President sat in a large stuffed arm chair, dressed in a blue coat, black small-clothes, white stockings. And a cotton cap covered his bald head. When we were introduced he held out his hand & welcomed us. We told him he must let us come & join our Congratulations to those of the nation on the happiness of his house. He thanked us & said "I am rejoiced because the nation is happy. The time of gratulations & congratulations is nearly over with me. I am astonished that I have lived to see & know of this event. I have lived now nearly a century (He will be ninety next October) a long harrassed & distracted life." I said, the world thinks a good deal of joy has been mixed with it. "The world does not know" he said "how much toil anxiety & sorrow I have suffered." I asked if Mr Adams' letter of acceptance had been read to him. Yes, he said, and then added, My son has more political prudence than any man that I know who has existed in my time. He never was put off his guard. And I hope he will continue so. But what effect age may work in diminishing the power of his mind, I do not know; it has been very much on the stretch ever since he was born. He has always been laborious child & man from infancy. When Mr J. Q. Adams' age was mentioned he said he was 58, or would be in July, and mentioned that all the Presidents were of the same age. Gen Washington was about 58, and I was about 58, & Mr Jefferson & Mr Madison, & Mr Monroe. We asked him when he expected to see Mr Adams, he said, "never; Mr Adams will not come to Quincy but to my funeral. It would be a great satisfaction to me to see him but I don't wish him to come on my account." He spoke of Mr Lechmere whom he well remembered "to come down daily at great age to walk in the old townhouse, and I wish I could walk as well as he. He was collector of the customs for many years under the royal government." Edward said, "I suppose, Sir, you wouldn't have taken his place even to walk as well as he." "No," he said, "*that* was not what I wanted." He talked of Whitefield and remembered when he was Freshman in College to have come in to the Old South (I think) to hear him, but could not get in; he however saw him thro' a window & distinctly heard all. "He had a voice such as I never heard before or since. He *cast* it out so that you might hear it at the meeting house (pointing towards Quincy Meeting house) and had the grace of a dancing master, of an actor of plays. His voice & his manner helped him more than his sermons. I went with Jonathan Sewall." And you were pleased with him, Sir? "Pleased, I was delighted

beyond measure." We asked if at Whitefield's return the same popular-
ity continued, "Not the same fury," he said, "not the same wild enthusiasm as before, but a greater esteem as he became more known. He did
not terrify, but was admired."

We spent about an hour in his room. He talks very distinctly for so
old a man—enters bravely into long sentences which are interrupted by
want of breath but carries them invariably to a conclusion without ever
correcting a word. He spoke of the new novels of Cooper, & Peep at the
Pilgrims & Saratoga with approbation & named with accuracy the characters in them. He likes to have a person always reading to him or company talking in his chamber, and is better the next day we were told
after having visitors in his chamber from morning till night. He received
a premature report of his son's election on Sunday afternoon without
any excitement and calmly told the reporter he had been hoaxed for it
was not yet time for any news to arrive. The informer however something damped in his heart insisted on repairing to the Meetinghouse &
the Congregation in the midst of service were so overjoyed that they
rose in their seats & cheered thrice. Mr. Whitney dismissed them immediately. We were told that his son Judge Adams can at any time excite
him in a moment to great indignation. He mentioned to us that he had
spoken to the President of the late Plymouth oration & said Mr Everett
had ambition enough to publish it doubtless. The old gentleman exclaimed with great vehemence "I would to God there were more ambition in the country, ambition of that laudable kind to excel."

June 1825?

A man's *style* is his intellectual Voice only in part under his controul.
It has its own proper tone & manner which when he is not thinking of it,
it will always assume. He can mimic the voices of others, he can modu-
late it with the occasion & the passion, but it has its own individual nature.

1825?

I have heard Shakespeare's Blow winds & crack your cheeks, &c. &
the rest, accused of false taste & bombast. I do not find this fault. And
tho' I might not allow it in another, even in his mad king, yet I am not
offended by this passage in Lear. For as the Romans were so idolatrous
of Cato's virtue that when he had drunk wine they would rather believe
that intemperance was virtue than that Cato was guilty of a vice, so I am
afraid to circumscribe within rhetorical rules, the circuits of such a
towering & majestic mind, and a taste the most exquisite that God ever
informed among men.

Jan. 8, 1826

I come with mended eyes to my ancient friend & consoler. Has the interval of silence made the writer wiser? Does his mind teem with well weighed judgments? The moral & intellectual universe has not halted because the eye of the observer was closed. . . .

Since I wrote before, I know something more of the grounds of hope & fear for what is to come. But if my knowledge is greater so is my courage. I know that I *know* next to nothing but I know too that the amount of probabilities is vast, both in mind & in morals. It is not certain that God exists but that he does not is a most bewildering & improbable chimera.

I rejoice that I live when the world is so old. There is the same difference between living with Adam & living with me as in going into a new house unfinished damp & empty, & going into a long occupied house where the time & taste of its inhabitants has accumulated a thousand useful contrivances, has furnished the chambers, stocked the cellars and filled the library. In the new house every comer must do all for himself. In the old mansion there are butlers, cooks, grooms, & valets. In the new house all must work & work with the hands. In the old one there are poets who sing, actors who play & ladies who dress & smile. O ye lovers of the past, judge between my houses. I would not be elsewhere than I am.

Jan.? 1826

The world is clothed by our imaginations in beautiful delusions. Who would rise from his sluggish couch if the colours were withdrawn & we beheld the ghastly reality of things?

March 16, 1826

My external condition may to many seem comfortable, to some enviable but I think that few men ever suffered *more genuine misery than I have suffered.

March 27, 1826

My years are passing away. Infirmities are already stealing on me that may be the deadly enemies that are to dissolve me to dirt and little is yet done to establish my consideration among my contemporaries & less to get a memory when I am gone. I confess the foolish ambition to be valued, with qualification. I do not want to be known by them that know me not but where my name is mentioned I would have it re-

---

*in degree not in amount. [RWE]

spected. My recollections of early life are not very pleasant. I find or imagine in it a meanness, a character of unfounded pride cleaving to certain passages which might come to many ears that death has not yet shut. I would have the echoes of a good name come to the same ears to remove such imputation. I do fully disclaim the vulgar hunger to be known, to have one's name hawked in great capitals in the street.

April 12, 1826

Most men who have given their attention to the prayers publicly offered in a Christian Congregation have felt in the institution an unsuitableness to their feelings. They have found themselves ready in their own exculpation to accuse a certain stubbornness of sympathy in their natural disposition or else their past lives of such discontinuance of the offices of piety as has issued in a total incapacity of joining their fellowmen in this venerable service. Disuse has made their contemplations of their Creator cold & ungrateful to their understandings. The man who prays is in quite another mood from the man who hears—and tones & language which we have once become accustomed to regard with suspicion or at best with admiration, it will be long ere we learn to listen to them with sympathy. The truth is public prayer is rather the offspring of our notions of what *ought* to be, than of what *is*. It has grown out of the sentiment of a few rather than the reason of many. Indeed we have said all—and I am sorry to say it—in characterizing it as an appeal to our veneration instead of our sympathy.

Aug. 3, 1826

Yesterday I attended the funeral solemnities in Fanueil Hall in honor of John Adams & Thomas Jefferson. The Oration of Mr Webster was worthy of his fame & what is much more was worthy of the august occasion. Never I think were the awful charms of person, manners, & voice outdone. For tho' in the beginning unpromising & in other parts imperfect in what was truly grand he fully realized the boldest conception of eloquence.

Sept. 23, 1826

Health, action, happiness. How they ebb from me! Poor Sisyphus saw his stone stop once at least when Orpheus chaunted. I must roll mine up & up & up how high a hill.... It would give me very great pleasure to be well.

Sept.–Oct. 1826

Die? what should you die for? Maladies? What maladies? Dost not know that Nature has her course as well as Disease? that Nature has not only helps & facilities for all beneficial operations but fangs and weapons for her enemies also? Die? pale face, lily liver! go about your business and when it comes to the point then die like a gentleman.

1826?

I pursue my speculations with confidence & tho' I can discern no remoter conclusion I doubt not the train I commence extends farther than I see as the first artificer of glass did not know he was instructing men in astronomy & restoring sight to those from whom nature had taken it. There is no thought which is not seed as well as fruit. It spawns like fish.

Dec. 13, 1826   Charleston, S.C.

I have for a fortnight past writ nothing. My bosom's lord sits somewhat drowsily on his throne. It is because I think not at all that I write not at all. There is to me something alarming in these *periods* of mentality. One day I am a doctor, & the next I am a dunce, that is so far as relates to my own resources.... The true account of the scarecrow is this. At sea a fortnight elapses in which I always remember myself to have been in times past a channel thro' which flowed bright & lofty thought. But I find in me no disposition, no power to recreate for myself the same brilliant entertainment. I come to land & the weary days succeed each other as on the desolate sea, but this coveted power does not return, & every attempt to force the soul is heavily baffled. Now suppose it should never return; the causes are concealed, the sun & the moon are hidden which affect the ebbs & flowings of the intellectual tides. They are determined by something out of me & higher than me.... This is our boasted human dignity & majesty & so forth. We are such bubbles that when we mount, we see not how; and when we grow great we cannot commend ourselves. Much less can we discern the secret of life (I speak of the soul) or confide with the approbation of reason in its continuance. Peace then to the pride of man—there are states of feeling in which it must appear either laughable or disgusting. And yet the cinders will live in its ashes & make the man glad with a foolish gladness, that they are not utterly extinct. It is the leading idea of Pascal's Religious Meditations to contrast what is grand & pitiful in human nature. And I can't write a page in one tone of sentiment tho' that tone be grounded in truth without doing injustice to the *whole* of Man. God has balanced us. And you remember Luther's comparison of human nature to a drunkard on horseback; put it up on one side it falls on t'other. 'Tis a lobsided thing.

Dec. 16? 1826 Charleston, S.C.

Manners seem to be more closely under the influence of climate. They belong more to the body than the soul, & so come under the influence of the sun. They are accomodations of the motions of the body to moods of the mind. In Lapland men are savage; in Norway they are plain spoken and use no ceremony; in England some; in France much; in Spain more. In like manner no man has travelled in the United States from the North to the South without observing the change & amelioration of manners. In this city, it is most observable, the use of the conventions of address among the lowest classes which are coarsely neglected by the labouring classes at the North. Two negroes recognize each other in the street tho' both in rags & both it may be balancing a burden on their heads with the same graduated advances of salutation, that well bred men who are strangers to each other would use in Boston. They do not part before they have shaken hands & bid Goodbye with an inclination of the head. There is a grace & perfection too about these courtesies which could not be imitated by a northern labourer where he designed to be extremely civil. Indeed I have never seen an awkward Carolinian.

Jan. 4, 1827 Charleston, S.C.

A new year has opened its bitter cold eye upon me, here where I sought warm weather. A new year has opened on me & found my best hopes set aside, my projects all suspended. A new year has found me perchance no more fit to live & no more fit to die than the last. But the eye of the mind has at least grown richer in its hoard of observations. It has detected some more of the darkling lines that connect past events to the present, and the present to the future.

Jan. 1827

If an ingenious man lived long enough, he might learn to talk by system, in a manner out of all comparison better than men now use. Suppose him to keep a book of commonplaces & as his knowledge grew to put down on the page of each the theories that occurred. It is clear that in process of time it would embrace all the ordinary subjects of human discourse. He wouldn't talk so well as those who have the natural talent. Nature has fetches which art cannot reach; bewitching felicities, affecting pauses that the mere practice of a moderate genius wouldn't attain. But something would doubtless be accomplished that would put to shame the cheap extemporaneous draggletail dialogue that takes place in our evening companies even among men of letters & ambition from candlelight till the bell strikes nine & breaks up the company.

* * *

We generalize very fast. I very readily learned the Jew face. And am prone to detect a likeness in people of the same name; as *Webbs.*

It is the rare fortune of those who are born in these times and this country to be born for the blessing of the world.

St. Augustine, E. Florida

And what is the amount of all that is called religion in the world? Who is he that has seen God of whom so much is known or where is one that has risen from the dead? Satisfy me beyond the possibility of doubt of the certainty of all that is told me concerning the other world and I will fulfil the conditions on which my salvation is suspended. The believer tells me he has an evidence historical & internal which make the presumption so strong that it is almost a certainty that it rests on the highest of probabilities. Yes; but change that imperfect to perfect evidence & I too will be a Christian. But now it must be admitted I am not certain that any of these things are true. The nature of God may be different from what he is represented. I never beheld him. I do not know that he exists. This good which invites me now is visible & specific. I will at least embrace it this time by way of experiment, & if it is wrong certainly God can in some manner signify his will in future. Moreover I will guard against evil consequences resulting to others by the vigilance with which I conceal it.

Jan.–Feb. 1827
Peculiarities of the present Age

1. Instead of the systematic pursuit of science men cultivate the knowledge of anecdotes.
2. It is said to be the age of the first person singular.
3. The reform of the Reformation.
4. Transcendentalism. Metaphysics & ethics look inwards—and France produces Mad. de Stael; England, Wordsworth; America, Sampson Reed; as well as Germany, Swedenborg.
5. The immense extent of the English language & influence. The Eng. tongue is spreading over all N. America except Mexico, over Demerary &c, Jamaica &c, Indostan, New Holland & the Australian islands.
6. The paper currency.
   Joint stock companies.
7. The disposition among men of *associating* themselves to promote any purpose. (Millions of societies.)

Feb. 2, 1827   St. Augustine

With a little thinking, passive almost amidst our sensations, & rounding our lives with a little sleep, we count off our days with a prodigal hand. The months depart & soon I shall measure back my way to my own people. But I feel how scanty is the addition I have made to my knowledge or my virtue. Day by day I associate with men to whom my society yields no noticeable amount of advantage or pleasure. I have heard of heights of virtue & lives of philanthropy. I am cold & solitary & lead a life comfortable to myself & useless to others. Yet I believe myself to be a moral agent of an indestructible nature & designed to stand in sublime relations to God & to my fellow men; to contribute in my proper enjoyments to the general welfare. What then, young pilot, who by chart & compass point out to others the shoals they must shun & the haven they must seek—art not thyself a castaway? Will you say you have no call to more austere virtue than you daily exhibit? Have you computed the moral influences of this quiescence, this waking torpor of the soul & found them adequate to what may in equity be demanded of you? Young pilot! you dare not say Aye.

Feb. 16, 1827   My weight is lb. 141½.

It is not those speculations which are most abstruse that either deserve or receive the best reward from fame. The only dispensers of fame are the middle class of mankind & they will not value the far sought abstraction, no matter how inaccessible or sublime, more than the fowl on the dung hill regards the pearl. It came from distant climes, it was got with toil, it was hoarded with care yet having no suitableness to the wants of the finder is less valued than a kernel of corn.

But those writings which indicate valuable genius treat of common things. Those minds which God has formed for any powerful influence over men, have never effeminately shrunk from intercourse with unnurtured minds. They scorned to be tender & squeamish. Human destiny is not nice. They have taken hold with manly hand on its vulgar wants; on poverty & riches; on pain of body & pain of mind, on the inconveniences of goodness & the compensating hope. Besides the advantage of being understood, it is a groundless fear that the author loses a jot of true dignity by this humility in the choice of topics; for, the high & low points of human life are so nearly allied that no man of powerful sense ever found himself on any subject far removed from the sources of what is deeper in human thought. It is a near neighbourhood, that of greatness, of destiny & lowness of lot; that of mind & matter; that of man & God. It is like our natural existence. Though we be pigmies of a few feet it is not a dungeon wall which confines us to the earth. There is nothing between us & the infinite Universe. So our life which had its beginning a few summers ago from a sorry succession of some dull material causes, walks with God on the other side thro' time & chance, thro' the fall of suns & systems, through unbounded ages, unhurt & immortal. 'Tis the rich treasure in earthen vessels. Such being the character of our life such must also be the character of its descriptions.

Feb. 25, 1827

I attended mass in the Catholic Church. The mass is in Latin & the sermon in English & the audience who are Spaniards understand neither. The services have been recently interrupted by the imprisonment of the worthy father for debt in the Castle of St Marks.

March 1, 1827

I found here a gentleman from N. Carolina who gave me some account of the monstrous absurdities of the Methodists at their Camp Meetings in that state. He related an instance of several of these fanatics jumping about on all fours, imitating the barking of dogs & surrounding a tree in which they pretended they had *"treed Jesus!"*

March 1827

The negroes in Charleston have a new theory of the seasons viz that the number of people from the North bring the cold with them.

April 6, 1827   Charleston   25 March weighed 152 lb.

A new event is added to the quiet history of my life. I have connected myself by friendship to a man who with as ardent a love of truth as that which animates me, with a mind surpassing mine in the variety of its research, & sharpened & strengthened to an energy for *action*, to which I have no pretension by advantages of birth & practical connexion with mankind beyond almost all men in the world—is, yet, that which I had ever supposed a creature only of the imagination—a consistent Atheist, and a disbeliever in the existence, &, of course, in the immortality of the soul. My faith in these points is strong & I trust, as I live, indestructible. Meantime I love & honour this intrepid doubter. His soul is noble, & his virtue as the virtue of a Sadducee must always be, is sublime.

April 17, 1827   Charleston

Let the glory of the world go where it will, the mind has its own glory. What it doth, endures. No man can serve many masters. And often the choice is not given you between greatness in the world & greatness of soul which you will choose, but both advantages are not compatible. The night is fine; the stars shed down their severe influ-

Achille Murat (1801–1847): "I love & honour this intrepid
doubter."

ences upon me and I feel a joy in my solitude that the merriment of vulgar society can never communicate. There is a pleasure in the thought
that the particular tone of my mind at this moment may be new in the
Universe; that the emotions of this hour may be peculiar & unexampled
in the whole eternity of moral being. I lead a new life. I occupy new
ground in the world of spirits, untenanted before. I commence a career
of thought & action which is expanding before me into a distant & daz-
zling infinity. Strange thoughts start up like angels in my way & beckon
me onward. I doubt not I tread on the highway that leads to the Divinity. And why shall I not be content with these thoughts & this being
which give a majesty to my nature & forego the ambition to shine in the
frivolous assemblies of men where the genuine objects of my ambition
are not revered or known?

May 19, 1827   Alexandria

Mr Adams went out aswimming the other day into the Potomac and went near to a boat which was coming down the river. Some rude blackguards were in it who not knowing the character of the swimmer amused themselves with laughing at his bald head as it poppled up & down in the water & as they drew nearer threatened to crack open his round pate if he came nigh them. The President of the United States was I believe compelled to wave the point of honour & seek a more retired bathing place.

Sept.–Oct. 1827

Aunt Mary used her thimble twice as a seal to once for her needle & I have heard my mother remark that her own was too much worn ever to make the indented impression on wax that Aunt Mary's did.

Dec.? 1827

Robinson Crusoe when in any perplexity was wont to retire to a part of his cave which he called his thinking corner. Devout men have found a stated spot so favorable to a habit of religious feeling that they have worn the solid rock of the oratory with their knees. I have found my ideas very refractory to the usual bye laws of Association. In the graveyard my muscles were twitched by some ludicrous recollections and I am apt to be solemn at a ball. But whilst places are alike to me I make great distinction between states of mind. My days are made up of the irregular succession of a very few different tones of feeling. These are my feasts & fasts.

It is said public opinion will not bear it. Really? Public opinion, I am sorry to say, will bear a great deal of nonsense. There is scarce any absurdity so gross whether in religion, politics, science, or manners, which it will not bear. . . . It will bear Andrew Jackson for President. . . . It will bear the obscenities of the Boston Theatre. Lord Bacon never spoke truer word than when he said There's more of the fool in the world than the wise.

1827?

There's a great difference between good poetry & everlasting poetry.

Shakespeare alludes to himself nowhere in his drama. The sonnets. Homer keeps out of sight except in two places. A grand trait. It is like Providence. . . . A different age. In antiquity nature towered above all man had done: it sunk the personal importance of man. The bard taught as the Minister preaches & felt an impertinence in introducing self. Now

Man has grown bigger, a commercial, political, canalling, writing animal. Philosophy inverts itself & poetry grows egotistical.

Shakespeare immortalizes his characters. They live to every age & as we say of Christianity have a prospective adaptation. Ben Jonson's are all dead. Read Alchemist & the rest. They are all in brocade.

Jan. 8, 1828

I have once or twice been apprehensive that I was reading in vain, that the cultivation of my mind did not turn to any good account in my intercourse with men. I am now satisfied of the contrary. I have every inch of my merits. More is conceded to me than I have a just title to. I am oftener compelled to deplore my ignorance than to be pleased with my knowledge. I have no knowledge that I do not want.

In Concord, N.H. I visited the prison & went into the cells. At this season, they shut up the convicts in these little granite chambers at about 4 o'clock P.M. & let them out, about 7 o'clock A.M.—15 dreadful hours.

Jan. 16, 1828

The main difficulty of life is to strike the balance betwixt contending claims. I am embarrassed by doubts in all my purposes, & in all my opinions. The best & surest advantages in the world are thought by large numbers of people & on very plausible grounds to be evils. The freedom of thought & action in this country often appears tending to the worst & most malignant results, chaos come again. The expediency of publishing truth is daily denied. The best manner of employing the mind whether in study or in invention who will determine even for himself?

For me I fear I lose days in determining how hours should be spent. A scholar is perplexed by the necessity of choosing between many books & many studies and a shade of sorrow thrown over his meditation by the comparison between the magnitude of the work to be done & the shortness of life. I regard them all, these doubts of ours, as hints God has interwoven in our condition to remind us of the temper that becomes us; that diffidence & candor suit us better than arrogance & dogmatism & to quicken our curiosity (a curiosity always respectable) to know the secrets of the other world.

Feb. 14, 1828   Divinity Hall

Burnap was very witty tonight. He said There was one man who had the queerest reputation—Dr Watts—such a mixture of heathenism & scholastic learning & Calvinism & love & despair & mullygrubs—he was the funniest old cock in the theological walk; that that old Betty should be one of the three legs that support the Trinity & that the Church should go chanting his hymns for centuries mistaking the effusions of belly ache for the inspirations of David—was the greatest phenomenon. Then that he should write a treatise on Logic, & then one on the Improvement of the mind! Then, that his sun should set clear after being foggy all day! And Dr Doddridge! who owed all his fame to his getting up at five o'clock every morning & writing for two hours what every body knew & said before.

July 1828

It is a peculiarity (I find by observation upon others) of humour in me, my strong propensity for strolling. I deliberately shut up my books in a cloudy July noon, put on my old clothes & old hat & slink away to the whortleberry bushes & slip with the greatest satisfaction into a little cowpath where I am sure I can defy observation. This point gained, I solace myself for hours with picking blue berries & other trash of the woods far from fame behind the birch trees. I seldom enjoy hours as I do these. I remember them in winter; I expect them in spring. I do not know a creature that I think has the same humour or would think it respectable. . . .

When I consider the constitutional calamity of my family which in its falling upon Edward has buried at once so many towering hopes— with whatever reason I have little apprehension of my own liability to the same evil. I have so much mixture of *silliness* in my intellectual frame that I think Providence has tempered me against this. My brother lived & acted & spoke with preternatural energy. My own manner is sluggish; my speech sometimes flippant, sometimes embarrassed & ragged; my actions (if I may say so) are of a passive kind. Edward had always great power of face. I have none. I laugh; I blush; I look ill tempered; against my will & against my interest. But all this imperfection as it appears to me . . . is a ballast—as things go—is a defence.

I like to have a man's knowledge comprehend more than one class of topics, one row of shelves. I like a man who likes to see a fine barn as well as a good tragedy.

Dec. 1828

Is it not true what we so reluctantly hear that men are but the mouthpieces of a great progressive destiny in as much as regards literature. I had rather asked is not the age gone by of the great splendour of English poetry, & will it not be impossible for any age soon to vie with the pervading etherial poesy of Herbert, Shakspeare, Marvell, Herrick,

Milton, Ben Jonson, at least to represent any thing like their peculiar form of ravishing verse? It is the head of human poetry. Homer & Virgil & Dante & Tasso & Byron & Wordsworth have powerful genius whose amplest claims I cheerfully acknowledge.—But 'tis a pale ineffectual fire when theirs shines. They would lie on my shelf in undisturbed honour for years, if these Saxon lays stole in my ear. I have for them an affectionate admiration I have for nothing else. They set me on speculations. They move my wonder at myself. They suggest the great endowments of the spiritual man. They open glimpses of the heaven that is in the intellect. When I am caught by a magic word & drop the book to explore the infinite charm—to run along the line of that ray—I feel the longevity of the mind; I admit the evidence of the immortality of the soul. Well, as I said, I am afraid the season of this rare fruit is irrecoverably past; that the earth has made such a mutation of its nodes, that the heat will never reach again that Hesperian garden in which alone these apricots & pomegranates grew.

Dec. 21, 1828   Concord, N.H.

I have now been four days engaged to Ellen Louisa Tucker. Will my Father in Heaven regard us with kindness, and as he hath, as we trust, made us for each other, will he be pleased to strengthen & purify & prosper & eternize our affection! Sunday Morning.

Jan. 17, 1829

She has the purity & confiding religion of an angel. Are the words common? the words are true. Will God forgive me my sins & aid me to deserve this gift of his mercy.

My history has had its important days within a brief period. Whilst I enjoy the luxury of an unmeasured affection for an object so deserving of it all & who requites it all, I am called by an ancient & respectable church to become its pastor. I recognize in these events, accompanied as they are by so many additional occasions of joy in the condition of my family, I recognize, with acute sensibility, the hand of my heavenly Father. This happiness awakens in me a certain awe: I know my imperfections: I know my ill-deserts; & the bounty of God makes me feel my own sinfulness the more. I throw myself with humble gratitude upon his goodness. I feel my total dependance. O God direct & guard & bless me, & those, & especially *her*, in whom I am blessed.

July? 1829

Oh Ellen, I do dearly love you—

July 3, 1829

My weight is 144 lb.

Oct. 15, 1829

The way for us to be wise is to foresee the great tendencies & currents of the universe in the leanings & motions of the little straws which our eyes can see. We live among eggs, embryos, & seminal principles & the wisest is the most prophetic eye.

Oct. 31, 1829

We must beware of the nature of the spiritual world. It has this terrible power of self change, self accommodation to whatsoever we do that Ovid's Metamorphoses take place continually. The nymph who wept became a fountain; the nymph who pined became an echo. They who do good become angels. They who do deformities become deformed. We are not immoveably moored as we are apt to think to any bottom. And if we do wrong & don't succeed we think we can come back to where we were. That where is gone. I can not live over my childhood. No more can I do right when I have vitiated all the springs of feeling & action.

Jan. 1830

I read in Plutarch's Political Precepts, that when Leo Bizantinus went to Athens to appease the Dissensions in that city—when he arose to speak he perceived that they laughed on account of the littleness of his stature. "What would you do," he exclaimed "if you saw my wife who scarce reaches to my knees?" And they laughing the more he said "yet as little as we are, when we fall out, the city of Byzantium is not big enough to hold us."

March 3, 1830

Read with admiration & delight Mr Webster's noble speech in answer to Hayne. What consciousness of political rectitude & what confidence in his intellectual treasures must he have to enable him to take this master's tone! Mr Channing said he had 'great Self Subsistence.' The beauty & dignity of the spectacle he exhibits should teach men the beauty & dignity of *principles*. This is one that is not blown about by every wind of opinion, but has mind great enough to see the majesty of moral nature & to apply himself in all his length & breadth to it & magnanimously trust thereto.

June 1830

A man is known by the books he reads, by the company he keeps, by the praise he gives, by his dress, by his tastes, by his distastes, by the stories he tells, by his gait, by the motion of his eye, by the look of his house, of his chamber; for nothing on earth is solitary but every thing hath affinities infinite.

July 1, 1830
    Brookline 12 o'clock Windows open   Mercury in the chamber in the shade 80°.—average heat of many days.
16 July 3 o'clk PM same place—mercury 85°.
      Great Heats   17 July. do do 86°
                 22   do do 90
                 24   84

July 20? 1830
    Don't say that qualities are so radical in us that the fickle man can never persevere let him try as he will, nor the selfish man ever distribute—for on the contrary any quality of a man may be taken advantage of to lead him to any other that is desireable. I hate steady labour from morn till night & therefore am not a learned man but I have an omnivorous curiosity & facility of new undertaking. In voluntary exertions to gratify it may I not become learned & acquire the habits of steady toil?

July 24, 1830
    It seems to me there are degrees in religion & much is religion that is not called by that name in minds that do oppose themselves to what they call religion. A man of honour & generosity who would rather die than speak falsely has an aversion to religion, treats it with a degree of contempt. Now I think this man is religious in the lowest degree. What he does well he does from his religious nature.

Aug. 18, 1830
    We never ask the reason of what is good. The sun shines & warms & lights us & we have no curiosity to know why this is so; but we ask the reason of all evil, of pain, & hunger, & musquitoes, & silly people.

Aug. 28, 1830
    Alii disputent, ego mirabor,* said Augustin. It shall be my speech to the Calvinist & the Unitarian.

Sept. 6–7, 1830
    Every thing a man knows & does enters into & modifies his expression of himself & therefore every character is different & expresses itself

---

*"Let others wrangle, I will wonder." [*JMN*]

differently when it speaks with freedom. If a man loves the city so will his writings love the city, & if a man loves sweet fern & roams much in the pastures, his writings will smell of it.

Sept. 8, 1830

Here is a man whom a melon & a glass of wine will make happy. Here is one of another temper—a fantastic book will serve his turn. Here is one whom power will make happy. And here is one who has got hold of his bible, & must have the Universe, & God himself to satisfy him.

Sept. 10, 1830

It is my purpose to methodize my days. I wish to study the scriptures, in a part of every day, that I may be able to explain them to others & that their light may flow into my life. I wish not to be strait laced in my own rules but to wear them easily & to make wisdom master of them. It is a resolving world, but God grant me persistency enough, so soon as I leave Brookline & come to my books, to do as I intend.

Sept. 27–28, 1830

It seems to be true that the more exclusively idiosyncratic a man is, the more general & infinite he is, which though it may not be a very intelligible expression means I hope something intelligible. In listening more intently to our own reason, we are not becoming in the ordinary sense more selfish, but are departing more from what is small, & falling back on truth itself & God. For it is when a man does not listen to himself but to others, that he is depraved & misled. The great men of the world, the teachers of the race, moralists, Socrates, Bacon, Newton, Butler, & the like, were those who did not take their opinions on trust, but explored themselves and that is the way ethics & religion were got out.

Nov. 3, 1830

Is it possible for religious principle to overcome the fear of death? It is commonly overcome, as Bacon observes, by every passion & humor in turn, love, honour, revenge, fun, &c. The instances are familiar of men habitually encountering the greatest risks—sailor & soldier marching up to a battery for sixpence a day. And multitudes of the lower classes of mankind die continually with almost no exhibition of fear. In all these instances, I apprehend it is not a conquest of the fear, but a setting it aside. It is want of thought. It is a dogged attention to the facts next them & not a consideration of the event of death.

On the contrary spiritual men exhibit not unfrequently strong apprehension—great gloom as Dr Johnson, at the thought of dissolution.

Ellen Louisa Tucker Emerson (1811–1831): "She has the purity
& confiding religion of an angel."

The more delicate the structure of the mind the stronger this emotion I
suppose. And this for two reasons: first, because such persons have more
to lose in losing life & secondly because they are not yet spiritual
enough to overcome the fear.

Nov. 5, 1830

When a man has got to a certain point in his career of truth he becomes conscious forevermore that he must take himself for better for
worse as his portion, that what he can get out of his plot of ground by
the sweat of his brow is his meat, & though the wide universe is full of

"I am called by an ancient & respectable church to become its pastor."

good, not a particle can he add to himself but through his toil bestowed on this spot. It looks to him indeed a little spot, a poor barren possession, filled with thorns and a lurking place for adders & apes & wolves. But cultivation will work wonders. It will enlarge to his eye as it is explored. That little nook will swell to a world of light & power & love.

Nov. 19, 1830

'Tis a good definition Coleridge gives in the "Friend," of Talent, that it pursues by original & peculiar means vulgar conventional ends. 'Tis dexterity intellectual applied to the purpose of getting power & wealth.

Genius on the contrary finds its end in the means. It concerns our peace to learn this distinction as quick as we can.

Nov. 1830
The speech that a man repeats which is not his own but was borrowed from another with the hope to pass for original is like a flower held in the hand or a dead feather in the cap manifestly cut off from all life & can deceive none but a child into the belief that it is a part of himself.

Dec. 11, 1830
Internal evidence outweighs all other to the inner man. If the whole history of the New Testament had perished & its teachings remained— the spirituality of Paul, the grave, considerate, unerring advice of James would take the same rank with me that now they do. I should say as now I say this certainly is the greatest height to which the religious principle of human nature has ever been carried. And it has the total suffrage of my soul to its truth whether the miracle was wrought as is pretended or not. If it had not, I should yield to Hume or any one that this, like all other miracle accounts, was probably false. As it is true the miracle falls in with & confirms it.

Feb. 13, 1831
Ellen Tucker Emerson died 8th February. Tuesday morning . . .

Five days are wasted since Ellen went to heaven to see, to know, to worship, to love, to intercede. God be merciful to me a sinner & repair this miserable debility in which her death has left my soul. Two nights since, I have again heard her breathing, seen her dying. O willingly, my wife, I would lie down in your tomb. But I have no deserts like yours, no such purity, or singleness of heart. Pray for me Ellen & raise the friend you so truly loved, to be what you thought him. When your friends or mine cross me, I comfort myself by saying, you would not have done so. Dear Ellen (for that is your name in heaven) shall we not be united even now more & more, as I more steadfastly persist in the love of truth & virtue which you loved? Spirits are not deceived & now you know the sins & selfishness which the husband would fain have concealed from the confiding wife—help me to be rid of them; suggest good thoughts as you promised me, & show me truth. Not for the world, would I have left you here alone; stay by me & lead me upward. Reunite us, o thou Father of our Spirits.

There is that which passes away & never returns. This miserable apathy, I know, may wear off. I almost fear when it will. Old duties will present themselves with no more repulsive face. I shall go again among my friends with a tranquil countenance. Again I shall be amused, I shall stoop again to little hopes & little fears & forget the graveyard. But will the dead be restored to me? Will the eye that was closed on Tuesday ever beam again in the fulness of love on me? Shall I ever again be able to connect the face of outward nature, the mists of the morn, the star of eve, the flowers, & all poetry, with the heart & life of an enchanting friend? No. There is one birth & one baptism & one first love and the affections cannot keep their youth any more than men.

Her end was blessed & a fit termination to such a career. She prayed that God would speedily release her from her body & that she might not make this prayer to be rid of her pains "but because thy favor is better than life." "Take me o God to thyself" was frequently on her lips. Never any one spake with greater simplicity or cheerfulness of dying. She said, 'I pray for sincerity & that I may not talk, but may realize what I say.' She did not think she had a wish to get well, & told me "she should do me more good by going than by staying; she should go first & explore the way, & comfort me." She prayed earnestly & suitably for me.

A little after 2 o'clock on Tuesday morn, she said she felt that she was going soon & having asked if Mother, Margaret, & Paulina were all present she wished them to be still & she would pray with them. And truly & sweetly did she pray for herself & for us & infused such comfort into my soul as never entered it before & I trust will never escape out of it. After this she kissed all, & bid her nurses, 'love God;' & then sunk very fast, occasionally recovering her wandering mind. One of the last things she said after much rambling & inarticulate expression was 'I have not forgot the peace & joy.' And at nine o'clock she died. Farewell blessed Spirit who hast made me happy in thy life & in thy death make me yet happy in thy disembodied state.

She frequently requested me that I would be with her when she died.

March 4, 1831

The Religion that is afraid of science dishonours God & commits suicide. It acknowledges that it is not equal to the whole of truth, that it legislates, tyrannizes over a village of God's empire but is not the immutable universal law. Every influx of atheism, of skepticism is thus made useful as a mercury pill assaulting & removing a diseased religion & making way for truth ... Who knows that he has got all the truth he might have? Who dares to think he has got all the good he might have? We dip our finger tips in the sea that would make us invulnerable if we would plunge & swim. Out upon the cold hardeyed zealot whose whole religion & whole sect & all his missions & all his prodigality of means go to stifle the flame of holy love which young & heroic minds are nourishing, go to traduce the spirit of man.

Dear Ellen do you despise knowledge, or through holier organs does the soul fill her thirst & add to her appetite? Do you despise goodness? Oh no never here did you underrate a miser's mite, & not there, not there, my love. O suggest, coming from God's throne, suggest to this lone heart some hint of him. O forget me not, think with me, pray with me.

March–April 1831

The imputation to which priests have always been subjected is that their private & their public discourses differ, that whilst they say one thing formally they sympathize fully with other men in private & reason & apprehend or regret the same trivial inconveniences as they. Whereas they should theologize in boots & shoes, they should remember the primal law if to their souls it is such at breakfast & dinner, when they make & receive visits, when they settle an estate, when they are threatened sickness, when they go to ride.

April 1, 1831

The spring is wearing into summer & life is wearing into death; our friends are forsaking us, our hopes are declining; our riches are wasting; our mortifications are increasing and is the question settled in our minds, what objects we pursue with undivided aim? Have we fixed ourselves by principles? Have we planted our stakes?

April 4, 1831

The days go by, griefs, & simpers, & sloth, & disappointments. The dead do not return, & sometimes we are negligent of their image. Not of yours Ellen—I know too well who is gone from me. And here come on the formal duties which are to be formally discharged, and in our sluggish minds no sentiment rises to quicken them.

April 4? 1831

Let us not be such coxcombs as to dishonour the gray hairs of the Puritans. I think of them as men whom God honoured with great usefulness. That solid sense, that expansion of the inner man, that greater reverence for history, for law which they had, may compensate for thrift & mechanical improvements & fine houses which they had not. He that thinks so much, he that acts mainly in reference to principles of the greatest class as to give all his face & manners the expression of simple gravity may be excused if he have little playfulness in his conversation or elegance in his furniture. There are some serious things in life. & seriousness may be forgiven to the redeemers of suffering Liberty, to the defenders of Religion, to the pious men who kept their integrity in an unholy age.

May 20, 1831

All things take their character from the state of the spectator. Do not complain that the world is barren of interest or destitute of goodness. These curses come home to roost. These arrows rebound on the archer. Blind men in Rome complained that the streets grew dark. To the dull mind all nature is leaden. To the illuminated mind the whole world burns & sparkles with light.

June 15, 1831

After a fortnight's wandering to the Green Mountains & Lake Champlain yet finding you dear Ellen nowhere & yet everywhere I come again to my own place, & would willingly transfer some of the pictures that the eyes saw, in living language to my page; yea translate the fair & magnificent symbols into their own sentiments. But this were to antedate knowledge. It grows into us, say rather, we *grow wise* & not take wisdom; and only in God's own order & by my concurrent effort can I get the abstract sense of which mountains, sunshine, thunder, night, birds, & flowers are the sublime alphabet.

June 20, 1831

I suppose it is not wise, not being natural, to belong to any religious party. In the bible you are not directed to be a Unitarian or a Calvinist or an Episcopalian. Now if a man is wise, he will not only not profess himself to be a Unitarian, but he will say to himself I am not a member of that or of any party. I am God's child, a disciple of Christ or in the eye of God a fellow disciple with Christ. Now let a man get into a stage coach with this distinct understanding of himself divorcing himself in his heart from every party & let him meet with religious men of every different sect, & he will find scarce any proposition uttered by them to which he does not assent—& none to the sentiment of which he does not assent though he may insist on varying the language. As fast as any man becomes great, that is, thinks, he becomes a new party. Socrates, Aristotle, Calvin, Luther, Abelard, what are these but names of parties? Which is to say, as fast as we use our own eyes, we quit these parties or Unthinking Corporations & join ourselves to God in an unpartaken relation.

A Sect or Party is an elegant incognito devised to save a man from the vexation of thinking.

Since to govern my passions with absolute sway is the work I have to do I cannot but think that the sect for the suppression of Intemperance or a sect for the suppression of loose behaviour to women would be a more reasonable & useful society than the orthodox sect which is a society for the suppression of Unitarianism or the Unitarian which is a society for the diffusion of useful knowledge.

Religion is the relation of the Soul to God, & therefore the progress of Sectarianism marks the decline of religion. For, looking at God instantly reduces our disposition to dissent from our brother. A man may die by a fever as well as by consumption & religion is as effectually destroyed by bigotry as by indifference.

June 25, 1831

No love without sympathy. Minds must be alike. All love a seeking in another what is like self. Difference of opinion separates, common thought ties us. If we find a person esteems excellence that we have loved we love him. No bond of kindness to me that A is a keen hunter or B fond of horses or C a great driver of business but if D is fond of flowers or of books, of poems, of De Stael, of Platonism, then I find a tie nearer & nearer as his tastes approach or unite with mine. And the higher is the principle on which we sympathize the more the love. The fact that we both drink hyson tea or both walk before breakfast—or delight in swimming are low points of union that do not create any permanent kindness but that we are both admirers of a great & good man is a very strong bond. If we both love God we shall be wholly alike & wholly love each other.

June 1831?

Wherever goes a man, there goes a great soul. I never more fully possess myself than in slovenly or disagreeable circumstances. When I stamp thro' the mud in dirty boots, I hug myself with the feeling of my immortality.

July 6, 1831

President Monroe died on the fourth of July—a respectable man, I believe.

July 8, 1831

No man can write well who thinks there is any choice of words for him. The laws of composition are as strict as those of sculpture & architecture. There is always one line that ought to be drawn or one proportion that should be kept & every other line or proportion is wrong, & so far wrong as it deviates from this. So in writing, there is always a right word, & every other than that is wrong. There is no beauty in words except in their collocation. The effect of a fanciful word misplaced is like that of a horn of exquisite polish growing on a human head.

July 10, 1831

Old English writers are the standards not because they are old but simply because they wrote well. They deviated every day from other people but never from truth & so we follow them. If we write as well we may deviate from them & our deviations shall be classical.

July 15? 1831

The things taught in schools & colleges are not an education but the means of education.

July 21, 1831

God cannot be intellectually discerned.

July 1831

All possessions that end in self are odious. The man who shuts himself up in solitary splendor hath much of the devil in him. The Exclusive in fashionable life is as bad as the Religious Exclusionist. Books are to be read, & every library should be a circulating library. Pictures are to be seen & are as if they were not when unseen, & palaces have no other use. . . . Riches are a trust.

July 26, 1831

There happened to me yesterday morning a little incident very pleasing & singular. I started from sleep thinking that a bedbug was creeping on my breast & at the moment I thought I saw the insect. But on opening my eyes fully & thoroughly examining my clothes & the bed I found there was none. I looked at my watch & found it wanted 20 minutes of five o'clock. It immediately occurred to me that the night before as I sat on the front doorstep Charles had expressed his wish to get up early to go & swim, & if possible to set out by 5 o'clock. I told him "well, I will give it in commission to one of the red rovers to wake me" as I had been complaining an hour before that I had found such inmates. The moment I remembered this conversation I ceased to look for a carnal bug & rose & dressed me. It was 30 minutes earlier than my usual waking time.

July 26, 1831

Dined with President Adams yesterday at Dr Parkman's.

Mr —— said to a woman doubting—'Do you not fear God? does not the feeling that your whole future destinies for happiness or misery are in his hands terrify you?' She said 'no, she wished it did.' The question was false theology. It does not recognize an immutable God. It was for the woman to become happy or miserable, not for God to make her so.

July 29, 1831

Suicidal is this distrust of reason; this fear to think; this doctrine that 'tis pious to believe on others' words, impious to trust entirely to yourself. To think is to receive.

Aug. 16, 1831

Every composition in prose or verse should contain in itself the reason of its appearance. Thousands of volumes have been written & mould in libraries of which this reason is yet to seek—does not appear. Then comes Adam Smith, Bacon, Burke, Milton, then comes any good sentence & its apology is its own worth. It makes its pertinence.

Aug. 26, 1831

Yesterday I heard John Quincy Adams deliver an Eulogy upon President Monroe. But he held his notes so close to his mouth that he could be ill heard. There was nothing heroic in the subject, & not much in the feelings of the orator, so it proved rather a spectacle than a speech.

Sept. 13, 1831

Education is the drawing out the Soul.

Sept. 15, 1831

I often make the criticism on my friend Herbert's diction that his thought has that heat as actually to fuse the words so that language is wholly flexible in his hands & his rhyme never stops the progress of the sense. And, in general, according to the elevation of the soul will the power over language always be, & lively thoughts will break out into spritely verse. No measure so difficult but will be tractable so that you only get up the temperature of the thought. To this point I quote gladly my old gossip Montaigne "For my part I hold, & Socrates is positive in it, That whoever has in his mind a spritely & clear imagination, he will express it well enough in one kind or another, & tho' he were dumb, by signs."

Nov. 25, 1831

May I not value my griefs, & store them up. I am imprisoned in the forms & uses of every day, & cannot surrender myself to the sweet bitterness of lamenting my beauty, my glory, the life of my life.

Dec. 28, 1831

The year hastens to its close. What is it to me? What I am that is all that affects me. That I am 28 or 8 or 58 years old is as nothing. Should I mourn that the spring flowers are gone, that the summer fruit has ripened, that the harvest is reaped, that the snow has fallen?

Jan. 10, 1832

It is the best part of the man, I sometimes think, that revolts most against his being the minister. His good revolts from official goodness. If he never spoke or acted but with the full consent of his understanding, if the whole man acted always, how powerful would be every act & every word. Well then or ill then how much power he sacrifices by conforming himself to say & do in other folks' time instead of in his own! The difficulty is that we do not make a world of our own but fall into institutions already made & have to accomodate ourselves to them to be useful at all. & this accommodation is, I say, a loss of so much integrity & of course of so much power.

Jan. 20, 1832

Don't trust children with edged tools, Don't trust man, great God, with more power than he has, until he has learned to use that little better. What a hell should we make of the world, if we could do what we would! Put a button on the foil till the young fencers have learned not to put each other's eyes out.

Jan. 1832

Dreams & beasts are two keys by which we are to find out the secrets of our own nature. All mystics use them. They are like comparative anatomy. They are test objects.

Feb. 18, 1832

What can we see, read, acquire, but ourselves? Cousin is a thousand books to a thousand persons. Take the book, my friend, & read your eyes out; you will never find there what I find.

March 10, 1832

Temperance is an estate. . . . A good way to look at the matter is to see how it figures in the ledger. Bacon says—Best spend in the most permanent ways, such as buying Plato. This year I have spent, say $20 in wine & liquors which are drunk up, & the drinkers are the worse. It would have bought a beautiful print that would have pleased for a century; or have paid a debt that makes me wince whenever I remember the person & may make me wince this hundred years. And so on.

> 28 March my food per diem weighed 14¼ oz
> 29 —   —   —   13 oz
> 2 April   12½

March 29, 1832
I visited Ellen's tomb & opened the coffin.

May 16, 1832
Shakspear's creations indicate no sort of anxiety to be understood. There is the Cleopatra, an irregular, unfinished, glorious, sinful character, sink or swim—there she is—& not one in the thousand of his readers apprehends the noble dimensions of the heroine. Then Ariel, Hamlet, & all—all done in sport with the free daring pencil of a Master of the World. He leaves his children with God.

May 23–25, 1832
Every thing is a monster till we know what it is for; a ship, a telescope, a surgical instrument are puzzles & painful to the eye until we have been shown successively the use of every part & then the thing tells its story at sight & is beautiful. A lobster is monstrous but when we have been shown the reason of the case & the color & the tentacula & the proportion of the claws & seen that he has not a scale nor a bristle nor any quality but fits to some habit & condition of the creature he then seems as perfect & suitable to his sea house as a glove to a hand. A man in the rocks under the sea would be a monster but a lobster is a most handy & happy fellow there.

May 26, 1832
Calvinism suited Ptolemaism. The irresistible effect of Copernican Astronomy has been to make the great scheme for the salvation of man absolutely incredible. Hence great geniuses who studied the mechanism of the heavens became unbelievers in the popular faith: Newton became a Unitarian. Laplace in a Catholic country became an infidel, substituting Necessity for God but a self intelligent necessity is God.

Thus Astronomy proves theism but disproves dogmatic theology. The Sermon on the Mount must be true throughout all the space which the eye sees & the brain imagines but St Paul's epistles, the Jewish

Christianity, would be unintelligible. It operates steadily to establish the moral laws, to disconcert & evaporate temporary systems. At the touch of time errors scatter; in the eye of Eternity truth prevails.

June 2, 1832

I have sometimes thought that in order to be a good minister it was necessary to leave the ministry. The profession is antiquated. In an altered age, we worship in the dead forms of our forefathers. Were not a Socratic paganism better than an effete superannuated Christianity?

July 6, 1832   Conway N.H.

Here among the mountains the pinions of thought should be strong and one should see the errors of men from a calmer height of love & wisdom. What is the message that is given me to communicate next Sunday? Religion in the mind is not credulity & in the practice is not form. It is a life. It is the order & soundness of a man. It is not something else *to be got*, to be *added*, but is a new life of those faculties you have. It is to do right. It is to love, it is to serve, it is to think, it is to be humble.

July 14, 1832

I would think—I would feel. I would be the vehicle of that divine principle that lurks within & of which life has afforded only glimpses enough to assure me of its being. We know little of its laws—but we have observed that a north wind clear cold with its scattered fleet of drifting clouds braced the body & seemed to reflect a similar abyss of spiritual heaven between clouds in our minds; or a brisk conversation moved this mighty deep or a word in a book was made an omen of by the mind & surcharged with meaning or an oration or a southwind or a college or a cloudy lonely walk.

July 15, 1832   White Mountains

A few low mountains, a great many clouds always covering the great peaks, a circle of woods to the horizon, a peacock on the fence or in the yard, & two travellers no better contented than myself in the plain parlor of this house make up the whole picture of this unsabbatized Sunday. But the hours pass on—creep or fly—& bear me and my fellows to the decision of questions of duty; to the crises of our fate; and to the solution of this mortal problem. . . .

The hour of decision. It seems not worth while for them who charge others with exalting forms above the moon to fear forms themselves with extravagant dislike. I am so placed that my aliquid ingenii* may be

---

*"Something of genius." [*JMN*]

brought into useful action. Let me not bury my talent in the earth in my indignation at this windmill. But though the thing may be useless & even pernicious, do not destroy what is good & useful in a high degree rather than comply with what is hurtful in a small degree. The Communicant celebrates on a foundation either of authority or of tradition an ordinance which has been the occasion to thousands—I hope to thousands of thousands—of contrition, of gratitude, of prayer, of faith, of love, & of holy living. Far be it from any of my friends—God forbid it be in my heart—to interrupt any occasion thus blessed of God's influences upon the human mind. I will not, because we may not all think alike of the means, fight so strenuously against the means, as to miss of the end which we all value alike. I think Jesus did not mean to institute a perpetual celebration, but that a commemoration of him would be useful. Others think that Jesus did establish this one. We are agreed that one is useful, & we are agreed I hope in the way in which it must be made useful, viz, by each one's making it an original Commemoration.

I know very well that it is a bad sign in a man to be too conscientious, & stick at gnats. The most desperate scoundrels have been the over refiners. Without accomodation society is impracticable. But this ordinance is esteemed the most sacred of religious institutions & I cannot go habitually to an institution which they esteem holiest with indifference & dislike.

Aug. 12, 1832
I would draw characters, not write lives. I would evoke the spirit of each and their relics might rot. Luther, Milton, Newton, Shakspear. Alfred a light of the world. Adams. I would walk among the dry bones & wherever on the face of the earth I found a living man I would say here is life & life is communicable. Jesus Christ truly said my flesh is meat indeed. I am the bread. For of his life or character have the nations of the earth been nourished. Socrates I should like well if I dared to take him. I should repeat Montaigne though. I wouldn't. . . . I would make Milton shine. I would mourn for Bacon. I would fly in the face of every cockered prejudice, feudal or vulgar, & speak as Christ of their good & evil.

Aug. 1832
What we say however trifling must have its roots in ourselves or it will not move others. No speech should be separate from our being like a plume or a nosegay, but like a leaf or a flower or a bud though the topmost & remotest, yet joined by a continuous line of life to the trunk & the seed.

Aug. 17, 1832

Cholera times. . . . When our own hour comes, when every medicine & means has been exhausted we are then to say to the Angel Hail! All hail! & pass to whatever God has yet to reveal to the conscious spirit. Why should we dread to die when all the good & the beautiful & the wise have died & earth holds nothing so good as that which it has lost?

But oh let not life be valued when that which makes the value of life is lost. It is only a clean conscience, the knowledge that we are beloved by our friends & deserve to be beloved that can persuade an honorable mind to pray that its being may be prolonged an hour, but to out live your own respect, to live when your acquaintance shall shrug their shoulders & count it a disgrace to you the breath that is yet in your nostrils. I shall be glad to be told what is the pleasure what is the profit that is worth buying at such a price.

Aug. 18, 1832

To be genuine. Goethe they say was wholly so. The difficulty increases with the gifts of the individual. A ploughboy can be, but a minister, an orator, an ingenious thinker, how hardly! George Fox was. "What I am in words," he said, "I am the same in life." Swedenborg was. "My writings will be found," he said, "another self." George Washington was; 'the irreproachable Washington.' Whoever is genuine, his ambition is exactly proportioned to his powers. The height of the pinnacle determines the breadth of the base.

Sept. 14? 1832

"Think of living." Don't tell me to get ready to die. I know not what shall be. The only preparation I can make is by fulfilling my present duties. This is the everlasting life. To think of mortality makes us queasy—the flesh creeps at sympathy with its kind. What is the remedy? to ennoble it by animating it with love & uses. Give the Soul its ends to pursue & death becomes indifferent. It saith, What have I to do with death?

Sept. 17, 1832

I would gladly preach to the demigods of this age (& why not to the simple people?) concerning the reality of truth & the greatness of believing in it & seeking after it. It does not shock us when ordinary persons discover no craving for truth & are content to exist for years exclusively occupied with the secondary objects of house & lands & food & company & never cast up their eyes to inquire whence it comes & what it is for, wholly occupied with the play & never ask after the design. But we cannot forgive it in the Everetts & Cannings that they who have souls to comprehend the magnificent secret should utterly neglect it & seek only huzzas & champagne. My quarrel with the vulgar great men is that they do not generously give themselves to the measures which they meddle with; they do not espouse the things they would do; live in the life of the cause they would forward & faint in its failure, but they are casting sheep's eyes ever upon their own by-ends; their pert individuality is ever & anon peeping out to see what way the wind blows & where this boat will land them, whether it is likely they will dine nicely & sleep warm.

Oct. 1, 1832

Has the doctrine ever been fairly preached of man's moral nature? The whole world holds on to formal Christianity, & nobody teaches the essential truth, the heart of Christianity for fear of shocking &c. Every teacher when once he finds himself insisting with all his might upon a great truth turns up the ends of it at last with a cautious showing *how* it is agreeable to the life & teaching of Jesus—as if that was any recommendation. As if the blessedness of Jesus' life & teaching were not because they were agreeable to the truth. Well this cripples his teaching. It bereaves the truth he inculcates of more than half its force by representing it as something secondary that can't stand alone. The truth of truth consists in this, that it is selfevident, selfsubsistent. It is light. You don't get a candle to see the sun rise. Instead of making Christianity a vehicle of truth you make truth only a horse for Christianity. It is a very operose way of making people good. You must be humble because Christ says, 'Be humble'. 'But why must I obey Christ?' 'Because God sent him.' But how do I know God sent him? 'Because your own heart teaches the same thing he taught.' Why then shall I not go to my own heart at first?

Oct. 9? 1832

I will not live out of me
I will not see with others' eyes
My good is good, my evil ill
I would be free—I cannot be
While I take things as others please to rate them
I dare attempt to lay out my own road
That which myself delights in shall be Good
That which I do not want,—indifferent,
That which I hate is Bad. That's flat
Henceforth, please God, forever I forego
The yoke of men's opinions. I will be
Lighthearted as a bird & live with God.

Oct. 17? 1832

All true greatness must come from internal growth.

If it be agreed that I am always to express my thought, what forbids me to tell the company that a flea bites me or that my occasions call me behind the house?

Oct. 27, 1832

"Luther's words were half battles." At Worms to the Diet he said "Till such time as either by proofs from Holy Scripture or by fair reason & argument I have been confuted & convicted I cannot & will not recant. It is neither safe nor prudent to do aught against conscience. Here stand I, I cannot otherwise. God assist me. Amen!"

Oct. 28? 1832

I propose to myself to read Schiller of whom I hear much. What shall I read? His Robbers? oh no, for that was the crude fruit of his immature mind. He thought little of it himself. What then: his Aesthetics? oh no, that is only his struggle with Kantean metaphysics. His poetry? oh no, for he was a poet only by study. His histories? & so with all his productions, they were the fermentations by which his mind was working itself clear, they were the experiments by which he got his skill & the fruit, the bright pure gold of all was—Schiller himself.

Nov. 11, 1832

Mr Walker preached today on the government of the thoughts. Thought I, what thunders mutter in these commonplaces. Suppose he had rolled back the cloud of ceremony & decency & showed us how bad the smooth plausible people we meet every day in society would be if they durst, nay how *we* should behave if we acted our thoughts—not how devils would do, but how good people that hope to be saved would do if they dared—I think it would shake us. There are the real terrors.

Dec. 1, 1832

I never read Wordsworth without chagrin. A man of such great powers & ambition, so near to the Dii majores to fail so meanly in every attempt. A genius that hath epilepsy, a deranged archangel. The Ode to Duty conceived & expressed in a certain high severe style does yet miss of greatness & of all effect by such falsities or falses as "And the most Ancient heavens thro thee are fresh & strong" which is throwing dust in your eyes because they have no more to do with duty than a dung cart has. So that fine promising passage about "the mountain winds being free to blow upon thee" &c flats out into *"me & my benedictions."* If he had cut in his Dictionary for words he could hardly have got worse.

Reorientation
1833-1834

THOUGH EMERSON WOULD later declare that "traveling is a fool's paradise," he set off on his first European tour in a hopeful and adventurous mood. He was indeed running for his life—for renewed energy, new enthusiasms, new ideas, and a fresh sense of direction and purpose. Despite the "nausea, darkness, unrest, uncleanness" that were the inevitable companions of a month on the Atlantic in 1832–33, he was preparing once again to find the universe hospitable. As the brig *Jasper* headed south, he noted the change of latitude and pronounced it preferable to his "bitter native 42 °." It was in fact the New England chill in a broader sense—its constricted manners, harsh opinions, and benumbed aesthetic sensibility—that Emerson was attempting to shuck off along with the "corpse-cold" Unitarianism of Cambridge and Boston. That would not prove easy for a man of his temperament and training, but surely his Puritan ancestors would have been perplexed and dismayed at the likes of a Waldo Emerson who could "hope they will carve & paint & inscribe the walls of our churches in New England" after his first taste of Europe's shrines. "How could any body who had been in a catholic church," he wrote, "devise such a deformity as a pew?" He wondered whether "the men of America never entered these European churches that they build such mean edifices at home." As we might expect, however, Emerson's prickly Americanism quickly reacted to his own overly enthusiastic introduction to the Old World. "Who cares?" he exclaims in response to the beauty of Naples. "Here's for the plain old Adam, the simple genuine Self against the whole world." His pure and upright Protestant

soul refused to be imposed upon by a gaudiness he considered
merely external, though his aesthetically starved senses reached
out eagerly for nourishment.

Thus early in his European *Wanderjahr*, we see the characteristic ebb and flow of Emerson's nature, as he attempts to attain
an approximation to personal truth through a dialectic of oppo-
sites. It was not so much conversion to a new way of thinking he
sought as a repositioning or redirecting of his own fundamental
stance. Emerson was not prepared to accept what he conceived to
be the superstitious trappings of the Roman Catholic Church any
more than he could continue to function within the worn-out
forms of Unitarianism, but he was prepared to extract basic truth
from all experience. Perhaps the representative anecdote, in this
regard, is the one Emerson records on May 25, 1833—his thir-
tieth birthday and the feast day of San Zenobio. Having observed
priests in the Duomo at Florence blessing flowers and using a silver bust of the saint as protection against headaches, Emerson
predictably questioned his landlady about the efficacy of such a
rite. Her response—"it depends on one's faith"—clearly impressed even this skeptical Protestant, since it touched a vital
chord in his own heart. What mattered was not the superstition,
but the personal imperative it symbolized: faith is self-ratifying.

Emerson journeyed north to Milan (where he admired the
Cathedral) and to Geneva (where he noted—reminder of
home—that the Unitarians had ousted the Calvinists). He went
reluctantly to visit Voltaire's chateau at Ferney but admitted, in
his determination to be fair-minded, that "it would be a sin
against faith & philosophy to exclude Voltaire from toleration."
He reached Paris on June 20 and immediately pronounced himself disappointed by this "loud modern New York of a place,"
but the Cabinet of Natural History in the Jardin des Plantes re-
deemed the experience for him. Moved by "strange sympathies"
at this impressive evidence of order and development in the universe, Emerson determined to become "a naturalist." Perhaps his
strong interest in science—especially the evolutionary sciences—
dates from this encounter.

The final leg of Emerson's tour, six weeks in England and
Scotland, was devoted mainly to his seeking out some of the great
figures whose innovative thinking and writing had helped reshape

his own career. Though the visits with Coleridge and Wordsworth were somewhat disappointing (Coleridge, himself a former
Unitarian, had grown conservative and discoursed on the Trinity), Emerson declared his time with Thomas Carlyle "a white
day in my years." Their friendship, occasionally stormy because
of Carlyle's reactionary ideas, would last over forty years and
produce one of the great epistolary exchanges of the nineteenth
century.

Emerson's return voyage in September 1833 was a time for
serious stock taking as well as occasional tippling. For all the
human value of the great men he had met, he pronounced them
deficient "in insight into religious truth." They lacked what he
called "the first philosophy"—a fundamental grasp of truth that
he had come to realize he would find only in his own heart. His
trip to the "schoolroom" of Europe had in fact mainly served to
center him in his own beliefs. He understood now that he had
gone abroad really for the purpose of regathering the scattered
fragments of his personality. A year and a half after his return, remembering a passage in Coleridge's writings, Emerson would articulate a happy formula for this very process of reorientation: the
mind must discover a rule whereby at any moment it can "*east
itself, & find the sun.*"

Back in Boston by early October 1833, Emerson began to
put his new intellectual enthusiasm to work by preparing lectures
on natural history. Lecturing was to be his major profession
henceforth, and Emerson thought a good deal about his vocation
for public speaking. Within the year he would be reaching for
"the high prize of eloquence . . . the joy of uttering what no other
can utter & what all must receive." Most important, he reminded
himself to continue to trust his instincts. His project was to look
at every object in its relation to himself: not to ask, "what must be
said in a Lyceum?" but rather, "what discoveries or stimulating
thoughts have I to impart? . . . not what they will expect to hear
but what is fit for me to say." Emerson was coming into full possession of that creative subjectivity which lay at the heart of the
Romantic impulse. As early as 1827 he had observed that one of
the peculiarities of his time was that it was "said to be the age of
the first person singular." Now he was trying that truth on his
own pulse and soon would pass it along to those within reach of

his voice—including, eventually, Thoreau and Whitman and Dickinson.

Emerson issued his manifesto in November 1834: "Henceforth I design not to utter any speech, poem, or book that is not entirely & peculiarly my work."

Jan. 2, 1833   At Sea

Sailed from Boston for Malta Dec. 25, 1832 in Brig Jasper, Capt Ellis, 236 tons laden with logwood, mahogany, tobacco, sugar, coffee, beeswax, cheese, &c.

A long storm from the second morn of our departure consigned all the five passengers to the irremediable chagrins of the stateroom, to wit, nausea, darkness, unrest, uncleanness, harpy appetite & harpy feeding, the ugly sound of water in mine ears, anticipations of going to the bottom, & the treasures of the memory. I remembered up nearly the whole of Lycidas, clause by clause, here a verse & there a word, as Isis in the fable the broken body of Osiris.

Out occasionally crawled we from our several holes, but hope & fair weather would not, so there was nothing for it but to wriggle again into the crooks of the transom. Then it seemed strange that the first man who came to sea did not turn round & go straight back again. Strange that because one of my neighbors had some trumpery logs & notions which would sell for a few cents more here than there he should thrust forth this company of his poor countrymen to the tender mercies of the northwest wind.

We study the sailor, the man of his hands, man of all work; all eye, all finger, muscle, skill, & endurance; a tailor, a carpenter, cooper, stevedore, & clerk & astronomer besides. He is a great saver, and a great quiddle by the necessity of his situation.

The Captain believes in the superiority of the American to every other countryman. "You will see, he says, when you get out here how they manage in Europe; they do everything by main strength & ignorance. Four truckmen & four stevedores at Long Wharf will load my brig quicker than 100 men at any port in the Mediterranean." It seems the Sicilians have tried once or twice to bring their fruit to America in their own bottoms, & made the passage, he says, in 120 days.

Jan. 3, 1833

I rose at sunrise & under the lee of the spencer sheet had a solitary thoughtful hour. All right thought is devout. 'The clouds were touched

& in their silent faces might be read unutterable love.' They shone with light that shines on Europe, Afric, & the Nile, & I opened my spirit's ear to their most ancient hymn. What, they said to me, goest thou so far to seek—painted canvass, carved marble, renowned towns? But fresh from us, new evermore, is the creative efflux from whence these works spring. You now feel in gazing at our fleecy arch of light the motions that express themselves in Arts. You get no nearer to the principle in Europe. It animates man. It is the America of America. It spans the ocean like a handbreadth. It smiles at Time & Space. Yet welcome young man! the Universe is hospitable. The great God who is Love hath made you aware of the forms & breeding of his wide house. We greet you well to the place of History as you please to style it; to the mighty Lilliput or ant hill of your genealogy, if, instructed as you have been, you must still be the dupe of shows, & count it much, the three or four bubbles of foam that preceded your own on the Sea of Time. This strong-winged sea gull & striped sheer-water that you have watched as they skimmed the waves under our vault—they are works of art better worth your enthusiasm, masterpieces of Eternal power strictly eternal because now active & ye need not go so far to seek what ye would not seek at all if it were not within you. Yet welcome & hail! So sang in my ear the silver grey mists & the winds & the sea said Amen.

Thursday 3 Jan. N. lat 37.53. Dr Johnson rightly defends conversation upon the weather. With more reason we at sea beat that topic thin. We are pensioners of the wind. The weather cock is the wisest man. All our prosperity, enterprize, temper come & go with the fickle air. If the wind should forget to blow we must eat our masts. Sea farmers must make hay when the sun shines. The gale collects plenty of work for the calm. Now we are all awaiting a smoother sea to stand at our toilette. A headwind makes grinning Esaus of us. Happy that there is a time for all things under the moon, so that no man need give a dinner party in a brig's cabin, nor shave himself by the gulf lightning.

Jan. 5, 1833

I like the latitude of 37° better than my bitter native 42°. We have sauntered all this calm day at one or two knots the hour & nobody on board well pleased but I. And why should I be pleased? I have nothing to record. I have read little. I have done nothing. What then? Need we be such barren scoundrels that the whole beauty of heaven, the main, & man cannot entertain us unless we too must needs hold a candle & daub God's world with a smutch of our own insignificance? Not I, for one. I will be pleased though I do not deserve it.

Jan. 6, 1833

Storm, storm; ah we! the sea to us is but a lasting storm. We have had no fine weather to last an hour. Yet I must thank the sea & rough weather for a truckman's health & stomach—how connected with celestial gifts!

Jan. 7, 1833

Though I do not find much attraction in the seaman yet I can discern that the naval hero is a hero. It takes all the thousand thousand European voyages that have been made to stablish our faith in the practicability of this our hodiurnal voyage. But to be Columbus, to steer WEST steadily day after day, week after week, for the first time, and wholly alone in his opinion, shows a mind as solitary & self-subsistent as any that ever lived.

Jan. 14, 1833

Well blithe traveller what cheer?

What have the sea & the stars & the moaning winds & your discontented thoughts sung in your attentive ears? Peeps up old Europe yet out of his eastern main? hospitably ho! Nay the slumberous old giant cannot bestir himself in these his chair days to loom up for the pastime of his upstart grandchildren as now they come shoal after shoal to salute their old Progenitor, the old Adam of all. Sleep on, old Sire, there is muscle & nerve & enterprise enow in us your poor spawn who have sucked the air & ripened in the sunshine of the cold West to steer our ships to your very ports & thrust our inquisitive American eyes into your towns & towers & keeping-rooms. Here we come & mean to be welcome. So be good now, clever old gentleman.

Jan. 15, 1833

I learn in the sunshine to get an altitude & the latitude but am a dull scholar as ever in real figures. Seldom I suppose was a more inapt learner of arithmetic, astronomy, geography, political economy than I am as I daily find to my cost. It were to brag much if I should there end the catalogue of my defects. My memory of history—put me to the pinch of a precise question—is as bad; my comprehension of a question in technical metaphysics very slow, & in all arts practick, in driving a bargain, or hiding emotion, or carrying myself in company as a man for an hour, I have no skill. What under the sun canst thou do then, pale face! Truly not much, but I can hope.

Jan. 16, 1833

The inconvenience of living in a cabin is that people become all eye. 'Tis a great part of wellbeing to ignorize a good deal of your fellowman's history & not count his warts nor expect the hour when he shall wash his teeth.

Jan. 25, 1833

Head winds are sore vexations & the more passengers the sorer. Yesterday the Captain killed a porpoise & I witnessed the cutting up of my mammiferous fellow creature. . . . In this little balloon of ours, so far from the human family and their sages & colleges & manufactories every accomplishment, every natural or acquired talent, every piece of information is some time in request. And a short voyage will show the difference between the man & the apprentice as surely as it will show the superior value of beef & bread to lemons & sugarplums. Honour evermore aboard ship to the man of action—to the brain in the hand. Here is our stout master worth a thousand philosophers—a man who can strike a porpoise, & make oil out of his blubber, & steak out of his meat; who can thump a mutineer into obedience in two minutes; who can bleed his sick sailor, & mend the box of his pump; who can ride out the roughest storm on the American coast, & more than all, with the sun & a three cornered bit of wood, & a chart, can find his way from Boston across 3000 miles of stormy water into a little gut of inland sea 9 miles wide with as much precision as if led by a clue.

Feb. 2, 1833

So here we are in Malta, in the renowned harbor of Marsa Muscette the Quarantine roads for a fortnight, imprisoned for poor dear Europe's health lest it should suffer prejudice from the unclean sands & mountains of America. . . . This P.M. I visited the Parlatorio where those in quarantine converse with those out across barriers. It looked to me like the wildest masquerade. There jabbered Turks, Moors, Sicilians, Germans, Greeks, English, Maltese, with friars & guards & maimed & beggars. And such grotesque faces! It resembled more some brave antique picture than a congregation of flesh & blood. The human family can seldom see their own differences of color & form so sharply contrasted as in this house. I noticed however that all the curiosity manifested was on our part. Our cousins of Asia & Europe did not pay us the compliment of a second glance.

In Quarantine, our acquaintance has been confined chiefly to the Maltese boatmen, a great multitude of poor, swarthy, goodnatured people, who speak their own tongue, not much differing from the Arabic, & most of them know very few words of Italian & less of English.

Feb. 16, 1833

La Valetta. . . . found lodgings once more on dry ground with great joy. All day with my fellow travellers I perambulated this little town of stone. It is from end to end a box of curiosities. & though it is very green & juvenile to express wonder, I could not hinder my eyes from rolling continually in their sockets nor my tongue from uttering my pleasure & surprize. It is an advantage to enter Europe at the little end so we shall admire by just degrees from the Maltese architecture up to St Peter's. . . . I went to the churches of St Popilius & St Thomas. The first is no other than 'Publius, the chief man of the island' in Acts XXVIII & much honor hath he in Malta at least on the walls of his church.

In all these churches there were many worshippers continually coming in, saying their prayers, & going their way. I yielded me joyfully to the religious impression of holy texts & fine paintings & this soothfast faith though of women & children. How beautiful to have the church always open, so that every tired wayfaring man may come in & be soothed by all that art can suggest of a better world when he is weary with this.

I hope they will carve & paint & inscribe the walls of our churches in New England before this century, which will probably see many grand granite piles erected there, is closed. To be sure there is plenty of superstition.

Feb. 17, 1833

Visited St John's again & attended mass. . . . The music of the organ & chaunting friars very impressive, especially when we left the kneeling congregation in the nave, & heard it at distance, as we examined the pictures in a side oratory. I went into several churches which were all well attended. How could any body who had been in a catholic church, devise such a deformity as a pew?

Feb. 20, 1833

The Maltese milkman drives his goats through the street & milks you a pint at your door. Asses & mules *passim.*

Feb. 21, 1833

At 8 o'clock P.M. we embarked for Syracuse in a Sicilian brigantine "Il Santissimo Ecce Homo," and a most ridiculous scene our ship's company offered, they to us & we to them. The little brig was manned with 14 men who were all on a perfect level with each other. The steersman sat down at the helm & when they brought him his supper the captain affectionately took his post whilst he ate. The boy was employed in sit-

ting down by the steersman & watching the hour glass so that he might
turn it when it ran out. But the whole interest of master & men was
concentrated on us his five passengers. We had hired for $30 the whole
cabin, so they put all their heads into the scuttle & companionway to
behold all that we did, the which seemed to amuse them mightily. When
any thing was to be done to sails or spars they did it who had a mind to
it & the captain got such obedience as he could. In the morning the mate
brought up his gazetteer to find Boston the account of which he read
aloud, and all the crew gathered round him whilst he read. They
laughed heartily at the captain & passed jokes upon him & when the little boy did something amiss every body gave him a knock. A cask of
blood red wine was on tap, from which every body drank when it
pleased him in a quart measure. Their food was a boiled fish called
purpo (which looks like an eel & tastes like lobster) with bread & green
onions eaten raw. Their little vessel sailed fast & in 16 hours we saw the
ancient city of Syracuse. Abundance of fuss & vexation did the Sanita &
the Dogana give us before we were suffered to land our baggage but our
Captain & mate helped us all they could, & our money opened all the
gates at last.

Feb. 23, 1833   Syracuse
     What is a passenger? He is a much enduring man who bends under
the load of his leisure. He fawns upon the Captain, reveres the mate, but
his eye follows the Steward; scans accurately as symptomatic, all the
motions of that respectable officer.
     The species is contemplative, given to imitation, viciously inquisi-
tive, immensely capable of sleep, large eaters, swift digesters, their
thoughts ever running on men & things ashore & their eye usually
squinting over the bulwark, to estimate the speed of the bubbles. . . .
     Abundance of examples here of great things turned to vile uses. The
fountain Arethuse, to be sure, gives name to the street Via Aretusa in
which it is found: but an obscure dark nook it is & we walked up &
down & looked in this & that court yard in vain for some time. Then we
asked a soldier on guard Where it was? He only knew that "Questa e la
batteria"—nothing more. At last an old woman guided us to the spot
and I grieve—I abhor to tell—the fountain was bubbling up in its world
renowned waters within four black walls serving as one great washing
tub to fifty or sixty women who were polluting it with all the filthy
clothes of the city.
     It is remarkable now as of old for its quantity of water springing up
out of the earth at once as large as a river. Its waters are sweet & pure &
of the colour of Lake George.

Feb. 24, 1833

Visited the Latomié of the Gardens of the Capuchins—a strange place. It is a large & beautiful garden full of oranges & lemons & pomegranates in a deep pit, say 120 feet below the surrounding grounds. . . .

Went into the Convent & the Fathers set before us bread, olives, & wine. Our conductor then showed us the dormitories (over each of which was a latin inscription from the bible or the Fathers), the Chapel, &c. of the House. There is no better spot in the neighborhood of Syracuse than the one they have chosen. The air, the view, the long gallery of the chambers, the peace of the place quite took me & I told the Padre that I would stay there always if he would give me a chamber. He said, 'I should have his,' which he opened—a little neat room, with a few books, "Theologia Thomea ex Charmes," & some others. My friend's whipcords hung by the bed side.

There are only 22 or 23 persons in this fine old house. We saw but 4 or 5. I am half resolved to spend a week or fortnight there. They will give me board, I am informed, on easy terms. How good & pleasant to stop & recollect myself in this worn out nook of the human race, to turn over its history & my own. But, ah me!

March 1, 1833   Catania

Fine strange ride & walk yesterday coming by mules from Syracuse hither, 42 miles, thirteen hours. Our party (3 gentlemen 2 ladies) were accomodated with seven beasts, 2 for the Lettiga containing the ladies, 2 for the baggage, one for each saddle. The morning road led us by catacombs without number. What are they but evidences of an immense ancient population that every rock should be cut into sepulchres. The road, a mere mule-path through very stony soil, was yet not so rough but that I preferred walking to riding, & for an hour or two kept up easily with the caravan. Fine air, clear sun, Mount Aetna right before us, green fields—laborers ploughing in them, many flowers, all the houses of stone. Passed the trophy of Marcellus, a pile of broken masonry and yet it answers its purpose as well as Marcellus could have hoped. Did he think that Mr Emerson would be reminded of his existence & victory this fine spring day 2047 years to come?

March 1-4, 1833

Signor Ricciardi of Syracuse gave me a letter to Padre Anselmo Adorno, the Celleraio of this monastery & this morn I waited upon his reverence in his cell, & the kings of France & England, I think, do not live in a better house. The Padre with great courtesy showed us the church & its paintings, & its organ, here reputed the finest in Europe. It imitates sackbut, harp, psaltery, & all kinds of music. The Monk Donatus who built it, begged that he might be buried under it, & there he lies. To my ignorance, however, the organ neither appeared very large nor very richly toned. But the Church shall be St Peter's to me till I behold a fairer shrine. Have the men of America never entered these European churches that they build such mean edifices at home?

I have been to the Opera, & thought three taris, the price of a ticket, rather too much for the whistle. It is doubtless a vice to turn one's eyes inward too much, but I am my own comedy & tragedy. Did ye ever hear of a magnet who thought he had lost his virtue because he had fallen into a heap of shavings? Our manners are sometimes so mean, our blunders & improprieties so many and mulish that it becomes a comfort to think that people are too much occupied with themselves to remember even their neighbor's defects very long.

March 5, 1833   Messina
From Catania my ride to this city was charming. The distance is but 60 miles but that is two days' journey here. Mount Etna was the grand spectacle of the first day & a fine sight it is. This monarch of mountains they say supports a population of 115000 souls, & is 180 miles in circuit. And its ample sides are belted with villages & towers up almost to the snow. As the wind blew fresh I *smelt* the snowbanks. Village of Giarre; old country; catholic all over; scarce a house or a fence but hath a shrine or cross or inscription. "Basta a chi non ha. Basta a chi morra." Another, "Viva la Divina Providenza," & a thousand more. It is a poor philosophy that dislikes these sermons in stones. But what green fields, & trees in bloom, & thick villages the turns in the road showed; & my Sicilian companions would break out "O che bella veduta!"

March 7, 1833
At the Viceroy's Palace, I saw nothing but a small chapel which they vaunted much. I went to the Capuchin Convent. That pleased me better. I like these Capuchins, who are the most esteemed of the Catholic clergy. Their profession is beggary but they distribute large alms to the poor. You approach their houses thro' a regiment of beggars. The Fathers were at dinner so I took a turn in their sober garden. Then came a monk & led me down into their Cemetery. A strange spectacle enough. Long aisles the walls of which on either side are filled with niches & in every niche the standing skeleton of a dead Capuchin; the skull & the hands appearing, the rest of the anatomy wrapped in cearments. Hundreds & hundreds of these grinning mortalities were ranged along the

walls, here an abbot, there a General of the Convent. Every one had his label with his name, when in the body, hanging at his breast. One was near 300 years old. On some the beard remained, on some the hair. I asked the monk how many there were? He said, since 300 years half a million; and he himself would stand there with his brothers in his turn.

March 11, 1833

I tried last night in my berth to recal what had occurred at the opera.... I could not help pitying the performers in their fillets & shields & togas, & saw their strained & unsuccessful exertions & thought on their long toilette & personal mortification at making such a figure. There they are—the same poor Johns & Antonios they were this morning, for all their gilt & pasteboard. But the moment the Prima donna utters one tone or makes a gesture of natural passion, it puts life into the dead scene. I pity them no more. It is not a ghost of departed things, not an old Greece & Rome but a Greece & Rome of this moment. It is living merit which takes ground with all other merit of whatever kind—with beauty, nobility, genius, & power. O trust to Nature, whosoever thou art, even though a strutting tragedy-prince. Trust your simple self & you shall stand before genuine princes. The play was tedious, & so are the criticisms.

March 12, 1833

And what if it is Naples, it is only the same world of cake & ale—of man & truth & folly. I won't be imposed upon by a name. It is so easy, almost so inevitable to be overawed by names that on entering this bay it is hard to keep one's judgment upright, & be pleased only after your own way. Baiae & Misenum & Vesuvius, Procida & Pausilippo & Villa Reale sound so big that we are ready to surrender at discretion & not stickle for our private opinion against what seems the human race. Who cares? Here's for the plain old Adam, the simple genuine Self against the whole world. Need is, that you assert yourself or you will find yourself overborne by the most paltry things. A young man is dazzled by the stately arrangements of the hotel & jostled out of his course of thought & study of men by such trumpery considerations. The immense regard paid to clean shoes & a smooth hat impedes him, & the staring of a few dozens of idlers in the street hinders him from looking about him with his own eyes; & the attention which he came so far to give to foreign wonders, is concentrated instead, on these contemptible particulars. Therefore it behooves the traveller to insist first of all upon his simple human rights of seeing & of judging here in Italy as he would in his own farm or sitting room at home.

March 23, 1833

Tired am I with a visit to Vesuvius. But it is well paid fatigue. I left the coach at Resina & was accommodated with a braying ass who but for his noise was a good beast & thus ascended about a mile above the Hermitage. Thence we climbed with good staves straight up thro' the loose soil wholly composed of lava & cinders. The guide showed us the limits of the different eruptions down to that of December 1832. Presently we came to the top of the old crater. Out of this has risen a new mass which is fast filling up & will soon probably obliterate the old crater. The soil was warm & smoking all around & above us. The ascent from this point to the summit looked dangerous & was not easy. The wind blows the smoke & fumes in your face almost to suffocation & the smoke hides all your party much of the time from your sight. We got to the top & looked down into the red & yellow pits, the navel of this volcano. I had supposed there was a chasm opening downward to unknown depths, but it was all closed up; only this hollow of salt & sulphur smoking furiously beneath us. We put paper between the stones & it kindled & blazed immediately. We found many parties going up & down the mountain & ladies are carried in chairs to the top.

March 27, 1833

It is even so; my poor feet are sore with walking all this day amongst the ruins of Rome.

March 28, 1833

I went to the Capitoline hill then to its Museum & saw the Dying Gladiator, The Antinous, the Venus—to the Gallery, then to the Tarpeian Rock, then to the vast & splendid museum of the Vatican. A wilderness of marble. After traversing many a shining chamber & gallery I came to the Apollo & soon after to the Laocoon. 'Tis false to say that the casts give no idea of the originals. I found I knew these fine statues already by heart & had admired the casts long since, much more than I ever can the originals.

Here too was the Torso Hercules, as familiar to the eyes as some old revolutionary cripple. On we went from chamber to chamber through galleries of statues & vases & sarcophagi & bas reliefs & busts & candelabra—through all forms of beauty & richest materials—till the eye was dazzled & glutted with this triumph of the arts. Go & see it, whoever you are. It is the wealth of the civilized world. It is a contribution from all ages & nations of what is most rich & rare. He who has not seen it does not know what beautiful stones there are in the planet.

March 29, 1833

Rome is very pleasant to me, as Naples was not, if only from one circumstance, that here I have pleasant companions to eat my bread with & there I had none.

March 31, 1833

I have been to the Sistine Chapel to see the Pope bless the palms & hear his choir chaunt the Passion. The Cardinals came in one after another, each wearing a purple robe, an ermine cape, & a small red cap to cover the tonsure. A priest attended each one to adjust the robes of their Eminences. As each Cardinal entered the chapel, the rest rose. One or two were fine persons. Then came the Pope in scarlet robes & a bishop's mitre. After he was seated the cardinals went in turn to the throne & kneeled & kissed his hand. After this ceremony the attendants divested the cardinals of their robes & put on them a gorgeous cope of cloth of gold. When this was arranged a sort of ornamental baton made of the dried palm leaf was brought to his holiness & blessed and each of the cardinals went again to the throne & received one of these from the hands of the pope. They were supplied from a large pile at the side of the papal chair. After the Cardinals, came other dignitaries, bishops, deans, canons, I know them not—but there was much etiquette, some kissing the hand only, & some the foot also of the pope. Some received Olive branches. Lastly several officers performed the same ceremony. When this long procession of respect was over and all the robed multitude had received their festal palms & olives his Holiness was attended to a chair of state & being seated was lifted up by bearers & preceded by the long official array & by his chaunting choir he rode out of the chapel.

It was hard to recognize in this ceremony the gentle Son of Man who sat upon an ass amidst the rejoicings of his fickle countrymen. Whether from age or from custom, I know not, but the pope's eyes were shut or nearly shut as he rode. After a few minutes he reentered the chapel in like state. And soon after retired & left the Sacred College of Cardinals to hear the Passion chaunted by themselves. The chapel is that whose walls Michel Angelo adorned with his 'Last Judgment.' But today I have not seen the picture well.

All this pomp is conventional. It is imposing to those who know the customs of courts & of what wealth & of what rank these particular forms are the symbols. But to the eye of an Indian I am afraid it would be ridiculous. There is no true majesty in all this millinery & imbecility. Why not devise ceremonies that shall be in as good & manly taste as their churches & pictures & music?

I counted twenty one cardinals present. Music at St Peter's in the afternoon & better still at Chiesa Nuova in the evg. Those mutilated wretches sing so well it is painful to hear them.

April 2, 1833

What is more pathetic than the Studio of a young Artist? Not rags & disease in the street move you to sadness like the lonely chamber littered round with sketches & canvass & colourbags. There is something so gay in the art itself that these rough & poor commencements contrast more painfully with it. Here another enthusiast feeds himself with hope & rejoices in dreams & smarts with mortifications. The melancholy artist told me that if the end of painting was to please the eye, he would throw away his pallet. And yet how many of them not only fail to reach the soul with their conceptions, but fail to please the eye.

These beggarly Italians! If you accept any hospitality at an Italian house a servant calls upon you the next day & receives a fee, & in this manner, the expense of your entertainment is defrayed. In like manner, if you are presented to the Pope, it costs you five dollars.

April 3, 1833

The famous Miserere was sung this afternoon in the Sistine chapel. The saying at Rome is that it cannot be imitated not only by any other choir but in any other chapel in the world. The Emperor of Austria sent Mozart to Rome on purpose to have it sung at Vienna with like effect, but it failed.

Surely it is sweet music & sounds more like the Eolian harp than any thing else. The pathetic lessons of the day relate the treachery of Judas & apply select passages from the prophets & psalms to the circumstances of Jesus. Then whilst the choir chaunt the words "Traditor autem dedit eis signum, dicens, Quem osculatus fuero, ipse est, tenete eum," all the candles in the chapel are extinguished but one. During the repetition of this verse, the last candle is taken down & hidden under the altar. Then out of the silence & the darkness rises this most plaintive & melodious strain, (the whole congregation kneeling) "Miserere mei, Deus," &c. The sight & the sound are very touching.

Every thing here is in good taste. The choir are concealed by the high fence which rises above their heads. We were in a Michel Angelo's chapel which is full of noblest scriptural forms & faces.

April 4, 1833

These forms strike me more than I expected, & yet how do they fall short of what they should be. Today I saw the Pope wash the feet of thirteen pilgrims, one from each nation of Christendom. One was from Kentucky. After the ceremony he served them at dinner; this I did not

see. But Gregory XVI is a learned & able man; he was a monk & is reputed of pure life. Why should he not leave one moment this formal
service of fifty generations & speak out of his own heart, the Father of
the Church to his Children, though it were but a single sentence or a
single word? One earnest word or act to this sympathetic audience
would overcome them. It would take all hearts by storm.

April 6, 1833
I did not go to the baptism of the Jew today. Usually it is a weary
farce. 'Tis said they buy the Jews at 150 scudes the head, to be sprin-
kled. This man was respectable. This P.M. I heard the Greek Mass. The
chaunts are in Armenian.

April 7, 1833
This morng the Pope said Mass at St Peter's. Rich dresses, great
throngs, lines of troops, but not much to be said for the service. It is
Easter & the curtains are withdrawn from the pictures & statues to my
great joy & the Pope wears his triple crown instead of a mitre.
At twelve o clock the benediction was given. A canopy was hung
over the great window that is above the principal door of St Peter's &
there sat the Pope. The troops were all under arms & in uniform in the
piazza below, & all Rome & much of England & Germany & France &
America was gathered there also. The great bell of the Church tolled,
drums beat, & trumpets sounded over the vast congregation.
Presently, at a signal, there was silence and a book was brought to
the Pope, out of which he read a moment & then rose & spread out his
hands & blessed the people. All knelt as one man. He repeated his action
(for no words could be heard), stretching his arms gracefully to the
north & south & east & west—pronouncing a benediction on the whole
world. It was a sublime spectacle. Then sounded drums & trumpets,
then rose the people, & every one went his way.

April 7-8, 1833
I love St Peter's Church. It grieves me that after a few days I
shall see it no more. It has a peculiar smell from the quantity of
incense burned in it. The music that is heard in it is always good &
the eye is always charmed. It is an ornament of the earth. It is not
grand, it is so rich & pleasing; it should rather be called the sublime
of the beautiful.

April 13, 1833
Rome fashions my dreams. All night I wander amidst statues &
fountains, and last night was introduced to Lord Byron!

April 17? 1833

What pleasant fountains all over Rome in every villa, garden, & piazza. An eye for beauty is nature's gift to this people; they delight in bright colours & in all ornaments. As we sat in the Caffé, we agreed that it was decorated & furnished with a beauty & good taste which could not be rivalled in America.

No man should travel until he has learned the language of the country he visits. Otherwise he voluntarily makes himself a great baby—so helpless & so ridiculous.

April 20, 1833

I have paid a last visit to the Capitoline Museum & Gallery. One visit is not enough, no, nor two to learn the lesson. The dying Gladiator is a most expressive statue but it will always be indebted to the muse of Byron for fixing upon it forever his pathetic thought. Indeed Italy is Byron's debtor, and I think no one knows how fine a poet he is who has not seen the subjects of his verse, & so learned to appreciate the justness of his thoughts & at the same time their great superiority to other men's. I know well the great defects of Childe Harold.

In the Gallery I coveted nothing so much as Michel Angelo's Portrait by himself.

April 21, 1833

I went this morn to the Church of Trinita di Monte to see some nuns take the veil. Can any ceremony be more pathetic than to see youth, beauty, rank thus self devoted to mistaken duty?

I went this afternoon to see Michel Angelo's statue of Moses at the Church of San Pietro in Vinculo, and it is grand. It seems he sought to embody the Law in a man. Directly under the statue, at the side where the whole face is seen, the expression is terrible. I could wish away those emblematic horns. "Alzati, parla!" said the enthusiastic sculptor.

May 1, 1833

And how do you like Florence? Why, well. It is pleasant to see how affectionately all the artists who have resided here a little while speak of getting home to Florence. And I found at once that we live here with much more comfort than in Rome or Naples. Good streets, industrious population, spacious well furnished lodgings, elegant & cheap Caffés, the cathedral & the Campanile, the splendid galleries and no beggars— make this city the favorite of strangers.

How like an archangel's tent is this great Cathedral of many-coloured marble set down in the midst of the city and by its side its wondrous campanile! I took a hasty glance at the gates of the Baptistery which Angelo said ought to be the gates of paradise "degne chiudere il Paradiso" and then of his own David & hasted to the Tribune & to the Pitti Palace. I saw the statue that enchants the world. And truly the Venus deserves to be visited from far. It is not adequately represented by the plaster casts as the Apollo & the Laocoon are. I must go again & see this statue. Then I went round this cabinet & gallery & galleries till I was well nigh "dazzled & drunk with beauty." I think no man has an idea of the powers of painting until he has come hither. Why should painters study at Rome? Here, here.

May 2? 1833

How bare & poor are these Florentine churches after the sumptuous temples of Naples & Rome. Ah! ah! for St Peter's, which I can never more behold. Close by my door is the Church of Santa Maria Novella which Michel Angelo called his *bride;* my eye has not yet learned why; it still looks naked & unfinished to me. The Church of St John's in Malta, he might well have distinguished by such a name.

Evg. Beautiful days, beautiful nights. It is today one of the hundred festas of this holiday people; so was yesterday; so is tomorrow. The charming Cascina, & the banks of the Arno are thronged, but moonshine or sunshine are indispensable to a festa; as they say in France, "there will be no revolution today, for it rains."

May 11, 1833

Last night I went to the Pergola, and to my eyes, unused to theatres, it was a glorious show. The prima donna, Signora Delsere, is a noble Greek beauty, full of dignity, & energy of action & when she sang the despair of Agnes, she was all voice. She had moreover so striking a resemblance to a valued friend in America, that I longed to know who & what Signora Delsere was, much more than the issue of the play. But nobody knew. The whole scenery & the dresses of the performers were in admirable taste, everything good but the strutting of the actors. Is it penal for an actor to *walk?* Before the play was done, my eyes were so dazzled with the splendor of light & colors that I was obliged to rest them & look at my shoes for half an hour, that I might keep them for the last act.

May 11, 1833

Cannot a lesson of wisdom & glory be got even from the hapless prima donna of an Italian opera? At least one is informed of the extent of female powers & warned not to be too easily satisfied with the accomplishments of vulgar pretty women.

May 18, 1833

When I walk up the piazza of Santa Croce I feel as if it were not a Florentine no nor an European church but a church built by & for the human race. I feel equally at home within its walls as the Grand duke, so *hospitably* sound to me the names of its mighty dead. Buonaroti & Galileo lived for us all. As Don Ferrante says of Aristotle, "non è nè antico nè moderno; è il filosofo, senza piu." . . .

The Italians use the Superlative too much. Mr Landor calls them the nation of the *issimi*. A man to tell me that this was the same thing I had before, said "E l'istessissima cosa;" and at the trattoria, when I asked if the cream was good, the waiter answered, "Stupendo." They use three negatives; it is good Italian to say, 'Non dite nulla a nessuno'.

I like the sayers of No better than the sayers of Yes.

May 19, 1833

Miss Anna Bridgen said very wittily, "that so inveterate were her Dutch instincts, that she sees almost no work of art in Italy, but she wants to give it a good scrubbing; the Duomo, the Campanella, & the statues."

May 25, 1833

We come out to Europe to learn what man can—what is the uttermost which social man has yet done. And perhaps the most satisfactory & most valuable impressions are those which come to each individual casually & in moments when he is not on the hunt for wonders. To make any sincere good use, I mean what I say, of what he sees, he needs to put a double & treble guard upon the independency of his judgments. The veriest Luther might well suspect his own opinion upon the Venus or the Apollo.

It is the Festa of San Zenobio once bishop of Florence. And at the churches, the priests bless the roses & other flowers which the people bring them, & they are then esteemed good for the cure of head ache & are laid by for that purpose. Last night in the Duomo I saw a priest carrying a silver bust of San Zenobio which he put upon the head of each person in turn who came up the barrier. This ceremony also protects him from the head ache for a year. But, asked I of my landlady, do you believe that the bust or the roses do really cure the head ache of any person? "Secondo alla fede di ciascuno," she replied.

It is my Festa also.

* * *

"Comanda niente Signore?"—Niente.—"Felice notte, Signore."—
Felice notte. Such is the dialogue which passes every evening betwixt
Giga & me when the worthy woman lights my lamp, & leaves me to
Goethe & Sismondi, to pleasant study hours, & to sound sleep.

June 1–3, 1833
I am speedily satisfied with Venice. It is a great oddity—a city for
beavers—but to my thought a most disagreeable residence. You feel always in prison, & solitary. Two persons may live months in adjoining
streets & never meet, for you go about in gondolas and all the gondolas
are precisely alike & the persons within commonly concealed; then there
are no Newsrooms; except St Mark's piazza, no place of public resort. It
is as if you were always at sea. And though, for a short time, it is very
luxurious to lie on the eider down cushions of your gondola & read or
talk or smoke, drawing to now the cloth lined shutter, now the venetian
blind, now the glass window, as you please, yet there is always a slight
smell of bilgewater about the thing, & houses in the water remind me of
a freshet & of desolation—any thing but comfort. I soon had enough
of it.

June 2, 1833
Sometimes I would hide myself in the dens of the hills, in the
thickets of an obscure country town, I am so vexed & chagrined with
myself—with my weakness, with my guilt. Then I have no skill to live
with men, that is, with such men as the world is made of, & such as I
delight in, I seldom find. It seems to me, no boy makes so many blunders or says such awkward, contrary, disagreeable speeches as I do. In
the attempt to oblige a person I wound & disgust him. I pity the hapless
folks that have to do with me. But would it not be cowardly to flee out of
society & live in the woods?

I collect nothing that can be touched or tasted or smelled, neither
cameo, painting, nor medallion; nothing in my trunk but old clothes, but
I value much the growing picture which the ages have painted & which
I reverently survey. It is wonderful how much we see in five months, in
how short a time we learn what it has taken so many ages to teach.

June 5, 1833
To Verona 30 miles. . . . We do not make many miles in a day but
our journey has many alleviations & we are very companionable travellers and some of our Tuscan conversations with the Vetturino ludicrous
enough. "Vetturino!" shouted my friend Stewardson from within the

coach, "Vetturino! Perché non arrangiate questo window?" Then we find a hospitable Caffé every evening where we find an ice and the oriental narcotic & Wall & Stewardson their cigar.

June 6, 1833

Today from Verona to Brescia, 40 miles. . . . We passed today many beautiful villas and what was new & pleasant we saw no beggars. The women in this country universally wear in their hair silver pins with heads as large as eggs: they remind one of an electrical machine. All the way they were stripping the mulberry trees of leaves for the food of the silkworms which are in every house. I went into a house & begged to see the animals; the padrona led me up stairs & showed the creatures in every age & state. She had given up the whole of the primo piano or what we call the second story to them.

Then to Brescia. All the Italian towns are different & all picturesque, the well paved Brescia. The Church of the Madonna dei Miracoli—how daintily it is carved without to the very nerves of the strawberry & vine leaf! Italy is the country of beauty but I think specially in the northern part. Every thing is ornamented. A peasant wears a scarlet cloak. If he has no other ornament he ties on a red garter or knee band. They wear flowers in the hat or the buttonhole. A very shabby boy will have the eye of a peacock's feather in his hat. In general the great coats & jackets of the common people are embroidered. And the other day I saw a cripple leaning on a crutch very finely carved. Every fountain, every pump, every post is sculptured, and not the commonest tavern room but its ceiling is painted. Red is a favorite color and on a rainy morning at Messina the streets blazed with red umbrellas.

June 9–10, 1833

There is an advantage which these old cities have over our new ones that forcibly strikes an American. Namely that the poorest inhabitants live in good houses. In process of time a city is filled with palaces, the rich ever deserting old ones for new, until beggars come to live in what were costly & well accommodated dwellings. Thus all the trattorias, even of little pretension, have their carved work & fresco painting, as this of the Marino where I dine with my companions.

June 16, 1833

Yesterday to oblige my companions & protesting all the way upon the unworthiness of his memory I went to Ferney to the chateau, the saloon, the bed chamber, the gardens of Voltaire, the king of the scorners. His rooms were modest & pleasing & hung with portraits of his friends. Franklin & Washington were there. The view of the lake &

mountains commanded by the lawn behind the chateau is superior to
that of Gibbon's garden at Lausanne. The old porter showed us some
pictures belonging to his old master & told a story that did full justice to
his bad name. Yet it would be a sin against faith & philosophy to exclude Voltaire from toleration. He did his work as the bustard & taran-
tula do theirs.

June 16? 1833
    The Established Church of Geneva is now Unitarian & the three
Calvinistic clergymen of the city are ejected.

June 17–20, 1833
    France France. It is not only a change of name—the cities, the lan-
guage, the faces, the manners have undergone a wonderful change in
three or four days. The running fight we have kept up so long with the
fierté of postillions & padroni in Italy is over & all men are complaisant.
The face of the country is remarkable, not quite a plain but a vast undulating champaign without a hill, and all planted like the Connecticutt
intervales. No fences, the fields full of working women.

June 20, 1833   Paris
    I arrived in Paris at noon on Thursday 20 June. The eye is satisfied
on entering the city with the unquestionable tokens on every side of a
vast, rich, old capital. I crossed the Seine by the Pont Neuf and was very
glad to see my old acquaintance Henry IV very respectably mounted in
bronze upon his own bridge—but a little mortified to see that the saucy
faction of the hour has thrust a tricolor into the monarch's hand as into a
doll's & in spite of time & decency & the grave the old monarch must be
Vicar of Bray in the whirligig politics of his city. From the bridge saw
the Louvre & the Thuilleries.
    We were presently lodged in the Hotel Montmorenci on the Boule-
vard Mont Martre. I have wandered round the city but I am not well
pleased. I have seen so much in five months that the magnificence of
Paris will not take my eye today. The gardens of the Louvre looked
pinched & the wind blew dust in my eyes and before I got into the
Champs Elysees I turned about & flatly refused to go farther. I was
sorry to find that in leaving Italy I had left forever that air of antiquity &
history which her towns possess & in coming hither had come to a loud
modern New York of a place.

July 11, 1833
    Does any man render written account to himself of himself? I think
not. Those who have anything worth repeating, ah! the sad confession!

Those who are innocent have been employed in tape & pins. When will good work be found for great spirits? When shall we be able without a blush & without harm to utter to the world our inmost thought?

July 12, 1833
Be cheerful. What an insane habit is this of groping always into the past months & scraping together every little pitiful instance of awkwardness & misfortune & keeping my nervous system ever on the rack. It is the disease of a man who is at the same time idle & too respectful to the opinions of others.

July 1833
Walk along the Boulevards here & see how men live. One man has live snakes crawling round him & sells soap & essences. Another man has books lying on the ground for sale. Another carries watchchains. Half a dozen beseige me every day with an armful of canes. A little further on one man sells cane tassels at 5 sous. Next sits Boots brandishing his brush at every dirty shoe that walks by. Then several great tubs of gold fish. Another sits at his table cleaning gold & silver spoons with emery & descanting upon its merits. Another has a little table of card puppets which he makes crawl. Then a hand organ. Then a wooden figure which can put an apple in its mouth whenever a child buys an almond. Then a flower merchant.Then a birdshop with perhaps twenty parrots, four swans, hawks, & nightingales. Then the exhibition of the boy with four legs.

July 13, 1833
I carried my ticket from Mr Warden to the Cabinet of Natural History in the Garden of Plants. How much finer things are in composition than alone. 'Tis wise in man to make Cabinets. When I was come into the Ornithological Chambers, I wished I had come only there. The fancy-coloured vests of these elegant beings make me as pensive as the hues & forms of a cabinet of shells, formerly. It is a beautiful collection & makes the visiter as calm & genial as a bridegroom. The limits of the possible are enlarged, & the real is stranger than the imaginary. Some of the birds have a fabulous beauty. One parrot of a fellow, called *Psittacus erythropterus* from New Holland, deserves as special mention as a picture of Raphael in a Gallery. He is the beau of all birds. Then the hummingbirds little & gay. Least of all is the Trochilus Niger. I have seen beetles larger. The *Trochilus pella* hath such a neck of gold & silver & fire! Trochilus Delalandi from Brazil is a glorious little tot—la mouche magnifique. . . .
In the other rooms I saw amber containing perfect musquitoes,

grand blocks of quartz, native gold in all its forms of crystallization, threads, plates, crystals, dust; & silver black as from fire. Ah said I this is philanthropy, wisdom, taste—to form a Cabinet of natural history. Many students were there with grammar & note book & a class of boys with their tutor from some school. Here we are impressed with the inexhaustible riches of nature. The Universe is a more amazing puzzle than ever as you glance along this bewildering series of animated forms—the hazy butterflies, the carved shells, the birds, beasts, fishes, insects, snakes—& the upheaving principle of life everywhere incipient in the very rock aping organized forms. Not a form so grotesque, so savage, nor so beautiful but is an expression of some property inherent in man the observer—an occult relation between the very scorpions and man. I feel the centipede in me—cayman, carp, eagle, & fox. I am moved by strange sympathies, I say continually "I will be a naturalist."

July 15, 1833
I have just returned from Pere le Chaise. It well deserves a visit & does honour to the French. But they are a vain nation. The tombstones have a beseeching importunate vanity and remind you of advertisements. But many are affecting. One which was of dark slate stone had only this inscription, 'Mon Pere.' I prefer the "Ci git" to the "Ici repose" as the beginning of the inscriptions but take the cemetery through I thought the classics rather carried the day. One epitaph was so singular, or so singular to be read by *me*, that I wrote it off.

"Ici repose Auguste Charles Collignon mort plein de confiance dans la bonte de Dieu à l'age de 68 ans et 4 mois le 15 Avril 1830. Il aima et chercha à faire du bein et mena une vie douce et heureuse, en suivant autant qu'il put, la morale et les lecons des essais de Montaigne et des Fables de la Fontaine."—I notice that, universally, the French write as in the above, *"Here lies Augustus, &c."* & we write, *"Here lies the body of, &c"* a more important distinction than *roi de France* & *roi des Francais.*

July 15–17, 1833
Young men are very fond of Paris, partly, no doubt, because of the perfect freedom—freedom from observation as well as interference—in which each one walks after the sight of his own eyes; & partly because the extent & variety of objects offers an unceasing entertainment. So long as a man has francs in his pocket he needs consult neither time nor place nor other men's convenience; wherever in the vast city he is, he is within a stone's throw of a patissier, a cafe, a restaurant, a public garden, a theatre & may enter when he will. If he wish to go to the Thuilleries, perhaps two miles off, let him stop a few minutes at the window of a

printshop or a bookstall, of which there are hundreds & thousands, and
an Omnibus is sure to pass in the direction in which he would go, & for
six sous he rides two or three miles. Then the streets swarm with Cabinets de Lecture where you find all the journals & all the new books. I
spend many hours at Galignani's & lately at the English Reading Room
in the Rue Neuve Augustine where they advertise that they receive 400
journals in all languages & have moreover a very large library.

Lastly the evening need never hang heavy on the stranger's hands,
such ample provision is made here for what the newspapers call "nos
besoins recreatifs." More than twenty theatres are blazing with light &
echoing with fine music every night from the Academie Royale de la
Musique, which is the French Opera, down to the Children's Drama;
not to mention concerts, gardens, & shows innumerable.

The Theatre is the passion of the French & the taste & splendour of
their dramatic exhibitions can hardly be exceeded. The Journal in
speaking of the opera last night, declares that "Mme D. was received by
the dilettanti of Paris with not less joy than the lost soul by the angels in
heaven."

July 15–17, 1833
I have been to the Faubourg St. Martin to hear the Abbe Chatel, the
founder of the Eglise Catholique Francaise. It is a singular institution
which he calls his church with newly invented dresses for the priests &
martial music performed by a large orchestra, relieved by interludes of a
piano with vocal music. His discourse was far better than I could expect
from these preliminaries.

Sometimes he is eloquent. He is a Unitarian but more radical than
any body in America who takes that name.

I was interested in his enterprize for there is always something pathetic in a new church struggling for sympathy & support. He takes
upon himself the whole pecuniary responsibilities of the undertaking, &
for his Chapel in the Rue St Honoré pays an annual rent of 40,000
francs.

July 1833
At Boulogne on Saturday Morn 19th took the steam-boat for London. After a rough passage of 20 hours we arrived at London & landed at
the Tower Stairs.

We know London so well in books & pictures & maps & traditions
that I saw nothing surprizing in this passage up the Thames. A noble
navigable stream lined on each side by a highly cultivated country, full
of all manner of good buildings. Then Greenwich & Deptford, hospital,

docks, arsenals, fleets of shipping, & then the mighty metropolis itself, old, vast, & still. Scarce any body was in the streets. It was about 7 o'clock Sunday Morning & we met few persons until we reached St Paul's. A porter carried our baggage, & we walked through Cheapside, Newgate St., High Holborn, and found lodgings (according to the direction of my friend in Paris) at Mrs. Fowler's No 63 Russell Square. It was an extreme pleasure to hear English spoken in the streets; to understand all the words of Children at play, & to find that we must not any longer express aloud our opinion of every person we met, as in France & Italy we had been wont to do.

Aug. 26, 1833   Carlisle in Cumberland
    I am just arrived in merry Carlisle from Dumfries. A white day in my years. I found the youth I sought in Scotland & good & wise & pleasant he seems to me. Thomas Carlyle lives in the parish of Dunscore 16 miles from Dumfries amid wild & desolate heathery hills & without a single companion in this region out of his own house. There he has his wife a most accomplished & agreeable woman. Truth & peace & faith dwell with them & beautify them. I never saw more amiableness than is in his countenance. He speaks broad Scotch with evident relish.

Aug. 28, 1833   Ambleside
    This morng. I went to Rydal Mt & called upon Mr Wordsworth. His daughters called in their father, a plain looking elderly man in goggles & he sat down & talked with great simplicity. A great deal to say about America, the more so that it gave occasion for talk upon his favorite topic, which is this, that Society is being enlightened by a superficial tuition out of all proportion to its being restrained by moral Culture. Schools do no good. Tuition is not education. He thinks far more of the education of circumstances than of tuition. It is not whether there are offences of which the law takes cognisance but whether there are offenses of which the law does not take cognisance. Sin, sin, is what he fears. & how society is to escape without greatest mischiefs from this source he cannot see.
    He has even said what seemed a paradox, that they needed a civil war in America to teach them the necessity of knitting the social ties stronger.
    There may be in America some vulgarity of manner but that's nothing important; it comes out of the pioneer state of things; but, 1. I fear they are too much given to making of money & secondly to politics; that they make political distinction the end & not the means. And I fear they lack a class of men of leisure—in short of gentlemen to give a tone of

Thomas Carlyle (1795-1881): " 'Tis curious, the magnificence of
his genius, & the poverty of his aims."

honor to the community. I am told that things are boasted of in the second class of society there that in England (God knows are done in
England every day) but never would be spoken of here.

Carlyle he thinks insane sometimes. (I stoutly defended Carlyle.)

Goethe's Wilhelm Meister he abused with might & main—all manner of fornication. It was like flies crossing each other in the air. He had
never got further than the first book, so disgusted was he. I spoke *for* the
better parts of the book & he promised to look at it again.

Carlyle he said wrote the most obscurely. Allowed he was clever &
deep but that he defied the sympathies of everybody. Even Mr Coleridge wrote more clearly though he always wished Coleridge would
write more to be understood. . . .

I hoped he would publish his promised poems. He said he never was in haste to publish, partly because he altered his poetry much & every alteration is ungraciously received but what he wrote would be printed whether he lived or died. I said Tintern Abbey was the favorite poem but that the more contemplative sort preferred the Excursion & the sonnets. He said yes they were better to him. He preferred himself those of his poems which touched the affections to any others.

Sept. 1, 1833   Liverpool

I thank the great God who has led me through this European scene, this last schoolroom in which he has pleased to instruct me from Malta's isle, thro' Sicily, thro' Italy, thro' Switzerland, thro' France, thro' England, thro' Scotland, in safety & pleasure & has now brought me to the shore & the ship that steers westward. He has shown me the men I wished to see—Landor, Coleridge, Carlyle, Wordsworth—he has thereby comforted & confirmed me in my convictions. Many things I owe to the sight of these men. I shall judge more justly, less timidly, of wise men forevermore. To be sure not one of these is a mind of the very first class, but what the intercourse with each of these suggests is true of intercourse with better men, that they never *fill the ear*—fill the mind—no, it is an *idealized* portrait which always we draw of them. Upon an intelligent man, wholly a stranger to their names, they would make in conversation no deep impression—none of a world-filling fame—they would be remembered as sensible well read earnest men— not more. Especially are they all deficient all these four—in different degrees but all deficient—in insight into religious truth. They have no idea of that species of moral truth which I call the first philosophy. (Peter Hunt* is as wise a talker as either of these men. Don't laugh.)

The comfort of meeting men of genius such as these is that they talk sincerely. They feel themselves to be so rich that they are above the meanness of pretending to knowledge which they have not & they frankly tell you what puzzles them. But Carlyle. Carlyle is so amiable that I love him. But I am very glad my travelling is done. A man not old feels himself too old to be a vagabond. The people at their work, the people whose avocations I interrupt by my letters of introduction accuse me by their looks for leaving my business to hinder theirs.

These men make you feel that fame is a conventional thing & that man is a sadly 'limitary' spirit. You speak to them as to children or per- sons of inferior capacity whom it is necessary to humor; adapting our tone & remarks to their known prejudices & not to our knowledge of the truth.

---

*One of Emerson's pupils in 1825. [*JMN*]

I believe in my heart it is better to admire too rashly, as I do, than to be admired too rashly as the great men of this day are. They miss by their premature canonization a great deal of necessary knowledge, & one of these days must begin the world again (as to their surprize they will find needful) poor. I speak now in general & not of these individuals. God save a great man from a little circle of flatterers. I know it is sweet, very sweet, rats bane.

Sept. 2, 1833   Liverpool
No sailing today, so you may know what I have seen & heard in the four days I have been here. Really nothing external, so I must spin my thread from my bowels. It must be said this is the least agreeable city to the traveller in all England—a good packet office—no more. Glad I bid adieu to England, the old, the rich, the strong nation, full of arts & men & memories; nor can I feel any regret in the presence of the best of its sons that I was not born here. I am thankful that I am an American as I am thankful that I am a man. It is its best merit to my eye that it is the most resembling country to America which the world contains.—The famous burden of English taxation is bearable. Men live & multiply under it, though I have heard a father in the higher rank of life speak with regret of the increase of his family.

Sept. 6, 1833
Fair fine wind, still in the Channel—off the coast of Ireland but not in sight of land. This morning 37 sail in sight.
I like my book about nature & wish I knew where & how I ought to live. God will show me. I am glad to be on my way home yet not so glad as others & my way to the bottom I could find perchance with less regret for I think it would not hurt me, that is the ducking or drowning.

Sept. 8, 1833   At Sea
I wrote above my conviction that the great men of England are singularly ignorant of religion. . . . Carlyle almost grudges the poor peasant his Calvinism. Must I not admit in the same moment that I have practical difficulties myself? I see or believe in the wholesomeness of Calvinism for thousands & thousands. I would encourage or rather I would not discourage their scrupulous religious observances. I dare not speak lightly of usages which I omit. And so with this hollow obeisance to things I do not myself value I go on not pestering others with what I do believe & so I am open to the name of a very loose speculator, a faint heartless supporter of a frigid & empty theism, a man of no rigor of manners, of no vigor of benevolence.

Sept. 9, 1833

The road from Liverpool to New York as they who have travelled it well know is very long, crooked, rough, & eminently disagreeable. Good company even, Heaven's best gift, will scarce make it tolerable. Four meals a day is the usual expedient (& the wretchedness of the expedient will show the extremity of the case) & much wine & porter—these are the amusements of wise men in this sad place. The purest wit may have a scurvy stomach.

Sept. 11, 1833

I have been nihilizing as usual & just now posting my Italian journal. . . . Never was a regular dinner with all scientific accompaniments so philosophic a thing as at sea. I tipple with all my heart here. May I not?

Sept. 16, 1833

Dull stormday yesterday. I kept Sunday with Milton & a Presbyterian magazine. Milton says, "if ever any was ravished with moral beauty, he is the man."

It occurred with sad force how much we are bound to be true to ourselves—(the old string)—because we are always judged by others as *ourselves* & not as those whose example we would plead. . . . The truth is, you can't find any example that will suit you, nor could, if the whole family of Adam should pass in procession before you, for you are a new work of God.

Sept. 17, 1833

Milton describes himself in his letter to Diodati as enamoured of moral perfection. He did not love it more than I. That which I cannot yet declare has been my angel from childhood until now. It has separated me from men. It has watered my pillow; it has driven sleep from my bed. It has tortured me for my guilt. It has inspired me with hope. It cannot be defeated by my defeats. It cannot be questioned though all the martyrs apostatize. It is always the glory that shall be revealed; it is the 'open secret' of the universe; & it is only the feebleness & dust of the observer that makes it future, the whole *is* now potentially in the bottom of his heart. It is the soul of religion. Keeping my eye on this I understand all heroism, the history of loyalty & of martyrdom & of bigotry, the heat of the methodist, the nonconformity of the dissenter, the patience of the Quaker. But what shall the hour say for distinctions such as these—this hour of southwest gales & rain dripping cabin? As the law of light is fits of easy transmission & reflexion such is also the soul's law.

She is only superior at intervals to pain, to fear, to temptation, only in raptures unites herself to God and Wordsworth truly said

> Tis the most difficult of tasks to keep
> Heights which the soul is competent to gain.

Sept. 1833

In this world, if a man sits down to think, he is immediately asked if he has the headache.

Sept.–Oct. 1833

Men seem to be constitutionally believers & unbelievers. There is no bridge that can cross from a mind in one state to a mind in the other. All my opinions, affections, whimsies, are tinged with belief—incline to that side. All that is generous, elegant, rich, wise, looks that way. But I cannot give reasons to a person of a different persuasion that are at all adequate to the force of my conviction. Yet when I fail to find the reason, my faith is not less.

It will take you long to learn another tongue so as to make yourself fully understood by those who speak it but your actions are easy of translation. They understand what you do. Temperance is good English & good French & good Italian. Your courage, your kindness, your honesty are as plain to a Turk as his own alphabet.

In Boston they have an eye for improvement, a thing which does not exist in Asia nor in Africa.

Oct. 20, 1833   Newtown

A Sabbath in the country but not so odoriferous as I have imagined. Mr. Bates a plain, serious Calvinist not winning but not repelling: one of the useful police which God makes out of the ignorance & superstition of the youth of the world. I dare not & wish not speak disrespectfully of these good, abstemious, laborious men. Yet I could not help asking myself how long is the society to be taught in this dramatic or allegorical style? When is religious truth to be distinctly uttered—what it is, not what it resembles? Thus every Sunday ever since they were born this congregation have heard tell of *Salvation,* and of going to the door of heaven & knocking, & being answered from Within, "Depart, I Never Knew You" & of being sent away to eternal ruin. What hinders that instead of this parable the naked fact be stated to them? Namely that as long as they offend against their conscience they will seek to be happy but they shall not be able, they shall not come to any true knowledge of

God, they shall be avoided by good & by wise men, they shall become
worse & worse.

Oct. 24, 1833   Newton

The teacher of the coming age must occupy himself in the study &
explanation of the moral constitution of man more than in the elucida-
tion of difficult texts. He must work in the conviction that the Scripture
can only be interpreted by the same spirit that uttered them. And that as
long as the heart & the mind are illumined by a spiritual life there is no
dead letter but a perpetual Scripture.

Nov.–Dec. 1833

This Book is my Savings Bank. I grow richer because I have somewhere to deposit my earnings; and fractions are worth more to me because corresponding fractions are waiting here that shall be made integers by their addition.

Dec. 14, 1833

I please myself with contemplating the felicity of my present situation. May it last. It seems to me singularly free & it invites me to every
virtue & to great improvement.

Jan. 19, 1834

What is it that interests us in biography? Is there not always a silent
comparison between the intellectual & moral endowments portrayed &
those of which we are conscious? The reason why the Luther, the
Newton, the Bonaparte concerning whom we read, was made the subject of panegyric, is, that in the writer's opinion, in some one respect this
particular man represented the idea of Man. And as far as we accord
with his judgment, we take the picture for a standard Man, and so let
every line accuse or approve our own ways of thinking & living by
comparison.

Jan. 21, 1834

Is not the use of society to educate the Will which never would acquire force in solitude? We mean Will, when we say that a person has a
good deal of character. Women generally have weak wills, sharply expressed perhaps, but capricious unstable. When the will is strong we inevitably respect it, in man or woman. I have thought that the perfection
of female character seldom existed in poverty, at least where poverty
was reckoned low. Is not this because the rich are accustomed to be
obeyed promptly & so the will acquires strength & yet is calm & graceful? I think that involuntary respect which the rich inspire in very inde-

pendent & virtuous minds, arises from the same circumstance, the irresistible empire of a strong will. There is not nor ever can be any competition between a will of words & a real will. Webster, Adams, Clay, Calhoun, Chatham, and every statesman who was ever formidable are wilful men. But Everett & Stanley & the Ciceros are not; want this backbone. Meantime a great many men in society speak strong but have no oak, are all willow. And only a virtuous will is omnipotent.

Jan. 22, 1834

Luther & Napoleon are better treatises on the Will than Edwards's.

Different faces things wear to different persons. Whole process of human generation how bifronted! To one it is bawdy, to another wholly pure. In the mother's heart every sensation from the nuptial embrace through the uncertain symptoms of the quickening to the birth of her child is watched with an interest more chaste & wistful than the contemplations of the nun in her cloister. Yet the low minded visiter of a woman in such circumstances has the ignorant impertinence to look down & feel a sort of shame.

Jan. 23, 1834

I cannot read of the jubilee of Goethe, & of such a velvet life without a sense of incongruity. Genius is out of place when it reposes fifty years on chairs of state & inhales a continual incense of adulation. Its proper ornaments & relief are poverty & reproach & danger. & if the grandduke had cut Goethe's head off, it would have been much better for his fame than his retiring to his rooms after dismissing the obsequious crowds to arrange tastefully & contemplate their gifts & honorary inscriptions.

Feb. 10–11, 1834

How imbecile is often a young person of superior intellectual powers for want of acquaintance with his powers; bashful, timid, he shrinks, retreats, before every confident person & is disconcerted by arguments & pretensions he would be ashamed to put forward himself. Let him work as many merchants do with the forces of millions of property for months & years upon the wills of hundreds of persons & you shall see him transformed into an adroit fluent masterful gentleman, fit to take & keep his place in any society of men. This is the account to be given of the fine manners of the young Southerners brought up amidst slaves, & of the concession that young Northerners make to them, yes, & old Northerners to old Southerners. . . .

This part of education is conducted in the nursery & the playground, in fights, in frolics, in business, in politics. My manners & history would have been very different, if my parents had been rich, when I was a boy at school.

Feb. 12, 1834   New Bedford
The days & months & years flit by, each with his own black riband, his own sad reminiscence. Yet I looked at the Almanack affectionately as a book of Promise. These last three years of my life are not a chasm—I could almost wish they were—so brilliantly sometimes the vision of Ellen's beauty & love & life come out of the darkness. Pleasantly mingled with my sad thoughts the sublime religion of Miss Rotch yesterday. She was much disciplined, she said, in the years of Quaker dissension and driven inward, driven home, to find an anchor, until she learned to have *no choice*, to acquiesce without understanding the reason when she found an obstruction to any particular course of acting. She objected to having this spiritual direction called an impression, or an intimation, or an oracle. It was none of them. It was so simple it could hardly be spoken of. . . .
Can you believe, Waldo Emerson, that you may relieve yourself of this perpetual perplexity of choosing? & by putting your ear close to the soul, learn always the true way.

Feb. 19, 1834
A seaman in the coach told the story of an old sperm whale which he called a white whale which was known for many years by the whalemen as Old Tom & who rushed upon the boats which attacked him & crushed the boats to small chips in his jaws, the men generally escaping by jumping overboard & being picked up. A vessel was fitted out at New Bedford, he said, to take him. And he was finally taken somewhere off Payta head by the Winslow or the Essex. He gave a fine account of a storm which I heard imperfectly. Only 'the whole ocean was all feather white.'

Feb. 22, 1834
It were well to live purely, to make your word worth something. Deny yourself cake & ale to make your testimony irresistible. Be a pure reason to your contemporaries for God & truth. What is good in itself can be bad to nobody. As I went to Church I thought how seldom the present hour is seized upon as a new moment. To a soul alive to God every moment is a new world. A new audience, a new Sabbath affords an opportunity of communicating thought & moral excitement that shall surpass all previous experience, that shall constitute an epoch a revolution in the minds on whom you act & in your own. The awakened soul,

the man of genius makes every day such a day, by looking forward only but the professional mob look back only to custom & their past selves.

April 10, 1834

Is it possible that in the solitude I seek I shall have the resolution the force to work as I ought to work—as I project in highest most farsighted hours? Well, & what do you project? Nothing less than to look at every object in its relation to Myself.

April 11, 1834

Went yesterday to Cambridge & spent most of the day at Mount Auburn, got my luncheon at Fresh Pond, & went back again to the woods. After much wandering & seeing many things, four snakes gliding up & down a hollow for no purpose that I could see—not to eat, not for love, but only gliding; then a whole bed of Hepatica triloba, cousins of the Anemone all blue & beautiful but constrained by niggard Nature to wear their last year's faded jacket of leaves; then a black capped titmouse who came upon a tree & when I would know his name, sang *chick a dee dee;* then a far off tree full of clamorous birds, I know not what, but you might hear them half a mile. I forsook the tombs & found a sunny hollow where the east wind could not blow & lay down against the side of a tree to most happy beholdings. At least I opened my eyes & let what would pass through them into the soul. I saw no more my relation how near & petty to Cambridge or Boston, I heeded no more what minute or hour our Massachusetts clocks might indicate—I saw only the noble earth on which I was born, with the great Star which warms & enlightens it. I saw the clouds that hang their significant drapery over us.—It was Day, that was all Heaven said. The pines glittered with their innumerable green needles in the light & seemed to challenge me to read their riddle. The drab-oak leaves of the last year turned their little somersets & lay still again. And the wind bustled high overhead in the forest top. This gay & grand architecture from the vault to the moss & lichen on which I lay, who shall explain to me the laws of its proportions & adornments?

April 12, 1834

We are always on the brink of an ocean of thought into which we do not yet swim. We are poor lords—have immense powers which we are hindered from using. I am kept out of my heritage. I talk of these powers of perceiving & communicating truth, as my powers. I look for respect as the possessor of them. & yet, after exercising them for short & irregular periods, I move about without them—quite under their sphere— quite unclothed. " 'Tis the most difficult of tasks to keep Heights—

which the soul is competent to gain." A prophet waiting for the word of
the Lord. Is it the prophet's fault that he waits in vain? Yet how mysterious & painful these laws. Always in the precincts—never admitted; always preparing—vast machinery—plans of life—travelling—studies—
the country—solitude—and suddenly in any place, in the street, in the
chamber will the heaven open & the regions of boundless knowledge be
revealed; as if to show you how thin the veil, how null the circumstances. The hours of true thought in a lifetime how few! . . .

All the mistakes I make arise from forsaking my own station & trying to see the object from another person's point of view. I read so resolute a self-thinker as Carlyle & am convinced of the riches of wisdom
that ever belong to the man who utters his own thought with a divine
confidence that it must be true if he heard it there.

April 13–14, 1834

It occurs how much friction is in the machinery of society. . . . A
young man is to be educated & schools are built & masters brought together & gymnasium erected & scientific toys & Monitorial Systems & a
College endowed with many professorships & the apparatus is so enormous & unmanageable that the e-ducation or *calling out of his faculties*
is never accomplished, he graduates a dunce.

April 20, 1834

The whole secret of the teacher's force lies in the conviction that
men are convertible. And they are. They want awakening. Get the soul
out of bed, out of her deep habitual sleep, out into God's universe, to a
perception of its beauty & hearing of its Call and your vulgar man, your
prosy selfish sensualist awakes a God & is conscious of force to shake the
world.

April 26, 1834

Rain rain. The good rain like a bad preacher does not know when to
leave off.

April 29, 1834

A ship, a locomotive, a cotton factory is a wonder until we see how
these Romes were not built in a day but part suggested part & complexity became simplicity. The poem, the oration, the book are superhuman,
but the wonder is out when you see the manuscript. Homer how wonderful until the German erudition discovered a cyclus of homeric
poems. It is all one; a trick of cards, a juggler's sleight, an astronomical
result, an algebraic formula, amazing when we see only the result, cheap
when we are shown the means.

*   *   *

G. P. Bradford tells a ridiculous story about the boy learning his alphabet. This letter is A; says the teacher. A—drawls the boy. "That is B," says the teacher. "B," drawls the boy, & so on, "That letter is W," says the teacher. "The Devil! Is that W?" enquires the pupil.—Now I say that this story hath an alarming sound. It is the essence of Radicalism. It is Jack Cade himself. Or is it not exquisite ridicule upon our learned Linnaean Classifications? What shell is this? "It is a strombus." "The devil! is that a strombus?" would be the appropriate reply.

April 30, 1834

Every common place we utter is a formula in which is packed up an uncounted list of particular observations. And every man's mind at this moment is a formula condensing the result of all his conclusions.

May 3, 1834

We have no Theory of animated Nature. When we have, it will be itself the true Classification. Perhaps a study of the cattle on the mountainside as they graze, is more suggestive of truth than the inspection of their parts in the dissection-room. . . .

I wrote once before that the true philosophy of man should give a theory of Beasts & Dreams. A German dispatched them both by saying that Beasts are dreams, or "the nocturnal side of Nature."

May 16, 1834

I remember when I was a boy going upon the beach & being charmed with the colors & forms of the shells. I picked up many & put them in my pocket. When I got home I could find nothing that I gathered—nothing but some dry ugly mussel & snail shells. Thence I learned that Composition was more important than the beauty of individual forms to effect. On the shore they lay wet & social by the sea & under the sky.

May 21, 1834

I will thank God of myself & for that I have. I will not manufacture remorse of the pattern of others, nor feign their joys. I am born tranquil, not a stern economist of Time but never a keen sufferer. I will not affect to suffer. Be my life then a long gratitude. I will trust my instincts. For always a reason halts after an instinct, & when I have deviated from the instinct, comes somebody with a profound theory teaching that I ought to have followed it. Some Goethe, Swedenborg, or Carlyle. I stick at scolding the boy, yet conformably to rule, I scold him. By & by the reprimand is a proven error. "Our first & third thought coincide." I was the

true philosopher in college, & Mr Farrar & Mr Hedge & Dr Ware the
false. Yet what seemed then to me less probable?

May 30, 1834
Languages as discipline, much reading as an additional atmosphere
or two, to gird the loins & make the muscles more tense. It seems time
lost for a grown man to be turning the leaves of a dictionary like a boy to
learn German, but I believe he will gain tension & creative power by so
doing. Good books have always a prolific atmosphere about them &
brood upon the spirit.

June 5, 1834
There are persons both of superior character & intellect whose superiority quite disappears when they are put together. They neutralize,
anticipate, puzzle, & belittle each other.

June 1834
Webster's speeches seem to be the utmost that the unpoetic West has
accomplished or can. We all lean on England, scarce a verse, a page, a
newspaper but is writ in imitation of English forms, our very manners &
conversation are traditional & sometimes the life seems dying out of all
literature & this enormous paper currency of Words is accepted instead.
I suppose the evil may be cured by this rank rabble party, the Jackson-
ism of the country, heedless of English & of all literature—a stone cut
out of the ground without hands—they may root out the hollow dilet-
tantism of our cultivation in the coarsest way & the new-born may
begin again to frame their own world with greater advantage. Meantime
Webster is no imitator but a true genius for his work if that is not the
highest. But every true man stands on the top of the world.

June 26, 1834
Next door to us lives a young man who is learning to drum. He studies hard at his science every night. I should like to reward his music with
a wreath of smilax peduncularis.*

July 15, 1834
In our plans of life an apparent confusion. We seem not to know
what we want. Why, it is plain we can do best something which in the
present form of society will be misconstrued & taken for another thing. I
wish to be a true & free man, & therefore would not be a woman, or a
king, or a clergyman, each of which classes in the present order of things

---

* A kind of stinkweed.

is a slave. Mr Canning judged right in preferring the title of *Mister*, in the company of Alexander & Napoleon, to *My Lord*. The simple untitled unofficed citizen possessing manners, power, cultivation, is more formidable & more pleasing than any dignitary whose condition & etiquette only makes him more vulnerable & more helpless.

July 18? 1834

What is there of the divine in a load of bricks? What is there of the divine in a barber's shop or a privy? Much. All.

Aug. 10, 1834

At Mr Grafton's church this P.M. and heard the eloquent old man preach his Jewish sermon dryeyed. Indeed I felt as a much worse spirit might feel among worshippers—as if the last link was severed that bound him to their traditions & he ought to go out hence. Strange that such fatuity as Calvinism is now, should be able to stand yet—mere shell as it is—in the face of day. At every close of a paragraph it almost seemed as if this devout old man looked intelligence & questioned the whole thing. What a revival if St Paul should come & replace these threadbare rags with the inexhaustible resources of sound Ethics. Yet they are so befooled as to call this sucked eggshell hightoned orthodoxy, & to talk of anything true as *mere morality*. Is it not time to present this matter of Christianity exactly as it is, to take away all false reverence from Jesus, & not mistake the stream for the source? 'It is no more according to Plato than according to me.' God is in every man. God is in Jesus but let us not magnify any of the vehicles as we magnify the Infinite Law itself. We have defrauded him of his claim of love on all noble hearts by our superstitious mouth honor. We love Socrates but give Jesus the Unitarian Association.

Aug. 16, 1834

Saturday Eve. King Lear & Ant. & Cleopatra still fill me with wonder. Every scene is as spirited as if writ by a fresh hand of the first class and there is never straining; sentiments of the highest elevation are as simply expressed as the stage directions. They praise Scott for taking kings & nobles off their stilts & giving them simple dignity but Scott's grandees are all turgid compared with Shakspear's. There is more true elevation of character in Prince Hal's sentence about the pleached doublet than in any king in the romances. Another mastership of Shakspear is the immortality of the style; the speeches of passion are writ for the most part in a style as fresh now as it was when the play was published. The remarkable sentences of Lear, Hamlet, Othello, Macbeth, might as naturally have been composed in 1834 as in 1600.

Aug. 17, 1834

Milton was too learned, though I hate to say it. It wrecked his originality. He was more indebted to the Hebrew than even to the Greek. Wordsworth is a more original poet than he. That seems the poet's garland. He speaks by the right that he has somewhat yet unsaid to say. Scott & Coleridge & such like are not poets, only professors of the art. Homer's is the only Epic. He is original yet he separates before the German telescopes into two, ten, or twenty stars. Shakspeare by singular similarity of fortune undeniably an original & unapproached bard—first of men—is yet infolded in the same darkness as an individual Writer. His best works are of doubted authenticity and what was his, & what his novelist's, & what the players', seems yet disputed. A sharp illustration of that relentless disregard of the individual in regard for the race which runs through history. It is not an individual but the general mind of man that speaks from time to time quite careless & quite forgetful of what mouth or mouths it makes use. Go to the bard or orator that has spoken & ask him if what he said were his own? No. He got it he knows not where, but it is none of his.

Aug. 19–20, 1834

We sit down with intent to write truly & end with making a book that contains no thought of ours but merely the tune of the time. Here am I writing a ΦBK poem free to say what I choose & it looks to me now as if it would scarce express thought of mine but be a sort of fata Morgana reflecting the images of Byron, Shakspear, & the newspapers.

We do what we can, & then make a theory to prove our performance the best.

Aug. 30, 1834

Were it not a heroic adventure in me to insist on being a popular speaker & run full tilt against the Fortune who with such beautiful consistency shows evermore her back? . . . my entire success, such as it is, is composed wholly of particular failures—every public work of mine of the least importance, having been (probably without exception) noted at the time as a failure. The only success (agreeably to common ideas) has been in the country & there founded on the false notion that here was a Boston preacher. I will take Miss Barbauld's line for my motto "And the more falls I get, move faster on."

Aug.–Sept. 1834

It is extremely disagreeable, nay, a little fiendish to laugh amid dreams. In bed I would keep my countenance, if you please.

Sept. 15, 1834

A man in the New Bedford coach told me a story of a lady who took an egg in her hand & the warmth of her body hatching it the little serpents came out & ran all over her hand.

Oct. 6, 1834

The high prize of eloquence may be mine, the joy of uttering what no other can utter & what all must receive.

Oct. 29–30, 1834

How different is one man in two hours! Whilst he sits alone in his studies & opens not his mouth he is God manifest in flesh. Put him in a parlor with unfit company and he shall talk like a fool.

Nov. 5, 1834

The elections. Whilst it is notorious that the Jackson party is the *Bad* party in the cities & in general in the country except in secluded districts where a single Newspaper has deceived a well disposed community, still, on all the banners equally of tory & whig good professions are inscribed. The Jackson flags say "Down with corruption!" "We ask for nothing but our Right." "The Constitution, the Laws," "the Laboring Classes," "Free trade," &c &c. So that they have not yet come to the depravity that says, "Evil be thou my good." Should the Whig party fail, which God avert! the patriot will still have some confidence in the redeeming force of the latent i.e. deceived virtue that is contained within the tory party; and yet more in the remedial regenerative Nature of Man which ever reproduces a healthful moral sense even out of stupidity & corruption. Thus the children of the Convicts at Botany Bay are found to have sound moral sentiments.

Nov. 15, 1834

Hail to the quiet fields of my fathers! Not wholly unattended by supernatural friendship & favor let me come hither. Bless my purposes as they are simple & virtuous. . . . Henceforth I design not to utter any speech, poem, or book that is not entirely & peculiarly my work. I will say at Public Lectures & the like, those things which I have meditated for their own sake & not for the first time with a view to that occasion. If otherwise you select a new subject & labor to make a good appearance on the appointed day, it is so much lost time to you & lost time to your hearer. It is a parenthesis in your genuine life. You are your own dupe. & for the sake of conciliating your audience you have failed to edify them & winning their ear you have really lost their love and gratitude.

Nov. 21, 1834

When we have lost our God of tradition & ceased from our God of rhetoric then may God fire the heart with his presence.

Dec. 2, 1834   Concord

The age of puberty is a crisis in the life of the man worth studying. It is the passage from the Unconscious to the Conscious; from the sleep of the Passions to their rage; from careless receiving to cunning providing; from beauty to use; from omnivorous curiosity to anxious stewardship; from faith to doubt; from maternal Reason to hard short-sighted Understanding; from Unity to disunion . . .

A real interest in your fellow creatures is of necessity reciprocal. For want of it how tragic is the solitude of the old man.* No prayer, no good wish out of the whole world follows him into his sick chamber. It is as frightful a solitude as that which cold produces round the traveller who has lost his way. This comes of management, of cunning, & of vanity. Never held he intercourse with any human being with thorough frankness, man to man but always with that imp-like second thought. And so hath no friend. Yet I forget not his generosity, his tenderness to Ellen. And his faults have not descended to his children.

Dec. 3, 1834

The poor Irishman—a wheelbarrow is his country.

Dec. 6, 1834

Do you imagine that because I do not say Luther's creed all his works are an offence to me? Far otherwise. I can animate them all that they shall live to me. I can worship in that temple as well as in any other. I have only to translate a few of the leading phrases into their equivalent verities, to adjust his almanack to my meridian & all the conclusions, all the predictions shall be strictly true. Such is the everlasting advantage of truth. Let a man work after a pattern he really sees & every man shall be able to find a correspondence between these works & his own & to turn them to some account in Rome, London, or Japan, from the first to the hundredth century.

Dec. 8, 1834

Pray heaven that you may have a sympathy with all sorts of excellence even with those antipodal to your own. If any eye rest on this page

---

*Dr. Ezra Ripley, Emerson's step-grandfather. [*JMN*]

let him know that he who blotted it, could not go into conversation with any person of good understanding without being presently gravelled. The slightest question of his most familiar proposition disconcerted him—eyes, face, & understanding, beyond recovery. Yet did he not the less respect & rejoice in this daily gift of vivacious common sense which was so formidable to him. May it last as long as the World.

Dec. 9? 1834

There is great delight in learning a new language. When the day comes in the scholar's progress unawares when he reads pages without recurrence to his dictionary, he shuts up his book with that sort of fearful delight with which the bridegroom sits down in his own house with the bride, saying, 'I shall now live with you always.'

Dec. 14, 1834

Yesterday I sealed & despatched my letter to Carlyle. Today, riding to East Sudbury, I pleased myself with the beauties & terrors of the snow; the oak-leaf hurrying over the banks is fit ornament. Nature in the woods is very companionable. There, my Reason & my Understanding are sufficient company for each other. I have my glees as well as my glooms, alone. Confirm my faith (& when I write the word, Faith looks indignant), pledge me the word of the Highest that I shall have my dead & my absent again, & I could be content & cheerful alone for a thousand years. . . . The moment we indulge our affections, the earth is metamorphosed; all its tragedies & ennuis vanish, all duties even, nothing remains to fill eternity with but two or three persons. But then a person is a *cause*. What is Luther but Protestantism? or Columbus but Columbia? And were I assured of meeting Ellen tomorrow would it be less than a world, a personal world? Death has no bitterness in the light of that thought.

Dec. 15-16, 1834

House of Seem & house of Be. Coleridge's four classes of Readers. 1. the Hour glass sort, all in & all out; 2. the Sponge sort, giving it all out a little dirtier than it took in; 3. of the Jelly bag, keeping nothing but the refuse; 4. of the Golconda, sieves picking up the diamonds only.

Dec. 18, 1834

Loathsome lecture last eve. on precocity, & the dissection of the brain, & the distortion of the body, & genius, &c. A grim compost of blood & mud. Blessed, thought I, were those who, lost in their pursuits, never knew that they had a body or a mind.

Ezra Ripley (1751–1841): "I remember his pleading almost reproachful
looks at the sky when the thundergust was coming up to spoil his
hay—'We are in the Lord's hand,' he said & seemed to say 'You
know me: this field is mine, Dr Ripley's thine own servant.' "

Dec. 21, 1834

Blessed is the day when the youth discovers that Within and Above
are synonyms.

Dec. 22, 1834

If I were more in love with life & as afraid of dying as you seem to
insinuate I would go to a Jackson Caucus or to the Julien Hall & I doubt
not the unmixed malignity, the withering selfishness, the impudent vulgarity that mark those meetings would speedily cure me of my appetite
for longevity. In the hush of these woods I find no Jackson placards af-
fixed to the trees.

Dec. 23, 1834

Do, dear, when you come to write Lyceum lectures, remember that
you are not to say, What must be said in a Lyceum? but what discover-

ies or stimulating thoughts have I to impart to a thousand persons? not what they will expect to hear but what is fit for me to say.

Dec. 27, 1834

There is in every man a determination of character to a peculiar end, counteracted often by unfavorable fortune, but more apparent the more he is left at liberty. This is called his genius, or his nature, or his turn of mind. The object of Education should be to remove all obstructions & let this natural force have free play & exhibit its peculiar product. It seems to be true that no man in this is deluded. This determination of his character is to something in nature; something real. This object is called his Idea. It is that which rules his most advised actions, those especially that are most his, & is most distinctly discerned by him in those days or moments when he derives the sincerest satisfaction from his life.

Dec. 29? 1834

Extremes meet. Misfortunes even may be so accumulated as to be ludicrous. To be shipwrecked is bad; to be shipwrecked on an iceberg is horrible; to be shipwrecked on an iceberg in a snowstorm, confounds us; to be shipwrecked on an iceberg in a storm and to find a bear on the snow bank to dispute the sailor's landing which is not driven away till he has bitten off a sailor's arm, is rueful to laughter.

Some people smile spite of themselves in communicating the worst news.

Concord and Discord

1835–1838

E MERSON HAILED HIS return to the "quiet fields" of his fathers in the fall of 1834, when he went with his mother to live in the ancestral home (Hawthorne's "Old Manse") that his grandfather William had built in north Concord before the Revolution. By January he was engaged to Lydia Jackson of Plymouth, and in September he brought his bride—now called Lidian (and sometimes in the journal Asia, the Queen of Sheba, or Queenie)—to the house he had bought on the Cambridge Turnpike in Concord. The Emersons' home soon filled with new friends—Bronson Alcott, Margaret Fuller, Henry Thoreau—who helped compensate Emerson for the deaths of his brothers Edward (in 1834) and Charles (in 1836).

Though now eclipsed by his daughter Louisa May, Alcott was considered an orphic genius in the Concord circle, and Emerson came to depend more and more on his spiritual companionship, despite his exasperating vaporousness (by 1840 Emerson had to concede that Alcott was a "tedious archangel"). The passionately intellectual Margaret Fuller spent three weeks with Waldo and Lidian in the summer of 1836 and quickly became, and remained, a fascination and a fear to Emerson. As for Henry Thoreau, who was a member of the class of 1837 at Harvard and probably heard Emerson's Phi Beta Kappa address at his commencement, it seems he made *his* first journal entry in October 1837 as a result of Emerson's asking "What are you doing now ... Do you keep a journal?" In line with his own Transcendental theory of friendship, Emerson would treat each of these three indispensable companions as "a sort of beautiful enemy" whose best function was to keep him on the stretch, provoking him to higher states of thought and feeling. In this extraordinary Massachusetts village, friendship—to borrow Dr. Johnson's definition of Metaphysical wit—was a kind of *discordia concors.*

Emerson continued to preach occasionally in this period while he prepared and delivered lecture series on such subjects as the biography of great men, English literature, the philosophy of history, and human culture. In September 1836 Emerson's first book, *Nature*—part philosophical treatise, part rhapsody on the powers of the imagination—was published anonymously in Boston, and by the end of the next month he had a first child as well. He pronounced little Waldo "a lovely wonder . . . which makes the Universe look friendly to me." Only five months before, when his beloved brother Charles died, Emerson feared that he was entering a "gloomy epoch" of his life. "Every body leads two or three lives, has two or three consciousnesses which he nimbly alternates," he had noted in 1835. Now he found himself unpredictably on the high side of the seesaw.

In the spring of 1837 America was struck by financial panic and declined into a severe depression, but Emerson was about to receive the second half of his Tucker inheritance, which altogether would provide him with a yearly income of about $1200. In an understandably ebullient mood, he delivered his "American Scholar" address at Harvard on August 31, exhorting the graduating class to trust themselves and cheer, raise, and guide their countrymen in an exciting age of change. This was the nation's "intellectual declaration of independence," in Oliver Wendell Holmes's phrase. Emerson's aim was to unite all Americans under the banner of a common hope, and he was much gratified when, at a dinner following his address, one of the speakers rose with this toast: "Mr. President . . . I suppose all know where the orator comes from; and I suppose all know what he has said. I give you *The Spirit of Concord. It makes us all of One Mind.*"

Emerson would surely have been happy to see the continuance of such genial agreement, but he also believed that harmony cloys without the provocation of creative discord. He had noted in 1835 that the mind vibrates like a pendulum between two objects—the desire of truth and the desire of repose: "He in whom the love of Repose predominates, will accept the first creed he meets . . . he gets rest & reputation; but he shuts the door of

Truth." Though Emerson did indeed love his comfort and his reputation, he had chosen the way of truth. Now it was time to cross the threshold. Responding to an invitation in the spring of 1838 from the graduating class in divinity at Harvard, he gave much thought to an address that would justify his decision to leave the church and would call for a religion first of soul, "and second, soul, and evermore, soul." Feeling in a rather violent mood and determined to speak out ("I ought to go upright & vital & say the truth in all ways"), however contentiously, he filled many journal pages with talk of Napoleon and revolution and prepared for the storm that he knew would follow his address. Part of his anger at the establishment he directed, in May, to President Van Buren in a strongly worded letter denouncing the government's plan to remove the Cherokee nation from its ancestral lands. Emerson considered his letter more a scream than a thesis, but he was in fact primed for screaming.

The Divinity School Address was delivered on July 15, 1838. It delighted his fellow Transcendentalists but outraged the faculty. Emerson had predicted that all the old grannies would "squeak & gibber," and so they did. A senior professor in divinity, Andrews Norton, attacked Emerson's discourse as the "latest form of infidelity," and some members of his own family—especially his Aunt Mary Moody Emerson—agreed. But Emerson held his ground. "We cannot easily be reconciled," he notes in the journal, "for I have a great deal more to say that will shock you." His address at Dartmouth on July 24 was not very shocking, perhaps because he himself was in a state of shock, but he did invoke Napoleon once again and asserted, with rich meaning, that he would "essay to be." If that was partially a statement about his projected work as a writer, Emerson took a decisive step to abandon his old career by preaching his last sermon in January 1839.

As the air of controversy cleared and Emerson's world returned to normal, he prepared to celebrate the birth of his second child in February. When the "soft, quiet, swarthy little creature" arrived, Emerson noted with satisfaction that the mother had decided to name her daughter Ellen, after Emerson's first wife. "Lidian . . . magnanimously makes my gods her gods," he wrote. Personally, a least, it was a happy conclusion to a year of theological debate.

Jan. 14, 1835

The great value of Biography consists in the perfect sympathy that exists between like minds. Space & time are an absolute nullity to this principle. An action of Luther's that I heartily approve I do adopt also. . . . Socrates, St Paul, Antoninus, Luther, Milton have lived for us as much as for their contemporaries if by books or by tradition their life & words come to my ear. We recognize with delight a strict likeness between their noblest impulses & our own. We are tried in their trial. By our cordial approval we conquer in their victory. We participate in their act by our thorough understanding of it.

Jan. 15, 1835

My Grandfather William Emerson left his parish & joined the Northern Army in the strong hope of having great influence on the men. He was bitterly disappointed in finding that the best men at home became the worst in the camp, vied with each other in profanity, drunkenness & every vice, & degenerated as fast as the days succeeded each other & instead of much influence he found he had none. This so affected him that when he became sick with the prevalent distemper he insisted on taking a dismission not a furlough, & as he died on his return his family lost, it is said, a major's pension.

We are all glad of warm days they are so economical & in the country in winter the back is always cold.

Feb. 2, 1835

Let Christianity speak ever for the poor & the low. Though the voice of society should demand a defence of slavery from all its organs that service can never be expected from me. My opinion is of no worth, but I have not a syllable of all the language I have learned, to utter for the planter. If by opposing slavery I go to undermine institutions, I confess I do not wish to live in a nation where slavery exists. The life of this world has but a limited worth in my eyes & really is not worth such a price as the toleration of slavery. Therefore though I may be so far restrained by unwillingness to cut the planter's throat as that I should refrain from denouncing him, yet I pray God that not even in my dream or in madness may I ever incur the disgrace of articulating one word of apology for the slave trader or slave-holder.

Feb. 16, 1835

If Milton, if Burns, if Bryant, is in the world we have more tolerance & more love for the changing sky, the mist, the rain, the bleak overcast day, the indescribable sunrise & the immortal stars. If we believed no poet survived on the planet, nature would be tedious.

Feb. 25, 1835
On Visits. If I had any thing to say to you, you would find me in your house pretty quick.

March 19, 1835
In talking weeks ago with Mary Moody Emerson I was ready to say that a severest truth would forbid me to say that ever I had made a sacrifice. That which we are, in healthy times seems so great that nothing can be taken from us that seems much. I loved Ellen, & love her with an affection that would ask nothing but its indulgence to make me blessed. Yet when she was taken from me, the air was still sweet, the sun was not taken down from my firmament, & however sore was that particular loss, I still felt that it was particular, that the Universe remained to us both, that the Universe abode in its light & in its power to replenish the heart with hope. Distress never, trifles never abate my trust. Only this Lethean stream that washes through us, that gives sometimes a film or haze of unreality, a suggestion that, as Charles said of Concord society, 'we are on the way back to Annihilation', only this threatens my Trust. But not that would certify me that I had ever suffered. Praise! Praise & Wonder! And oft we feel so wistful & babe-like that we cannot help thinking that a correspondent sentiment of paternal pleasantry must exist over us in the bosom of God.

March 29, 1835
Certainly a man would be glad to do his country service but he cannot cram his service down its throat. It is time enough if he come when he is called. It is enough for him that he has eyes to see that he is infinite spectator without hurrying uncalled to be infinite doer. Let him brood on his immortality . . .

April 10, 1835
I fretted the other night at the Hotel at the stranger who broke into my chamber after midnight claiming to share it. But after his lamp had smoked the chamber full & I had turned round to the wall in despair the man blew out his lamp, knelt down at his bedside & made in low whisper a long earnest prayer. Then was the relation entirely changed between us. I fretted no more but respected & liked him.

April 11, 1835

Glad to hear music in the village last evening under the fine yellow moon: it sounds like cultivation, domestication. In America where all are on wheels one is glad to meet with a sign of adorning our own town. It is a consecrated beautifying of our place. A bugle, clarionet, & flute are to us a momentary Homer & Milton. Music is sensuous poetry.

April 14, 1835

Rev. Dr Freeman consoled my father on his deathbed by telling him he had not outlived his teeth, &c. & bid my mother expect now to be neglected by society.

April 19, 1835

It is a happy talent to know how to play. Some men must always work if they would be respectable; for the moment they trifle, they are silly. Others show most talent when they trifle. Be it said of W that his excess of reverence made it impossible for him to realize ever that he was a man; he never assumed equality with strangers but still esteemed them older than himself though they were of his own age or younger. He went through life postponing his maturity & died in his error.

May 10–12, 1835

Hard Times. In this contradictory world of Truth the hard times come when the good times are in the world of commerce; namely, sleep, fulleating, plenty of money, care of it, & leisure; these are the hard times. Nothing is doing & we lose every day.

May 13, 1835

What a benefit if a rule could be given whereby the mind could at any moment *east* itself, & find the sun. . . .

The truest state of mind, rested in, becomes false. Thought is the manna which cannot be stored. It will be sour if kept, & tomorrow must be gathered anew. Perpetually must we East ourselves, or we get into ir-recoverable error, starting from the plainest truth & keeping as we think the straightest road of logic. It is by magnifying God, that men become Pantheists; it is by piously personifying him, that they become idolaters.

No human wit unaided is equal to the production at one time of such a result as the Hamlet or Lear, but by a multitude of trials & a thousand rejections & the using & perusing of what was already written, one of those tragedies is at last completed—a poem made that shall thrill the world by the mere juxtaposition & inter-action of lines & sentences that singly would have been of little worth & short date. Rightly is this art named composition & the composition has manifold the effect of the component parts. The orator is nowise equal to the evoking on a new subject of this brilliant chain of sentiments, facts, illustrations whereby he now fires himself & you. Every link in this living chain he found separate; one, ten years ago; one, last week; some of them he found in his father's house or at school when a boy; some of them by his losses; some of them by his sickness; some by his sins.

May 14, 1835

When will you mend Montaigne? When will you take the hint of nature? Where are your Essays? Can you not express your one conviction that moral laws hold? Have you not thoughts & illustrations that are your own; the parable of geometry & matter; the reason why the atmosphere is transparent; the power of Composition in nature & in man's thoughts; the Uses & uselessness of travelling; the law of Compensation; the transcendant excellence of truth in character, in rhetoric, in things; the sublimity of Self-reliance; and the rewards of perseverance in the best opinion? Have you not a testimony to give for Shakspear, for Milton? one sentence of real praise of Jesus, is worth a century of legendary Christianity. Can you not write as though you wrote to yourself & drop the token assured that a wise hand will pick it up?

"My entrails I lay open to men's view." I recorded worse things in my Italian Journal than one I omitted; that a lady in Palermo invited me to come & ride out with her in her barouche which I did, though the day was rainy & so the coach was covered. She did not invite me to dine, so I made my obeisance, when on our return I had waited upon her into the house; then I *walked* home through a drenching rain in a city where I was an entire stranger, but not until I had paid her coachman my half dollar who waylaid me on the stairs.

May 15, 1835

My niedrig man* playing with a beautiful child could think of nothing but to ask the child whether it is careful to keep its head clean of creatures. And when it is mentioned that a red cloth irritates the cow, 'Yes,' he replies, 'they think of their calf,' forcing on the ladies the allusion to poor Nature's rags of parturition.

May 29, 1835

He weakens who means to confirm his speech by vehemence, feminine vehemence.

---

*Emerson's farmhand.

May 30, 1835

The whole of Virtue consists in substituting *being* for *seeming*, & therefore God properly saith *I AM.*

June 3, 1835

Mr Alston would build a very plain house & have plain furniture because he would hold out no bribe to any to visit him who had not similar tastes to his own. A good Ascetic.

If a conversation be prolonged which is not exactly on my key, I become nervous, & need to go out of the room, or to eat. And when my friend is gone, I am unfit for work. Society suffocates, as Lidian said, and irritates.

June 20, 1835

When we read a book in a foreign language we suppose that an English version of it would be a transfusion of it into our own consciousness. But take Coleridge or Bacon or many an English book besides & you immediately feel that the English is a language also & that a book writ in that tongue is yet very far from being transfused into your own consciousness. There is every degree of remoteness from the line of things in the line of words. . . .

The good of publishing one's thoughts is that of hooking to you likeminded men, and of giving to men whom you value, such as Wordsworth or Landor, one hour of stimulated thought. Yet, how few! Who in Concord cares for the first philosophy in a book? The woman whose child is to be suckled? the man at Nine-Acre-Corner who is to cart 60 loads of gravel on his meadow? the stageman? the gunsmith? O No! Who then?

June 24? 1835

I will no longer confer, differ, refer, defer, prefer, or suffer. I renounce the whole family of *Fero.* I embrace absolute life.

June 27, 1835

Between cultivated minds the first interview is the best, & it is surprizing in how few hours the results of years are exhausted. Besides though it seem ungrateful to friends whom the heart knoweth by name yet the value of the conversation is not measured according to the wisdom of the company but by quite other & indefinable causes, the fortunate moods. I think we owe the most recreation & most memorable thoughts to very unpromising gossips.

June 29, 1835

I replied this morn. to the Committee that I would do what I could to prepare a Historical Discourse for the Town Anniversary. Yet why notice it? Centuries pass unnoticed. The Saxon King was told that man's life was like the swallow that flew in at one window, fluttered around, & flew out at another. So is this population of the spot of God's earth called Concord. For a moment they fish in this river, plow furrows in the banks, build houses on the fields, mow the grass. But hold on to hill or tree never so fast they must disappear in a trice.

July 4? 1835

The arts languish now because all their scope is exhibition; when they originated it was to serve the gods. The Catholic Religion has turned them to continual account in its service. Now they are mere flourishes. Is it strange they perish?

I study the art of solitude. I yield me as gracefully as I can to my destiny. Why cannot one get the good of his doom, & since it is from eternity a settled thing that he & society shall be nothing to each other, why need he blush so, & make wry faces & labor to keep up a poor beginner's place, a freshman's seat in the fine world?

July 15, 1835

Why do I still go to pasture where I never find grass, to these actors without a purpose unless a poor mechanical one, these talkers without method, & reasoners without an idea? At the Divinity School this morning I heard what was called the best performance but it was founded on nothing & led to nothing & I wondered at the patience of the people.

July 1835

It is droll enough that when I had been groping for months after the natural process which I felt sure resembled in my experience the freedom with which at a certain height of excitement, thoughts pour into the mind, I should at last recognize it in so mean a fact as the passage of bile into the mouth in the retchings of seasickness.

It seems as if every body was insane on one side & the Bible makes them as crazy as Bentham or Spurzheim or politics. The ethical doctrines of these theosophists are true & exalting, but straightway they run upon their Divine Transformation, the Death of God &c & become

horn mad. To that point they speak reason then they begin to babble. &
so this man cries out Wo to them that do not believe &c &c. This obstinate Orientalism that God is a petty Asiatic King & will be very angry if
you do not prostrate yourself, they cannot get rid of.

July 24–26, 1835

Ephraim Slow, says the newspaper, "was born on the last day of the
year which gave occasion to a parish wit to remark that he came near not
being born at all."

July 27–29, 1835

Manners. There are occasions on which it seems not much can be
said. Dr Ripley says he has been eating an apple of which he sent the
graft to Waterford and he would give me a piece but that he has just eat
it up.

July 30, 1835

I know nothing of the source of my being but I will not soil my nest.
I know much of it after a high negative way, but nothing after the understanding. God himself contradicts through me & all his creatures the
miserable babble of Kneeland & his crew* but if they set me to affirm in
propositions his character & providence as I would describe a mountain
or an Indian, I am dumb. Oft I have doubted of his person, never that
truth is divine.

July 31, 1835

When shall I be tired of reading? When the moon is tired of waxing
& waning, when the sea is tired of ebbing & flowing, when the grass is
weary of growing, when the planets are tired of going.

Aug. 1, 1835

After thirty a man wakes up sad every morning excepting perhaps
five or six until the day of his death.

Aug. 2, 1835

Charles wonders that I don't become sick at the stomach over my
poor journal yet is obdurate habit callous even to contempt. I must
scribble on if it were only to say in confirmation of Oegger's doctrine
that I believe I never take a step in thought when engaged in conversation without some material symbol of my proposition figuring itself in-
cipiently at the same time. My sentence often ends in babble from a vain
effort to represent that picture in words.

---

*Abner Kneeland was a notorious atheist.

* * *

It is pleasant to have a book come down to us of which the author has, like Homer, lost his individual distinctness, is almost a fabulous personage, so that the book seems to come rather out of the spirit of humanity & to have the sanction of human nature than to totter on the two legs of any poor Ego.

Who can make a good sentence can make a good book. . . . If you find a good thing in the writing of a mediocre man be sure he stole it.

Aug. 3, 1835

One of the poorest employments of the country gentleman is to sit sentinel at his window to watch every cow, baker, or boy that comes in at his gate. Better be asleep.

Aug. 3–4, 1835

Ah Homer! Ah Chaucer! ah Shakspear! But we live in the age of Propriety. Their elegance is intrinsic, ours superadded. Their cleanness is sunshine, ours painting & gilding.

Aug. 5, 1835

If you read much at a time you have a better sight of the plan & connexion of the book but you have less lively attention. If you read little fine things catch your eye & you read accurately but all proportion & ulterior purpose are at an end.

Aug. 8, 1835

Yesterday I delighted myself with Michel de Montaigne. With all my heart I embrace the grand old sloven. He pricks & stings the sense of Virtue in me, the wild gentile stock I mean, for he has no Grace. But his panegyric of Cato & of Socrates in his essay of Cruelty (Vol II) do wind up again for us the spent springs & make virtue possible without the discipline of Christianity or rather do shame her of her eyeservice & put her upon her honor. I read the Essays in Defence of Seneca & Plutarch; on Books; on Drunkenness; & on Cruelty.

Aug. 15, 1835

I bought my house & two acres six rods of land of John T. Coolidge for 3500 dollars.

Aug. 31, 1835

Use of Harvard College to clear the head of much nonsense that gathers in the inferior colleges.

Sept. 14, 1835

I was married to Lydia Jackson.

Oct. 5, 1835

I like that poetry which without aiming to be allegorical, is so. Which sticking close to its subject & that perhaps trivial can yet be applied to the life of man & the government of God & be found to hold.

Oct. 10, 1835

The oak is magnificent from the acorn up. The whortle berry no pruning or training can magnify. Who can believe in the perfectibility of this race of man, or in the potency of Education? Yet compare the English nation with the Esquimaux tribe, & who can underestimate the advantages of culture?

Oct. 10–12, 1835

The minister in these days, how little he says! Who is the most decorous man? & no longer, who speaks the most truth? Look at the orations of Demosthenes & Burke, & how many irrelevant things—sentences, words, letters—are there? Not one. Go into one of our cool churches, & begin to count the words that might be spared, & in most places, the entire sermon will go. One sentence kept another in countenance, but not one by its own weight could have justified the saying of it. 'Tis the age of Parenthesis. You might put all we say in brackets & it would not be missed.

Oct. 21, 1835

Last Saturday night came hither Mr Alcott & spent the Sabbath with me. A wise man, simple, superior to display. & drops the best things as quietly as the least. Every man, he said, is a Revelation, & ought to write his Record. But few with the pen.

Oct. 22, 1835

What can be truer than the doctrine of inspiration? of fortunate hours? Things sail dim & great through my head. Veins of rich ore are in me, could I only get outlet & pipe to draw them out. How unattainable seem to me these wild pleasantries of Shakspear yet not less so seem to me passages in old letters of my own.

What platitudes I find in Wordsworth. "I poet bestow my verse on this & this & this." Scarce has he dropped the smallest piece of an egg, when he fills the barnyard with his cackle.

Oct. 28–29, 1835

I read nothing in St John or St Paul concerning the planting of America or the burning of Anthracite coal. Yet as I sit here in America by my anthracite coal fire, I cannot help thinking that there has been somewhere a design that one should be inhabited & the other burned.

'Tis a good thing for man that I am obliged to pick my words of low trades with so much care. In England you may say a sweep, a blacksmith, a scavenger, as synonym for a savage in civil life. But in this country I must look about me. I perhaps speak to persons who occasionally or regularly work at these works & yet do take as they ought their place as Men in places of manly culture & entertainment.

Oct. 30, 1835

How hard it is to impute your own best sense to a dead author! The very highest praise we *think* of any writer, or painter, or sculptor, or builder is that he actually possessed the thought or feeling with which he has inspired us. We hesitate at doing Spenser so great an honor as to think that he meant by his allegory the sense which we affix to it.

Oct.–Nov. 1835

To the chaste man the white skin of the woman with whom he talks, appears to be distant by some miles.

Nov. 6, 1835

Burke's imagery is much of it got from books & so is a secondary formation. Webster's is all primary. Let a man make the woods & fields his books then at the hour of passion his thoughts will invest themselves spontaneously with natural imagery.

Dec. 7? 1835

In Shakspear I actually shade my eyes as I read for the splendor of the thoughts.

Feb. 8? 1836

Women have less accurate measure of time than men. There is a clock in Adam: none in Eve.

Feb.–March 1836

Strange is this alien despotism of Sleep which takes two persons lying in each other's arms & separates them leagues, continents, asunder.

"Here's for the plain old Adam, the simple genuine Self against
the whole world."

March 5–8, 1836

Last week I went to Salem. At the Lafayette hotel where I lodged, every five or ten minutes the barkeepers came into the sitting room to arrange their hair & collars at the looking glass. So many joys has the kind God provided for us dear creatures.

Other men wait upon their bowels most of the day.*

May 16, 1836

And here I am again at home but I have come alone. My brother, my friend, my ornament, my joy & pride has fallen by the wayside, or rather has risen out of this dust. Charles died at New York Monday afternoon, 9 May. His prayer that he might not be sick was granted him. He was never confined to a bed. He rode out on Monday afternoon with Mother, promised himself to begin his journey with me on my arrival, the next day; on reaching home, he stepped out of the carriage alone, walked up the steps & into the house without assistance, sat down on the stairs, fainted, & never recovered. Beautiful without any parallel, in my experience of young men, was his life, happiest his death. Miserable is my own prospect from whom my friend is taken. Clean & Sweet was his life, untempted almost, and his action on others all-healing, uplifting, & fragrant. I read now his pages, I remember all his words & motions without any pang, so healthy & humane a life it was, & not like Edward's, a tragedy of poverty & sickness tearing genius. His virtues were like the victories of Timoleon, & Homer's verses, they were so easy & natural. I cannot understand why his mss. journal should have so bitter a strain of penitence & deprecation. I mourn that in losing him I have lost his all, for he was born an orator, not a writer. His written pages do him no justice, and as he felt the immense disparity between his power of conversation & his blotted paper, it was easy for him to speak with scorn of written composition.

Now commences a new & gloomy epoch of my life. I have used his society so fondly & solidly. It was pleasant to unfold my thought to so wise a hearer. It opened itself genially to his warm & bright light, and borrowed color & sometimes form from him. Besides my direct debt to him of how many valued thoughts—through what orbits of speculation have we not travelled together, so that it would not be possible for either of us to say, This is my thought, That is yours.

I have felt in him the inestimable advantage, when God allows it, of finding a brother and a friend in one. The mutual understanding is then perfect, because Nature has settled the constitution of the amity on soli-

---

*Emerson crossed out this sentence.

dest foundations; and so it admits of mercenary usefulness & of unsparing censure; there exists the greatest convenience inasmuch as the same persons & facts are known to each, and an occult hereditary sympathy underlies all our intercourse & extends farther than we know.

Who can ever supply his place to me? None. I may live long. I may (tho' 'tis improbable) see many cultivated persons, but his elegance, his wit, his sense, his worship of principles, I shall not find united—I shall not find them separate. The eye is closed that was to see Nature for me, & give me leave to see; the taste & soul which Shakspear satisfied; the soul that loved St John, & St Paul, Isaiah & David; the acute discernment that divided the good from the evil in all objects around him, in society, in politics, in church, in books, in persons; the hilarity of thought which awakened good humor wherever it came, and laughter without shame; and the endless endeavor after a life of ideal beauty; —these are all gone from my actual world & will here be no more seen.

I read with some surprise the pages of his journal. They show a nocturnal side which his diurnal aspects never suggested—they are melancholy, penitential, self accusing; I read them with no pleasure: they are the creepings of an eclipsing temperament over his abiding light of character.

May 16–18, 1836

Charles said, There were two ways of living in the world, viz. either to postpone your own ascetic entirely, & live among people as among aliens; or, to lead a life of endless warfare by forcing your Ideal into act. In either of these ways the wise man may be blameless.

June 14–15, 1836

Power is one great lesson which Nature teaches Man. The secret that he can not only reduce under his will, that is, conform to his character, particular events but classes of events & so harmonize all the outward occurrences with the states of mind, that must he learn.

Worship, must he learn.

Is the pretension of the Ideal Theory enormous? Every possible statement of the connexion between the world & you involves pretensions as enormous.

July 1836

Make your own Bible. Select & Collect all those words & sentences that in all your reading have been to you like the blast of trumpet out of Shakspear, Seneca, Moses, John, & Paul.

Aug. 6, 1836

The grey past, the white future.

A year ago I studied Ben Jonson a good deal. You may learn much from so complete records of one mind as his works are. There is something fearful in coming up against the walls of a mind on every side & learning to describe their invisible circumference.

"I know not what you think of me", said my friend. Are you sure? You know all I think of you by those things I say to you. You know all which can be of any use to you. If I, if all your friends should draw your portrait to you—faults & graces, it would mislead you, embarrass you; you must not ask how you please me for curiosity. You must not look in the glass to see how handsome you are but to see if your face is clean. Certainly I know what impression I made on any man, by remembering what communications he made to me.

Aug. 12, 1836

Yesterday Margaret Fuller returned home after making us a visit of three weeks—a very accomplished & very intelligent person.

All our experience helps us very little directly, except in getting bread & doing the work of the world. But if you have learned with years of pain how to treat an annoying relative as a foolish father or wife & you hug yourself at your acquired skill, let that person die or depart & you shall find all your fancied experience useless in the first new relation you enter, as marriage, paternity, or care of an insane, or vicious person. . . . Each new relation finds us, maugre all our experience & all our talent, mere babies. Our progress in the particular never helps us in the particular. There is only out of the particular a general growth of the soul from year to year.

Fathers wish to be fathers of the mind as well as of the body of their children. But in my experience they seem to be merely the occasion of new beings coming into the world than parents of their life or seers of their own affection incarnated as Alcott would think.

The best Service which history renders us is to lead us to prize the present.

Aug. 27, 1836

Today came to me the first proof-sheet of "Nature" to be corrected, like a new coat, full of vexations; with the first sentences of the chapters perched like mottoes aloft in small type! The peace of the author cannot be wounded by such trifles, if he sees that the sentences are still good. A good sentence can never be put out of countenance by any blunder of compositors. It is good in text or note, in poetry or prose, as title or corollary. But a bad sentence shows all his flaws instantly by such dislocation.

Sept. 13, 1836

I went to the College Jubilee on the 8th instant. A noble & well thought of anniversary. The pathos of the occasion was extreme & not much noted by the speakers. Cambridge at any time is full of ghosts; but on that day the anointed eye saw the crowd of spirits that mingled with the procession in the vacant spaces, year by year, as the classes proceeded; and then the far longer train of ghosts that followed the company, of the men that wore before us the college honors & the laurels of the state—the long winding train reaching back into eternity. But among the living was more melancholy reflection, namely the identity of all the persons with that which they were in youth, in college halls. I found my old friends the same; the same jokes pleased, the same straws tickled; the manhood & offices they brought hither today seemed masks; underneath, we were still boys.

Sept. 13? 1836

The babe is formed in the womb of the mother quite outside of her system. It is carefully guarded from any interference with her constitution. So if you go into a family where you supposed a perfect understanding & intimate bonds subsisted, you find with surprise that all are in a degree strangers to each other, that father has one interest & you another, that husband & wife observe each other's acts & words with much of a stranger's curiosity.

Sept. 20? 1836

A rail road, State street, Bunker Hill monument are genuine productions of the age but no art.

The reason is manifest. They are not wanted. The statue of Jove was to be worshipped. The Virgin of Titian was to be worshipped. Jesus, Luther were reformers; Moses, David did something, the builders of cathedrals feared. Love & fear laid the stones in their own order.

What interest has Greenough to make a good statue? Who cares whether it is good? A few prosperous gentlemen & ladies, but the Universal Yankee nation roaring in the Capitol to approve or condemn would make his eye & hand & heart go to a new tune.

* * *

Mr Webster never loses sight of his relation to Nature. The Day is always part of him. "But, Mr President, the shades of evening which close around us, admonish me to conclude," he said at Cambridge.

I notice George Herbert's identification of himself with Jewish genius. "List, you may hear great Aaron's bell"—"Aaron's drest!" & the like. It reminds me of that criticism I heard in Italy of Michel Angelo, viz. that he painted prophets & patriarchs like a Hebrew; that they were not merely old men in robes & beards, but a sanctity & the character of the pentateuch & the prophecy was conspicuous in them.

Sept. 28? 1836

A very good discourse on Marriage might be written by him who would preach the nature of things. Let him teach how fast the frivolous external fancying fades out of the mind. Let him teach both husband & wife to mourn for the rapid ebb of inclination not one moment, to yield it no tear. As this fancy picture, these fata-Morgana, this cloud scenery fades forever the solid mountain chains whereupon the sky rests in the far perspective of the soul begin to appear. The parties discover every day the deep & permanent character each of the other as a rock foundation on which they may safely build their nuptial bower. They learn slowly that all other affection than that which rests upon what they are is superstitious & evanescent, that all concealment, all pretension is wholly Vain, that to the amiable & useful & heroic qualities which inhere in the other belong a certain portion of love, of pleasure, of veneration which is as exactly measured as the attraction of a pound of iron, that there is no luck nor witchcraft nor destiny nor divinity in marriage that can produce affection but only those qualities that by their nature extort it, that all love is mathematical.

The fine prints & pictures which the dentist hangs in his anteroom have a satirical air to the waiting patient.

Oct. 6, 1836

Transcendentalism means, says our accomplished Mrs B., with a wave of her hand, *A little beyond.*

Oct. 19, 1836

As long as the soul seeks an external God, it never can have peace, it always must be uncertain what may be done & what may become of it. But when it sees the Great God far within its own nature, then it sees that always itself is a party to all that can be, that always it will be informed of that which will happen and therefore it is pervaded with a great Peace.

Oct. 21, 1836

As History's best use is to enhance our estimate of the present hour, so the value of such an observer as Goethe who draws out of our consciousness some familiar fact & makes it glorious by showing it in the light of thought is this, that he makes us prize all our being by suggesting its inexhaustible wealth; for we feel that all our experience is thus convertible into jewels. He moves our wonder at the mystery of our life.

Oct. 24–26, 1836

The love that is in me, the justice, the truth can never die & that is all of me that will not die. All the rest of me is so much death—my ignorance, my vice, my corporeal pleasure. But I am nothing else than a capacity for justice, truth, love, freedom, power. I can inhale, imbibe them forevermore. They shall be so much to me that I am nothing, they all. Then shall God be all in all. Herein is my Immortality.

Oct. 29–30, 1836

There is one advantage which every man finds in setting himself a literary task as these my lectures, that it gives him the high pleasure of reading which does not in other circumstances attain all its zest. When the mind is braced by the weighty expectations of a prepared work, the page of whatever book we read, becomes luminous with manifold allusion. Every sentence is doubly significant & the sense of our author is as broad as the world. There is creative reading as well as creative writing.

Oct. 31, 1836

Last night at 11 o'clock, a son was born to me. Blessed child! a lovely wonder to me, and which makes the Universe look friendly to me. How remote from my knowledge, how alien, yet how kind does it make the Cause of Causes appear! The stimulated curiosity of the father sees the graces & instincts which exist, indeed, in every babe, but unnoticed in others; the right to see all, know all, to examine nearly, distinguishes this relation, & endears this sweet child. Otherwise I see nothing in it of mine; I am no conscious party to any feature, any function, any perfection I behold in it. I seem to be merely a brute occasion of its being & nowise attaining to the dignity even of a second cause no more than I taught it to suck the breast.

Please God, that "he, like a tree of generous kind, By living waters set," may draw endless nourishment from the fountains of Wisdom & Virtue!

Now am I Pygmalion.

Every day a child presents a new aspect, Lidian says, as the face of the sky is different every hour, so that we never get tired.

The truth seems to be that every child is infinitely beautiful, but the father alone by position & by duty is led to look near enough to see. He looks with microscope. But what is most beautiful is to see the babe & the mother together, the contrast of size makes the little nestler appear so *cunning*, & its tiny beseeching weakness is compensated so perfectly by the happy patronizing look of the mother, who is a sort of high reposing Providence toward it—that they make a perfect group.

Nov. 3–4, 1836

It seemed yesterday morn as the snow fell, that the adult looks more sourly than the child at the phenomena of approaching Winter. The child delights in the first snow & sees with it the spruce & hemlock boughs they bring for Christmas with glee. The man sees it all sourly expecting the cold days & inconvenient roads & labors of Winter. But the experience of a thousand years has shown him that his faculties are quite equal to master these inconveniences & despite of them to get his bread & wisdom. Therefore the child is the wiser of the two.

This age will be characterized as the era of Trade, for every thing is made subservient to that agency. The very savage on the shores of the N.W. America, holds up his shell & cries 'a dollar!' Government at home is conducted on such principles. Superstition gives way; Patriotism; Martial Ardor; Romance in the people; but avarice does not.

Meantime, it is also a social era; the age of associations, the powers of Combination are discovered. & hence of course the age of Constitutions, of Universal suffrage, of schools, of revision of laws, abolition of imprisonment, of railroads.

I ought not to forget in characterising Charles the things he remarked & loved in nature. George Barrell Emerson truly said We shall think of him when the June birds return. The birds he loved & discriminated & showed them us. So the pleasing effect of the grey oakleaf on the snow pleased him well; next it was he said in liveliness to green & white of pine tree & snow. Like my brother Edward, Charles had a certain severity of Character which did not permit him to be silly—no not for moments, but always self possessed & elegant whether morose or playful; no funning for him or for Edward. It was also remarkable in

C. that he contemplated with satisfaction the departure of a day. Another day is gone, I am thankful he said. And to E.H. "Put me by the world wheels, & if I wouldn't give them a twirl!"

Nov. 5, 1836

The reality which the Ancient mind attributed to all things equally, to the fictions of the poets & to the facts observed by their own eyes, is most remarkable. . . . They seem to be no Transcendentalists—to rest always in the spontaneous consciousness.

I find my measures of the value of time differ strangely. At the close of the day, at the close of the week I am quite incompetent to say if it have been well or ill spent. When I have least to show for my time, no reading in English or German, no writing in Journal, & no work in the world, I have yet philosophised best, and arrived at some solid conclusions that become conspicuous thoughts in the following months & years.

This day I have been scrambling in the woods & with help of Peter Howe I have got six hemlock trees to plant in my yard which may grow whilst my boy is sleeping.

Nov. 8, 1836

I dislike to hear the patronizing tone in which the self sufficient young men of the day talk of ministers "adapting their preaching to the great mass." Was the sermon good? "O yes, good for you & me, but not understood by the great mass." Don't you deceive yourself, say I, the great mass understand what's what, as well as the little mass. The self-conceit of this tone is not more provoking than the profound ignorance it argues is pitiable.

The fit attitude of a man is humble Wonder & gratitude, a meek watching of the marvels of the Creation to the end that he may know & do what is fit. But these pert gentlemen assume that the whole object is to manage "the great mass" & they forsooth are behind the curtain with the Deity and mean to help manage. They know all & will now smirk & manoeuvre & condescendingly yield the droppings of their wisdom to the poor people.

Nov. 10, 1836

Language clothes nature as the air clothes the earth, taking the exact form & pressure of every object. Only words that are new fit exactly the thing, those that are old like old scoriae that have been long exposed to the air & sunshine, have lost the sharpness of their mould & fit loosely.

But in new objects & new names one is delighted with the plastic nature of man as much as in picture or sculpture.

Nov. 12, 1836

How many attractions for us have our passing fellows in the streets both male & female, which our ethics forbid us to express which yet infuse so much pleasure into life. A lovely child, a handsome youth, a beautiful girl, a heroic man, a maternal woman, a venerable old man, charm us though strangers & we cannot say so, or look at them but for a moment.

Nov. 19–20, 1836

The poet, the moralist have not yet rendered us their entire service when they have written & published their books. The book & its direct influence on my mind, are one fact, but a more important fact is the verdict of humanity upon it, a thing not suddenly settled, &, in the case of great works, not for an age.

Nov. 24, 1836

I told Miss Peabody last night that Mr Coleridge's churchmanship is thought to affect the value of his criticism &c. I do not feel it. It is a harmless freak & sometimes occurs in a wrong place, as when he refuses to translate some alleged blasphemy in Wallenstein. Some men are affected with hemorrhage of the nose; it is of no danger but unlucky when it befals where it should not as at a wedding or in the rostrum. But Coleridge's is perfectly separable. I know no such critic. Every opinion he expresses is a canon of criticism that should be writ in steel, & his italics are italics of the mind.

Nov. 28, 1836

I see plainly the charm which belongs to Alienation or Otherism. "What wine do you like best, O Diogenes?" "Another's," replied the sage. What fact, thought, word, like we best? Another's. The very sentiment I expressed yesterday without heed, shall sound memorable to me tomorrow if I hear it from another. My own book I read with new eyes when a stranger has praised it.

Edward Taylor is a noble work of the divine cunning who suggests the wealth of Nature.* If he were not so strong, I should call him lovely.

---

*Taylor, a Methodist minister who maintained a chapel for seamen in Boston, is said to have been the model for Melville's Father Mapple in *Moby-Dick*.

What cheerfulness in his genius & what consciousness of strength. "My voice is thunder," he said in telling me how well he was. And what teeth & eyes & brow & aspect—I study him as a jaguar or an Indian for his untamed physical perfections. He is a work, a man not to be predicted. His vision poetic & pathetic; sight of love, is unequalled. How can he transform all those whiskered shaggy untrim tarpaulins into sons of light & hope? By seeing the man within the sailor, seeing them to be sons, lovers, brothers, husbands.

Dec. 2, 1836

The present state of the colony at Liberia is a memorable fact. It is found that the black merchants are so fond of their lucrative occupations that it is with difficulty that any of them can be prevailed upon to take office in the colony. They dislike the trouble of it. Civilized arts are found to be as attractive to the wild negro, as they are disagreeable to the wild Indian.

Dec. 3, 1836

I have been making war against the superlative degree in the rhetoric of my fair visiter. She has no positive degree in her description of characters & scenes. You would think she had dwelt in a museum where all things were extremes & extraordinary. Her good people are very good, her naughty so naughty that they cannot be eaten. But beside the superlative of her mind she has a superlative of grammar which is suicidal & defeats its end. Her minds are "most perfect" "most exquisite" & "most masculine." I tell her the positive degree is the sinew of speech, the superlative is the fat. "Surely all that is simple is sufficient for all that is good" said Mme. de Stael. And when at a trattoria at Florence I asked the waiter if the cream was good, the man replied 'yes, sir, stupendous': *Si, signore, stupendo.*

Dec. 10, 1836

Pleasant walk yesterday, the most pleasant of days. At Walden Pond, I found a new musical instrument which I call the ice-harp. A thin coat of ice covered a part of the pond but melted around the edge of the shore. I threw a stone upon the ice which rebounded with a shrill sound, & falling again & again, repeated the note with pleasing modulation. I thought at first it was the 'peep' 'peep' of a bird I had scared. I was so taken with the music that I threw down my stick & spent twenty minutes in throwing stones single or in handfuls on this crystal drum.

I cannot hear a sermon without being struck by the fact that amid drowsy series of sentences what a sensation a historical fact, a biographical name, a sharply objective illustration makes! . . . A preacher should be a live coal to kindle all the church.

Jan. 14, 1837

Lidian's grandmother had a slave Phillis whom she freed. Phillis went to the little colony on the outside of Plymouth which they called New Guinea. Soon after, she visited her old mistress. "Well, Phillis, what did you have for dinner on Thanksgiving Day?" "Fried 'taturs, Missy;" replied Phillis. "And what had you to fry the potatoes in?" said Mrs Cotton. "Fried in Water, Missy;" answered the girl. "Well Phillis," said Mrs Cotton, "how can you bear to live up there, so poor, when here you used to have every thing comfortable, & such good dinner at Thanksgiving?"—"Ah Missy, Freedom's sweet," returned Phillis.

Jan. 21, 1837

I either read or inferred today in the Westminster Review that Shakspear was not a popular man in his day. How true & wise. He sat alone & walked alone a visionary poet & came with his piece, modest but discerning, to the players, & was too glad to get it received, whilst he was too superior not to see its transcendant claims.

Jan. 25, 1837

This evening the heavens afford us the most remarkable spectacle of Aurora Borealis. A deep red plume in the East & west streaming almost from the horizon to the zenith, forming at the zenith a sublime coronet; the stars peep delicately through the ruddy folds & the whole landscape below covered with snow is crimsoned. The light meantime equal nearly to that of full moon, although the moon was not risen.

Jan. 29, 1837

One has patience with every kind of living thing but not with the dead alive. I, at least, hate to see persons of that lumpish class who are here they know not why, & ask not whereto, but live as the larva of the ant or the bee to be lugged into the sun & then lugged back into the cell & then fed. The end of nature for such, is that they should be fatted. If mankind should pass a vote on the subject, I think they would throw them in sacks into the sea.

Feb. 1837

In these Lectures which from week to week I read, each on a topic which is a main interest of man, & may be made an object of exclusive interest I seem to vie with the brag of Puck "I can put a girdle round about the world in forty minutes." I take fifty.

March 14, 1837

Edward Taylor came last night & gave us in the old church a Lecture on Temperance. A wonderful man; I had almost said, a perfect orator. The utter want & loss of all method, the ridicule of all method, the bright chaos come again of his bewildering oratory, certainly bereaves it of power but what splendor! what sweetness! what richness what depth! what cheer! How he conciliates, how he humanizes! how he exhilarates & ennobles! Beautiful philanthropist! godly poet! the Shakspeare of the sailor & the poor. God has found one harp of divine melody to ring & sigh sweet music amidst caves & cellars.

He spent the night with me. He says "he lives a monarch's life, he has none to control him, or to divide the power with him." His word is law for all his people & his coadjutors. He is a very charming object to me. I delight in his great personality, the way & sweep of the man which like a frigate's way takes up for the time the centre of the ocean, paves it with a white street, & all the lesser craft "do curtsey to him, do him reverence." Every body plays a second part in his presence, & takes a deferential & apologetic tone. In the church, likewise, every body—the rich, the poor, the scoffer, the drunkard, the exquisite, & the populace, acknowledge the Man, & feel that to be right & lordly which he doth—so that his prayer is a winged ship in which all are floated forward. The wonderful & laughing life of his illustration keeps us broad awake. A string of rockets all night. He described his bar-room gentry as "hanging like a half dead bird over a counter." He describes Helen Loring as out on her errands of charity, & "running through the rain like a beech-bird." He speaks of poor ministers coming out of divinity schools, &c. as "poor fellows hobbling out of Jerusalem." "We'll give you hypocrites for honest men, two for one, & trade all night." "The world is just large enough for the people. There is no room for a partition wall."

March 19, 1837

Yesterday I read many of C.C.E.'s letters to E.H. I find them noble but sad. Their effect is painful. I withdrew myself from the influence. So much contrition, so much questioning, so little hope, so much sorrow, harrowed me. I could not stay to see my noble brother tortured even by himself. No good or useful air goes out of such scriptures, but cramp & incapacity only. I shall never believe that any book is so good to read as that which sets the reader into a working mood, makes him feel his strength, & inspires hilarity.

Such are Plutarch, & Montaigne & Wordsworth.

But also Charles would say this, & his conversation was of this character; but when he shut his closet door, "a quality of darkness" haunted him.

Edward Thompson Taylor (1793–1871): "I delight in his great
personality, the way & sweep of the man which like a frigate's
way takes up for the time the centre of the ocean, paves it
with a white street . . . his prayer is a winged ship in
which all are floated forward."

March 1837

Every man has hydrophobia the first time in summer he goes into
the salt water baths. Life.

March 29–31, 1837

[Carlyle] is a worshipper of strength, heedless much whether its
present phase be divine or diabolic. Burns, Geo. Fox, Luther, and those
unclean beasts Diderot, Danton, Mirabeau, whose sinews are their own
& who trample on the tutoring & conventions of society he loves. For he
believes that every noble nature was made by God, & contains—if savage passions—also fit checks & grand impulses within it, hath its own
resources, &, however erring, will return from far. Then he writes
English & crowds meaning into all the nooks & corners of his sentences.
Once read he is but half read.

* * *

I rode well. My horse took hold of the road as if he loved it. I saw in Boston my fair young L. but so rashly grown that her sweet face was like a violet on the top of a pole.

Carlyle again. I think he has seen as no other in our time how inexhaustible a mine is the language of Conversation. He does not use the *written* dialect of the time in which scholars, pamphleteers, & the clergy write, nor the parliamentary dialect, in which the lawyer, the statesman, & the better newspapers write, but draws strength & motherwit out of a poetic use of the *spoken* vocabulary, so that his paragraphs are all a sort of splendid conversation.

April 8, 1837

Ah! my darling boy, so lately received out of heaven leave me not now! Please God, this sweet symbol of love & wisdom may be spared to rejoice, teach, & accompany me.

April 10, 1837

Love is fabled to be blind, but to me it seems that kindness is necessary to perception, that love is not an ophthalmia but an electuary.

Slavery is an institution for converting men into monkeys.

April 12, 1837

I find it the worst thing in life that I can put it to no better use. One would say that he can have little to do with his time who sits down to so slow labor & of such doubtful return as studying Greek or German; as he must be an unskilful merchant who should invest his money at three per cent. Yet I know not how better to employ a good many hours in the year. If there were not a general as well as a direct advantage herein we might shoot ourselves.

April 12–15, 1836

In life all finding is not that thing we sought, but something else. The lover on being accepted, misses the wildest charm of the maid he dared not hope to call his own. The husband loses the wife in the cares of the household. Later, he cannot rejoice with her in the babe for by becoming a mother she ceases yet more to be a wife. With the growth of children the relation of the pair becomes yet feebler from the demands children make, until at last nothing remains of the original passion out of which all these parricidal fruits proceeded; and they die because they are superfluous.

April 20, 1837

Mine Asia grudges the time she is called away from her babe because he grows so fast that each look is new & each is never to be repeated.

April 21, 1837

I learn evermore. In smooth water I discover the motion of my boat by the motion of trees & houses on shore, so the progress of my mind is proved by the perpetual change in the persons & things I daily behold.

April 22, 1837

Cold April; hard times; men breaking who ought not to break; banks bullied into the bolstering of desperate speculators; all the newspapers a chorus of owls. . . . Loud cracks in the social edifice. Sixty thousand laborers, says rumor, to be presently thrown out of work, and these make a formidable mob to break open banks & rob the rich & brave the domestic government.

There is a crack in every thing God has made. Fine weather!—yes but cold. Warm day!—'yes but dry.'—'You look well'— 'I am very well except a little cold.' The case of damaged hats—one a broken brim; the other perfect in the rim, but rubbed on the side; the third whole in the cylinder, but bruised on the crown.

I say to Lidian that in composition the *What* is of no importance compared with the *How*. The most tedious of all discourses are on the subject of the Supreme Being.

May 4, 1837

Margaret Fuller left us yesterday morning. Among many things that make her visit valuable & memorable, this is not the least that she gave me five or six lessons in German pronunciation never by my offer and rather against my will, each time, so that now spite of myself I shall always have to thank her for a great convenience—which she foresaw.

May 6, 1837

Sad is this continual postponement of life. I refuse sympathy & intimacy with people as if in view of some better sympathy & intimacy to come. But whence & when? I am already thirtyfour years old. Already my friends & fellow workers are dying from me. Scarcely can I say that I see any new men or women approaching me; I am too old to regard fashion; too old to expect patronage of any greater or more powerful. Let me suck the sweetness of those affections & consuetudes that grow near

me—that the Divine Providence offers me. These old shoes are easy to
the feet.

May 7, 1837

The Sabbath reminds me of an advantage which education may give,
namely a normal piety, a certain levitical education which only rarely
devout genius could countervail. I cannot hear the young men whose
theological instruction is exclusively owed to Cambridge & to public institution, without feeling how much happier was my star which rained
on me influences of ancestral religion. The depth of the religious sentiment which I knew in my Aunt Mary imbuing all her genius & derived
to her from such hoarded family traditions, from so many godly lives &
godly deaths of sainted kindred at Concord, Malden, York, was itself a
culture, an education. I heard with awe her tales of the pale stranger
who at the time her grandfather lay on his death bed tapped at the window & asked to come in. The dying man said, 'Open the door;' but the
timid family did not; & immediately he breathed his last, & they said
one to another It was the angel of death. Another of her ancestors when
near his end had lost the power of speech & his minister came to him &
said, 'If the Lord Christ is with you, hold up your hand'; and he
stretched up both hands & died. With these I heard the anecdotes of the
charities of Father Moody & his commanding administration of his holy
office. When the offended parishioners would rise to go out of the
church he cried "Come back, you graceless sinner, come back!" And
when his parishioners ventured into the ale house on a Saturday night,
the valiant pastor went in, collared them, & dragged them forth & sent
them home. Charity then went hand in hand with zeal. They gave alms
profusely & the barrel of meal wasted not. Who was it among this venerable line who whilst his house was burning, stood apart with some of
his church & sang "There is a house not made with hands." Another
was wont to go into the road whenever a traveller past on Sunday & entreat him to tarry with him during holy time, himself furnishing food
for man & beast. In my childhood Aunt Mary herself wrote the prayers
which first my brother William & when he went to college I read aloud
morning & evening at the family devotions, & they still sound in my ear
with their prophetic & apocalyptic ejaculations. Religion was her occu-
pation, and when years after, I came to write sermons for my own
church I could not find any examples or treasuries of piety so hightoned, so profound, or promising such rich influence as my remem-
brances of her conversation & letters.

This day my boy was baptized in the old church by Dr Ripley.
They dressed him in the selfsame robe in which twentyseven years ago

my brother Charles was baptised. Lidian has a group of departed Spirits in her eye who hovered around the patriarch & the babe.

May 14, 1837
  Harder times. . . . The true medicine for hard times seems to be sleep. Use so much bodily labor as shall ensure sleep, then you arise refreshed and in good spirits and in Hope. That have I this morn. Yesterday afternoon I stirred the earth about my shrubs & trees & quarreled with the piper-grass and now I have slept, & no longer am morose nor feel twitchings in the muscles of my face when a visiter is by. The humble-bee & the pine warbler seem to me the proper objects of attention in these disastrous times. I am less inclined to ethics, to history, to aught wise & grave & practick, & feel a new joy in nature. I am glad it is not my duty to preach these few sundays & I would invite the sufferers by this screwing panic to recover peace through these fantastic amusements during the tornado.

May 19, 1837
  Is it not pathetic that the action of men on men is so partial? We never touch but at points. The most that I can have or be to my fellow man, is it the reading of his book, or the hearing of his project in conversation? I approach some Carlyle with desire & joy. I am led on from month to month with an expectation of some total embrace & oneness with a noble mind, & learn at last that it is only so feeble & remote & hiant action as reading a Mirabeau or a Diderot paper, & a few the like. This is all that can be looked for. More we shall not be to each other. Baulked soul! It is not that the sea & poverty & pursuit separate us. Here is Alcott by my door—yet is the union more profound? No, the Sea, vocation, poverty, are seeming fences, but Man is insular, and cannot be touched. Every man is an infinitely repellent orb, & holds his individual being on that condition.

May 20, 1837
  Is the world sick? Bankruptcy in England & America: Tardy rainy season; snow in France; plague in Asia & Africa; these are the morning's news.

May 22, 1837
  The black times have a great scientific value. It is an epoch so critical a philosopher would not miss. As I would willingly carry myself to be played upon at Faneuil Hall by the stormy winds & strong fingers of the enraged Boston so is this era more rich in the central tones than many

languid centuries. What was, ever since my memory, solid continent, now yawns apart and discloses its composition and genesis.

Among provocatives, the next best thing to good preaching is bad preaching. I have even more thoughts during or enduring it than at other times.

I wrote above that life wants worthy objects: the game is not worth the candle: It is not that not I—it is that *nobody* employs it well. The land stinks with suicide.

May 25, 1837

"My dear Sir, clear your mind of cant," said Dr Johnson. Wordsworth, whom I read last night, is garrulous & weak often, but quite free from cant. I think I could easily make a small selection from his volumes which should contain all their poetry. It would take Fidelity, Tintern Abbey, Cumberland Beggar, Ode to Duty, September, The force of prayer, Lycoris, Lines on the death of Fox, Dion, Happy Warrior, Laodamia, the Ode.

Still hard times. Yet how can I lament, when I see the resources of this continent in which three months will anywhere yield a crop of wheat or potatoes. On the bosom of this vast plenty, the blight of trade & manufactures seems to me a momentary mischance.

May 26, 1837

Who shall define to me an Individual? I behold with awe & delight many illustrations of the One Universal Mind. I see my being imbedded in it. As a plant in the earth so I grow in God. I am only a form of him. He is the soul of Me. I can even with a mountainous aspiring say, *I am God*, by transferring my *Me* out of the flimsy & unclean precincts of my body, my fortunes, my private will, & meekly retiring upon the holy austerities of the Just & the Loving—upon the secret fountains of Nature. That thin & difficult ether, I also can breathe. The mortal lungs & nostrils burst & shrivel, but the soul itself needeth no organs—it is all element & all organ. Yet why not always so? How came the Individual thus armed & impassioned to parricide, thus murderously inclined ever to traverse & kill the divine life? Ah wicked Manichee! Into that dim problem I cannot enter. A believer in Unity, a seer of Unity, I yet behold two.

I behold; I bask in beauty; I await; I wonder; Where is my Godhead now? This is the Male & Female principle in Nature. One Man, male &

female created he him. Hard as it is to describe God, it is harder to describe the Individual.

A certain wandering light comes to me which I instantly perceive to be the Cause of Causes. It transcends all proving. It is itself the ground of being; and I see that it is not one & I another, but this is the life of my life. That is one fact, then; that in certain moments I have known that I existed directly from God, and am, as it were, his organ. And in my ultimate consciousness Am He. Then, secondly, the contradictory fact is familiar, that I am a surprised spectator & learner of all my life. This is the habitual posture of the mind—beholding. But whenever the day dawns, the great day of truth on the soul, it comes with awful invitation to me to accept it, to blend with its aurora.

Cannot I conceive the Universe without a contradiction?

May 31, 1837
We have had two peerless summer days after all our cold winds & rains. I have weeded corn & strawberries, intent on being fat & have forborne study. The Maryland yellow-throat pipes to me all day long, seeming to say extacy! Extacy! and the Bobo'lincoln flies & sings.

I read during the heat of the day Beppo & Manfred. What famine of meaning! Manfred is ridiculous for its purposeless raving. Not all the genuine love of nature nor all the skill of utterance can save it. It is all one circular proposition.

June 29, 1837
Almost one month lost to study by bodily weakness & disease.

July 19, 1837
If you go into the garden & hoe corn or kill bugs on the vines or pick pease, when you come into the house you shall still for some time see simulacra of weeds, vines, or peapods as you see the image of the sun sometime after looking at the sun. Both are disagreeable phenomena, as bad as laughing.

July 27–28, 1837
Many trees bear only in alternate years. Why should you write a book every year?

Aug. 14–16, 1837
I like not to have the day hurry away under me whilst I sit at my desk; I wish not reveries; I like to taste my time & spread myself through all the hour.

*   *   *

The least effect of the oration is on the orator. Yet it is something; a faint recoil; a kicking of the gun.

Aug. 18, 1837

The hope to arouse young men at Cambridge to a worthier view of their literary duties prompts me to offer the theory of the Scholar's function. He has an office to perform in society. What is it? To arouse the intellect; to keep it erect & sound; to keep admiration in the hearts of the people; to keep the eye open upon its spiritual aims.

Aug. 19, 1837

I please myself with getting my nail box set in the snuggest corner of the barn chamber & well filled with nails & gimlet pincers, screw driver, & chisel. Herein I find an old joy of youth, of childhood which perhaps all domestic children share—the cat-like love of garrets, barns, & corn chambers and of the conveniences of long housekeeping. It is quite genuine. When it occurs today, I ask—Have others the same? Once I should not have thought of such a question. What I loved, I supposed all children loved & knew, & therefore I did not name them. We were at accord. But much conversation, much comparison apprises us of difference. The first effect of this new learning is to incline us to hide our tastes. As they differ, we must be wrong. Afterwards some person comes & wins eclat by simply describing this old but concealed fancy of ours. Then we immediately learn to value all the parts of our nature, to rely on them as Self-authorised and that to publish them is to please others. So now the nailbox figures for its value.

Aug. 20, 1837

Lidian remembers the religious terrors of her childhood when *Young* tinged her day & night thoughts, and the doubts of *Cowper* were her own; when every lightning seemed the beginning of conflagration, & every noise in the street the crack of doom. I have some parallel recollections at the Latin School when I lived in Beacon street. Afterwards what remained for me to learn was cleansed by books & poetry & philosophy & came in purer forms of literature at College. These spiritual crises no doubt are periods of as certain occurrence in some form of agitation to every mind as dentition or puberty.

The babe cheers me with his hearty & protracted laugh which sounds to me like thunder in the woods.

Aug. 21, 1837

What means all the monitory tone of the world of life, of literature, of tradition? Man is fallen, Man is banished; an exile; he is in earth whilst there is a heaven. What do these apologues mean? These seem to him traditions of memory. But they are the whispers of hope and Hope is the voice of the Supreme Being to the Individual.

We say Paradise was; Adam fell; the Golden Age; & the like. We mean man is not as he ought to be; but our way of painting this is on Time, and we say *Was.*

Sept. 6, 1837

Not a word inscribed for ten days.

And now we bask in warm & yellow light of three pearly days— corn, beans, & squashes ripening every hour, the garden, the field an Indian paradise.

Sept. 13? 1837

The American artist who would carve a wood-god and who was familiar with the forest in Maine where enormous fallen pine trees "cumber the forest floor", where huge mosses depending from the trees and the mass of the timber give a savage & haggard strength to the grove—would produce a very different statue from the sculptor who only knew an European woodland—the tasteful Greek, for example.

It occurred the other day in hearing some clapping of hands after a speech, that the orator's value might be measured by every additional round after the three first claps, just as jockeys are wont to pay ten dollars for every additional roll of a horse who rolls himself on the ground. For in both cases the first & second roll come very easily off, but it gets beyond the third very hardly.

Sept. 19, 1837

I should like very well to get the data of the good story which Lidian tells of the stout soldier who persisted in wearing his military queue when the reforming major ordered all queues to be cut off in the regiment; the soldier held fast to his own & dying required that a hole should be made underneath his head in his coffin and the dear queue should project decent & honorable thereout.

C.C.E. talking of Mrs ———, said that she had two faces, and when conversing with her, you looked up & would suddenly find that instead of talking with the beautiful Mrs ———, you were talking with a ghoul.

Sept. 19? 1837

On the 29 August, I received a letter from the Salem Lyceum signed I.F Worcester, requesting me to lecture before the institution next winter and adding "The subject is of course discretionary with yourself 'provided no allusions are made to religious controversy, or other exciting topics upon which the public mind is honestly divided.'" I replied on the same day to Mr W. by quoting these words & adding "I am really sorry that any person in Salem should think me capable of accepting an invitation so encumbered."

It was the happiest turn to my old thrum which Charles H Warren gave as a toast at the ΦBK Dinner. "Mr President," he said, "I suppose all know where the orator comes from; and I suppose all know what he has said. I give you *The Spirit of Concord. It makes us all of One Mind.*"

Sept. 21, 1837

The autumnal equinox comes with sparkling stars and thoughtful days. I think the principles of the Peace party sublime and that the opposers of this philanthropy do not sufficiently consider the positive side of the spiritualist but only see his negative or abstaining side. But if a nation of men is exalted to that height of morals as to refuse to fight & choose rather to suffer loss of goods & loss of life than to use violence, they must be not helpless but most effective and great men; they would overawe their invader, & make him ridiculous; they would communicate the contagion of their virtue & inoculate all mankind.

Sept. 30, 1837

The child delights in shadows on the wall. The child prattles in the house, but if you carry him out of doors, he is overpowered by the light & extent of natural objects & is silent. But there was never child so lovely but his mother was glad to get him asleep.

Oct. 1, 1837

The young preacher preached from his ears & his memory, & never a word from his soul. His sermon was loud & hollow. It was not the report so much as the rimbombo, the reverberation of Calvinism. A solemn conclusion of a Calvinistic discourse imitated at the end of a Unitarian sermon, is purely ludicrous like grandfather's hat & spectacles on a rogue of six years. Alas, I could not help thinking how few prophets are left: There are five or six seers & sayers in the land: all the rest of the preaching is the reverberation of theirs.

*   *   *

The young man relying on his instincts who has only a good intention is apt to feel ashamed of his inaction & the slightness of his virtue when in the presence of the active & zealous leaders of the philanthropic enterprizes of Universal Temperance, Peace, & Abolition of Slavery. He only loves like Cordelia after his duty. Trust it nevertheless. A man's income is not sufficient for all things. If he spend here, he must save there.

Lidian grieves aloud about the wretched negro in the horrors of the middle passage; and they are bad enough. But to such as she, these crucifixions do not come. They come to the obtuse & barbarous to whom they are not horrid but only a little worse than the old sufferings. They exchange a cannibal war for a stinking hold. They have gratifications which would be none to Lidian.

Oct. 2, 1837
Consumption kills the Speakers. Speaking is apt to engender a worse consumption within. Blessed are they that hear.

I have read the second volume of Bancroft's History of U.S. It is very pleasing. He does not I think ever originate his views, but he imports very good views into his book, & parades his facts by the brave light of his principles. A very pleasant book, for here lo! the huge world has at last come round to Roger Williams, George Fox, & William Penn; & time-honored John Locke receives kicks. An objection to the book is the insertion of a boyish hurra every now & then for each State in turn, which resembles the fortune of the good Professor of Mathematics in a Southern College who was not permitted to go on with his exercise on Election day without interposing in his demonstration A B F equal G H I (Hurra for Jackson!) and so on.

The pagan theology of our churches treats Heaven as an inevitable evil which as there is no help against, the best way is to put the best face on the matter we can. "From whence," said the good preacher yesterday in his prayer, "we shall not be able to return". Truth will out.

Oct. 3, 1837
The very naming of a subject by a man of genius is the beginning of insight.
We do not love the man who gives us thoughts in conversation. We do not love that act. Why? does it violate our thinking? does it accuse

our unthinking? We like the company of him whose manners or unconscious talk sets our own minds in action & we take occasions of rich
opinions from him as we take apples off a tree without any thanks.

Oct. 5, 1837

I suppose there was seldom a person of my age & advantages whom
so little people could pull down & overcrow. The least people do most
entirely demolish me. I always find some quarter, & some orts of respect
from the mediocre. But a snippersnapper eats me whole.

There is no activity but accomplishes somewhat. A man is sometimes offended at the superfluous supererogatory order & nicety of a
woman who is the good housewife. But he must bear with little extremities & flourishes of a quality that makes comfort for all his senses
throughout his house. He must look at a virtue *whole*, & not only at the
skirt of its garment where it gathers up a little dust.

Oct. 6, 1837

Laban Turner told me that the musicians of the Brigade Band are
paid six dollars a day, & their expenses, & that some of them are employed almost every day of the year. Several of them are men of good estate; & they are not dissipated.

Oct. 8, 1837

The young Southerner comes here a spoiled child with graceful
manners, excellent self command, very good to be spoiled more, but
good for nothing else, a mere parader. He has conversed so much with
rifles, horses, & dogs that he is become himself a rifle, a horse, & a dog
and in civil educated company where anything human is going forward
he is dumb & unhappy; like an Indian in a church. Treat them with
great deference as we often do, and they accept it all as their due without
misgiving. Give them an inch & they take a mile. They are mere blad-
ders of conceit. Each snippersnapper of them all undertakes to speak for
the entire Southern states. "At the South, the reputation of Cambridge"
&c. &c. which being interpreted, is, In my negro village of Tuscaloosa
or Cheraw or St Marks I supposed so & so. "We, at the South," forsooth. They are more civilized than the Seminoles, however, in my
opinion; a little more. Their question respecting any man is like a
Seminole's, How can he fight? In this country, we ask, What can he do?
His pugnacity is all they prize, in man, dog, or turkey. The proper way
of treating them is not deference but to say as Mr Ripley does "Fiddle
faddle" in answer to each solemn remark about "The South." "It must
be confessed" said the young man, "that in Alabama, we are dead to

every thing, as respects politics." "Very true," replied Mr Ripley, "leaving out the last clause."

Oct. 1837

A good coat is always respected, they say, in the stage coach. Good reason; a good coat stands for Something, implies a small history: it shows that the wearer had some kind of a coat before, probably a good one & will have another when this is worn out; it shows that the wearer lives among people who wear good coats. Beside a man's coat money is usually only a small proportion to his food & fire & house & travelling money & by the outlay he can afford in the coat, we infer what outlay he can make in all.

The common complaint is of the dulness of life. I do not know but it must be confessed that the glance we give at the world in a leisure hour is melancholy: that melancholy cleaves to the English mind as to the Aeolian harp. But I maintain that all melancholy belongs to the exterior of man; I claim to be a part of the All.

We are carried by destiny along our life's course looking as grave & knowing as little as the infant who is carried in his wicker coach thro' the street.

Oct. 13, 1837

With much to say I put off writing until perhaps I shall have nothing in my memory. Now too soon then too late. I must try the pen & make a beginning.

At Boston Thursday I found myself nearly alone in the Athenaeum & so dropt my book to gaze at the Laocoon. The main figure is great: the two youths work harmoniously on the eye producing great admiration, so long as the eye is directed at the old man, but look at them & they are slight & unaffecting statues. No miniature copy and no single busts can do justice to this work. Its mass & its integrity are essential. At the Athenaeum, you cannot see it unless the room is nearly empty. For you must stand at the distance of nearly the whole hall to see it and interposing bystanders eclipse the statue. How is time abolished by the delight I have in this old work and without a name I receive it as a gift from the Universal Mind.

Then I read with great content the August number of the Asiatic Journal. Herein is always the piquancy of the meeting of civilization & barbarism. Calcutta or Canton are twilights where Night & Day contend. A very good paper is the Narrative of Lord Napier's mission to

China (who arrived at Macao 15 July 1834 and died 11 October). There stand in close contrast the brief wise English despatches with the mountainous nonsense of the Chinese diplomacy. The "red permit" writ by the vermilion pencil of the emperor, the superafrican ignorance with which England is disdained as out of the bounds of civilization, & her king called "reverently submissive" &c, &c. There is no farce in fiction better than this historical one of John Bull & the Yellow Man: albeit it ends tragically, as Lord Napier died of vexation apparently. I must get that book again.

Then I read an ascent of the Himmaleh mounts and the terror of the cold & the river seen bursting through caves of snow, and the traveller finding all over the desolate mountains bears' dung. Then, a duel: pistols for two and coffee for the survivor. Then an escape from a tiger in a cane-brake.

Then thinking of the trees which draw out of the air their food by their aerial roots the leaves, I mused on the strange versatility of the mind's appetite & food. Here were in the Reading Room some four or five men besides me, feeding on newspapers & Journals, unfolding our being thereby. Secluded from War, from trade, & from tillage, we were making amends to ourselves by devouring the descriptions of these things & atoning for the thinness by the quantity of our fare.

Oct. 16, 1837
The babe stands alone today for the first time.

In the present moment all the past is ever represented. The strong roots of ancient trees still bind the soil. The Provencal literature is not obsolete for me, for I have Spenser's Faerie Queen to read and all that faded splendor revives again in him for some centuries yet. Nor will Homer or Sophocles let me go though I read them not for they have formed those whom I read. Nor will the Egyptian designer die to me; my chair & tables forget him not.

Oct. 20, 1837
Margaret Fuller talking of Women, said, "Who would be a goody that could be a genius?"

Oct 21, 1837
I said when I awoke, After some more sleepings & wakings I shall lie on this mattrass sick; then, dead; and through my gay entry they will carry these bones. Where shall I be then? I lifted my head and beheld the spotless orange light of the morning beaming up from the dark hills into the wide Universe.

Oct. 21–22, 1837

A man may find his words mean more than he thought when he uttered them & be glad to employ them again in a new sense.

Oct. 23, 1837

In conversing with a lady it sometimes seems a bitterness & unnecessary wound to insist as I incline to, on this self sufficiency of man. There is no society say I; there can be none. 'Very true but very mournful,' replies my friend; we talk of courses of action. But to women my paths are shut up and the fine women I think of who have had genius & cultivation who have not been wives but muses have something tragic in their lot & I shun to name them.

Oct. 24, 1837

I find in town the ΦBK Oration, of which 500 copies were printed, all sold, in just one month.

Oct. 27, 1837

Let the air in. The Advertising is one of the signs of our times: the hanging out a showy sign with the hitherto unheard of name of the huckster flourished in letters more gorgeous than ever the name of Pericles or of Jove was writ in. They do wisely who do thus. It is a petty title of nobility. The man is made one of the public in a small way. What he doth is of some more importance; he is more responsible. His gay sign & far flying advertisement hold him at least to decency. So the publishing names of boys who have won school medals illustrates them, & bringing a petty Broad street scuffle into court lets the air in, & purges blind alleys.

Oct. 28, 1837

The event of death is always astounding; our philosophy never reaches, never possesses it; we are always at the beginning of our catechism; always the definition is yet to be made, What is Death? I see nothing to help beyond observing what the mind's habit is in regard to that crisis. Simply, I have nothing to do with it. It is nothing to me. After I have made my will & set my house in order, I shall do in the immediate expectation of death the same things I should do without it.

But more difficult is it to know the death of another. Mrs Ripley says that her little Sophia told the Mantuamaker this morning that "in heaven she was going to ask Dod to let her sit by Mother, all the time." And if this little darling should die, Mrs R thinks she could not live. So with the expectation of the death of persons who are conveniently situated, who have all they desire, & to whom death is fearful, she looks in

Lidian Jackson Emerson (1802–1892): "Asia makes my gods hers."

vain for a consolation. In us there ought to be remedy. There ought to be, there can be nothing, to which the soul is called, to which the soul is not equal. And I suppose that the roots of my relation to every individual are in my own constitution & not less the causes of his disappearance from me.

Nov. 2, 1837

Immense curiosity in Boston to see the delegation of the Sacs & Foxes, of the Sioux & the Ioways. I saw the Sacs & Foxes at the State-

house on Monday—about 30 in number. Edward Everett addressed
them & they replied. One chief said "They had no land to put their
words upon, but they were nevertheless true." One chief wore the skin
of a buffaloe's head with the horns attached, on his head, others birds
with outspread wings. Immense breadth of shoulder & very muscular
persons. Our Picts were so savage in their headdress & nakedness that it
seemed as if the bears & catamounts had sent a deputation. They danced
a war-dance on the Common, in the centre of the greatest crowd ever
seen on that area. The Governor cautioned us of the gravity of the tribe
& that we should beware of any expression of the ridiculous; and the
people all seemed to treat their guests gingerly as the keepers of lions &
jaguars do those creatures whose taming is not quite yet trustworthy.

Certainly it is right & natural that the Indian should come & see the
civil White man, but this was hardly genuine but a show so we were not
parties but spectators. . . .

At Faneuil Hall they built a partition between the two tribes because the tribes are at war.

Nov. 3–5, 1837

It is the right economy of time to do nothing by halves, nothing for
show, nothing perfunctorily. If you write a letter, put your earnest
meaning in, & God shall reward you by enlarging your sight. But save
your thought & you shall find it worthless & your wordy letter worthless also. In writing a review, put in only that you have to say, only the
things, & leave the consideration of the Greeks & Romans & the Universal History quite out. Stop when you have done. And stop when you
have begun if it is not something to you.

Nov. 6, 1837

Fuller at Providence explained to me his plans, "that he was to keep
the school 5 years—income so much; outlay so much; then he should be
able to go to Europe; &c, &c." When I repeated all this to Alcott, he expressed chagrin & contempt. For Alcott holds the School in so high regard that he would scorn to exchange it for the Presidency of the United
States. The School is his Europe. And this is a just example of the true
rule of Choice of Pursuit. You may do nothing to get money which is
not worth your doing on its own account. This is the sense of "he that
serves at the altar shall live by it." Every vocation is an altar. There must
be injury to the constitution from all false, from all half-action. Nor will
the plainly expressed wishes of other people be a reason why you should
do to oblige them what violates your sense, what breaks your integrity
& shows you falsely not the man you are.

* * *

The ultra benevolence of mine Asia reminds me of the pretty fable of the seven cedar birds sitting on the bough who passed the morsel which one had taken from bird to bird with courtesy until it returned again to the first. None cared for the morsel: All are fed with love. Asia makes my gods hers.

Perhaps in the village we have manners to paint which the city life does not know. Here we have Mr S. who is man enough to turn away the butcher who cheats in weight & introduce another butcher into town. The other neighbors could not take such a step. Here is Mr. E. who when the Moderator of the Townmeeting is candidate for representative & so stands in the centre of the box inspecting each vote & each voter dares carry up a vote for the opposite candidate & put it in. There is the hero who will not subscribe to the flag staff or the engine though all say it is mean. There is the man who gives his dollar but refuses to give his name though all other contributors are set down. There is Mr H. who never loses his spirits though always in the minority & though the people behave as bad as if they were drunk, he is just as determined in opposition & just as cheerful as ever. Here is Mr C. who says "Honor bright" & keeps it so. Here is Mr S. who warmly assents to what ever proposition you please to make & Mr M. who roundly tells you he will have nothing to do with the thing. The high people in the village are timid, the low people are bold & nonchalant; negligent too of each other's opposition for they see the amount of it & know its uttermost limits which the more remote proprietor does not. Here too are not to be forgotten our two companies, the Light Infantry & the Artillery who brought up one the Brigade Band & one the Brass Band from Boston, set the musicians side by side under the great tree on the common, & let them play two tunes & jangle & drown each other & presently got the companies into actual hustling & kicking.

Nov. 7, 1837

It needs a well read variously informed man to read Carlyle, from his infinite allusion. He knows every joke that ever was cracked.

Nov. 8, 1837

I believe the man & the writer should be one & not diverse, as they say Bancroft, as we know Bulwer is. Wordsworth gives us the image of the truehearted man, as Milton, Chaucer, Herbert do; not ruffled fine gentlemen who condescend to write like Shaftesbury, Congreve, & greater far, Walter Scott. Let not the author eat up the man, so that he shall be a balcony & no house. Let him not be turned into a dapper clerical anatomy to be assisted like a lady over a gutter or a stone wall. In meeting Milton, I feel that I should encounter a real man but Coleridge is a writer, & Pope, Waller, Addison & Swift & Gibbon though with attributes are too modish. It is not Man but the fashionable wit they would be. Yet Swift has properties. Allston is respectable to me. Novalis, Schiller are only voices, no men. Dr Johnson was a man though he lived in unfavorable solitude & society of one sort so that he was an unleavened lump at last on which a genial unfolding had only begun. Humanity cannot be the attribute of these people's writing. Humanity which smiles in Homer, in Chaucer, in Shakspear, in Milton, in Wordsworth. Montaigne is a Man.

Milton's expression of "Music smoothing the raven down of darkness till it smiled" has great beauty. Nothing in nature has the softness of darkness. Ride in the night through a wood, and the overhanging boughs shall become to the eye lumps of darkness and of an unutterable gentleness to the sense.

Nov. 9–10, 1837
How graceful & lively a spectacle is a squirrel on a bough cracking a nut! how sylvan beautiful a stag bounding through Plymouth Woods! how like a smile of the earth is the first violet we meet in spring! Well, it was meant that I should see these & partake this agreeable emotion. Was it not? And was it not further designed that I should thereby be prompted to ask the relation of these natures to my own, & so the great word Comparative Anatomy has now leaped out of the womb of the Unconscious. I feel a cabinet in my mind unlocked by each of these new interests. Wherever I go, the related objects crowd on my Sense & I explore backward & wonder how the same things looked to me before my attention had been aroused.

Rightminded men have recently been called to decide for Abolition.

Nov. 23, 1837
A fine paper ascribed to Parsons in the Daily Advertiser, not so much for the things said, as for the masterly tone. It is as hard to get the right tone as to say good things. One indicates character the other intellect.

Nov. 24, 1837
The selfsubsistent shakes like a reed before a sneering paragraph in the Newspaper or even at a difference of opinion concerning something

to be done expressed in a private letter from just such another shaking bulrush as himself. He sits expecting a dinner guest with a suspense which paralyses his inventive or his acquiring faculties. He finds the solitude of two or three entire days when mother, wife, & child are gone, tedious & dispiriting. Let him not wrong the truth & his own experience by too stiffly standing on the cold & proud doctrine of self sufficiency.

In the woods this afternoon, the bud on the dry twig appeared to reach out unto & prophesy an eternity to come.

When a zealot comes to me & represents the importance of this Temperance Reform my hands drop—I have no excuse—I honor him with shame at my own inaction.

Then a friend of the slave shows me the horrors of Southern slavery—I cry guilty guilty! Then a philanthropist tells me the shameful neglect of the Schools by the Citizens. I feel guilty again.

Then I hear of Byron or Milton who drank soda water & ate a crust whilst others fed fat & I take the confessional anew.

Then I hear that my friend has finished Aristophanes, Plato, Cicero, & Grotius, and I take shame to myself.

Then I hear of the generous Morton who offers a thousand dollars to the cause of Socialism, and I applaud & envy.

Then of a brave man who resists a wrong to the death and I sacrifice anew.

I cannot do all these things but these my shames are illustrious tokens that I have strict relations to them all. None of these causes are foreigners to me. My Universal Nature is thus marked. These accusations are parts of me too. They are not for nothing.

Nov. 26, 1837

How can such a question as the Slave Trade be agitated for forty years by the most enlightened nations of the world without throwing great light on ethics into the general mind? The fury with which the slaveholder & the slavetrader defend every inch of their plunder, of their bloody deck, & howling Auction, only serves as a Trump of Doom to alarum the ear of Mankind, to wake the sleepers, & drag all neutrals to take sides & listen to the argument & to the Verdict which Justice shall finally pronounce. The loathsome details of the kidnapping; of the middle passage; six hundred living bodies sit for thirty days betwixt death & life in a posture of stone & when brought on deck for air cast themselves into the sea—were these details merely produced to harrow the nerves of the susceptible & humane or for the purpose of engraving the question on the memory that it should not be dodged or obliterated & securing to it the concentration of the whole conscience of Christendom?

Dec. 10, 1837

I could not help remarking at church how much humanity was in the preaching of my good Uncle, Mr S. Ripley. The rough farmers had their hands at their eyes repeatedly. But the old hardened sinners, the arid educated men, ministers & others, were dry as stones.

Dec. 1837

In the sunset against the sky, the stone wall looked like a locket of black beads.

Feb. 3, 1838

Five days ago came Carlyle's letter & has kept me warm ever since with its affection & praise. It seems his friend John Sterling loves Waldo Emerson also, by reason of reading the book "Nature." I am quite bewitched maugre all my unamiableness with so dainty a relation as a friendship for a scholar & poet I have never seen, and he Carlyle's friend. I read his papers immediately in Blackwood & see a thinker if not a poet. Thought he has & right in every line, but Music he cares not for. I had certainly supposed that a lover of Carlyle & of me must needs love rhythm & music of style.

So pleasant a piece of sentiment as this new relation, it does not seem very probable that any harsh experience will be allowed to disturb. It is not very probable that we shall meet bodily to put the oetherial web we weave to the test of any rending or straining. And yet God knows I dare & I will boldly impawn his temper that he dares meet & cooperate until we are assayed & proven. I am not a sickly sentimentalist though the name of a friend warms my heart & makes me feel as a girl, but must & will have in my companion sense & virtue.

Feb. 5, 1838

But the Lecture must be writ—friend or no friend. And it seems as if Condition might be treated. Fate, fortune, Love, Demonology, Sleep; Death—what deities or demons environ man; Nothing but aids him.

Feb. 9, 1838

In Boston, Wednesday Night, I read at the Masonic Temple the tenth & last lecture of my Course on Human Culture. . . .

The pecuniary advantage of the Course has been considerable.

Season tickets sold 319	for	$620
Single tickets sold 373	for	186
		806
deduct error somewhere		13
		793
deduct expenses		225
		$568. net profit

The attendance on this course adding to the above list 85 tickets distributed by me to friends, will be about 439 persons on the average of an
evening—& as it was much larger at the close than at the beginning I
think 500 persons at the closing lectures.

A very gratifying interest on the part of the audience was evinced in
the views offered—which were drawn chiefly out of the materials already collected in this Journal. The ten lectures were read on ten pleasant winter evenings on consecutive Wednesdays. Thanks to the Teacher
of me & of all, the Upholder, the Health giver; thanks & lowliest wondering acknowledgment.

Feb. 9–10, 1838

You must love me as I am. Do not tell me how much I should love
you. I am content. I find my satisfactions in a calm considerate reverence
measured by the virtues which provoke it. So love me as I am. When I am
virtuous, love me; when I am vicious, hate me; when I am lukewarm,
neither good nor bad, care not for me.

But do not by your sorrow or your affection solicit me to be somewhat else than I by nature am.

Feb. 11, 1838

At the "teachers' meeting" last night my good Edmund after dis-
claiming any wish to difference Jesus from a human mind suddenly
seemed to alter his tone & said that Jesus made the world & was
the Eternal God. Henry Thoreau merely remarked that "Mr Hosmer
had kicked the pail over." I delight much in my young friend, who
seems to have as free & erect a mind as any I have ever met. He told
as we walked this afternoon a good story about a boy who went to
school with him, Wentworth, who resisted the school mistress' command that the children should bow to Dr Heywood & other gentlemen as they went by, and when Dr Heywood stood waiting & cleared
his throat with a Hem! Wentworth said, "You need not hem, Doctor; I
shan't bow."

Feb. 17, 1838

My good Henry Thoreau made this else solitary afternoon sunny with his simplicity & clear perception. How comic is simplicity in this doubledealing quacking world. Every thing that boy says makes merry with society though nothing can be graver than his meaning. I told him he should write out the history of his College life as Carlyle has his tutoring. We agreed that the seeing the stars through a telescope would be worth all the Astronomical lectures. Then he described Mr Quimby's electrical lecture here & the experiment of the shock & added that "College Corporations are very blind to the fact that that twinge in the elbow is worth all the lecturing."

Feb. 19, 1838

Solitude is fearsome & heavy hearted. I have never known a man who had so much good accumulated upon him as I have. Reason, health, wife, child, friends, competence, reputation, the power to inspire, & the power to please. Yet leave me alone a few days, & I creep about as if in expectation of a calamity. My mother, my brother are at New York. A little farther—across the sea—is my friend Thomas Carlyle. In the islands I have another friend, it seems. I will love you all & be happy in your love. My gentle wife has an angel's heart; & for my boy, his grief is more beautiful than other people's joy.

March 2, 1838

"Society," said M.M.E. in speaking of the malignity & meanness of conversation, "Society is like a corpse that purges at the mouth."

March 4, 1838

Last night a remembering & remembering talk with Lidian. I went back to the first smile of Ellen on the door stone at Concord. I went back to all that delicious relation to feel as ever how many shades, how much reproach. Strange is it that I can go back to no part of youth, no past relation without shrinking & shrinking. Not Ellen, not Edward, not Charles. Infinite compunctions embitter each of those dear names & all who surrounded them. Ah could I have felt in the presence of the first, as now I feel my own power & hope, & so have offered her in every word & look the heart of a man humble & wise, but resolved to be true & perfect with God, & not as I fear it seemed, the uneasy uncentred joy of one who received in her a good—a lovely good—out of all proportion to his deserts, I might haply have made her days longer & certainly sweeter & at least have recalled her seraph smile without a pang. I console myself with the thought that if Ellen, if Edward, if Charles could have read my entire heart they should have seen nothing but rectitude of purpose & generosity conquering the superficial coldness & prudence. But I ask now why was not I made like all these beatified mates of mine *superficially* generous & noble as well as *internally* so. They never needed to shrink at any remembrance; & I—at so many sad passages that look to me now as if I had been blind & mad. Well O God I will try & learn, from this sad memory to be brave & circumspect & true henceforth & weave now a web that will not shrink. This is the thorn in the flesh.

March 5, 1838

We acquire courage by our success daily & have a daring from experience which we had not from genius. I regret one thing omitted in my late Course of Lectures; that I did not state with distinctness & conspicuously the great error of modern Society in respect to religion & say, You can never come to any peace or power until you put your whole reliance in the moral constitution of man & not at all in a historical Christianity. The Belief in Christianity that now prevails is the Unbelief of men. They will have Christ for a lord & not for a brother. Christ preaches the greatness of Man but we hear only the greatness of Christ.

March 6, 1838

Montaigne is spiced throughout with rebellion as much as Alcott or my young Henry T.

March 6–8, 1838

I like, to be sure, Mrs Hoar's good saying that when that transcendant beggar Ma'am Bliss received the beefsteaks she had sent her, saying, "Yes, you can leave it; Mrs D. has sent me some turkey, but this will do for the cat;" Mrs H. told Elizabeth, that, "it would do her as much good as if she thanked us". Very true & noble, Mrs H! and yet I grudged the dollar & a half paid to my stupid beggar-mannered thankless, Mrs W. because all that I gave to this lump of tallow was so much taken from my friend & brother whom I ought to go labor on daywages to help.

March 9–10, 1838

Of droll word blunders Lidian could never cure Mrs W. of calling mashed, *smashed.* "Oh yes she had fed Baby with a smashed potato."

March 18, 1838

At Church all day but almost tempted to say I would go no more. Men go where they are wont to go else had no soul gone this afternoon. The snowstorm was real, the preacher merely spectral. Vast contrast to look at him & then out of the window. Yet no fault in the good man. Evidently he thought himself a faithful searching preacher, mentioned that he thought so several times; & seemed to be one of that large class, *sincere persons based on shams; sincere persons who are bred & do live in shams.* He had lived in vain. He had no one word intimating that ever he had laughed or wept, was married or enamoured, had been cheated, or voted for, or chagrined. If he had ever lived & acted we were none the wiser for it. It seemed strange they should come to church. It seemed as if their own houses were very unentertaining that they should prefer this thoughtless clamorous young person. . . .

The Church is a good place to study Theism by comparing the things said with your Consciousness.

There is no better subject for effective writing than the Clergy. I ought to sit & think & then write a discourse to the American clergy showing them the ugliness & unprofitableness of theology & churches at this day & the glory & sweetness of the Moral Nature out of whose pale they are almost wholly shut.

Present Realism as the front face. & remind them of the fact that I shrink & wince as soon as the prayers begin & am very glad if my tailor has given me a large velvet collar to my wrapper or cloak, the prayers are so bad. A good subject, because we can see always the good ideal, the noble Ethics of Nature, as contrast to the poverty stricken pulpit. Tell them that a true preacher can always be known by this, that he deals them out his life, life metamorphosed; as Taylor, Webster, Scott, Carlyle do. But of the bad preacher, it could not be told from his sermon, what age of the world he fell in, whether he had a father or a child, whether he was a freeholder or a pauper, whether he was a citizen or a countryman, or any other fact of his biography. But a man's sermon should be rammed with life.

The men I have spoken of above—sincere persons who live in shams, are those who accept another man's consciousness for their own, & are in the state of a son who should always suck at his mother's teat. I think Swedenborg ought so to represent them or still more properly, as permanent embryos which received all their nourishment through the umbilical cord & never arrived at a conscious & independent existence. . . .

See how easily these old worships of Moses, of Socrates, of Zoroaster, of Jesus, domesticate themselves in my mind. It will be admitted I have great susceptibility to such. Will it not be as easy to say they are other Waldos?

A man comes now into the world a slave, he comes saddled with twenty or forty centuries. Asia has arrearages & Egypt arrearages; not to mention all the subsequent history of Europe & America. But he is not his own man but the hapless bondman of Time with these continents & aeons of prejudice to carry on his back. It is now grown so bad that he cannot carry the mountain any longer & be a man. There must be a Revolution.

March 24, 1838

I have been led yesterday in to a rambling exculpatory talk on Theism. I say that here we feel at once that we have no language; that words are only auxiliary & not adequate; are suggestions and not copies of our cogitation. I deny Personality to God because it is too little not too much. Life, personal life is faint & cold to the energy of God. For Reason & Love & Beauty, or, that which is all these, is the life of life, the reason of reason, the love of love.

March 26, 1838

Thought is only to be answered by thought not by authority, not by wishes. I tell men what I find in my consciousness. They answer me. "It is wrong; it is false; for we wish otherwise." I report to them from my thought how little we know of God, and they reply "We think you have no Father. We love to address the Father." Yes, I say, the Father is a convenient name & image to the affections; but drop all images if you wish to come at the elements of your thought & use as mathematical words as you can. We must not be so wise. We must not affect as all mankind do, to know all things & to have quite finished & done God & Heaven. We must come back to our real initial state & see & own that we have yet beheld but the first ray of Being. In strict speech it seems fittest to say, *I Become* rather than *I am*. I am a *Becoming*.

April 1, 1838

Cool or cold windy clear day. The Divinity School youths wished to talk with me concerning theism. I went rather heavyhearted for I always find that my views chill or shock people at the first opening. But the conversation went well & I came away cheered. I told them that the preacher should be a poet smit with love of the harmonies of moral nature: and yet look at the Unitarian Association & see if its aspect is poetic. They all smiled No. A minister nowadays is plainest prose, the prose of prose. He is a Warming-pan, a Night-chair at sick beds & rheumatic souls; and the fire of the minstrel's eye & the vivacity of his word is exchanged for intense grumbling enunciation of the Cambridge sort, & for scripture phraseology.

April 1? 1838

How well the newspapers illustrate the truth that only biography, not nations interest. The Reporters tell us nothing but of Calhoun, Clay,

& Webster, not the Sub Treasury Bill but the personal controversy absorbs them.

April 1838

Preaching especially false preaching is for able men a sickly employment. Study of books is also sickly & the garden & the family, wife, mother, son, & brother are a balsam. There is health in table talk & nursery play. We must wear old shoes & have aunts & cousins.

April 20, 1838

Last night, ill dreams. Dreams are true to nature & like monstrous formations (e.g. the horsehoof divided into toes) show the law. Their double consciousness, their sub- & ob-jectiveness is the wonder. I call the phantoms that rise the creation of my fancy but they act like volunteers & counteract my inclination. They make me feel that every act, every thought, every cause, is bipolar & in the act is contained the counteract. If I strike, I am struck. If I chase, I am pursued. If I push, I am resisted.

April 23, 1838

This tragic Cherokee business which we stirred at a meeting in the church yesterday will look to me degrading & injurious do what I can. It is like dead cats around one's neck. It is like School Committees & Sunday School classes & Teachers' meetings & the Warren street chapel & all the other holy hurrahs. I stir in it for the sad reason that no other mortal will move & if I do not, why it is left undone.

The amount of it, be sure, is merely a Scream but sometimes a scream is better than a thesis.

April 26–28, 1838

Yesterday P.M. I went to the Cliff with Henry Thoreau. Warm, pleasant, misty weather which the great mountain amphitheatre seemed to drink in with gladness. A crow's voice filled all the miles of air with sound. A bird's voice, even a piping frog enlivens a solitude & makes world enough for us. At night I went out into the dark & saw a glimmering star & heard a frog & Nature seemed to say Well do not these suffice? Here is a new scene, a new experience. Ponder it, Emerson, & not like the foolish world hanker after thunders & multitudes & vast landscapes, the sea or Niagara.

April 29? 1838

Lidian came into the study this afternoon & found the towerlet that Wallie had built half an hour before, of two spools, a card, an awl-case,

& a flourbox top—each perpendicularly balanced on the other, & could scarce believe that her boy had built the pyramid, & then fell into such a fit of affection that she lay down by the structure & kissed it down, & declared she could possibly stay no longer with papa, but must go off to the nursery to see with eyes the lovely creature; & so departed.

May 1, 1838

The advantage of the Napoleon temperament, impassive, unimpressible by others, is a signal convenience over this other tender one which every aunt & every gossipping girl can daunt & tether. This weakness be sure is merely cutaneous, & the sufferer gets his revenge by the sharpened observation that belongs to such sympathetic fibre. As even in college I was already content to be *"screwed"* in the recitation room, if, on my return, I could accurately paint the fact in my youthful Journal.

May 5, 1838

Last night E.H described the apathy from which she suffers. I own I was at a loss to prescribe as I did not sufficiently understand the state of mind she paints.

May 22, 1838

Dr Jackson once said that the laws of disease were as beautiful as the laws of health. Our good Dr Hurd came to me yesterday before I had yet seen Dr Ripley (yesterday represented as in a dying condition)— with joy sparkling in his eyes. "And how is the Doctor, sir," I said. "I have not seen him today," he replied, "but it is the most correct apoplexy I have ever seen, face & hands livid, breathing sonorous, & all the symptoms perfect" & he rubbed his hands with delight.

May 26, 1838

Nettled again & nervous (as much as sometimes by flatulency or piddling things) by the wretched Sunday's preaching of Mr H. You Cambridge men affect to think it desireable that there should be light in the people. But the elevation of the people by one degree of thought would blow to shreds all this nightmare preaching. How miserable is that which stands only in the wooden ignorance of villages. As the dull man droned & droned & wound his stertorous horn upon the main doctrine of Xty the resurrection, namely, & how little it was remembered in modern preaching, & modern prayers, I could not help thinking that there are two emphases that distinguish the two sorts of teachers: 1. *Human life.* 2. *Thought.* Those who remain fast in the first, respect facts supremely; & thought is but a tool for them. Those who dwell in the second, respect principles; & facts & persons & themselves they regard only as slovenly unperfect manifestations of these; they care not for Christ, nor for Death, nor for resurrection, except as illustrations.

June 6, 1838
When I told Alcott that I would not criticise his compositions; that it would be as absurd to require them to conform to my way of writing & aiming, as it would be to reject Wordsworth because he was wholly unlike Campbell; that here was a new mind & it was welcome to a new style;—he replied, well pleased, "That is criticism."

June 8, 1838
A man must have aunts & cousins, must buy carrots & turnips, must have barn & woodshed, must go to market & to the blacksmith's shop, must saunter & sleep & be inferior & silly.

June 9, 1838
Whilst I behold the holy lights of the June sunset last evening or tonight I am raised instantly out of fear & out of time, & care not for the knell of this coughing body. Strange the succession of humors that pass through this human spirit. Sometimes I am the organ of the Holy Ghost & sometimes of a vixen petulance.

June 12, 1838
Solitude is naught & society is naught. Alternate them & the good of each is seen. You can soon learn all that society can teach you for one while. A foolish routine, an indefinite multiplication of balls, concerts, rides, theatres, can teach you no more than a few can. Then retire & hide; & from the valley behold the mountain. Have solitary prayer & praise. Love the garden, the barn, the pasture, & the rock. There digest & correct the past experience, blend it with the new & divine life, & grow with God. After some interval when these delights have been sucked dry, accept again the opportunities of society. The same scenes revisited shall wear a new face, shall yield a higher culture. And so on. Undulation, Alternation, is the condition of progress, of life.

June 13–15, 1838
It is the distinction of genius that it is always inconceivable—once & ever a surprise. Shakspeare we cannot account for, no history, no "life & times" solves the insoluble problem. I cannot slope things to him so as to make him less steep & precipitous; so as to make him one of many, so as to know how I should write the same things. Goethe, I can see, wrote

things which I might & should also write, were I a little more favored, a little cleverer man. He does not astonish. But Shakspear, as Coleridge says, is as unlike his cotemporaries as he is unlike us. His style is his own. And so is Genius ever total & not mechanically composable. It stands there a beautiful unapproachable whole like a pinetree or a strawberry—alive, perfect, yet inimitable; nor can we find where to lay the first stone, which given, we could build the arch. Phidias or the great Greeks who made the Elgin marbles & the Apollo & Laocoon belong to the same exalted category with Shakspeare & Homer. And I imagine that we see somewhat of the same possibility boundless in countrymen & in plain motherwit & unconscious virtue as it flashes out here & there in the corners.

When I read the North American Review, or the London Quarterly, I seem to hear the snore of the muses, not their waking voice.

I was in a house where tea comes like a loaded wagon very late at night.

Read & think. Study now, & now garden. Go alone, then go abroad. Speculate awhile, then work in the world. Yours affectionately.

June 16? 1838
    Elizabeth Palmer Peabody brought me yesterday Hawthorne's Footprints on the seashore to read. I complained that there was no inside to it. Alcott & he together would make a man.

The Unbelief of the age is attested by the loud condemnation of trifles. Look at our silly religious papers. Let a minister wear a cane, or a white hat, go to a theatre, or avoid a sunday school, let a school book with a Calvinistic sentence or a sunday schoolbook without one, be heard of, & instantly all the old grannies squeak & gibber & do what they call sounding an alarm, from Bangor to Mobile. Alike nice & squeamish is its ear; you must on no account say "stink" or "damn."

This afternoon, the foolishest preaching—which bayed at the moon. Go, hush, old man, whom years have taught no truth.* The hardness & ignorance with which the threat that the son of man when he cometh in clouds will be ashamed of A. & B. because they are not members of Concord Church must have suggested to them 'Be it so: then I also will be ashamed of Him.' Such Moabitish darkness, well typified in the

---

*Emerson seems to be referring to his step-grandfather, Ezra Ripley.

perplexity about his glasses, reminded one of the squashbugs who stupid stare at you when you lift the rotten leaf of the vines.

June 17, 1838

A cool damp day, a cool evening, the first interruption we have had to the energy of the heat of the last 8 or 10 days wherein the mercury has ranged from 70 to 90. When the cool wind blows, the serene muse parts her fragrant locks, & looks forth.

What canst thou say, high daughter of God! to the waiting son of man? What canst thou teach to elevate these low relations, or to interpret them; to fill the day; to dispel the languor & dulness; & bring heaven into the house-door? Ah! say it, & to me.

June 18, 1838

C[aroline] S[turgis] protests. That is a good deal. In these times you shall find a small number of persons of whom only that can be affirmed that they protest. Yet is it as divine to say no, as to say yes. You say they go too much alone. Yea, but they shun society to the end of finding society. They repudiate the false out of love of the true. Extravagance is a good token. In an Extravagance, there is hope; in Routine, none.

The art of writing consists in putting two things together that are unlike and that belong together like a horse & cart. Then have we somewhat far more goodly & efficient than either.

I think we cannot safely argue. I think it needs a saint to dispute. If he set out to contend, almost St Paul will lie, almost St John will hate. What low, poor, paltry, hypocritical people, an argument on religion will make of the pure & select souls. Shuffle they will & crow, crook & hide, feign to confess here, only that they may brag & conquer there; & not a thought has enriched either party, & oh! not one sweet emotion of bravery, of modesty, of kindness, or of hope, for all the mouthing they have mouthed concerning humility, love of truth, & listening to the God within. I see plainly it will not do for me to pretend anything. But how I heard it in silent thunders one Sunday in my pew that all nature helps him who speaks the truth. Speak the truth & the very roots of the grass underground there, move & stir to bear you witness. Speak the truth & the innocent day loves you & serves you.

June 19, 1838

Forget the past. Be not the slave of your own past. In your prayer, in your teaching cumber not yourself with solicitude lest you contradict somewhat you have stated in this or that public place. So you worship the dull God Terminus & not the Lord of Lords. But dare rather to quit the platform, plunge into the sublime seas, dive deep, & swim far, so shall you come back with self respect, with new power, with an advanced experience, that shall explain & overlook the old. Trust your emotion. If perchance you say in a metaphysical analysis I cannot concede personality to the Deity, yet when the devout motions of the soul come, yield to them heart & soul if they should clothe God with garments of shape & color.

June 21, 1838

Have you had doubts? Have you struggled with coldness; with apathy; with selfcontempt that made you pale & thin? George Fox perambulated England in his perplexity. In elegant Cambridge, have you walked a mile in perturbation of the spirit? Yet somehow you must come to the bottom of those doubts or the human soul in its great ebbs & flows asking you for its law will call you, Boy! Life, authentic life, you must have or you can teach nothing. There is more to be learned by the poor passions which have here exercised many a pale boy in the little strife for the college honors, in the incommunicable irritations of hope & fear; of success, but still more of defeat; the remorse, the repentance, the resolution, that belong to conscientious youths in the false estimate they are apt to form here of duty & ambition, than there is in all the books of divinity.

They call it Christianity, I call it Consciousness.

Day creeps after day each full of facts—dull, strange, despised things that we cannot enough despise—call heavy, prosaic, & desart. And presently the aroused intellect finds gold & gems in one of these scorned facts, then finds that the day of facts is a rock of diamonds, that a fact is an Epiphany of God, that on every fact of his life he should rear a temple of wonder, joy, & praise.

June 22, 1838

You must treat the men & women of one idea, the Abolitionist, the Phrenologist, the Swedenborgian, as insane persons with a continual tenderness & special reference in every remark & action to their known state, which reference presently becomes embarrassing & tedious. "I am tired of fools," said once my sharpwitted Aunt to me with wondrous emphasis.

June 23, 1838

I hate goodies. I hate goodness that preaches. Goodness that preaches undoes itself. A little electricity of virtue lurks here & there in kitchens & among the obscure—chiefly women, that flashes out occasional light & makes the existence of the thing still credible. But one had as lief curse & swear as be guilty of this odious religion that watches the beef & watches the cider in the pitcher at table, that shuts the mouth hard at any remark it cannot twist nor wrench into a sermon, & preaches as long as itself & its hearer is awake. Goodies make us very bad. We should, if the race should increase, be scarce restrained from calling for bowl & dagger. We will almost sin to spite them. Better indulge yourself, feed fat, drink liquors, than go strait laced for such cattle as these.

June 24, 1838

Nothing is so shallow as dogmatism. Your soaring thought is only a point more, a station more whence you draw triangles for the survey of the illimitable field: and the event of each moment, the harvest, the shower, the steamboat disaster, the bankruptcy, the amour of Julia, the apoplexy of Dr Sawdust, are tests to try your theory, your truth, the approximate result you call Truth, & reveal its defects. If I have renounced the search, come into a port of some pretending dogmatism, some New Church or Old Church, some Schelling or Cousin, I have died to all use of these new events that are born out of prolific time into multitude of life every hour, I am as a bankrupt to whom brilliant opportunities offer in vain. He has just foreclosed his freedom, tied his hands, locked himself up, & given the key to another to keep. Thou Awful Father! who so slowly uncoverest my nature & hope to my curiosity & faith, I lowly strive to keep thy law, to bow no knee to the Baals fine with what jewels, mystic with what poetry soever, but to keep erect that head which thou gavest me erect against the solicitations, &, if it should so be, against the physical & metaphysical terrors of the Universe. This it is to have immortal youth.

Alcott has the great merit of being a believer in the soul. I think he has more faith in the Ideal than any man I have known. Hence his welcome influence. A wise woman said to me that he has few thoughts, too few. She could count them all. Well. Books, conversation, discipline will give him more. But what were many thoughts if he had not this distinguishing Faith, which is a palpable proclamation out of the deeps of nature that God yet is? With many thoughts, & without this, he would be only one more of a countless throng of lettered men; but now you cannot spare the fortification that he is.

* * *

It seems clear that it will be the distinction of the new age, the refusal of authority. Men will not now say as the emigrant French noblesse on their return under Napoleon, "You know we must serve somebody." But it will be the point of honor in literature & in life, & the principle in the church to imbibe God without medium.

July 1, 1838

Most of the Commonplaces spoken in churches every Sunday respecting the Bible & the life of Christ, are grossly superstitious. . . . Do let the new generation speak the truth, & let our grandfathers die. Let go if you please the old notions about responsibility for the souls of your parishioners but do feel that Sunday is their only time for thought & do not defraud them of that, as miserably as two men have me today. Our time is worth too much than that we can go to church twice, until you have something to announce there.

There is a limit to the effect of written eloquence. It may do much, but the miracles of eloquence can only be expected from the man who thinks on his legs; he who thinks may thunder; on him the Holy Ghost may fall & from him pass.

July 16, 1838

Little Waldo cheers the whole house by his moving calls to the cat, to the birds, to the flies—"Pussy cat come see Waddow! Liddel Birdy come see Waddo! Pies! pies! come see Waddo!" His mother shows us the two apples that his Grandfather gave him, & which he brought home one in each hand & did not begin to eat till he got nearly home. "See where the dear little Angel has gnawed them. They are worth a barrel of apples that he has not touched."

July 17, 1838

In preparing to go to Cambridge with my speech to the young men, day before yesterday, it occurred with force that I had no right to go unless I were equally willing to be prevented from going.

Aug. 14, 1838

Sanity is very rare: every man almost & every woman has a dash of madness, & the combinations of society continually detect it. See how many experiments at the perfect man. One thousand million, they say, is the population of the globe. So many experiments then. Well a few times in history a well mixed character transpires. Look in the hundreds of persons that each of us knows. Only a few whom we regard with great complacency, a few sanities.

"I have a great deal more to say that will shock you."

Aug. 15–16, 1838

The little girl comes by with a brimming pail of whortleberries, but the wealth of her pail has passed out of her little body, & she is spent & languid. So is it with the toiling poet who publishes his splendid composition, but the poet is pale & thin.

Aug. 17, 1838

Saw beautiful pictures yesterday. Miss Fuller brought with her a portfolio of Samuel Ward, containing a chalk sketch of one of Raphael's Sibyls, of Cardinal Bembo, & the Angel in Heliodorus' profanation; and Thorwaldsen's Entry of Alexander, &c, &c. I have said sometimes that it depends little on the object, much on the mood, in art. I have enjoyed more from mediocre pictures casually seen when the mind was in equilibrium, & have reaped a true benefit of the art of painting—the stimulus of color, the idealizing of common life into this gentle, elegant, unoffending fairy-land of a picture, than from many masterpieces seen with much expectation & tutoring, & so not with equipoise of mind. The mastery of a great picture comes slowly over the mind. If I see a fine picture with other people, I am driven almost into inevitable affectations. The scanty vocabulary of praise is quickly exhausted, & we lose our common sense, & much worse our reason, in our *superlative degrees*. But these pictures I looked at with leisure & with profit.

Aug. 18, 1838

It would give me new Scope to write on topics proper to this age & read discourses on Goethe, Carlyle, Wordsworth, Canova, Thorwaldsen, Tennyson, O'Connell, Baring, Channing, & Webster. To these I must write up. If I arrived at causes & new generalizations, they would be truly valuable, & would be telescopes into the Future. Elizabeth Hoar says, add the topic of the rights of Woman; & Margaret Fuller testifies that women are Slaves.

Dr Ripley prays for rain with great explicitness on Sunday & on Monday the showers fell. When I spoke of the speed with which his prayers were answered, the good man looked modest.

Aug. 21, 1838

The Address to the Divinity School is published & they are printing the Dartmouth Oration. The correction of these two pieces for the press has cost me no small labor, now nearly ended. There goes a great deal of work into a correct literary paper, though of few pages. Of course, it cannot be overseen & exhausted except by analysis as faithful as this synthesis. But negligence in the author is inexcusable. I know & will know no such thing as haste in composition. All the foregoing hours of a man's life do stretch forth a finger & a pen & inscribe their several line or word into the page he writes today.

Aug. 22, 1838

I decline invitations to evening parties chiefly because beside the time spent, commonly ill, in the party, the hours preceding & succeeding the visit, are lost for any solid use, as I am put out of tune for writing or reading. That makes my objection to many employments that seem trifles to a bystander as packing a trunk, or any small handiwork, or correcting proof sheets, that they put me out of tune.

Aug. 27, 1838

There is history somewhere worth knowing; as, for example, Whence came the negro? Who were those primeval artists that in each nation converted mountains of earth or stone into forms of architecture or sculpture? What is the genealogy of languages? & When & What is the Genesis of Man?

Aug. 31, 1838

Yesterday at ΦBK anniversary. Steady, steady. I am convinced that if a man will be a true scholar, he shall have perfect freedom. The young people & the mature hint at odium, & aversion of faces to be presently encountered in society. I say no: I fear it not. No scholar need fear it. For if it be true that he is merely an observer, a dispassionate reporter, no partisan, a singer merely for the love of music, his is a position of perfect immunity: to him no disgusts can attach; he is invulnerable. The vulgar think he would found a sect & would be installed & made much of. He knows better & much prefers his melons & his woods. Society has no bribe for me, neither in politics, nor church, nor college, nor city. My resources are far from exhausted. If they will not hear me lecture, I shall have leisure for my book which wants me. Beside, it is an universal maxim worthy of all acceptation that a man may have that allowance which he takes. Take the place & attitude to which you see your unquestionable right, & all men acquiesce. Who are these murmurers, these haters, these revilers? Men of no knowledge, & therefore no stability. The scholar on the contrary is sure of his point, is fast-rooted, & can securely predict the hour when all this roaring multitude shall roar *for* him. Analyze the chiding opposition & it is made up of such timidities, uncertainties, & no opinions, that it is not worth dispersing.

It is one of the blessings of old friends that you can afford to be stupid with them.

Sept. 3-4, 1838

I have usually read that a man suffered more from one hard word than he enjoyed from ten good ones. My own experience does not confirm the saying. The censure (I either know or fancy) does not hit me; and the praise is very good.

Sept. 5, 1838

How rare is the skill of writing! I detected a certain unusual unity of purpose in the paragraph levelled at me in the Daily Advertiser, & I now learn it is the old tyrant of the Cambridge Parnassus himself, Mr Norton, who wrote it.

Sept. 5–7, 1838

There is a fire in many men which demands an outlet in some vigorous action. They betray their impatience of quiet in an irregular Catalinarian walk; in irregular, faltering, disturbed speech too emphatic for the occasion. They do trifles with a tragic air. This is not beautiful. Let them split wood & work off this superabundant irritability.

Sept. 8, 1838

That which is individual & remains individual in my experience is of no value. What is fit to engage me & so engage others permanently, is what has put off its weeds of time & place & personal relation. Therefore all that befals me in the way of criticism & extreme blame & praise drawing me out of equilibrium—putting me for a time in false position to people, & disallowing the spontaneous sentiments, wastes my time, bereaves me of thoughts, & shuts me up within poor personal considerations. Therefore I hate to be conspicuous for blame or praise. It spoils thought.

Henry Thoreau told a good story of Deacon Parkman, who lived in the house he now occupies, & kept a store close by. He hung out a salt fish for a sign, & it hung so long & grew so hard, black, & deformed, that the deacon forgot what thing it was, & nobody in town knew, but being examined chemically it proved to be salt fish. But duly every morning the deacon hung it on its peg.

Sept. 12, 1838

Alcott wants a historical record of conversations holden by you & me & him. I say how joyful rather is some Montaigne's book which is full of fun, poetry, business, divinity, philosophy, anecdote, smut, which dealing of bone & marrow, of cornbarn & flour barrel, of wife, & friend, & valet, of things nearest & next, never names names, or gives you the glooms of a recent date or relation, but hangs there in the heaven of letters, unrelated, untimed, a joy & a sign, an autumnal star.

Sept. 13–14, 1838

To pack a trunk for a journey is to me one of the most dispiriting employments. Another is to feel a necessity to laugh at fun & jokes which do not amuse you. I went to New Bedford & Mr D. was in a frolicsome mood, & got up from supper in the evening, & said, "Come let us have some fun," & went about to tickle his wife & his sisters. I grew grave, &, do what I could, I felt that I looked like one appointed to be hanged.

* * *

After thirty a man is too sensible of the strait limitations which his physical constitution sets to his activity. The stream feels its banks, which it had forgotten in the run & overflow of the first meadows.

Sept. 15, 1838

There must be somewhat unfair in entire literature. For every writer avoids of course to say what all think & say around him. This is his endeavor in every sentence—to say that which is not thought & said. Because it is *not* said, therefore he says it. Of course that which he skipped, is precisely that which it now concerns us to know. He shunned the things of garish day & gave us the shades. He shunned the obvious & seized the rare & recondite.

Sept. 16, 1838

It does seem as if history gave no intimation of any society in which despondency came so readily to heart as we see it & feel it in ours. Young men, young women at thirty & even earlier seem to have lost all spring & vivacity, & if they fail in their first enterprize the rest is rock & shallow. Is the Stoic in the soul dead in these late ages? I cannot understand it. Our people are surrounded with a greater external prosperity & general well-being than Indians or Saxons; more resources, outlets, asylums: Yet we are sad & these were not. Why should it be? Has not Reflection any remedy for her own diseases?

Sunday Eve. I went at sundown to the top of Dr Ripley's hill & renewed my vows to the Genius of that place. Somewhat of awe, somewhat grand & solemn mingles with the beauty that shines afar around. In the west, where the sun was sinking behind clouds, one pit of splendor lay as in a desert of space—a deposite of *still light*, not radiant. Then I beheld the river like God's love journeying out of the grey past on into the green future. Yet sweet & native as all those fair impressions on that summit fall on the eye & ear, they are not yet mine. I cannot tell why I should feel myself such a stranger in nature. I am a tangent to their sphere, & do not lie level with this beauty. And yet the dictate of the hour is to forget all I have mislearned; to cease from man, & to cast myself again into the vast mould of nature.

Sept. 18, 1838

Forget as fast as you can that you exist, if you would be beautiful & beloved. You do not tell me, young maiden, in words that you wish to be admired, that not to be lovely but to be courted, not to be mistress of yourself but to be mistress of me, is your desire. But I hear it, an ugly harlot sound in the recesses of your song, in the niceties of your speech, in the lusciousness (forgive the horrid word) of your manners. Can you not possibly think of any thing that you really & heartily want & can say so, & go the *straight* way in the face of God & men to effect, if it were only to raise a cucumber, or own a cat, or make a scratch cradle?

This P.M. the Eclipse. Peter Howe did not like it for his rowan would not make hay: and he said "the sun looked as if a nigger was putting his head into it."

Sept. 19, 1838
I found in the wood this afternoon the drollest mushroom—tall, stately, pretending, uprearing its vast dome as if to say "Well I am something! Burst, ye beholders! thou lucky beholder! with wonder." Its dome was a deep yellow ground with fantastic starlike ornaments richly over wrought; so shabby genteel, so negro fine, the St Peter's of the beetles & pismires. Such ostentation *in petto* I never did see. I touched the white column with my stick—it nodded like old Troy, & so eagerly recovered the perpendicular as seemed to plead piteously with me not to burst the fabric of its pride. Shall I confess it? I could almost hear my little Waldo at home begging me as when I have menaced his little block house, and the little puffball seemed to say "Don't, papa, pull it down!" So, after due admiration of this blister, this cupola of midges, I left the little scaramouch alone in its glory. Goodbye Vanity, Goodbye Nothing! Certainly there is Comedy in the Divine Mind when these little Vegetable Selfconceits front the day as well as Newton or Goethe, with such impressive emptiness.

Sept. 20, 1838
They say Dr Palfrey lost his countenance once at the baptismal font when the affectionate father whispered in his ear the name of his babe Jacob Adonis. 'Tis poor fun but sometimes resistless—odd names. Zephaniah Tearsheet; Belzabub Edwards, not the distinguished Belzebub.

Sept. 21, 1838
The greatest expression of limitation in the human frame is in the teeth. "Thus far," says the face; "No farther," say the teeth. I mean that whilst the face of the child expresses an excellent possibility; as soon as he opens his mouth, you have an expression of defined qualities. I like him best with his mouth shut.

Tennyson is a beautiful half of a poet.

Sept. 28, 1838

Our health is our sound relation to external objects; our sympathy with external being. A man wakes in the morning sick with fever; & he perceives at once he has lost his just relation to the world. Every sound in the lower parts of the house, or in the street, falls faint & foreign on his ear. He begins to hear the frigid doom of Cold Obstruction, 'Thou shalt have no part in any thing that is done under the Sun.'

A foolish formula is "the Spirit of faction," as it is used in books old & new. Can you not get any nearer to the fact than that, you old granny? It is like the answer of children, who, when you ask them the subject of the sermon, say, it was about Religion.

Sept. 29, 1838

Blessed be the wife that in the talk tonight shared no vulgar sentiment, but said, In the gossip & excitement of the hour, be as one blind & deaf to it. Know it not. Do as if nothing had befallen. And when it was said by the friend, The end is not yet: wait till it is done; she said, "It is done in Eternity." Blessed be the wife! I, as always, venerate the oracular nature of woman. The sentiment which the man thinks he came unto gradually through the events of years, to his surprise he finds woman dwelling there in the same, as in her native home.

Oct. 5, 1838

Once I thought it a defect peculiar to me, that I was confounded by interrogatories & when put on my wits for a definition was unable to reply without injuring my own truth: but now, I believe it proper to man to be unable to answer in terms the great problems put by his fellow: it is enough if he can live his own definitions. A problem appears to me. I cannot solve it with all my wits: but leave it there; let it lie awhile: I can by patient faithful truth live at last its uttermost darkness into light.

Oct. 5–8, 1838

How soon the sunk spirits rise again, how quick the little wounds of fortune skin over & are forgotten. I am sensitive as a leaf to impressions from abroad. And under this night's beautiful heaven I have forgotten that ever I was *reviewed*. It is strange how superficial are our views of these matters, seeing we are all writers & philosophers. A man thinks it of importance what the great sheet or pamphlet of today proclaims of him to all the reading town; and if he sees graceful compliments, he relishes his dinner; & if he sees threatening paragraphs & odious nicknames, it becomes a solemn depressing fact & sables his whole thoughts until bedtime. But in truth the effect of these paragraphs is mathematically measureable by their depth of thought. How much water do they draw? If they awaken you to think—if they lift you from your feet with the great voice of eloquence—then their effect is to be wide, slow, permanent over the minds of men: but if they instruct you not, they will die like flies in an hour.

Oct. 9, 1838

Vanburenism. I passed by the shop & saw my spruce neighbor the dictator of our rural jacobins teaching his little circle of villagers their political lessons. And here thought I is one who loves what I hate; here is one wholly reversing my code. I hate persons who are nothing but persons. I hate numbers. He cares for nothing but numbers & persons. All the qualities of man, all his accomplishments, affections, enterprises except solely the ticket he votes for, are nothing to this philosopher. Numbers of majorities are all he sees in the newspaper. All of North or South, all in Georgia, Alabama, Pennsylvania, or New England that this man considers is what is the relation of Mr Clay or of Mr Van Buren to those mighty mountain chains, those vast fruitful champaigns, those expanding nations of men. What an existence is this to have no home, no heart, but to feed on the very refuse & old straw & chaff of man, the numbers & names of voters.

Oct. 12, 1838

It seems not unfit that the Scholar should deal plainly with society & tell them that he saw well enough before he spoke the consequence of his speaking, that up there in his silent study by his dim lamp he foreheard this Babel of outcries. The nature of man he knew, the insanity that comes of inaction & tradition, & knew well that when their dream & routine were disturbed, like bats & owls & nocturnal beasts they would howl & shriek & fly at the torch bearer. But he saw plainly that under this their distressing disguise of bird-form & beast-form, the divine features of man were hidden, & he felt that he would dare to be so much their friend as to do them this violence to drag them to the day & to the healthy air & water of God, that the unclean spirits that had possessed them might be exorcised & depart. The taunts & cries of hatred & anger, the very epithets you bestow on me are so familiar long ago in my reading that they sound to me ridiculously old & stale. The same thing has happened so many times over, (that is, with the appearance of every original observer) that if people were not very ignorant of literary history they would be struck with the exact coincidence. And whilst I see this that you must have been shocked & must cry out at what I have

said I see too that we cannot easily be reconciled for I have a great deal
more to say that will shock you out of all patience.

Oct. 13, 1838

Do not be a night chair, a warming pan at sick beds & rheumatic
souls. Do not let them make a convenience of you. Do not be a pastry
cook either & give parties.

Oct. 16, 1838

Here came on Sunday Morning (14th) Edward Palmer & departed
today, a gentle, faithful, sensible, well-balanced man for an enthusiast.
He has renounced since a year ago last April the use of money. When he
travels he stops at night at a house & asks if it would give them any satisfaction to lodge a traveller without money or price? If they do not give
him a hospitable answer he goes on but generally finds the country people free & willing. When he goes away he gives them his papers or
tracts. He has sometimes found it necessary to go 24 hours without food
& all night without lodging. Once he found a wagon with a good buffalo
under a shed & had a very good nap. By the seashore he finds it difficult
to travel as they are inhospitable. He presents his views with great gentleness; & is not troubled if he cannot show the way in which the destruction of money is to be brought about; he feels no responsibility to
show or know the details. It is enough for him that he is sure it must fall
& that he clears himself of the institution altogether.

Why should not I if a man comes & asks me for a book give it him? if
he ask me to write a letter for him write it? if he ask me to write a poem
or a discourse which I can fitly write, why should I not? And if my
neighbor is as skilful in making cloth, why should not all of us who have
wool, send it to him to make for the common benefit, & when we want
ten yards or twenty yards go to him & ask for so much & he like a gentleman give us exactly what we ask without hesitation? And so let every
house keep a store-room in which they place their superfluity of what
they produce, & open it with ready confidence to the wants of the
neighborhood, & without an account of debtor & credit. E. P. asks
if it would be a good plan for a family of brothers & sisters to keep
an account of Dr. & Cr. of their good turns, & expect an exact balance? And is not the human race a family? Does not kindness dis-
arm? It is plain that if perfect confidence reigned, then it would be
possible and he asks how is confidence to be promoted but by reposing
confidence?

It seems to me that I have a perfect claim on the community for the
supply of all my wants if I have worked hard all day, or if I have spent

my day well, have done what I could, though no meat, shoes, cloth, or utensils, have been made by me, yet if I have spent my time in the best manner I could, I must have benefitted the world in some manner that will appear & be felt somewhere. If we all do so, we shall all find ourselves able to ask & able to bestow with confidence. It seems too that we should be able to say to the lazy "You are lazy; you should work & cure this disease. I will not give you all you ask, but only a part. Pinch yourself today & ask me for more when you have labored more, as your brothers do, for them."

However I incline to think that among angels the money or certificate system might have some important convenience not for thy satisfaction of whom I borrow, but for my satisfaction that I have not exceeded carelessly my proper wants—have not overdrawn.

Oct. 19, 1838

It is a poor-spirited age. The great army of cowards who bellow & bully from their bed chamber windows have no confidence in truth or God. Truth will not maintain itself, they fancy, unless they bolster it up & whip & stone the assailants; and the religion of God, the being of God, they seem to think dependent on what we say of it. The feminine vehemence with which the Andrews Norton of the Daily Advertiser beseeches the dear people to whip that naughty heretic is the natural feeling in the mind whose religion is external. It cannot subsist, it suffers shipwreck if its faith is not confirmed by all surrounding persons. A believer, a mind whose faith is consciousness, is never disturbed because other persons do not yet see the fact which he sees. It is plain that there are two classes in our educated community; first; Those who confine themselves to the facts in their consciousness; & secondly; Those who superadd sundry propositions. The aim of a true teacher now would be to bring men back to a trust in God & destroy before their eyes these idolatrous propositions: to teach the doctrine of the perpetual revelation.

Oct. 20, 1838

What said my brave Asia concerning the paragraph writers, today? that "this whole practice of self justification & recrimination betwixt literary men seemed every whit as low as the quarrels of the Paddies." Then said I, But what will you say, excellent Asia, when my smart article comes out in the paper, in reply to Mr A & Dr B? "Why, then," answered she, "I shall feel the first emotion of fear & of sorrow on your account." But do you know, I asked, how many fine things I have thought of to say to these fighters? They are too good to be lost.— "Then" rejoined the queen, "there is some merit in being silent."

* * *

It is plain from all the noise that there is Atheism somewhere. The only question is now, Which is the Atheist?

Oct. 21–25, 1838

I have no joy so deep as the stings of remorse.

Edward Palmer asked me if I liked two services in a sabbath. I told him—Not very well. If the sermon was good, I wished to think of it; if it was bad, one was enough.

Oct. 26, 1838

Every word, every striking word that occurs in the pages of an original genius will provoke attack & be the subject of twenty pamphlets & a hundred paragraphs. Should he be so duped as to stop & listen? Rather, let him know that the page he writes today will contain a new subject for the pamphleteers, & that which he writes tomorrow, more. Let him not be misled to give it any more than the notice due from him, viz. just that which it had in his first page, before the controversy. The exaggeration of the notice is right for them, false for him. Every word that he quite naturally writes is as prodigious & offensive. So write on, & by & by will come a reader and an age that will justify all your context. Do not even look behind. Leave that bone for them to pick & welcome.

Let me study & work contentedly & faithfully, I do not remember my critics. I forget them—I depart from them by every step I take. If I think then of them, it is a bad sign.

Superlatives in conversation have the effect of diminutives or negatives. "An exquisite delightful angel of a child," probably means a child not engaging.

O worthy Mr Graham! poet of branbread & pumpkins: There is a limit to the revolutions of a pumpkin, project it along the ground with what force soever. It is not a winged orb like the Egyptian symbol of dominion, but an unfeathered, ridgy, yellow pumpkin, & will quickly come to a standstill.

Oct. 30, 1838

There is no terror like that of being known. The world lies in night of sin. It hears not the cock crowing: it sees not the gray streak in the East. At the first entering ray of light, society is shaken with fear & anger from side to side. Who opened that shutter? they cry, Wo to him! They belie it, they call it darkness that comes in, affirming that they were in light before. Before the man who has spoken to them the dread word, they tremble & flee. They flee to new topics, to their learning, to the solid institutions about them, to their great men, to their windows, & look out on the road & passengers, to their very furniture, & meats, & drinks, anywhere, anyhow to escape the apparition. The wild horse has heard the Whisper of the Tamer: the maniac has caught the glance of the Keeper. They try to forget the memory of the speaker, to put him down into the same obscure place he occupied in their minds before he spake to them. It is all in vain. They even flatter themselves that they have killed & buried the enemy when they have magisterially denied & denounced him. But vain, vain, all vain. It was but the first mutter of the distant storm they heard—it was the first cry of the Revolution—it was the touch, the palpitation that goes before the Earthquake. Even now Society is shaken because a thought or two have been thrown into the midst. The sects, the colleges, the church, the statesmen all have forebodings. It now works only in a handful. What does State street and Wall street and the Royal Exchange & the Bourse at Paris care for these few thoughts & these few men? Very little; truly; most truly. But the doom of State street, & Wall street, of London, & France, of the whole world, is advertised by those thoughts: is in the procession of the Soul which comes after those few thoughts.

Oct. 31, 1838

Yesterday eve. Lidian's soirée. As soon as the party is broken up, I shrink, & wince, & try to forget it. There is no refuge but in oblivion of such misdemeanors.

Nov. 3, 1838

I should not dare to tell all my story. A great deal of it I do not yet understand. How much of it is incomplete. In my strait & decorous way of living, native to my family & to my country, & more strictly proper to me, is nothing extravagant or flowing. I content myself with moderate, languid actions, & never transgress the staidness of village manners. Herein I consult the poorness of my powers. More culture would come out of great virtues & vices perhaps, but I am not up to that. Should I obey an irregular impulse, & establish every new relation that my fancy prompted with the men & women I see, I should not be followed by my faculties; they would play me false in making good their very suggestions. They delight in inceptions, but they warrant nothing else.

I told Jones Very that I had never suffered, & that I could scarce bring myself to feel a concern for the safety & life of my nearest friends that would satisfy them: that I saw clearly that if my wife, my child, my mother, should be taken from me, I should still remain whole with the same capacity of cheap enjoyment from all things. I should not grieve enough, although I love them. But could I make them feel what I feel— the boundless resources of the soul—remaining entire when particular threads of relation are snapped—I should then dismiss forever the little remains of uneasiness I have in regard to them.

Nov. 4–6, 1838

I am very sensible to beauty in the human form, in children, in boys, in girls, in old men, & old women. No trait of beauty, I think escapes me. So am I to beauty in Nature; a clump of flags in a stream, a hill, a wood, a path running into the woods, captivate me as I pass. If you please to tell me that I have no just relish for the beauty of man or of nature, it would not disturb me certainly. I do not know but it may be so, & that you have so much juster, deeper, richer knowledge, as that I, when I come to know it, shall say the same thing. But now your telling me that I do not love nature will not in the least annoy me. I should still have a perfect conviction that, love it, or love it not, every bough that waved, every cloud that floated, every water ripple is & must remain a minister to me of mysterious joy. But I hear occasionally young people dwelling with emphasis on beauties of nature which may be there or may not, but which I do not catch, & blind, at the same time, to the objects which give me most pleasure. I am quite unable to tell the difference, only I see that they are less easily satisfied than I; that they talk where I would be silent, & clamorously demand my delight where it is not spontaneous. I fancy the love of nature of such persons is rhetorical. If however, I tell them, as I am moved to do, that I think they are not susceptible of this pleasure, straightway they are offended, & set themselves at once to prove to me with many words that they always had a remarkable delight in solitude & in nature. They even affirm it with tears. Then can I not resist the belief that the sense of joy from every pebble, stake, & dry leaf is not yet opened in them.

Nov. 7, 1838

I will, I think, no longer do things unfit for me. Why should I act the part of the silly women who send out invitations to many persons, & receive each billet of acceptance as if it were a pistol shot? Why should I read lectures with care & pain & afflict myself with all the meanness of ticket mongering, when I might sit, as God in his goodness has enabled me, a free poor man with wholesome bread & warm clothes though without cakes or gewgaws, & write & speak the beautiful & formidable words of a free man? If you cannot be free, be as free as you can.

Nov. 8, 1838

Let me never fall into the vulgar mistake of dreaming that I am per-
secuted whenever I am contradicted. No man, I think, had ever a
greater well being with a less desert than I. I can very well afford to be
accounted bad or foolish by a few dozen or a few hundred persons—I
who see myself greeted by the good expectation of so many friends far
beyond any power of thought or communication of thought residing in
me. Besides, I own, I am often inclined to take part with those who say I
am bad or foolish, for I fear I am both. I believe & know there must be a
perfect compensation. I know too well my own dark spots. Not having
myself attained, not satisfied myself, far from a holy obedience—how
can I expect to satisfy others, to command their love? A few sour faces, a
few biting paragraphs—is but a cheap expiation for all these shortcom-
ings of mine.

Nov. 9, 1838

Read Lear yesterday & Hamlet today with new wonder & mused
much on the great soul whose authentic signs flashed on my sight in the
broad continuous *day light* of these poems. Especially I wonder at the
perfect reception this wit & immense knowledge of life & intellectual superiority find in us all in connexion with our utter incapacity to produce
anything like it. The superior tone of Hamlet in all the conversations
how perfectly preserved without any mediocrity much less any dulness
in the other speakers. How real the loftiness! an inborn gentleman; &
above that, an exalted intellect. What incessant growth & plenitude of
thought—pausing on itself never an instant—and each sally of wit sufficient to save the play. How true then & unerring the *earnest* of the dialogue, as when Hamlet talks with the Queen! How terrible his discourse! What less can be said of the perfect mastery as by a superior
being of the conduct of the drama as the free introduction of this capital
advice to the players; the commanding good sense which never retreats
except before the godhead which inspires certain passages—the more I
think of it the more I wonder. I will think nothing impossible to man.
No Parthenon, no sculpture, no picture, no architecture can be named
beside this. All this is perfectly visible to me & to many—the wonderful
truth & mastery of this work, of these works—yet for our lives could not
I, or any man, or all men, produce any thing comparable to one scene in
Hamlet or Lear. With all my admiration of this life-like picture, set me
to producing a match for it, & I should instantly depart into mouthing
rhetoric. Now why is this that we know so much better than we do? that
we do not yet possess ourselves, & know at the same time that we are
much more? I feel the same truth how often in my merely trivial conversation or dealing with my neighbors, that somewhat higher in each of

us overlooks this by-play, & Jove nods to Jove from behind each of us. Men descend to meet. They seem to me to resemble those Arabian sheikhs who dwell in mean houses & affect an external poverty to escape the rapacity of the pacha, & reserve all their display of wealth for their interior & guarded retirements.

I find no good lives. I would live well. I seem to be free to do so, yet I think with very little respect of my way of living; it is weak, partial, not full & not progressive. But I do not see any other that suits me better. The scholars are shiftless & the merchants are dull.

Nov. 10–11, 1838
Shakspeare fills us with wonder the first time we approach him. We go away, & work, & think, for years, & come again, he astonishes us anew. Then having drank deeply & saturated us with his genius, we lose sight of him for another period of years. By & by we return, & there he stands immeasureable as at first. We have grown wiser, but only that we should see him wiser than ever. He resembles a high mountain which the traveller sees in the morning & thinks he shall quickly near it & pass it & leave it behind. But he journeys all day till noon, till night. There still is the dim mountain close by him, having scarce altered its bearings since the morning light.

My brave Henry Thoreau walked with me to Walden this P.M. and complained of the proprietors who compelled him to whom as much as to any the whole world belonged, to walk in a strip of road & crowded him out of all the rest of God's earth. He must not get over the fence: but to the building of that fence he was no party. Suppose, he said, some great proprietor, before he was born, had bought up the whole globe. So had he been hustled out of nature. Not having been privy to any of these arrangements he does not feel called on to consent to them & so cuts fishpoles in the woods without asking who has a better title to the wood than he. I defended of course the good Institution as a scheme not good but the best that could be hit on for making the woods & waters & fields available to Wit & Worth, & for restraining the bold bad man. At all events, I begged him, having this maggot of Freedom & Humanity in his brain, to write it out into good poetry & so clear himself of it. He replied, that he feared that that was not the best way; that in doing justice to the thought, the man did not always do justice to himself: the poem ought to sing itself: if the man took too much pains with the expression he was not any longer the Idea himself. I acceded & confessed that this was the tragedy of Art that the Artist was at the expense of the Man; & hence, in the first age, as they tell, the Sons of God printed no epics,

Henry David Thoreau (1817–1862): "I delight much in my young
friend, who seems to have as free & erect a mind as any I
have ever met."

carved no stone, painted no picture, built no railroad; for the sculpture,
the poetry, the music, & architecture, were in the Man. And truly Bolts
& Bars do not seem to me the most exalted or exalting of our institutions. And what other spirit reigns in our intellectual works? We have
literary property. The very recording of a thought betrays a distrust
that there is any more or much more as good for us. If we felt that the
Universe was ours, that we dwelled in eternity & advance into all wisdom we should be less covetous of these sparks & cinders. Why should

we covetously build a St Peter's, if we had the seeing Eye which beheld all the radiance of beauty & majesty in the matted grass & the overarching boughs? Why should a man spend years upon the carving an Apollo who looked Apollos into the landscape with every glance he threw?

Nov. 12, 1838

I could forgive your want of faith if you had any knowledge of the uttermost that man could be & do, if arithmetic could predict the last possibilities of instinct. But men are not made like boxes, a hundred, a thousand to order, & all exactly alike, of known dimension, & all their properties known; but no they come into nature through a nine months' astonishment & of a character each one incalculable & of extravagant possibilities; out of darkness & out of the Awful Cause they come to be caught up into this vision of a seeing, partaking, acting & suffering life, not foreknown, not fore-estimable but slowly or speedily they unfold new, unknown, mighty traits. Not boxes but these machines are alive, agitated, fearing, sorrowing.

Nov. 13, 1838

'Fire', Aunt Mary said, 'was a great deal of company;' & so is there company, I find, in Water. It animates the solitude. Then somewhat nearer to human society is in the hermit birds that harbor in the wood. I can do well for weeks with no other society than the partridge & the jay, my daily company.

Nov. 13–14, 1838

Gladly I would solve if I could this problem of a Vocabulary which like some treacherous wide shoal waylays the tall bark, the goodly soul & there it founders & suffers shipwreck. In common life every man is led by the nose by a verb. Even the great & gifted do not escape but with great talents & partial inspiration have local cramps, withered arms, & mortification. Proportion is not. Every man is lobsided and even holding in his hands some authentic token & gift of God holds it awry. It must be from everlasting & from the infinitude of God, that when God speaketh he should then & there exist; should fill the world with his voice; should scatter forth light, nature, time, souls, from the centre of the Present thought; & new date & new create the Whole. Whenever therefore a soul is true, is simple, & expelling all wilfulness consents to God, & receives the Soul of the Soul into itself, then old things pass away, then means, teachers, texts, temples, fall. . . . If a man claims to know & speak of God & carries you backward to the phraseology of some old mouldered nation in another country in another world, believe him not: he does not speak for God: God does not speak to him. If he interposes betwixt you & your Maker, himself or some other person or persons, believe him not: God has better things for you. This should be plain enough;—yet see how great & vivacious souls, with grand truths in their keeping, do fail in faith to see God face to face, to see Time pass away & be no more, & to utter directly from him that which he would give them to say, but rather imprison it in the old Hebrew language, mimick David, Jeremiah, & Paul & disbelieve that God who maketh the stars & stones sing, can speak our English tongue in Massachusetts & give as deep & glad a melody to it as shall make the whole world & all coming ages ring with the sound.—Be assured we shall not always set so great a price on a few texts, on a few lives. When we were young, we repeated by rote the words of our grandames, of our tutors—&, as we grew older, of the men of talents & character we met, & painfully recollected & recited the exact words they spake. But as we advanced, & came into the selfsame point of view which they had, when they uttered these sayings, we understand them perfectly, & are willing at once to let the words go; for, at any time, we can use words as good, as occasion comes. So will it continue to be, if we proceed. If we live truly, we shall see truly. It is as easy for the strong man to be strong, as it is for the weak to be weak. With new perception, we shall disburthen our Memory of all its trumpery when we can create. When a man lives with God, his voice shall be as sweet as is now the murmur of the brook & the rustle of the corn.

This palsy of tradition goes so far that when a Soul in which the intellectual activity is a balance for the Veneration (whose excess seems to generate this love of the old word) renounces the superstition out of love for the primary teaching in his heart, the doctors of the church are not glad as they ought to be that a new & original confirmation comes to the truth, but they curse & swear because he scorns their idolatry of the nouns & verbs, the vellum & ink in which the same teaching was anciently conveyed. And now at last the highest truth on this subject remains unsaid, probably cannot be said; for, all that we say is the far off description merely, of the awful truth which in moments of life flashes on us, & bids us go months & years feeding on the remembrance of that light & essaying to tell what we saw. That thought, by what I can nearest approach to say it, is this. When good is near you, when you have life in yourself it is not by any known or appointed way; you shall not discern the footprints of any other; you shall not see the face of man; you shall not hear any name; the way, the thought, the good, shall be wholly strange & new. It shall exclude all other being. There shall be no fear in it. To climb that most holy mountain, you must tread on Fear. You take the way *from* man not *to* man. Quit the shore & go out to sea. Christian, Jew, Pagan, leave all behind you & rush.

Nov. 14, 1838

What is the hardest task in the world? To think. I would put myself where I have so often been in the attitude of meeting as it were face to face an abstract truth—& I cannot; I blench; I withdraw on this side, on that. I seem to know what he meant who said, "No man can see God face to face & live."

I think sometimes that my lack of musical ear, is made good to me through my eyes. That which others hear, I *see*. All the soothing, plaintive, brisk, or romantic moods which corresponding melodies waken in them, I find in the carpet of the wood, in the margin of the pond, in the shade of the hemlock grove, or in the infinite variety & rapid dance of the treetops as I hurry along.

Nov. 16, 1838

You are wrong in demanding of the Bible more than can be in a book. Its only defect is that it is a book & not alive.

Seek ye first the kingdom of God, & all these things shall be added unto you. What!—Art? Hamlets? Ballads?

Nov. 18, 1838

The manners of young men who are still engaged heart & soul in uttering their Protest against society as they find it, are perchance disagreeable; their whole being seems rough & unmelodious; but have a little patience. And do not exaggerate the offence of that particular objection which with such undue and absurd dogmatism they make every day from morn till dewy eve. The institutions of society come across each ingenuous & original soul in some different point. One feels the jar in Marriage; one in Property; one in Money; one in Church; one in social Conventions; one in Slavery; one in War; each feels it in some one & a different point according to his own circumstance & history & for a long time does not see that it is a central falsehood which he is contending against, & that his protest against a particular superficial falsehood will surely ripen with time & insight into a deeper & Universal grudge.

Nov. 25, 1838

I remember that when I preached my first sermon in Concord, "on showing piety at home," Dr Ripley remarked on the frequent occurrence of the word *Virtue* in it, and said his people would not understand it, for the largest part of them when Virtue was spoken of, understood *Chastity*. I do not imagine however that the people thought any such thing. It was an old-school preacher's contractedness.

A Self on Trial

1839-1841

EMERSON'S BREAK WITH the ministry was now complete and he would no longer (if he ever did) relish being called "Reverend." He had reverence only for the uncompromised and uncompromising self. In the years leading up to the publication of his first book of *Essays* (March 1841), Emerson would give much thought to developing and testing his literary voice and vocation. Whether in the lecture hall or on paper, he had few viable models—in America particularly—for his peculiar calling. He was engaged, in fact, in creating for himself the role of man of letters—that is, of a nonacademic scholar and thinker capable of representing the genius of his day "so well as to write the laws of Criticism, of Ethics, of History." He was concerned not to be pegged simply as a poet or philosophical belletrist but rather to be welcomed as a perpetual innovator in lecture and essay. "Why should we write dramas, & epics, & sonnets, & novels in two volumes?" he asked in 1839. "Why not write as variously as we dress & think?" He was interested in shaping "a new literature, which leaves aside all tradition, time, place, circumstance" and speaks directly to the human perplexities and needs of its audience. He thought of himself as presenting a sort of personal inventory of the world. "What shall be the substance of my shrift? Adam in the garden, I am to new name all the beasts in the field & all the gods in the Sky."

On a less exalted level, though, Emerson was well aware that other authors before him had devoted themselves to the fine art of essay writing. Two obvious examples, extremely important in his development, were Montaigne and Bacon. Of the latter, an early favorite, Emerson noted in a lecture devoted to Bacon that his work had the advantage "that it allowed of perpetual amendment and addition." It was precisely this feature, the provision for "gradual growth" rather than fixity in form and content, that appealed to Emerson. As he had suggested in "The American Scholar," he was less interested in exhibiting his thoughts than he was in presenting *himself* in the act of thinking. Here, undoubtedly, was one reason for his special fondness for Montaigne, whose essays were unabashedly personal, eccentric, and self-indulgent. "Montaigne," Emerson noted affectionately in 1837, "was an unbuttoned sloven"—meaning, it seems, that he was not ashamed to reveal himself in his writing. Emerson too was passionately devoted to the notion of personal honesty in writing, though he knew well enough (and long before F. Scott Fitzgerald's Nick Carraway) that confessional utterances are frequently compromised by plagiarism and the impulse to self-dramatization.

As early as 1835 Emerson was calling upon himself to "mend Montaigne" and produce his own essays. He hoped in some fashion to open his entrails to public inspection, to enact his thought without concealment, to lay himself out "utterly—large, enormous, prodigal," on whatever his subject was. This was his ideal and his dream, but he found, as his book of essays actually took shape under his hand, that his genius seemed to desert him in the mechanical work of writing and he was left with "a cold exhibition of dead thoughts." As he sent his book to the printer on New Year's Day, 1841, he still found the work imperfect and hoped that it might be "filled with the character not with the skill of the writer."

Indeed, in these years we see Emerson worrying a good deal over his constitutional tendency to preserve and protect himself despite his desire to be expansive and expressive. New demands were being made that he found it difficult to meet. Margaret Fuller, among others, was asking for a more direct and human expression of his affection. "Your courage, your enterprize, your budding affection, your opening thought, your prayer, I can love," he exclaims, "but what else?" They were both perplexed by their feelings and by the relationship of love to the physical needs of the body. Emerson, in particular, feared that if he dissipated his "vital force" in a "flowing & friendly life" he would "die of consumption in three months." It appears that even as a husband Emerson generally led what he delicately calls a "bachelor life." At all events, he and Margaret seem to have agreed that the best of Emerson was to be found in his work, and they accordingly turned away from the "porcupine impossibility of contact" and invested their energies in a joint literary venture—*The Dial*—the first number of which appeared in July 1840.

In October, Emerson's theories of self-reliance and self-culture were once again put to the test when George and Sophia Ripley, Margaret Fuller, and Alcott tried to persuade him to join them in the utopian community that came to be known as Brook Farm. Though Emerson was deeply sympathetic—and indeed was already projecting ways of reforming his own household—he saw that such an experiment could only compromise his essentially solitary nature. "A man is stronger than a city," is the justification or rationalization he offers in his journal. "His solitude is more prevalent & beneficent than the concert of crowds." By way of a private gesture toward socialism, however, he invited the Alcotts to live in his home and also tried to get his domestic help to join the family at meals, but nothing came of either plan. More happily, the Emersons persuaded Henry Thoreau to become a member of the household, which he did in the spring of 1841. Though Thoreau thought the situation one of "dangerous prosperity" for such an ascetic bachelor of the woods as he, he remained two years, during which he ran the greater risk, it appears, of falling in love alternately with the Emerson children's governess and Lidian herself. It well may be that Lidian needed Henry's devotion, if a cryptic notation in Emerson's journal for May 1841 has personal reference: "I gave you enough to eat & I never beat you: what more can the woman ask? said the Good Husband." Transcendental marriage may have been a trial for other selves besides Emerson's.

But, as usual, he was his own sharpest critic. "I am awkward, sour, saturnine, lumpish, pedantic, & thoroughly disagreeable & oppressive to the people around me," he claimed toward the end of 1841. "Yet if I am born to write a few good sentences or verses, these shall endure & my disgraces utterly perish out of memory." Emerson was undoubtedly exaggerating his disgraces, but his great strength as a writer would in fact rest on his willingness to put himself unremittingly to the test. He had already confessed in his essay "Circles" that he sometimes felt like God in nature and sometimes like a "weed by the wall." Perhaps this was why he noted in December 1841 that Transcendentalism could be represented as a "winged serpent."

Jan. 1, 1839
Adjourned the promised lecture on Genius until Wednesday week on account of my unaccountable vigils now for four or five nights, which destroy all power of concentration by day.

Jan. 12? 1839
In my dealing with my child, my Latin & Greek, my accomplishments and my money stead me nothing. They are all lost on him; but as much Soul as I have, avails. If I am merely wilful, he gives me a Rowland for an Oliver; sets his will against mine; tit for tat. But if I renounce my will & act for the soul, setting that up as umpire between us two, his young eyes look with soul also; he reveres & loves with me.

Feb. 7, 1839
The drunkard retires on a keg & locks himself up for a three days' debauch. When I am sick, I please myself not less in retiring on a salamander stove, heaping the chamber with fuel, & inundating lungs, liver, head, & feet, with floods of caloric, heats on heats. It is dainty to be sick if you have leisure & convenience for it. How bland the aspect of all things! One sees the colors of the carpet & the paper hangings. All the housemates have a softer fainter look to the debilitated retina.

Feb. 15, 1839
In the morning a man walks with his whole body; in the evening, only with his legs; the trunk is carried along almost motionless.

"A lovely child! I promise you he will be a great scholar." A dear little child with soft hair. Tomorrow he will defy you.

Feb. 22–24, 1839
The pathetic lies usually not in miseries but petty losses & disappointments as when the poor family have spent their little utmost upon a wedding or a christening festival, & their feast is dishonored by some insult or petty disaster—the falling of the salver, or the spoiling of a

carpet. When I was a boy, I was sent by my mother with a dollar bill to buy me a pair of shoes at Mr Baxter's shop, & I lost the bill; & remember being sent out by my disappointed mother to look among the fallen leaves under the poplar trees opposite the house for the lost bank note.

When I was in College, Robert Barnwell, the first scholar in my class put his hand on the back of my head to feel for the bump of ambition, & pronounced that it was very very small.

"Where's the cover that lives in this box?" asks little Waldo. When he saw the dead bird, he said "he was gone By-By"; then he said, "he was broke." When Dr Jackson smoked a cigar, Waldo said "See the cobwebs go up out of the gentleman's mouth."

Feb. 25, 1839

Yesterday morning, 24 Feb. at 8 o'clock a daughter was born to me, a soft, quiet, swarthy little creature, apparently perfect & healthy. My second child. Blessings on thy head, little winter bud! & comest thou to try thy luck in this world & know if the things of God are things for thee? Well assured & very soft & still, the little maiden expresses great contentment with all she finds, & her delicate but fixed determination to stay where she is, & grow. So be it, my fair child! Lidian, who magnanimously makes my gods her gods, calls the babe Ellen. I can hardly ask more for thee, my babe, than that name implies. Be that vision & remain with us, & after us.

March 8, 1839

We all wish to be of importance in one way or another. The child coughs with might & main, since it has no other claims on the company.

No Age in Talk. I make no allowance for youth in talking with my friends. If a youth or maiden converses with me I forget they are not as old as I am.

March 22, 1839

Each work of art excludes the world, concentrates attention on itself. For the time it is the only thing worth doing—to do just that; be it a sonnet, a statue, a landscape, an outline head of Caesar, or an oration. Presently we return to the sight of another that globes itself into a Whole as did the first, for example, a beautiful garden; and nothing seems worth doing in life but laying out a garden.

March 22–25, 1839

A man must consider what a rich realm he abdicates when he becomes a conformist. I hear my preacher announce his text & topic as for instance the expediency of the institution of Fast with a coldness that approaches contempt. For do I not know beforehand that not possibly can he say a new or spontaneous word? Do I not know that with all this affectation of *examining the grounds* of the institution he will do no such thing? Do I not know that he is pledged to himself beforehand not to look at but one side; the permitted side; not as a man, but as a parish minister in Concord? What folly then to say *let us examine,* & purse the mouth with the wrinkles of a judge. He is a retained attorney; and this air of *judgeship* is mere affectation. Even so is it with newspapers; & so with most politicians.

April 11–12, 1839

I told S[arah] M[argaret] F[uller] that I was a cross of Plato & Aristotle.

April 14, 1839

The philosopher has a good deal of knowledge which cannot be abstractly imparted, which needs the combinations & complexity of social action to paint it out, as many emotions in the soul of Handel and Mozart are thousand voiced & utterly incapable of being told in a simple air on a lute, but must ride on the mingling whirlwinds & rivers & storms of sound of the great orchestra of organ, pipe, sackbut, dulcimer, & all kinds of music. As the musician avails himself of the concert, so the philosopher avails himself of the drama, the epic, the novel, & becomes a poet; for these complex forms allow of the utterance of his knowledge of life by *indirections* as well in the didactic way, & can therefore express the fluxional quantities & values which the thesis or dissertation could never give.

April 15–16, 1839

The simple knot of Now & Then will give an immeasureable value to any sort of catalogue or journal kept with common sense for a year or two. See in the Merchant's compting room for his peddling of cotton & indigo, the value that comes to be attached to any Blotting book or Leger; and if your aims & deeds are superior, how can any record of yours (suppose, of the books you wish to read, of the pictures you would see, of the facts you would scrutinize)—any record that you are genuinely moved to begin & continue—not have a value proportionately superior? It converts the heights you have reached into table land. That book or literary fact which had the whole emphasis of attention a month ago stands here along with one which was as important in preceding months, and with that of yesterday; &, next month, there will be another. Here they will occupy but four lines & I cannot read these together without juster views of each than when I read them singly.

April 17, 1839
Am I a hypocrite who am disgusted by vanity everywhere, & preach self trust every day?

April 17–20, 1839
Philosophy teaches how to be personal without being unparliamentary.

May 23, 1839
The poor madman—whipped through the world by his thoughts.

May 26, 1839
At Waltham I repeated with somewhat more emphasis perhaps than was needed the impression the Allston gallery makes on me; that whilst Homer, Phidias, Dante, Shakspeare, Michel Angelo, Milton, Raphael, make a positive impression, Allston does not. It is an eyeless face. It is an altar without fire. Beautiful drawing there is—a rare merit; taste there is; the blandest, selectest forms & circumstance; a highly cultivated mind; a beneficent genial atmosphere; but no man. And this it does not seem unreasonable or ungrateful to demand, that the artist should pierce the soul; should command; should not sit aloof & circumambient merely, but should come & take me by the hand & lead me somewhither.... Allston's pictures are Elysian; fair, serene, but unreal.

I extend the remark to all the American geniuses; Irving, Bryant, Greenough, Everett, Channing, even Webster in his recorded Eloquence, all lack nerve & dagger.

May 27, 1839
A great genius must come & preach self reliance. Our people are timid, desponding, recreant whimperers. If they fail in their first enterprises they lose all heart. If the young merchant fails, men say he is RUINED. If the finest genius studies at the Cambridge Divinity College, and is not ordained within a year afterwards in Boston, or New York, it seems to his friend & himself that he is justified in being disheartened & in complaining for the rest of his life.

A sturdy New Hampshire man or Vermonter who in turn tries *all* the professions, who *teams it, farms it, peddles,* keeps a school, preaches, edits a newspaper, goes to Congress, & so forth, in successive years, and always like a cat falls on his feet, is worth a hundred of these Boston dolls. My brave Henry here who is content to live now, & feels no shame in not studying any profession, for he does not postpone his life but lives already—pours contempt on these crybabies of routine & Boston. He has not one chance but a hundred chances. Now let a stern preacher arise who shall reveal the resources of Man, & tell men they are not leaning willows, but can & must detach themselves, that a man, a woman, is a sovereign eternity, born to shed healing to the nations; that he should be ashamed of our compassion; & that the moment he acts from himself, tossing the laws, the books, the idolatries, the customs, out of the window, we pity him, we pity her no more, but thank & revere them; that with the exercise of self trust new powers shall appear.

May 28, 1839

There is no history: There is only Biography. The attempt to perpetuate, to fix a thought or principle, fails continually. You can only live for yourself: Your action is good only whilst it is alive—whilst it is in you. The awkward imitation of it by your child or your disciple, is not a repetition of it, is not the same thing but another thing. The new individual must work out the whole problem of science, letters, & theology for himself, can owe his fathers nothing. There is no history; only biography.

May 30, 1839

'Tis pity we should leave with the children all the romance, all that is daintiest in life, and reserve for ourselves as we grow old, only the prose. Goethe fell in love in his old age, and I would never lose the capacity of delicate & noble sentiments.

May–June 1839

Language is made up of the Spoils of all actions, trades, arts, games, of men. Every word is a metaphor borrowed from some natural or mechanical, agricultural or nautical process. The poorest speaker is like the Indian dressed in a robe furnished by a half a dozen animals. It is like our marble footslab made up of countless shells & exuviae of a foregone World.

June 3, 1839

Our young scholars read newspapers, smoke, & sleep in the afternoons. Goethe, Gibbon, Bentley, might provoke them to industry. Undoubtedly the reason why our men are not learned ... is because the Genius of the age does not tend that way. This old learning of Bentley &

Gibbon, was the natural fruit of the Traditional age in philosophy & religion. Ours is the Revolutionary Age, when man is coming back to Consciousness, & from afar this mind begets a disrelish for lexicons. Alcott therefore, and Very, who have this spirit in great exaltation, abhor books. But at least it behoves those who reject the new ideas, the sticklers of tradition to be learned. But they are not.

June 12, 1839

I know no means of calming the fret & perturbation into which too much sitting, too much talking brings me so perfect as labor. I have no animal spirits; therefore when surprised by company & kept in a chair for many hours, my heart sinks, my brow is clouded, & I think I will run for Acton Woods, & live with the squirrels henceforward.

But my garden is nearer, and my good hoe as it bites the ground revenges my wrongs & I have less lust to bite my enemies. I confess I work at first with a little venom, lay to a little unnecessary strength. But by smoothing the rough hillocks, I smooth my temper; by extracting the long roots of the piper grass, I draw out my own splinters; & in a short time I can hear the Bobalink's song & see the blessed deluge of light & colour that rolls around me.

June 22, 1839

It is one of the signs of our time, the ill health of all people. All the young people are near sighted in the towns.

June 28-29, 1839

Belief. The man I saw believed that his suspenders would hold up his pantaloons & that his straps would hold them down. His creed went little farther.

June 30, 1839

It is proposed to form a very large Society to devise & execute means for propping in some secure & permanent manner this planet. It has long filled the minds of the benevolent & anxious part of the community with lively emotion, the consideration of the exposed state of the globe; the danger of its falling & being swamped in absolute space; the danger of its being drawn too near the sun & roasting the race of mankind & the daily danger of its being overturned & if a stage coach overset costs valuable lives what will not ensue on the upset of this Omnibus? It has been thought that by a strenuous & very extensive concert aided by a committee of master builders & blacksmiths, a system of booms & chains might be set round the exterior surface & that it might be underpinned in such a manner as to enable the aged & the women & children to sleep & eat with greater security henceforward. It is true that there is not a perfect unanimity on this subject at present & it is much to be regretted. A pert & flippant orator remarked to the meeting last Sunday, that the World could stand without linch pins & that even if you should cut all the ropes & knock away the whole underpinning, it would swing & poise perfectly for the poise was in the globe itself. But this is Transcendentalism.

July 5-6, 1839
     Why should we write dramas, & epics, & sonnets, & novels in two volumes? Why not write as variously as we dress & think? A lecture is a new literature, which leaves aside all tradition, time, place, circumstance, & addresses an assembly as mere human beings—no more—It has never yet been done well. It is an organ of sublime power, a panharmonicon for variety of note. But only then is the orator successful when he is himself agitated & is as much a hearer as any of the assembly. In that office you may & shall (please God!) yet see the electricity part from the cloud & shine from one part of heaven to the other.

July 7, 1839
     Reform. The objection to conforming to usages that have become dead to you, is, that it scatters your force: loses your time, blears the impression of your character. If you maintain the church, join the Bible society, vote with the Whig or Government party, spread your table like other housekeepers, under all these screens I have difficulty to detect the precise man you are. Do your thing & I shall know you.

July 7-8, 1839
     Extempore speaking can be good, & written discourses can be good. A tent is a very good thing, but so is a cathedral.

     Ah could I hope to enact my thought! Do not covet nor hide nor sneak in relation to MSS. or thoughts or Literature.

     We want all the elements of our being. High culture cannot spare one. We want the Exact & the Vast; we want our Dreams and our Mathematics; we want our Folly & Guilt.
     Yet a majestic soul never unfolds all these in speech. They lie at the base of what is said & colour the word but are reserved.

July 9? 1839
     I like my boy with his endless sweet soliloquies & iterations and his utter inability to conceive why I should not leave all my nonsense, busi-

ness, & writing & come to tie up his toy horse, as if there was or could be any end to nature beyond his horse. And he is wiser than we when he threatens his whole threat 'I will not love you.'

Nature delights in punishing stupid people. The very strawberry vines are more than a match for them with all their appetites, & all their fumbling fingers. The little defenceless vine coolly hides the best berry now under this leaf, then under that, & keeps the treasure for yonder darling boy with the bright eyes when Booby is gone.

July 14, 1839
I desire that my housekeeping should be clean & sweet & that it should not shame or annoy me. I desire that it should appear in all its arrangements that human Culture is the end to which that house is built & garnished. I wish my house to be a college open as the air to all to whom I spiritually belong, & who belong to me. But it is not open to others or for other purposes. I do not wish that it should be a confectioner's shop wherein eaters & drinkers may get strawberries & champagne. I do not wish that it should be a playground or house of entertainment for boys. They do well to play; I like that they should, but not with me, or in these precincts. Nor do I wish that it should be a hospital for the sick excepting only *my* sick. Nor do I wish that it should be a tavern or house of convenience to harbour any one—neither unwise, neither wise—beyond the limit of their stay for the express end of conversation & study. All these other wants are, I know, natural & necessary, but they must be satisfied elsewhere: as potatoes, fuel, & broadcloth must be had, yet you would not go to a church to buy them. I do not wish to hear such words or sounds at my table as to overpersuade me that there is a pig sitting there in the disguise of a fine lady or a fine gentleman.

July 20, 1839
Night in this enchanting Season is not night but a miscellany of lights. The journeying twilight, the half-moon, the kindling Venus, the beaming Jove—Saturn & Mars something less bright, and, fainter still, "the common people of the sky," as Crashaw said; then below, the meadows & thickets flashing with the fireflies, and all around the farms the steadier lamps of men compose the softest warmest illumination.

Aug. 27, 1839
Yesterday ascended Red Hill & saw our Lake & Squam Lake, Ossipee, Conway, Gunstock, & one dim summit which stood to us for the White Hills. Mrs Cook lives in this Red mountain half a mile from the

top & a mile from the bottom. We asked her what brought her here 51 years ago. She said "Poverty brought & poverty kept her here." For our parts, we thought that a poor man could not afford to live here, that it was to increase poverty tenfold to set one's cabin at this helpless height. Her son makes 1000 lb. of maple sugar in a year. They use the coffee bean for coffee, and the Fever bush for tea.

The Hedysarum which they call wild-bean was the principal food of the cows when they first came here until grass grew.

There is no man in mountain or valley but only abortions of such, and a degree of absurdity seems to attach to nature.

On Sunday we heard sulphurous Calvinism. The preacher railed at Lord Byron. I thought Lord Byron's vice better than Rev. Mr M's Virtue. He told us of a man he had seen on Lake Michigan who saw his ship in danger & said, "If the Almighty would only stand neuter six months, it was all he asked." In his horror at this sentiment the preacher did not perceive that it was the legitimate inference from his own distorting creed; that it was the *reductio ad absurdum* of Calvinism.

Sept. 12, 1839

How to spend a day nobly, is the problem to be solved, beside which all the great reforms which are preached seem to me trivial. If any day has not the privilege of a great action, then at least raise it by a wise passion. If thou canst not do, at least abstain. Now the memory of the few past idle days so works in me that I hardly dare front a new day when I leave my bed. When shall I come to the end of these shameful days, & *organize* honour in every day?

Sept. 14, 1839

An education in things is not: we all are involved in the condemnation of words, an Age of words. We are shut up in schools & college recitation rooms for ten or fifteen years & come out at last with a bellyfull of words & do not know a thing. We cannot use our hands or our legs or our eyes or our arms. We do not know an edible root in the woods. We cannot tell our course by the stars nor the hour of the day by the sun. It is well if we can swim & skate. We are afraid of a horse, of a cow, of a dog, of a cat, of a spider. Far better was the Roman rule to teach a boy nothing that he could not learn standing. Now here are my wise young neighbors who instead of getting like the wordmen into a railroad-car where they have not even the activity of holding the reins, have got into a boat which they have built with their own hands, with sails which they have contrived to serve as a tent by night, & gone up the river Merrimack to live by their wits on the fish of the stream & the berries of the wood. My worthy neighbor Dr Bartlett expressed a true parental instinct when he desired to send his boy with them to learn something. The farm, the farm is the right school. The reason of my deep respect for the farmer is that he is a realist & not a dictionary. The farm is a piece of the world, the School house is not. The farm by training the physical rectifies & invigorates the metaphysical & moral nature.

Sept. 14–17, 1839

I hate preaching whether in pulpits or Teachers' meetings. Preaching is a pledge & I wish to say what I think & feel today with the proviso that tomorrow perhaps I shall contradict it all. Freedom boundless I wish. I will not pledge myself not to drink wine, not to drink ink, not to lie, & not to commit adultery lest I hanker tomorrow to do these very things by reason of my having tied my hands. Besides Man is so poor he cannot afford to part with any advantages or bereave himself of the functions even of one hair. I do not like to speak to the Peace Society if so I am to restrain me in so extreme a privilege as the use of the sword & bullet. For the peace of the man who has forsworn the use of the bullet seems to me not quite peace, but a canting impotence: but with knife & pistol in my hands, if I, from greater bravery & honor, cast them aside, then I know the glory of peace.

The mob are always interesting. We hate editors, preachers, & all manner of scholars, and fashionists. A blacksmith, a truckman, a farmer we follow into the barroom & watch with eagerness what they shall say, for such as they, do not speak because they are expected to, but because they have somewhat to say.

It seems as if the present age of words should naturally be followed by an age of silence when men shall speak only through facts & so regain their health. We die of words. We are hanged, drawn, & quartered by dictionaries. We walk in the vale of shadows. It is an age of hobgoblins. Public Opinion is a hobgoblin, Christianity a hobgoblin, the God of popular worship a hobgoblin. When shall we attain to be real & be born into the new heaven & earth of nature & truth?

It is a disgrace to remember as we do. All our life is the pitifullest remembering. Memory is an indigestion, a flatulency of mind which eats over again its dinner all night with feverish disgust. Each man does but six or seven new things in all his lifetime; the smith, the joiner, the farmer repeat every day the same manipulations. The singer repeats his old song, the preacher his old sermon, the talker his old fact.

It is not good sense to repeat an old story to the same child. Yet the pulpit thinks there is some piquancy or rag of meat in his paragraph about the traitor Judas or the good Samaritan.

Sept. 18–23, 1839

All conversation among literary men is muddy. I derive from literary meetings no satisfaction. Yet it is pity that meetings for conversation should end as quickly as they ordinarily do. They end as soon as the blood is up, & we are about to say daring & extraordinary things. They adjourn for a fortnight & when we are reassembled we have forgot all we had to say.

It is no easy matter to write a dialogue. Cooper, Sterling, Dickens, & Hawthorne cannot.

Sept. 24? 1839

I have read Oliver Twist in obedience to the opinions of so many intelligent people as have praised it. The author has an acute eye for costume; he sees the expression of dress, of form, of gait, of personal deformities; of furniture, of the outside & inside of houses; but his eye rests always on surfaces; he has no insight into Character. For want of key to the moral powers the Author is fain to strain all his stage trick of grimace, of bodily terror, of murder, & the most approved performances of Remorse. It all avails nothing. There is nothing memorable in the book except the *flash*, which is got at a police office, & the dancing of the madman which strikes a momentary terror. Like Cooper & Hawthorne he has no dramatic talent. The moment he attempts dialogue the improbability of life hardens to wood & stone. And the book begins & ends without a poetic ray & so perishes in the reading.

Sept. 28, 1839

The life of Raffaello is the Catalogue of his works. The life of a great artist always is thus inward, a life of no events. Shakspeare has no biography worth seeking. Dante by how much he had a biography is by so much the worse artist.

I love the Sunday Morning. I hail it from afar. I wake with gladness & a holiday feeling always on that day.

Mr Dewey said to me that W. C. promised to be a great man twenty years hence. Mr Felt, then one of the parish Committee in the First Church in N.Y., observed "Yes but we want a minister ready grown. He must have his growing elsewhere." So it is with us all. Only fathers

& mothers may contentedly be present at the growing. I hate to hear a singer who is learning, let her voice be never so sweet. I wish not to be asked in every note whether I will allow it; I wish every note to command me with sweet yet perfect empire.

Also I hate Early Poems.

A lovely Saturday afternoon & I walked toward Fairhaven with H. T. & admired autumnal red & yellow and as of old Nature's wonderful boxes in which she packs so workmanlike her pine seed & oak seed & not less the keys of frost & rain & wind with which she unlocks them by & by.

Sept. 29–30? 1839
A walk in the woods is only an exalted dream.

When I was thirteen years old, my uncle Samuel Ripley one day asked me, "How is it, Ralph, that all the boys dislike you & quarrel with you, whilst the grown people are fond of you?"—Now am I thirty six and the fact is reversed—the old people suspect & dislike me, & the young love me.

The whole world is in conspiracy against itself in religious matters. The best experience is beggarly when compared with the immense possibilities of man. Divine as the life of Jesus is, what an outrage to represent it as tantamount to the Universe! To seize one accidental good man that happened to exist somewhere at some time and say to the new born soul, Behold thy pattern; aim no longer to possess entire Nature, to fill the horizon, to fill the infinite amplitude of being with great life, to be in sympathy & relation with all creatures, to lose all privateness by sharing all natural action, shining with the Day, undulating with the Sea, growing with the tree, instinctive with the animals, entranced in beatific vision with the human reason. Renounce a life so broad & deep as a pretty dream & go in the harness of that past individual, assume his manners, speak his speech—this is the madness of christendom. The little bigots of each town & neighborhood seek thus to subdue the manly & freeborn. But for this poor dependent fraction of a life they bereave me of that magnificent destiny which the young soul had embraced with auguries of immeasurable hope. I turn my back on these insane usurpers. The soul always believes in itself.

Oct. 11, 1839
At Waltham, last Sunday, on the hill near the old meeting-house, I heard music so soft that I fancied it was a pianoforte in some neighbor-

ing Farmhouse, but on listening more attentively I found it was the church bells in Boston, nine miles distant, which were playing for me this soft tune.

Oct. 16–17, 1839

Said Lidian, How we covet insensibility! My boy whines & wails if I wake him. We are Buddhists all.

Oct. 18, 1839

In these golden days it behoves me once more to make my annual inventory of the world. For the five last years I have read each winter a new course of lectures in Boston, and each was my creed & confession of faith. Each told all I thought of the past, the present, & the future. Once more I must renew my work and I think only once in the same form though I see that he who thinks he does something for the last time ought not to do it at all. Yet my objection is not to the thing but to the form; & the concatenation of errors called *society* to which I still consent, until my plumes be grown, makes even a duty of this concession also. So I submit to sell tickets again. But the form is neither here nor there. What shall be the substance of my shrift? Adam in the garden, I am to new name all the beasts in the field & all the gods in the Sky. I am to invite men drenched in time to recover themselves & come out of time, & taste their native immortal air. I am to fire with what skill I can the artillery of sympathy & emotion. I am to indicate constantly, though all unworthy, the Ideal and Holy Life, the life within life—the Forgotten Good, the Unknown Cause in which we sprawl & sin. I am to try the magic of sincerity, that luxury permitted only to kings & poets. I am to celebrate the spiritual powers in their infinite contrast to the mechanical powers & the mechanical philosophy of this time. I am to console the brave sufferers under evils whose end they cannot see by appeals to the great optimism self-affirmed in all bosoms.

Oct. 21–22, 1839

Trust thy time also. What a fatal prodigality to contemn *our* Age. One would say we could well afford to slight all other Ages if only we value this one. . . .

The very time sees for us, thinks for us; it is a microscope such as philosophy never had. Insight is for us which was never for any. And doubt not the moment & the opportunity are divine. He who shall represent the genius of this day, he who shall, standing in this great cleft of Past and Future, understand the dignity & power of his position so well as to write the laws of Criticism, of Ethics, of History will be found an

"I am sometimes discontented with my house because it lies on a
dusty road and with its sills & cellar almost in the water of the
meadow."

age hence neither false nor unfortunate but will rank immediately &
equally with all the masters whom we now acknowledge.

Oct. 23, 1839

Fact is better than fiction if only we could get pure fact. Do you
think any rhetoric or any romance would get your ear from one who
could tell straight on the real history of man, who could reconcile your
moral character & your natural history, who could explain your misfortunes, your fevers, your debts, your temperament, your habits of
thought, your tastes, & in every explanation not sever you from the
Whole but unite you to it?

Oct. 23–25, 1839

See a knot of country people working out their road-tax or laying a
new bridge. How close are they to their work. How they sympathize

with every log & foreknow its every nod & stir with chain & crowbar & seem to see through the ground all the accidents of preservation & decay.

Oct. 26, 1839

There are two elements of which our nature is mixed, most unequally in different individuals. The first is Rest, predominant in manifold facts from the vision of reason, the contemplation of the infinite, to the simple satisfaction in permanence, the love of what is old, Old Age itself, Sleep and Death. The second is Love.

Oct. 27, 1839

In our modern reforms there's a little too much commentary on the movement by the mover.

Oct. 28–30, 1839

We ought never to lose our youth. In all natural & necessary labors as in the work of a farm, in digging, splitting, rowing, drawing water, a man always appears young—is still a boy. So in doing anything which is still above him; which asks all his strength & more; somewhat commensurate with his ability, so that he works up to it, not down upon it—he is still a youth. But if his work is unseasonable, as botany & shells or the Greek verbs at 80 years of age, or playing Blindman's Buff, we say, Go up thou baldhead!

Nov. 3–5, 1839

It is only known to Plato that we can do without Plato.

Nov. 9–12, 1839

It is very hard to find an ideal in history. By courtesy we call saints & heroes such but they were very defective characters. I cannot easily find a man I would be.

Nov. 13, 1839

I dare not look for a friend to me who have never been one.

A good sentence, a noble verse which I meet in my reading are an epoch in my life. From month to month, from year to year they remain fresh & memorable. Yet when we once in our writing come out into the free air of thought, we seem to be assured that nothing is easier than to continue this communication at pleasure indefinitely. Up, down, around, the kingdom of thought has no enclosures, but the Muse makes us free of her city. Well the world has a million writers. One would think then that thought would be as familiar as the air & water & the gifts of each new hour exclude the repetition of those of the last. Yet I remember a beautiful verse for twenty years.

Nov. 14, 1839

S[arah] M[argaret] F[uller] writes me that she waits for the Lectures seeing well after much intercourse that the best of me is there. She says very truly; & I thought it a good remark which somebody repeated here from S. S. that I "always seemed to be on stilts". It is even so. Most of the persons whom I see in my own house I see across a gulf. I cannot go to them nor they come to me. Nothing can exceed the frigidity & labor of my speech with such. You might turn a yoke of oxen between every pair of words; and the behavior is as awkward & proud. I see the ludicrousness of the plight as well as they. But having never found any remedy I am very patient with this folly or shame, patient of my churl's mask, in the belief that this privation has certain rich compensations inasmuch as it makes my solitude dearer & the impersonal God is shed abroad in my heart more richly & more lowly welcome for this porcupine impossibility of contact with men. And yet in one who sets his mark so high, who presumes so vast an elevation as the birthright of man, is it not a little sad to be a mere mill or pump yielding one wholesome product at the mouth in one particular mode but as impertinent & worthless in any other place or purpose as a pump or a coffee mill would be in a parlor or a chapel? I make rockets: Must I therefore be a good senator?

I need hardly say to any one acquainted with my thoughts that I have no System. When I was quite young I fancied that by keeping a Manuscript Journal by me, over whose pages I wrote a list of the great topics of human study, as, *Religion, Poetry, Politics, Love, &c* in the course of a few years I should be able to complete a sort of Encyclopaedia containing the net value of all the definitions at which the world had yet arrived. But at the end of a couple of years my Cabinet Cyclopaedia though much enlarged was no nearer to a completeness than on its first day. Nay somehow the whole plan of it needed alteration nor did the following months promise any speedier term to it than the foregoing. At last I discovered that my curve was a parabola whose arcs would never meet, and came to acquiesce in the perception that although no diligence can rebuild the Universe in a model by the best accumulation or disposition of details, yet does the World reproduce itself in miniature in every event that transpires, so that all the laws of nature may be read in the smallest fact. So that the truth speaker may dismiss all solicitude as to the proportion & congruency of the aggregate of his thoughts so long as he is a faithful reporter of particular impressions.

Nov. 17, 1839
Why should they call me good natured? I too like puss have a re-
tractile claw.

Women see better than men. Men see lazily if they do not expect to
act. Women see quite without any wish to act. Men of genius are said to
partake of the masculine & feminine traits. They have this feminine eye,
a function so rich that it contents itself without asking any aid of the
hand. Trifles may well be studied by him for he sees nothing insulated,
the plaid of a cloak, the plaits of a ruffle, the wrinkles of a face absorb his
attention & lead it to the root of these matters in Universal Laws.

Nov. 19, 1839
Society quarrels with the clerisy or learned class if they sell their
wisdom for money. But Society compels them to this course. Once, before Malthus was in vogue, the world thought its health & grace consisted in its clerisy. The state magnificently maintained them. No one
could spend money so well, of course, as the most cultivated. The state
took care that the best qualified should be the richest Benefactors. But
times are changed. The Church is not now the resort of all or almost all
this class. They are gone out hence, & the ecclesiastics are not drawn to
the church by their nature but by convenience. Of course the church
has lost the veneration of the people & they do not like to pay for its
support. Meantime the Scholars out of the church have the same needs as
before; the same fitness to be the almoners of the State; for all the expenditure of a truly cultivated man is like the expenditure of a temple,
religious & public. They have a right, have they not? in proportion to
their enlarged sight to exert a larger power, to direct the means of the
Community, to select & aid & enrich the youth of genius & virtue. Shall
they then, since the state is no state, gives them no place, desert also
their function in the commonwealth, untimely deny themselves & those
whom they ought to serve the first means of education? Shall they kill
through a fatal economy every generous proposition of culture to the
community, forbear assembling themselves together, grudge the miles
of travel that will bring them face to face with poets & sages, deny
themselves the sight of a picture, a statue, & a concert of music, a correspondence with distant philosophers & the interchange of books & apparatus? Or shall they forsake their duties since they are so straitened
by your penury, & go dig in the fields & buy & sell in the markets to the
detriment of all learning & civility in the Commonwealth, in order that
they may have that share of external power which their insight has made
a higher need to them? If not, then leave open to them the resource of
selling the works which are the only vendible product of so many

laborious days & watching nights, & whose price ought to be esteemed sacred & not vile.

Nov. 20, 1839

O Lord! Unhappy is the man whom man can make unhappy.

Burton's Anatomy of Melancholy is a wonderful work of a man. To read it however is much like reading in a dictionary. I think we read it as an inventory to be reminded how many classes & species of facts exist &, by observing in to what strange & multiplex byways learning hath strayed, agreeably infer our opulence. A dictionary however is not a bad book to read. There is no cant in it. No excess of explanation. And it is very suggestive, full of inferences undrawn. There is all poetry & all prose & needs nothing but a little combination. See what hosts of forgotten scholars he feeds us withal.

Nov. 21, 1839

You teach your boy to walk but he learns to run himself.

Nov. 27, 1839

Happy is he who in looking at the compositions of an earlier date knows that the moment wrote them, & feels no more call or right to alter them than to alter his recollections of a day or a fact.

When once & again the regard & friendship of the nobleminded is offered me, I am made sensible of my disunion with myself. The head is of gold, the feet are of clay. In my *worthiness* I have such confidence, that I can court solitude. I know that if my aspirations should demonstrate themselves, angels would not disdain me. Of my *unworthiness*, the first person I meet shall apprize me. I shall have so little presence, such pitiful gingerbread considerations, so many calculations, & such unconcealable weariness of my company—that in my heart I beseech them to begone & I flee to the secretest hemlock shade in Walden Woods to recover my selfrespect.

Nov. 28, 1939

It seems a matter of indifference what, & how, & how much, you write, if you write poetry. Poetry makes its own pertinence and a single stanza outweighs a book of prose. One stanza is complete. But one sentence of prose is not.

Dec. 1–3, 1839

Rob was tender & timid as a fawn in his affections, yet he passed for a man of calculation & cold heart. He assumed coldness only to hide his *woman's heart.* There is a play in which the sister is enamoured of her brother & when they embrace, she exclaims, "J'ai froid."

Dec. 4, 1839

In Boston ... I read the first lecture of my course on the Present Age; with the old experience that when it was done, & the time had come to read it, I was then first ready to begin to write.

Dec. 1839

I say how the world looks to me without reference to Blair's Rhetoric or Johnson's Lives. And I call my thoughts The Present Age, because I use no will in the matter, but honestly record such impressions as things make. So transform I myself into a Dial, and my shadow will tell where the sun is.

Dec. 22, 1839

I do not care what you write, but only that you show yourself a man by writing.

Dec. 22–23, 1839

It is the necessity of my nature to shed all influences. Who can come near? ... Neither the rain, neither the warm ray of love, nor the touch of human hand. It seemed, as I mused in the street, in Boston, on the unpropitious effect of the town on my humor, that there needs a certain deliberation & tenacity in the entertainment of a thought—a certain longanimity to make that confidence & stability which can meet the demand others make on us. I am too quickeyed & unstable. My thoughts are too short, as they say my sentences are. I step along from stone to stone over the Lethe which gurgles around my path, but the odds are that my companion encounters me just as I leave one stone & before my foot has well reached the other & down I tumble into Lethe water. But the man of long wind, the man who receives his thought with a certain phlegmatic entertainment & unites himself to it for the time as a sailor to his boat has a better principle of poise & is not easily moved from the perpendicular.

In my dream I saw a man reading in the library at Cambridge, and one who stood by said, "He readeth advertisements," meaning that he read for the market only & not for truth. Then I said—Do I read advertisements?

In some hours I walk in a world of glass. I see then the equivalence of all circumstances, that each life is a repetition of every other, so that there is no presumption, but good reason, in assuming to paint the Age from one man's routine.

Every thing should be treated poetically—law, politics, housekeeping, money. A judge and a banker must drive their craft poetically as well as a dancer or a scribe. That is, they must exert that higher vision which causes the object to become fluid & plastic. Then they are inventive, they detect its capabilities. If they do not this they have nothing that can be called success, but the work & the workman become blockish & near the point of everlasting congelation. All human affairs need the perpetual intervention of this elastic principle to preserve them supple & alive as the earth needs the presence of caloric through its pores to resist the tendency to absolute solidity. If you would write a code or logarithms or a cook-book you cannot spare the poetic impulse. We must not only have hydrogen in balloons and steel springs under coaches but we must have fire under the Andes at the core of the world. No one will doubt that battles must be fought poetically who reads Plutarch or Las Casas. Economy must be poetical, inventive, alive: that is its essence, and therein is it distinguished from mere parsimony, which is a poor, dead, base thing: but economy inspires respect—is clean & accomplishes much.

Dec. 25, 1839
All life is a compromise. We are haunted by an ambition of a celestial greatness & baulked of it by all manner of paltry impediments. But each of us can do somewhat marked—either lucrative or graceful or kind or wise or formidable. That we do, as an apology to others & ourselves for not reaching the mark of a good & equal life. But that feat does not satisfy *us*, whilst we obtrude it on the notice of our comrades. Although it succeed in throwing dust in their eyes, it does not smooth our own brow or give us the tranquillity of the pure when we walk in the street. We do penance as we go. We feel that our talent itself is but a sort of expiation, and so we are constrained to reflect on our splendid hour with a certain humiliation as somewhat too fine & not as one moment of many moments, a fair expression of our permanent energy.

Jan.–Feb. 1840
Guy wished all his friends dead on very slight occasion. Whoever was privy to one of his gaucheries, had the honour of this Stygian optation. Had Jove heard all his prayers, the planet would soon have been unpeopled.

* * *

I can't forgive you that you do not see A nor hear him *whilst you think you do.*

I marry you for better but not for *worse.* I marry impersonally.

The capital crime with which the church stands charged is its poverty. Truth is always rich, all-related, all explaining. But our church is a little bye way, an eddy, a nook wherein you hear some words & notions you will hear of nowhere else and which will not explain to the handcartman his cart nor to me my pen & ink, my sex, my form, & face.

Feb. 19, 1840

I closed last Wednesday, 12th instant, my Course of Lectures in Boston, "On the Present Age". . .

These lectures give me little pleasure. I have not done what I hoped when I said, I will try it once more. I have not once transcended the coldest selfpossession. I said I will agitate others, being agitated myself. I dared to hope for extacy & eloquence. A new theatre, a new art, I said, is mine. Let us see if philosophy, if ethics, if chiromancy, if the discovery of the divine in the house & the barn, in all works & all plays, cannot make the cheek blush, the lip quiver, & the tear start. I will not waste myself. On the strength of Things I will be borne, and try if Folly, Custom, Convention, & Phlegm cannot be made to hear our sharp artillery. Alas! alas! I have not the recollection of one strong moment. A cold mechanical preparation for a delivery as decorous—fine things, pretty things, wise things—but no arrows, no axes, no nectar, no growling, no transpiercing, no loving, no enchantment.

And why?

I seem to lack constitutional vigor to attempt each topic as I ought. I ought to seek to lay myself out utterly—large, enormous, prodigal, upon the subject of the week. But a hateful experience has taught me that I can only expend, say, twenty one hours on each lecture, if I would also be ready & able for the next. Of course, I spend myself prudently; I economize; I cheapen: whereof nothing grand ever grew. Could I spend sixty hours on each, or what is better, had I such energy that I could rally the lights & mights of sixty hours into twenty, I should hate myself less, I should help my friend.

April 1840

At Providence Mr G. is quite too much an artist. If he tells the best story I see so much preparation that the fun always falls short. I grow grave in my efforts to meet so much display.

It was well said of Mr F. by one of his neighbors, "He strikes twelve the first time."

Ah my poor countrymen! Yankees & Dollars have such inextricable association that the words ought to rhyme. In New York, in Boston, in Providence, you cannot pass two men in the street without the word escaping them in the very moment of encounter, "dollars," "two & a half per cent," "three per-cent."

April 7? 1840

I see with great pleasure this growing inclination in all persons who aim to speak the truth, for manual labor & the farm. It is not that commerce, law, & state employments are unfit for a man, but that these are now all so perverted & corrupt that no man can right himself in them, he is lost in them, *he* cannot move hand or foot in them. Nothing is left him but to begin the world anew, as he does who puts the spade into the ground for food. When many shall have done so, when the majority shall admit the necessity of reform, of health, of sanity in all these institutions, then the way will be open again to the great advantages that arise from division of labor. & a man will be able to select employments fittest for him without losing his selfdirection & becoming a tool.

In all my lectures, I have taught one doctrine, namely, the infinitude of the private man. This, the people accept readily enough, & even with loud commendation, as long as I call the lecture, Art; or Politics; or Literature; or the Household; but the moment I call it Religion—they are shocked, though it be only the application of the same truth which they receive everywhere else, to a new class of facts.

April 9, 1840

We walked this P.M. to Edmund Hosmer's & Walden Pond—The south wind blew & filled with bland & warm light the dry sunny woods. The last year's leaves flew like birds through the air. As I sat on the bank of the Drop or God's Pond & saw the amplitude of the little water, what space what verge the little scudding fleets of ripples found to scatter & spread from side to side & take so much time to cross the pond, & saw how the water seemed made for the wind, & the wind for the water, dear playfellows for each other—I said to my companion, I declare this world is so beautiful that I can hardly believe it exists. At Walden Pond, the waves were larger and the whole lake in pretty uproar. Jones Very said, "See how each wave rises from the midst with an original force, at the same time that it partakes the general movement!"

April 27, 1840

My little boy says, 'I want something to play with which I never saw before'. And thus lives over already in his experience the proclamation of Xerxes advertising a reward for a new pleasure. I tell him that the sun & moon are good playthings still, though they are very old; they are as good as new. So are Eating & drinking, though rather dangerous toys, very good amusements though old ones; so is water which we wash & play with; but he is not persuaded by my eloquence.

April 27–29, 1840

There is an important *équivoque* in our use of the word Unconscious, a word which is much displayed upon in the psychology of the present day. We say that our virtue & genius are unconscious, that they are the influx of God, & the like. The objector replies that to represent the Divine Being as an unconscious somewhat, is abhorrent, &c. But the unconsciousness we spake of was merely relative to *us*; we speak, we act from we know not what higher principle, and we describe its circumambient quality by confessing the subjection of our perception to it, we cannot overtop, oversee it—not see at all its channel into us. But in saying this, we predicate nothing of its consciousness or unconsciousness in relation to itself. We see at once that we have no language subtle enough for distinctions in that inaccessible region. That air is too rare for the wings of words. We cannot say God is self conscious, or not self-conscious; for the moment we cast our eye on that dread nature, we see that it is the wisdom of wisdom, the love of love, the power of power, & soars infinitely out of all definition & dazzles all inquest.

April 30, 1840

Waldo looks out today from my study window & says, "These are not the woods I like to look at."—And what woods do you like to look at?—"Those that I see from the window of the Nursery."

May 3, 1840

Our friends die—husbands, wives, children—and the finest things are said to console us. Presently the man is consoled, but not by the fine things; no, but perhaps by very foul things, namely, by the defects of the dead from which he shall no more suffer; or, what often happens, by being relieved from relations & a responsibility to which he was unequal. The willingness to lose a man shows us what a sad dog he is.

May 4–5, 1840

Waldo says, "God is very glorious, he always says his prayers, and never 'haves (behaves) naughty."

May 6, 1840
 A. What did he say to you of me?
 B. Ask him.

May 10, 1840
 If you have no talent for scolding, do not scold; if none for explaining, do not explain; if none for giving parties, do not give parties, however graceful or needful these acts may appear in others.

 I begin to dislike animal food. I had whimsies yesterday after dinner which disgusted me somewhat. The man will not be much better than the beast he eats.

May 17, 1840
 The earth is gay in these days with the blossoming of all fruit trees. An apple tree near at hand is a great awkward flower but seen at some distance it gives a wonderful softness to the landscape.

May 18, 1840
 We have more traditions than the most resolute skeptic has yet interrogated or even guessed. How few cosmogonies have we. A few have got a kind of classical character & we let them stand, for a world-builder is a rare man. And yet what ghosts & hollow formless dream-gear these theories are; how crass & inapplicable! how little they explain; what a poor handful of facts in this plentiful Universe they touch; Let me see.—Moses, Hesiod, Egyptian lore of Isis & Osiris, Zoroaster, Menu—With these few rude poems or extracts from rude poems the nations have been content when any clever boy black or white has anywhere interrupted the stupid uproar by a sharp question—"Would any one please to tell me whence I came hither?" To be sure that question is contrary to the rules of good society in all countries. For society is always secondary not primary & delights in secondaries. It is gregarious & parasitic & loves to lay its egg like the cowtroopial in a nest which other birds have built & to build no nest itself. Absolute truths, previous questions, primary natures, society loathes the sound of & the name of. "Can you not as well say Christ as say truth?" it asks. "Who are you, child, that you must needs ask so many questions? See what a vast procession of your Uncles & Aunts who never asked any. Can't you eat your dinner & read in the books? besides; I hate conversation, it makes my head ache."—But if the urchin has wild eyes & can neither be coaxed nor chidden into silence & cares not a pin for the Greeks & Romans, for art or antiquity, for Bible or Government, for politics or money, & keeps

knocking soundly all night at the gate, then at last the good world con-
descends to unroll for him these solemn scrolls as the reports of the
Commissioners from the East, from the South, from the North & the
West, to whom his question had been formerly referred. If the poor lad
got no answer before, he has got none now.—What birth do these famous books of Genesis reveal? Do they explain so much as the nest of a
blue bird or the hum of a fly? Can they tell him the pedigree of the
smallest effect? Can they detect the virtue of the feeblest Cause? Can
they give him the least hint of the history of the eyes he has worshipped,
or disclose his relations to the summer brook & the waving corn? And
yet every man is master of the whole Fact & shall one day find himself so.

May 25–27, 1840
    I went to the circus & saw a man ride standing on the back of two
galloping horses, a third horse being interposed between the two. As he
rode, the sinews of his limbs played like those of his beasts. One horse
brought a basket in his teeth, picked up a cap, & selected a card out of
four. All wonder comes of showing an effect at two or three removes
from the cause. Show us the two or three steps by which the horse was
brought to fetch the basket, and the wonder would cease. But I & Waldo
were of one mind when he said, "It makes me want to go home."

May 28–29, 1840
    Old Age. Sad spectacle that a man should live & be fed that he may
fill a paragraph every year in the newspapers for his wonderful age, as
we record the weight & girth of the Big Ox or Mammoth girl. We do not
count a man's years until he has nothing else to count.

May 30, 1840
    Wordsworth's Excursion awakened in every lover of nature the right
feeling. We saw stars shine, we felt the awe of mountains, we heard the
rustle of the wind in the grass, & knew again the sweet secret of solitude.
It was a great joy. It was nearer to nature & verse that more commanded
nature than aught we had before. But the promise was not fulfilled. The
whole book was dull.

June 1–3, 1840
    Our American letters are, we confess, in the optative mood; but
whoso knows these seething brains, these admirable radical projects,
these talkers who talk the sun & moon away will believe that this generation cannot pass away without leaving its mark.

June 1840

Waldo says, "the flowers talk when the wind blows over them." My little boy grows thin in the hot summer & runs all to eyes & eyelashes.

June 11, 1840

I finish this morning transcribing my old Essay on Love, but I see well its inadequateness. I cold because I am hot—cold at the surface only as a sort of guard & compensation for the fluid tenderness of the core—have much more experience than I have written there, more than I will, more than I can write. In silence we must wrap much of our life, because it is too fine for speech, because also we cannot explain it to others, and because somewhat we cannot yet understand.

June 14? 1840

It is a superstition to insist on vegetable or animal or any special diet. All is made up at last of the same chemical atoms. The Indian rule shames the Graham rule—A man can eat anything: cats, dogs, snakes, frogs, fishes, roots, & moss. All the religion, all the reason in the new diet is that animal food costs too much. We must spend too much time & thought in procuring so varied & stimulating diet & then we become dependent on it.

June 18, 1840

I like Henry Thoreau's statement on Diet. "If a man does not believe that he can thrive on board nails, I will not talk with him."

June 19? 1840

It makes no difference what a saintly soul eats or drinks; let him eat venison or roots, let him drink champagne or water, nothing will harm him or intoxicate or impoverish him: he eats as though he eat not, & drinks as though he drank not. But we are Skeptics over our dinner table & therefore our food is noxious & our bodies fat or lean. Looking as we do at means, & not at grand ends, being in our action disunited, our bodies have come to be detached also from our souls, & we speak of our health.

June 24–28, 1840

The language of the street is always strong. What can describe the folly & emptiness of scolding like the word *jawing?* I feel too the force of the double negative, though clean contrary to our grammar rules. And I confess to some pleasure from the stinging rhetoric of a rattling oath in the mouth of truckmen & teamsters. How laconic & brisk it is by the side of a page of the North American Review. Cut these words &

they would bleed; they are vascular & alive; they walk & run. Moreover they who speak them have this elegancy, that they do not trip in their speech. It is a shower of bullets, whilst Cambridge men & Yale men correct themselves & begin again at every half sentence. I know nobody among my contemporaries except Carlyle who writes with any sinew & vivacity comparable to Plutarch & Montaigne. Yet always this profane swearing & bar-room wit has salt & fire in it. I cannot now read Webster's speeches. Fuller & Brown & Milton are quick, but the list is soon ended. Goethe seems to be well alive, no pedant. Luther too. *Guts* is a stronger word than intestines.

Now for near five years I have been indulged by the gracious Heaven in my long holiday in this goodly house of mine entertaining & entertained by so many worthy & gifted friends and all this time poor Nancy Barron the madwoman has been screaming herself hoarse at the poorhouse across the brook & I still hear her whenever I open my window.

June 29, 1840
Today at the Cliff we held our villegiatura. I saw nothing better than the passage of the river by the dark clump of trees that line the bank in one spot for a short distance. There nature charmed the eye with her distinct & perfect painting. As the flowing silver reached that point, it darkened, & yet every wave celebrated its passage through the shade by one sparkle. But ever the direction of the sparkles was onward, onward. Not one receded. At one invariable pace like marchers in a procession to solemn music, in perfect time, in perfect order, they moved onward, onward, & I saw the Warning of their eternal flow. Then the rock seemed good to me. I think we can never afford to part with Matter. How dear & beautiful it is to us! As water to our thirst, so is this rock to our eyes & hands & feet. It is firm water; it is cold flame. What refreshment, what health, what magic affinity! ever an old friend, ever like a dear friend or brother when we chat affectedly with strangers comes in this honest face whilst we prattle with men & takes a grave liberty with us & shames us out of our nonsense.

June/July/Aug.? 1840
What is so bewitching as the experiments of young children on grammar & language? The purity of their grammar corrects all the anomalies of our irregular verbs & anomalous nouns. They carry the analogy thorough. *Bite* makes *bited,* and *eat eated* in their preterite. Waldo says there is no "telling" on my microscope meaning no name of the maker as he has seen on knifeblades, &c. "Where is the wafer that *lives* in this box?" &c. They use the strong double negative which we

English have lost from our books, though we keep it in the street. "I wish you would not dig your leg," said Waldo to me. Ellen calls the grapes "green berries" & when I asked Does it rain this morning? she said "There's tears on the window."

Waldo asks if the strings of the harp open when he touches them!

You fancy the stout woodchopper is thinking always of his poverty compared with the power & money of the capitalist who makes the laws. I will not deny that such things have passed thro' his mind for he has been at a Caucus with open mouth & ears. But now he is thinking of a very different matter, for his horse has started in the team & pulled with such a spring that he has cleared himself of the harness—hames & all— and he, as he mends the broken tackle is meditating revenge on the horse—"Well you may draw as fast as you like up the mile hill: you shall have enough of it if you like to draw, Damn you"—the horse, that is, and not the capitalist.

Let every man shovel out his own snow and the whole city will be passable.

July 10, 1840
Nature invites to repose, to the dreams of the oriental sages; there is no petulance, no fret; there is eternal resource and a long tomorrow rich & strong as yesterday. We should be believers in Necessity and Compensation and a man would have the air of pyramids & mountains, if we forsook our petulant mates & kept company with leaves & waters.

July 10-12, 1840
All diseases run into one, namely, Old Age. We grizzle every day. I see no need of it. Whilst we converse with what is above us, we do not grow old but grow young. Infancy, youth, receptive, aspiring, with religious eye looking upward, counts itself nothing & abandons itself to the flowing instruction, flowing from all sides. But the man & woman of seventy assume to know all, throw up their hope, renounce aspiration, accept the actual for the Necessary & talk down to the young. Let them then become organs of the Holy Ghost. Let them be in love. Let them behold truth & instantly their eyes are lifted again, their wrinkles smoothed, they are perfumed again with hope & power. Is it possible a man should not grow old? I will not answer for his crazy body. It seems to be a ship which carries him through the waves of this world & whose timbers contract barnacles & dry rot & will not serve for a second cruise. But I refuse to admit this appeal to the old people we know as valid

against a good hope. For do we know one who is an organ of the holy ghost?

July 13–14, 1840
We are all boarders at one table—White man, black man, ox and eagle, bee, & worm.

July 26, 1840
I often hear the remark made that there is great pleasure in giving up all care, when we find that we are really sick. And one wishes for a good fit of dyspepsia or hemorrhage to procure him leisure & freedom. Is this a trait of New England & Eighteen-hundred-forty-dom, or should I have found the same satire on daily life in Rome & in Thebes?

July 26? 1840
Shall the scholar write every word in his mind—how bad as well as how good he is—like Rabelais & Goethe; or shall he be an Eclectic in his experience? Is there not then cant when he writes more chastely than he speaks if you should hear his whispers? Let him then mend his manners & bring them within the mark which he trusts his pen to draw.

July 31, 1840
A newspaper in Providence contains some notice of Transcendentalism, & deplores Mr Emerson's doctrine that the argument for immortality betrays weakness. The piece seems to be written by a woman. It begins with round sentences but ends in Oh's & Ah's. Yet cannot society come to apprehend the doctrine of One Mind? Can we not satisfy ourselves with the fact of living for the Universe, of lodging our beatitude therein? Patriotism has been thought great in Sparta, in Rome, in New England even, only sixty years ago. How long before *Universalism* or Humanity shall be creditable & beautiful?

Aug. 9? 1840
Waldo rolled over in the night on his trundle bed until he got quite under my bed & off his own. Then he broke out into loud cries, telling me, "I tried to get away from the bed, and the bed came."

The poet cannot spare any grief or pain or terror in his experience; he wants every rude stroke that has been dealt on his irritable texture. I need my fear & my superstition as much as my purity & courage, to construct the glossary which opens the Sanscrit of the world.

Aug. 16, 1840
After seeing Anna Barker I rode with Margaret Fuller to the plains.

She taxed me, as often before, so now more explicitly with inhospitality of soul. She & Caroline would gladly be my friends, yet our intercourse is not friendship, but literary gossip. I count & weigh but do not love. They make no progress with me, but however often we have met, we still meet as strangers. They feel wronged in such relation, & do not wish to be catechised & criticised. I thought of my experience with several persons which resembled this: and confessed that I would not converse with the divinest person more than one week. M. insisted that it was no friendship which was so soon thus exhausted, & that I ought to know how to be silent & companionable at the same moment. She would surprise me—she would have me say & do what surprised myself. I confess to all this charge with humility unfeigned. I can better converse with George Bradford than with any other. Elizabeth Hoar & I have a beautiful relation not however quite free from the same hardness & fences. Yet would nothing be so grateful to me as to melt once for all these icy barriers, & unite with these lovers. But great is the law. I must do nothing to court their love which would lose my own. Unless that which I do to build up myself, endears me to them, our covenant would be injurious. Yet how joyfully would I form permanent relations with the three or four wise & beautiful whom I hold so dear, and dwell under the same roof or in a strict neighborhood. That would at once ennoble life. And it is practicable. It is easier than things which others do. It is easier than to go to Europe, or to subdue a forest farm in Illinois. But this survey of my experience taught me anew that no friend I have surprises, none exalts me. This then is to be set down, is it not? to the requirements we make of the friend, that he shall constrain us to sincerity, & put under contribution all our faculties.

Sept. 1, 1840

One fact the fine conversations of the last week—now already fast fading into oblivion—revealed to me not without a certain shudder of joy—that I must thank what I am & not what I do for the love my friends bear me. I, conscious all the time of the short coming of my hands, haunted ever with a sense of beauty which makes all I do & say pitiful to me, & the occasion of perpetual apologies, assure myself to disgust those whom I admire, and now suddenly it comes out that they have been loving me all this time, not at all thinking of my hands or my words, but only of that love of something more beautiful than the world, which, it seems, being in my heart, overflowed through my eyes or the tones of my speech.

Gladly I learn that we have these subterranean—say rather, these supersensuous channels of communication, and that spirits can meet in their pure upper sky without the help of organs.

Sept. 10, 1840

Strange history this of *abolition*. The negro must be very old & belongs, one would say, to the fossil formations. What right has he to be intruding into the late & civil daylight of this dynasty of the Caucasians & Saxons? It is plain that so inferior a race must perish shortly like the poor Indians. Sarah Clarke said, "the Indians perish because there is no place for them". That is the very fact of their inferiority. There is always place for the superior. Yet pity for these was needed, it seems, for the education of this generation in ethics. Our good world cannot learn the beauty of love in narrow circles & at home in the immense Heart, but it must be stimulated by somewhat foreign & monstrous, by the simular man of Ethiopia.

Sept. 11, 1840

Would it not be a good cipher for the seal of the Lonely Society which forms so fast in these days, Two Porcupines meeting with all their spines erect, and the motto, "We converse at the *quill's* end."

Sept. 12, 1840

Sarah Clarke who left us yesterday is a true & high minded person, but has her full proportion of our native frost.

She remarked of the Dial, that the spirit of many of the pieces was lonely.

Sept. 16? 1840

A sleeping child gives me the impression of a traveller in a very far country.

Sept. 20–23, 1840

I have no quarrel with the universe. My heart, when the noble love me, beats peacefully. If I am bashful I am serene.

Between narrow walls we walk: insanity on one side, & fat dulness on the other.

Sept. 24, 1840

The victories of the Arabs after Mahomet interest me. They did they knew not what. The naked Derar horsed on an idea was an overmatch to a troop of cavalry. The women fought & conquered men. To read this, causes fear, or something like it. That is to say I am so effeminate at this moment that the staves of those women do reach unto & hit me too. This force is not in Arabs but in all women. Every noble maiden & dame will take up into herself the same might, although in proportioned

& cultivated souls it will cease to be terrible and will become endurance
& overcoming love.

Sept. 26, 1840

You would have me love you. What shall I love? Your body? The
supposition disgusts you. What you have thought & said? Well, whilst
you were thinking & saying them, but not now. I see no possibility of
loving any thing but what now is, & is becoming; your courage, your
enterprize, your budding affection, your opening thought, your prayer,
I can love—but what else?

Oct. 7, 1840

I have been writing with some pains Essays on various matters as a
sort of apology to my country for my apparent idleness. But the poor
work has looked poorer daily as I strove to end it. My genius seemed to
quit me in such a mechanical work, a seeming wise—a cold exhibition of
dead thoughts. When I write a letter to any one whom I love, I have no
lack of words or thoughts: I am wiser than myself & read my paper with
the pleasure of one who receives a letter, but what I write to fill up the
gaps of a chapter is hard & cold, is grammar & logic; there is no magic in
it; I do not wish to see it again. Settle with yourself your accusations of
me. If I do not please you, ask me not to please you, but please yourself.
What you call my indolence, nature does not accuse; the twinkling
leaves, the sailing fleets of waterflies, the deep sky like me well enough
and know me for their own. With them I have no embarrassments, dif-
fidences, or compunctions: with them I mean to stay. You think it is because I have an income which exempts me from your day-labor, that I
waste (as you call it) my time in sungazing & stargazing. You do not
know me. If my debts, as they threaten, should consume what money I
have, I should live just as I do now: I should eat worse food & wear a
coarser coat and should wonder in a potato patch instead of in the
wood—but it is I & not my Twelve Hundred dollars a year, that love
God.

Oct. 1840

I do not give you my time, but I give you that which I have put my
time into, namely my letter or my poem, the expression of my opinion,
or better yet an act which in solitude I have learned to do.

Oct. 17, 1840

Yesterday George & Sophia Ripley, Margaret Fuller & Alcott dis-
cussed here the new social plans. I wished to be convinced, to be
thawed, to be made nobly mad by the kindlings before my eye of a new

Margaret Fuller (1810–1850): "Talking of Women, [she] said,
'Who would be a goody that could be a genius?' "

dawn of human piety. But this scheme was arithmetic & comfort; this
was a hint borrowed from the Tremont House & U.S. Hotel; a rage in
our poverty & politics to live rich & gentlemanlike, an anchor to leeward
against a change of weather; a prudent forecast on the probable issue of
the great questions of pauperism & property. And not once could I be
inflamed—but sat aloof & thoughtless, my voice faltered & fell. It was
not the cave of persecution which is the palace of spiritual power, but
only a room in the Astor House hired for the Transcendentalists. I do

not wish to remove from my present prison to a prison a little larger. I wish to break all prisons. I have not yet conquered my own house. It irks & repents me. Shall I raise the siege of this hencoop & march baffled away to a pretended siege of Babylon? It seems to me that so to do were to dodge the problem I am set to solve, & to hide my impotency in the thick of a crowd. I can see too afar that I should not find myself more than now—no, not so much, in that select, but not by me selected, fraternity. Moreover to join this body would be to traverse all my long trumpeted theory, and the instinct which spoke from it, that one man is a counterpoise to a city—that a man is stronger than a city, that his solitude is more prevalent & beneficent than the concert of crowds.

Oct. 1840

I wish to be approved but as soon as any approves me I distrust him.

The old experiences still return. Society when I rarely enter the company of my well dressed & well bred fellow creatures, seems for the time to bereave me of organs or perhaps only to acquaint me with my want of them. The soul swells with new life and seeks expression with painful desire, but finds no outlets. Its life is all incommunicable. There was a man who put a hat on his head, and a vizor on his face, and gloves on his hands, & shoes on his feet—and could not take them off, for they grew to him. Those who are to me lovely & dear seem for that reason to multiply & tighten the folds that envelope & smother my speech.

Oct. 18, 1840

Dr Ripley is no dandy, but speaks with the greatest simplicity & gravity. He preaches however to a congregation of Dr Ripleys; and Mr Frost to a supposed congregation of Barzillai Frosts; & Daniel Webster to an assembly of Websters. Could this belief of theirs be verified in the audience, each would be esteemed the best of all speakers.

Oct. 18? 1840

Today is always trivial.

The history of Jesus is only the history of every man written large. The names he bestows on Jesus, belong to himself—Mediator, Redeemer, Saviour.

Oct. 25, 1840

What a pity that we cannot curse & swear in good society. Cannot the stinging dialect of the sailors be domesticated? It is the best rhetoric and for a hundred occasions those forbidden words are the only good ones. My page about "Consistency" would be better written thus; Damn Consistency. And to how many foolish canting remarks would a sophomore's ejaculation be the only suitable reply, "The devil you do;" or, "You be damned."

I dreamed that I floated at will in the great Ether, and I saw this world floating also not far off, but diminished to the size of an apple. Then an angel took it in his hand & brought it to me and said "This must thou eat." And I ate the world.

Dec. 1840

I hear much that is ridiculous in music. You would laugh to know all that passes through my head in hearing a concert.

A. [Alcott] is a tedious archangel.

Waldo declines going to church with Mrs Mumford "because Mrs M. is not beautiful. She has red hands & red face." The next week when reminded that he does not like Mrs M. he tells Louisa "I have made a little prayer that Mrs Mumford might be beautiful, & now I think her beautiful."

Louisa proposed to carry W. to church with her & he replies, 'I do not wish to go to church with you because you live in the kitchen.'

Dec? 1840

A droll dream last night, whereat I ghastly laughed. A congregation assembled, like some of our late Conventions, to debate the Institution of Marriage; & grave & alarming objections stated on all hands to the usage; when one speaker at last rose & began to reply to the arguments, but suddenly extended his hand & turned on the audience the spout of an engine which was copiously supplied from within the wall with water & whisking it vigorously about, up, down, right, & left, he drove all the company in crowds hither & thither & out of the house. Whilst I stood watching astonished & amused at the malice & vigor of the orator, I saw the spout lengthened by a supply of hose behind, & the man suddenly brought it round a corner & drenched me as I gazed. I woke up relieved to find myself quite dry, and well convinced that the Institution of Marriage was safe for tonight.

Jan. 1, 1841

I begin the year by sending my little book of Essays to the press. What remains to be done to its imperfect chapters I will seek to do justly. I see no reason why we may not write with as much grandeur of spirit as we can serve or suffer. Let the page be filled with the character not with the skill of the writer.

Jan. 11, 1841

Does Nature, my friend, never show you the wrong side of the tapestry? never come to look dingy & shabby? Do you never say "Old Stones! Old rain! old landscape! you have done your best; there is no more to be said. Praise wearies: you have pushed your joke a little too far."—Or, on the other hand, do you find nature always transcending and as good as new every day? I know, I know, how nimble it is—the good monster; You have quite exhausted its power to please & today you come into a new thought & lo! in an instant there stands the entire world converted suddenly into the cipher or exponent of that very thought & chanting it in full chorus from every leaf & drop of water. It has been singing that song ever since the creation in your deaf ears.

Jan. 31, 1841

Bancroft writes with research faithful no doubt the "Synopsis of the Indian Families"—but the ungrateful reader asks "Wherefore? Is it history, to give me facts which do not involve the reason of their being told?" Bancroft does not know any more than he tells. He sees no reason why these barren facts should be preserved in modern ink. There is a kind of mockery in printing out in Boston in 1841, these withered marrowless facts, like the dead body of an officer I saw at Naples dressed out in his regimentals, powdered & pomatumed, & sitting up in the bier, going to his own funeral.

All my thoughts are foresters. I have scarce a day-dream on which the breath of the pines has not blown, & their shadows waved. Shall I not then call my little book Forest Essays?

Jan.-Feb. 1841

To find a story which I thought I remembered in Quentin Durward, I turned over the volume until I was fairly caught in the old foolish trap & read & read to the end of the novel. Then as often before I feel indignant to have been duped & dragged after a foolish boy & girl, to see them at last married & portioned & I instantly turned out of doors like a beggar that has followed a gay procession into the castle.... These novels will give way by & by to diaries or autobiographies;—captivating books if only a man knew how to choose among what he calls his experiences that which is really his experience, and how to record truth truly!

Feb. 4, 1841

I am dispirited by the lameness of an organ: if I have a cold, and the thought I would utter to my friend comes forth in stony sepulchral tones, I am disgusted, & will not speak more. But, as the drunkard who cannot walk can run, so I can speak my oration to an assembly, when I cannot without pain answer a question in the parlor. But lately it is a sort of general winter with me. I am not sick that I know, yet the names & projects of my friends sound far off & faint & unaffecting to my ear, as do, when I am sick, the voices of persons & the sounds of labor which I overhear in my solitary bed. A puny limitary creature am I, with only a small annuity of vital force to expend, which if I squander in a few feast days, I must feed on water & moss the rest of the time.

Feb. 4-5, 1841

If I judge from my own experience I should unsay all my fine things, I fear, concerning the manual labor of literary men. They ought to be released from every species of public or private responsibility. To them the grasshopper is a burden. I guard my moods as anxiously as a miser his money. For, company, business, my own household-chores untune & disqualify me for writing. I think then the writer ought not to be married, ought not to have a family. I think the Roman Church with its celibate clergy & its monastic cells was right. If he must marry, perhaps he should be regarded happiest who has a shrew for a wife, a sharp-tongued notable dame who can & will assume the total economy of the house, and having some sense that her philosopher is best in his study suffers him not to intermeddle with her thrift. He shall be master but not mistress, as Elizabeth Hoar said.

Feb. 10, 1841

What right have I to write on Prudence whereof I have but little & that of the negative sort? My prudence consists in avoiding & going without, not in the inventing of means & methods, not in adroit steering, not in gentle repairing. I have no skill to make money spend well, no genius in my economy & whoever sees my garden discovers that I must have some other garden. Yet I love facts & hate lubricity & people without perception. Then I have the same title to write on prudence that I have to write on poetry or holiness. We write from aspiration & antagonism as well as experience. We paint those qualities which we do not possess. The poet admires the man of energy & tactics; the merchant breeds his son for the church or the bar; & where a man is not vain & egotistic, you shall find what he has not, by his praise.

Feb. 12, 1841

In the Feejee islands, it appears, cannibalism is now familiar. They eat their own wives and children. We only devour widows' houses, & great merchants outwit & absorb the substance of small ones and every man feeds on his neighbor's labor if he can. It is a milder form of cannibalism; a varioloid.

March 1, 1841

In March many weathers. March always comes if it do not come till May. May generally does not come at all.

March? 1841

Away with your prismatics, I want a spermatic book. Plato, Plotinus, & Plutarch are such.

April 19, 1841

I am tempted lately to wish, for the benefit of our literary society, that we had the friendly institution of the Café. How much better than Munroe's bookshop, would be a coffee room wherein one was sure at one o'clock to find what scholars were abroad taking their walk after the morning studies were ended.

April 22, 1841

America & not Europe is the rich man. According to De Tocqueville, the column of our population on the western frontier from Lake Superior to the Gulf of Mexico (1200 miles as the bird flies) advances every year a mean distance of seventeen miles. He adds "This gradual & continuous progress of the European race towards the Rocky Mountains has the solemnity of a providential event; it is like a deluge of men rising unabatedly & daily driven onward by the hand of God."

April 23, 1841

For this was I born & came into the world to deliver the self of myself to the Universe from the Universe; to do a certain benefit which Nature could not forego, nor I be discharged from rendering, & then immerge again into the holy silence & eternity, out of which as a man I arose. God is rich & many more men than I, he harbors in his bosom, biding their time & the needs & the beauty of all. Or, when I wish, it is permitted me to say, these hands, this body, this history of Waldo Emerson are profane & wearisome, but I, I descend not to mix myself with that or with any man. Above his life, above all creatures I flow down forever a sea of benefit into races of individuals. Nor can the stream ever roll backward or the sin or death of a man taint the immutable energy which distributes itself into men as the sun into rays or the sea into drops.

April 24? 1841

I frequently find the best part of my ride in the Concord coach from my house to Winthrop Place to be in Prince street, Charter street, Ann street, & the like places at the North End of Boston. The dishabille of both men & women, their unrestrained attitudes & manners make pictures greatly more interesting than the clean shaved & silk robed procession in Washington & Tremont streets. I often see that the attitudes of both men & women engaged in hard work are more picturesque than any which art & study could contrive, for the Heart is in these first. I say *picturesque;* because when I pass these groups, I instantly know whence all the fine pictures I have seen had their origin: I feel the painter in me: these are the traits which make us feel the force & eloquence of *form* & the sting of color. But the painter is only *in* me; it does not come to the fingers' ends.

May 6, 1841

I doubt if the interior & spiritual history of New England could be truelier told than through the exhibition of family history such as this, the picture of this group of M.M.E. & the boys, mainly Charles. The genius of that woman, the key to her life, is in the conflict of the new & the old ideas in New England. The heir of whatever was rich & profound & efficient in thought & emotion in the old religion which planted & peopled this land, she strangely united to this passionate piety the fatal gift of penetration, a love of philosophy, an impatience of words, and was thus a religious skeptic. She held on with both hands to the faith of the past generation as to the palladium of all that was good & hopeful in the physical & metaphysical worlds, and in all companies, & on all occasions, & especially with these darling nephews of her hope & pride, extolled & poetised this beloved Calvinism. Yet all the time she doubted & denied it, & could not tell whether to be more glad or sorry to find that these boys were irremediably born to the adoption & furtherance of the new ideas. . . . These combined traits in M.M.E.'s character gave the new direction to her hope; that these boys should be richly & holily qualified & bred to purify the old faith of what narrowness & error adhered to it & import all its fire into the new age—such a gift should her Prometheus bring to men. She hated the poor, low, thin, unprofitable, unpoetical Humanitarians as the devastators of the Church & robbers of the soul & never wearies with piling on them new terms of slight & weariness. "Ah!" she said, "what a poet would Byron have been, if he had been born & bred a Calvinist!"

May 1841

General Harrison was neither Whig nor Tory, but the Indignation President; and, what was not at all surprising in this puny generation, he could not stand the excitement of seventeen millions of people but died of the Presidency in one month. A man should have a heart & a trunk vascular and on the Scale of the Aqueducts or the Cloaca Maxima of Rome to bear the friction of such a Missisippi stream.

May 28, 1841

I gave you enough to eat & I never beat you: what more can the woman ask? said the Good Husband.

June 6, 1841

I am sometimes discontented with my house because it lies on a dusty road and with its sills & cellar almost in the water of the meadow. But when I creep out of it into the Night or the Morning and see what majestic & what tender beauties daily wrap me in their bosom, how near to me is every transcendant secret of Nature's love & religion, I see how indifferent it is where I eat & sleep. This very street of hucksters & taverns the moon will transform to a Palmyra, for she is the apologist of all apologists & will kiss the elm-trees alone & hides every meanness in a silver edged darkness. Then the good river-god has taken the form of my valiant Henry Thoreau here & introduced me to the riches of his shadowy starlit, moonlit stream, a lovely new world lying as close & yet as unknown to this vulgar trite one of streets & shops as death to life or poetry to prose. Through one field only we went to the boat & then left all time, all science, all history behind us and entered into Nature with one stroke of a paddle. Take care, good friend! I said, as I looked west into the sunset overhead & underneath, & he with his face toward me rowed towards it—take care; you know not what you do, dipping your wooden oar into this enchanted liquid, painted with all reds & purples & yellows which glows under & behind you. Presently this glory faded & the stars came & said "Here we are," & began to cast such private & ineffable beams as to stop all conversation.

June? 1841

We are too civil to books. For a few golden sentences we will turn over & actually read a volume of 4 or 500 pages. Even the great books. 'Come,' say they, 'we will give you the key to the world'—Each poet each philosopher says this, & we expect to go like a thunderbolt to the centre, but the thunder is a superficial phenomenon, makes a skin-deep cut, and so does the Sage—whether Confucius, Menu, Zoroaster, Socrates; striking at right angles to the globe his force is instantly diffused laterally & enters not. The wedge turns out to be a rocket. I have found this to be the case with every book I have read & yet I take up a new writer with a sort of pulse beat of expectation.

July? 1841

I value my welfare too much to pay you any longer the compliment of attentions. I shall not draw the thinnest veil over my defects, but if you are here, you shall see me as I am. You will then see that though I am full of tenderness, and born with as large hunger to love & to be loved as any man can be, yet its demonstrations are not active & bold, but are passive & tenacious. My love has no flood & no ebb, but is always there under my silence, under displeasure, under cold, arid, and even weak behaviour.

July 1841

If I were a preacher, I should carry straight to church the remark Lidian made today, that "she had been more troubled by piety in her *help* than with any other fault." The girls that are not pious, she finds kind & sensible, but the church members are scorpions, too religious to do their duties, and full of wrath & horror at her if she does them.

If I should or could record the true experience of my late years, I should have to say that I skulk & play a mean, shiftless, subaltern part much the largest part of the time. Things are to be done which I have no skill to do, or are to be said which others can say better, and I lie by, or occupy my hands with something which is only an apology for idleness until my hour comes again. Thus how much of my reading & all my labor in house or garden seems mere waiting: any other could do it as well or better. It really seems to me of no importance—so little skill enters into these works, so little do they mix with my universal life— what I do, whether I hoe, or turn a grindstone, or copy manuscript, or eat my dinner. All my virtue consists in my consent to be insignificant which consent is founded on my faith in the great Optimism, which will justify itself to me at last.

Lidian says that the only sin which people never forgive in each other is a difference of opinion.

July–Aug. 1841

The Church aerates my good neighbors & serves them as a somewhat stricter & finer ablution than a clean shirt or a bath or a shampooing. The minister is a functionary & the meetinghouse a functionary: they are one and when they have spent all their week in private & selfish

action the Sunday reminds them of a need they have to stand again in
social & public & ideal relations—beyond neighborhood—higher than
the town-meeting—to their fellow men. They marry, & the minister
who represents this high Public, celebrates the fact; their child is baptized & again they are published by his intervention. One of their family
dies, he comes again, & the family go up publicly to the Church to be
publicised or churched in this official sympathy of mankind. It is all
good as far as it goes. It is homage to the Ideal Church, which they have
not; which the actual Church so foully misrepresents. But it is better so
than nohow. These people have no fine arts, no literature, no great men
to boswellize, no fine speculation to entertain their family board or their
solitary toil with. Their talk is of oxen & pigs & hay & corn & apples.
Whatsoever liberal aspirations they at any time have, whatsoever spiritual experiences, have looked this way, and the church is their fact for
such things. It has not been discredited in their eyes as books, lectures,
or living men of genius have been. It is still to them the accredited symbol of the religious Idea. The Church is not to be defended against any
spiritualist clamoring for its reform, but against such as say it is expedient to shut it up & have none, thus much may be said. It stands in the
history of the present time as a high school for the civility & mansue-
tude of the people.

The Metamorphosis of nature shows itself in nothing more than this
that there is no word in our language that cannot become typical to us of
nature by giving it emphasis. The world is a Dancer; it is a Rosary; it is a
Torrent; it is a Boat; a Mist; a Spider's Snare; it is what you will; and the
metaphor will hold, & it will give the imagination keen pleasure. Swifter
than light the World converts itself into that thing you name & all things
find their right place under this new & capricious classification. There is
no thing small or mean to the soul. It derives as grand a joy from sym-
bolizing the Godhead or his Universe under the form of a moth or a gnat
as of a Lord of Hosts. Must I call the heaven & the earth a maypole &
country fair with booths or an anthill or an old coat in order to give you
the shock of pleasure which the imagination loves and the sense of spiritual greatness? Call it a blossom, a rod, a wreath of parsley, a tamarisk-
crown, a cock, a sparrow, the ear instantly hears & the spirit leaps to the
trope; and hence it is that men of eloquence like Chatham have found a
Dictionary very suggestive reading when they were disposed to speak.

We all know enough to be endless writers. Those who have written
best are not those who have known most, but those to whom writing
was natural & necessary.

Let us answer a book of ink with a book of flesh & blood.
All writing comes by the grace of God.

Aug. 1841

I remember when a child in the pew on Sundays amusing myself
with saying over common words as "black," "white," "board," &c
twenty or thirty times, until the word lost all meaning & fixedness, & I
began to doubt which was the right name for the thing, when I saw that
neither had any natural relation, but all were arbitrary. It was a child's
first lesson in Idealism.

How readily we join certain persons in our thought. Among my
friends I couple particular names as naturally as I say apples & pears.

Long ago I said, I have every inch of my merits allowed me, & was
sad because my success was more than I deserved—sad for others who
had less. Now the beam trembles, & I see with some bitterness the slender claims I can make on fortune & the inevitable parsimony with which
they will be answered.

When we are old, we have not an assurance that we are wanted. We
need a continual reinforcement of compliments to certify us.

I saw a young man who had a rare gift for pulpit eloquence: his
whole constitution seemed to qualify him for that office and to see &
hear him produced an effect like a strain of music: not what he said but
the pleasing efflux of the spirit of the man through his sentences & gesture, suggested a thousand things, and I enjoyed it as I do painting or
poetry, & said to myself, "Here is creation again." I was touched &
taken out of my numbness & unbelief & wished to go out & speak &
write all things. After months I heard the favored youth speak again.
Perhaps I was critical, perhaps he was cold. But too much praise I fancied had hurt him, had given to his flowing gesture the slightest possible
fixedness; to his glowing rhetoric an artful return; it was later in the season yet the plant was all in flower still & no signs of fruit. Could the
flowers be barren or was an artificial stimulus kept upon the plant to
convert all the leaves & fruitbuds to flowers? We love young bachelors
& maidens but not old bachelors & old maids. It seemed to me that I had
seen before an example of the finest graces of youthful eloquence hardened by the habit of haranguing into grimace. It seemed that if instead
of the certainty of a throng of admirers the youth had felt assured every
Sunday that he spoke to hunger & debt, to lone women & poor boys, to
grief & to the friends of some sick or insane or felonious person, he
would have lopped some of these redundant flowers, & given us with all

the rest one or two plain & portable propositions. Praise is not so safe as austere exactors. And of all teachers of eloquence the best is a man's own penitence & shame.

Our forefathers walked in the world & went to their graves tormented with the fear of sin & the terror of the Day of Judgment. We are happily rid of those terrors, and our torment is the utter uncertainty & perplexity of what we ought to do; the distrust of the value of what we do; and the distrust that the Necessity which we all at last believe in, is Fair.

Aug.–Sept. 1841

It is strange that this world should be a world of approximations. Every vessel has a false bottom. Every end is temporary, a make-shift, & a round & final success nowhere. Our literatures make some figure, but have not a square inch of firm immortal texture. Our music is an effort merely, and is good only to the dull ear. Our appetites are never satisfied for so much as a moment. Hunger & thirst lead us on to eat & to drink; but bread & wine, vary & cook them how you will, leave us hungry & thirsty after the belly is full. In all things the promise outruns the performance.

At Cambridge, the last Wednesday I met twenty members of my college class & spent the day with them. . . . It was strange how fast the company returned to their old relation and the whole mass of college nonsense came back in a flood. They all associated perfectly, were an unit for the day—men who now never meet. Each resumed his old place. The change in them was really very little in 20 years although every man present was married & all but one fathers. I too resumed my old place & found myself as of old a spectator rather than a fellow. I drank a great deal of wine (for me) with the wish to raise my spirits to the pitch of good fellowship, but wine produced on me its old effect, & I grew graver with every glass. Indignation & eloquence will excite me, but wine does not. One poor man came whom fortune had not favored, & we carried round a hat, & collected $115.00 for him in two minutes.

Almost all these were prosperous men, but there was something sad and affecting in their prosperity. Very easy it was to see that each owed his success to some one trait or talent not supported by his other properties. There is no symmetry in great men of the first or of the tenth class. Often the division of talents is very minute. One man can pronounce well; another has a voice like a bell and the "orotund tone." Edward Everett's beautiful elocution & rhetoric had charms for the dull. I remember Charles Jarvis in my class who said "he did not care what the subject was, he would hear him lecture on Hebrew or Persian." There is this pleasure in a class meeting: Each has been thoroughly measured & known to the other as a boy, and they are not to be imposed upon by later circumstances & acquisitions. One is a governor of a state, one is a President of a college, one is President of a senate, two or three are Bank Presidents. They have removed from New Hampshire or from Massachusetts or from Vermont into the state where they live. Well all these are imposing facts in the new neighborhood, in the imaginations of the young men among whom they come; but not for us. When they come into the presence of either of their old mates, off goes every disguise, & the boy meets the boy as of old. This was ludicrously illustrated in the good story Wood told us of his visit to Moody in his office among his clients at Bangor. "How are you, Moody," with a slap on the back. "How do you do, sir," with a stare & a civil but formal bow. "Sir you have the advantage of me." "Yes and I mean to keep it. But I am in no hurry. Go on with your business. I will sit here & look at this newspaper until your client is gone." M. looked up every now & then from his bond & his bondsman but could not recollect the stranger. By & by they were left alone. "Well" said Wood "And you have not found me out?" "*Hell!*" cried Moody with the utmost prolongation of accent, "it's Wood!"

For me, what I may call the autumnal style of Montaigne keeps all its old attraction.

Waldo's diplomacy in giving account of Ellen's loud cries declares that she put her foot into his sand house & *got pushed.*

Sept. 4–8, 1841
I suppose there is no more abandoned Epicure or opium eater than I. I taste every hour of these autumn days. Every light from the sky, every shadow on the earth ministers to my pleasure. I love this gas. I grudge to move or to labor or to change my book or to will, lest I should disturb the sweet dream.

Sept. 9, 1841
Rightly says Elizabeth Hoar, that we do not like to hear our authors censured, for we love them by sympathy as well as for cause, and do not wish to have a reason put in the mouth of their enemies.

Sept. 12–20, 1841
We are all of us very near to sublimity. As one step freed Wordsworth's Recluse on the mountains from the blinding mist & brought him to the view of "Glory beyond all glory ever seen" so near are we all

to a vision of which Homer & Shakspeare are only hints & types and yet cannot we take that one step. It does not seem worth our while to toil for anything so pitiful as skill to do one of the little feats we magnify so much, when presently the dream will scatter & we shall burst into universal power. The reason of all idleness & of all crime is the same. Whilst we are waiting we beguile the time, one with jokes, one with sleep, one with eating, one with crimes.

Sept. 21, 1841

Dr Ripley died this morning. The fall of this oak of ninety years makes some sensation in the forest old & doomed as it was. He has identified himself with the forms at least of the old church of the New England Puritans; his nature was eminently loyal, not in the least adventurous or democratical & his whole being leaned backward on the departed so that he seemed one of the rearguard of this great camp & army which have filled the world with fame & with him passes out of sight almost the last banner & guide's flag of a mighty epoch. For these men however in our last days they have declined into ritualists, solemnized the heyday of their strength by the planting & the liberating of America.

Great, grim, earnest men I belong by natural affinity to other thoughts & schools than yours but my affection hovers respectfully about your retiring footprints, your unpainted churches, street platforms & sad offices, the iron-gray deacon & the wearisome prayer rich with the diction of ages. Well the new is only the seed of the old. What is this abolition & non-resistance & temperance but the continuation of Puritanism tho' it operate inevitably the destruction of the church in which it grew, as the new is always making the old superfluous.

Dr R. was a gentleman, no dandy: courtly, hospitable, manly, public spirited: his nature social, his house open to all men. Mr R. H., I remember, said "No horse from the eastern country would go by his gate." His brow serene & open for he had no studies, no occupations which company could interrupt. To see his friends unloosed his tongue & talents: they were his study. His talk was chiefly narrative: a man of anecdote he told his stories admirably well. Indeed all his speech was form & pertinence itself. There was no architect of sentences who built them so well. In private discourse or in debate of a more public kind the structure of his speech was perfect, so neat, so natural, so terse, no superfluous clause, his words fell like stones. & commonly tho' quite unconscious of it his speech was a satire on the loose, voluminous, draggletail periods of other speakers. He sat down when he had done. A foresight he had when he opened his mouth of all that he would say & he marched straight to the conclusion. E.B.E. used to say that "a man who could tell a story so well was company for kings & John Quincy Adams." His knowledge was an external experience, an Indian wisdom, the observation of such facts as country life for nearly a hundred years could supply. He sympathized with the cow, the horse, the sheep, & the dog whose habits he had watched so long & so friendly. For those who do not separate poetry blend it with things. His eye was always on the horizon & he knew the weather like a sea captain. All the plain facts of humanity—birth, marriage, sickness, death, the common temptations, the common ambitions—he knew them all & sympathized so well that as long as the fact was quite low & external he was very good company & counsel, but he never divined, never speculated, & you might as well ask his hill to understand or sympathize with an extraordinary state of mind, an enthusiasm or an Idea as ask him. What he did not, he affected not to do. There was no nonsense about him. He was always sincere, & true to his mark & his mark was never remote. But his conversation was always strictly personal & apt to the party & the occasion. An eminent skill he had in saying difficult & unspeakable things, saying to a man or woman that which all his other friends abstained from saying, uncovering the bandages from the sore place & applying the surgeon's knife with a truly surgical skill. Was a man a sot or too long a bachelor, or suspected of some secret crime or had he quarreled with his wife or collared his father or was there any cloud or suspicious circumstance in his behavior the doctor leaped on the quarry like hunter on his game. He thought himself entitled to an explanation & whatever relief to one or both parties plain speech could effect that was procured. Right manly he was & the manly thing he could always say. When Put. Meriam that graduate of the State Prison had the effrontery to call within the last year on the Doctor as an old acquaintance, in the midst of general conversation Mr Frost came in & the Doctor presently said, "Mr Meriam, here is my brother & colleague Mr Frost, has come to take tea with me. I regret very much the causes which you know very well, that make it impossible for me to ask you to stay & take bread with us." For the man had for years been setting at defiance every thing which the Doctor esteemed social & sacred. Another man might easily have taken another view of his duty but with the doctor's views it was a matter of religion to say thus much. I liked very well his speech to Charles Miles at the funeral of his father. Mr Miles was supposed to be in bad habits when his father died. "Sir, I condole with you; Madam I condole with you; Sir, I knew your great grandfather. When I came to this town, your great grandfather was a substantial farmer in this very place & an excellent citizen. Your grandfather followed him & was a virtuous man. Now your father has gone to his grave full of labors & virtues. There is none of that large family left, but you, and it rests with you to bear up the good name & usefulness of your ancestors. If you fail—Ichabod—the glory is departed. &c. &c.

He was the more competent to these searching discourses from his long family knowledge. He knew everybody's grandfather. This day has perished more history, more local & personal anecdote for this village & vicinity than in any ten men who have died in it before. He was the patriarch of all the tribe and his manners had a natural dignity that comported with his office. The same skill of speech made him incomparable in his parochial visits and in his exhortations & prayers with the sick & mourners. He gave himself up to his feeling & said the best things in the world . . . Many & many a felicity he had in his prayer now forever lost which eclipsed all the rules of all the rhetoricians. He did not know when he was good in prayer or sermon, for he had no literature & no art. But he believed & therefore spoke. He was sincere in his attachment to forms & he was the genuine fruit of a ritual church. The incarnation of the platform of the Puritan Church. A modern Israelite, a believer in the Genius or Jehovah of the Jews to the very letter. His prayers for rain & against the lightning, "that it may not lick up our spirits," and for good weather & against "these violent sudden changes" and against sickness & insanity & the like, all will remember. I remember his pleading almost reproachful looks at the sky when the thundergust was coming up to spoil his hay—"We are in the Lord's hand," he said & seemed to say "You know me: this field is mine, Dr Ripley's thine own servant." He was a punctual fulfiller of all duties. What order! what prudence! no waste, & no stint. Always open handed; just & generous. My little boy a week ago carried him a peach in a calabash but the calabash brought home two pears. I carried him melons in a basket but the basket came home with apples. He subscribed to all charities; he was the most public spirited citizen in this town; he gave the land for the monument. He knew the value of a dollar as well as another man. Yet he always sold cheaper than any other man. If the fire bell rang he was on horseback in a minute & away with his buckets & bag.

Wo that the linden & the vine should bloom
And a just man be gathered to the tomb.

But out of his own ground he was not good for aught. To talk with the insane he was as mad as they; to speculate with the thoughtful & the haters of forms he was lost & foolish. He was credulous & the dupe of Colonizationist or Antipapist or any charlatan of iron combs or tractors or phrenology or magnetism who went by. Credulous & opinionative, a great brow beater of the poor old fathers who still survived from the Nineteenth of April in order to make them testify to his history as he had written it. A man of no enthusiasm, no sentiment. His horror at the doctrine of non-resistance was amusing, for he actually believed that once abrogate the laws, promiscuous union of the sexes would instantly take place!

He was a man very easy to read, for his whole life & conversation was consistent & transparent: all his opinions & actions might be certainly predicted by any one who had good opportunities of seeing him. In college, F King told me from Governor Gore who was the Doctor's classmate, he was called "Holy Ripley," perhaps in derision, perhaps in sadness. And now in his old age when all the antique Hebraism & customs are going to pieces it is fit he too should depart, most fit that in the fall of laws a loyal man should die.

Shall I not say in general, of him, that, given his constitution, his life was harmonious & perfect.

His body is a handsome & noble spectacle. My mother was moved just now to call it "the beauty of the dead." He looks like a sachem fallen in the forest, or rather like "a warrior taking his rest with his martial cloak around him". I carried Waldo to see him & he testified neither repulsion nor surprise, but only the quietest curiosity. He was ninety years old the last May, yet this face has the tension & resolution of vigorous manhood. He has been a very temperate man.

Sept. 28, 1841

Every man, no doubt, is eloquent once in his life. The only difference betwixt us is that we boil at different degrees of the thermometer. This man is brought to the boiling point by the excitement of conversation in the parlor; that man requires the additional caloric of a large meeting, a public debate; and a third needs an antagonist or a great indignation; a fourth must have a revolution; and a fifth nothing less than the grandeur of absolute Ideas, the splendors of Heaven & Hell, the vastness of truth & love.

Sept.? 1841

Queenie (who has a gift to curse & swear) will every now & then in spite of all manners & christianity rip out on Saints, reformers, & Divine Providence with the most edifying zeal. In answer to the good Burrill Curtis who asks whether trade will not check the free course of love she insists "it shall be said that there is no love to restrain the course of, & never was, that poor God did all he could, but selfishness fairly carried the day."

* * *

I told H.T. that his freedom is in the form, but he does not disclose new matter. I am very familiar with all his thoughts—they are my own quite originally drest. But if the question be, what new ideas has he thrown into circulation, he has not yet told what that is which he was created to say. I said to him what I often feel, I only know three persons who seem to me fully to see this law of reciprocity or compensation—himself, Alcott, & myself: and 'tis odd that we should all be neighbors, for in the wide land or the wide earth I do not know another who seems to have it as deeply & originally as these three Gothamites.

Oct. 1841

I would have my book read as I have read my favorite books not with explosion & astonishment, a marvel and a rocket, but a friendly & agreeable influence stealing like the scent of a flower or the sight of a new landscape on a traveller. I neither wish to be hated & defied by such as I startle, nor to be kissed and hugged by the young whose thoughts I stimulate.

The sum of life ought to be valuable when the fractions & particles are so sweet. A man cannot resist the sweet excitements of opium or brandy. Well then, the universe must be worth somewhat.

The *Daguerrotype* is good for its authenticity. No man quarrels with his shadow, nor will he with his miniature when the sun was the painter. Here is no interference and the distortions are not the blunders of an artist, but only those of motion, imperfect light, & the like.

The view taken of Transcendentalism in State Street is that it threatens to invalidate contracts.

Men shall not, like poultry, eat all day.

Plutarch's heroes are my friends & relatives.

Oct. 12, 1841

I would that I could, I know afar off that I cannot give the lights & shades, the hopes & outlooks that come to me in these strange, cold-warm, attractive-repelling conversations with Margaret, whom I always admire, most revere when I nearest see, and sometimes love, yet whom I freeze, & who freezes me to silence, when we seem to promise to come nearest. Yet perhaps my old motto holds true here also

"And the more falls I get, move faster on."

Oct. 14, 1841

It is not the proposition but the tone that signifies. Is it a man that speaks, or the mimic of a man? Universal Whiggery is tame & weak. Every proclamation, dinner-speech, report of victory, or protest against the government it publishes betrays its thin & watery blood. It is never serene nor angry nor formidable, neither cool nor red hot. Instead of having its own aims passionately in view, it cants about the policy of a Washington & a Jefferson. It speaks to expectation and not the torrent of its wishes & needs, waits for its antagonist to speak that it may have something to oppose, and, failing that, having nothing to say is happy to hurrah. What business have Washington or Jefferson in this age? You must be a very dull or a very false man if you have not a better & more advanced policy to offer than they had. They lived in the greenness & timidity of the political experiment. The kitten's eyes were not yet opened. They shocked their contemporaries with their daring wisdom: have you not something which would have shocked *them*? If not, be silent, for others have.

Oct. 16, 1841

I saw in Boston Fanny Elsller in the ballet of Nathalie. She must show, I suppose, the whole compass of her instrument and add to her softest graces of motion or "the wisdom of her feet"—the feats of the rope dancer & tumbler: and perhaps on the whole the beauty of the exhibition is enhanced by this that is strong & strange, as when she stands erect on the extremities of her toes, or on one toe, or "performs the impossible" in attitude, but the chief beauty is in the extreme grace of her movement, the variety & nature of her attitude, the winning fun & spirit of all her little coquetries, the beautiful erectness of her body & the freedom & determination which she can so easily assume, and what struck me much the air of perfect sympathy with the house and that mixture of deference and conscious superiority which puts her in perfect spirits & equality to her part. When she courtesies, her sweet & slow & prolonged Salam which descends & still descends whilst the curtain falls, until she seems to have invented new depths of grace & condescension, she earns well the profusion of bouquets of flowers which are hurled on to the stage. . . .

But over & above her genius for dancing are the incidental vices of this individual, her own false taste or her meretricious arts to please the groundlings & which must displease the judicious. The immorality the immoral will see, the very immoral will see that only, the pure will not heed it, for it is not obtrusive, perhaps will not see it at all. I should not think of danger to young women stepping with their father or brother out of happy & guarded parlors into this theatre to return in a few hours to the same; but I can easily suppose that it is not the safest resort for college boys who have left Metaphysics, Conic Sections, or Tacitus to see these tripping satin slippers and they may not forget this graceful silvery swimmer when they have retreated again to their baccalaureate cells.

It is a great satisfaction to see the best in each kind, and as a good student of the world, I desire to let pass nothing that is excellent in its own kind unseen, unheard.

Oct. 16? 1841

I saw Webster in the street—but he was changed since I saw him last—black as a thunder cloud, & care worn: the anxiety that withers this generation among the young & thinking class had crept up also into the great lawyer's chair, & too plainly, too plainly he was one of us. I did not wonder that he depressed his eyes when he saw me, and would not meet my face. The canker worms have crawled to the topmost bough of the wild elm & swing down from that. No wonder the elm is a little uneasy.

Every body, old men, young women, boys, play the doctor with me & prescribe for me. They always did so.

Oct. 1841

I told Garrison that I thought he must be a very young man or his time hang very heavy on his hands who can afford to think much & talk much about the foibles of his neighbors, or 'denounce' and play 'the son of thunder' as he called it. I am one who believe all times to be pretty much alike and yet I sympathize so keenly with this. We want to be expressed, yet you take from us War, that great opportunity which allowed the accumulations of electricity to stream off from both poles, the positive & the negative. Well, now you take from us our cup of alcohol as before you took our cup of wrath. We had become canting moths of peace, our helm was a skillet, & now we must become temperance watersops. You take away, but what do you give me? Mr Jefts has been preached into tipping up his barrel of rum into the brook, but day after tomorrow when he ·vakes up cold & poor, will he feel that he has somewhat for somewhat? No, this is mere thieving hypocrisy & poaching. If I could lift him by happy violence into a religious beatitude, or into a Socratic trance & imparadise him in ideas, or into the pursuit of human beauty a divine lover, then should I have greatly more than indemnified him for what I have taken. I should not take, he would put away, or rather ascend out of this litter & sty, in which he had rolled, to go up clothed & in his right mind into the assembly & conversation of men. I fight in my fashion but you, o paddies & roarers, must not fight in yours. I drink my tea & coffee, but as for you & your cups, here is the pledge & the Temperance Society. I walk on Sundays & read Aristophanes & Rabelais in church hours; but for you, go to Church. Good vent or bad we must have for our nature, somewhere we must let out all the length of all the reins. Make love a crime & we shall have lust. If you cannot contrive to raise us up to the love of science & make brute matter our antagonist which we shall have joy in handling, mastering, penetrating, condensing to adamant, dissolving to light, then we must brawl, carouse, gamble, or go to bullfights. If we can get no full demonstration of our heart & mind we feel wronged & incarcerated: the philosophers & divines we shall hate most, as the upper turnkeys. We wish to take the gas which allows us to break through your wearisome proprieties, to plant the foot, to set the teeth, to fling abroad the arms, & dance & sing.

H. is a person of extraordinary health & vigor, of unerring perception, & equal expression; and yet he is impracticable, and does not flow through his pen or (in any of our legitimate aqueducts) through his tongue. A. stands for Spirit itself & yet when he writes, he babbles. When he acts, the ladies find something very unsightly which he can very well explain to himself and which I like well enough but they set their faces like a flint against him, and that makes him feel uncomfortable, then is he less himself, is belligerent, unhappy, & thoughtless.

Nobody can oppress me but myself. Once more, the degradation of that black race, though now lost in the starless spaces of the past, did not come without sin. The condition is inevitable to the men they are, & nobody can redeem them but themselves. An infusion from God of new thought & grace can retrieve their loss, but nothing less. The exertions of the abolitionist are nugatory except for themselves. As far as they can emancipate the North from Slavery, well.

Mrs B. inquires whether Transcendentalism does not mean Sloth, for the moment people are classed under that name they sit down & do nothing. I think that the virtue of some persons is now to sit & wait—though all the saints should wonder. "She had as lief hear that they were dead as that they were Transcendentalists—they are paralysed & never do anything for humanity" said Mrs B.

"What are you doing Zek?" said Judge Webster to his eldest boy. "Nothing."
"What are you doing, Daniel?"

"Helping Zek."
A tolerably correct account of most of our activity today.

It seems to me sometimes that we get our education ended a little too quick in this country. As soon as we have learned to read & write & cipher, we are dismissed from school & we set up for ourselves. We are writers & leaders of opinion & we write away without check of any kind, play whatsoever mad prank, indulge whatever spleen or oddity or obstinacy comes into our dear head and even feed our complacency thereon and thus fine wits come to nothing as good horses spoil themselves by running away & straining themselves. I cannot help seeing that Dr Channing would have been a much greater writer had he found a strict tribunal of writers, a graduated intellectual empire established in the land & knew that bad logic would not pass & that the most severe exaction was to be made on all who enter these lists. Now if a man can write a paragraph for a newspaper, next year he writes what he calls a history and reckons himself a classic incontinently. Nor will his contemporaries in Critical Journal or Review question his claims. It is very easy to reach the degree of culture that prevails around us, very hard to pass it and Dr C. had he found Wordsworth, Southey, Coleridge, & Lamb around him would as easily have been severe with himself & risen a degree higher as he has stood where he is. I mean of course a genuine intellectual tribunal not a literary junto of Edinburg Wits or dull conventions of Quarterly or Gentleman's Reviews. . . . I wish that the writers of this country would begin where they now end their culture.

Every young person writes a journal into which when the hours of prayer & penitence arrive he puts his soul. The pages which he has written in the rapt moods are to him burning & fragrant. He reads them on his knees by midnight & by the morning star he wets them.

Oct. 21, 1841
And why not draw for these times a portrait gallery? . . . A camera! A camera! cries the century, that is the only toy. Come let us paint the agitator and the dilettante and the member of Congress and the college professor, the Unitarian minister, the editor of the newspaper, the fair contemplative girl, the aspirant for fashion & opportunities, the woman of the world who has tried & knows better—let us examine how well she knows. Good fun it would be for a master who with delicate finger in the most decisive yet in the most parliamentary & unquestionable manner should indicate all the lions by traits not to be mistaken yet so that none should dare wag his finger whilst the shadow of each well known form flitted for a moment across the wall. So should we have at last if it

were done well a series of sketches which would report to the next ages the color & quality of ours.

Yet is it not ridiculous this that we do in this languid idle trick that we have gradually fallen into of writing & writing without end. After a day of humiliation & stripes if I can write it down I am straightway relieved & can sleep well. After a day of joy the beating heart is calmed again by the diary.

Oct. 22, 1841

A nightmare is very bad company as long as it stays: a shower-bath, a shampooing, a sea voyage may be prescribed.

Immanuel Kant said Detestable is the company of literary men.

Margaret is "a being of unsettled rank in the Universe". So proud & presumptuous yet so meek; so worldly and artificial & with keenest sense & taste for all pleasures of luxurious society, yet living more than any other for long periods in a trance of religious sentiment; a person who according to her own account of herself, expects everything for herself from the Universe.

Oct. 23, 1841

We forget in taking up a cotemporary book that we see the house that is building & not the house that is built. A glance at my own MSS. might teach me that all my poems are unfinished, heaps of sketches but no masterpiece, yet when I open a printed volume of poems, I look imperatively for art.

I think Society has the highest interest in seeing that this movement called the Transcendental is no boys' play or girls' play but has an interest very near & dear to them. That it has a necessary place in history is a Fact not to be overlooked, not possibly to be prevented, and however discredited to the heedless & to the moderate & conservative persons by the foibles or inadequacy of those who partake the movement yet is it the pledge & the herald of all that is dear to the human heart, grand & inspiring to human faith.

I think the genius of this age more philosophical than any other has been, righter in its aims, truer, with less fear, less fable, less mixture of any sort.

Oct. 24, 1841

Life in Boston: A play in two acts, Youth & Age. Toys, dancing school, *Sets*, parties, picture galleries, sleighrides, Nahant, Saratoga

Springs, lectures, concerts, *sets* through them all, solitude & poetry, friendship, ennui, desolation, decline, meanness, plausibility, old age, death.

Oct. 30, 1841

On this wonderful day when Heaven & earth seem to glow with magnificence & all the wealth of all the elements is put under contribution to make the world fine as if Nature would indulge her offspring it seemed ungrateful to hide in the house. Are there not dull days enough in the year for you to write & read in that you should waste this glittering season when Florida & Cuba seem to have left their seats & come to visit us with all their shining Hours and almost we expect to see the jasmine & the cactus burst from the ground instead of these last gentians & asters which have loitered to attend this latter glory of the year. All insects are out, all birds come forth, the very cattle that lie on the ground seem to have great thoughts & Egypt & India look from their eyes.

Oct.–Nov. 1841

Shelley is wholly unaffecting to me. I was born a little too soon: but his power is so manifest over a large class of the best persons, that he is not to be overlooked.

The Yankee in Ohio could he keep the habits of the Yankee in Massachusetts would be a very rich man. But the easiness of securing a subsistence keeps him always poor. In like manner we learn here to write & spell & then finding that we know as much as our neighbors, shut our books & cut our quills into toothpicks. Our vast ignorance & incuriosity rest like this thin religion of the day on a yawning gulf of skepticism. We do not believe in Man or in God, in no high & hopeful destiny, & so we console us with the first trifles that appear, an invitation to dinner, or three weeks at Nahant.

Great causes are never tried, assaulted, or defended on their merits: they need so long perspective and the habits of the race are marked with so strong a tendency to particulars. The stake is Europe or Asia & the battle is for some contemptible village or doghutch. A man shares the new light that irradiates the world & promises the establishment of the kingdom of heaven and ends with champing unleavened bread or devoting himself to the nourishment of a beard or making a fool of himself about his hat or his shoes.

And where did you pick up all this heap of fripperies, Messer Lodovico Ariosto? said the duke to the poet. "Here in your court, your

Highness" he replied. I own that all my universal pictures are nothing but very private sketches; that I live in a small village, and am obliged to guess at the composition of society from very few & very obscure specimens, and to tell Revolutions of France by anecdotes, &c. &c. yet I supposed myself borne out in my confidence that each individual stands for a class by my own experience.

I have sympathy with war & sin, with pleasure & insanity, with sleep & death.

We are very near to greatness: one step & we are safe: can we not take the leap?

'Tis certain that the Daguerrotype is the true Republican style of painting. The Artist stands aside & lets you paint yourself. If you make an ill head, not he but yourself are responsible and so people who go Daguerrotyping have a pretty solemn time. They come home confessing & lamenting their sins. A Daguerrotype Institute is as good as a national Fast.

This discontent—this Ennui for which we Saxons had no name, this word of France—has become a word of terrific significance, a disease which shortens life & bereaves the day of its light.

Nov.-Dec. 1841
All writing is by the grace of God. People do not deserve to have good writing, they are so pleased with bad. In these sentences that you show me I can find no beauty, for I see death in every clause & every word. There is a fossil or a mummy character which pervades this book. The best sepulchres, the vastest catacombs, Thebes, & Cairo pyramids are sepulchres to me. I like gardens and nurseries. Give me initiative, spermatic, prophesying man-making words.

It is never worthwhile to worry people with your contritions. We shed our follies & absurdities as fast as the rosebugs drop off in July & leave the apple tree which they so threatened. Nothing dies so fast as a fault & the memory of a fault. I am awkward, sour, saturnine, lumpish, pedantic, & thoroughly disagreeable & oppressive to the people around me. Yet if I am born to write a few good sentences or verses, these shall endure & my disgraces utterly perish out of memory.

Dec. 1841
Mr Frost thought that there would not be many of these recusants who declared against the state &c. I told him he was like the good man of

Waldo Emerson (1836–1842): "A boy of early wisdom, of a grave
& even majestic deportment, of a perfect gentleness."

Noah's neighbors who said "Go to thunder with your old ark! I don't
think there'll be much of a shower."

Was any man ever all the time solid, and never a shrunken heap of
dry leaves or ashes? Today this restless being seems so perplexed &
mean, it has no future, it is a document of weakness & sin; and I can remember that I have been calm & great, or, at least called myself so.

Dec. 18, 1841

The reason offered why the legislature should not give money to
Harvard College to build their Library, was that Harvard had so much
already. But that is the very reason why it should have more: that certainly is its strongest claim at this moment. If I have a valuable antique
in my possession, I should not give it to a stage driver, but to some collector who had already a cabinet. Better yet, to a state- or national-cab-
inet, for then it would be sure to be seen by the greatest number of those
whom it concerned.

Experience
1842-1846

ONCE EMERSON HAD A DREAM that an angel brought him the world "diminished to the size of an apple" and bade him eat, which he did. If this dream symbolizes Emerson's hope that he might be equal to the task of digesting worldly experience, he was now entering a darker period of his life when that hope would be severely tested. By the middle of 1841 he could wonder whether "people expect the world to drop into their mouths like a peach." Six months later, on January 27, 1842, Emerson had a tragic response to that query when his beloved son Waldo, his namesake and firstborn, died from scarlet fever at the age of five. Emerson, to be sure, was no stranger to such grief. But the loss of Waldo was different from that of Ellen or his brothers. He learned that the death of one's child is the most terrible of all personal disasters. As he wrote later in "Threnody,"

> . . . this losing is true dying;
> This is lordly man's down-lying,
> This his slow but sure reclining,
> Star by star his world resigning.

Emerson tried hard to assimilate this crushing blow to his affirmative philosophy, asserting in April, for example, that he was born to victory despite the perpetual defeat of his hopes. Yet he seemed to "comprehend nothing of this fact but its bitterness." Two years later, in January 1844, he admitted to Margaret Fuller that he had "no experiences nor progress" to reconcile himself to the "calamity" whose second anniversary he was marking. The atmosphere in the Emerson household must have continued to be gloomy, if one is to judge by this canceled journal entry in 1843 (presumably quoting Lidian): "Dear husband, I wish I had never been born. I do not see how God can compensate me for the sorrow of existence."

Emerson himself had already argued for the sureness of "compensation" in his first book of essays, but now he seemed much less certain. Filled with a sense of the ephemerality of all things, he wrote the great essay "Experience" (published in his second series of *Essays* in 1844) in which he said that "the results of life are uncalculated and uncalculable." In his general mood of lapse and loss, Emerson conceived of the Fall of Man in existential terms as "the discovery we have made that we exist." Our painful awareness of the treacheries of experience, he now saw, defines the human condition. And even that awareness is partial and disjointed, for we are not constituted so as to be able to get our minds around the whole of experience. "I know better than to claim any completeness for my picture," he continues. "I am a fragment, and this is a fragment of me."

In April of 1842 Emerson had noted that if he were to write an "honest diary" it would have to show "that Life has halfness, shallowness." His journal for these years in fact became largely a record of diminishment and lack of clear direction. Life frequently looked mean and he felt himself "dying of miscellany." The world seemed filled with "snivelling nobodies," and he wondered that anyone managed to keep on going with so little aim. He dreamt—and awoke believing it to be true—that he was "living in the morning of history amidst barbarians, that right & truth had yet no voice, no letters, no law"; it was simply every man for himself. Or he could turn the fantasy around, as in an 1846 entry, and see himself living at the end of time, shorn of his wings by the "sins of our predecessors," which lie "on us like a mountain of obstruction."

Although the major reason for this obscuring of Emerson's Transcendental vision was obviously the weight of his own harsh experience, public events also played a part. The slavery issue was heating up, and Emerson was disgusted by the cravenness of Whig politics. He had hoped that the victory of William Henry Harrison over Van Buren in 1840 might signal a return to principle in American politics, but Harrison's death after only one month in office left John Tyler free to fall in line with his fellow

Southerners. Emerson was dismayed at Tyler's annexation of Texas, and he attended an indignation meeting in Concord in September 1845. In 1846 he predicted that the United States would conquer Mexico, "but it will be as the man swallows the arsenic, which brings him down in turn. Mexico will poison us." At all events, he did what he could to counteract the vicious drift of affairs by lecturing against slavery and supporting abolitionist speakers at the Concord Lyceum. He himself refused to lecture at the New Bedford Lyceum in November 1845 when he discovered that Negroes were excluded from membership. Emerson's remark, in his 1846 journal, that the question of slavery finally came down to the issue of private property, makes him sound like a proto-Marxist: "every man must do his own work, or, at least, receive no interest for money."

In these years, Emerson's dominant posture was that of the skeptic, and his patron saint was Montaigne, whom he lectured on in his "Representative Men" series in 1845–46. He no longer believed in great men; all finally were made of the same "common pottery." The gods had departed, and Emerson was learning to appreciate the fitful gleams of divinity that occasionally sparkle over human nature. The stance of Montaigne, the "considerer," epitomized Emerson's new position. He would carefully sift and weigh all the evidence and abstain from drawing rash conclusions. His denials, he insisted, would be made out of honesty. He would "rather stand charged with the imbecility of skepticism, than with untruth." Since the world is so enigmatic, he notes, we must learn to take things, not "literally, but genially." Lectures should not be approached as the gospel and the law handed down from Mt. Sinai, but simply as "a few reasonable words to keep us in mind of truth amidst our nonsense." The wise man will always be willing to weigh one definition, one point of view, against another. Thus, in this period of dubiety, Emerson could entertain both a multiplicity of skepticisms and an ultimate faith. One day he would observe that "the universe is like an infinite series of planes, each of which is a false bottom, and when we think our feet are planted now at last on the Adamant, the slide is drawn out from under us"; another day he would reply to his own bleak view by saying, "skepticism & again skepticism? Well, let abyss open under abyss, they are all contained & bottomed at last, & I have only to endure."

Jan. 28, 1842

Yesterday night at 15 minutes after eight my little Waldo ended his life.

Jan. 30, 1842

What he looked upon is better, what he looked not upon is insignificant. The morning of Friday I woke at 3 oclock, & every cock in every barnyard was shrilling with the most unnecessary noise. The sun went up the morning sky with all his light, but the landscape was dishonored by this loss. For this boy in whose remembrance I have both slept & awaked so oft, decorated for me the morning star, & the evening cloud, how much more all the particulars of daily economy; for he had touched with his lively curiosity every trivial fact & circumstance in the household, the hard coal & the soft coal which I put into my stove; the wood of which he brought his little quota for grandmother's fire, the hammer, the pincers, & file, he was so eager to use; the microscope, the magnet, the little globe, & every trinket & instrument in the study; the loads of gravel on the meadow, the nests in the henhouse and many & many a little visit to the doghouse and to the barn—For every thing he had his own name & way of thinking, his own pronunciation & manner. And every word came mended from that tongue. A boy of early wisdom, of a grave & even majestic deportment, of a perfect gentleness.

Every tramper that ever tramped is abroad but the little feet are still.

He gave up his little innocent breath like a bird.

He dictated a letter to his cousin Willie on Monday night to thank him for the Magic Lantern which he had sent him, and said I wish you would tell Cousin Willie that I have so many presents that I do not need that he should send me any more unless he wishes to very much.

The boy had his full swing in this world. Never I think did a child enjoy more. He had been thoroughly respected by his parents & those around him & not interfered with; and he had been the most fortunate in respect to the influences near him for his Aunt Elizabeth had adopted him from his infancy & treated him ever with that plain & wise love which belongs to her and, as she boasted, had never given him sugar plums. So he was won to her & always signalized her arrival as a visit to him & left playmates playthings & all to go to her. Then Mary Russell had been his friend & teacher for two summers with true love & wisdom. Then Henry Thoreau had been one of the family for the last year, & charmed Waldo by the variety of toys whistles boats popguns & all kinds of instruments which he could make & mend; & possessed his love & respect by the gentle firmness with which he always treated him.

Margaret Fuller & Caroline Sturgis had also marked the boy & caressed & conversed with him whenever they were here. Meantime every day his Grandmother gave him his reading lesson & had by patience taught him to read & spell; by patience & by love for she loved him dearly.

Sorrow makes us all children again, destroys all differences of intellect. The wisest knows nothing.

It seems as if I ought to call upon the winds to describe my boy, my fast receding boy, a child of so large & generous a nature that I cannot paint him by specialties, as I might another.

"Are there any other countries?" Yes. "I wish you to name the other countries"; so I went on to name London, Paris, Amsterdam, Cairo, &c. But HDT well said in allusion to his large way of speech that "his questions did not admit of an answer; they were the same which you would ask yourself."

He named the parts of the toy house he was always building by fancy names which had a good sound as "the Interspeglium" & "the Coridaga" which names he told Margaret "the children could not understand."

If I go down to the bottom of the garden it seems as if some one had fallen into the brook.

Every place is handsome or tolerable where he has been. Once he sat in the pew.

His house he proposed to build in summer of burs & in winter of snow.

"My music," he said, "makes the thunder dance;" for it thundered when he was blowing his willow whistle.

Mamma, may I have this bell which I have been making, to stand by the side of my bed.

Yes it may stand there.

But Mamma I am afraid it will alarm you. It may sound in the middle of the night and it will be heard over the whole town, it will be louder than ten thousand hawks it will be heard across the water, and in all the countries. It will be heard all over the world.

It will sound like some great glass thing which falls down & breaks all to pieces.

Jan.? 1842

I have seen the poor boy when he came to a tuft of violets in the wood, kneel down on the ground, smell of them, kiss them, & depart without plucking them.

For marriage find somebody that was born near the time when you were born.

> 28 January 1842
> Yesterday night at 15 minutes after eight my little Waldo ended his life.

Feb. 4, 1842

I have read that Sheridan made a good deal of *experimental writing* with a view to take what might fall, if any wit should transpire in all the waste pages. I in my dark hours may scratch the page if perchance any hour of recent life may project a hand from the darkness & inscribe a record. Twice today it has seemed to me that Truth is our only armor in all passages of life & death. Wit is cheap & anger is cheap, but nothing is gained by them.

Feb. 21, 1842

Home again from Providence to the deserted house. Dear friends find I, but the wonderful Boy is gone. What a looking for miracles have I! As his walking into the room where we are, would not surprise Ellen, so it would seem to me the most natural of all things.

March 18, 1842

Home from New York where I read six lectures on the Times viz. *Introductory;* The Poet; The Conservative; the Transcendentalist; Manners; Prospects. . . . My Lectures had about the same reception there as elsewhere: very fine & poetical but a little puzzling. One thought it "as good as a kaleidoscope". Another, a good Staten Islander, would go hear, "for he had heard I was a *rattler.*"

March 20, 1842

The Dial is to be sustained or ended & I must settle the question, it seems, of its life or death. I wish it to live but do not wish to be its life. Neither do I like to put it in the hands of the Humanity & Reform Men, because they trample on letters & poetry; nor in the hands of the Scholars, for they are dead & dry.

March 20–23, 1842

In New York lately, as in cities generally, one seems to lose all substance, & become surface in a world of surfaces. Every thing is external, and I remember my hat & coat, and all my other surfaces, & nothing else. If suddenly a reasonable question is addressed to me, what refreshment & relief! I visited twice & parted with a most polite lady without giving her reason to believe that she had met any other in me than a worshipper of surfaces, like all Broadway. It stings me yet.

This beloved and now departed Boy, this Image in every part beautiful, how he expands in his dimensions in this fond Memory to the dimensions of Nature!

March 23, 1842

Ellen asks her Grandmother "whether God can't stay alone with the angels a little while & let Waldo come down?"

And Amy Goodwin too thinks that "if God has to send any angel for anything to this world, he had better send Waldo."

The chrysalis which he brought in with care & tenderness & gave to his Mother to keep is still alive and he most beautiful of the children of men is not here.

I comprehend nothing of this fact but its bitterness. Explanation I have none, consolation none that rises out of the fact itself; only diversion; only oblivion of this & pursuit of new objects.

Ellen says, I believe God has a feeding-tire for Waldo up in heaven.

March–April 1842

Tecumseh: a Poem. A wellread clerical person with a skilful ear and with Scott & Campbell in full possession of his memory has written this poem in the feeling that the delight he has experienced from Scott's effective lists of names might be reproduced in America from the enumeration of the sweet or sonorous Indian names. The costume as is usual in all such essays crowds the man out of nature. The most Indian thing about the Indian is surely not his moccasins or his calumet, his wampum or his stone hatchet, but traits of character & sagacity, skill, or passion which would be intelligible to all men and which Scipio or Sidney or Col Worth or Lord Clive would be as likely to exhibit as Osceola & Black Hawk. As Johnson remarked that there was a middle style in English above vulgarity & below pedantry which never became obsolete & in which the plays of Shakspeare were written, so is there in human language a middle style proper to all nations & spoken by Indians & by Frenchmen so they be men of personal force.

Here prepares now the good A B Alcott to go to England after so long & strict acquaintance as I have had with him for seven years. I saw him for the first time in Boston in 1835. What shall we say of him to the wise Englishman? . . .

He delights in speculation, in nothing so much and is very well endowed & weaponed for that work with a copious, accurate, & elegant vocabulary; I may say poetic; so that I know no man who speaks such good English as he, and is so inventive withal. He speaks truth truly; or the expression is adequate. Yet he knows only this one language. He hardly needs an antagonist—he needs only an intelligent ear. Where he is greeted by loving & intelligent persons his discourse soars to a wonderful height, so regular, so lucid, so playful, so new & disdainful of all boundaries of tradition & experience, that the hearers seem no longer to have bodies or material gravity, but almost they can mount into the air at pleasure, or leap at one bound out of this poor solar system. I say this of his speech exclusively, for when he attempts to write, he loses, in my judgment, all his power, & I derive more pain than pleasure from the perusal. The Boston Post expressed the feeling of most readers in its rude joke when it said of his Orphic Sayings that they "resembled a train of 15 railroad cars with one passenger." . . .

It must be conceded that it is speculation which he loves & not action. Therefore he dissatisfies everybody & disgusts many. When the conversation is ended, all is over. He lives tomorrow as he lived today for further discourse, not to begin, as he seemed pledged to do, a New Celestial life. The ladies fancied that he loved cake; very likely; most people do. Yet in the last two years he has changed his way of living which was perhaps a little easy & selfindulgent for such a Zeno, so far as to become ascetically temperate. He has no vocation to labor, and, although he strenuously preached it for a time, & made some efforts to practise it, he soon found he had no genius for it, and that it was a cruel waste of his time. It depressed his spirits even to tears. . . .

Another circumstance marks this extreme love of speculation. He carries all his opinions & all his condition & manner of life in his hand, &, whilst you talk with him, it is plain he has put out no roots, but is an air-plant, which can readily & without any ill consequence be transported to any place. He is quite ready at any moment to abandon his present residence & employment, his country, nay, his wife & children, on very short notice, to put any new dream into practice which has bubbled up in the effervescence of discourse. If it is so with his way of living, much more so is it with his opinions. He never remembers. He never affirms anything today because he has affirmed it before. You are rather astonished, having left him in the morning with one set of opinions, to find him in the evening totally escaped from all recollection of them, as confident of a new line of conduct, & heedless of his old advocacy. *Sauve qui peut.* . . .

His vice, an intellectual vice, grew out of this constitution, & was that to which almost all spiritualists have been liable—a certain brooding on the private thought which produces monotony in the conversation, & egotism in the character. Steadily subjective himself, the variety of facts which seem necessary to the health of most minds, yielded him no variety of meaning, & he quickly quitted the play on objects, to come to *the Subject*, which was always the same, viz. *Alcott in reference to the World of Today.* . . .

Unhappily, his conversation never loses sight of his own personality. He never quotes; he never refers; his only illustration is his own biography. His topic yesterday is Alcott on the 17 October; today, Alcott on the 18 October; tomorrow, on the 19th. So will it be always. The poet rapt into future times or into deeps of nature admired for themselves, lost in their law, cheers us with a lively charm; but this noble genius discredits genius to me. I do not want any more such persons to exist. Part of this egotism in him is a certain comparing eye which seems to sour his view of persons prosperously placed, & to make his conversation often accusing & minatory. He is not selfsufficing & serene.

What for the visions of the Night? Our life is so safe & regular that we hardly know the emotion of terror. Neither public nor private violence, neither natural catastrophes, as earthquake, volcano, or deluge; nor the expectation of supernatural agents in the form of ghosts or of purgatory & devils & hellfire, disturb the sleepy circulations of our blood in these calm, well spoken days. And yet dreams acquaint us with what the day omits. Eat a hearty supper, tuck up your bed tightly, put an additional bedspread over your three blankets, & lie on your back, & you may, in the course of an hour or two, have this neglected part of your education in some measure supplied. Let me consider: I found myself in a garret disturbed by the noise of some one sawing wood. On walking towards the sound, I saw lying in a crib an insane person whom I very well knew, and the noise instantly stopped: there was no saw, a mere stirring among several trumpery matters, fur-muffs, & empty baskets that lay on the floor. As I tried to approach, the Muffs swelled themselves a little as with wind, & whirled off into a corner of the garret, as if alive, and a kind of animation appeared in all the objects in that corner. Seeing this, and instantly aware that here was Witchcraft, that here was a devilish Will which signified itself plainly enough in the stir & the sound of the wind, I was unable to move; my limbs were frozen with fear; I was bold & would go forward, but my limbs I could not move; I mowed the defiance I could not articulate & woke with the ugly sound I made. After I woke and recalled the impressions, my brain tingled with repeated vibrations of terror—and yet was the sensation pleasing, as it was a sort of rehearsal of a Tragedy.

April 6, 1842
Having once learned that in some one thing although externally small, greatness might be contained, so that in doing that, it was all one as if I had builded a world; I was thereby taught, that everything in nature should represent total nature; & that whatsoever thing did not represent to me the sea & sky, day & night, was something forbidden or wrong.

April 6–12, 1842
The history of Christ is the best document of the power of Character which we have. A youth who owed nothing to fortune & who was "hanged at Tyburn"—by the pure quality of his nature has shed this epic splendor around the facts of his death which has transfigured every

particular into a grand universal symbol for the eyes of all mankind ever since.

He did well. This great Defeat is hitherto the highest fact we have. But he that shall come shall do better. The mind requires a far higher exhibition of character, one which shall make itself good to the senses as well as to the soul; a success to the senses as well as to the soul. This was a great Defeat. We demand Victory. More character will convert judge & jury, soldier & king; will rule human & animal & mineral nature; will command irresistibly and blend with the course of Universal Nature.

In short there ought to be no such thing as Fate. As long as we use this word, it is a sign of our impotence & that we are not yet ourselves. There is now a sublime revelation in each of us which makes us so strangely aware & certain of our riches that although I have never since I was born for so much as one moment expressed the truth, and although I have never heard the expression of it from any other, I know that the whole is here—the wealth of the Universe is for me. Every thing is explicable & practicable for me. And yet whilst I adore this ineffable life which is at my heart, it will not condescend to gossip with me, it will not announce to me any particulars of science, it will not enter into the details of my biography, & say to me why I have a son & daughters born to me, or why my son dies in his sixth year of joy. Herein then I have this latent omniscience coexistent with omnigorance. Moreover, whilst this Deity glows at the heart, & by his unlimited presentiments gives me all power, I know that tomorrow will be as this day, I am a dwarf, & I remain a dwarf. That is to say, I believe in Fate. As long as I am weak, I shall talk of Fate; whenever the God fills me with his fulness, I shall see the disappearance of Fate.

I am *Defeated* all the time; yet to Victory I am born.

But the objection to idolatry of which all Christendom is guilty, why do you not feel, viz. that it is retrospective, whilst all the health & power of man consists in the prospective eye. A saint, an angel, a chorus of saints, a myriad of Christs, are alike worthless & forgotten by the soul as the leaves that fell or the fruit that was gathered in the garden of Eden in the golden age. A new day, a new harvest, new duties, new men, new fields of thought, new powers call you, and an eye fastened on the past unsuns nature, bereaves me of hope, & ruins me with a squalid indigence which nothing but death can adequately symbolize.

The school boys went on with their game of baseball without regard to the passenger, & the ball struck him smartly in the back. He was angry. Little cared the boys. If you had learned how to play when you was at school, they said, you would have known better than to be hit.

If you did not learn then, you had better stop short where you are, & learn now. Hit him again, Dick!

Last night I read many pages in *Chester Dewey's Report of Herbaceous Plants in Massachusetts*. With what delight we always come to these images! the mere names of reeds & grasses, of the milk weeds, of the mint tribe & the gentians, of mallows & trefoils, are a lively pleasure. The odorous waving of these children of beauty soothes & heals us. The names are poems often. *Erigeron* because it grows old early, is thus named *The Old man of the Spring*. The Pyrola umbellata is called *Chimaphila, Lover of Winter* because of its bright green leaves in the snow; called also Princes' Pine. The Plantain (splantago major) which follows man wherever he builds a hut, is called by the Indians "White man's foot." And it is always affecting to see Lidian or one of her girls stepping outside the door with a lamp at night to gather a few plantain leaves to dress some slight wound or inflamed hand or foot. What acres of Houstonia whiten & ripple before the eye with innumerable pretty florets at the mention of May. My beloved Liatris in the end of August & September acquires some added interest from being an approved remedy for the bite of serpents, & so called "Rattlesnake's Master."

These are our Poetry. What I pray thee O Emanuel Swedenborg have I to do with jasper, sardonyx, beryl, & chalcedony? What with tabernacles, arks, ephahs & ephods, what with lepers & emeroids, what with midnight bridal processions, with chariots of fire? with dragons crowned & horned, or Behemoth or Unicorn?

Good for orientals, these are nought to me. The more learning you bring to explain them the more glaring the impertinence. My learning is in my birth & habits, in the delight of my eyes, and not another man's. Of all the absurdities of men this of some foreigner proposing to take away my poetry & substitute his own & amuse me with pelican & stork instead of robin & thrush; palm trees & shittim wood instead of sugar maple & sassafras—seems the most needless & insulting. One would think that God made fig trees & dates, grapes & olives but the devil made Baldwin apples & pound pears, cherries & whortleberries, Indian corn & Irish potatoes. I tell you, I love the peeping of a Hyla in a pond in April, or the evening cry of a whip-poor-will, better than all the bellowing of the Bulls of Bashan or all the turtles of whole Palestina. The County of Berkshire is worth all Moab, Gog, & Kadesh, put together.

April 14, 1842
If I should write an honest diary what should I say? Alas that Life has halfness, shallowness. I have almost completed thirty nine years and

I have not yet adjusted my relation to my fellows on the planet, or to my own work. Always too young or too old, I do not satisfy myself; how can I satisfy others?

April 1842
    I am not united, I am not friendly to myself, I bite & tear myself. I am ashamed of myself. When will the day dawn of peace & reconcilement when self-united & friendly I shall display one heart & energy to the world?

    When I saw the sylvan youth I said, "very good promise but I cannot now watch any more buds: Like the good Grandfather when they brought him the twentieth babe he declined the dandling, he had said 'Kitty, Kitty' long enough."

    Queenie says, "Save me from magnificent souls. I like a small common sized one."

May 1, 1842
    "And the most difficult of tasks to keep
    Heights which the soul is competent to gain."

These lines of Wordsworth are a sort of elegy on these times.

June 14, 1842
    A highly endowed man with good intellect & good conscience is a Man-woman & does not so much need the complement of Woman to his being, as another. Hence his relations to the sex are somewhat dislocated & unsatisfactory. He asks in Woman, sometimes the Woman, sometimes the Man.

June 26, 1842
    Nelly waked & fretted at night & put all sleep of her seniors to rout. Seniors grew very cross, but Nell conquered soon by the pathos & eloquence of childhood & its words of fate. Thus after wishing it would be morning, she broke out into sublimity; "Mother, it must be morning." Presently, after, in her sleep, she rolled out of bed; I heard the little feet running round on the floor, and then, "O dear! where's my bed?"
    She slept again, and then woke; "Mother I am afraid; I wish I could sleep in the bed be side of you. I am afraid I shall tumble into the waters—It is all water." What else could papa do? He jumped out of bed & laid himself down by the little mischief, & soothed her the best he might.

June–July 1842

I hear with pleasure that a young girl in the midst of rich decorous Unitarian friends in Boston is well nigh persuaded to join the Roman Catholic Church. Her friends who are also my friends, lamented to me the growth of this inclination. But I told them that I think she is to be greatly congratulated on the event.

She has lived in great poverty of events. In form & years a woman, she is still a child, having had no experiences, and although of a fine liberal susceptible expanding nature, has never yet found any worthy object of attention; has not been in love, nor been called out by any taste except lately by music, and sadly wants adequate objects. In this church perhaps she shall find what she needs, in a power to call out the slumbering religious sentiment. It is unfortunate that the guide who has led her into this path is a young girl of a lively forcible but quite external character who teaches her the historical argument for the Catholic faith. I told A. that I hoped she would not be misled by attaching any importance to that. If the offices of the Church attract her, if its beautiful forms & humane spirit draw her, if St Augustine & St Bernard, Jesu & Madonna, Cathedral, Music & Masses, then go, for thy dear heart's sake, but do not go out of this icehouse of Unitarianism all external, into an icehouse again of externals. At all events I charged her to pay no regard to dissenters but to suck that orange thoroughly.

In Boston I saw the new second volume of Tennyson's Poems. It had many merits but the question might remain whether it has *the* merit. One would say it was the poetry of an exquisite; that it was prettiness carried out to the infinite, but with no one great heroic stroke; a too rigorous exclusion of all mere natural influences.

In town I also talked with Sampson Reed, of Swedenborg & the rest. "It is not so in your experience, but is so in the other world."—"Other world?" I reply, "there is no other world; here or nowhere is the whole fact; all the Universe over, there is but one thing—this old double, Creator-creature, mind-matter, right-wrong." He would have devils, objective devils. I replied, That pure malignity exists, is an absurd proposition. Goodness & Being are one. Your proposition is not to be entertained by a rational agent: it is atheism; it is the last profanation. In regard to Swedenborg, I commended him as a grand poet: Reed wished that if I admired the poetry, I should feel it as a fact. I told him All my concern is with the subjective truth of Jesus's or Swedenborg's or Homer's remark, not at all with the object. To care too much for the object were low & gossipping. He may & must speak to his circumstance and the way of events & of belief around him; he may speak of angels or jews or gods or Lutherans or Gypsies, or whatsoever figures come next to his hand; I can readily enough translate his rhetoric into mine.

July 12–14, 1842
It is sad to outgrow our preachers, our friends, & our books and find them no longer potent. Proclus & Plato last me still, yet I do not read them in a manner to honor the writer, but rather as I should read a dictionary for diversion & a mechanical help to the fancy & the Imagination. I read for the lustres as if one should use a fine picture in a chromatic experiment merely for its rich colours. It is not Proclus but a piece of Nature & Fate that I explore.

Yes Carlyle represents very well the literary man; makes good the place of & function of Erasmus & Johnson, of Dryden & Swift, to our generation. He is thoroughly a gentleman and deserves well of the whole fraternity of scholars, for sustaining the dignity of his profession of author in England. Yet I always feel his limitation, & praise him as one who plays his part well according to his light, as I praise the Clays & Websters. For Carlyle is worldly, and speaks not out of the celestial region of Milton & Angelo.

July–Aug. 1842
Fate takes in the holidays & the work minutes; it was writ on your brow before you were born; the watch was wound up to go seventy years & here to stop & there to hasten. Just this neuralgia & that typhus fever, this good October & that most auspicious friendship were all rolled in. The little barrel of the music box revolves until all its ditties are played.

Aug. 1842
The only poetic fact in the life of thousands & thousands is their death. No wonder they specify all the circumstances of the death of another person.

The doctrine in which the world has acquiesced (has it not?) on this much agitated question of the Classic & Romantic is that it is not a question of times nor of forms but of methods; that the Classic is creative & the Romantic is aggregative; that the Greek in the Christian Germany would have built a Cathedral; and that the Romantic in our time builds a Parthenon Custom House.

Sept. 1–3, 1842

You say perhaps Nature will yet give me the joy of friendship. But our pleasures are in some proportion to our forces. I have so little vital force that I could not stand the dissipation of a flowing & friendly life; I should die of consumption in three months. But now I husband all my strength in this bachelor life I lead, & no doubt shall be a well preserved old gentleman.

Sept. 1842

The poor Irish Mary Corbet whose five weeks' infant died here 3 months ago, sends word to Lidian that "she cannot send back her bandbox (in which the child's body was carried to Boston): she must plase give it to her; & she cannot send back the little hand-kerchief (with which its head was bound up): she must plase give it to her."

N. Hawthorn's reputation as a writer is a very pleasing fact, because his writing is not good for anything, and this is a tribute to the man.

Intellect always puts an interval between the subject & the object. Affection would blend the two. For weal or for woe I clear myself from the thing I contemplate: I grieve, but am not a grief: I love, but am not a love.

White Lies. It shall be the law of this society that no member shall be reckoned a liar who is a sportsman and indicates the wrong place when asked where he shot his partridge; or who is an angler, & misremembers where he took his trout; or who is an engineer, and misdirects his inquiring friends as to the best mill-privilege; or who is a merchant, & forgets in what stock he proposes to invest; or who is an author, and being asked if he wrote an anonymous book, replies in the negative.

GHOST (*under the floor*). It shall not be the law.

Sept. 27 was a fine day, and Hawthorn & I set forth on a walk. We went first to the Factory where Mr Demond makes Domett cloths, but his mills were standing still, his houses empty. Nothing so small but comes to honour & has its shining moment somewhere; & so was it here with our little Assabet or North Branch; it was falling over the rocks into silver, & above was expanded into this tranquil lake. After looking about us a few moments we took the road to Stow. The day was full of sunshine and it was a luxury to walk in the midst of all this warm & coloured light. The days of September are so rich that it seems natural to walk to the end of one's strength, & then fall prostrate saturated with the fine floods, & cry *Nunc dimittis me*. Fringed gentians, a thornbush with red fruit, wild apple trees whose fruit hung like berries, and grapevines were the decorations of the path. We scarcely encountered man or boy in our road nor saw any in the fields. This depopulation lasted all day. But the outlines of the landscape were so gentle that it seemed as if we were in a very cultivated country, and elegant persons must be living just over yonder hills. Three or four times, or oftener, we saw the entrance to their lordly park. But nothing in the farms or in the houses made this good. And it is to be considered that when any large brain is born in these towns it is sent, at sixteen or twenty years, to Boston or New York, and the country is tilled only by the inferior class of the people, by the second crop or *rowan* of the men. Hence all these shiftless poverty-struck pig-farms. In Europe where society has an aristocratic structure, the land is full of men of the best stock, & the best culture, whose interest & pride it is to remain half of the year at least on their estates & to fill these with every convenience & ornament. Of course these make model-farms & model-architecture, and are a constant education to the eye & hand of the surrounding population. Our walk had no incidents. It needed none, for we were in excellent spirits, had much conversation, for we were both old collectors who had never had opportunity before to show each other our cabinets, so that we could have filled with matter much longer days. We agreed that it needed a little dash of humor or extravagance in the traveller to give occasion to incident in his journey. Here we sober men easily pleased kept on the outside of the land & did not by so much as a request for a cup of milk creep into any farmhouse. If want of pence in our pocket or some vagary in our brain drove us into these "huts where poor men lie" to crave dinner or night's lodging, it would be so easy to break into some mesh of domestic romance, learn so much pathetic private history, perchance see the first blush mantle on the cheek of the young girl when the mail stage came or did not come, or even get entangled ourselves in some thread of gold or grey. Then again the opportunities which the taverns once offered the traveller of witnessing & even sharing in the joke & the politics of the teamster & farmers on the road, are now no more. The Temperance Society emptied the bar-room; it is a cold place. H. tried to smoke a cigar, but I observed he was soon out on the piazza. After noon we reached Stow, and dined, then continued our journey towards Harvard, making our day's walk, according to our best computation, about 20 miles. The last mile, however, we rode in a wagon, having been challenged by a friendly fatherly gentleman, who knew my name, & my father's name & history, & who insisted on doing the honours of his town to us, & of us to his townsmen; for he fairly installed us at the tavern, introduced us to the Doctor, & to General ——, & bespoke the land-lord's best attention to our wants. We get the view of the Nashua River valley from the top of Oak-Hill, as we enter Harvard village. Next morning, we begun our walk at 6½ o'clock for the Shaker Village distant 3½ miles. Whilst the good Sisters were getting ready our breakfast, we had a conversation with Seth Blanchard & Cloutman of the Brethren, who gave an honest account by yea & by nay of their faith & practice. They were not stupid like some whom I have seen of their society, & not worldly like others. The conversation on both parts was frank enough; with the downright I will be downright, thought I, and Seth showed some humour. I doubt not we should have had our own way with them to a good extent . . . if we could have staid twenty four hours: although my powers of persuasion were crippled by a disgraceful barking cold, & Hawthorn inclined to play Jove more than Mercurius. After breakfast Cloutman showed us the farm, vineyard, orchard, barn, herb room, pressing room &c. The vineyard contained two noble arcades of grapes, both White & Isabella, full of fruit; the orchard fine varieties of pears, & peaches & apples.

They have 1500 acres here, a tract of wood-land in Ashburnham, and a sheep pasture somewhere else, enough to supply the wants of the 200 souls in this family. They are in many ways an interesting Society, but at present have an additional importance as an experiment of Social-ism which so falls in with the temper of the times. What improvement is made is made for ever, this capitalist is old & never dies, his subsistence was long ago secured, & he has gone on now for long scores of years in adding easily, compound interests to his stock. Moreover, this settle-ment is of great value in the heart of the country as a model farm, in the absence of that rural nobility we talked of yesterday. Here are improve-ments invented or adopted from the other Shaker Communities which the neighboring farmers see & copy. From the Shaker Village we came to Littleton, & thence to Acton, still in the same redundance of splen-dour. It was like a day of July, and from Acton we sauntered leisurely homeward to finish the nineteen miles of our second day before four in the afternoon.

Oct. 8? 1842

Ellen H. spoke of the voracity of our Americans for food, for news, for money, for excitement. In England, Alcott told her, he partook of the repose of the people; but in this climate, at once felt the instigating, inciting restlessness & eagerness. Hunger for objects. All men look hungry.

Oct. 1842

The merit of a poem or tragedy is a matter of experience. An intelligent youth can find little wonderful in the Greeks or Romans. These tragedies, these poems are cold & tame. Nature & all the events passing in the street are more to him, he says, than the stark unchangeable crisis of the Iliad or the Antigone; and as for thoughts, his own thoughts are better and are more numerous. So says one, so say all. Presently, each of them tries his hand at expressing his thought; but there is a certain stiffness, or a certain extravagance in it. All try, and all fail, each from some peculiar & different defect. The whole age of authors tries; many ages try; and in millions & millions of experiments these confessedly tame & stark poems of the Ancient are still the best. It seems to be certain that they will go on discontenting yet excelling the intelligent youths of the generations to come.

The sannup & the Squaw do not get drunk at the same time. They take turns in keeping sober & husband & wife should never be low-spirited at the same time, but each should be able to cheer the other.

We learn with joy & wonder this new & flattering art of language deceived by the exhilaration that accompanies the attainment of each new word. We fancy we gain somewhat; we gain nothing. It seemed to men that words came nearer to the thing; described the fact; were the fact. They learn later that they only suggest it. It is an operose circuitous way of putting us in mind of the thing—of flagellating our attention. But this was slowly discovered. With what good faith these old books of barbarous men record the genesis of the world. Their best attempts to narrate how it is that star & earth & man exist, run out into some gigantic mythology, which, when it is ended, leaves the beautiful simple facts where they were, & the stupid gazing fabulist just as far from them as at first. Garrulity is our religion & philosophy. They wonder and are angry that some persons slight their book, & prefer the thing itself. But with all progress this happens, that speech becomes less, & finally ceases in a nobler silence.

Cheerfulness is so much the order of nature that the superabundant glee of a child lying on its back & not yet strong enough to get up or to sit up, yet cooing, warbling, laughing, screaming with joy is an image of independence which makes power no part of independence. Queenie looks at Edie kicking up both feet into the air, & thinks that Edie says "The world was made on purpose to carry round the little baby; and the world goes round the sun only to bring titty-time and creeping-on-the-floor-time to the Baby."

*   *   *

I told Hawthorn yesterday that I think every young man at some-time inclines to make the experiment of a dare-God & daredevil original-ity like that of Rabelais. He would jump on the top of the nearest fence & crow. He makes the experiment, but it proves like the flight of pig-lead into the air which cannot cope with the poorest hen. Irresistible custom brings him plump down, and he finds himself instead of odes, writing gazettes & leases. Yet there is imitation & model or suggestion to the very archangels if we knew their history, and if we knew Rabe-lais's reading we should see the rill of the Rabelais river. Yet his hold of his place in Parnassus is as firm as Homer's. A jester, but his is the jest of the world, & not of Touchstone or Clown or Harlequin. His wit is uni-versal, not accidental, and the anecdotes of the time which made the first butt of the satire & which are lost, are of no importance, as the wit tran-scends any particular mark, & pierces to permanent relations & inter-ests. His joke will fit any town or community of men.

In these Indian summers, of which we have eight or ten every year, you can almost see the Indians under the trees in the wood. These are the reconciling days which come to graduate the autumn into winter, & to comfort us after the first attacks of the cold. Soothsayers, prediction as well as memory, they look over December & January into the crepus-cular lights of March & April.

This feeling I have respecting Homer & Greek, that in this great empty continent of ours stretching enormous almost from pole to pole with thousands of long rivers and thousands of ranges of mountains, the rare scholar who under a farmhouse roof reads Homer & the Tragedies adorns the land. He begins to fill it with wit, to counterbalance the enor-mous disproportion of unquickened earth. He who first reads Homer in America is its Cadmus & Numa, and a subtle but unlimited benefactor.

Rabelais is not to be skipped in literary history as he is source of so much proverb, story, & joke which are derived from him into all modern books in all languages. He is the Joe Miller of modern literature.

You shall have joy, or you shall have power, said God, you shall not have both.

Oct. 26, 1842
Boston is not quite a mean place since in walking yesterday in the street I met George Bancroft, Horatio Greenough, Sampson Reed, Sam

Ward, Theodore Parker, George Bradford, & had a little talk with each of them.

Ibrahim is a wise man at home but when Ibrahim rides in the stage coach his commonplaces are much like those of a child of four years; he absolutely prattles, which is not graceful after 25 years.

Oct.? 1842

Men of aim must always rule the aimless. And yet there will always be singing-birds.

The Englishmen remarked that the greatest interior advantage which they observed in our community over theirs was in the women. In England the women were quite obtuse to any liberal thought; whilst here, they are intelligent & ready.

Oct.–Nov. 1842

A poor man had an insufficient stove which it took him a great part of the winter to tend: he was up early to make the fire and very careful to keep it from going out. He interrupted his work at all hours of the day to feed it: he kept it late into the night that the chamber walls need not get hopelessly cold, but it never warmed the room; he shivered over it hoping it would be better, but he lost a great deal of time & comfort.

Once Latin & Greek had a strict relation to all the science & culture there was in Europe, and the Mathematics had a momentary importance at some era of activity in physical science. These things became stereotyped as *Education*, as the manner of men is. The good *Spirit of the World* never cared for the colleges, and though all men & boys were now drilled in Latin, Greek, & the Mathematics, he had quite left these shells high & dry on the beach, & was now creating & feeding other matters at other ends of the world. So it happened & still happens in a hundred high schools & colleges that this petty drivelling warfare against nature & life, is still waged. Four or six or ten years the pupil is parsing Greek & Latin, and, as soon as he leaves the *University*, as it is ludicrously called, he shuts those books for the last time. Some thousands of young men are graduated at our colleges in this country every year, and the persons who at 40 years still read Greek can all be counted on your hand. I never met with ten. Three persons I have seen who read Plato.

But is not this absurd—that the whole liberal talent of this country should be dedicated in all its best years to these studies which lead to nothing? What was the consequence? Some intelligent persons said or

thought, Is that Greek & Latin a barbaric talisman, a spell to conjure
with, & not words of reason? If you never use it for your ends, perhaps I
need never learn it, to come at your ends. I will omit the conjuring, and
go straight to business. So they jumped the Greek & Latin, & studied
law, medicine, or sermons, without it. To the astonishment of all society, these self-made men, as they were called, took even ground at once
with the oldest of the regular troops, and in a few months the most conservative circles of Boston & New York had quite forgotten who was
college-bred, & who not, of its gownsmen.

Our young Abolitionists vapor at the North, and in the streets of
Boston with Massachusetts at their back, they are hot for an encounter
with Mr Gray of Virginia. Him they will shove, him they will hustle,
him they will utterly vanquish & drive out of the city. But if they go
into the southern country, these young men are at once hushed by the
"chivalry" which they sneer at, at home. For these southerners are
haughty, selfish, wilful, & unscrupulous men, who will have their way,
& have it. The people of New England with a thousand times more
talent, more worth, more ability of every kind, are timid, prudent,
calculating men who cannot fight until their blood is up, who have consciences & many other obstacles betwixt them & their wishes. The Vir-
ginian has none, & so always beats them today, & is steadily beaten by
them year by year.

Nov. 1842
The young people, like Brownson, Channing, Green, Elizabeth
Palmer Peabody, & possibly Bancroft think that the vice of the age is to
exaggerate individualism, & they adopt the word *l'humanité* from Le
Roux, and go for *"the race."* Hence the Phalanx, Owenism, Simonism,
the Communities. The same spirit in theology has produced the Puseyism which endeavours to rear "the Church" as a balance and over-
poise to the Conscience.

I think four walls one of the best of our institutions. A man comes to
me, & oppresses me by his presence: he looks very large & unanswerable: I cannot dispose of him whilst he stays; he quits the room, & passes
not only out of the house but, as it were, out of the horizon; he is a mere
phantasm or ghost, I think of him no more. I recover my sanity, the Universe dawns on me again.

Do not be too timid & squeamish about your actions. All life is an
experiment. The more experiments you make, the better. What if they

are a little coarse, & you may get your coat soiled or torn? What if you do fail, & get fairly rolled in the dirt once or twice? Up again, you shall never more be so afraid of a tumble. This matter of the lectures, for instance. The engagement drives your thoughts & studies to a head, & enables you to do somewhat not otherwise practicable; that is the action. Then there is the reaction; for when you bring your discourse to your auditory, it shows differently. You have more power than you had thought of, or less. The thing fits, or does not fit; is good or detestable.

Last night Henry Thoreau read me verses which pleased if not by beauty of particular lines, yet by the honest truth, and by the length of flight & strength of wing; for, most of our poets are only writers of lines or of epigrams. These of H.T. at least have rude strength, & we do not come to the bottom of the mine. Their fault is, that the gold does not yet flow pure, but is drossy & crude. The thyme & marjoram are not yet made into honey; the assimilation is imperfect. . . . But it is a great pleasure, to have poetry of the second degree also, & mass here as in other instances is some compensation for superior quality for I find myself stimulated & rejoiced like one who should see a cargo of sea-shells discharged on the wharf, whole boxes & crates of conchs, cypraeas, cones, neritas, cardiums, murexes, though there should be no pearl oyster nor one shell of great rarity & value among them.

I was a little chubby boy trundling a hoop in Chauncey Place and spouting poetry from Scott & Campbell at the Latin School. But Time the little grey man has taken out of his vest pocket a great aukward house (in a corner of which I sit & write of him) some acres of land, several fullgrown & several very young persons, & seated them close beside me; then he has taken that chubbiness & that hoop quite away (to be sure he has left the declamation & the poetry) and here left a long lean person threatening soon to be a little grey man, like himself.

Nov. 19? 1842
You ask, O Theanor, said Amphitryon that I should go forth from this palace with my wife & my children, and that you & your family may enter & possess it. The same request in substance has been often made to me before by numbers of persons. Now I also think that I & my wife ought to go forth from this house, & work all day in the fields, & lie at night under some thicket, but I am waiting where I am, only until some god shall point out to me which among all these applicants, yourself or some other, is the rightful claimant.

Nov. 25, 1842

Yesterday I read Dickens's American Notes. It answers its end very well, which plainly was to make a readable book, nothing more. Truth is not his object for a single instant, but merely to make good points in a lively sequence, and he succeeds very well. As an account of America it is not to be considered for a moment: it is too short, & too narrow, too superficial, & too ignorant, too slight, & too fabulous, and the man totally unequal to the work. A very lively rattle on that nuisance a sea voyage is the first chapter. And a pretty fair example of the historical truth of the whole book. We can hear throughout every page the dialogue between the author & his publisher, "Mr Dickens the book must be entertaining—that is the essential point. Truth! damn truth. I tell you it must be entertaining." As a picture of American manners nothing can be falser. No such conversations ever occur in this country in real life, as he relates. He has picked up & noted with eagerness each odd local phrase that he met with and, when he had a story to relate, has joined these together, so that the result is the broadest caricature; and the scene might as truly have been laid in Wales or in England as in the States. Monstrous exaggeration is an easy secret of romance. But Americans who, like some of us Massachusetts people, are not fond of spitting, will go from Maine to N. Orleans, & meet no more annoyance than we should in Britain or France. So with "yes," so with "fixings," so with soap & towels; & all the other trivialities which this trifler detected in travelling over half the world. The book makes but a poor apology for its author who certainly appears in no dignified or enviable position. He is a gourmand & a great lover of wines & brandies, & for his entertainment has a cockney taste for certain charities. He sentimentalizes on every prison & orphan asylum, until dinner time. But science, art, Nature, & charity itself all fade before us at the great hour of Dinner.

Nov.–Dec. 1842

Buddhism, transcendentalism, life delights in reducing it ad absurdum. The child, the infant is a transcendentalist & charms us all: We try to be, & instantly run in debt, lie, steal, commit adultery, go mad, & die. Each practical mistake that we add to our sins, reacts on us, & spoils our tune & temper, steals away all our edge & manhood, & we are eunuchs & women. Narrow & narrower grows the line on which we must walk; deep the gulf on either hand, the man is weary of labor & mere repetition of tasks, & would willingly exchange some of this rude health for some intellectual culture. Instantly we say, how hollow—how white he is, a man of verbs & nouns! God is grown but a noun; & philosophy, spirit, & heaven a grammar exercise. Well, the man of letters takes to the field, & very soon the field enters him, & he grows cloddy & rude. Disgusts on both sides. I hate books, they are an usurpation & impertinence. I cannot once go home to truth & Nature for this perpetual clatter of words & dust of libraries. Yet take me at my word & burn my books &, like poor Petrarch, I might come to insanity for want of this fine wine of the gods.

Dec.? 1842

I hear the whistle of the locomotive in the woods. Wherever that music comes it has a sequel. It is the voice of the civility of the Nineteenth Century saying "Here I am." It is interrogative: it is prophetic: and this Cassandra is believed: "Whew! Whew! Whew! How is real estate here in the swamp & wilderness? Swamp & Wilderness, ho for Boston! Whew! Whew! Down with that forest on the side of the hill. I want ten thousand chestnut sleepers. I want cedar posts and hundreds of thousands of feet of boards. Up my masters, of oak & pine! You have waited long enough—a good part of a century in the wind & stupid sky. Ho for axes & saws, and away with me to Boston! Whew! Whew! I will plant a dozen houses on this pasture next moon and a village anon; and I will sprinkle yonder square mile with white houses like the broken snow-banks that strow it in March."

Dec. 1842–Jan. 1843

The Yankee is one who if he once gets his teeth set on a thing, all creation can't make him let go; who if he can get hold any where of a rope's end or a spar, will not let it go but will make it carry him; if he can but find so much as a stump or a log, will hold on to it & whittle out of it a house & barn, a farm & stock, a mill-seat & a village, a railroad & a bank and various other things equally useful & entertaining, a seat in Congress or a foreign mission for example. But these no doubt are inventions of the enemy.

The harvest will be better preserved & go farther laid up in private bins, in each farmer's corn barn, & each woman's basket, than if it were kept in national granaries. In like manner, an amount of money will go farther if expended by each man & woman for their own wants, & in the feeling that this is their all, than if expended by a great Steward, or National Commissioners of the Treasury. Take away from me the feeling that I must depend on myself, give me the least hint that I have good friends & backers there in reserve who will gladly help me, & instantly I relax my diligence & obey the first impulse of generosity that is to cost me nothing, and a certain slackness will creep over all my conduct of my affairs. Here is a bank note found of 100 dollars. Let it fall into the hands of an easy man who never earned the estate he spends, & see how little difference it will make in his affairs. At the end of the year he is just as much behindhand as ever, & could not have done at all without that hundred. Let it fall into the hands of a poor & prudent woman, and every shilling & every cent of it tells, goes to reduce debt or to add to instant & constant comfort, mends a window, buys a blanket or a pelisse, gets a stove instead of the old cavernous fireplace all chimney.

The Standing Committee of the Antislavery Society are said to have been lavish spenders.

First we eat, then we beget; first we read, then we write; have you a better appetite? then you will do well. I have no thoughts today; What then? What difference does it make? It is only that there does not chance today to be an antagonism to evolve them, the electricity is the more accumulated, & a week hence you shall meet somebody or some thing that shall draw from you a shower of sparks.

There is a comparative innocence in this country & a correspondent health. We do not often see bald boys & grayhaired girls, children victims of gout & apoplexy; the street is not full of nearsighted & deaf people; nor do we see those horrid mutilations & disgusting forms of disease as leprosy & undescribed varieties of plague which European streets exhibit, stumps of men. Alcott remarked in England that he saw a great deal of hereditary disease & not the innocent New Hampshire complexions which abound here.

How often in Rome & Naples one sees a fragment of a man sitting all day on a stone in some public crossing place to beg with a plate with his head covered, and only some sign of dreadful meaning peeping under his cowl as if day was not to see nor mankind his rottenness.

Feb. 7? 1843

Webster is very dear to the Yankees because he is a person of very commanding understanding with every talent for its adequate expression. The American, foreigners say, always reasons, and he is the most American of the Americans. They have no abandonment, but dearly love logic, as all their churches have so long witnessed. His external advantages are very rare & admirable; his noble & majestic frame, his breadth & projection of brows, his coalblack hair, his great cinderous eyes, his perfect self possession, and the rich & well modulated thunder of his voice (to which I used to listen sometimes, abstracting myself from his sense merely for the luxury of such noble explosions of sound) distinguish him above all other men. In a million you would single him out. In England, he made the same impression by his personal advan-

tages as at home, & was called the Great Western. In speech he has a
great good sense—is always pertinent to time & place, and has an eye to
the simple facts of nature—to the place where he is, to the hour of the
day, to the Sun in heaven, to his neighborhood, to the sea or to the
mountains—but very sparingly notices these things, & clings closely to
the business part of his speech with great gravity & faithfulness. "I do
not inflame," he said on one occasion, "I do not exaggerate, I avoid all
incendiary allusion." He trusts to his simple strength of statement, in
which he excels all men—for the attention of his assembly. His statement is lucid throughout, & of equal strength. He has great fairness &
deserves all his success in debate, for he always carries a point from his
adversary by really taking superior ground, as in the Hayne debate.
There are no puerilities, no tricks, no academical play in any of his
speeches—they are all majestic men of business. Every one is a first-rate
Yankee.

He has had a faithful apprenticeship to his position for he was born
in New Hampshire a farmer's son & his youth spent in those hardships
& privations which add such edge to every simple pleasure & every lib-
eralizing opportunity. The Almanac does not come unnoticed but is
read & committed to heart by the farmer's boys. And when it was announced to him by his father that he would send him to college he could
not speak. The struggles. Brothers & sisters in poor men's houses in
New England are dear to each other & the bringing up of a family involves many sacrifices each for the other.

The faults that shade his character are not such as to hurt his popu-
larity. He is very expensive, and always in debt; but this rather recom-
mends him, as he is known to be generous, & his countrymen make for
him the apology of Themistocles that to keep treasure undiminished is
the virtue of a chest & not of a man. Then there is in him a large share of
good nature & a sort of bonhommie. It is sometimes complained of him
that he is a man of pleasure & all his chosen friends are easy epicures &
debauchees. But this is after Talleyrand's taste, who said of his foolish
wife that he found nonsense very refreshing: so Webster, after he has
been pumping his brains in the Courts & the Senate, is no doubt heartily glad to get among cronies & gossips where he can stretch himself at
his ease & drink his mulled wine. They also quote as his *three rules* of
living: 1. Never to pay any debt that can by any possibility be avoided;
2. Never to do anything today that can be put off till tomorrow; 3.
Never to do anything himself which he can get any body else to do for
him.

And here is Carlyle's portrait of 24 June 1839: "Not many days ago,
I saw at breakfast the notablest of all your notabilities, Daniel Webster.

He is a magnificent specimen; you might say to all the world, This is our Yankee Englishman, such limbs *we* make in Yankeeland! As a logic fencer, Advocate, or Parliamentary Hercules, one would incline to back him, at first sight, against all the extant world. The tanned complexion, that amorphous craglike face; the dull black eyes under their precipice of brows, like dull anthracite furnaces needing only to be *blown;* the mastiff mouth, accurately closed, I have not traced as much of *silent Berserkir rage,* that I remember of, in any other man. 'I guess I should not like to be *your* nigger.' Webster is not loquacious, but is pertinent, conclusive; a dignified, perfectly bred man, tho' not English in breeding; a man worthy of the best reception from us, & meeting such I understand."

Earth Spirit, living, a black river like that swarthy stream which rushes through the human body, is thy nature, demoniacal, warm, fruitful, sad, nocturnal.

Feb. 7, 1843

I am greatly pleased with the merchants. In railcar & hotel it is common to meet only the successful class, & so we have favorable specimens: but these discover more manly power of all kinds than scholars; behave a great deal better, converse better, and have independent & sufficient manners.

Dreamlike travelling on the railroad. The towns through which I pass between Phila. & New York, make no distinct impression. They are like pictures on a wall. The more, that you can read all the way in the car a French novel.

Feb.–March 1843

It is very funny to go into a family where the father & mother are devoted to the children. You flatter yourself for an instant that you have secured your friend's ear, for his countenance brightens; then you discover that he has just caught the eye of his babe over your shoulder, & is chirruping to him.

In N.Y. men get a good living by collecting ends of cigars which have been thrown away by the smoker, cutting off the unconsumed part & selling it to the tobacconist for pipe tobacco.

Others by collecting cinders out of coal ashes, Others by raking for rags & dishcloths in the gutters which they sell to the papermaker. Others by collecting dog & hog manure.

A man going out of Constantinople met the Plague coming in, who said he was sent thither for 20,000 souls. Forty thousand persons were swept off, and when the traveller came back, he met the Plague coming out of the city. "Why did you kill Forty thousand?" he asked. "I only killed twenty," replied the Pest; "Fear killed the rest."

Mr Adams chose wisely & according to his constitution, when on leaving the Presidency he went into Congress. He is no literary old gentleman, but a bruiser, & loves the melée. When they talk about his age & venerableness & nearness to the grave, he knows better, he is like one of those old Cardinals who as quick as he is chosen pope, throws away his crutches & his crookedness, and is as straight as a boy. He is an old roué who cannot live on slops, but must have sulphuric acid in his tea.

Cheap literature makes new markets. We have thought only of a box audience, or at most of box & pit; but now it appears there is also slip audience, & galleries one, two, three; & backstairs, & street listeners, besides. Greeley tells me that Graham's Magazine has 70,000 subscribers. And I may write a lecture, if I will, to 70,000 readers.

March 1843

At the Five Points, I heard a woman swearing very liberally, as she talked with her companions; but when I looked at her face, I saw that she was no worse than other women; that she used the dialect of her class, as all others do, & are neither better nor worse for it; but under this bad costume was the same repose, the same probity as in Broadway. Nor was she misinterpreted by her mates. There is a virtue of vice as well as of virtue.

March? 1843

I thank the translators & it is never my practice to read any Latin, Greek, German, Italian, scarcely any French book, in the original which I can procure in an English translation. I like to be beholden to the great metropolitan English speech, the sea which receives tributaries from every region under heaven, the Rome of nations, and I should think it in me as much folly to read all my books in originals when I have them rendered for me in my mother's speech by men who have given years to that labor, as I should to swim across Charles River when ever I wished to go to Charlestown.

Queenie's epitaph: "Do not wake me."

"Dear husband, I wish I had never been born. I do not see how God can compensate me for the sorrow of existence."*

---

*This entry has been heavily canceled.

March 23, 1843

Two brave chanticleers go up & down stripping the plumes from all the fine birds, showing that all are not in the best health. It makes much unhappiness on all sides; much crowing it occasions on the part of the two cockerels who so shrewdly discover & dismantle all the young beaux of the aviary. But alas the two valiant cocks who strip, are no better than those who are stripped, only they have sharper beak & talons. In plain prose, I grieved so much to hear the most intellectual youth I have met, Charles Newcomb, so disparaged, & our good & most deserving scholar Theodore Parker threatened as a morsel to be swallowed when he shall come tomorrow, & all this by my brave friends who are only brave, not helpful, not rejoicing, not humble, not loving, not creative—that I said, Cursed is preaching—the better it is, the worse. A preacher is a bully: I who have preached so much—by the help of God will never preach more.

March–April 1843

To live with, good taste seems more necessary than freedom from vice. One could easilier live with a person who did not respect the truth, or chastity, than with a filthy person.

Margaret. A pure & purifying mind, selfpurifying also, full of faith in men, & inspiring it. Unable to find any companion great enough to receive the rich effusions of her thought, so that her riches are still unknown & seem unknowable. It is a great joy to find that we have underrated our friend, that he or she is far more excellent than we had thought. All natures seem poor beside one so rich, which pours a stream of amber over all objects clean & unclean that lie in its path, and makes that comely & presentable which was mean in itself. We are taught by her plenty how lifeless & outward we were, what poor Laplanders burrowing under the snows of prudence & pedantry. Beside her friendship, other friendships seem trade, and by the firmness with which she treads her upward path, all mortals are convinced that another road exists than that which their feet know. The wonderful generosity of her sentiments pours a contempt on books & writing at the very time when one asks how shall this fiery picture be kept in its glow & variety for other eyes. She excels other intellectual persons in this, that her sentiments are more blended with her life; so the expression of them has greater steadiness & greater clearness. I have never known any example of such steady progress from stage to stage of thought & of character. An inspirer of courage, the secret friend of all nobleness, the patient waiter for the realization of character, forgiver of injuries, gracefully waiving aside folly, & elevating lowness—in her presence all were apprised of their fettered estate & longed for liberation, of ugliness & longed for their beauty; of meanness, & panted for grandeur.

Her growth is visible. All the persons whom we know, have reached their height, or else their growth is so nearly at the same rate with ours, that it is imperceptible, but this child inspires always more faith in her. She rose before me at times into heroical & godlike regions, and I could remember no superior women, but thought of Ceres, Minerva, Proserpine, and the august ideal forms of the Foreworld. She said that no man gave such invitation to her mind as to tempt her to a full expression; that she felt a power to enrich her thought with such wealth & variety of embellishment as would no doubt be tedious to such as she conversed with. And there is no form that does seem to wait her beck—dramatic, lyric, epic, passionate, pictorial, humourous.

She has great sincerity, force, & fluency as a writer, yet her powers of speech throw her writing into the shade. What method, what exquisite judgment, as well as energy, in the selection of her words, what character & wisdom they convey! You cannot predict her opinion. She sympathizes so fast with all forms of life, that she talks never narrowly or hostilely nor betrays, like all the rest, under a thin garb of new words, the old droning castiron opinions or notions of many years standing. What richness of experience, what newness of dress, and fast as Olympus to her principle. And a silver eloquence, which inmost Polymnia taught. Meantime, all the pathos of sentiment and riches of literature & of invention and this march of character threatening to arrive presently at the shores & plunge into the sea of Buddhism & mystic trances, consists with a boundless fun & drollery, with light satire, & the most entertaining conversation in America.

Her experience contains, I know, golden moments, which, if they could be fitly narrated, would stand equally beside any histories of magnanimity which the world contains; and whilst Dante's 'Nuova Vita' is almost unique in the literature of sentiment, I have called the imperfect record she gave me of two of her days, 'Nuovissima Vita.'

I confess that Plato seems to me greatly more literary than strong—weak inasmuch as he is literary. Shakspeare is not literary, but the strong earth itself. Veracity is that which we want in poets that they shall say how it was with them & not what might be said.

It is a great joy to get away from persons, & live under the dominion of the Multiplication Table.

Form always stands in dread of power. What the devil will he do next?

* * *

The world must be new as we know it, for see how lately it has bethought itself of so many articles of the simplest convenience; as, for example, wooden clothespins to pinch the clothes to the line, instead of metallic pins were introduced since the peace of 1783.

My mother remembers when her sister Mrs Inman returned from England at that time, & brought these articles with her furniture, then new in this country; then the India rubber shoe; the rail-road; the steam boat; and the airtight stove; the friction match; and cut nails.

No man believes any more than he has experienced.

The difference between talent & genius, is, that talent says things which he has never heard but once, & genius things which he has never heard.

Genius is power; Talent is applicability. A human body, an animal, is an applicability; the Life, the Soul, is Genius.

E.H says, "I love Henry, but do not like him." Young men like Henry Thoreau owe us a new world & they have not acquitted the debt: for the most part, such die young, & so dodge the fulfilment. One of our girls . . . said, that Henry never went through the kitchen without colouring.

Much poor talk concerning woman which at least had the effect of revealing the true sex of several of the party who usually go disguised in the form of the other sex. Thus Mrs B is a man. The finest people marry the two sexes in their own person. Hermaphrodite is then the symbol of the finished soul. It was agreed that in every act should appear the married pair: the two elements should mix in every act.

To me it sounded hoarsely the attempt to prescribe didactically to woman her duties. Man can never tell woman what her duties are: he will certainly end in describing a man in female attire, as Harriet Martineau a masculine woman solved her problem of woman. No. Woman only can tell the heights of feminine nature, & the only way in which man can help her, is by observing woman reverentially & whenever she speaks from herself & catches him in inspired moments up to a heaven of honor & religion, to hold her to that point by reverential recognition of the divinity that speaks through her.

I can never think of woman without gratitude for the bright revelations of her best nature which have been made to me unworthy. The angel who walked with me in younger days, shamed my ambition & prudence by her generous love in our first interview. I described my prospects; She said, I do not wish to hear of your prospects.

April 10, 1843

The slowly retreating snow blocks the roads & woodpaths & shuts me in the house. But yesterday the warm southwind drew me to the top of the hill like the dove from the ark to see if these white waters were abated, & there was place for the foot. The grass springs up already between the holes in the snow, and I walked along the knolls & edges of the hill wherever the winter bank was melted but I thrust my cane into the bank two feet perpendicular. I greeted the well known pine-grove which I could not reach; the pine tops seemed to cast a friendly gold-green smile of acquaintance toward me, for it was in my heart that I had not yet quite got home from my late journey, until I had revisited & rejoined these vegetable daemons. The air was kind & clear, the sky southward was full of comets, so white & fanshaped & ethereal lay the clouds as if the late visit of this foreign wonder had set the fashion for the humbler meteors. And all around me the new come sparrows, robins, bluebirds & blackbirds were announcing their arrival with great spirit.

April 10? 1843

I told Mr Means that he need not consult the Germans, but, if he wished at any time to know what the Transcendentalists believed, he might simply omit what in his own mind he added from the tradition, & the rest would be Transcendentalism.

Buddhism. Winter, Night, Sleep, are all the invasions of eternal Buddh, and it gains a point every day. Let be, *Laissez faire*, so popular now in philosophy & in politics, that is bald Buddhism; & then very fine names has it got to cover up its chaos withal, namely trances, raptures, abandonment, ecstasy, all Buddh, naked Buddh.

April 17, 1843

How sincere & confidential we can be, saying all that lies in the mind, & yet go away feeling that we have spun a rope of sand, that all is yet unsaid, from the incapacity of the parties to know each other *although they use the same words.* My companion assumes to know my mood & habit of thought, and so we go on from explanation to explanation, until all is said which words can, & we leave matters just as they were at first, because of that vicious assumption. Is it that every man believes every other to be a fatal partialist, & himself an universalist? I fear this is the history of our conversation at the cottage yesterday, when we all behaved well & frankly as we could. I endeavoured to show my good men that I loved every thing by turns & nothing long; that I loved the Centre, but doted on the superficies, that I loved Man, but men seemed to me mice & rats, that I revered saints but woke up glad that the dear old Devil kept his state in Boston, that I was glad of men of every gift & nobility, but would not live in their arms. Now could they but once understand that I loved to know that they existed & heartily wished them Godspeed, yet out of my poverty of life & thought, had no word or welcome for them when they came to see me and could well consent to their living in another town for any claim that I felt on them—it would be great satisfaction. Not this, but something like this, I said . . .

And now, I said, will you not please to pound me a little, before I go, just by way of squaring the account, that I may not remember that I alone was saucy. Alcott contented himself with quarreling with the injury done to greater qualities in my company, by the tyranny of my taste—which certainly was very soft pounding. And so I parted from the divine lotos-eaters.

April 17? 1843

Intellectual race are the New Englanders. S.R. at Brook Farm said that the young women who came thither from farms & elsewhere would work faithfully & do whatever was given them without grumbling, but there was no heart in it, but their whole interest was in their intellectual culture.

May 2? 1843

In America out of doors all seems a market; in-doors, an air tight stove of conventionalism. Every body who comes into the house savors of these precious habits, the men, of the market; the women, of the custom. In every woman's conversation & total influence mild or acid lurks the *conventional devil.* They look at your carpet, they look at your cap, at your saltcellar, at your cook & waiting maid, conventionally—to see how close they square with the customary cut in Boston & Salem & New Bedford.

May 7–9, 1843

Yesterday English visitors, and I waited all day when they should go.

If we could establish the rule that each man was a guest in his own house, and when we had shown our visitors the passages of the house, the way to fire, to bread, & water, & thus made them as much at home as the inhabitant, did then leave them to the accidents of intercourse, & went about our ordinary business, a guest would no longer be formidable.

May 18, 1843

Extremes meet: there is no straight line. Machinery & Transcendentalism agree well.

Our American lives are somewhat poor & pallid, Franklins & Washingtons, no fiery grain. Staid men like our pale & timid Flora. We have too much freedom, need an austerity, need some iron girth. Sunday Schools not friendly to heroism. But our census increases, ten or twelve young persons already appear. But why go to Europe? Best swallow this pill of America which Fate brings you & sing a land unsung. Here stars, here birds, here trees, here hills abound and the vast tendencies concur of a new Order.

The poets, the great, have been illustrious wretches who have beggared the world which has beggared them.

The young men complain that here in America is no past, no traditions; only shopkeeping, no ghost, no god in the landscape, no stimulus.

May 19, 1843

A youth of the name of Ball, a native as he told me of Concord, came to me yesterday who towered away in such declamatory talk that at first I thought it rhodomontade & we should soon have done with each other. But he turned out to be a prodigious reader, and writer too (for he spoke of whole volumes of prose & poetry barreled away) and discovered great sagacity & insight in his criticisms—a great impatience of our strait New England ways, and a wish to go to the Ganges, or at the least to live in Greece & Italy. There was little precision in his thinking, great discontent with metaphysics and he seemed of a musical, rather than a mathematical structure. With a little more repose of thought, he would be a great companion. He thought very humbly of most of his contemporaries & Napoleon he thought good to turn periods with, but that he could see through him; but Lord Bacon he could not pardon for not seeing Shakspeare, for said he, "as many Lord Bacons as could stand in Concord could find ample room in Shakspeare's brain," and Pope's mean thought & splendid rhetoric he thought "resembled rats' nests in kings' closets, made up in a crown & purple robe & regalia." He knows Greek well & reads Italian, German, & Spanish. He spent five hours with me & carried off a pile of books. He had never known but one person of extraordinary promise, a youth at Dartmouth of the name of Hobart.

May 1843

Shakspeare's speeches in Lear are in the very dialect of 1843.

May–June 1843

I enjoy all the hours of life. Few persons have such susceptibility to pleasure; as a countryman will say "I was at sea a month & never missed a meal" so I eat my dinner & sow my turnips yet do I never, I think, fear death. It seems to me so often a relief, a rendering up of responsibility, a quittance of so many vexatious trifles.

A soft lovely child always truer & better, unhurt amidst the noxious influences of wealth & ultra whiggism, & can resist everything unless it were the vitriolic acid of marriage.

It is folly to imagine that there can be anything very bad in the position of woman compared with that of man, at any time; for since every woman is a man's daughter & every man is a woman's son, every woman is too near to man, was too recently a man, than that possibly any wide disparity can be. As is the man will be the woman; and as is the woman, the man.

Life
If any of us knew what we were doing, or whither we were going! We are all dying of miscellany.

June 10, 1843

Hawthorne & I talked of the number of superior young men we have seen. H. said, that he had seen several from whom he had expected much, but they had not distinguished themselves; and he had inferred that he must not expect a popular success from such; he had in nowise lost his confidence in their power.

June 18, 1843

Yesterday at Bunker Hill, a prodigious concourse of people but a village green could not be more peaceful, orderly, sober, & even affectionate. Webster gave us his plain statement like good bread, yet the oration was feeble compared with his other efforts, and even seemed poor & Polonius like with its indigent conservatisms. When there is no antagonism as in these holiday speeches, & no religion, things sound not heroically. It is a poor oration that finds Washington for its highest mark. The audience give one much to observe, they are so light headed & light timbered, every man thinking more of his inconveniences than of the objects of the occasion, & the hurrahs are so slight & easily procured. Webster is very good—America himself. Wonderful multitudes; on the top of a house I saw a company protecting themselves from the

sun by an old large map of the United States. A charitable lumber merchant near the Bridge had chalked up over his counting room door "500
seats for ladies, free" and there the five hundred sat in white tiers. The
ground within the square at the monument was arranged to hold 80,000
persons.

June 22, 1843
It was evident that there was the monument & here was Webster,
and he knew well that a little more or less of rhetoric signified nothing:
he was only to say plain & equal things, grand things if he had them, and
if he had them not, only to abstain from saying unfit things, & the whole
occasion was answered by his presence. It was a place for behaviour
much more than speech, & Mr Webster behaved well or walked through
his part with entire success. He was there as the representative of the
American continent, there in his Adamitic capacity, and that is the basis
of the satisfaction the people have in hearing him that he alone of all men
does not disappoint the eye & ear but is a fit figure in the landscape.

June–July 1843
The Chinese are as wonderful for their etiquette as the Hebrews for
their piety.

Those men who are noised all their life time as on the edge of some
great discovery, never discover anything. But nobody ever heard of M.
Daguerre until the Daguerrotype appeared. And now I do not know
who invented the railroad.

We used to read in our textbooks of natural philosophy an illustration of the porosity of bodies, from a barrel of cannon balls, whose interstices were filled with grapeshot, whose interstices again were filled
with small shot, and theirs again with powder. It is an emblem of nature
whose problem seems to have been to see how she could crowd in the
most life into the world & for every class of eaters which she inserted,
she adds another class of eaters to prey on them, & tucked in musquitoes
among the last like an accommodating stage-coachman, who, when
twelve insides are jammed down solid, puts in a child at the window, &
guesses there will be room for that.

Fools & clowns & sots make the fringes of every one's tapestry of
life, & give a certain reality to the picture. What could we do in Concord
without Bigelow's & Wesson's barrooms & their dependencies? What

without such fixtures as Uncle Sol and old Moore who sleeps in Dr
Hurd's barn? And the red charity house over the brook? Tragedy &
comedy always go hand in hand.

July 10, 1843
W. E. C. railed an hour in good set terms at the usurpation of the
past, at the great hoaxes of the Homers & Shakspeares, hindering the
books & the men of today of their just meed. Oh certainly, I assure him,
that oaks & horse-chestnuts are entirely obsolete, that the horticultural
society are about to recommend the introduction of cabbages as a shade
tree, so much more convenient & every way comprehensible; all grown
from the seed upward to its most generous crumpled extremity within
one's own short memory; past contradiction the ornament of the world,
& then so good to eat, as acorn & horsechestnuts are not. Shadetrees for
breakfast!

July 10? 1843
Ellery, who hopes there will be no cows in heaven, has discovered
what cows are for, namely, to give the farmers something to do in summer time. All this haying comes at midsummer between planting &
harvest, when all hands would be idle, but for this cow & ox, which
must be fed & mowed for; and thus Intemperance & the progress of
Crime is prevented!

July–Aug. 1843
I have got in my barn a carpenter's bench & two planes, a shave, a
saw, chisel, a vice, & a square. These planes seem to me great institutions, whose inventor no man knoweth, yet what a stroke of genius was
each of these tools! When you have them, you must watch a workman
for a month, or a year, or seven years, as our boys do, to know all his
tricks with them. Great is Tubal Cain. A good pen is a finer stronger instrument and a language, an algebra, a calculus, music, or poetic metre,
more wondrous tools yet, for this polygon or pantagon that is called
man. Thanks too to Pythagoras for the multiplication table.

Aug. 5, 1843
Home from Plymouth where I spent a fine day in an excursion to
Half Way Pond dining at the house of Mrs Raymond, Mary & Lucia
Russell made the party for us and Abraham Jackson, & Helen Russell
accompanied us. Mrs R. was a genuine Yankee and so fluent in her pro-
vincial English that Walter Scott or Dickens could not desire a better
sample of local life. Mr Faunce, Mr Swift, & Mr Stetson, her ministers

at Ponds (meaning Monument P.), baptism by immarsion & by sprin-
kling, Mr Whitfield's "sarmons," the "Univarsallers," the schools, & the
Reformation in the church at Ponds & elsewhere, and the drowning of
her son Allen in a vessel loaded with pavingstones which sunk in a tempest near Boston Light, and the marriage of her son's widow, were the
principal events of her life, & the topics of her conversation. She lives
alone in this pleasing tranquil scene at the head of a pond, and never is
uneasy except in a tempest in the night.

I cannot well say what I found at Plymouth, beyond the uneasiness
of seeing people. Every person of worth, man or woman whom I see,
gives me a pain as if I injured them, because of my incapacity to do them
justice in the intercourse that passes between us. Two or more persons
together deoxygenate the air, apathize & paralyze me, I twist like the
poor eel in the exhausted receiver,* and my conviction of their sense &
virtue only makes matters worse for me by accusing my injustice. I am
made for chronic relations not for moments, and am wretched with fine
people who are only there for an hour. It is a town of great local & social
advantages, Plymouth; lying on the sea with this fine broken inland
country pine-covered & scooped into beds of two hundred lakes. Their
proverb is that there is a pond in P. for every day of the year. Billington
Sea is the best of all, & yet this superb chain of lakes which we pass in
returning from Half Way Pond might content one a hundred years. The
botany of the region is rare. The Epigaea named Mayflower at P. is now
found elsewhere. The beautiful & fragrant Sabbatia, the Empetrum, the
sundew, the Rhinanthus or yellow-rattle, and other plants are almost
peculiar to this spot. Great linden trees lift their green domes above the
town as seen from the Sea, and the graveyard hill shows the monuments
of the Pilgrims & their children as far out to sea as we could see anything of the town. The virtues of the Russells are as eminent & fragrant
here at this moment, as ever were the glories of that name in England:
and Lucia is a flower of the sweetest & softest beauty which real life ever
exhibited. These people know so well how to live, and have such perfect
adjustment in their tastes and their power to gratify them, that the ideal
life is necessarily thrown into the shade, and I have never seen a strong
conservatism appear so amiable & wise. We saw their well built houses
which an equal & generous economy warmed & animated; and their
good neighborhood was never surpassed: the use of the door bell &
knocker seem unknown. And the fine children who played in the yards
& piazzas appeared to come of a more amiable & gentle stock. I went
also over the new house of Mr A. J. and afterwards went with L. to his

---

* Vacuum jar.

comptinghouse, & took a lesson in arithmetic, as he showed us our inventory & our bad debts. What L. told of her youth struck us all as still true, that "she liked the apples very well, but never knew where the orchard was."

Aug. 17, 1843

Mr Webster loses nothing by comparison with brilliant men in the legal profession: he is as much before them as before the ordinary lawyer. At least I thought he appeared among these best lawyers of the Suffolk bar, like a schoolmaster among his boys. His wonderful organization, the perfection of his elocution, and all that thereto belongs, voice, accent, intonation, attitude, manner, are such as one cannot hope to see again in a century; then he is so thoroughly simple & wise in his rhetoric. Understanding language, & the use of the positive degree, all his words tell, and his rhetoric is perfect, so homely, so fit, so strong. Then he manages his matter so well, he hugs his fact so close, & will not let it go, & never indulges in a weak flourish, though he knows perfectly well how to make such exordiums & episodes & perorations as may give perspective to his harangue, without in the least embarrassing his plan or confounding his transitions. What is small, he shows as small, & makes the great, great. In speech he sometimes roars. And his words are like blows of an axe. His force of personal attack is terrible, he lays out his strength so directly in honest blows, and all his powers of voice, arm, eye, & whole man are so heartily united & bestowed on the adversary that he cannot fail to be felt.

Elizabeth Hoar says that she talked with him as one likes to go behind the Niagara Falls, so she tried to look into these famed caverns of eyes, & see how deep they were, and the whole man was magnificent.

It seems to me the Quixotism of criticism to quarrel with Webster because he has not this or that fine evangelical property. He is no saint, but the wild olive wood, ungrafted yet by grace, but according to his lights a very true & admirable man. His expansiveness seems to be necessary to him. Were he too prudent a Yankee it would be a sad deduction from his magnificence. I only wish he would never truckle, I do not care how much he spends.

Aug.–Sept. 1843

In the points of good breeding, what I most require & insist upon is deference. I like that every chair should be a throne & hold a king. And what I most dislike is a low sympathy of each with his neighbor's palate & belly at table, anticipating without words what he wishes to eat &

drink. If you wish bread, ask me for bread, & if you wish anchovies or lobster, ask me for them, & do not hold out your plate as if I knew already. I respect cats, they seem to have so much else in their heads besides their mess. Yet every natural function can be dignified by deliberation & privacy. I prefer a tendency to stateliness to an excess of fellowship. In all things I would have the island of a man inviolate. No degree of affection is to invade this religion. Lovers should guard their strangeness. As soon as they surrender that, they are no more lovers.

Society always values inoffensive people susceptible of conventional polish. The clergyman who would live in Boston must have taste.
The new gospel is, By taste are ye saved.*

H. D. T. sends me a paper with the old fault of unlimited contradiction. The trick of his rhetoric is soon learned. It consists in substituting for the obvious word & thought its diametrical antagonist. He praises wild mountains & winter forests for their domestic air; snow & ice for their warmth; villagers & wood choppers for their urbanity; and the wilderness for resembling Rome & Paris. With the constant inclination to dispraise cities & civilization, he yet can find no way to honour woods & woodmen except by paralleling them with towns & townsmen. W. E. C. declares the piece is excellent: but it makes me nervous & wretched to read it, with all its merits.

The thinker looks for God in the direction of the consciousness, the churchman out of it. If you ask the former for his definition of God, he would answer, "my possibility;" for his definition of man, "my actuality."

Is life a thunderstorm that we can see now by a flash the whole horizon, and then cannot see our right hand?

Never strike a king unless you are sure you shall kill him.

Sept. 3–12, 1843
Any form of government would content me in which the rulers were gentlemen, but it is in vain that I have tried to persuade myself that Mr Calhoun or Mr Clay or Mr Webster were such; they are underlings, & take the law from the dirtiest fellows. In England it usually appears as if the power were confided to persons of superior sentiment, but they have

---

*This sentence is crossed out.

not treated Russia as they ought in the affair of Poland. It is time these fellows should hear the truth from other quarters than the antislavery papers and Whig papers & Investigators & all other committed organs. We have allowed them to take a certain place in private society as if they were at the head of their countrymen: they must be told that they have dishonoured themselves & it can be allowed no longer; they are not now to be admitted to the society of scholars.

The relation of parents & children is usually reversed. The children become at last the parents of their parents.

I am in the habit of surrendering myself to my companion, so that it may easily happen that my companion finds himself some what tasked to meet the occasion. But the capital defect of my nature for society (as it is of so many others) is the want of animal spirits. They seem to me a thing incredible, as if God should raise the dead. I hear of what others perform by their aid, with fear. It is as much out of my possibility as the prowess of Coeur de Lion or an Irishman's day's work on the railroad.

Has the South European more animal spirits than we, that he is so joyous a companion? I well remember my stay at the *Hotel Giaccheri,* in Palermo, where I listened with pleasure to the novelty of the melo-dramatic conversation of a dozen citizens of the world. They mimicked in telling a story the voice & manner of the persons they described. They crowed like cocks, they hissed, cackled, barked, & screamed, and were it only by the physical strength they exerted in telling the story, kept the table in sympathetic life.

I think it will soon become the pride of this country to make gardens & adorn country houses. That is the fine art which especially fits us. Sculpture, painting, music, architecture do not thrive with us, but they seem as good as dead, & such life as they show is a sort of second child-hood. But land we have in greater extent than ever did any people of the same power, and the new modes of travelling are making it easy to culti-vate very distant tracts & yet remain in strict intercourse with the great centres of trade & population. And the whole force of all the arts goes to facilitate the decoration of lands & dwellings. A garden has this advan-tage, that it makes it indifferent where you live. If the landscape around you is pleasing, the garden shows it: if tame, it excludes it. A little grove which any farmer can find or cause to grow, will in a few years so fill the eye & mind of the inhabitant, as to make cataracts & chains of moun-tains quite unnecessary, and he is so contented with his alleys, his brook, his woodland, his orchard, his baths, & his piazza, that Niagara and the

Notch of the White Hills and Nantasket Beach are superfluities. The
other day came Caroline Sturgis with eyes full of Naushon & Nahant &
Niagara, dreaming by day & night of canoes, & lightning, & deer-parks,
& silver waves, & could hardly disguise her disdain for our poor cold
low life in Concord, like rabbits in a warren. Yet the interiors of our
woodland, which recommend the place to us, she did not see. And the
capital advantage which we possess here, that the whole town is permeable, that I can go through it like a park, distinguishes it above towns
built on three or four New Hampshire hills, having each one side at 45
degrees & the other side perpendicular. Then as the Indians dwell
where they can find good water, so my wife values her house because of
the pump in the kitchen above all palaces.

Sept. 13–25, 1843
   A poet in his holidays, or vacations rather, should write Criticism.

   'Tis a great convenience to be educated for a time in a countingroom
or attorney's business; then you may safely be a scholar the rest of your
life & will find the use of that partial thickening of the skin every day as
you will of your shoes or your hat. What mountains of nonsense will
you have cleared your brain of forever!

Sept. 26, 1843
   This morning Charles Lane left us after a two days' visit. He was
dressed in linen altogether, with the exception of his shoes, which were
lined with linen, & he wore no stockings. He was full of methods of an
improved life: valued himself chiefly just now on getting rid of the animals; thinks there is no economy in using them on a farm. He said, that
they could carry on their Family at Fruitlands in many respects better,
no doubt, if they wished to play it well. He said that the clergy for the
most part opposed the Temperance Reform, and conspicuously this
simplicity in diet, because they were alarmed, as soon as such nonconformity appeared, by the conviction that the next question people would
ask, would be, "Of what use are the clergy?"

Sept.–Nov. 1843
   Read Montaigne's Journey into Italy, which is an important part of
his biography. I like him so well that I value even his register of his disease—Is it that the valetudinarian gives the assurance that he is not
ashamed of himself? Then what a treasure, to enlarge my knowledge of
his friend by his narrative of the last days & the death of Etienne de la
Boetie. In Boston when I heard lately Chandler Robbins preach so well
the funeral sermon of Henry Ware, I thought of Montaigne, who would

also have felt how much this surface called Unitarianism admits of being opened & deepened, and that this was as good & defensible a post of life to occupy as any other. It was a true cathedral music & brought chancels & choirs, surplices, ephods, & arks & hierarchies into presence. Certainly Montaigne is the antagonist of the fanatic reformer. Under the oldest mouldiest conventions he would prosper just as well as in the newest world.

George Barrell Emerson read me a criticism on Spenser, who makes twenty trees of different kinds grow in one grove, wherein the critic says it was an imaginary grove. G. B. E., however, doubts not it was after nature, for he knows a piece of natural woodland near Boston, wherein twentyfour different trees grow together in a small grove.

Hard clouds, & hard expressions, & hard manners, I love.

In Salem, the aristocracy is of the merchants, even the lawyers are a second class. In Boston is aristocracy of families which have inherited their wealth & position, and of lawyers & of merchants. In Charleston, the Merchants are an inferior class, the Planters are the aristocracy. In England the aristocracy, incorporated by law & education, degrades life for the unprivileged classes. Long ago they wrote on placards in the streets "Of what use are the lords?" And now that the misery of Ireland & of the English manufacturing counties famishes & growls around the park fences of Lord Shannon, Lord Cork, & Sir Robert Peel, a park and a castle will be a less pleasant abode. The only compensation to the embittered feeling of a proud commoner, is in the reflection that the worthless lord who by the magic of a title paralyzes his arm & plucks from him half the graces & rights of a man, is himself also an aspirant excluded with the same ruthlessness from higher circles, for there is no end to the wheels within wheels of this spiral heaven. Philip II of Spain rated his Ambassador for neglecting business of great importance in Italy, whilst he debated some *pundonore* with the French Ambassador, "How have you left a business of importance for a ceremony!" The Ambassador replied, "How? for a ceremony? Your majesty's self is but a ceremony." In the East, where the religious sentiment comes in to the support of the aristocracy, & in the Romish Church also, there is a grain of sweetness in the tyranny, but in England the fact seems to me intolerable that no man of letters is received into the best society except as a lion. I must nevertheless respect this *Order* as "a part of the order of Providence," as my good Aunt used to say of the rich, when I see, as I do everywhere, a class born with these attributes of rule. The class of officers I recognize everywhere in town or country. . . . These gallants come into the world to ruffle it & by rough or smooth to find their way to the top. When I spoke to Nathaniel Hawthorne of the class who hold the keys of State street & are yet excluded from the best Boston circles, he said "Perhaps he has a heavy wife."

Queenie thinks the Fruitlands people far too gross in their way of living. She prefers to live on snow.

Let me live in America, & until I am very good or very able not creep into England to cast another foolsweight to the side of flattery & servility. Yet am I sure that worth & personal power must sit crowned in all companies, nor will Lord Herbert of Cherbury, or Daniel Webster or Edward Taylor or Bronson Alcott, so long as they are themselves, be slighted or affronted in any company of civilized men. Our people creep abroad that they may ruffle it at home. But one part of their apprenticeship, their compliances to the foreign great, they quite omit to report in their book of travels. In solitude, in the woods, for example, every man is a noble, and we cannot prize too highly the staid & erect & plain manners of our farmers.

The only straight line in nature that I remember is the spider swinging down from a twig.
The rainbow & the horizon seen at sea are good curves.
The hair on a cat's back is a straight line.

Yankee. John Richardson got a living by buying odd bits of land near good dwelling houses & removing on to them some old crazy barn or wretched shop & keeping it there until the proprietor of the house paid him a round sum for the land.

In Montaigne, man & thinker are inseparable: you cannot insert the blade of a pen knife betwixt the man & his book.

Ellery says, Wordsworth writes like a man who takes snuff.

Tennyson is a master of metre but it is as an artist who has learned admirable mechanical secrets. He has no woodnotes. Great are the dangers of education—skepticism. Tennyson a cosmetic poet.

My great grandfather was Rev. Joseph Emerson of Malden, son of Edward Emerson, Esq. of Newbury(port). I used often to hear that when William, son of Joseph, was yet a boy walking before his father to church, on a Sunday, his father checked him, "William, you walk as if the earth was not good enough for you." "I did not know it, sir," he replied with the utmost humility. This is one of the household anecdotes in which I have found a relationship. 'Tis curious but the same remark was made to me, by Mrs Lucy Brown, when I walked one day under her windows here in Concord.

We come down with freethinking into the dear institutions & at once make carnage amongst them. We are innocent of any such fell purpose as the sequel seems to impute to us. We were only smoking a cigar, but it turns out to be a powder mill that we are promenading.

My divine Thomas Taylor in his translation of Cratylus ... calls Christianity "a certain most irrational & gigantic impiety."

People came, it seems, to my lectures with expectation that I was to realize the Republic I described, & ceased to come when they found this reality no nearer. They mistook me. I am & always was a painter. I paint still with might & main, & choose the best subjects I can. Many have I seen come & go with false hopes & fears, and dubiously affected by my pictures. But I paint on. I count this distinct vocation, which never leaves me in doubt what to do but in all times, places, & fortunes, gives me an open future, to be the great felicity of my lot.

The condition of participation in any man's thought is entering the gate of that life. No man can be intellectually apprehended. As long as you see only with your eyes, you do not see him. You must be committed, before you shall be entrusted with the secrets of any party.

Alcott came, the magnificent dreamer, brooding as ever on the renewal or reedification of the social fabric after ideal law, heedless that he had been uniformly rejected by every class to whom he has addressed himself and just as sanguine & vast as ever; the most cogent example of the drop too much which nature adds of each man's peculiarity. To himself he seems the only realist, & whilst I & other men wish to deck the dulness of the months with here & there a fine action or hope, he would weave the whole a new texture of truth & beauty. Now he spoke of marriage & the fury that would assail him who should lay his hand on that institution, for reform: and spoke of the secret doctrines of Fourier. I replied, as usual—that, I thought no man could be trusted with it; the formation of new alliances is so delicious to the imagination, that St Paul & St John would be riotous; and that we cannot spare the coarsest muniment of virtue. Very pathetic it is to see this wandering emperor from year to year making his round of visits from house to house of such as do not exclude him, seeking a companion, tired of pupils.

Nov. 5-8, 1843

The Reformers wrote very ill. They made it a rule not to bolt their flour & unfortunately neglected also to sift their thoughts. . . .

Alcott & Lane want feet; they are always feeling of their shoulders to find if their wings are sprouting; but next best to wings are cowhide boots, which society is always advising them to put on.

Married women uniformly decided against the communities. It was to them like the brassy & lackered life in hotels. The common school was well enough, but the common nursery they had grave objections to. Eggs might be hatched in ovens, but the hen on her own account greatly preferred the old way. A hen without chickens was but half a hen.

Nov.–Dec. 1843

Each man reserves to himself alone the right of being tedious.

Dec. 25, 1843

At the performing of Handel's Messiah I heard some delicious strains & understood a very little of all that was told me. My ear received but a little thereof. But as the master overpowered the littleness & incapableness of the performers, & made them conductors of his electricity, so it was easy to see what efforts nature was making through so many hoarse, wooden, & imperfect persons to produce beautiful voices, fluid & soulguided men & women. The genius of nature could well be discerned. By right & might we should become participant of her invention, & not wait for morning & evening to know their peace, but prepossess it. I walked in the bright paths of sound, and liked it best when the long continuance of a chorus had made the ear insensible to the music, made it as if there was none, then I was quite solitary & at ease in the melodious uproar. Once or twice in the solos, when well sung, I could play tricks, as I like to do, with my eyes, darken the whole house & brighten & transfigure the central singer, and enjoy the enchantment.

This wonderful piece of music carries us back into the rich historical past. It is full of the Roman Church & its hierarchy & its architecture. Then further it rests on & requires so deep a faith in Christianity that it seems bereft of half & more than half its power when sung today in this unbelieving city.

Dec. 31, 1843

The year ends, and how much the years teach which the days never know! The individuals who compose our company converse, & meet, & part, & variously combine, and somewhat comes of it all, but the individual is always mistaken. He designed many things, drew in others, quarrelled with some or all, blundered much, & something is done; all are a little advanced; but the individual is always mistaken.

Jan. 1844

We rail at trade, but the historian of the world will see that it was the principle of liberty, that it settled America, & destroyed feudalism, and made peace & keeps peace, that it will abolish slavery.

Kant, it seems, searched the Metaphysics of the Selfreverence which is the favourite position of modern ethics, & demonstrated to the Consciousness that itself alone exists.

The two parties in life are the believers & unbelievers, variously named. The believer is poet, saint, democrat, theocrat, free-trade, no-church, no capital punishment, idealist.

The unbeliever supports the church, education, the fine arts, &c as *amusements* . . .

But the unbelief is very profound: who can escape it? I am nominally a believer: yet I hold on to property: I eat my bread with unbelief. I approve every wild action of the experimenters. I say what they say concerning celibacy or money or community of goods and my only apology for not doing their work is preoccupation of mind. I have a work of my own which I know I can do with some success. It would leave that undone if I should undertake with them and I do not see in myself any vigour equal to such an enterprise. My Genius loudly calls me to stay where I am, even with the degradation of owning bankstock and seeing poor men suffer whilst the Universal Genius apprises me of this disgrace & beckons me to the martyr's & redeemer's office.

Jan. 26, 1844

Finish each day before you begin the next, and interpose a solid wall of sleep between two. This you cannot do without temperance.

Jan. 30, 1844

I wrote to M. F. that I had no experiences nor progress to reconcile me to the calamity whose anniversary returned the second time last Saturday. The senses have a right to their method as well as the mind; there should be harmony in facts as well as in truths. Yet these ugly breaks happen there, which the continuity of theory does not compensate. The amends are of a different kind from the mischief.

Jan.–March 1844

That idea which I approach & am magnetized by—is my country.

We read in youth a great many true proverbs concerning the narrowness & inconsistency of men but we are very tardy in verifying them on our own respectable neighbors of whom they are accurately descriptive. I knew a Dr S., a pious Swedenborgian in the country, from whom I heard much truth. He is now a tippler. We have accustomed ourselves to respect our dignified fellow citizens so much that their exceeding narrowness & selfishness puzzles us & we are slow at calling it by its proper name.

I am sorry to say that the Numas & Pythagorases have usually a spice of charlatanism & that abolition Societies & Communities are dangerous fixtures. The manliness of man is a frail & exquisite fruit which does not keep its perfection twenty four hours. Its sweet fragrance cannot be bottled or barreled or exported. Carlyle is an eloquent writer but his recommendations of emigration & education appear very inadequate. Noble as it seems to work for the race, & hammer out constitutions for phalanxes, it can only be justly done by mediocre thinkers, or men of practical, not theoretic faculty. As soon as a scholar attempts it, I suspect him. Good physicians have least faith in medicine. Good priests the least faith in church-forms.

It is not enough to say that we are bundles of moods, for we always rank our mental states. The graduation is exquisite. We are not a bundle but a house.

When I address a large assembly, as last Wednesday, I am always apprised what an opportunity is there: not for reading to them as I do, lively miscellanies, but for painting in fire my thought, & being agitated to agitate. One must dedicate himself to it and think with his audience in his mind, so as to keep the perspective & symmetry of the oration, and enter into all the easily forgotten secrets of a great nocturnal assembly & their relation to the speaker. But it would be fine music & in the present well rewarded; that is, he should have his audience at his devotion and all other fames would hush before his. Now eloquence is merely fabulous. When we talk of it, we draw on our fancy. It is one of many things which I should like to do, but it requires a seven years' wooing.

* * *

Now when at any time I take part in a public debate, I wish on my return home to be shampooed & in all other ways aired & purified.

Precisely what the painter or the sculptor or the epic rhapsodist feels, I feel in the presence of this house, which stands to me for the human race, the desire, namely, to express myself fully, symmetrically, gigantically to them, not dwarfishly & fragmentarily. H. D. T., with whom I talked of this last night, does not or will not perceive how natural is this, and only hears the word Art in a sinister sense. But I speak of instincts. I did not make the desires or know anything about them: I went to the public assembly, put myself in the conditions, & instantly feel this new craving—I hear the voice, I see the beckoning of this Ghost. To me it is vegetation, the pullulation & universal budding of the plant man. Art is the path of the creator to his work. The path or methods are ideal and eternal, though few men ever see them: not the artist himself for years, or for a lifetime, unless he come into the conditions. Then he is apprised with wonder what herds of daemons hem him in. He can no more rest: he says, 'By God, it is in me & must go forth of me.' I go to this place and am galvanized, and the torpid eyes of my sensibility are opened. I hear myself speak as a stranger—Most of the things I say are conventional; but I say something which is original & beautiful. That charms me. I would say nothing else but such things. In our way of talking, we say, that is mine, that is yours; but this poet knows well that it is not his, that it is as strange & beautiful to him as to you; he would fain hear the like eloquence at length.

Once having tasted this immortal ichor, we cannot have enough of it. Our appetite is immense. And, as "an admirable power flourishes in intelligibles," according to Plotinus, "which perpetually fabricates," it is of the last importance that these things get spoken. What a little of all we know, is said! What drops of all the sea of our science are baled up! And by what accident it is that these are spoken, whilst so many thoughts sleep in nature!

Hence the oestrum of speech: hence these throbs & heart beatings at the door of the assembly to the end, namely, that the thought may be ejaculated as Logos or Word.

The text of our life is accompanied all along by this commentary or gloss of dreams.

The question of the annexation of Texas is one of those which look very differently to the centuries and to the years. It is very certain that the strong British race which have now overrun so much of this continent, must also overrun that tract, & Mexico & Oregon also, and it will in the course of ages be of small import by what particular occasions & methods it was done. It is a secular* question. It is quite necessary & true to our New England character that we should consider the question in its local & temporary bearings, and resist the annexation with tooth & nail.

It is a measure which goes not by right nor by wisdom but by feeling.

It would be a pity to dissolve the union & so diminish immensely every man's personal importance. We are just beginning to feel our oats.

H. D. T. said he knew but one secret, which was to do one thing at a time, and though he has his evenings for study, if he was in the day inventing machines for sawing his plumbago, he invents wheels all the evening & night also; and if this week he has some good reading & thoughts before him, his brain runs on that all day, whilst pencils pass through his hands. I find in me an opposite facility or perversity, that I never seem well to do a particular work, until another is due. I cannot write the poem though you give me a week, but if I promise to read a lecture day after tomorrow, at once the poem comes into my head & now the rhymes will flow. And let the proofs of the Dial be crowding on me from the printer, and I am full of faculty how to make the Lecture.

Pure intellect is the pure devil when you have got off all the masks of Mephistopheles. It is a painful symbol to me that the index or forefinger is always the most soiled of all the fingers.

March 12, 1844

On Sunday evening, 10th inst. at the close of the fifteenth year since my ordination as minister in the Second Church, I made an address to the people on the occasion of closing the old house, now a hundred & twenty three years old, and the oldest church in Boston. Yesterday they begun to pull it down.

March–April 1844

It is curious that intellectual men should be most attractive to women. But women are magnetic; intellectual men are unmagnetic: therefore as soon as they meet, communication is found difficult or impossible. Various devices are tried in the villages to *wont* them, such as candy parties, nut-crackings, picnics, sleighrides, charades, but with slender success.

---

*Of long duration.

* * *

I have always found our American day short. The constitution of a Teutonic scholar with his twelve, thirteen, or fourteen hours a day, is fabulous to me. I become nervous & peaked with a few days editing the Dial, & watching the stagecoach to send proofs to printers. If I try to get many hours in a day, I shall not have any.

In America I grieve to miss the strong black blood of the English race: ours is a pale diluted stream. What a company of brilliant young persons I have seen with so much expectation! the sort is very good, but none is good enough of his sort. Every one an imperfect specimen, respectable not valid. Irving thin, & Channing thin, & Bryant & Dana, Prescott & Bancroft. There is Webster, but he cannot do what he would; he cannot do Webster. Then the youth, as I said, are all promising failures. No writing is here, no redundant strength, but declamation, straining, correctness, & all other symptoms of debility.

Alcott has been writing poetry, he says, all winter. I fear there is nothing for me in it. His overpowering personality destroys all poetic faculty.

Unhappily no knife is long enough to reach to the heart of any enemy we have. If what we hate was murderable, that would be some comfort.

"My dear sir," said my friend to her suitor, "I cannot realize you."

May 8, 1844
This morn the air smells of vanilla & oranges.

May? 1844
Our people are slow to learn the wisdom of sending character instead of talent to Congress. Again & again they have sent a man of great acuteness, a fine scholar, a fine forensic orator, and some master of the brawls has crunched him up in his hand like a bit of paper. At last they sent a man with a back and he defied the whole southern delegation when they attempted to smother him & has conquered them. Mr Adams is a man of great powers, but chiefly he is a sincere man & not a man of the moment and of a single measure. And besides the success or failure of the measure there remains to him the respect of all men for his earnestness. When Mr Webster argues the case there is the success or the failure, and the admiration of the unerring talent & intellectual nature, but no respect for an affection to a principle. Could Mr

Webster have given himself to the cause of Abolition of Slavery in Congress, he would have been the darling of this continent, of all the youth, all the genius, all the virtue in America. Had an angel whispered in his young ear, Never mind the newspapers, Fling yourself on this principle of freedom, Show the legality of freedom; though they frown & bluster they are already half convinced & at last you shall have their votes; the tears of the love & joy & pride of the world would have been his.

Ole Bull a dignifying civilizing influence. Yet he was there for exhibition, not for music; for the wonders of his execution, not as St. Cecilia incarnated, who would be there to carry a point, & degrading all her instruments into meekest means. Yet he played as a man who found a violin in his hand, & so was bent to make much of that; but if he had found a chisel or a sword or a spyglass or a troop of boys, would have made much of them. It was a beautiful spectacle. I have not seen an artist with manners so pleasing. What a sleep as of Egypt on his lips in the midst of his rapturous music!

H. T.'s conversation consisted of a continual coining of the present moment into a sentence & offering it to me. I compared it to a boy who from the universal snow lying on the earth gathers up a little in his hand, rolls it into a ball, & flings it at me.

Spring 1844

The finest women have a feeling we cannot sympathize with in regard to marriage. They cannot spare the exaltation of love & the experiences of marriage from their history. But shall a virgin descend & marry below her? Does she not see that Nature may be trusted for completing her own circle? The true Virgin will raise herself by just degrees into a goddess admirable & helpful to all beholders.

H. D. T. said that the other world was all his art; that his pencils would draw no other; that his jackknife would cut nothing else. He does not use it as a means.

Henry is a good substantial childe, not encumbered with himself. He has no troublesome memory, no wake, but lives extempore, & brings today a new proposition as radical & revolutionary as that of yesterday, but different. The only man of leisure in the town. He is a good Abbot Samson: & carries counsel in his breast. If I cannot show his performance much more manifest than that of the other grand promisers, at least I can see that with his practical faculty, he has declined all the kingdoms of this world. Satan has no bribe for him.

* * *

In America we are such rowdies in church & state, and the very boys are so soon ripe, that I think no philosophical skepticism will make much sensation. Spinosa pronounced that there was but one substance—yea, verily; but that boy yonder told me yesterday he thought the pinelog was God, & that God was in the jakes. What can Spinoza tell the boy?

Even Dickens is doubtless of much use to this country, though in so humble a way as to circulate into all towns & into the lowest classes the lesson which is pasted in the waterclosets of public houses—*Do not spit, & please close the covers.*

In America, we drag a pine-log to a mill, turn a crank, & it comes out at the other end chairs & tables.

I read a little in Behmen. In reading there is a sort of half & half mixture. The book must be good, but the reader must also be active. I have never had good luck with Behmen before today. And now I see that his excellence is in his comprehensiveness, not like Plato in his precision. His propositions are vague, inadequate, & straining. It is his aim that is great. He will know not one thing, but all things. He is like those great swaggering country geniuses that come now & then down from New Hampshire to college & soon demand to learn not Horace & Homer but also Euclid and Spinoza, and Voltaire, and Palladio, & Columbus, & Bonaparte, and Linnaeus.

Woman. It is the worst of her condition that its advantages are permissive. Society lives on the system of money and woman comes at money & money's worth through compliment. I should not dare to be woman. Plainly they are created for that better system which supersedes money. But today—In our civilization her position is often pathetic. What is she not expected to do & suffer for some invitation to strawberries & cream. Mercifully their eyes are holden that they cannot see.

Pythagoras was right who used music as a medicine. I lament my want of ear, but never quite despair of becoming sensible to this discipline. We cannot spare any stimulant or any purgative, we lapse so quickly into flesh & sleep. We must use all the exalters that will bring us into an expansive & productive state, or to the top of our condition. But to hear music, as one would take an ice-cream or a bath, & to forget it the next day, gives me a humble picture.

* * *

I think the best argument of the conservative is this bad one; that he is convinced that the angry democrat who wishes him to divide his park & chateau with him will, on entering into the possession, instantly become conservative, & hold the property & spend it as selfishly as himself. For a better man, I might dare to renounce my estate; for a worse man, or for as bad a man as I, why should I? All the history of man with unbroken sequence of examples establishes this inference. Yet is it very low & degrading ground to stand upon. We must never reason from history, but plant ourselves on the ideal.

June 15, 1844

A second visit to the Shakers with Mr Hecker. Their family worship was a painful spectacle. I could remember nothing but the Spedale dei Pazzi at Palermo; this shaking of their hands like the paws of dogs before them as they shuffled in this dunce-dance seemed the last deliration. If there was anything of heart & life in this it did not appear to me: and as Swedenborg said that the angels never look at the back of the head so I felt that I saw nothing else. My fellow men could hardly appear to less advantage before me than in this senseless jumping. The music seemed to me dragged down nearly to the same bottom. And when you come to talk with them on their topic, which they are very ready to do, you find such exaggeration of the virtue of celibacy, that you might think you had come into a hospital-ward of invalids afflicted with priapism. Yet the women were well dressed and appeared with dignity as honoured persons. And I judge the whole society to be cleanly & industrious but stupid people. And these poor countrymen with their nasty religion fancy themselves *the Church* of the world and are as arrogant as the poor negroes on the Gambia river.

Fourier said, Man exists to gratify his twelve passions: and he proposes to remove the barriers which false philosophy & religion & prudence have built against indulgence. Some of the old heroic legislators proposed to open public brothels as safety-valves to defend virtuous women from the occasional extravagances of desire in violent persons & to yield a resort of less danger to young men in the fury of passion. And in Amsterdam & other cities, the governments have authorized the stews. Well, Swedenborg too wandered through the Universe and found not only heavenly societies but horrid cavernous regions where imps & dragons delighted themselves in all bestialities and he said these too enjoyed their condition & recreations, as well as the cherubim theirs. Fourier too has a sacred Legion and an order called sacred, of Chastity, Virgins & bachelors; a lower order of husband & wife; a lower of free companions & harlots. In having that higher order he gives all up. For the vulgar world not yet emancipated from prejudice replies to his invitation, Well, I will select only that part from your system, and leave the sty to those who like it. I have observed that indulgence always effeminates. I have organs also & delight in pleasure, but I have experience also that this pleasure is the bait of a trap.

June? 1844
   If I made laws for Shakers or a School, I should gazette every Saturday all the words they were wont to use in reporting religious experience as 'Spiritual life,' 'God,' 'soul,' 'cross,' &c. and if they could not find new ones next week they might remain silent.

   Be an opener of doors for such as come after thee and do not try to make the Universe a blind alley.

Spring–Summer 1844
   Society is babyish. Talleyrand's question is the main one to be asked; not, is he honest? is he rich? is he committed? is he of the movement, or, is he of the establishment? but, "Is he any body?" We want fire; a little less mutton and a little more genius.

   It is by means of my vices that I understand yours.

   The abolitionists with their holy cause; the Friends of the Poor; the ministers at large; the Prison Discipline Agents; the Soup Societies, the whole class of professed Philanthropists—it is strange & horrible to say—are an altogether odious set of people, whom one would be sure to shun as the worst of bores & canters.

   · Henry described Hugh as saving every slip & stone & seed, & planting it. He picks up a peach stone & puts it in his pocket to plant. That is his vocation in the world, to be a planter of plants. Not less is a writer to heed his vocation of reporting. Whatever he beholds or experiences, he is to daguerrotype. It is all nonsense that they say that some things rebuke literature, & are undescribable; he knows better, & would report God himself or attempt it. Nothing so sudden, nothing so broad, nothing so subtle, nothing so dear, but it comes therefore commended to his pen, & he will write. In his eyes a man is the faculty of reporting, & the universe is the possibility of being reported.

   Life is so affirmative that I can never hear of personal vigour of any kind, great power of performance, without lively sympathy & fresh resolutions.

* * *

When at last in a race a new principle appears, an idea, that con-
serves it. Ideas only save races. If the black man is feeble & not important to the existing races, not on a par with the best race, the black man
must serve & be sold & exterminated. But if the black man carries in his
bosom an indispensable element of a new & coming civilization, for the
sake of that element no wrong nor strength nor circumstance can hurt
him, he will survive & play his part. So now it seems to me that the arrival of such men as Toussaint if he is pure blood, or of Douglas if he is
pure blood, outweighs all the English & American humanity. The Antislavery of the whole world is but dust in the balance, a poor squea-
mishness & nervousness; the might & the right is here. Here is the
Anti-Slave. Here is Man; & if you have man, black or white is an insignificance. Why at night all men are black. The intellect, that is miraculous, who has it has the talisman, his skin & bones are transparent, he is
a statue of the living God, him I must love & serve & perpetually seek &
desire & dream on: and who has it not is superfluous. But a compassion
for that which is not & cannot be useful & lovely, is degrading & maud-
lin, this towing along as by ropes that which cannot go itself. Let us not
be our own dupes; all the songs & newspapers & subscriptions of money
& vituperation of those who do not agree with us will avail nothing
against eternal fact. I say to you, you must save yourself, black or white,
man or woman. Other help is none. I esteem the occasion of this jubilee
to be that proud discovery that the black race can begin to contend with
the white; that in the great anthem of the world which we call history, a
piece of many parts & vast compass, after playing a long time a very low
& subdued accompaniment they perceive the time arrived when they
can strike in with force & effect & take a master's part in the music. The
civilization of the world has arrived at that pitch that their moral quality
is becoming indispensable, & the genius of this race is to be honoured
for itself. For this they have been preserved in sandy desarts, in rice
swamps, in kitchens & shoeshops so long. Now let them emerge clothed
& in their own form. I esteem this jubilee & the fifty years' movement
which has preceded it to be the announcement of that fact & our antislavery societies, boastful as we are, only the shadow & witness to that
fact. The negro has saved himself, and the white man very patronisingly
says, I have saved you. If the negro is a fool all the white men in the
world cannot save him though they should die.

Does not he do more to abolish Slavery who works all day steadily in
his garden, than he who goes to the abolition meeting & makes a speech?
The antislavery agency like so many of our employments is a suicidal
business. Whilst I talk, some poor farmer drudges & slaves for me. It requires a just costume then, the office of agent or speaker, he should sit

very low & speak very meekly like one compelled to do a degrading thing. Do not then, I pray you, talk of the work & the fight, as if it were any thing more than a pleasant oxygenation of your lungs. It is easy & pleasant to ride about the country amidst the peaceful farms of New England & New York &, sure every where of a strict sympathy from the intelligent & good, argue for liberty, & browbeat & chastise the dull clergyman or lawyer that ventures to limit or qualify our statement. This is not work. It needs to be done but it does not consume heart & brain, does not shut out culture, does not imprison you as the farm & the shoeshop & the forge. There is really no danger & no extraordinary energy demanded; it supplies what it wants. I think if the witnesses of the truth would do their work symmetrically, they must stop all this boast & frolic & vituperation, & in lowliness free the slave by love in the heart. Let the diet be low, & a daily feast of commemoration of their brother in bonds. Let them eat his corn cake dry, as he does. Let them wear negrocloths. Let them leave long discourses to the defender of slavery, and show the power of true words which are always few. Let them do their own work. He who does his own work frees a slave. He who does not his own work, is a slave-holder. Whilst we sit here talking & smiling, some person is out there in field & shop & kitchen doing what we need, without talk or smiles. Therefore, let us, if we assume the dangerous pretension of being abolitionists, & make that our calling in the world, let us do it symmetrically. The world asks, do the abolitionists eat sugar? do they wear cotton? do they smoke tobacco? Are they their own servants? Have they managed to put that dubious institution of servile labour on an agreeable & thoroughly intelligible & transparent foundation? It is not possible that these purists accept the accommodations of hotels, or even of private families, on the existing profane arrangements? If they do, of course, not conscience, but mere prudence & propriety will seal their mouths on the inconsistences of churchmen. Two tables in every house! Abolitionists at one & *servants* at the other! It is a calumny that you utter. There never was, I am persuaded, an asceticism so austere as theirs, from the peculiar emphasis of their testimony. The planter does not want slaves: give him money: give him a machine that will provide him with as much money as the slaves yield, & he will thankfully let them go: he does not love whips, or usurping overseers, or sulky swarthy giants creeping round his house & barns by night with lucifer matches in their hands & knives in their pockets. No; only he wants his luxury, & he will pay even this price for it. It is not possible then that the abolitionist will begin the assault on his luxury, by any other means than the abating of his own. A silent fight without warcry or triumphant brag, then, is the new abolition of New England sifting the thronging ranks of the champions, the speakers, the poets, the editors, the subscribers, the givers, & reducing the armies to a handful of just men & women. Alas! alas! my brothers, there is never an abolitionist in New England.

Fall–Winter 1844
It is a great happiness to escape a religious education. Calvinism destroys religion of character.

A gentleman may have many innocent propensities but if he chances to have the habit of slipping arsenic into the soup of whatever persons sit next him at table he must expect some inconvenience. He may call it his peculiar institution, a mere way of his, he never puts it in his own soup, only in the soup of his neighbour, & even only in some of his neighbours', for example he is partial to light hair, & only spices the dish of such as have black hair, & he may persuade his chaplain to find him a text & be very indignant & patriotic & quarrelsome & moral & religious on the subject & swear to die in defence of this old & strong habit he has contracted.

The conscience of the white & the improvement of the black cooperated, & the Emancipation became inevitable. It is a great deed with great sequel & cannot now be put back. The same movement goes forward with advantage; the conscience is more tender & the black more respectable. Meantime the belly is also represented & the ignorant & sensual feel the danger & resist, so it goes slower. But it gains & the haters of Garrison have lived to rejoice in that grand world-movement which every age or two casts out so masterly an agent of good. I cannot speak of that gentleman without respect.

I wish that Webster & Everett & also the young political aspirants of Massachusetts should hear Wendell Phillips speak, were it only for the capital lesson in eloquence they might learn of him. This, namely, that the first & the second & the third part of the art is to keep your feet always firm on a fact. They talk about the Whig party. There is no such thing in nature. They talk about the Constitution. It is a scorned piece of paper. He feels after a fact & finds it in the money-making, in the commerce of New England, and in the devotion of the Slave states to their interest, which enforces them to the crimes which they avow or disavow, but do & will do. He keeps no terms with sham churches or shamming legislatures, and must & will grope till he feels the stones. Then his other & better part, his subsoil, is the *morale,* which he solidly shows. Eloquence, poetry, friendship, philosophy, politics, in short all power must & will have the real or they cannot exist.

* * *

Alcott does not do justice to the merits of labour: The whole human
race spend their lives in hard work from simple & necessary motives,
and feel the approbation of their conscience; and meet with this talker at
their gate, who, as far as they see, does not labour himself, & takes up
this grating tone of authority & accusation against them. His unpopularity is not at all wonderful. There must be not a few fine words, but
very many hard strokes every day, to get what even an ascetic wants.

Putnam pleased the Boston people by railing at Goethe in his ΦBK
oration because Goethe was not a New England Calvinist. If our lovers
of greatness & goodness after a local type & standard could expand their
scope a little they would see that a worshipper of truth and a most subtle
perceiver of truth like Goethe with his impatience of all falsehood &
scorn of hypocrisy was a far more useful man & incomparably more
helpful ally to religion than ten thousand lukewarm churchmembers
who keep all the traditions and leave a tithe of their estates to establish
them. But this clergyman should have known that the movement which
in America created these Unitarian dissenters of which he is one, begun
in the mind of this great man he traduces; that he is precisely the individual in whom the new ideas appeared & opened to their greatest extent & with universal application, which more recently the active scholars in the different departments of Science, of State, & of the Church
have carried in parcels & thimblefuls to their petty occasions. Napoleon
I join with him as being both representatives of the impatience & reaction of nature against the morgue of conventions, two stern realists.
They want a third peer who shall stand for sentiment as they for truth &
power.

Jan.–March? 1845

In January 1845 arose the question again in our village Lyceum
whether we should accept the offer of the Ladies who proposed to contribute to the Course a Lecture on Slavery by Wendell Phillipps. I
pressed the acceptance on the part of the Curators of this proffer, on two
grounds; 1. because the Lyceum was poor, & should add to the length &
variety of their Entertainment by all innocent means, especially when a
discourse from one of the best speakers in the Commonwealth was vol-
unteered; 2. because I thought in the present state of this country the
particular subject of Slavery had a commanding right to be heard in all
places in New England in season & sometimes out of season, that as in
Europe the partition of Poland was an outrage so flagrant that all European men must be willing once in every month or two to be plagued
with hearing over again the horrid story; so this iniquity of Slavery

in this country was a ghost that would not down at the bidding of Boston merchants, or the best democratic drill-officers; but the people must consent to be plagued with it from time to time until something was done, & we had appeased the negro blood so.

Feb. 26, 1845

A thaw for more than a week & three days of heavenly weather bringing all mythology on their breezy dawns. Down falls the water from the steeps; up shoots the northern-light after sunset from the horizon. But nature seems a dissipated hussey. She seduces us from all work, listen to her rustling leaves—to the invitations which each blue peak, and rolling river, & fork of woodland road offers, & we should never wield the shovel or the trowel.

March 15, 1845

How gladly, after three months sliding on snow, our feet find the ground again!

Jan.–March 1845

Very great was the inconvenience in the country of finding domestics, but the darker the night the nearer the dawn. When at last we could absolutely get none, our deliverance was suddenly achieved: we instantly simplified in good earnest our modes of living: we disused fifty luxuries and our health & wealth & morals were improved.

A despair has crept over the Whig party in this country. They the active, enterprizing, intelligent, well meaning, & wealthy part of the people, the real bone & strength of the American people, find themselves paralysed & defeated everywhere by the hordes of ignorant & deceivable natives & the armies of foreign voters who fill Pennsylvania, N. Y., & New Orleans, and by those unscrupulous editors & orators who have assumed to lead these masses. The creators of wealth and conscientious, rational, & responsible persons, those whose names are given in as fit for jurors, for referees, for offices of trust, those whose opinion is public opinion, find themselves degraded into observers, & violently turned out of all share in the action & counsels of the nation.

The position of Massachusetts seems to me to be better for Mr Hoar's visit to S. Carolina, in this point, that one illusion is dispelled.*

---

*Samuel Hoar, an agent of Massachusetts, had gone to South Carolina in December, 1844, to take measures for the protection of Negro seamen who were citizens of Massachusetts and faced imprisonment and sale when they entered the port of Charleston. On a request to the governor from the legislature of South Carolina, Hoar was expelled. [*JMN*]

Massachusetts was dishonoured before; but she was credulous in the protection of the Constitution & either did not believe or affected not to believe that she was dishonoured. Now all doubt on that subject is removed, & every Carolina boy will not fail to tell every Massachusetts boy, whenever they meet, how the fact stands. The Boston merchants would willingly salve the matter over, but they cannot hereafter receive Southern gentlemen at their tables, without a consciousness of shame. I do not like very well to hear a man say he has been in Carolina. I know too well what men she suffers in her towns. He is no freeman.

In every government there are wild lawless provinces where the constituted authorities are forced to content themselves with such obedience as they can get. Turkey has its Algiers & Morocco, Naples its Calabria, Rome its Fondi, London its Alsatia, & Bristol County its Slab Bridge, where the life of a man is not worth insuring. South Carolina must be set down in that infamous category, and we must go there in disguise & with pistols in our pockets leaving our pocketbooks at home, making our wills before we go.

Good manners require a great deal of time, as does a wise treatment of children. Orientals have time, the desert, & stars; the occidentals have not.

The state is our neighbors; our neighbors are the state. It is a folly to treat the state as if it were some individual arbitrarily willing thus and so. It is the same company of poor devils we know so well, of William & Edward & John & Henry, doing as they are obliged to do, & trying hard to do conveniently what must & will be done. They do not impose a tax. God & the nature of things imposes the tax, requires that the land shall bear its burden, of road, & of social order, & defence; & I confess I lose all respect for this tedious denouncing of the state by idlers who rot in indolence, selfishness, & envy in the chimney corner.

Eve softly with her womb
Bit him to death

Lightly was woman snared, herself a snare.

Once you saw phoenixes, and now you see such no longer, but the world is not therefore disenchanted. The vessels on which you read sacred emblems have turned out to be common pottery, but the sacred pictures are transferred to the walls of the world. You no longer see phoenixes; men are not divine individuals; but you learn to revere their social & representative character. They are not gods, but the spirit of God sparkles on & about them.

After this generation one would say mysticism should go out of fashion for a long time.

Of what use is it that I should take the chair, and glibly rattle off theories of society, religion, & nature, when I know so well that three or four of my worthy neighbors will each of them pin me to my seat & reduce me to silence by objections & arguments unanswerable by me?

I am far from wishing that Mass. should retaliate. If we could bring down the N. Eng. culture to the Carolina level, if we were cartwhip gentlemen, it might be possible to retaliate very effectively, and to the apprehensions of Southerners. Shut up Mr Calhoun and Mr Rhett when they come to Boston as hostages for the mulattoes & negroes they have kidnapped from the caboose & the cabin of our ships. But the N. Eng. culture is not so low. Ours is not a brutal people, but intellectual & mild. Our land is not a jail; we keep open house; we have taken out the bolt & taken off the latch & taken the doors off the hinges. Does S.C. warn us out & turn us out, and then come hither to visit us? She shall find no bar. We are not afraid of visiters. We do not ring curfews nor give passes nor keep armed patroles; from Berkshire to the sea our roads are open; from N.H. to Connecticutt the land is without a guard; we have no secrets, no fears. For her flying slave & for his degraded master here is rest & plenty and wisdom & virtue which he cannot find at home.

But new times have come & new policy subtler & nobler & more strong than any before. It is the inevitable effect of culture—it cannot be otherwise—to dissolve the animal ties of brute strength, to insulate, to make a country of men, not one strong officer but a thousand strong men, ten thousand. In all S.C. there is but one opinion, but one man: Mr Calhoun. Its citizens are but little Calhouns. In Massachusetts there are many opinions, many men. It is coming I hope to a pass when there shall not be the Atlas and the Post, the Daily Advertiser & the Courier, but these voices shall lose their importance in a crowd of equal & superior men.

Let us not pretend an union where union is not. Let us not cowardly say that all is right where all is damnable. Let us not treat with fawning hospitalities & deceive others by harbouring as a gentleman a felon & a manstealer but let us put all persons on their guard & say this dog will bite. Come not into his company, he will kidnap & burk you.

March–June 1845

Is it not strange that the transcendent men, Homer, Plato, Shakspeare, confessedly unrivalled, should have questions of identity & of genuineness raised respecting their writings? Was there such a man as Homer? Here a Scholiast on Plato avers that Homer learned all his epic of some Creophilus of Chios whose daughter he married. Several of Plato's pieces are reckoned spurious. Who knows who wrote the book of Job, or of Genesis, or the Gospel of St Matthew? Of Shakspeare, we have many dubious remains, & touching him many questions. The architect who designed the Cathedral of Cologne, has left his plans, but not his name.

The only use which the country people can imagine of a scholar, the only compliment they can think of to pay him, is, to ask him to deliver a Temperance Lecture, or to be a member of the School Committee.

It is but a few years ago that Swedenborgism was exhibited to our people in a pamphlet of garbled extracts from Swedenborg's writings as a red rag of whoredom. Dr Ripley lived & died in the belief that it was a horrible libertinism. Now Fourier is represented in the same light by the Swedenborgians, who get their revenge so.

It is easy to see what must be the fate of this fine system in any very serious & comprehensive enterprise to set it on foot in this country. As soon as our people got wind of the doctrine of sexual relations of this master, it would fall at once into the hands of the rowdies, who would flock in troops & gangs to so fair a game. "Who would see fun must be on hand!" And like the dreams of poetic people on the first outbreak of the old French Revolution they must disappear in a slime of mire & blood.

No, it is not the part & merit of a man to make his stove with his own hands, or cook & bake his own dinner: Another can do it better & cheaper; but it is his essential virtue to carry out into action his own dearest ends, to dare to do what he believes & loves. If he thinks a sonnet the flower & result of the world, let him sacrifice all to the sonnet; if he loves the society of one or of several friends, more than life, let him so arrange his living & make everything yield to the procuring him that chief good. Now, we spend our money for that which is not bread, for paint & floor-cloths, for newspapers, & male and female servants that yield us the very smallest fraction of direct advantage. The friction of this social machine is grown enormous, & absorbs almost all the power applied.

Fourier, in his talk about women, seems one of those salacious old men who are full of the most ridiculous superstitions on this matter. In their head, it is the universal rutting season. Any body who has lived with women will know how false & prurient this is; how serious nature always is; how chaste is their organization, & how lawful a class of people women are.

The Native American party resembles a dog which barks at all strangers.*

There is always room for a man of force, and not only so, but he makes room for many. There is always room for a man of force, if it were only as Buonaparte replied to Bourrienne when he showed the difficulty of getting acknowledged by the old reigning families of Europe, "If it comes to that, I will dethrone them all, & then I shall be the oldest sovereign among them." For really society is at any time only a troop of thinkers, and the best heads among them take the best seats. It is with the prizes of power & place as it is with estates. A feeble man can only see the farms that are fenced & tilled; the houses that are built. At the end of the town, he is at the end of the world. The strong man sees not only the actual but the possible houses & farms. His eye makes estates & villages, as fast as the sun breeds clouds.

There is always room for a man of force as I think even swindlers & imposters show. A man of more talent than Cagliostro or Monroe Edwards would take the wind out of the sails of kings & governors, cotton-lords & Rothschilds and make asses of the heads of Society. For, as these are the slaves of appearance also, & not of truth, they have not an intrinsic defence to make, but only stand on opinion. But the lover of truth is invulnerable.

Yet a bully cannot lead the age.

Another distinction should be made. It is obvious that the two Parties I describe as dividing modern society—conservative & democratic—differ only as young & old. The democrat is a young conservative, & conservative is an old democrat. It is then not two Parties but one, and Bonaparte represents the whole history of this Party—its youth & its age—and needs a counterpart who has not yet appeared, in the shape of a lover and a transcendentalist.

---

*The Native American Party (originally the American Republican Party), founded in 1843, was anti-Catholic and anti-immigrant. [*JMN*]

* * *

The puny race of Scholars in this country have no counsel to give, and are not felt. Every wretched partisan, every village brawler, every man with talents for contention, every clamourous place hunter makes known what he calls his opinion, all over the country, that is, as loud as he can scream. Really, no opinions are given, only the wishes of each side are expressed, of the spoils party, that is, & of the malcontents. But the voice of the intelligent & the honest, of the unconnected & independent, the voice of truth & equity is suppressed. In England, it is not so. You can always find in their journals & newspapers, a better & a best sense as well as the low coarse party cries.

I have now arrived at a perfect selfishness on the most enforced consideration. For I am constrained by many lapses & failures to proportion my attempts to my means. Now I receive daily just so much vital energy as suffices to put on my clothes, to take a few turns in my garden & in my study with a book or a pen in my hand. If I attempt anything beyond this, if I so much as stretch out my hand to help my neighbor in his field, the stingy Genius leaves me faint & sprawling; and I must pay for this vivacity by a prostration for two or three days following. These are costly experiments to try, I cannot afford two or three days when I count how many days it requires to finish one of my tasks; so I grow circumspect & disobliging beyond the example of all the misers.

What argument, what eloquence can avail against the power of that one word *niggers?* The man of the world annihilates the whole combined force of all the antislavery societies of the world by pronouncing it.

Society at all times has the same want, namely, of one sane man with adequate powers of expression to hold up each new object of monomania in its right relations. The ambitious & the mercenary bring their last new mumbo-jumbo, whether it be Tariff or Texas or Mesmerism or Phrenology or Antimasonry or Trade in Eastern lands or Puseyism, and by detaching this one object from its relations easily succeed in making it seen insanely: and a great multitude go suddenly mad on the subject; and they are not to be reproved or cured by the opposite multitude, who are kept from this particular insanity only by an equal frenzy on another crotchet. But let one man have so comprehensive an eye that he can replace this isolated wonder in its natural neighborhood & relations, it loses instantly all illusion, and the returning reason of the community thanks the reason of the monitor.

*   *   *

I woke this morn with a dream which perchance was true that I was living in the morning of history amidst barbarians, that right & truth had yet no voice, no letters, no law, every one did what he would & grasped what he could.

The girl likes the ice cream but does not wish therefore to marry the confectioner.

Is not a small house best? Put a woman into a small house, and after five years she comes out large & healthy, and her children are so. Put her into a large house, & after the same time, she shall be haggard, sickly, with a sharp voice, & a wrinkled careful countenance, & her children suffer with her.

Writing should be the settlement of dew on the leaf, of stalactites on the wall of the grotto, the deposite of flesh from the blood, of woody fibre in the tree from the sap.

Our virtue runs in a narrow rill: we have never a freshet. We ought to be subject to enthusiasms. One would like to see Boston & Massachusetts agitated like a wave with some generosity, mad for learning, for music, for philosophy, for association, for freedom, for art; but now it goes like a pedlar with its hand ever on its pocket, cautious, calculating.

How hard to find a man. It would take as Taylor said the lamp of Diogenes added to the splendour of the noonday sun. Otis talked too much. Webster has no morale. Choate wants weight. Alcott is unlimited & unballasted. Bound, bound, let there be bound! But let there not be too strict bound.

It is easy to read Plato, difficult to read his commentators.

I avoid the Stygian anniversaries at Cambridge, those hurrahs among the ghosts, those yellow, bald, toothless meetings in memory of red cheeks, black hair, and departed health. Most forcible Feeble made the only oration that fits the occasion that contains all these obituary eloquences.

June 1845

Against low assailants we have also low defenders. As I came home by the brook, I saw the carcass of a snake which the mud-turtles were eating at both ends.

* * *

All conversation, as all literature, appears to me the pleasure of rhetoric, or, I may say, of metonomy. "To make the great little, & the little great," Isocrates said, "was the orator's part." Well that is what poetry & thinking do. I am a reader & writer, please myself with the parallelism & the relation of thoughts, see how they classify themselves on the more fundamental & the resultant & then again the new & newer result. I go out one day & see the mason & carpenters busy in building a house, and I discover with joy the parallelism between their work & my construction, and come home glad to know that I too am a housebuilder. The next day I go abroad & meet hunters, and, as I return, accidentally discover the strict relation between my pursuit of truths & theirs of forest game.

June 23, 1845

It was a pleasure yesterday to hear Father Taylor preach all day in our country church. Men are always interested in a man, and the whole various extremes of our little village society were for once brought together. Black & white, poet & grocer, contractor & lumberman, methodist & preacher joined with the regular congregation in rare union.

The speaker instantly shows the reason in the breadth of his truly social nature. He is mighty nature's child, another Robert Burns trusting heartily to her power as he has never been deceived by it and arriving unexpectedly every moment at new & happiest deliverances. How joyfully & manly he spreads himself abroad. It is a perfect Punch & Judy affair, his preaching. The preaching quite accidental & ludicrously copied & caricatured from the old style, as he found it in some Connecticutt tubs. As well as he can he mimics & exaggerates the parade of method & logic of text & argument but after much threatening to exterminate all gainsayers by his syllogisms he seldom remembers any of the divisions of his plan after the first, and the slips & gulfs of his logic would involve him in irreparable ridicule if it were not for the inexhaustible wit by which he dazzles & conciliates & carries away captive the dullest & the keenest hunter. He is perfectly sure in his generous humanity. He rolls the world into a ball & tosses it from hand to hand. He says touching things, plain things, grand things, cogent things, which all men must perforce hear. He says them with hand & head & body & voice; the accompaniment is total & ever varied. "I am half a hundred years old, & I have never seen an unfortunate day. There are none"— "I have been in all the four quarters of the world, and I never saw any men I could not love."

"We have sweet conferences & prayer meetings. We meet every day. There are not days enough in the year for us."

Everything is accidental to him: his place, his education, his church, his seamen, his whole system of religion a mere confused rigmarole of refuse & leavings of former generations—all has a grinning absurdity, *except* the sentiment of the man. He is incapable of thought; he cannot analyse or discriminate; he is a singing dancing drunkard of his wit— Only he is sure of the sentiment. That is his mother's milk, that he feels in his bones, heaves in his lungs, throbs in his heart, walks in his feet, and gladly he yields himself to the sweet magnetism & sheds it abroad on the people rejoicing in his power. Hence he is an example—I, at this moment say—the single example we have of an inspiration; for a wisdom not his own, not to be appropriated by him, which he cannot recall or ever apply, sails to him on the gale of this sympathetic communication with his auditory. There is his closet, there his college, there his confessional, he discloses secrets there, & receives informations there, which his conversation with thousands of men (and he knows every body in the world almost) and his voyages to Egypt & journeys in Germany & in Syria never taught him. Indeed I think that all his talk with men and all his much visiting & planning for the practical in his "Mariners' House," &c &c, is all very fantastic, all stuff; I think his guardians & overseers & treasurers will find it so. Not the smallest dependence is to be put on his statement of facts. Arithmetic is only one of the nimble troop of dancers he keeps. No; this free happy expression of himself & of the deeps of human nature, of the happier sunny facts of life, of things connected & lying amassed & grouped in healthy nature, that is his power and his teacher. He is so confident, that his security breathes in all his manners, & gestures, in his tones, & the expressions of his face, & he lies all open to men a man, & disarms criticism & malignity by perfect frankness. We open our arms too & with half closed eyes enjoy this rare sunshine. A wondrous beauty swims all the time over the picture gallery & touches points with an ineffable lustre.

June–Aug. 1845

Men go through the world each musing on a great fable dramatically pictured & rehearsed before him. If you speak to the man, he turns his eyes from his own scene, & slower or faster endeavors to comprehend what you say. When you have done speaking, he returns to his private music. Men generally attempt early in life to make their brothers first, afterwards their wives, acquainted with what is going forward in their private theatre, but they soon desist from the attempt on finding that they also have some farce or perhaps some ear- & heart-rending tragedy forward on their secret boards on which they are intent, and all parties acquiesce at last in a private box with the whole play performed before himself *solus*.

Even for those whom I really love I have not animal spirits.

Literature has been before us, wherever we go. When I come in the secretest recess of a swamp, to some obscure, and rare, & to me unknown plant, I know that its name & the number of its stamens, every bract & awn, is carefully described & registered in a book in my shelf. So is it with this young soul wandering lonely, wistful, reserved, unfriended up & down in nature. These mysteries which he ponders, which astonish & entrance him, this riddle of liberty, this dream of immortality, this drawing to love, this trembling balance of motive, and the centrality whereof these are rays, have all been explored to the recesses of consciousness, to the verge of Chaos & the Néant, by men with grander steadfastness & subtler organs of search than any now alive; so that when this tender philosopher comes from his reverie to literature, he is alarmed (like one whose secret has been betrayed) by the terrible fidelity, with which, men long before his day, have described all & much more than all he has just seen as new Continent in the West.

Aug. 19, 1845
We do not expect the tree to bear but one harvest in the year, but a man we expect to yield his fruit of wit & action every day.

Aug. 1845
Lectures are a few reasonable words to keep us in mind of truth amidst our nonsense.

See how many cities of refuge we have. Skepticism & again skepticism? Well, let abyss open under abyss, they are all contained & bottomed at last, & I have only to endure. I am here to be worked upon.

What a luck in teaching! The tutor aims at fidelity, the pupil strives to learn, but there is never a coincidence, but always a diagonal line drawn partaking of the genius of the tutor & the genius of the pupil. This, when there is success, but that how capricious! Two precious madmen who cannot long conspire.

I know that the slaveholding is not the only manstealing and that white men are defrauded & oppressed as well as black but this stealing is not so gross & is not so legalized & made hopeless.

"After thirty a man wakes up sad every morning excepting perhaps five or six until the day of his death."

Aug. 25, 1845

I heard last night with some sensibility that the question of slavery has never been presented to the south with a kind & thoroughly scientific treatment, as a question of pure political economy in the largest sense.

Aug.–Sept. 1845

Bronson Alcott told me that when he saw Cruikshank's drawings, he thought him a fancy caricaturist, but when he went to London he saw that he drew from nature without any exaggeration.

The old dramatists wrote the better for the great quantity of their writing and knew not when they wrote well. The playhouse was low enough to have entire interests for them; they were proprietors; it was low & popular; and not literary. That the scholars scorned it, was its saving essence. Shakspeare & his comrades, Shakspear evidently thought the mass of old plays or of stage plays *corpus vile,* in which any experiment might be freely tried. Had the prestige which hedges about a modern tragedy or other worthless literary work existed, nothing could have been done. The coarse but warm blood of the living England circulated in the play as in street ballads, & gave body to his airy & majestic fancy. For the poet peremptorily needs a basis which he cannot supply; a tough chaos-deep soil, or main, or continent, on which his art may work, as the sculptor a block of stone, and this basis the popular mind supplies: otherwise all his flowers & elegances are transcendental & mere nuisance.

You are here to chant the hymn of Destiny, to be worked upon, here for miracle, here for resignation, here for intellect, love, & being; here to know the awful secret of genius, here to become not readers of poetry but Dante, Milton, Shakspeare, Homer, Swedenborg, in the fountain through that: here to foresee India & Persia & Judaea & Europe in the old paternal mind.

If I could reach to initiate you, if I could prevail to communicate the incommunicable mysteries, you should see the breadth of your realm; that even as you ascend inward your radiation is immense; that you receive the keys of history & of nature.

You assimilate the remote, & rise on the same stairs to science & to piety.

Sept. 1845

Plato & the great intellects have no biography. If he had wife, children, we hear nothing of them; he ground them all into paint. As a good chimney burns up all its own smoke, so a good philosopher consumes all his own events in his extraordinary intellectual performances.

Sept. 23, 1845
In the convention yesterday it was easy to see the drunkenness of eloquence. As I sat & listened, I seemed to be attending at a medical experiment where a series of patients were taking nitrous oxide gas. Each patient, on receiving it in turn, exhibited similar symptoms; redness in the face, volubility, violent gesticulation, the oddest attitudes, occasional stamping, a loss of perception of the passage of time, a selfish enjoyment of the sensation, & loss of perception of the suffering of the audience. Plato says that the punishment which the wise suffer who refuse to take part in the government, is to live under the government of worse men. That is the penalty of abstaining to speak in a public meeting, that you shall sit & hear wretched & currish speakers. I have a bad time of it on these occasions, for I feel responsible for every one of the speakers, & shudder with cold at the thinness of the morning audience, & with fear lest all will fail at every bad speech. Mere ability & mellowness is then inestimable. . . .
An orator is a thief of belief.

Sept.–Oct. 1845
Health is genius, the higher tone. Potentially all wise enow, wine is what we want, wine of wine, excitement, opportunity, an initiative. Is the solar system good art & architecture? The same wise achievment is in my brain; can you only wile me from interference & marring. The poetic gift we want, but not the poetic profession; poetic gift, as the health & supremacy of man, but not rhymes & sonneteering, not book-making & bookselling, not cold spying & authorship.

Whiggism, a feast of shells, idolatrous of the forms of legislature; like a cat loving the house, not the inhabitant.

There is a XIX-Century or secular disease which infects all those who stand on or near the dividing line between conservatism & absolutism. Many are born of conservative parents, hedged round with conservative connexions, & are themselves by genius absolutists. In proportion to their nearness to this line, the conflict of energies in them is exasperated, & the distemper acute. You see them without visible cause or any organic ail, thin, dyspeptic, irritable, melancholy, & imbecile.

You cannot say God, blood, & hell too little. Always suppose God. The Jew named him not.

*   *   *

We know in one mood that which we are ignorant of in another mood, like mesmerised patients who are clairvoyant at night & in the day know nothing of that which they told.

Vigilance or anxiety is required of us. We do not eat for pleasure. We go to the table at least for necessity, and when there, eat too much, for pleasure; but how gladly we would eat exactly enough, if there were a measured & scaled Enough: if a cubic inch of pemmican per day would keep us at the top of our condition, how gladly we would swallow it & go about our business. But every sane man in turn has tried starving, tried parched corn, tried grass, & found that it did not give him blood but that we were faint & dispirited. If it could be settled once for all that coffee & wine & all stimulus were bad.

The greatest man underlies the human nature. The longest wave quickly is lost in the sea. No individualism can make any head against the swallowing universality. Plato would willingly have a Platonism, a known & accurate expression for the world, and it should be adequate: it shall be—the world passed through the mind of Plato—nothing less; every atom shall have the Platonic tinge. Every atom, every relation, every quality you knew before, you shall know again, & find here, but now, ordered; not nature, but art, & you shall feel that Alexander indeed overran with some men & horses some countries of the planet—but countries, & things of which countries are composed—elements—planet itself, & laws of planet, & of men, thoughts, truths, all actual & possible things, have passed through this man as bread into his body & become no longer bread but body; so all this mammoth mouthful has become Plato.

Well this is the ambition of Individualism: but the mouthful proves too great. Boa Constrictor has good will to eat it, but he is foiled. He falls abroad in the attempt and, biting, gets strangled, & the bitten world holds him fast by his own teeth. There he perishes, & the Unconquered Nature goes on & forgets him. Alas, alas, Plato turns out to be philosophical exercitations. He argues now on this side, now on that. The acutest searcher, the lovingest disciple could never tell what Platonism was; indeed admirable texts can be quoted on both sides of every great question, from him.

It would be so easy to draw two pictures of the literary man, as of one possessed & led by muses, or, as of one ridden by some dragon, or dire distemper. A mechanic is driven by his work all day, but it ends at night; it has an end. But the scholar's work has none. That which he has

learned is that there is much more to be learned. He feels only his in-
competence. A thousand years, tenfold, a hundredfold his faculties,
would not suffice: the demands of the task are such, that it becomes om-
nipresent; he studies in his sleep, in his walking, in his meals, in his
pleasures. He is but a fly or a worm to this mountain. He becomes anxious: if one knock at his door, he scowls: if one intimate the purpose of
visiting him, he looks grave.

In Spenser (Book III Canto XI) is the Castle of Busyrane on whose
gate is writ Be bold, on the second gate, Be bold, be bold, and the inner
iron door, Be not too bold.

One service which this age has rendered to men, is, to make the life
& wisdom of every past man accessible & available to all. Mahomet is no
longer accursed; Voltaire is no longer the scarecrow; Plato is no longer a
pagan. Even Rabelais is citable.

The worst day is good for something. All that is not love, is knowledge, and all that is not good today, is a store laid up for the wants of
distant days.

I hate the narrowness of the Native American party. It is the dog in
the manger. It is precisely opposite to all the dictates of love & magnanimity: & therefore, of course, opposite to true wisdom. It is the result of
science that the highest simplicity of structure is produced, not by few
elements, but by the highest complexity. Man is the most composite of
all creatures, the wheel-insect, *volvox globator*, is at the beginning.
Well, as in the old burning of the Temple at Corinth, by the melting &
intermixture of silver & gold & other metals, a new compound more
precious than any, called the Corinthian Brass, was formed so in this
Continent—asylum of all nations, the energy of Irish, Germans,
Swedes, Poles, & Cossacks, & all the European tribes—of the Africans,
& of the Polynesians, will construct a new race, a new religion, a new
State, a new literature, which will be as vigorous as the new Europe
which came out of the smelting pot of the Dark Ages, or that which earlier emerged from the Pelasgic & Etruscan barbarism.

People who live together grow alike & if they should live long
enough we should not know them apart.

Every age has its objects & symbol, & every man. Why not then
every epoch of our life its own; & a man should journey through his own
zodiack of signs.

Oct. 27, 1845

In this finest of all Indian summer days it seems sad that each of us can only spend it once. We sigh for the thousand heads & thousand bodies of the Indian gods, that we might celebrate its immense beauty in many ways & places, & absorb all its good.

Oct.–Nov. 1845

As for King Swedenborg I object to his cardinal position in Morals that evils should be shunned as sins. I hate preaching. I shun evils as evils. Does he not know—Charles Lamb did—that every poetic mind is a pagan, and to this day prefers Olympian Jove, Apollo, & the Muses & the Fates, to all the barbarous indigestion of Calvin & the Middle Ages?

We are very clumsy writers of history. We tell the chronicle of parentage, birth, birthplace, schooling, companions, acquisition of property, marriage, publication of books, celebrity, & death, and when we have come to an end of this external history, the reader is no whit instructed, no ray of relation appears between all this lumber & the goddess-born, and it really appears as if, had we dipped at random into the modern Plutarch or Universal Biography, & read any other life there, it would have fitted to the poems quite as well. It is the very essence of Poetry to spring like the rainbow daughter of Wonder from the invisible: to abolish the Past, & refuse all history. . . . What can any biography biographize the wonderful world into which the Midsummer Night's dream admits me? Did Shakspeare confide to any Notary or Parish Recorder, sacristan or surrogate in Stratford upon Avon, the genesis of that delicate creation? The forest of Arden, the air of Scone Castle, the moonlight of Portia's villa; where is the third cousin or grandnephew, the prompter's book or private letter that has heard one word of those transcendant secrets? Shakspeare is the only biographer of Shakspeare. And ah, what can Shakspeare tell in any way but to the Shakspeare in us?

The Indian teaching through its cloud of legends has yet a simple & grand religion like a queenly countenance seen through a rich veil. It teaches to speak the truth, love others as yourself, & to despise trifles. The East is grand—& makes Europe appear the land of trifles. Identity, identity! friend & foe are of one stuff, and the stuff is such & so much that the variations of surface are unimportant. All is for the soul, & the soul is Vishnu; & animals & stars are transient paintings; & light is whitewash; & durations are deceptive; and form is imprisonment and heaven itself a decoy. That which the soul seeks is resolution into Being above form, out of Tartarus & out of Heaven; liberation from existence is its name. Cheerful & noble is the genius of this cosmogony. Hari is always gentle & serene—he translates to heaven the hunter who has accidentally shot him in his human form; he pursues his sports with boors & milkmaids at the cow-pens; all his games are benevolent, and he enters into flesh to relieve the burdens of the world.

One said, "if the hand had not been divided into fingers, man would be still a beast roaming in the desert." The like if the tongue had not been fitted for sharp articulation. Children cry & scream & stamp with fury unable to express their desires. As soon as they can speak & plainly tell their want & the reason, they become gentle. It is the same with adults. Whilst the perceptions are blunt, men & women talk vehemently & superlatively, & overgo the mark. Their manners are full of desperation, their speech is full of oaths. As soon as a little clearness of perception is added, they desist from that weak & brutish vehemence, & accurately express their meaning.*

Nov. 5, 1845
Yesterday evening, saw Robert Owen at Mr Alcott's. His four elements are Production, Distribution, Formation of Character, and Local & General governing. His *Three Errors,* on which society has always been based, & is now, are, 1. That we form ourselves. 2. That we form our opinions. 3. That we form our feelings. The Three Truths which he wishes should replace these, are, 1. That we proceed from a creating power; 2. That our opinions come from conviction; 3. That our feelings come from our instincts.

The five Evils which proceed from our Three Errors & which make the misery of life are
  1 Religious perplexities
  2 Disappointment in affections
  3 Pecuniary difficulties
  4 Intemperance
  5 Anxiety for offspring. . . .
You are very external with your evils, Mr Owen: let me give you some real mischiefs:
  Living for show

---

*Same weakness & want on a higher plane occurs in history of all interesting young men & women. "Ah you don't understand me;" and, "I have never met with any body that understands me," & so they sob & sigh, write poetry, & walk alone, fault of power to express their precise meaning. In a month or two they meet some one so related as to assist their volcanic estate and good communication once established they are thenceforward good citizens. [RWE]

    Losing the whole in the particular
    Indigence of vital power
I am afraid these will appear in a phalanstery or in a tub.

Nov. 1845–March 1846
    We are made of contradictions—our *freedom* is *necessary*.

    Locke said, "God, when he makes the prophet, does not unmake the
man." Swedenborg's history confirms & points the remark. A poor little
narrow pragmatical Lutheran for whom the heavens are opened, so that
he sees with eyes & in the richest symbolic forms the awful truth of
things, and utters again in his endless books the indisputable secrets
of moral nature, remains with all these grandeurs resting upon him,
through it all, & after all, a poor little narrow pragmatical Lutheran.
His judgments are those of a Swedish polemic, and his vast enlargements seem purchased by adamantine limitations. He reminds me
again & again of our Jones Very, who had an illumination that enabled him to excel every body in wit & to see farthest in every company & quite easily to bring the proudest to confession: & yet he
could never get out of his Hebraistic phraseology & mythology, &,
when all was over, still remained in the thin porridge or cold tea of
Unitarianism.

    It is the largest part of a man that is not inventoried. He has many
enumerable parts: he is social, professional, political, sectarian, literary,
& of this or that set & corporation. But after the most exhausting census
has been made, there remains as much more which no tongue can tell.
And this remainder is that which interests. This is that which the
preacher & the poet & the musician speak to. This is that which the
strong genius works upon; the region of destiny, of aspiration, of the unknown. Ah they have a secret persuasion that as little as they pass for in
the world, they are immensely rich in expectancy & power. Nobody has
ever yet dispossessed this adhesive self to arrive at any glimpse or guess
of the awful Life that lurks under it.
    For the best part, I repeat, of every mind is not that which he knows,
but that which hovers in gleams, suggestions, tantalizing unpossessed
before him. His firm recorded knowledge soon loses all interest for him.
But this dancing chorus of thoughts & hopes is the quarry of his future,
is his possibility, & teaches him that his man's life is of a ridiculous brev-
ity & meanness, but that it is his first age & trial only of his young
wings, but that vast revolutions, migrations, & gyres on gyres in the celestial societies invite him.

*   *   *

Shakspeare's fault that the world appears so empty. He has educated you with his painted world, & this real one seems a huckster's shop.

It is sad to see people reading again their old books, merely because they don't know what new books they want.

How is it, I say in my bed, that the people manage to live along, so aimless as they are? After their ends (& they so petty) are gained, it seems as if the lime in their bones alone held them together, & not any worthy purpose. And how do I manage it? A house, a bargain, a debt, some friends, some book, some names & deeds of heroes, or of geniuses, these are the toys I play with, these intercept between me & heaven, or these are they that devastate the soul.

The world is enigmatical, every thing said & every thing known & done, & must not be taken literally, but genially. We must be at the top of our condition to understand any thing rightly.

March 24, 1846

Why should people make such a matter of leaving this church & going into that? They betray so their want of Faith, or spiritual perception. The holy principles discredit & accredit all churches alike. God builds his temple in the heart on the ruins of churches & religions. It is not otherwise with social forms. A. or B. refuses the tax or some tax with solemnity, but eats & drinks & wears & perspires taxation all day. Let them not hew down the state with axe & gunpowder, but supersede it by irresistible genius; huddle it aside as ridiculous & obsolete by their quantity of being. Eloquence needs no constable.

April–May 1846

You must treat the days respectfully, you must be a day yourself, and not interrogate life like a college professor. Every thing in the universe goes by indirection. There are no straight lines.

I grow old, I accept conditions; thus far—no farther; to learn that we are not the first born, but the latest born; that we have no wings; that the sins of our predecessors are on us like a mountain of obstruction.

What a discovery I made one day that the more I spent the more I grew, that it was as easy to occupy a large place & do much work as an obscure place & do little; and that in the winter in which I communicated all my results to classes, I was full of new thoughts.

*   *   *

Queenie came it over Henry last night when he taxed the new astro-
nomers with the poverty of their discoveries & showings—not strange
enough. Queenie wished to see with eyes some of those strange things
which the telescope reveals, the satellites of Saturn, &c. H. said that
stranger things might be seen with the naked eye. "Yes," said Queenie
"but I wish to see some of those things that are not quite so strange."

I see not how we can live except alone. Trenchant manners, a sharp
decided way will prove a lasting convenience. Society will coo & claw &
caress. You must curse & swear a little: They will remember it, & it will
do them good. What if they are wise & fine people. I do not want your
silliness, though you be Socrates, and if you indulge them, all people are
babyish. Curse them.

Understand me when I say, I love you, it is your genius & not you. I
like man, but not men. The genius of humanity is very easily & accurately to be made out by the poet-mind, but it is not in Miss Nancy nor
in Adoniram with any sufficiency.

May 1, 1846

I was at Cambridge yesterday to see Everett inaugurated. His political brothers came as if to bring him to the convent door, & to grace with
a sort of bitter courtesy his taking of the cowl. It is like the marriage of a
girl: not until the wedding & the departure with her husband, does it
appear that she has actually & finally changed homes & connexions &
social caste. Webster I could so willingly have spared on this occasion.
Everett was entitled to the entire field; & Webster came, who is his evil
genius, & has done him incalculable harm by Everett's too much admiration of his iron nature; warped him from his true bias all these
twenty years, & sent him cloud-hunting at Washington & London, to
the ruin of all solid scholarship, & fatal diversion from the pursuit of his
right prizes. It is in vain that Everett makes all these allusions to his
public employments; he would fain deceive me & himself; he has never
done any thing therein, but has been, with whatever praises & titles &
votes, a mere dangler & ornamental person. It is in vain for sugar to try
to be salt. Well, this Webster must needs come into the house just at the
moment when Everett was rising to make his Inaugural Speech. Of
course, the whole genial current of feeling flowing towards him was ar-
rested, & the old Titanic Earth-son was alone seen. The house shook
with new & prolonged applause, & Everett sat down, to give free course
to the sentiment. . . .

The satisfaction of men in this appointment is complete. Boston is
contented because he is so creditable, safe, & prudent, and the scholars

because he is a scholar, & understands the business. Old Quincy with all his worth & a sort of violent service he did the College, was a lubber & a grenadier among our clerks.

Quincy made an excellent speech, so stupid good, now running his head against a post, now making a capital point; he has motherwit, & great fund of honour & faithful serving. And the faults of his speech increased my respect for his character.

The Latin allusions flew all day; "Sol occubuit, nulla nox sequitur," said Webster. "Uno avulso, non deficit aureus alter," said Winthrop.

It is so old a fault that we have now acquiesced in it, that the complexion of these Cambridge feasts is not literary, but some what bronzed by the colours of Washington & Boston. The aspect is political, the speakers are political, & Cambridge plays a very pale & permitted part in its own halls. A man of letters—who was purely that—would not feel attracted, & would be as much out of place there as at the Brokers' Board. Holmes's poem was a bright sparkle, but Frothingham, Prescott, Longfellow, old Dana, Ward, Parker, Hedge, Clark, Judd the author of "Margaret," & whoever else is a lover of letters, were absent or silent; & Everett himself, richly entitled on grounds of scholarship to the chair, used his scholarship only complimentarily.

The close of Everett's Inaugural Discourse was chilling & melancholy. With a coolness indicating absolute skepticism & despair, he deliberately gave himself over to the corpse-cold Unitarianism & Immortality of Brattle street & Boston.

May 1846

Daguerrotype gives the sculpture of the face, but omits the expression, the painter aims at the expression & comes far short of Daguerre in the form & organism. But we must have sea and shore, the flowing & the fixed, in every work of art. On the sitter the effect of the Daguerrotypist is asinizing.

Language. Words borrowed from animals
- to dog
- to raven
- to cow
- to ram
- to ape
- to horse
- to rabbit
- to snake
- to badger
- to worm
- to rat

*   *   *

American idea, Emancipation, appears in our freedom of intellection, in our reforms, & in our bad politics; has, of course, its sinister side, which is most felt by the drilled & scholastic. But, if followed, leads to heavenly places.

A man who can speak well to a public assembly, I must respect, and he is *ipso facto* ennobled. Like a great general or a great poet, or a millionaire, he may wear his coat out at elbows, and his shoes & his hat as he will. He has established relation, representativeness, that he is a good apple of his kind, proved by the homage of the apples, and not merely like your lonely man of genius, that he is an apple shaped like a cucumber. He is not a curiosity but capable of yielding aid & comfort to men.

Autobiography & allo-biography go abreast; with every new insight we discover a new man.

We live with such different velocity. We are not timed with our contemporaries. We cannot keep step. One man is thinking of Plato & his companion is thinking of lobsters.

When summer opens, I see how fast it matures, & fear it will be short; but after the heats of July & August, I am reconciled, like one who has had his swing, to the cool of autumn. So will it be with the coming of death.

Men quarrel with your rhetoric. Society chokes with a trope, like a child with the croup. They much prefer Mr Prose, & Mr Hoarse-as-Crows, to the dangerous conversation of Gabriel and the archangel Michael perverting all rules, & bounding continually from earth to heaven.

Walking one day in the fields I met a man.
We shall one day talk with the central man, and see again in the varying play of his features all the features which have characterised our darlings, & stamped themselves in fire on the heart: then, as the discourse rises out of the domestic & personal, & his countenance waxes grave & great, we shall fancy that we talk with Socrates, & behold his countenance: then the discourse changes, & the man, and we see the face & hear the tones of Shakspeare—the body & the soul of Shakspeare living & speaking with us, only that Shakspeare seems below us. A change again, and the countenance of our companion is youthful & beardless, he talks of form & colour & the riches of design; it is the face of the painter Raffaelle that confronts us with the visage of a girl, & the easy audacity

of a creator. In a moment it was Michel Angelo; then Dante; afterwards it was the Saint Jesus, and the immensities of moral truth & power embosomed us. And so it appears that these great secular* personalities were only expressions of his face chasing each other like the rack of clouds. Then all will subside, & I find myself alone. I dreamed & did not know my dreams.

No man deserves a patron until first he has been his own. What do you bring us slipshod verses for? no occasional delicacy of expression or music of rhythm can atone for stupidities. Here are lame verses, false rhymes, absurd images, which you indulge yourself in, which is as if a handsome person should come into a company with foul hands or face. Read Collins. Collins would have cut his hand off before he would have left from a weak selfesteem a shabby line in his ode.

The Indians and the old monks chose their dwellingplace for beauty of scenery. The Indians have a right to exist in this world: they are (like Monadnoc & the Ocean) a part of it, & fit the other parts, as Monadnoc & the sea, which they understand & live with so well, as a rider his horse. The teamster, the farmer, are jocund & hearty, & stand on their legs: but the women are demure and subdued, as Shaker Women, &, if you see them out of doors, look, as H. T. said, "as if they were going for the Doctor." Has our Christianity saddled & bridled us?

That none but a writer should write, & that he should not dig.
Tell children what you say about writing & laboring with the hands. I know better. Can you distil rum by minding it at odd times? or analyse soils? or carry on the Suffolk Bank? or the Greenwich observatory? or sail a ship through the Narrows by minding the helm when you happen to think of it? or serve a glass-house, or a steam-engine, or a telegraph, or a rail-road express? or accomplish anything good or anything powerful in this manner? Nothing whatever. And the greatest of all arts, the subtlest, & of most miraculous effect, you fancy is to be practised with a pen in one hand & a crowbar or a peat-knife in the other. All power is of geometrical increase.
And to this painting the education is the costliest, & mankind cannot afford to throw away on ditching or wood-sawing the man on whom choicest influences have been concentrated, its Baruch or scribe. Just as much & just such exercise as this costly creature needs, he may have; & he may breathe himself with a spade, or a rapier, as he likes, not as you like: & I should rather say, bad as I think the rapier, that it were as much

---

*Enduring.

to his purpose as the other implement. Both are bad, are only rare & medicinal resorts. The writer must live & die by his writing. Good for that, & good for nothing else. A war; an earthquake, the revival of letters, the new dispensation by Jesus, or by Angels, Heaven, Hell, power, science, the Neant—exist only to him as colours for his brush. That you think he can write at odd minutes only shows what your knowledge of writing is. American writing can be written at odd minutes—Unitarian writing, Charlatan writing, Congress speeches, Railroad novels.

Hawthorn invites his readers too much into his study, opens the process before them. As if the confectioner should say to his customers Now let us make the cake.

If I were a member of the Massachusetts legislature, I should propose to exempt all coloured citizens from taxation because of the inability of the government to protect them by passport out of its territory. It does not give the value for which they pay the tax.

In the city of Makebelieve is a great ostentation bolstered up on a great many small ostentations. I think we escape something by living in the villages. In Concord here, there is some milk of life, we are not so raving-distracted with wind & dyspepsia. The mania takes a milder form. People go a fishing & know the taste of their meat. They cut their own whippletree in the woodlot, they know something practically of the sun & the east wind, of the underpinning & the roofing of the house, of the pan & the mixture of the soils.

In the city of Makebelieve all the marble edifices were veneered & all the columns were drums.

May–June 1846

Boston or Brattle Street Christianity is a compound force or the best diagonal line that can be drawn between Jesus Christ & Abbott Lawrence.

I should say of the memorable moments of my life that I was in them & not they in me. I found myself by happy fortune in an illuminated portion or meteorous zone, & passed out of it again—so aloof was it from any will of mine. Law of that! To know the law of that, & to live in it! o thought too wild! o hope too fond!

Cotten thread holds the union together, unites John C. Calhoun & Abbott Lawrence. Patriotism for holidays & summer evenings with music & rockets, but cotten thread is the union.

* * *

I must feel that the speaker compromises himself to his auditory, comes for something; it is a cry on the perilous edge of fight, or let him be silent. Pillsbury, whom I heard last night, is that very gift from New Hampshire which we have long expected, a tough oak stick of a man not to be silenced or insulted or intimidated by a mob, because he is more mob than they; he mobs the mob. John Knox is come at last, on whom neither money nor politeness nor hard words nor rotten eggs nor kicks & brickbats make the slightest impression. He is fit to meet the barroom wits & bullies; he is a wit & a bully himself & something more, he is a graduate of the plough & the cedarswamp & the snowbank and has nothing new to learn of labor, or poverty, or the rough of farming. His hard head too had gone through in boyhood all the drill of Calvinism with text & mortification so that he stands in the New England Assembly a purer bit of New England than any, & flings his sarcasms right & left, sparing no name, or person, or party, or presence. The "Concord Freeman" of the last week he held in his hand (the Editor was in the audience) and read the paragraph on Mexican War from it, & then gave his own version of that fact.

What question could be more pertinent than his to the Church: "What is the Church for? if, whenever there is any moral evil to be grappled with, as Intemperance, or Slavery, or War, there needs to be originated an entirely new instrumentality?"

Every man in the presence of the orator is to feel that he has not only got the documents in his pocket to answer to all his cavils & to prove all his positions, but he has the eternal reason in his head; and that this man does not need any society or Governor or Army for he has latent but really present in himself in a higher form navy & artillery, judge & jury, farmer, mechanic, mob, & executioner. Danger is not so dangerous as he.

What a blessed world of snivelling nobodies we live in! There is no benefit like a war or a plague. The poor-smell has overpowered the roses & the aromatic fern. Oil of vitriol must be applied.

Life is a selection, no more. The work of the gardener is simply to destroy this weed, or that shrub, or that tree, & leave this other to grow. The library is gradually made inestimable by taking out from the superabounding mass of books all but the best. The palace is a selection of materials; its architecture, a selection of the best effects. Things collect very fast of themselves; the difference between house & house is the wise omissions.

*   *   *

Every reform is only a mask under cover of which a more terrible reform, which dares not yet name itself, advances. Slavery & Antislavery is the question of property & no property, rent & anti-rent; and Antislavery dare not yet say that every man must do his own work, or, at least, receive no interest for money. Yet that is at last the upshot.

The United States will conquer Mexico, but it will be as the man swallows the arsenic, which brings him down in turn. Mexico will poison us.

The Southerner is cool & insolent. "We drive you to the wall, & will again." Yes, gentlemen, but do you know why Massachusetts & New York are so tame? it is because we own you, and are very tender of our mortgages, which cover all your property.

June–July 1846

O Bacchus, make them drunk, drive them mad, this multitude of vagabonds, hungry for eloquence, hungry for poetry, starving for symbols, perishing for want of electricity to vitalize this too much pasture; &, in the long delay, indemnifying themselves with the false wine of alcohol, of politics, or of money. Pour for them, o Bacchus, the wine of wine. Give them, at last, Poetry.

Do they stand immoveable there, the sots, & laugh at your socalled poetry? They may well laugh; it does not touch them yet. Try a deeper strain. There is no makebelieve about these fellows; they are good tests for your skill; therefore, a louder yet, & yet a louder strain. There is not one of them, but will spin fast enough when the music reaches him, but he is very deaf, try a sharper string. Angels in satinette & calico—angels in hunting knives, & rifles—swearing angels, roarers with liquor—O poet, you have much to learn.

These rabble at Washington are really better than the snivelling opposition. They have a sort of genius of a bold & manly cast, though Satanic. They see, against the unanimous expression of the people, how much a little well directed effrontery can achieve, how much crime the people will bear, & they proceed from step to step & it seems they have calculated but too justly upon your Excellency, O Governor Briggs. Mr Webster told them how much the war cost, that was his protest, but voted the war, & sends his son to it. They calculated rightly on Mr

Webster. My friend Mr Thoreau has gone to jail rather than pay his tax. On him they could not calculate. The abolitionists denounce the war & give much time to it, but they pay the tax.

The State is a poor good beast who means the best: it means friendly. A poor cow who does well by you—do not grudge it its hay. It cannot eat bread as you can, let it have without grudge a little grass for its four stomachs. It will not stint to yield you milk from its teat. You who are a man walking cleanly on two feet will not pick a quarrel with a poor cow. Take this handful of clover & welcome. But if you go to hook me when I walk in the fields, then, poor cow, I will cut your throat.

July 31, 1846

Webster knows what is done in the shop & remembers & uses it in the Senate. He saw it in the shop with an eye supertabernal & supersenatorial or it would not have steaded. He is a ship that finds the thing where it is cheap, & carries it where it is dear. Knowledge is of some use in the best company. But the grasp is the main thing. Most men's minds do not grasp any thing. All slips through their fingers, like the paltry brass grooves that in most country houses are used to raise & drop the curtain, but are made to sell, & will not hold any curtain but cobweb. I have heard that idiot children are known from the birth by the circumstance that their hands do not close round any thing. Webster naturally & always grasps, & therefore retains some thing from every company & circumstance. One of these tenacities, it is no matter where it goes. It gets an education in a shanty, in an alehouse, over a cigar, or in a fishingboat, as good as it could find in Germany or in Sais: for the world is unexpectedly rich, & everywhere tells the same things. The grasp is much, but not quite all; the juggle of commerce never loses its power to astonish & delight us, namely, the unlooked for juxtaposition of things. Take the peaches from under the tree, & carry them out of sight of the tree, & their value is centupled.

Aug. 23, 1846

The teacher should be the complement of the pupil; now for the most part they are earth's diameters wide of each other. A college professor should be elected by setting all the candidates loose on a miscellaneous gang of young men taken at large from the street. He who could get the ear of these youths after a certain number of hours, or of the greatest number of these youths, should be professor. Let him see if he could interest these rowdy boys in the meaning of a list of words.

Oct. 1846

My friend William Emerson at Bangor told me that he thought "Judge Story might be a great man, O yes, a man of a good deal of talent & learning & fame," but he did not think so highly of him as a Judge, as many did; "that he had two failings as a Judge; first, in pint of judgment; & second, in pint of integrity—you take my idea."

Representing the Age
1847-1856

A FTER PUBLISHING his first book of poetry at the end of 1846, Emerson began the new year with a full lecture schedule and a determination to continue his education. He felt restless and eager for new experience, in need of "society, provocation, a whip for the top." He even thought he might be "set aglow" by a professorship or the pulpit—better yet, by an "Abolition-Campaign" or a "course of mobs." He was feeling the need to immerse himself more in the current of contemporary events. "In this emergency," he notes, "one advises Europe, & especially England." He believed that England had become the epitome of modern industrial civilization, and he needed to test the premises and fruits of that proposition if his own "autobiography" was to be adequate to his conception of such a document: "a book of answers from one individual to the main questions of the time." In the volume already growing under his hand—*Representative Men*, to be published in 1850—Emerson did offer essays on two nineteenth-century figures, Napoleon and Goethe, but that was not a response to the conditions of life as he knew them. Reading proofs of the book late in 1849, Emerson in fact criticized himself for continuing the "parrot echoes of the names of literary notabilities & mediocrities" while overlooking the "greatness of the common farmer & labourer."

Leaving Thoreau in charge of his family, Emerson set off on his second European journey in October 1847 and spent most of the next nine months touring and lecturing in England and Scotland. He was greatly impressed with the advances in science and technology that had enabled this small island to transform itself into a kind of mechanical paradise, but noticing that coal smoke had turned day into night, begrimed the livestock, and made the trees and even human spittle black, he wondered at the cost. He concluded that "Birmingham birminghamizes all," including the English mind and spirit. Emerson might praise England as the "best of actual nations," but not without qualification—"& so you see the poor best you have yet got." Perfection of the means of existence without a concomitant elevation of the spirit could not strike this moralist as unmitigated progress. There is no doubt, too, that Emerson was shocked by the revolution in sexual values that he found characteristic of modern cities. Spending a month in Paris in the spring of 1848, he noticed advertisements everywhere for "La Guerison des Maladies secretes" and had to conclude that "extremes of vice" and "animal indulgence" were also part of this charming urban scene. He had heard the same from Carlyle and Dickens at a dinner in April. They discoursed on the "shameful lewdness of the London streets at night" so forcefully that Emerson feared for English boyhood; but his companions insisted that male chastity was a thing of the past generally, in New York as well as Liverpool. He assured them that well-bred young men in America went "virgins to their nuptial bed, as truly as their brides," whereupon Dickens replied he would be worried if his son were "particularly chaste" for fear that "he could not be in good health." Emerson might console himself with the notion that these gentlemen were not idealists, but they had given him something to think about. After his return to America Emerson would conclude that the author who omits "inevitable facts in his view of life" fails to satisfy our expectations.

Emerson was learning that the writer must be willing to represent his age or run the risk of losing his audience. Early in 1850 he noted that all the regulars on the Lyceum circuit had reached the same conclusion: "Putnam, Whipple, Dewey, W. H. Channing, & I—and I know not how many more—are lecturing this winter on the *Spirit of the Times!*" Emerson marveled that even the misty-headed Bronson Alcott had attempted the same subject and attracted a good audience of men who "sympathized with engineers & Californians." This was navel gazing with modern microscopes; "mad contradictions," he noted, "flavor all our dishes." An even madder and more serious contradiction in the spirit of the times occurred in March when almost a thousand distinguished citizens of Boston published a letter praising Webster's infamous 7th of March speech in support of the Fugitive Slave Law, causing Emerson to feel that "the badness of the times is making death attractive." But it was this issue that brought him most vitally alive to the problems of his age, and he filled page after page of his journal with bitter denunciations of this "filthy enactment" and his once revered Daniel Webster. Emerson now became more outspoken publicly on the slave question and would not rest until the cleansing fire of civil war had rooted this evil out of the *respublica*. His patriotism was sorely tried by the realization that "Webster truly represents the American people just as they are, with their vast material interests, materialized intellect, & low morals." In such a circumstance he would have trouble advancing claims for America's superiority over a "birminghamized" England, though he would make a valiant attempt in *English Traits* (1856).

Beginning in 1853, Emerson extended his lecture tours to the western states, and in 1856 he noted that the rough climate and manners were "a new test for the wares of a man of letters." The age and American popular tradition demanded some representation of the comic impulse, and Emerson was prepared to oblige; indeed, he had already tried his hand at dry Yankeeisms and other forms of wit in his lectures and essays. (When Emerson was introduced to Abraham Lincoln in 1862, he was gratified at the President's remarking, "O Mr Emerson, I once heard you say in a lecture, that a Kentuckian seems to say by his air & manners, *'Here am I; if you don't like me, the worse for you.'* ") Emerson believed that "he is no master who cannot vary his forms, & carry his own end triumphantly through the most difficult," and this concession to popular taste occasionally caused friction between him and his refractory disciple, Henry Thoreau, who maintained that "whatever succeeded with the audience was bad." Emerson never turned himself into a crowd pleaser, however. He had simply come into closer contact with his audience and was willing to admit the value of that communion. He observed approvingly in 1853 that *Uncle Tom's Cabin* had the distinction of being "read equally in the parlour & the kitchen & the nursery of every house." No one could thereby impugn the seriousness of Mrs.

Stowe's intent; she had touched a chord at all levels of American society, demonstrating the universality and relevance of her message.

Emerson had long believed that America was a poem only waiting for the right meters. He therefore celebrated Whitman's *Leaves of Grass* in 1855 as the representative poetry of its time and place, *the* New World book he had been expecting—"indisputably American," as he wrote Carlyle. The fact that such a book might be explicitly carnal and sexual did not theoretically trouble him. He had after all argued, in his essay "The Poet," that "the vocabulary of an omniscient man would embrace words and images excluded from polite conversation." What might be considered base or even obscene could become "illustrious, spoken in a new connection of thought." Nevertheless, with his insistent flesh and appetites, Whitman was sometimes an embarrassment. "Whipple said of the author of 'Leaves of Grass,' that he had every leaf but the fig leaf," he notes in his 1856 journal, humorously acknowledging that among nice people Whitman was being dismissed as one of the roughs. Still, he *was* Emerson's American bard. The journal entry that immediately follows this one—"the audience that assembled to hear my lectures in these six weeks was called, 'the *effete* of Boston' "—suggests through its juxtaposition to Whipple's quip Emerson's complex awareness of the problem. If the elite of Boston truly were effete, they needed the raucous poet of the body as least as much as they needed Emerson's polite conversation. A true American taste would have to be ample enough to accept both the sublime master and his disorderly disciple. Such a seeming contradiction, Emerson knew, was another necessary ingredient of his rich Transcendental dish as it was coming to a boil in what Whitman would call a "strange, unloosened, wondrous time."

Jan. 10, 1847

Read Alfieri's Life: Who died the year I was born, was a dear lover of Plutarch & Montaigne, a passionate lover of beauty & of study. His rare opportunities & the determination to use them, make him a valuable representative. His temperament however isolated him, & he travels in a narrow track with high walls on either side. Yet he is most fortunate in his friendships, & at last in his love. The noble is seeking the same good as the republican, namely one or two companions of intelligence, probity, & grace, to wear out life with, & rebut the disparagement he reads in the sea & the sky. Gori, Caluso, & the Countess of Albany were sea & sky to him. One has many thoughts, in reading this book, of the uses of Aristocracy & Europe to the native scholar.

Jan.? 1847

I have tried to read Machiavelli's Histories but find it not easy. The Florentine factions are as tiresome as the history of the Philadelphia Fire Companies . . .

H. D. T. wants to go to Oregon, not to London. Yes surely; but what seeks he but the most energetic nature? & seeking that, he will find Oregon indifferently in all places; for it snows & blows & melts & adheres & repels all the world over.

Feb.–March 1847

Vice of men is setting up for themselves too early. I can't go into the quarrel or into the tavern, &c. because I am old; or into the abolition meeting at Faneuil Hall & attempt to speak, it won't do for me to fail!

But I look at wise men, & see that I am very young. I look over those stars yonder & into the myriads of the aspirant & ardent souls, & I see I am a stranger & a youth, & have yet my spurs to win. Too ridiculous are these airs of age.

Ancora imparo. I carry my satchel still.

See this terrible Atlantic stretching its stormy chaos from pole to pole terrible by its storms, by its cold, by its ice-bergs, by its Gulf stream, the desert in which no caravan loiters, but all hurry as thro' the valley of the Shadow of Death, as unpassable to the poor Indian through all ages as the finer ocean that separates him from the moon; let him stand on the shore & idly entreat the birds or the wind to transport him across the roaring waste. Yet see, a man arrives at the margin with 120 dollars in his pocket, and the rude sea grows civil, and is bridged at once for the long three thousand miles to England, with a carpeted floor & a painted & enamelled walls & roof, with books & gay company & feasting & music & wine.

The chief good of life seems, this morning, to be born with a cheerful happy temper, & well adjusted to the tone of the human race: for such a man feels himself in the harmony of things, & conscious of an infinite strength. He need not do any thing. But if he is not well mixed &

averaged, then he needs to achieve something, build a rail road, make a fortune, write an Iliad, as a compensation to himself for his abnormal position, & as we pinch ourselves to know that we are awake.

Health, south wind, books, old trees, a boat, a friend.

How can we hear children ask for a story or men for a novel or the theatre & not realize the necessity of the imagination in Education. We must have symbols.

March 3, 1847

At Lincoln, last night, read a lecture in the schoolhouse. The architect had a brighter thought than ordinary there. He had felicitously placed the door at the right of the desk, so that when the orator is just making a point and just ready to drive the last nail, the door opens at his side & Mr Hagar & Deacon Sanborn & Captain Peck come in, & amiably divide with him the attention of the company. Luckily the sleighbells, as they drove up to the door, were a premonitory symptom, & I was able to rein in my genius a little, whilst these late arrivers were bundling out & stamping their feet before they usurped the attention of the house.

March 1847

On the Beauties of Concealment. I have a question to propose to the company. Whether it is worth any man's while to relax any private rule. If he has drank water, why should he not drink wine? If he finds it best to add mortgages & securities to the good strength of love; to pray and also keep his powder dry; prayer, but also manure.

What is the harm of a little indulgence, so it be decent—that is—secret?

Why nothing; an imbecility is the only consequence. And that does not signify, does it? To remain a boy, an old boy at 50 years. He covered up all his particular frauds, but they made his face sharp. He concealed as well as he could all his effeminate & cowardly habits, but they made him cowering, & threw him on the Whig side, & he looked irritable & shy, & on his guard in public.

Concord had certain roads & waste places which were much valued for their beauty but which were difficult to find. There was one which whoso entered could not forget—but he had more than common luck if he ever found it again, let him search for it with his best diligence. Run boy from the swamp beside the lake to the big hemlock where a chestnut has been chopped down at twelve feet high from the ground then leave the high wood road & take the ox path to the right; pass one right hand turn, & take the second, & run down a valley with long prairie hay covering it close; an old felled pine-tree lies along the valley, follow it down till the birds do not retreat before you; then till the faint daymoon rides nearer; then till the valley is a ravine with the hills of Nobscot seen at the bottom of it across the Bay.

March 25, 1847

We must have society, provocation, a whip for the top. A Scholar is a candle which the love & desire of men will light. Let it not lie in a dark box. But here am I with so much all ready to be revealed to me as to others if only I could be set aglow. I have wished for a professorship. Much as I hate the church, I have wished the pulpit that I might have the stimulus of a stated task. N. P. Rogers spoke more truly than he knew, perchance, when he recommended an Abolition-Campaign to me. I doubt not, a course of mobs would do me much good. A snowflake will go through a pine board, if projected with force enough. I have almost come to depend on conversation for my prolific hours. I who converse with so few & those of no adventure, connexion, or wide information. A man must be connected. He must be clothed with society, or we shall feel a certain bareness & poverty, as of a displaced, disfurnished person. He is to be drest in arts, picture-galleries, sculpture, architecture, institutions, as well as in body garments. Pericles, Plato, Caesar, Shakspeare, will not appoint us an interview in a hovel. My friends would yield more to a new companion. In this emergency, one advises Europe, & especially England. If I followed my own advices—if I were master of a liberty to do so—I should sooner go toward Canada. I should withdraw myself for a time from all domestic & accustomed relations & command an absolute leisure with books—for a time.

I think I have material enough to serve my countrymen with thought & music, if only it were not scraps. But men do not want handfuls of gold dust, but ingots.

March–April 1847

The name of Washington City in the newspapers is every day of blacker shade. All the news from that quarter being of a sadder type, more malignant. It seems to be settled that no act of honor or benevolence or justice is to be expected from the American Government, but only this, that they will be as wicked as they dare. No man now can have any sort of success in politics without a streak of infamy crossing his name.

Things have another order in these men's eyes. Heavy is hollow & good is evil. A western man in Congress the other day spoke of the opponents of the Texan & Mexican plunder as "Every light character in the house," & our good friend in State street speaks of "the solid portion of the community" meaning, of course, the sharpers. I feel, meantime, that those who succeed in life, in civilized society, are beasts of prey. It has always been so.

Theology, Medicine, Law, Politics, Trade have their meetings & assembly rooms. Literature has none. See how magnificently the Merchants meet in State street. Every Bank & Insurance office is a Palace, & Literature has not a poor café, not a corner even of Mrs Haven's shop in which to celebrate its unions. By a little alliance with some of the rising parties of the time, as the Socialists, & the Abolitionists, and the Artists, we might accumulate a sufficient patronage to establish a good room in Boston. As Ellery Channing says there is not a chair in all Boston where I can sit down.

I hate vulnerable people.

It becomes those who want animal spirits to take the low tone; never to take the initiative. Such are chameleons, &, in the presence of the wise, they are transparent & serene; in the presence of the worldly, they are turbid & weak.

The virtue of Democrats is to rail against England, the Lowell companies, & Mr Webster's pension.

Centrality Centrality. "Your reading is irrelevant." Yes, for you, but not for me. It makes no difference what I read. If it is irrelevant, I read it deeper. I read it until it is pertinent to me & mine, to nature & to the hour that now passes. A good scholar will find Aristophanes & Hafiz & Rabelais full of American history.

I believe in Omnipresence & find footsteps in Grammar rules, in oyster shops, in church liturgies, in mathematics, and in solitudes & in galaxies. I am shamed out of my declamations against churches by the wonderful beauty of the English liturgy, an anthology of the piety of ages & nations.

A national man. Pericles, Caesar, Luther, Dr Johnson, Mirabeau, Goethe, Webster.

A large well-built brain with a great trunk below to supply it, as if a fine alembic were fed with liquor for its distillations from broad full vats in the vaults of the laboratory.

* * *

Nature loves crosses, as inoculations of barbarous races prove: and marriage is crossing.

Where two shadows cross, the darkness thickens: where two lights cross, the light glows.

Milton, Bacon, Gray, are crosses of the Greek & Saxon geniuses.

'Tis purposed to establish a new Quarterly Journal. Well, 'tis always a favorable time, & now is.

The essential ground of a new book is that there be a new spirit; that the authors really have a new idea, a higher life, see the direction of a more comprehensive tendency than others are aware of and this with that fulness or steadiness of perception as to falter never in affirming it, but take the victorious tone, as did the Edinburgh Review, the London Times, & the Boston Chronotype.

An autobiography should be a book of answers from one individual to the main questions of the time. Shall he be a scholar? the infirmities & ridiculousness of the scholar being clearly seen. Shall he fight? Shall he seek to be rich? Shall he go for the ascetic or the conventional life? he being aware of the double consciousness. Shall he value mathematics? Read Dante? or not? Aristophanes? Plato? Cosmogonies, & scholar's courage. What shall he say of Poetry? What of Astronomy? What of Religion?

Then let us hear his conclusions respecting government & politics. Does he pay taxes and record his title deeds? Does Goethe's Autobiography answer these questions? So of love, of marriage, so of playing providence. It should be a true Conversation's Lexicon for earnest men.

Novels, Poetry, Mythology must be well allowed for an imaginative being. You do us great wrong, Henry T., in railing at the novel reading. The novel is that allowance & frolic their imagination gets. Everything else pins it down. And I see traces of Byron & D'Israeli & Walter Scott & George Sand in the deportment of these stately young clerks in the streets & hotels. Their education is neglected but the ballroom & the circulating library, the fishing excursion & Trenton Falls make such amends as they can.

April 5, 1847

The best feat of Genius is to make an audience of the mediocre & the dull. They also feel addressed; they are for once fairly blended with the intelligent. The same things interest them which interest the wise; the iron boundary lines fade away, and the stupid & mean have become interesting also.

April 1847

A whip for our top! A cold sluggish blood thinks it has not quite facts enough to the purpose in hand and must decline its turn in the conversation. But they who speak have no more; have less; the best success of the day is without any new facts.

Heat, heat, is all. Heat puts you in rapport with magazines & worlds of facts.

My stories did not make them laugh, my facts did not quite fit the case, my arguments did not hit the white. Is it so? then warm yourself, old fellow, with hot mincepie and half a pint of port wine, & they will fit like a glove, & hit like a bullet.

Look at literary New England, one would think it was a national fast. All are sick with debility and want of object; so that the literary population wears a starved, puny, & piteous aspect.

May 23, 1847

Henry Truman Safford born at Royalton, Vt Jan 6, 1836. In 1846 was examined for 3 hours by Rev H W Adams of Concord N.H. & Rev C N Smith of Randolph Vt. and at last was bidden:

"Multiply in your head 365 365 365 365 365 365 by 365 365 365 365 365 365!" eighteen figures by eighteen. "He flew round the room like a top, pulled his pantaloons over the top of his boots, bit his hand rolled his eyes in their sockets sometimes smiling & talking & then seeming to be in agony until in not more than one minute, he said, 133,491,850, 208,566,925,016,658,299,941,583,225. The boy's father Rev C. N. Smith & myself had each a pencil & slate to take down the answer, & he gave it us in periods of three figures each as fast as it was possible for us to write them. And what was still more wonderful he began to multiply at the left hand & to bring out the answer from left to right giving first 123, 491 &c. Here confounded above measure I gave up the examination. The boy looked pale & said he was tired. He said, it was the largest sum he ever did."

May 24, 1847

The days come & go like muffled & veiled figures sent from a distant friendly party, but they say nothing, & if we do not use the gifts they bring, they carry them as silently away.

May–June 1847

On the seashore at Nantucket I saw the play of the Atlantic with the coast. Here was wealth: every wave reached a quarter of a mile along shore as it broke. There are no rich men, I said to compare with these.

Every wave is a fortune. One thinks of Etzlers and great projectors who will yet turn this immense waste strength to account and save the limbs of human slaves. Ah what freedom & grace & beauty with all this might. The wind blew back the foam from the top of each billow as it rolled in, like the hair of a woman in the wind. The freedom makes the observer feel as a slave. Our expression is so slender, thin, & cramp; can we not learn here a generous eloquence? This was the lesson our starving poverty wanted. This was the disciplinary Pythagorean music which should be medicine.

At Brook Farm one man ploughed all day, & one looked out of the window all day & drew his picture, and both received the same wages.

When I see my friend after a long time, my first question is, Has any thing become clear to you?

Loose the knot of the heart, says Hafiz. At the Opera I think I see the fine gates open which are at all times closed, and that tomorrow I shall find free & varied expression. But tomorrow I am mute as yesterday. Expression is all we want: Not knowledge, but vent: we know enough; but have not leaves & lungs enough for a healthy perspiration & growth. . . . An air of sterility, poor, thin, arid, reluctant vegetation belongs to the wise & the unwise whom I know. If they have fine traits, admirable properties, they have a palsied side. But an utterance whole, generous, sustained, equal, graduated-at-will, such as Montaigne, such as Beaumont & Fletcher so easily & habitually attain, I miss in myself most of all, but also in my contemporaries. A palace style of manners & conversation, to which every morrow is a new day, which exists extempore and is equal to the needs of life, at once tender & bold, & with great arteries like Cleopatra & Corinne, would be satisfying, and we should be willing to die when our time came, having had our swing & gratification. But my fine souls are cautious & canny, & wish to unite Corinth with Connecticutt. I see no easy help for it. Our virtues too are in conspiracy against grandeur, and are narrowing. Benvenuto Cellini. He had concentration and the right rage.
The true nobility has floodgates—an equal inlet & outgo.

"Keep the body open," is the hygeian precept, and the reaction of free circulations on growth & life. The fact that the river makes its own shores, is true for the artist.
Large utterance! The pears are suffering from *frozen sap-blight*, the sap being checked in its fullest flow, & not being able to form leaves &

fruit, which is the perspiration & utterance of the tree, becomes thick, unctuous & poisonous to the tree.

The jockey looks at the chest of the horse, the physician looks at the breast of the babe, to see if there is room enough for the free play of the lungs.

Arteries, perspiration. Shakspeare sweats like a haymaker—all pores.

June 1847

To a right aristocracy, to Hercules, Theseus, Odin, the Cid, and Napoleon; to Sir Robert Walpole, to Fox, Chatham, Webster, to the men, that is, who are incomparably superior to the populace in ways agreeable to the populace, showing them the way they should go, doing for them what they wish done, & cannot do; of course, every thing will be permitted & pardoned, gaming, drinking, adultery, fighting—these are the heads of party who can do no wrong—every thing short of incest & beastliness will pass.

Every thing teaches transition, transference, metamorphosis: therein is human power, in transference, not in creation; & therein is human destiny, not in longevity but in removal. We dive & reappear in new places.

American mind a wilderness of capabilities.

In Carlyle as in Byron, one is more struck with the rhetoric than with the matter. He has manly superiority rather than intellectuality, & so makes good hard hits all the time. There is more character than intellect in every sentence. Herein strongly resembling Samuel Johnson.

Alas for America as I must so often say, the ungirt, the diffuse, the profuse, procumbent, one wide ground juniper, out of which no cedar, no oak will rear up a mast to the clouds! it all runs to leaves, to suckers, to tendrils, to miscellany. The air is loaded with poppy, with imbecility, with dispersion, & sloth.

Eager, solicitous, hungry, rabid, busy-body America attempting many things, vain, ambitious to feel thy own existence, & convince others of thy talent, by attempting & hastily accomplishing much; yes, catch thy breath & correct thyself and failing here, prosper out there; speed & fever are never greatness; but reliance & serenity & waiting & perseverance, heed of the work & negligence of the effect.

America is formless, has no terrible & no beautiful condensation.

* * *

How attractive is land, orchard, hillside, garden, in this fine June!
Man feels the blood of thousands in his body and his heart pumps the
sap of all this forest of vegetation through his arteries. Here is work for
him & a most willing workman. He displaces the birch & chestnut, larch
& alder, & will set oak & beech to cover the land with leafy colonnades.
Then it occurs what a fugitive summer flower papilionaceous is he,
whisking about amidst these longevities. Gladly he could spread himself
abroad among them; love the tall trees as if he were their father; borrow
by his love the manners of his trees, and with nature's patience watch
the giants from the youth to the age of golden fruit or gnarled timber,
nor think it long.

Channing proposed that there should be a magnified Dollar, say as
big as a barrel head, made of silver or gold, in each village & Col. Shattuck or other priest appointed to take care of it & not let it be stolen;
then we should be provided with a local deity, & could bring it baked
beans or other offerings & rites, as pleased us.

Literature should be the counterpart of nature & equally rich. I find
her not in our books. I know nature, & figure her to myself as exuberant,
tranquil, magnificent in her fertility—coherent, so that every thing is an
omen of every other. She is not proud of the sea or of the stars, of space
or time; for all her kinds share the attributes of the selectest extremes.
But in literature her geniality is gone—her teats are cut off, as the Ama-
zons of old.

It is said that when manners are licentious, a revolution is always
near: the virtue of woman being the main girth or bandage of society;
because a man will not lay up an estate for children any longer than
whilst he believes them to be his own. I think, however, that it is very
difficult to debauch society. This chastity which people think so lightly
lost, is not so. 'Tis like the eye which people fancy is the most delicate
organ, but the oculist tells you it is a very tough & robust organ, & will
bear any injury; so the poise of virtue is admirably secured. Unchastity
with women is an acute disease, not a habit; the party soon gets through
it. Men are always being instructed more & more in the chastity of
women.

Contrarious temperament with chills, Muff, & buffalo when the
mercury reaches 90 degrees, and a fan at Zero and parasol. On going to
bed wants strong coffee as a soporific and when we must write at night
sup on baked beans, lettuce, and poppy-juice. He dislikes to hear night-

ingales hallooing all night but finds something soft & lulling in the voice of a pig.

In an evil hour I pulled down my fence & added Warren's piece to mine. No land is bad, but land is worse. If a man own land, the land owns him. Now let him leave home, if he dare. Every tree and graft, every hill of melons, every row of corn, every hedge-shrub, all he has done and all he means to do, stand in his way like duns when he so much as turns his back on his house. Then the devotion to these vines & trees & cornhills I find narrowing & poisonous. I delight in long free walks. These free my brain & serve my body. Long marches would be no hardship to me. My frame is fit for them. I think I compose easily so. But these stoopings & scrapings & fingerings in a few square yards of garden are dispiriting, drivelling, and I seem to have eaten lotus, to be robbed of all energy, & I have a sort of catalepsy, or unwillingness to move, & have grown peevish & poorspirited.

The garden is like those machineries which we read of every month in the newspapers which catch a man's coatskirt or his hand & draw in his arm, his leg, & his whole body to irresistible death.

June 22, 1847

An orientalist recommended to me who was a Hercules among the bugs and curculios, a Persian experiment of setting a lamp under the plum tree in a whitewashed tub with a little water in it, by night. But the curculio showed no taste for so elegant a death. A few flies & harmless beetles perished, & one genuine Yankee spider instantly wove his threads across the tub, thinking that there was likely to be a crowd & he might as well set up his booth & win something for himself. At night in the garden all bugdom & flydom is abroad.

This year is like Africa or New Holland, all surprising forms & masks of creeping, flying, & loathsomeness.

June 27, 1847

Irresistibility of the American; no conscience; his motto like nature's is, 'our country right or wrong.' He builds shingle palaces and shingle cities; yes, but in any altered mood perhaps this afternoon he will build stone ones, with equal celerity. Tall, restless Kentucky strength; great race, but tho' an admirable fruit, you shall not find one good sound well-developed apple on the tree. Nature herself was in a hurry with these hasters & never finished one.

Nature in this climate ardent; rushing up after a shower into a mass of vegetation.

June–July 1847

My young friend believed his calling to be musical, yet without jewsharp, catgut, or rosin. Yes, but there must be demonstration. Look over the fence yonder into Captain Abel's land. There's a musician for you, who knows how to make men dance for him in all weathers, & all sorts of men, paddies, felons, farmers, carpenters, painters, yes, and trees, & grapes & ice & stone, hot days, cold days. Beat that, Menetrier de Meudon! if you can! Knows how to make men saw, dig, mow, & lay stone wall, and how to make trees bear fruit God never gave them, and grapes from France & Spain yield pounds of clusters at his door. He saves every drop of sap as if it were his own blood. His trees are full of brandy. You would think he watered them with wine. See his cows, see his swine, see his horses and he, the musician that plays the jig which they all must dance, biped & quadruped & centipede, is the plainest, stupidest looking harlequin in a coat of no colours. But his are the woods & the waters, the hills & meadows.

An American in this ardent climate gets up early some morning & buys a river; & advertises for 12 or 1500 Irishmen; digs a new channel for it, brings it to his mills, and has a head of 24 feet of water: then, to give him an appetite for his breakfast, he raises a house; then carves out within doors a quarter township into streets & building lots, tavern, school, & methodist meeting house—sends up an engineer into New Hampshire, to see where his water comes from &, after advising with him sends a trusty man of business to buy of all the farmers such mill privileges as will serve him among their waste hill & pasture lots and comes home with great glee announcing that he is now owner of the great Lake Winnipiseosce, as reservoir for his Lowell mills at Midsummer.

The one event which never loses its romance is the alighting of superior persons at my gate.

My pear. This noble tree had every property which should belong to a plant. It was hardy and almost immortal. It accepted every species of nourishment & could live almost on none. It was free from every species of blight. Grubs, worms, flies, bugs, all attacked it. It yielded them all a share of its generous juices, but when they left their eggs on its broad leaves, it thickened the fiber & suffered them to dry up, & shook off the vermin. It grows like the ash Yggdrasil.

One other thing is to be remarked concerning the law of affinity. Every constitution has its natural enemies & poisons, which are to be avoided as ivy & dogwood are by those whom those plants injure.

There are those who, disputing, will make you dispute; and nervous and hysterical and animalized, will produce a like series of symptoms in you; though no other persons produce the like phenomena in you, & though you are conscious that they do not properly belong to you, but are a sort of extension of the diseases of the other party into you. I have heard that some men sympathize with their wives in pregnancy, as for example in the nauseas with which women are affected, a ridiculous & incredible circumstance, but it, no doubt, grew out of this observation.

July 1847

T. sometimes appears only as a gen d'arme, good to knock down a cockney with, but without that power to cheer & establish, which makes the value of a friend.

Goethe in this 3d vol. autobiography, which I read now in new translation, seems to know altogether too much about himself.

Luther, according to Mr Blecker, advises in one of his letters, a young scholar who cannot get rid of his doubts & spiritual fears, to get drunk.

Conversation that would really interest me would be those old conundrums which at Symposia the seven or seventy Wise Masters were wont to crack—What is intellect? What is time? What are the runners and what the goals?

But now there is no possibility of treating them well. Conversation on intellect & scholars becomes pathology. What a society it needs! I think you could not find a club at once acute & liberal enough in the world. Bring the best wits together and they are so impatient of each other, so worldly, or so babyish, there is so much more than their wit, so many follies & gluttonies & partialities, so much age & sleep & care that you have no academy. The questions that I incessantly ask myself as, What is our mythology? (which were a sort of test object for the power of our lenses) never come into my mind when I meet with clergymen; & what Academy has propounded this for a prize?

We have experience, reading, relatedness enough, o yes, & every other weapon, if only we had constitution enough. But, as the doctor said in my boyhood—"You have no *stamina.*"

C. Stow wanted his bog-meadow brought into grass. He offered Antony Colombe, Sol. Wetherbee, & whosoever else, seed & manure, & team, & the whole crop; which they accepted, & went to work, & re-

duced the tough roots, the tussucks of grass, the uneven surface & gave
the whole field a good rotting & breaking & sunning, and now Stow
finds no longer any difficulty in getting good English grass from the
smooth & friable land. What Stow does with his field, what the Creator
does with the planet, the Yankees are now doing with America. It will
be friable, arable, habitable, to men & angels yet.

Aug. 1847
     There came here, the other day, a pleasing child, whose face & form
were moulded into serenity & grace. We ought to have sat with her serene & thankfully with no eager demand. But she was made to run over
all the list of South Shore acquaintance. How is Mrs H's cholera-
morbus, & the Captain's rheumatism? When will Miss B. buy her carpets, and are there plums this year in Plymouth? When I got into the P.
coach in old times a passenger would ask me, "How's fish?"

     The superstitions of our age are,
          the fear of Catholicism
          the fear of Pauperism
          the fear of immigration
          the fear of manufacturing interests
          the fear of radicalism or democracy,
          and faith in the steam engine.

     I am always reminded, & now again by reading last night in Rous-
seau's Confessions, that it is not the events in one's life, but in the faculty of selecting & reporting them, that the interest lies. Mrs Marshall
over the way if she could write would make as interesting a life as Robinson Crusoe. And this because poetry needs little history. It is made of
one part history & ninety nine parts music; or, shall I say, fact & affection.

     Life consists in what a man is thinking of all day.

     The artist must be sacrificed. The child had her basket full of ber-
ries, but she looked sadly tired. The scholar is pale. Schiller shuns to
learn French that he may keep the purity of his German idiom. Herschel
must live in the observatory & draw on his night-cap when the sun rises,
& defend his eyes for nocturnal use. Michel Angelo must paint Sistine
Chapels, till he can no longer read except by holding the book over his
head. Nature deals with all her offspring so. See the poor moths & flies,
lately so vigorous, now on the wall or the trunk of the tree, exhausted,
dried up, & presently blown away. Men likewise. They must put their

lives into the sting they give. What is a man good for without enthusiasm? What is enthusiasm but this daring of ruin for its object? There are thoughts beyond the reaches of our souls; we are not the less drawn to them. The moth flies into the flame of the lamp, & Swedenborg must solve the problems though he be crazed & killed.

H. D. T. when you talked of art, blotted a paper with ink, then doubled it over, & safely defied the artist to surpass his effect.

Sept.–Oct. 1847

We go to Europe to see aristocratic society with as few abatements as possible. We go to be Americanized, to import what we can. This country has its proper glory, though now shrouded & unknown. We will let it shine.

Patriotism is balderdash. Our side, our state, our town is boyish enough. But it is true that every foot of soil has its proper quality, that the grape on either side of the same fence has its own flavor, and so every acre on the globe, every group of people, every point of climate has its own moral meaning whereof it is the symbol. For such a patriotism let us stand.

Why can we not let the broker, the grocer, the farmer, be themselves, and not addle their brains with sciolism & religion?

But the spiritualist needs a decided bias to the life of contemplation. Else what prices he pays! poor withered Ishmaelite, Jew in his Ghetto, disfranchised, odd one; what succors, what indemnities, what angels from the celestial side must come in to make him square!

All biography auto-biography.

I notice that the biography of each noted individual is really at last communicated by himself. The lively traits of criticism on his works are all confessions made by him from time to time among his friends & remembered & printed.

Do not imagine that I should work for the future, if my services were accepted or acceptable in the present. Immortality, as you call it, is my *pis aller*.

Remarkable trait in the American Character is the union not very infrequent of Yankee cleverness with spiritualism.

The beginning of wealth is in wealth of nature in the man. Sickness is poorspirited, & cannot serve any one, because it must husband its resources to live. It does not ask a question, or hazard a look at other people. But health or fulness answers its own needs & has to spare, & runs over, & inundates the neighborhoods & creeks of other men's necessities.

Oct. 14, 1847   At sea

The good ship darts thro' the water all night like a fish, quivering with speed. Sliding thro' space, sliding from horizon to horizon. She has passed Cape Sable; she has reached the Banks; gulls, haglets, ducks swim, dive, & hover around; no fishermen; she has passed the Banks, left five sail behind her, far on the edge of the west, at sundown, who were far east of us at morn, tho' they say at sea a stern chase is a long race. And still we fly for life. The ship cost $56 000.00. The shortest sea line from Boston to Liverpool is 2850 miles. This the steamer keeps, & saves by keeping her course 150 miles. Captain Caldwell says that he can never go in a shorter line than 3000 & usually much longer than that. The sailor is the practical ropedancer. The ship may weigh with all its freight 1500 tons. Every bound & plunge is taking us out of danger. If sailors were contented, if they had not resolved again & again never to go to sea any more, I should respect them. I can tell you what secrets the sea yielded me.

Oct. 18, 1847

In reading last night this old diary of Joseph Emerson of Malden ending in the year 1726, one easily sees the useful egotism of our old puritan clergy. The minister *experienced* life for his flock. He gave prominence to all his economy & history for the benefit of the parish. All his haps are providences. If he keeps school, marries, begets children, if his house burns, if his children have the measles, if he is thrown from his horse, if he buys a negro, & Dinah misbehaves, if he buys or sells his chaise, all his adventures are fumigated with prayer & praise, he preaches next Sunday on the new circumstance and the willing flock are contented with his consecration of one man's adventures for the benefit of them all, inasmuch as that one is on the right level & therefore a fair representative.

Oct. 1847

Carlyle. I found at Liverpool, after a couple of days, a letter which had been seeking me, from Carlyle, addressed to "R.W.E.—on the instant when he lands in England," conveying the heartiest welcome & urgent invitation to house & hearth. And finding that I should not be wanted for a week in the Lecture-rooms I came down to London, on Monday, &, at 10 at night, the door was opened to me by Jane Carlyle, and the man himself was behind her with a lamp in the hall. They were very little changed from their old selves of fourteen years ago (in August) when I left them at Craigenputtock. "Well," said Carlyle, "here we are shovelled together again!" The floodgates of his talk are quickly opened, & the river is a plentiful stream. We had a wide talk that night, until nearly 1 o'clock, & at breakfast next morning, again. At noon or later we walked forth to Hyde Park, & the palaces, about two miles from here to the National Gallery, & to the Strand, Carlyle melting all Westminster & London into his talk & laughter, as he goes. Here, in his house, we breakfast about 9, & Carlyle is very prone, his wife says to sleep till 10 or 11, if he has no company. An immense talker, and, altogether as extraordinary in that, as in his writing; I think, even more so. You will never discover his real vigor & range, or how much more he might do, than he has ever done, without seeing him. My few hours' discourse with him, long ago, in Scotland, gave me not enough knowledge of him; & I have now, at last, been taken by surprise, by him. He is not mainly a scholar, like the most of my acquaintances, but a very practical Scotchman, such as you would find in any saddler's or irondealer's shop—& then only accidentally, & by a surprising addition, the admirable scholar & writer. If you would know precisely how he talks, just suppose that our burly gardener, Hugh Whelan, had leisure enough, on the top of his day labor, to read Plato, Shakspeare, & Calvin, &, remaining Hugh Whelan all the time, should talk scornfully of all this nonsense of books he had been bothered with, & you shall have the tone & talk & laughter of Carlyle. I called him *a trip-hammer, with an Aeolian attachment.* He has, too, the strong religious tinge, in the way you find it in people of that burly temperament. That, & all his qualities have a certain virulence, coupled, tho' it be, in his case, with the utmost impatience of Christendom & Jewdom, & all existing presentments of the good old story. He talks like a very unhappy man, profoundly solitary, displeased & hindered by all men & things about him, & plainly biding his time & meditating how to undermine & explode the whole world of nonsense that torments him. He is respected here by all sorts of people—understands his own value quite as well as Webster—(of whom, his behavior sometimes reminds me, especially when he is with fine people) & can see society on his own terms.

Nov.? 1847

In Westminster Abbey, I was surprised to find the tombs cut & scrawled with penknives, and even in the coronation chair in which is contained the royal stone of Scone & in which for hundreds of years the Kings & Queens of England have been crowned, Mr Butter & Mr Light, and Mr Abbott have recorded their humble pretensions to be remembered: "I Butter slept in this chair" is explicitly recorded by that gentle-man's penknife on the seat.

Dec. 4, 1847

What a misfortune to America that she has not original names on the land but this whitewash of English names. Here every name is history. I was at Rochdale yesterday; I asked, where is the Rock? "That river down there." So at Sheffield, the Sheafe. Prestwick, Greenwich, is the Priest's vicus (street), the green vicus, so that all means somewhat. And poor America is born into cast-off clothes, and her alphabet is second-ary, & not organic.

Jan. 1848

In the minster I heard "God Save the King," of Handel, played by Dr Camidge on the grand organ. It was very great. I thought I had never heard anything so sublime. The music was made for the minster, & the minster for the music.

In the choir was service of evening prayer read & chanted. It was strange to hear the whole history of the betrothal of Rebekah & Isaac in the morning of the world read with all this circumstantiality in York minster, 13 Jan. 1848, to the decorous English audience just fresh from the Times Newspaper & their wine, and they listening with all the de-votion of national pride. That was binding old & new to some purpose. The reverence for the Scriptures is a powerful element of civilization, for thus has the history of the world been preserved, & is preserved. Every day a chapter of Genesis and a leader in the Times.

I see here continually the counterparts of faces, complexions, & manners well known to me at home, & have sometimes a sure key to the new man I talk with, through my experience of his antipode in America.

My Nights repeat my day, & I dream of gas light, heaps of faces, & darkness.

Jan.–Feb. 1848

The English have no curiosity about any foreign country. The Scotchman is as curious as an American. . . .

The English have stamina, can take the initiative in all companies. The foreigner is on the defensive & takes the low tone.

Feb. 1848

I find here a wonderful crop of mediocre and super-mediocre poets, they lie 3, 6, or 10 deep, instead of single as in America.

But, as at home, the merchants seem to me a greatly superior class to the clerisy. & they have a right to a great contempt of these.

English are trained to the highest inoffensiveness.

The Americans are sun-dried, the English are baked in the oven. The upper classes have only birth, say people here, & not thoughts; yes, but they have manners, & 'tis wonderful how much talent runs into manners. Nowhere & never so much as in England. And when they go into America & find that this gift has lost its power, the gold has become dry leaves, no wonder they are impatient to get away.

Every man in the carriage is a possible lord.

Yet they look alike & every man I meet in London I think I know. English have hard eyes.

Feb.–March? 1848

I stayed in London till I had become acquainted with all the styles of face in the street & till I had found the suburbs & their straggling houses on each end of the city. Then I took a cab, left my farewell cards, & came home.

March? 1848

I am sorry that all the French can say is ça va.

March–April 1848

A man must be in sympathy with society about him, or else, not wish to be in sympathy with it. If neither of these two, he must be wretched.

The Athenaeum excludes Guizot, when his name is proposed as an honorary member. They would be proud of his name, but the Englishman is not fickle, he really made up his mind to hate & to despise Guizot, & the altered position of the man, as an exile and a guest in the country, make no difference to him, as they would instantly to an American. The Englishman talks of politics & institutions, but the real thing which he values is his home, & that which belongs to it—that general culture & high polish which in his experience no man but the Englishman possesses, & which he naturally believes have some essential connexion with his throne & laws. That is what he does not believe resides in America, & therefore his contempt of America is only half-concealed. This English tenacity in strong contrast with our facility. The facile American sheds his Puritanism when he leaves Cape Cod, runs into all English & French vices with great zest & is neither Unitarian, nor Calvinist, nor Catholic nor stands for any known thought or thing; which is very distasteful to English honour. It is a bad sign that I have met with many Americans who flattered themselves that they pass for English. Levity, levity. I do not wish to be mistaken for an Englishman, more than I wish Monadnock or Nahant or Nantucket to be mistaken for Wales or the Isle of Wight.

Yes, there will be a new church founded on moral science, at first cold & naked, a babe in a manger again, a Copernican theory, the algebra & mathematics of Ethical law, the church of men to come without shawms or psaltery or sackbut, but it will have heaven & earth for its beams & rafters, all geology & physiology, botany, chemistry, astronomy for its symbol & illustration, and it will fast enough gather beauty, music, picture, poetry.

It was necessary that this roaring Babylon should fall flat, before the whisper that commands the world could be heard. It seems to every youth that he is alone, & left to fall abroad with too much liberty, when he is left with only God. He does not yet begin to see & to hear.

The English church being undermined by German criticism, had nothing left but tradition, & flung itself in to Roman church; distrusting the laws of the universe. The next step is now the ruin of Christendom.

The objection, the loud denial not less proves the reality & conquests of an idea, than the friends & advocates it finds. Thus communism now is eagerly attacked, and all its weak points acutely pointed out by British writers & talkers; which is all so much homage to the Idea, whose first inadequate expressions interest them so deeply, & with which they feel their fate to be mingled. If the French should set out to prove that three was four, would British journalism bestir itself to contradict them?

If I should believe the Reviews, and I am always of their opinion, I have never written any thing good. And yet, against all criticism, the books survive until this day.

People here expect a revolution. There will be no revolution, none that deserves to be called so. There may be a scramble for money. But as all the people we see want the things we now have, & not better things, it is very certain that they will, under whatever change of forms, keep the old system.

In the question of socialism, which now proposes the confiscation of France, one has only this guidance. You shall not so arrange property as to remove the motive to industry. If you refuse rent & interest, you make all men idle & immoral. As to the poor a vast proportion have made themselves so, and in any new arrangement will only prove a burden on the state. And there is a great multitude also whom the existing system bereaves forever of all culture & of all hope.

The masses—ah if you could read the biographies of those who compose them!

What is vulgar but the laying the emphasis on facts instead of on the quality of the fact? Mr Jones, in despair of getting your attention, tells you that his grandmother died this morning. Mr Giles, when there is a pause in the conversation, volunteers the information that he thinks himself dying in these weeks at the liver. Both fail of eliciting any remark.

Happy is he who looks only into his work to know if it will succeed, never into the times or the public opinion; and who writes from the love of imparting certain thoughts & not from the necessity of sale—who writes always to *the unknown friend.*

April? 1848

The British Museum holds the relics of ancient art, & the relics of ancient nature, in adjacent chambers. It is alike impossible to reanimate either.

The arrangement of the antique remains is surprisingly imperfect & careless, without order, or skilful disposition, or names or numbers. A warehouse of old marbles. People go to the Elgin chamber many times & at last the beauty of the whole comes to them at once like music. The figures sit like gods in heaven.

Coventry Patmore's remark was that to come out of the other room to this was from a room full of snobs to a room full of gentlemen.

St Paul's is, as I remembered it, a very handsome noble architectural exploit, but singularly unaffecting. When I formerly came to it from the Italian cathedrals, I said, "Well, here is New York." It seems the best of show-buildings, a fine British vaunt, but there is no moral interest attached to it.

In America we fancy that we live in a new & forming country but that England was finished long ago. But we find London & England in full growth, the British Museum not yet arranged, the boards only taken down the other day from the monument & fountains of Trafalgar Square.

Two poles here gather: all the wealth & all the poverty.

*   *   *

John will have you in the wrong.

I don't like him. He don't eat supper.

Yes but he has no appetite.

Well, if he had not stuffed himself so immoderately at dinner, he would have an appetite.

It is cold. If the snow had fallen two days ago, it would have lasted till now & given you as pretty a winter as we have in America.

Yes but it makes such a deal of dirt when it goes that we don't like it.

40 *per cent* of the English people cannot write their names. One half of one *per cent* of the Massachusetts people cannot, & these are probably Britons born.

It is certain that more people speak English correctly, in the United States, than in Britain.

April 25, 1848

Dined with John Forster, Esq. Lincoln's Inn Fields, & found Carlyle, & Dickens, & young Pringle. Forster, who has an obstreperous cordiality, received Carlyle with loud salutation, "My Prophet!" Forster called Carlyle's passion, Musket-worship. There were only gentlemen present, & the conversation turned on the shameful lewdness of the London streets at night. "I hear it," he [Carlyle] said, "I hear whoredom in the House of Commons. Disraeli betrays whoredom, & the whole H. of Commons universal incontinence, in every word they say." I said, that, when I came to Liverpool, I inquired whether the prostitution was always as gross in that city, as it then appeared? for, to me, it seemed to betoken a fatal rottenness in the state, & I saw not how any boy could grow up safe. But I had been told, it was not worse nor better, for years. C. & D. replied, that chastity in the male sex was as good as gone in our times; &, in England, was so rare, that they could name all the exceptions. Carlyle evidently believed that the same things were true in America. He had heard this & that, of New York, &c. I assured them that it was not so with us; that, for the most part, young men of good standing & good education with us, go virgins to their nuptial bed, as truly as their brides. Dickens replied, "that incontinence is so much the rule in England, that if his own son were particularly chaste, he should be alarmed on his account, as if he could not be in good health. Leigh Hunt," he said, "thought it indifferent." Dickens told me, that Miss Coutts had undertaken to establish an asylum for vicious girls taken out of the street. She had bed, clothed, schooled them, & had them taught to sew, & knit, & bake, that they might be wives for the Australians. Then she proposed to send them out, at her charge, & have them provided for until they married. They liked all this, very well, until it came to sailing for Australia. Then, they preferred going back to the Strand.

April–May? 1848
An artist spends himself, like the crayon in his hand, till he is all gone.

What games sleep plays with us! We wake indignant that we have been so played upon, & should have lent ourselves to such mountains of nonsense. All night I was scarifying with my wrath some conjuring miscreant, but unhappily I had an old age in my toothless gums, I was old as Priam, could not articulate, & the edge of all my taunts & sarcasms, it is to be feared, was quite lost. Yet, spite of my dumb palsy, I defied & roared after him, rattled in my throat, until wifey waked me up. Then I bit my lips. So one day we shall wake up from this longer confusion, & be not less mortified that we had lent ourselves to such rigmarole.

May 5? 1848
I saw Tennyson, first, at the house of Coventry Patmore, where we dined together. His friend Brookfield was also of the party. I was contented with him, at once. He is tall, scholastic-looking, no dandy—but a great deal of plain strength about him, &, though cultivated, quite unaffected. Quiet sluggish sense & strength, refined, as all English are—and good humoured. The print of his head in Horne's book is too rounded & handsome. There is in him an air of general superiority, that is very satisfactory. He lives very much with his college set, Spedding, Brookfield, Hallam, Rice, & the rest and has the air of one who is accustomed to be petted and indulged by those he lives with, like George Bradford. Take away Hawthorne's bashfulness, & let him talk easily & fast, & you would have a pretty good Tennyson. He had just come home from Ireland, where he had seen much vapouring of the Irish youth against England, & described a scene in some tavern, I think, where a hot young man was flourishing a drawn sword, & swearing that he would drive it to the hilt into the flesh & blood of Englishmen. Tennyson was disgusted, &, going up to the young man, took out his penknife, & offered it to him. "I am an Englishman," he said, "and there is my penknife, and, you know, you will not so much as stick that into me." The youth was disconcerted, & said, "he knew he was not an Englishman." "Yes, but I am." Hereupon the companions of the youth interfered, & apologized for him, he had been in drink, & was excited, &c.
Tennyson talked of Carlyle, & said If Carlyle thinks the Christian religion has lost all vitality, he is wholly mistaken. Tennyson & all Car-

lyle's friends feel the caprice & incongruity of his opinions. He talked of London as a place to take the nonsense out of a man. When "Festus" was spoken of, I said, that a poem must be made up of little poems, but that, in Festus, were no single good lines; you could not quote one line. Tennyson quoted

> "there came a hand between the sun & us,
> And its five fingers made five nights in air."

After dinner, Brookfield insisted that we should go to his house. So we stopped an omnibus, &, not finding room inside for all three, Tennyson rode on the box, & B. & I within. Brookfield, knowing that I was going to France, told me, that, if I wanted him, Tennyson would go. "That is the way we do with him," he said: "We tell him, he must go, & he goes. But you will find him heavy to carry." At Brookfield's house we found young Hallam, with Mrs Brookfield, a very pleasing woman. I told Tennyson, that I heard from his friends very good accounts of him, & I & they were persuaded that it was important to his health, an instant visit to Paris; & that I was to go on Monday, if he was ready. He was very goodhumoured, and affected to think that I should never come back alive from France, it was death to go. But he had been looking for two years for somebody to go to Italy with, & was ready to set out at once, if I would go there. I was tempted, of course, to pronounce for Italy; but now I had agreed to give my course in London.

May 13, 1848

The one thing odious to me now is joking. What can the brave & strong genius of C. himself avail? What can his praise, what can his blame avail me, when I know that if I fall or if I rise, there still awaits me the inevitable joke? The day's Englishman must have his joke, as duly as his bread. God grant me the noble companions whom I have left at home who value merriment less, & virtues & powers more. If the English people have owed to their House of Commons this damnable derision, I think they have paid an overprice for their liberties & empire. But when I balance the attractions of good & evil, when I consider what facilities, what talents a little vice would furnish, then rise before me not these laughers, but the dear & comely forms of honour & genius & piety in my distant home, and they touch me with chaste palms moist & cold, & say to me, You are ours.

The secret of Guy, the lucky & famous, was, to conceal from all mankind that he was a bore. It was wonderful how often & how long by skilful dispositions & timings he managed to make it believed, by clever people, too, that he was witty & agreeable.

May 1848

In Paris, my furnished lodgings, a very comfortable suite of rooms (15 Rue des Petits Augustins) on the second floor cost me 90 francs a month or 3 francs a day. My breakfast, which is brought to me at my chamber, & consists of bread, butter, one boiled egg, milk & coffee, costs one franc a day; my dinner at the Cafe "Cinq Arcades" in the Palais Royale costs 2 francs 2 sous and a cup of coffee in the evening 10 or 12 sous more. Say the expenses of living for a day, at my rate, are 6 francs 15 sous, or seven francs.

In Paris, the number of beggars does not compare with that in London, or in Manchester even.

I looked in all the shopwindows for toys this afternoon, and they are very many & gay; but the only one of all which I really wish to buy is very cheap, yet I cannot buy it, namely, their speech. I covet that which the vilest of the people possesses.

French poetry is peu de chose and in their character & performance is always prose, prose ornée, but never poesy.

Madame de Tocqueville, who is English, tells me, that the French is so beautiful a language, so neat, concise, & lucid, that she can never bear to speak English. 'Tis a peculiarity of the French that they assimilate all foreign words, & do not suffer them to be pronounced in the foreign manner. *libretto* is livret, *charivari* is *s*harivari, & so on, so that every blouse in the street speaks like an academician; which is not possible in England. I do not distinguish between the language of a blouse talking philosophy in a group, & that of Cousin.

The Boulevarts have lost their fine trees, which were all cut down for barricades in February. At the end of a year we shall take account, & see if the Revolution was worth the trees.

An eminent difference between Paris & London is the economy of water. In Paris the stranger is struck with the beautiful fountains on the Place de la Concorde & gives Paris the preference to London. But this water is not drinkable, & the houses in Paris have no wells or pumps & buy all their water by the bucket from water carriers who bring it from certain springs. In London every house has some kind of water privilege; as that in which I lived, received its water from Hertfordshire by an aquaduct which entered at the top of the house.

May–June 1848

Paris has great merits as a city. Its river is made the greatest pleasure to the eye by the quays & bridges: its fountains are noble & copious, its gardens or parks far more available to the pleasure of the people than those of London. What a convenience to the senses of men is the Palais Royal: the swarming Boulevards, what an animating promenade: the furnished lodgings have a seductive independence: the living is cheap & good; then what a luxury is it to have a cheap wine for the national beverage as uniformly supplied as beer in England. The manners of the people & probably their inferiority as individuals make it as easy to live with them as with so many shopkeepers whose feelings & convenience are nowise to be consulted. Meanwhile they are very civil & goodtempered, polite & joyous, and will talk in knots & multitudes in the streets all day for the entertainment of the passenger. Then they open their treasures of art & science so freely to the mere passport of the traveller & to all the world on Sunday. The University, the Louvre, the Hotel de Cluny, the Institute, the Gallery of the Luxembourg, Versailles. Then the Churches are always open, Notre Dame; La Sainte Chapelle, built by St Louis, & gorgeous within; St Sulpice; the Madeleine.

Then there is the Pantheon; and there is the Jardin des Plantes worthy of admiration. Everything odd & rare & rich can be bought in Paris; & by no means the least attractive of its shows is the immense bookstalls in the streets: maps, pictures, models, busts, sculptures, & libraries of old books spread abroad on tables or shelves at the side of the road. The manners of the people are full of entertainment so spirited, chatty, & coquettish, as lively as monkeys. And now the whole nation is bearded & in military uniform. I have no doubt also that extremes of vice are found here & that there is a liberty & means of animal indulgence hardly known by name or even by rumour in other towns. But any extremes are here also exceptional & are visited here by the fatal Nemesis who climbs all walls, dives into all cellars (and I notice that every wall in Paris is stigmatized with an advertisement of La Guerison des Maladies secretes) but also the social decorum seems to have here the same rigours as in England with a little variety in the application.

A special advantage which Paris has is in the freedom from aristocratic pride manifest in the tone of society. It is quite easy for any young man of liberal tastes to enter on a good footing the best houses. It is not easy in England. Then the customs are cheap & inexpensive; whilst it is a proverb almost, that, to live in England at all, you must have great fortune; which sounds to me as certain a prediction of revolution as musket shots in the streets.

So that on the whole I am thankful for Paris, as I am for the discovery of Ether & Chloroform; I like to know that, if I should need an amputation, there is this balm; and if hard should come to hard, & I should be driven to seek some refuge of solitude & independency, why here is Paris.

* * *

Paris & London have this difference, that Paris exists for the foreigner, serves him; whilst in London is the Londoner, who is much in the foreigner's way. England has built London for its own use. France has built Paris for the world.

June 1848

In England, every man is a castle. When I get into our first class cars on the Fitchburg Road, & see sweltering men in their shirt sleeves take their seats with some well drest men & women, & see really the very little difference of level that is between them all, and then imagine the astonishment that would strike the polished inmates of English first class carriages, if such masters should enter & sit beside them, I see that it is not fit to tell Englishmen that America is like England. No, this is the Paradise of the third class; here every thing is cheap; here every thing is for the poor. England is the Paradise of the first class; it is essentially aristocratic, and the humbler classes have made up their minds to this, & do contentedly enter into the system. In England, every man you meet is some man's son; in America, he may be some man's father.

July 1848

The road from Liverpool to New York is long, crooked, rough, rainy, & windy. Even good company will hardly make it agreeable. Four meals a day is the usual expedient, four & five (& the extreme remedy shows the exasperation of the case) & much wine & porter are the amusements of wise men in this sad place.

Never was a well-appointed dinner with all scientific belongings so philosophic a thing as at sea. Even the restless American finds himself, at last, at leisure.

July 23, 1848   At sea

One long disgust is the sea. No personal bribe would lure one who loves the present moment. Who am I to be treated in this ignominious manner, tipped up, shoved against the side of the house, rolled over, suffocated with bilge, mephitis, & stewing oil.

July–Aug. 1848

People eat the same dinner at every house in England. 1. soup; 2. fish; 3. beef, mutton, or hare; 4. birds; 5. pudding & pastry & jellies; 6. cheese; 7. grapes, nuts, & wine. During dinner, hock & champagne are offered you by the servant, & sherry stands at the corners of the table. Healths are not much drunk in fashionable houses. After the cloth is removed, three bottles, namely, port, sherry, claret invariably circulate. What rivers of wine are drunk in all England daily! One would say, every guest drinks six glasses.

But after much experience, we find literature the best thing; and men of thought, if still thinking, the best company. I went to England, &, after allowing myself freely to be dazzled by the various brilliancy of men of talent, in calm hours I found myself no way helped; my sequins were all yellow leaves, I said I have valued days (& must still) by the number of clear insights I get, and I must estimate my company so. Then I found I had scarcely had a good conversation, a solid dealing, man with man, in England. Only in such passages is a reason for human life given, and every such meeting puts a mortal affront on Kings & Governments by showing them to be of no account.

I spoke of friendship, but my friends & I are fishes in their habit. As for taking T.'s arm, I should as soon take the arm of an elm tree.

Henry Thoreau is like the woodgod who solicits the wandering poet & draws him into antres vast & desarts idle, & bereaves him of his memory, & leaves him naked, plaiting vines & with twigs in his hand. Very seductive are the first steps from the town to the woods, but the End is want & madness.

In England I found wine enough; as Dr Johnson said, "for once in his life he had as much wall fruit as he pleased." In France I had the privilege of leaving my papers all lying wide in my room; for nobody could read English.

H. D. T. working with A. B. A. on the summerhouse, said, he was nowhere, doing nothing.

Aug.–Sept. 1848
I observe that all the bookish men have a tendency to believe that they are unpopular. Parker gravely informs me by word & by letter that he is precisely the most unpopular of all men in New England. Alcott believes the same thing of himself, and I, no doubt, if they had not anticipated me in claiming this distinction, should have claimed it for myself.

The old writers, such as Montaigne, Milton, Browne, when they had put down their thoughts, jumped into their book bodily themselves, so that we have all that is left of them in our shelves; there is not a pinch of dust beside.

"I stayed in London till I had become acquainted with all the
styles of face in the street & till I had found the suburbs &
their straggling houses on each end of the city. Then I took
a cab, left my farewell cards, & came home."

Sept. 1848

None ever heard of a good marriage from Mesopotamia to Missouri
and yet right marriage is as possible tomorrow as sunshine. Sunshine is
a very mixed & costly thing as we have it, & quite impossible, yet we get
the right article every day. And we are not very much to blame for our
bad marriages. We live amid hallucinations & illusions, & this especial
trap is laid for us to trip up our feet with & all are tripped up, first or

last. But the Mighty Mother who had been so sly with us, feels that she owes us some indemnity, & insinuates into the Pandora-box of marriage, amidst dyspepsia, nervousness, screams, Christianity, "help," poverty, & all kinds of music, some deep & serious benefits & some great joys. We find sometimes a delight in the beauty & the happiness of our children that makes the heart too big for the body. And in these ill assorted connections there is ever some mixture of true marriage. The poorest Paddy & his jade, if well-meaning & welltempered, get some just & agreeable relations of mutual respect & kindly observation & fostering each of other. & they learn something, & would carry themselves wiselier if they were to begin life anew in another sphere.

Tennyson's poetry is as legitimate a fruit of the veneering or cabinetmaker style of English culture, as the Dinnertable.

The immense amount of valuable knowledge now afloat in society enriches the newspapers, so that one cannot snatch an old newspaper to wrap his shoes in, without his eye being caught by some paragraph of precious science out of London or Paris which he hesitates to lose forever. My wife grows nervous when I give her waste paper lest she is burning holy writ, & wishes to read it before she puts it under her pies.

George Sand is a great genius, & yet owes to her birth in France her entire freedom from the cant & snuffle of our dead Christianity.

I know what I shall find if Alcott brings me Mss. I shall have a Salisbury Plain full of bases of pyramids to each of which I am to build an apex.

I go twice a week over Concord with Ellery, &, as we sit on the steep park at Conantum, we still have the same regret as oft before. Is all this beauty to perish? Shall none remake this sun & wind, the skyblue river, the riverblue sky, the yellow meadow spotted with sacks & sheets of cranberry pickers, the red bushes, the irongray house with just the colour of the granite rock, the paths of the thicket, in which the only engineers are the cattle grazing on yonder hill; the wide straggling wild orchard in which nature has deposited every possible flavour in the apples of different trees. Whole zones & climates she has concentrated into apples. We think of the old benefactors who have conquered these fields; of the old man Moore who is just dying in these days, who has absorbed such volumes of sunshine like a huge melon or pumpkin in the sun— who has owned in every part of Concord a woodlot, until he could not find the boundaries of these, and never saw their interiors. But we say, where is he who is to save the present moment, & cause that this beauty be not lost? Shakspeare saw no better heaven or earth, but had the power & need to sing, & seized the dull ugly England, ugly to this, & made it amiable & enviable to all reading men, and now we are fooled into likening this to that; whilst, if one of us had the chanting constitution, that land would no more be heard of.

Oct. 1? 1848

Books are like rainbows to be thankfully received in their first impression & not examined & surveyed by theodolite & chain, as if they were part of the railroad. Perhaps it would be good in the tuition of an emperor that he should never read the same book twice. I owed—my friend & I—owed a magnificent day to the Bhagavat Geeta. It was the first of books; it was as if an empire spake to us, nothing small or unworthy but large, serene, consistent, the voice of an old intelligence which in another age & climate had pondered & thus disposed of the same questions which exercise us. Let us not now go back & apply a minute criticism to it, but cherish the venerable oracle.

Oct. 1848

We have a ridiculous wisdom like that which a man has of his corns, or of his gouty foot, & has become by experience cunning in setting it down so as not to hurt him, so we of our limitations. We have learned not to strut or talk of our wings, or affect angelic moods, but to keep the known ways, knowing that at the end of these fine streets is the Lunatic Asylum.

We say nothing against astronomy & vegetation, because we are roaring here in our bed with rheumatism, we doubt not there are bounding fawns, & lilies with graceful springing stem; so neither do we doubt or fail to love the eternal law of which we are such shabby practisers. A cripple was our father & an Ethiop was our mother. And we worship the Liberty which we shall not see with our eyes, nor help but with our prayer.

Our philosophy is to *wait*. We have retreated on patience, transferring our oft shattered hope now to larger & eternal good. We meant well, but our uncle was crazy & must be restrained from waking the house. The roof leaked, we were out of wood, our sisters were unmarried & must be maintained; there were taxes to pay, & notes, and, alas, a tomb to build: we were obliged continually to postpone our best action, and that which was life to do, could only be smuggled in to odd moments of the month & year.

* * *

H. T. sports the doctrines of activity: but I say, What do *we*? We want a sally into the regions of wisdom & do we go out & lay stone wall or dig a well or turnips? No, we leave the children, sit down by a fire, compose our bodies to corpses, shut our hands, shut our eyes, that we may be entranced & see truly.

There is in California a gold ore in great abundance in which the gold is in combination with such elements that no chemistry has yet been able to separate it without great loss. Alcott is a man of unquestionable genius, yet no doctrine or sentence or word or action of his which is excellent can be detached & quoted.

He is like Channing, who possesses a painter's eye, an appreciation of form & especially of colour, that is admirable, but who, when he bought pigments & brushes & painted a landscape on a barrel head could not draw a tree so that his wife could know it was a tree. So Alcott the philosopher has not an opinion or an apothegm to produce.

I shall write on his tomb, *Here lies Plato's reader.* Read he can with joy & naiveté inimitable, and the more the style rises, the more natural & current it seems to him. And yet his appetite is so various that the last book always seems to him the best. *Here lies the amateur.*

I notice that people who wash much, have a high mind about it, & talk down to those who wash little. Carlyle washes, & he has come to believe that the only religion left us is ablution, and that Chadwick, the man who is to bring water for the million, is the priest of these times. So at home I find the morning bathers are proud & haughty scorners, and I begin to believe that the composition of water must be one part hydrogen, & three parts conceit.

Edith, who until now has been quite superior to all learning, has been smitten with ambition at Miss Whiting's school and cannot be satisfied with spelling. She spells at night on my knees with fury & will not give over; asks new words like conundrums with nervous restlessness and, as Miss W. tells me, "will not spell at school for fear she shall miss."

Poor Edie struggled hard to get the white card called an "approbation" which was given out on Saturdays but one week she lost it by dropping out of a book on her way home her week's card on which her marks were recorded. This she tried hard to get safe home but she had no pocket so she put it in her book as the safest place. When half way home she looked in her book & it was there; but when she arrived at home it was gone. The next week she tried again to keep a clean bill but

Henry Frost pointed his jack-knife at her; Edie said, "Don't!" & lost her "approbation" again.

The Beatitude of Conversation. I am afraid books do stand in our way; for the best heads are writers, and when they meet & fall into profound conversation, they never quite lose all respects of their own economy & pour out the divinest wine, but each is a little wary, a little checked, by thought of the rare helps this hour might afford him to some page which he has written. Each is apt to become abstracted & lose the remark of the other through too much attention to his own.

Yet I have no book & no pleasure in life comparable to this. Here I come down to the shore of the Sea & dip my hands in its miraculous waves. Here I am assured of the eternity, & can spare all omens, all prophecies, all religions, for I see & know that which they obscurely announce. I seem rich with earth & air & heaven, but the next morning I have lost my keys. To escape this economy of writers, women would be better friends; but they have the drawback of the perplexities of sex.

Love is necessary to the righting the estate of woman in this world. Otherwise nature itself seems to be in conspiracy against her dignity & welfare; for the cultivated, high thoughted, beauty-loving, saintly woman finds herself unconsciously desired for her sex, and even enhancing the appetite of her savage pursuers by these fine ornaments she has piously laid on herself. She finds with indignation that she is herself a snare, & was made such. I do not wonder at her occasional protest, violent protest against nature, in fleeing to nunneries, & taking black veils. Love rights all this deep wrong, but who ever knew in real life a genuine instance of seasonable love?

I cannot tell you how many chatterers I see who exercise on me their airy genius for one real observer & honest reporter like my two or three friends. I should be very short & decisive with my visiters, but that I am not sure that I have private employment, when I shall have got rid of them. If my inspiration were only sure, I should disembarrass myself very fast of my company.

I knew an ingenious honest man who complained to me that all his dreams were servile, and, that, though he was a gentleman by day, he was a drudge, a miser, and a footman, by night. Civil war in our atoms, mutiny of the sub-daemons not yet subdued.

When I am walking in Boston, I think how much better had it been if I had stayed at home, & read such or such a book, written such letters, disposed of such affairs, &c. But if I stay at home, I do not those things. Why?

Oct. 29, 1848

Yesterday, 28 October, another walk with Ellery well worth commemoration if that were possible; but no pen could write what we saw: it needs the pencils of all the painters that ever existed, to aid the description. We went to White Pond, a pretty little Indian basin, lovely now as Walden once was; we could almost see the sachem in his canoe in a shadowy cove. But making the circuit of the lake on the shore, we came at last to see some marvellous reflections of the coloured woods in the water, of such singular beauty & novelty that they held us fast to the spot, almost to the going down of the sun. The water was very slightly rippled, which took the proper character from the pines, birches, & few oaks, which composed the grove; & the submarine wood seemed all made of Lombardy poplar, with such delicious green, stained by gleams of mahogany from the oaks, & streaks of white from the birches, every moment growing more excellent, it was the world seen through a prism, & set Ellery on wonderful Lucretian theories of "law" & "design".

Ellery, as usual, found the place with excellent judgment "where your house should be set," leaving the woodpaths as they were, which no art could make over; and, after leaving the pond, & a certain dismal dell, whither a man might go to shoot owls, or to do selfmurder in, we struck across an orchard to a steep hill of the right New Hampshire slope, newly cleared of wood, & came presently into rudest woodland landscapes, unknown, undescribed, & hitherto *unwalked* by us Saturday afternoon professors. The sun was setting behind terraces of pines disposed in groups unimaginable by Downings, or Loudons, or Capability Browns; but we kept our way & fell into the Duganne trail, as we had already seen the glimpse of his cabin in the edge of the barbarous district we had traversed. Through a clump of apple-trees, over a long ridge . . . with fair outsight of the river, & across the Nutmeadow brook, we came out upon the banks of the river just below James Brown's. Ellery proposed that we should send the Horticultural Society our notes, 'Took an apple near the White Pond fork of the Duganne trail—an apple of the *Beware of this* variety, a true *Touch me if you dare!—Seek no further of this.*' We had much talk of books & lands & arts & farmers. We saw the original *tumulus* or first barrow, which the fallen pine tree makes with its upturned roots, & which, after a few years, precisely resembles a man's grave. We talked of the great advantage which he has who can turn a verse, over all the human race. I read in Wood's A. Oxoniensis a score of pages of learned nobodies, of whose once odoriferous reputations not a trace remains in the air, & then I came to the name of some Carew, Herrick, Suckling, Chapman, whose name is as fresh & modern as those of our friends in Boston & London, and all because they could turn a verse. Only write a dozen lines, & rest on your oars forever, you are dear & necessary to the human race & worth all the old trumpery Plutarchs & Platos & Bacons of the world. I quoted Suckling's line, "a bee had stung it newly" to praise it, & E. said, "Yes, every body's poetry is good but your own." He declared that the modern books, Tennyson, Carlyle, Landor, gave him no standard, no measure of thought & life and he fancies that the only writing open for us is the Essay. . . .

In walking with Ellery you shall always see what was never before shown to the eye of man. And yet for how many ages of lonely days has that pretty wilderness of White Pond received the sun & clouds into its transparency, & woven each day new webs of birch & pine, shooting into wilder angles & more fantastic crossing of these coarse threads, which, in the water, have such momentary elegance.

Oct. 31, 1848

A good deal of thought & reading is no better than smoking, yet we give ourselves airs thereon, & not on our cigars. The difference between labor & indolence in the world of thought certainly points at a code and scale of reward as emphatic as the Christian heaven & hell. Yet with this difference, that Inspiration is very coy & capricious, we must lose many days to gain one, and, in order to win infallible verdicts from the inner mind, we must indulge & humour it in every way, & not too exactly task & harness it.

Oct.–Nov. 1848

How nature to keep her balance true invented a cat. What phantasmagoria in these animals! Why is the snake so frightful, which is the line of beauty, & every resemblance of it pleases? See what disgust & horror of a rat, loathsome in its food, loathsome in its form, & a tail which is villanous, formidable by its ferocity; yet interposed between this horror and the gentler kinds, is the cat, a beautiful horror, or a form of many bad qualities but tempered & thus strangely inserted as an offset, check, & temperament, to that ugly horror. See then the squirrel strangely adorned with his tail, which is his saving grace in human eyes.

Nov. 9, 1848

The whig party are what people would call *firstrate* in opposition, but not so good in government. Perhaps they have not sufficient fortitude. The same thing happens often in England.

Here has passed an Election, I think, the most dismal ever known in this country. Three great parties voting for three candidates whom they disliked. Next Monday there will be more heart.*

Nov. 1848

My friends begin to value each other, now that Alcott is to go; & Ellery declares, "that he never saw that man without being cheered," & Henry says, "He is the best natured man he ever met. The rats & mice make their nests in him."

The apple is our national fruit, & I like to see that the soil yields it; I judge of the country so. The American sun paints himself in these glowing balls amid the green leaves. Man would be more solitary, less friended, less supported, if the land yielded only the useful maize & potato, & withheld this ornamental & social fruit.

'Tis very certain that this almanack of the soul may be written as well as that of Greenwich. We have had our heights of sun & depths of shade, & it would be easy in the soul's year to recall & fix its 21 of June.

There is a sort of climate in every man's speech running from hot noon, when words flow like steam & perfume—to cold night, when they are frozen.

Nov. 19, 1848

'Tis the coldest November I have ever known. This morning the mercury is at 26. Yesterday afternoon cold fine ride with Ellery to Sudbury Inn, & mounted the side of Nobscot. Finest picture though wintry air of the russet Massachusetts. The landscape is democratic, not gathered into one city or baronial castle, but equally scattered into these white steeples, round which a town clusters in every place where six roads meet, or where a river branches or falls, or where the pan of soil is a little deeper. The horizon line marked by hills tossing like waves in a storm: firm indigo line. 'Tis a pretty revolution which is effected in the landscape by simply turning your head upside down, or, looking through your legs: an infinite softness & loveliness is added to the picture. It changes the landscape at once from November to June. Or as Ellery declared makes *Campagna* of it at once; so he said, Massachusetts is Italy upside down.

---

*Zachary Taylor (Whig), Lewis Cass (Democrat), and Martin Van Buren (Free Soil) were the candidates of the "great parties" in the Presidential election, Tuesday, November 7, 1848. [*JMN*]

Dec. 1848

Men live on the defensive, and go through life without an action, without one overt act, one initiated action. They buy stock, because others do, and stave off want & pain the best they can, defending themselves; but to carry the war into the enemy's country; to live from life within, & impress on the world their own form, they dare not. Thousands & thousands vegetate in this way, streets full, towns full, & never an action in them all.

All the talk that goes on is like chat on the way to church, to pass the time. When that is spoken which has a right to be spoken all this chattering will gladly stop.

Jan.–March 1849

Now that the man was ready, the horse was brought. The timeliness of this invention of the locomotive must be conceded. To us Americans, it seems to have fallen as a political aid. We could not else have held the vast North America together, which now we engage to do. It was strange, too, that when it was time to build a road across to the Pacific—a railroad, a shiproad, a telegraph, & in short a perfect communication in every manner for all nations—'twas strange to see how it is secured. The good World-Soul understands us well. How simple the means. Suddenly Californian soil is spangled with a little gold dust here & there, in a mill race, in a mountain cleft, an Indian picks up a little, a farmer, & a hunter, & a soldier, each a little; the news flies here & there, to New York, to Maine, to London, and an army of a hundred thousand picked volunteers, the ablest & keenest & boldest that could be collected instantly organize & embark for this desart bringing tools, instruments, books, & framed houses, with them. Such a well appointed Colony as never was planted before arrive with the speed of sail & steam on these remote shores, bringing with them the necessity that their government shall instantly proceed to make the road which they themselves are all intimately engaged to assist.

May 1849

I dismiss my labourer with saying "Well, Malachi, I shall send for you as soon as I cannot do without you." Malachi goes off contented with that assurance, for he knows well that the potatoes will grow & the weeds with them; the melons & squashes must be planted week after next. And however unwilling to pay his high wages I must send for him. I wish that all labour should be as real & valuable as his, & should stand on the same simple & surly market. If it is the best of its kind, it will. I want & must have painter, stable-keeper, locksmith, poet, gentleman, priest, doctor, cook, confectioner, carpet weaver, chairmaker, & so on each in turn in course of the year. If each really knows his craft, he cannot be spared. Political Economy rightly read, would be a consolation, like Christianity.

I meet in the street people full of life. I am, of course, at ebbtide; they at flood; they seem to have come from the south or from the west or from Europe. I see them pass with envy at this gift which includes all gifts.

The wisdom of words every day might surprise us. After a man has made great progress, & has come, as he fancies, to heights hitherto unscaled, the common words still fit his thought; nay, he only now finds for the first time how wise they were. *"Macrocosm," Reason, Conscience, Substance, Accidence, Nature, Relation, Fortune, Fate, Genius,* Element, Person . . .

There is the least deliberation in our life. We worry through the world, & do not unfold ourselves with leisure & dignity, & adorn our days suitably. Especially I observe that we have not learned the art to avail ourselves of the virtues & powers of our Companions. The day is gloomy with politics or bitter with debt.

Those who painted angels & nativities and descents from the cross, were also writing biographies & satires, though they knew it not. The history of humanity is no hopping squib, but all its discoveries in science, religion & art, consecutive & correlated.

Immortality. I notice that as soon as writers broach this question they begin to quote. I hate quotation. Tell me what you know.

May–June 1849
The children divide their waking time between school, fruit, & the cats.

I do not drink wine, but would have the name of drinking wine.

June 1849
New England Catholics disgusting. And the spread of Popery futile. As to fearing the Pope, we in America should as soon think of fearing a muskmelon.

July 1849
I cannot get enough alone to write a letter to a friend. I retreat & hide. I left the city, I hid myself in the pastures. When I bought a house,

the first thing I did was to plant trees. I could not conceal myself enough. Set a hedge here, set pines there, trees & trees, set evergreens, above all, for they will keep my secret all the year round.

I am afraid Alcott can as little as any man separate his drivelling from his divining.

'Tis very certain that the man must yield who has omitted inevitable facts in his view of life. Has he left out marriage & the σπερματος ουσιης συντηρησιν,* he has set a date to his fame. We are expecting another.

July 13, 1849
Yesterday, the day before, & today, another storm of heat, like that three weeks ago. The day is dangerous, the sun acts like a burningglass, on the naked skin, & the very slugs on the pear leaves seem broiled in their own fat.   Mercury at 94° at 3 p.m.

July 1849
I think if I were professor of Rhetoric, teacher of the art of writing well, to young men, I should use Dante for my text-book. Come hither, youth, & learn how the brook that flows at the bottom of your garden, or the farmer who ploughs the adjacent field—your father & mother, your debts & credits, & your web of habits are the very best basis of poetry, & the material which you must work up. Dante knew how to throw the weight of his body into each act, and is, like Byron, Burke, & Carlyle, the Rhetorician. I find him full of the *nobil volgare eloquenza;* that he knows "God damn", & can be rowdy if he please, & he does please. Yet is not Dante reason or illumination & that essence we were looking for, but only a new exhibition of the possibilities of genius. Here is an imagination that rivals in closeness & precision the senses. But we must prize him as we do a rainbow, we can appropriate nothing of him. Could we some day admit into our oyster heads the immense figure which these flagrant points compose when united, the hands of Phidias, the conclusion of Newton, the pantheism of Goethe, the all wise music of Shakspeare, the robust eyes of Swedenborg!

The cheap press & the universal reading, which have come in together, have caused a great many translations to be made from the Greek, the German, the Italian, & the French. Bohn's Library now fur-

---

*This phrase from Plutarch's "Advice about Keeping Well" (*Moralia* 129F) is trans- lated in the Loeb Classical Library edition as "observance of chastity," but Emerson seems to use it here to refer to sexuality generally.

nishes me with a new & portable Plato, as it had already done with new Goethes. And John Carlyle translates Dante. To me the command is loud to use the time by reading these books. And I should as soon think of foregoing the railroad & the telegraph, as to neglect these.

A feature of the times is this, that when I was born, private & family prayer was in the use of all well-bred people, & now it is not known.

Aug. 1, 1849
Correcting MSS & proofs for printing, makes apparent the value of perspective as essential to good writing. Once we said genius was health; but now we say genius is Time.

Aug. 1849
Trade is the lord of the world nowadays—& government only a parachute to this balloon.

Buna was engaged in writing a book on the conduct of life, & today in the chapter on Crickets. It could not be said of Buna, that she lived entirely for her dinner, though she was tenderly patiently absorbed in that capital event of the day, no, for she was not less dedicated to her supper, nor less to her breakfast. He had studied her character imperfectly who thought she lived in these. No, she wished to keep her feet warm, & she was addicted to a soft seat & expended a skill & generalship on securing the red chair & a corner out of the draft & in the air worthy of a higher seat in heaven. . . .

In a frivolous age Buna was earnest. She screamed, she groaned, she watched at night, she waited by day for her omelet & her lamp with smooth handle & when she went out of the house it was a perfect *row* for half an hour.

Buna had catarrh, pleurisy, rush of blood to the head, apoplexy, diabetes, diarrhea, sunstroke, atrophy, worms, palsy, erisypelas, consumption & dropsy.

It is no matter how fine is your rhetoric, or how strong is your understanding, no book is good which is not written by the Instincts. A fatal frost makes cheerless & undesireable every house where animal heat is not. Cold allegory makes us yawn whatever elegance it may have.

The Indian Squaw with a decisive hat has saved herself a world of vexation. The tragedy of our women begins with the bonnet. Only think of the whole Caucasian race damning the women to cover themselves with this frippery of rye straw & tags, that they may be at the mercy of every shower of rain. A meetinghouse full of women & a shower coming up—it is as if we had dressed them all in paper. Put on the squaw's man's hat, & you amputate so much misery.

Aug. 18, 1849
Yesterday a ride & walk with Thoreau to Acton. We climbed to the top of Nagog hill, & afterwards of Nashobah, the old domain of Tahatawan & his praying Indians. The wide landscape is one vast forest skirted by villages in the horizon.

The houses in Acton seemed to be filled with fat old people who looked like old tomatos, their faces crumpled into red collops, fatting & rotting at their ease.

Aug. 29? 1849
Love is the bright foreigner, the foreign self.

Parker thinks, that, to know Plato, you must read Plato thoroughly, & his commentators, &, I think, Parker would require a good drill in Greek history too. I have no objection to hear this urged on any but a Platonist. But when erudition is insisted on to Herbert or Henry More, I hear it as if to know the tree you should make me eat all the apples. It is not granted to one man to express himself adequately more than a few times: and I believe fully, in spite of sneers, in interpreting the French Revolution by anecdotes, though not every diner out can do it. To know the flavor of tanzy, must I eat all the tanzy that grows by the Wall? When I asked Mr Thom in Liverpool—who is Gilfillan? & who is Mac-Candlish? he began at the settlement of the Scotch Kirk in 1300 ? & came down with the history to 1848, that I might understand what was Gilfillan, or what was Edin. Review &c &c. But if a man cannot answer me in ten words, he is not wise.

Sept. 4? 1849
It is true that Webster has never done any thing up to the promise of his faculties. He is unmistakeably able, & might have ruled America, but he was cowardly, & has spent his life on specialties. When shall we see as rich a vase again! Napoleon, on the other hemisphere, obeyed his instincts with a fine audacity, dared all, went up to his line, & over his line, found himself confronted by Destiny, & yielded at last.

Sept. 1849
I think it as much a disease to be silenced when I do not wish it, as to have the measles when I do not wish it.

Sept.–Oct. 1849

In dreams, last night, a certain instructive race-horse was quite elaborately shown off, which seemed marvellously constructed for violent running, & so mighty to go, that he stood up continually on his hind feet in impatience & triumphant power. But my admiration was checked by some one's remarking behind me, that, "in New York they could not get up the smallest plate for him." Then I noticed, for the first time, that he was a show-horse, & had wasted all the time in this rearing on the hind legs, & had not run forward at all. I hope they did not mean to be personal.

Aunt Mary never liked to throw away any medicine; but, if she found a drop of laudanum here, & a pill or two there, a little quinine & a little antimony, mixed them up & swallowed them. So when she came to the tea-table—"O, no, she never took tea;"—"Can you get a little shells?" The cocoa came, & Aunty took cocoa, because it was soothing, & put a little tea in it to make her lively, & if there was a little coffee, that was good for getting rid of the taste.

Dr Patten of New York was challenged to continue the verses in the Primer;

In Adam's Fall
We sinned all.

Dr Patten proceeded;

In Cain's murder,
We sinned furder.

Today, carpets; yesterday, the aunts; the day before, the funeral of poor S; & every day, the remembrance in the library of the rope of work which I must spin; in this way life is dragged down & confuted. We try to listen to the hymn of gods, & must needs hear this perpetual cock-a-doodle-doo, & ke-tar-kut, right under the library windows. They the gods ought to respect a life, you say, whose objects are their own: But steadily they throw mud & eggs at us, roll us in the dirt, & jump on us.

Solitary Imprisonment is written on his coat & hat, on the lines of his face, & the limbs of his body, on his brow, & on the leaves of laurel on his brow. He wrestles hard with the judge, & does not believe he is in earnest. "Solitary Imprisonment," replies the Judge. Yet with some mitigation. Three times a day his keeper comes to the window, & puts bread & water on the shelf. The keeper's dog he may play with, if he will. Bow-wow-wow, says the dog. People may come from Asia to see him, if they like. He is only permitted to become his own friend.

For good reading, there must be, of course, a yielding, sometimes entire, but always some yielding to the book. Then the reader is refreshed with a new atmosphere & foreign habits. But many minds are incapable of any surrender; they are like knights of a Border Castle, who

> "Carve at the meal
> In gloves of steel,
> And drink the red wine thro the helmet barred."

&, of course, their dining is very unsatisfactory. How admirable a University is Plato's *Republic*; yet set P. to read it, he would read nothing in it but P.

In the conduct of life, let us not parade our rags, let us not, moved by vanity, confess, & tear our hair, at the corners of streets, or in the sitting room; but, as age & infirmity steal on us, contentedly resign the front seat & the games to these bright children, our better representatives, nor expect compliments or inquiries—much less, gifts or love—any longer (which to expect is ridiculous) and, not at all wondering why our friends do not come to us, much more wondering when they do, decently withdraw ourselves into modest & solitary resignation & rest.

In youth we clothe ourselves with rainbows, with hope & love, & go as brave as the Zodiack. In age we put out another sort of perspiration; gout, fever, rheumatism, caprice, doubt, fretting, and avarice.

Macaulay's History is full of low merits: it is like English manufactures of all kinds, neat, convenient, portable, saleable, made on purpose for the Harpers to print a hundred thousand copies of. So far can Birmingham go.

Macaulay is the Banvard of English history, good at drawing a Mississippi Panorama, but 'tis cheap work.* No memorable line has he written, no sentence. He is remembered by flippancy on one occasion against Plato & Bacon, but has no affirmative talent: he can write quantities of verses, too, to order, wrote "Lays," or something. No doubt wrote good nonsense verses at Eton, better than Virgil. His chef d'oeuvre was a riddle on the Cod-fish.

---

*John Banvard (1821–1891) painted a half-mile-long panorama of the Mississippi on canvas and exhibited it throughout the United States and abroad. [*JMN*]

Oct.–Nov. 1849

Bigendians	Littleendians
Plato	Alcott
Swedenborg	Very
Shakspere	Newcomb
Montaigne	Channing
Goethe	RWE
Napoleon	Thoreau

At this time we fell upon the design of establishing a club of the readers of Shakspeare's Sonnets, as the only Church still possible. The questions to be announced for the debate of this parliament were: Who is the author? To whom were they written? What do they mean?

Symbolism. What I want to know, is, the meaning of what I do; believing that any of my current Mondays or Tuesdays is Fatebook for me; & believing that hints & telegraphic signals are arriving to me every moment out of the interior eternity, I am tormented with impatience to make them out. We meet people who seem to overlook our game, & read us with a smile, but they do not tell us what they read.

Nov.–Dec. 1849

As for Germany, we have had no interest in it since the death of Goethe. All kinds of power usually develop themselves at the same time, and I look in the most active race for the idealism. The Americans went to Heidelberg to find Germany, & discovered with surprise that they had left it behind them in New York. Mr Scherb attempted last night to unfold Hegel for me and I caught somewhat that seemed cheerful & large, & that might, & probably did, come by Hindu suggestion. But all abstract philosophy is easily anticipated—it is so structural, or necessitated by the mould of the human mind. Schelling said, "the Absolute is the union of the Ideal and the Real."

[Alcott] is like a slate-pencil which has a sponge tied to the other end, and, as the point of the pencil draws lines, the sponge follows as fast, & erases them. He talks high & wide, & expresses himself very happily, and forgets all he has said. If a Skilful operator could introduce a lancet & sever the sponge, ABA would be the prince of writers.

I envied a young man in the cars who when his companion told him they had arrived at Waltham, by Massasoit House, was asleep, & his friend shook him, lifted him up, & called in his ear, in vain, he could not wake him, & the cars went on again to the next station before he could be fully aroused. Then I came home & counted every hour the clock struck all night.

Many after thoughts, as usual, with my printing, come just a little too late; & my new book seems to lose all value from their omission. Plainly one is the justice that should have been done to the unexpressed greatness of the common farmer & labourer. A hundred times I have felt the superiority of George, & Edmund, & Barrows, & yet I continue the parrot echoes of the names of literary notabilities & mediocrities, which, bring them (if they dared) into presence of these Concord & Plymouth Norsemen, would be as uncomfortable & ridiculous as mice before cats.

Dec. 14, 1849

Every day shows a new thing to veteran walkers. Yesterday reflections of trees in the ice; snowflakes, perfect rowels, on the ice; beautiful groups of icicles all along the eastern shore of Flint's Pond, in which, especially where encrusting the bough of a tree, you have the union of the most flowing with the most fixed. Ellery all the way squandering his jewels as if they were icicles, sometimes not comprehended by me, sometimes not heard. How many days can Methusalem go abroad & see somewhat new? When will he have counted the changes of the kaleidoscope?

Dec. 1849–Jan. 1850

When I see one of our young farmers in Sunday clothes, I feel the greatest respect for & joy in them, because I know what powers & utilities are so meekly worn. What I wish to know they know, what I would so gladly do, they can do. The cold gloomy day, the rough rocky pasture, the swamp, are invitations & opportunities to them. And yet there is no arrogance in their bearing, but a perfect gentleness, though they know how to take care of cattle, how to raise & cure & keep their crops. Why a writer should be vain, & a farmer not, though the writer admires the farmer, & the farmer does not admire the writer, does not appear.

The dinner, the wine, the homes of England look attractive to the traveller, but they are the poor utmost that illiberal wealth can perform. Alas! the halls of England are musty, the land is full of coal-smoke & carpet-smell: not a breath of mountain air dilates the languishing lungs . . .

Like the New England soil, my talent is good only whilst I work it. If I cease to task myself, I have no thoughts. This is a poor sterile Yankeeism. What I admire & love is the generous spontaneous soil which flowers & fruits at all seasons.

I easily distinguish three eras—

1. *the Greek;* when men deified nature; Jove was in the air, Neptune in the sea, Pluto in the earth, Naiads in the fountains, dryads in the woods, oreads on the mountain; happy beautiful beatitude of nature.

2. *the Christian;* when the Soul became pronounced, and craved a heaven out of nature & above it—looking on nature now as evil—the world was a mere stage & school, a snare, and the powers that ruled here were devils hostile to the soul.

and now lastly,

3. *the Modern;* when the too idealistic tendencies of the Christian period running into the diseases of cant, monachism, and a church, demonstrating the impossibility of Christianity, have forced men to retrace their steps, & rally again on Nature; but now the tendency is to marry mind to nature, to put nature under the mind, convert the world into the instrument of Right Reason. Man goes forth to the dominion of the world by commerce, by science, & by philosophy.

Chladni's experiment seems to me central. He strewed sand on glass, & then struck the glass with tuneful accords, & the sand assumed symmetrical figures. With discords the sand was thrown about amorphously. It seems, then, that Orpheus is no fable: You have only to sing, and the rocks will crystallize; sing, and the plant will organize; sing, & the animal will be born.

Jan.–Feb. 1850
Love is temporary & ends with marriage. Marriage is the perfection which love aimed at, ignorant of what it sought. Marriage is a good known only to the parties. A relation of perfect understanding, aid, contentment, possession of themselves & of the world—which dwarfs love to green fruit.

The English journals snub my new book; as indeed they have all its foregoers. Only now they say, that this has less vigour & originality than the others. Where then was the degree of merit that entitled my books to their notice? They have never admitted the claims of either of them. The fate of my books is like the impression of my face. My acquaintances, as long back as I can remember, have always said, "Seems to me you look a little thinner than when I saw you last."

Feb.–March 1850

Carlyle is wonderful for his rhetorical skill. This trick of rhyme, burden, or refrain, which he uses so well, he not only employs in each new paragraph, suddenly treating you with the last ritornello, but in each new Essay or Book quoting the Burden or Chorus of the last book.—You know me, & I know you; or, Here we are again, come take me up again on your shoulders—is the import of this. 'Tis curious, the magnificence of his genius, & the poverty of his aims. He draws his weapons from the skies, to fight the cause of some wretched English property or monopoly or prejudice or whim. A transcendental John Bull delighting in the music of Bow-bells, who cannot see across the channel, but has the skill to make divine oratorios in praise of the Strand, Kensington & Kew. I was to have said just now that he contrives in each piece to make out of his theme or lucky expression, a proverb before he has done; and this conclusion of the last is the exordium of the next Chapter.

He is no idealist in opinions. He is a protectionist in Political Economy, aristocrat in politics, epicure in diet, goes for slavery, murder, money, punishment by death, & all the pretty abominations, tempering them with epigrams.

It is not the least characteristic sign of the Times, that Alcott should have been able to collect such a good company of the best heads for two Monday Evenings, for the expressed purpose of discussing the Times. What was never done by human beings in another age, was done now; there they met to discuss their own breath, to speculate on their own navels, with eyeglass & solar microscope, and no man wondered at them. But these very men came in the cars by steam-ferry & locomotive to the meeting, & sympathized with engineers & Californians. Mad contradictions flavor all our dishes.

March–April 1850

Ellery C. thinks the merit of Irving's "Life of Goldsmith," is, that he has not had the egotism to put in a single new sentence. It is nothing but an agreeable repetition of Boswell, Johnson, & Company. And so Montaigne is good, because there is nothing that has not already been in books. A good book being a Damascus blade made by the welding of old nails & horseshoes. Every thing has seen service, & been proved by wear & tear in the world for centuries, & yet now the article is brand-new.

So Pope had but one good line, & that he got from Dryden, & therefore Pope is the best & only readable English poet.

* * *

Society disgusts and the poet resolves to go into retirement & indulge this great heart & feed his thought henceforwards with botany & astronomy. Behold, on the instant, his appetites are exasperated: he wants dinners & concerts, scholars & fine women, theatre & club. And life consists in managing adroitly these antagonisms to intensate each other. Life must have continence & abandonment.

Language is a quite wonderful city, which we all help to build. But each word is like a work of nature, determined a thousand years ago, & not alterable. We confer & dispute, & settle the meaning so or so, but it remains what it was in spite of us. The word beats all the speakers & definers of it, & stands to their children what it stood to their fathers.

As far as I know, the misfortune of New England is that the Southerner always beats us in Politics. And for this reason, that it comes at Washington to a game of personalities. The Southerner has personality, has temperament, has manners, persuasion, address & terror. The cold Yankee has wealth, numbers, intellect, material power of all sorts, but has not fire or firmness, & is coaxed & talked & bantered & shamed & scared, till he votes away the dominion of his millions at home. He never comes back quite the same man he went; but has been handled, tampered with. What is the remedy? Plainly I think, that we must borrow a hint from the military art. The Hungarians said, they could have easily beaten the Russians, if in any manner they could have made them run: but the Russian soldier is more afraid of his officers, than of the enemy: if he runs, he will assuredly be shot: if he fights, he has a chance of escape, and therefore he is cut down & butchered, but dares not run. So let our representative know that if he misrepresents his constituency there is no recovery from social damnation at home.

I heard a good speech, & a bad one, yesterday, at the town school; one boy in the name of the school presented the master with an escritoire of rosewood, & some books, & made a long speech to him, in which I remember something about "our posterity" that is, the boys' posterity! Another boy, Tolman, in the name of his schoolmates also, presented a portfolio & a book to the assistant, Miss Buttrick, and said, "he only hoped that she would have as much pleasure in receiving it, as they had in giving it."

The great man is the impressionable man, most irritable, most delicate, like iodine to light, so he feels the infinitesimal attractions. He obeys the main current, that is all his secret, the main current is so feeble a force as can be felt only by bodies delicately poised. He can orient himself. In the woods, I have one guide, namely, to follow the light—to go where the woods are thinnest; then at last I am sure to come out. So he cannot be betrayed or misguided, for he knows where the North is, knows painfully when he is going in the wrong direction.

Did one ever see a beautiful woman, & not wish to look again? Could one ever see enough of a beautiful woman?

Watson Haynes, the sailor, testifies that when he attempted to enlist the Clergy in his crusade against flogging in the navy, they replied, that their business was to preach the gospel, & not to interfere with the regulations of the navy.

And Webster thinks the gospel was to touch the heart, & not to abolish slavery.

April 1850

I have made no note of these long weary absences at New York & Philadelphia. I am a bad traveller, & the hotels are mortifications to all sense of well being in me. The people who fill them oppress me with their excessive virility, and would soon become intolerable, if it were not for a few friends, who, like women, tempered the acrid mass. Henry James was true comfort—wise, gentle, polished, with heroic manners, and a serenity like the sun.

The worst symptom I have noticed in our politics lately is the attempt to make a gibe out of Seward's appeal to a higher law than the Constitution, & Webster has taken part in it. I have seen him snubbed as "*Higher-law*-Seward." And now followed by Rufus Choate, in his phrase, "the trashy sentimentalism of our lutestring enthusiasts."

Lucretia Mott is the flower of Quakerism. That woman has a unity of sense, virtue, & good-meaning perfectly impressed on her countenance which are a guarantee of victory in all the fights to which her Quaker faith & connection lead her. She told exceedingly well the story of her contest with the mob at Dover & Smyrna in Delaware, she and the wife of Mr ———— attending him down to the place where the mob were to tar & feather him, & it was perfectly easy to see that she might safely go & would surely defend herself & him. No mob could remain a mob where she went. She brings domesticity & common sense, & that propriety which every man loves, directly into this hurly-burly, & makes every bully ashamed. Her courage is no merit, one almost says, where triumph is so sure.

* * *

I think there was never an event half so painful occurred in Boston as the letter with 800 signatures to Webster.* The siege of Boston was a day of glory. This was a day of petticoats, a day of imbecilities, the day of the old women La Veille. Many of the names very properly belong there—they are the names of aged & infirm people, who have outlived everything but their night cap & their tea & toast. But I observe some names of men under forty! I observe that very few lawyers have set their names. They are a prudent race though not very fond of liberty.

May–July 1850

Thackeray's "Vanity Fair" is pathetic in its name, & in his use of the name; an admission it is from a man of fashion in the London of 1850, that poor old Puritan Bunyan was right in his perception of the London of 1650. And yet now in Thackeray is the added wisdom or skepticism, that, though this be really so, he must yet live in tolerance of, & practically in homage & obedience to these illusions.

Men want wine, beer, & tobacco, to dull or stupefy a little the too tender papillae. The body is sore with the too quick & harsh impressions of nature. The edge of all objects must be taken off. Close the eyes partly; they are painfully wide open. Drop them to the floor, & do not see every ugly man that goes by.

It is the scholar's misfortune that his virtues are all on paper, & when the time comes to use them, he rubs his eyes & tries to remember what is it that he should do.

July–Aug. 1850

On Friday, 19 July, Margaret dies on rocks of Fire Island Beach within sight of & within 60 rods of the shore.† To the last her country proves inhospitable to her; brave, eloquent, subtle, accomplished, devoted, constant soul! If nature availed in America to give birth to many such as she, freedom & honour & letters & art too were safe in this new world. . . .

---

*Toward the end of March, 1850, nearly a thousand leading citizens of Boston, including Oliver Wendell Holmes, addressed a letter to Webster praising his Seventh of March speech in Congress supporting the Compromise of 1850, which included the infamous Fugitive Slave Law. [*JMN*]

†Margaret Fuller, her husband Giovanni Angelo Ossoli, and their child, Angelo Eugene Philip (born September 5, 1848), perished in the wreck of the merchantman *Elizabeth*, which sailed from Leghorn May 17. A gale on the night of July 18 off the New Jersey coast drove the ship off course; it sank about 4 o'clock the next morning. Only the body of the son was recovered. [*JMN*]

She had a wonderful power of inspiring confidence & drawing out of people their last secret.

The timorous said, What shall we do? how shall she be received, now that she brings a husband & child home? But she had only to open her mouth, & a triumphant success awaited her. She would fast enough have disposed of the circumstances & the bystanders. For she had the impulse, & they wanted it. Here were already mothers waiting tediously for her coming, for the education of their daughters. . . .

Her love of art, like that of many, was only a confession of sympathy with the artist in the mute condemnation which his work gave to the deformity of our daily life; her co-perception with him of the eloquence of Form; her aspiration with him to a life altogether beautiful.

"Her heart, which few knew, was as great as her mind, which all knew"—what Jung Stilling said of Goethe, E. H. says of Margaret; and, that she was the largest woman; & not a woman who wished to be a man.

I have lost in her my audience. I hurry now to my work admonished that I have few days left. There should be a gathering of her friends & some Beethoven should play the dirge.

She poured a stream of amber over the endless store of private anecdotes, of bosom histories which her wonderful persuasion drew out of all to her. When I heard that a trunk of her correspondence had been found & opened, I felt what a panic would strike all her friends, for it was as if a clever reporter had got underneath a confessional & agreed to report all that transpired there in Wall street.

[From a later entry.]

Her confidence in herself was boundless, & was frankly expressed. She told S. G. W. that she had seen all the people worth seeing in America, & was satisfied that there was no intellect comparable to her own.

[Around 1851 Emerson was reading through Fuller's papers.]

The unlooked for trait in all these journals to me is the Woman, poor woman: they are all hysterical. She is bewailing her virginity and languishing for a husband. "I need help. No, I need a full, a godlike embrace from some sufficient love." &c. &c. . . . This I doubt not was all the more violent recoil from the exclusively literary & "educational" connections in which she had lived. Mrs Spring told me that Margaret said to her, "I am tired of these literary friendships, I long to be wife & mother."

* * *

A larger dialectic, I said, conveys a sense of power & feeling of terror before unknown, & H. T. said, "that a thought would destroy like the jet of a blowpipe most persons," & yet we apologise for the power, & bow to the persons. I want an electrical machine. Slumbering power we have, but not excited, collected, & discharged. If I should be honest, I should say, my exploring of life presents little or nothing of respectable event or action, or, in myself, of a personality. Too composite to offer a positive unity, but it is a recipiency, a percipiency. And I, & far weaker persons, if it were possible, than I, who pass for nothing but imbeciles, do yet affirm by their percipiency the presence & perfection of Law, as much as all the martyrs.

Sept. 1, 1850
Yesterday took that secluded Marlboro road with W. E. C. in a wagon. Every rock was painted "Marlboro." & we proposed to take the longest day in the year, & ride to Marlboro, that flying Italy. We went to Willis's Pond in Sudbury & paddled across it, & took a swim in its water, coloured like sugarbaker's molasses. Nature, E. thought, is less interesting. Yesterday Thoreau told me it was more so, & persons less. I think it must always combine with man. Life is ecstatical, & we radiate joy & honour & gloom on the days & landscapes we converse with.

But I must remember a real or imagined period in my youth, when they who spoke to me of nature, were religious, & made it so, & made it deep: now it is to the young sentimentalists frippery; & a milliner's shop has as much reason & worth.

Sept.–Oct. 1850
Schelling's distinction, "Some minds speak about things, & some minds speak the things themselves" remains by far the most important intellectual distinction, as the quality is the important moral distinction. Amount and Quality. Searching tests these! What does he add? and What is the state of mind he leaves me in? . . . For Amount, I look back over all my reading, & think how few authors have given me *things*: Plato has, and Shakspeare, & Plutarch, & Montaigne, & Swedenborg.

Goethe abounds in things, & Chaucer & Donne & Herbert & Bacon had much to communicate. But the majority of writers had only their style or rhetoric, their claudelorraine glass. They were presentableness, Parliamentariness, Currency, Birmingham. Wordsworth almost alone in his times belongs to the giving, adding class, and Coleridge also has been a benefactor.

Oct. 24–26, 1850
Now that the *civil* Engineer is fairly established, I think we must have one day a Naturalist in each village as invariably as a lawyer or

doctor. It will be a new subdivision of the medical profession. I want to know what plant this is? Penthorum. What is it good for? in medical botany? in industrial botany? Now the Indian doctor, if there were one, & not the sham of one, would be more consulted than the diplomatic one. What bird is this? What hyla? What caterpillar? Here is a new bug on the trees. Cure the warts on the plum, & on the oak. How to attack the rosebug & the curculio. Show us the poisons. How to treat the cranberry meadow? The universal impulse toward natural science in the last twenty years promises this practical issue. And how beautiful would be the profession. . . . To have a man of Science remove into this town, would be better than the capitalist who is to build a village of houses on Nashawtuck. I would gladly subscribe to his maintenance. He is, of course, to have a microscope & a telescope.

Oct.-Nov. 1850

The world wears well. These autumn afternoons & well-marbled landscapes of green, & gold, & russet, & steel-blue river, & smoke-blue New Hampshire mountain, are & remain as bright & perfect pencilling as ever.

It occurred yesterday more strongly than I can now state it, that we must have an intellectual property in all property, & in all action, or they are naught. I must have children, I must have events, I must have a social state & history—or my thinking & speaking will have no body & background. But having these, I must also have them not (so to speak), or carry them as contingent and merely apparent possessions to give them any real value.

The one thing we watch with pathetic interest in our children is the degree in which they possess recuperative force. When they are wounded by us, or by each other, when they go down at school to the bottom of the class, when they fail in competitions of study or of play with their mates, if they lose their spirit, & remember the mischance in their chamber at home—it is all over with them, they have a check for life. But if they have that degree of buoyancy & resistance that makes light of these mishaps, & preoccupies them with ever new interest in the new moment, the scars rapidly cicatrize & the fibre is all the tougher for the wound.

Nov.-Dec. 1850

A Journal is to the author a book of constants, each mind requiring (as I have so often said) to write the whole of literature & science for itself.

* * *

Architecture, the skeleton, the resistance to gravity & the elements—make one extreme; florid petulant anthropomorphism which carves every pumphandle & doorknob into a human face is the other; midway between these is the sobriety & grace of art.

GAMES

What reason to think Charles I consented to his execution?
 They axed him whether he would or no.
Why is one playing blindman's buff, like sympathy?
 'Tis a *Fellow feeling for a fellow creature.*
What reason to think the Carthaginians had domestic animals?
 Virgil says, *"Dido et dux,"*
  "et pig-e-bit Elisa."
How could the Children of Israel sustain themselves for forty days in the desart?
 Because of the sand-wich-is there.
Why is a kiss like a sermon?
 two heads & an application.

Charlestown Versatility. Several years ago, how much we were entertained with Mr Tyler, whom I knew only because he had rare books, & the only copy in this country, of Taylor's Aristotle in the "Nobleman's Edition." But when, one day, he stopped at my door, his feats were by no means exclusively platonic. He was hale, stout, & ruddy; said he could lift a barrel of flour, & carry it farther than any of his men. He was immersed in politics, & knew how the elections were going, & was stumping it every night for Gen. Harrison. He was an efficient member of an Engine-Company, was a thriving broker, & had lately been on a visit to some religious relations in New Hampshire, where he met with a Baptist from Plaistow, who was so edified by his talk, that he mistook T. for a clergyman, & invited him to come over to Plaistow, & speak at a Conference—an invitation, which T. accepted, to the horror of his cousins, went over on the appointed day, spoke an hour & twenty minutes, left all the audience in tears, & heard, two days after, that he had awakened a revival in the town!

Dec. 1850–Jan. 1851
—— complained that life had lost its interest. 'Tis very funny, be sure, to hear this. For most of us the world is all too interesting, *l'embarras de richesses.* We are wasted with our versatility; with the eagerness to grasp on every possible side, we all run to nothing. I cannot open an agricultural paper without finding objects enough for Methusalem. I

jilt twenty books whenever I fix on one. I stay away from Boston, only because I cannot begin there to see those whom I should wish, the men, & the things. I wish to know France. I wish to study art. I wish to read laws.

Tennyson's *In Memoriam* is the commonplaces of condolence among good unitarians in the first week of mourning. The consummate skill of the versification is the sole merit. The book has the advantage that was Dr Channing's fortune, that all the merit was appreciable. He is never a moment too high for his audience.

In the streets I have certain darkenings which I call my nights.

I found when I had finished my new lecture that it was a very good house, only the architect had unfortunately omitted the stairs.

Jan.–Feb. 1851

To every reproach, I know now but one answer, namely, to go again to my own work.

"But you neglect your relations."

Yes, too true; then I will work the harder.

"But you have no genius." Yes, then I will work the harder.

"But you have no virtues." Yes, then I will work the harder.

"But you have detached yourself & acquired the aversation of all decent people. You must regain some position & relation." Yes, I will work harder.

Some persons are thrown off their balance, when in society; others are thrown on to balance; the excitement of company & the observation of other characters corrects their biases. Margaret Fuller always appeared to unexpected advantage in conversation with a circle of persons, with more commonsense & sanity than any other—though her habitual vision was through coloured lenses.

Feb.? 1851

Chasles thinks the rage for *illustrated Journals* all over Europe & the United States, a decided symptom of the decline of literature. Exciting novels, & pictures, in the room of ideas, have made literature a sensual pleasure.

The country boys & men have in their mind the getting a knowledge of the world as a thing of main importance. The New Hampshire man

in the cars said that. Somebody grew up at home & his father whipped
him for several years—he would fall on him in the field & beat him as he
would his cattle. But one day the boy faced him, & held his hands. Then
the boy had never been to school, & he thought he would go to California. There he was, a man grown, good, stout, well-looking fellow, six
feet, but as ignorant as a horse; *he had never had any chance;* how could
he know anything? So he went to California, & stayed there a year, &
has come back. He looks well, he has much improved in his appearance,
but he has not got a ninepence.

And really New Hampshire & Vermont look on California, & railroads, as formerly they did on a peddling trip to Virginia—as their education, as *giving them a chance* to know something.

Feb. 7, 1851   Rochester

Mr J A Wilder made me acquainted with the University of R. which
was extemporising here like a picnic. They had bought a hotel, once
a railroad terminus depot, for $8,500, turned the diningroom into
a chapel by putting up a pulpit on one side, made the barroom into a
Pythologian Society's Hall, & the chambers into Recitation rooms, Libraries, & professors' apartments, all for $700. a year. They had brought
an Omnibus load of professors down from Madison bag & baggage—
Hebrew, Greek, Chaldee, Latin, Belles Lettres, Mathematics, & all Sciences, called in a painter, sent him up a ladder to paint the title "University of Rochester" on the wall, and now they had runners on the road to
catch students. One lad came in yesterday; another, this morning;
"thought they should like it first rate", & now they thought themselves
ill used if they did not get a new student every day. And they are confident of graduating a class of Ten by the time green peas are ripe.

Feb.–March 1851

Nothing so marks a man as bold imaginative expressions. A complete statement in the imaginative form of an important truth arrests attention & is repeated & remembered. A phrase or two of that kind will
make the reputation of a man. Pythagoras's golden sayings were such;
and Socrates's, & Mirabeau's & Bonaparte's; and, I hope I shall not
make a sudden descent, if I say that Henry Thoreau promised to make
as good sentences in that kind as any body.

April–May 1851

Bad times. We wake up with a painful auguring, and after exploring
a little to know the cause find it is the odious news in each day's paper,
the infamy that has fallen on Massachusetts, that clouds the daylight,

& takes away the comfort out of every hour. We shall never feel well again until that detestable law is nullified in Massachusetts & until the Government is assured that once for all it cannot & shall not be executed here. All I have, and all I can do shall be given & done in opposition to the execution of the law.

Mr. Samuel Hoar has never raised his head since Webster's speech in last March, and all the interim has really been a period of calamity to New England. That was a steep step downward. I had praised the tone & attitude of the Country. My friends had mistrusted it. They say now, It is no worse than it was before; only it is manifest and acted out. Well I think *that* worse. It shows the access of so much courage in the bad, so much check of virtue, terror of virtue, withdrawn. The tameness is shocking. Boston, of whose fame for spirit & character we have all been so proud. Boston, whose citizen intelligent people in England told me they could always distinguish by their culture among Americans. Boston, which figures so proudly in Adams's diary, which we all have been reading: Boston, through the personal influence of this New Hampshire man, must bow its proud spirit in the dust, & make us irretrievably ashamed. I would hide the fact if I could, but it is done, it is debased. It is now as disgraceful to be a Bostonian as it was hitherto a credit. . . .

I met an episcopal clergyman, & allusion being made to Mr Webster's treachery, he replied "Why, do you know I think that the great action of his life?" I am told, they are all involved in one hot haste of terror, presidents of colleges & professors, saints & brokers, insurers, lawyers, importers, jobbers, there is not an unpleasing sentiment, a liberal recollection, not so much as a snatch of an old song for freedom dares intrude.

I am sorry to say it, But New-Hampshire has always been distinguished for the servility of its eminent men. Mr Webster had resisted for a long time the habit of his *compatriots*, I mean no irony, & by adopting the spirited tone of Boston had recommended himself—as much as by his great talents to the people of Massachusetts; but blood is thicker than water, the deep servility of New Hampshire politics which have marked all prominent statesmen from that district, with the great exception of Mr Hale, has appeared late in life with all the more strength that it had been resisted so long, & he has renounced, what must have cost him some perplexity, all the great passages of his past career on which his fame is built. . . .

I opened a paper today in which he pounds on the old strings in a letter to the Washington Birth Day feasters at N. Y. "Liberty! liberty!"

Pho! Let Mr Webster for decency's sake shut his lips once & forever on this word. The word *liberty* in the mouth of Mr Webster sounds like the word *love* in the mouth of a courtezan.

I may then add *the Union.* Nothing seems to me more bitterly futile than this bluster about the Union. A year ago we were all lovers & prizers of it. Before the passage of that law which Mr Webster made his own, we indulged in all the dreams which foreign nations still cherish of American destiny. But in the new attitude in which we find ourselves, the degradation & personal dishonour which now rests like miasma on every house in Massachusetts, the sentiment is entirely changed. No man can look his neighbor in the face. We sneak about with the infamy of crime in the streets, & cowardice in ourselves and frankly once for all the Union is sunk, the flag is hateful, & will be hissed.

The Union! o yes, I prized that, other things being equal; but what is the Union to a man self condemned, with all sense of self respect & chance of fair fame cut off—with the names of conscience & religion become bitter ironies, & liberty the ghastly nothing which Mr Webster means by that word? The worst mischiefs that could follow from secession, & new combination of the smallest fragments of the wreck were slight & medicable to the calamity your Union has brought us. Another year, and a standing army officered by Southern gentlemen, to protect the Commissioners & to hunt the fugitives will be illustrating the new sweets of Union in Boston, Worcester, & Springfield. It did not appear & it was incredible that the passage of the Law would make the Union odious; but from the day it was attempted to be executed in Massachusetts, this result has appeared that the Union is no longer desireable. Whose deed is that?

One more consideration occurs—the mischief of a legal crime. The demoralization of the Community. Each of these persons who touches it is contaminated. There has not been in our lifetime another moment when public men were personally lowered by their political action. But here are gentlemen whose names stood as high as any, whose believed probity was the confidence & fortification of all, who by fear of public opinion, or by that dangerous ascendency of Southern manners, have been drawn into the support of this nefarious business, and have of course changed their relations to men. We poor men in the country who might have thought it an honor to shake hands with them, would now shrink from their touch; nor could they enter our humblest doors.... Well, is not this a loss inevitable to a bad law?—a law which no man can countenance or abet the execution of, without loss of all self respect, & forfeiting forever the name of a gentleman....

The College, the churches, the schools, the very shops & factories are discredited. Every kind of property & every branch of industry & every avenue to power suffers injury, and the value of life is reduced. I had hardly written this before my friend said, "If this law should be repealed, I shall be glad that I have lived; if not, I shall be sorry that I was born." What kind of law is that which extorts this kind of language for a free civilized people?

I am surprised that lawyers can be so blind as to suffer the law to be discredited. The law rests not only in the instinct of all people, but, according to the maxims of Blackstone & the jurists, on equity, and it is the cardinal maxim that a statute contrary to natural right is illegal, is in itself null & void. The practitioners should guard this dogma well, as the palladium of the profession, as their anchor in the respect of mankind.

Against this all the arguments of Webster make no more impression than the spray of a child's squirt.

The fame of Webster ends in this nasty law.

And as for the Andover & Boston preachers . . . who deduce kidnapping from their Bible, tell the poor dear doctor if this be Christianity, it is a religion of dead dogs, let it never pollute the ears & hearts of noble children again. O bring back then the age when valour was virtue, since what is called morality means nothing but pudding. Pardon the spleen of a professed hermit.

Mr Webster cannot choose but regret his loss. Tell him that those who make fame, accuse him with one voice: those to whom his name was once dear & honoured as the manly statesman, to whom the choicest gifts of nature had been accorded—eloquence with a simple greatness; those who have no points to carry that are not those of public morals & of generous civilization, the obscure & private who have no voice & care for none as long as things go well, but who feel the infamy of his nasty legislation creeping like a fever into all their homes & robbing the day of its beauty. Tell him that he who was their pride in the woods & mountains of New England is now their mortification; that they never name him; they have taken his picture from the wall & torn it—dropped the pieces in the gutter; they have taken his book of speeches from the shelf & put it in the stove. . . .

It will be his distinction to have changed in one day by the most detestable law that was ever enacted by a civilized state, the fairest & most triumphant national escutcheon the sun ever shone upon, the free, the expanding, the hospitable, the irresistible America, home of the homeless & pregnant with the blessing of the world, into a jail or barracoon for the slaves of a few thousand Southern planters & all the citizens of this hemisphere into kidnappers & drivers for the same. Is that a name will feed his hungry ambition?

In the weakness of the Union the law of 1793 was framed, and much may be said in palliation of it. It was a law affirming the existence of two states of civilization or an intimate union between two countries, one civilized & Christian & the other barbarous, where cannibalism was still permitted. It was a little gross, the taste for boiling babies, but as long as this kind of cookery was confined within their own limits, we could agree for other purposes, & wear one flag. The law affirmed a right to hunt their human prey within our territory; and this law availed just thus much to affirm their own platform—to fix the fact, that, though confessedly savage, they were yet at liberty to consort with men; though they had tails, & their incisors were a little long, yet it is settled that they shall by courtesy be called men; we will all make believe they are Christians; & we promise not to look at their tails or incisors when they come into company. This was all very well. The convenient equality was affirmed, they were admitted to dine & sup, & profound silence on the subject of tails & incisors was kept. . . . But of course on their part all idea of boiling babies in our caboose was dropt; all idea of hunting in our yards fat babies to boil, was dropt; & the law became, as it should, a dead letter. It was merely there in the statute-book to soothe the dignity of the maneaters. And we Northerners had, on our part, indemnified & secured ourselves against any occasional eccentricity of appetite in our confederates by our own interpretation, & by offsetting state-law by state-laws. It was & is penal here in Massachusetts for any sheriff or town- or state-officer to lend himself or his jail to the slavehunter, & it is also settled that any slave brought here by his master, becomes free. All this was well. What Mr Webster has now done is not only to re-enact the old law, but *to give it force,* which it never had before, or to bring down the free & Christian state of Massachusetts to the cannibal level.

Webster & Choate think to discredit the higher law by personalities; they insinuate much about transcendentalists & abstractionists & people of no weight. It is the cheap cant of lawyers & of merchants in a failing condition, & of rogues. These classes usually defend an immorality by the practice of men of the world, & talk of dreamers & enthusiasts; every woman has been debauched by being made to believe that it is the mode, it is custom & none but the priest & a few devout visionaries ever think otherwise. People never bring their history into politics, or this thin smoke would deceive nobody.

*   *   *

Mr Everett, a man supposed aware of his own meaning, advises pathetically a reverence for the Union. Yes but hides the other horn under this velvet? Does he mean that we shall lay hands on a man who has escaped from slavery to the soil of Massachusetts & so has done more for freedom than ten thousand orations, & tie him up & call in the marshal, and say—I am an orator for freedom; a great many fine sentences have I turned—none has turned finer, except Mr Webster, in favour of plebeian strength against aristocracy; and, as my last & finest sentence of all, to show the young men of the land who have bought my book & clapped my sentences & copied them in their memory, how much I mean by them—Mr Marshal, here is a black man of my own age, & who does not know a great deal of Demosthenes, but who means what he says, whom we will now handcuff and commit to the custody of this very worthy gentleman who has come on from Georgia in search of him; I have no doubt he has much to say to him that is interesting & as the way is long I don't care if I give them a copy of my Concord & Lexington & Plymouth & Bunker Hill addresses to beguile their journey from Boston to the plantation whipping post? Does Mr Everett really mean this? that he & I shall do this? Mr Everett understands English, as few men do who speak it. Does he mean this? Union is a delectable thing, & so is wealth, & so is life, but they may *all* cost too much, if they cost honour. . . .

It is very remarkable how rare a bad law, an immoral law, is. Does Mr Everett know how few examples in Civil history there are of bad laws? I do not think it will be easy to parallel the crime of Mr Webster's law. But the crime of kidnapping is on a footing with the crimes of murder & of incest and if the Southern states should find it necessary to enact the further law in view of the too great increase of blacks that every fifth manchild should be boiled in hot water—& obtain a majority in Congress with a speech by Mr Webster to add an article to the Fugitive Slave Bill—that any fifth child so & so selected, having escaped into Boston should be seethed in water at 212 °, will not the mayor & alderman boil him? Is there the smallest moral distinction between such a law, & the one now enacted? How can Mr E. put at nought all manly qualities, all his claims to truth & sincerity, for the sake of backing up this cowardly nonsense?

Does he mean this, that he & I shall do this, or does he secretly know that he will die the death sooner than lift a finger in the matter, he or his son, or his son's son, and only hopes to persuade certain truckmen & constables to do this, that rich men may enjoy their estates in more security?

One way certainly the Nemesis is seen. Here is a measure of pacification & union. What is its effect? that it has made one subject, one only subject for conversation, & painful thought, throughout the Union, Slavery. We eat it, we drink it, we breathe it, we trade, we study, we wear it. We are all poisoned with it, & after the fortnight the symptoms appear, purulent, making frenzy in the head & rabidness.

What a moment was lost when Judge Lemuel Shaw declined to affirm the unconstitutionality of the Fugitive Slave Law!

But we must put out this poison, this conflagration, this raging fever of Slavery out of the Constitution. If Webster had known a true & generous policy, this would have made him. He is a spent ball. It is the combined wealth behind him that makes him of any avail. And that is as bad as Europe.

May? 1851
The old woman who was shown the telegraph & the railroad, said, "Well, God's works are great, but man's works are greater!"

Prudence. One of the cardinal rules is Timeliness. My neighbor the carriage maker, all summer is making Sleighs, and all winter is making light gay gigs & chariots for June & August; & so, on the first days of the new season is ready with his carriage, which is itself an invitation. And the putting the letter into the post one minute before the mail-bag is closed, is a great triumph over Fate. And in all our affairs the sense of being ready & up with the hour imparts to a man's countenance & demeanour a wonderful air of leisure & success. A man who is always behind time, is careworn & painful.

Danger of doing something. You write a discourse, &, for the next weeks & months, you are carted about the Country at the tail of that discourse simply to read it over & over.

But it does not seem to me much better, when the gross instincts are a little disguised, and the oestrum, gadfly, or brize of sex takes sentimental forms. I like the engendering of snails better than the same rut* masquerading in Watts's psalms to the Church, the bride of Christ, or an old girl forming sentimental friendships with every male thing that comes by, under the pretence of *"developing a new side."*

May–July 1851
Politics. Bear in mind the difference between the opponents & the defenders of the shameful statute, that the opposition will never end,

---

*This word is crossed out.

will never relax, whilst the statute exists: as long as grass grows, as long as there is summer & winter, night & day, world & man, so long the sentiments will condemn this. But your statute & its advocacy is a thing; is a phantasm, is a contrivance, a cat's cradle, a petty trap, a jackstraw that has no root in the world.

The absence of moral feeling in the whiteman is the very calamity I deplore. The captivity of a thousand negroes is nothing to me.

Webster truly represents the American people just as they are, with their vast material interests, materialized intellect, & low morals. Heretofore, their great men have led them, have been better than they, as Washington, Hamilton, & Madison. But Webster's absence of moral faculty is degrading to the country.

Of this fatal defect of course Webster himself has no perception. He does, as immoral men usually do, make very low bows to the Christian church, & goes through all the decorums of Sunday, but when allusion is made to Ethics, & the sanctions of morality, he very frankly replies, as at Albany the other day, "Some higher law somewhere between here & the third heaven, I do not know where."

July 22, 1851

Yesterday, Eddy & Edie going with me to bathe in Walden, Eddy was very brave with a sharp bulrush, & presently broke into this rhyme—

"With my sharp-pointed sword
I will conquer Concórd."

July–Oct. 1851

Thoreau wants a little ambition in his mixture. Fault of this, instead of being the head of American Engineers, he is captain of a huckleberry party.

I think Horace Greeley's career one of the most encouraging facts in our Whiggish age. A white haired man in the city of New York has adopted every benevolent crotchet, & maintained it, until he commands an army of a million now in the heart of the United States. Here we stand shivering on the North wall of opposition, we New-England idealists—& might have taken Boston long ago, "had we had the pluck of a louse," to use the more energetic than elegant expression of my travelling friend.

Daniel Webster (1782–1852): "It seems to me the Quixotism of
criticism to quarrel with Webster because he has not this or
that fine evangelical property. He is no saint, but the
wild olive wood, ungrafted yet by grace."

* * *

H. T. will not stick—he is not practically renovator. He is a boy, & will be an old boy. Pounding beans is good to the end of pounding Empires, but not, if at the end of years, it is only beans.

I fancy it an inexcusable fault in him that he is insignificant here in the town. He speaks at Lyceum or other meeting but somebody else speaks & his speech falls dead & is forgotten. He rails at the town doings & ought to correct & inspire them.

America is the idea of emancipation.

Abolish kingcraft, Slavery, feudalism, blackletter monopoly, pull down gallows, explode priestcraft, tariff, open the doors of the sea to all emigrants. Extemporize government, California, Texas, Lynch Law. All this covers selfgovernment. All proceeds on the belief that as the people have made a govt. they can make another, that their Union & law is not in their memory but in their blood. If they unmake the law they can easily make it again.

These thirty nations are equal to any work. They are to become 50 millions presently & should achieve something just & generous. Let them trample out this mischief before it has trampled out them. For the future of slavery is not inviting. But the destinies of nations are too great for our spanning & what are the instruments no policy can show, whether Liberia, whether flax, cotton, whether the working them out by Irish & Germans none can tell; or by what scourges God has guarded his law. But one thing is imperative, not to do unjustly, not to steal a man, or help steal him, or to call stealing honest.

S. Ward thinks 'Twill do for Carolina to be unreasonable & nullify. But not so with Massachusetts, which is the head: the toe may nullify, but the head must not nullify.

We are glad at last to get a clear case, one on which no shadow of doubt can hang. This is not meddling with other people's affairs—this is other people meddling with us. This is not going crusading after slaves who it is alieged are very happy & comfortable where they are: all that amiable argument falls to the ground, but defending a human being who has taken the risks of being shot or burned alive, or cast into the sea, or starved to death or suffocated in a wooden box—taken all this risk to get away from his driver & recover the rights of man. And this man the Statute says, you men of Massachusetts shall kidnap & send back again a thousand miles across the sea to the dog-hutch he fled from. And this filthy enactment was made in the 19th Century, by people who could read & write.

I will not obey it, by God.

The ancients most truly & poetically represented the incarnation or descent into nature of Pythagoras, his condescension to be born, as his first virtue.

It is indeed a perilous adventure, this serious act of venturing into mortality, swimming in a sea strewn with wrecks, where none indeed go undamaged.

It is as bad as going to Congress; none comes back innocent.

We would gladly think highly of Nature & Life but what a country-muster, what Vanity-Fair full of noise, squibs, & egg pop, it is! Pass your last week in review, & what figures move on the swelling scene! Mr Potter, Mr Minott, Mr Garfield, Tom Hazel, & the ticket master, are among the best. 'Tis a one-cent farce. Am I deceived, or is the low & absurd a little predominant in the piece?

Elizabeth Palmer Peabody ransacks her memory for anecdotes of Margaret's youth, her selfdevotion, her disappointments which she tells with fervency, but I find myself always putting the previous question. These things have no value, unless they lead somewhere. If a Burns, if a De Stael, if an artist is the result, our attention is preengaged; but quantities of rectitude, mountains of merit, chaos of ruins, are of no account without result—'tis all mere nightmare; false instincts; wasted lives.

Now, unhappily, Margaret's writing does not justify any such research. All that can be said, is, that she represents an interesting hour & group in American cultivation; then, that she was herself a fine, generous, inspiring, vinous, eloquent talker, who did not outlive her influence; and a kind of justice requires of us a monument, because crowds of vulgar people taunt her with want of position.

Shakspeare astonishes by his equality in every play, act, scene, & line. One would say, he must have been a thousand years old, when he wrote his first piece, so thoroughly is his thought familiar to him, so solidly worded, as if it were already a proverb, & not only hereafter to become one. Well, that millennium, in effect, is really only a little acceleration in his process of thought: his mill, his loom, is better toothed & cranked & pedalled than other people's. & he can turn off a hundred yards to their one. It is just as we see at school, now & then, a boy or girl who is a wonderful cipherer, wonderful remembering-machine of geography, Greek grammar, history, &c.

One chamber more, one cell more is opened in this brain, than is opened in all the rest, & what majestic results. I admire Thoreau, too, with his powerful arithmetic, & his whole body co-working. He can pace sixteen rods more accurately than another man can measure it by tape.

Where is the New Metaphysics? We are intent on Meteorology to find the law of the Variable Winds to the end that we may not get our hay wet. I also wish a Farmer's Almanac of the Mental Moods that I may farm my mind. There are undulations of power & imbecility & I lose days sitting at my table which I should gain to my body & mind if I knew beforehand that no thought would come that day. I see plainly enough that ordinarily we take counters for gold, that our eating & trading & marrying & learning are mistaken by us for ends & realities, whilst they are only symbols of true life; and, as soon as we have come by a divine leading into the inner firmament, we are apprised of the unreality or representative character of what we had esteemed solidest. Then we say, here & now! We then see that before this terrific beauty nature too is cheap; that geometry & astronomy also are its cheap effects, before this pure glory. Yet Ah! if we could once come in & plant our instruments, & take some instant measurement & inventory of this Dome, in whose light forms, & substances, & sciences are dissolved. But we never so much as enter—'tis a glimpse; 'tis a peeping through a chink; the dream in a dream. We play at Bo-peep with Truth, and cannot write the Chapter of Metaphysics. We write books, "How to Observe," &c yet the Kant or the Plato of the Inner World, which is Heaven, has not come. To describe adequately, is the high power & one of the highest enjoyments of man. This is Art.

Edith's opinion. Edith, when a little girl, whimpered when her mother described the joys of Heaven. She did not want to go there, she wanted to "stay" (& she looked round the room) "where there was a *door*, & folks, and *things.*"

Ellery thinks that he is the lucky man who can write in bulk, forty pages on a hiccough, ten pages on a man's sitting down in a chair; like Hawthorne, &c, that will go.

End of Culture, Self-creation.

In some sort, the end of life, is, that the man should take up the universe into himself, or, out of that quarry leave nothing unrepresented, and he is to create himself. Yonder mountain must migrate into his mind. Yonder magnificent astronomy he is at last to import, fetching away moon & planet lunation, solstice, period, comet, & binal star, by comprehending their relation & law. Instead of the timid stripling he was, he is to be the stalwart Archimedes, Pythagoras, Columbus, Jesus, of the physic, metaphysic, & ethics of the design.

Oct. 14, 1851

Today is holden at Worcester the "Woman's Convention."

I think that, as long as they have not equal rights of property & right of voting, they are not on a right footing. But this wrong grew out of the savage & military period, when, because a woman could not defend herself, it was necessary that she should be assigned to some man who was paid for guarding her. Now in more tranquil & decorous times it is plain she should have her property, &, when she marries, the parties should as regards property, go into a partnership full or limited, but explicit & recorded.

For the rest, I do not think a woman's convention, called in the spirit of this at Worcester, can much avail. It is an attempt to manufacture public opinion, & of course repels all persons who love the simple & direct method. I find the Evils real & great. If I go from Hanover street to Atkinson street—as I did yesterday—what hundreds of extremely ordinary, paltry, hopeless women I see, whose plight is piteous to think of. If it were possible to repair the rottenness of human nature, to provide a rejuvenescence, all were well, & no specific reform, no legislation would be needed. For, as soon as you have a sound & beautiful woman, a figure in the style of the Antique Juno, Diana, Pallas, Venus, & the Graces, all falls into place, the men are magnetised, heaven opens, & no lawyer need be called in to prepare a clause, for woman moulds the lawgiver. I should therefore advise that the Woman's Convention should be holden in the Sculpture Gallery, that this high remedy might be suggested.

"Women," Plato says, "are the same as men in faculty, only less." I find them all victims of their temperament. "I never saw a woman who did not cry," said E. Nature's end of maternity—maternity for twenty years—was of so supreme importance, that it was to be secured at all events, even to the sacrifice of the highest beauty. Bernhard told Margaret that every woman (whatever she says, reads, or writes) is thinking of a husband. And this excess of temperament remains not less in Marriage. Few women are sane. They emit a coloured atmosphere, one would say, floods upon floods of coloured light, in which they walk evermore, & see all objects through this warm tinted mist which envelopes them. Men are not, to the same degree, temperamented; for there are multitudes of men who live to objects quite out of them, as to politics, to trade, to letters, or an art, unhindered by any influence of constitution.

Oct. 1851

Fenimore Cooper said to a lady in conversation, "I can make any woman blush." The lady blushed with natural resentment. "I can lay it on deeper than that, madam," said the pitiless talker. Out of vexation at her own selfdistrust the lady crimsoned again to her neck & shoulders.—the power of impudence.

Mr Mackay said to little Marny Storer, "Why Marny! What is the matter with your eyes?" "Nothing is the matter with my eyes," said the little beauty, looking up earnestly. "Why Marney," said Mr Mackay, "they are getting to look deeper & deeper, and, by & by, I fear, they will be so deep, that somebody will fall in."

Oct. 27, 1851

It would be hard to recall the rambles of last night's talk with H. T. But we stated over again, to sadness, almost, the Eternal loneliness. . . . how insular & pathetically solitary, are all the people we know! Nor dare we tell what we think of each other, when we bow in the street. 'Tis mighty fine for us to taunt men of the world with superficial & treacherous courtesies. I saw yesterday, Sunday, whilst at dinner my neighbor Hosmer creeping into my barn. At once it occurred, 'Well, men are lonely, to be sure, & here is this able, social, intellectual farmer under this grim day, as grimly, sidling into my barn, in the hope of some talk with me, showing me how to husband my cornstalks. Forlorn enough!'

It is hard to believe that all times are alike & that the present is also rich. When this annual project of a Journal returns, & I cast about to think who are to be contributors, I am struck with a feeling of great poverty; my bareness! my bareness! seems America to say.

Oct. 27–31, 1851

Beware of Engagements. Learn to say no, & drop resolutely all false claims. I suppose, I have a letter, each week, asking an autograph; one, each quarter, asking antislavery lecture; one yesterday asking particulars of the life of Mr Carlyle, &c. &c. And every day is taxed by the garden, the orchard, the barn.

Jan.? 1852

I find one state of mind does not remember or conceive of another state. Thus I have written within a twelvemonth verses ("Days") which I do not remember the composition or correction of, & could not write the like today, & have only for proof of their being mine, various external evidences as, the MS. in which I find them, & the circumstance that I have sent copies of them to friends, &c &c. Well, if they had been better, if it had been a noble poem, perhaps it would have only more entirely taken up the ladder into heaven.

Jan.–April 1852

Jere. Mason said to R H Dana—"law school! a man must read law in the court house." And Mr A. took "Hoar's treatise on the Vine" into his garden, but could not find that kind of buds & eyes on his vines. And it is true that all the theory in the world is vain without the thumb of practice. What could Coke or Blackstone do against the bullies of the Middlesex Bar as F. & Butler? No, you must have equal spunk & face them down—ready witted, ready handed.

Few know how to read. Women read to find a hero whom they can love. Men for amusement. Editors, for something to *crib*. Authors, for something that supports their view: and hardly one reads comprehensively & wisely.

April 1852

When we have arrived at the question, the answer is already near.

The Purist who refuses to vote, because the govt does not content him in all points, should refuse to feed a starving beggar, lest he should feed his vices.

The Illustrations in modern books mark the decline of art. 'Tis the dramdrinking of the eye, & candy for food; as whales & horses & elephants, produced on the stage, show decline of drama.

Mr McDonald made me laugh with his account of lectures in Montreal. He said, if there were only two fellows left in Montreal one would deliver a lecture & the other would hear it.

May 1852

To what base uses we put this ineffable intellect! To reading all day murders & railroad accidents, to choosing patterns for waistcoats & scarfs.

Observe, that the whole history of the intellect is expansions & concentrations. The expansions are the claims or inspirations from heaven to try a larger sweep, a higher pitch than we have yet tried, and to leave all our past, for this enlarged scope. Present power, performance of any kind, on the other hand, requires concentration on the moment, & the thing doable.

But all this old song I have trolled a hundred times already, in better ways, only, last night, Henry Thoreau insisted much on "expansions," & it sounded new.

But of the congelation I was to add one word, that, by experience, having learned that this old inertia or quality of oak & granite inheres in us, & punishes, as it were, any fit of geniality, we learn with surprise that our fellow man or one of our fellowmen or fellowwomen is a doctor or enchanter, who snaps the staunch iron hoops that bind us, thaws the fatal frost, & sets all the particles dancing each round each. He must be inestimable to us to whom we can say what we cannot say to ourselves.

June 1, 1852

The belief of some of our friends in their duration suggests one of those musty householders who keep every broomstick & old grate, put in a box every old tooth that falls out of their heads; preserve their ancient frippery of their juvenile wardrobe. And they think God saves all the old souls which he has used up. What does he save them for?

June 7? 1852

Nature's best feat is enamouring the man of these children, like kissing the knife that is to cut his throat—they sucking, fretting, mortifying, ruining him, & upsetting him at last, because they want his chair, & he, dear old donkey, well pleased to the end.

June 12, 1852

Yesterday a walk with Ellery C. to the Lincoln Mill-Brook, to Nine Acre Corner, & Conantum. It was the first right day of summer. Air, cloud, river, meadow, upland, mountain, all were in their best. We took a swim at the outlet of the little brook at Baker-Farm. Ellery is grown an accomplished Professor of the Art of Walking, & leads like an Indian. He likes the comic surprise of his botanic information which is so suddenly enlarged. Since he knew Thoreau, he carries a little pocket-book, in which he affects to write down the name of each new plant or the first day on which he finds the flower. He admires viburnum & cornel, & despises dooryards with foreign shrubs.

June–July 1852

Miss Bridge, a mantuamaker in Concord, became a *Medium*, & gave up her old trade for this new one; & is to charge a pistareen a spasm, and nine dollars for a fit. This is the Rat-revelation, the Gospel that comes by taps in the wall, & thumps in the table-drawer. The spirits make themselves of no reputation. They are rats & mice of Society. And one of the demure disciples of the rat-tat-too, the other day, remarked, "that this, like every other communication from the spiritual world, began very low." It was not ill said; for Christianity began in a manger, & the Knuckle dispensation in a rat-hole.

July 6, 1852

The head of Washington hangs in my diningroom for a few days past, & I cannot keep my eyes off of it. It has a certain Apalachian strength, as if it were truly the first-fruits of America, & expressed the country. The heavy leaden eyes turn on you, as the eyes of an ox in a pasture. And the mouth has a gravity & depth of quiet, as if this man had absorbed all the serenity of America, & left none for his restless, rickety, hysterical countrymen. Noble aristocratic head, with all kinds of elevation in it, that come out by turns. Such majestical ironies, as he hears the day's politics, at table. We imagine him hearing the letter of General Cass, the letter of Gen. Scott, the letter of Mr Pierce, the effronteries of Mr Webster, recited. This man listens like a god to these low conspirators.*

July 1852

Henry T. rightly said, the other evening, talking of lightning-rods, that the only rod of safety was in the vertebrae of his own spine.

What Aeschylus will translate our heaventempting politics into a warning ode, strophe & antistrophe? A slave, son of a member of Congress, flees from the plantation-whip to Boston, is snatched by the marshal, is rescued by the citizens; an excited population; a strong chain is stretched around the Court House. Webster telegraphs from Washington urgent orders to prosecute rigorously. Whig orators & interests intervene. Whig wisdom of waiting to be last devoured. Slave is caught, tried, marched at midnight under guard of marshals & pike & swordbearing police to Long Wharf & embarked for Baltimore. "Thank-God-Choate" thanks God five times in one speech; Boston thanks God. Presidential Election comes on. Webster triumphant, Boston sends a thousand rich men to Baltimore: Convention meets: Webster cannot get one vote, from Baltimore to the Gulf—not one. The competitor is chosen. The Washington wine sour, dinners disturbed. The mob at Wash-

---

*Lewis Cass, Democratic candidate for President in 1848, was at this time a United States senator; Winfield Scott and Franklin Pierce were the Whig and Democratic candidates, respectively, for President in 1852. [*JMN*]

ington turns out, at night, to exult in Scott's election. Goes to Webster's house & raises an outcry for Webster to come out & address them. He resists; the mob is violent—will not be refused. He is obliged to come in his night-shirt, & speak from his window to the riff-raff of Washington in honor of the election of Scott. Pleasant conversation of the Boston delegation on their return home! The cars unusually swift.

A man avails much to us, like a point of departure to the seaman, or his stake & stones to the surveyor. I am my own man more than most men, yet the loss of a few persons would be most impoverishing—a few persons, who give flesh to what were, else, mere thoughts, and which, now, I am not at liberty to slight, or, in any manner, treat as fictions. It were too much to say that the Platonic world I might have learned to treat as cloud-land, had I not known Alcott, who is a native of that country, yet I will say that he makes it as solid as Massachusetts to me. And Thoreau gives me in flesh & blood & pertinacious Saxon belief, my own ethics. He is far more real, & daily practically obeying them, than I; and fortifies my memory at all times with an affirmative experience which refuses to be set aside.

I live a good while & acquire as much skill in literature as an old carpenter does in wood. It occurs, then, what pity, that now, when you know something, have at least learned so much good omission, your organs should fail you; your eyes, health, fire & zeal of work, should decay daily. Then I remember that it is the mind of the world which is the good carpenter, the good scholar, sailor, or blacksmith, thousand-handed, versatile, all-applicable. . . . In you, this rich soul has peeped, despite your horny muddy eyes, at books & poetry. Well, it took you up, & showed you something to the purpose; that there was something there. Look, look, old mole! there, straight up before you, is the magnificent Sun. If only for the instant, you see it. Well, in this way it educates the youth of the Universe; in this way, warms, suns, refines every particle; then it drops the little channel or canal, through which the Life rolled beatific—like a fossil to the ground—thus touched & educated by a moment of sunshine, to be the fairer material for future channels & canals, through which the old Glory shall dart again, in new directions, until the Universe shall have been shot through & through, *tilled* with light.

Lovejoy the preacher came to Concord, & hoped Henry T. would go to hear him. "I have got a sermon on purpose for him."—"No," the aunts said, "we are afraid not." Then he wished to be introduced to him at the house. So he was confronted. Then he put his hand behind

Henry, tapping his back, & said, "Here's the chap who camped in the woods." Henry looked round, & said, "And here's the chap who camps in a pulpit." Lovejoy looked disconcerted, & said no more.

The two Ingersolls in Illinois(?) joined different political parties, so that, whichever party won, the family were safe. The two Newmans in England are distinguished one as Papist, & one extreme liberalist. The two junior Quincys in Boston are, one, Hunker, & the other Abolitionist. These cases remind me of two brothers, one of whom, being a gardener, & suffering every year from the bugs, the other resolved to be entomologist, so that, the worse the case was for the garden, the better might his museum thrive.

July 18, 1852
H. T. makes himself characteristically the admirer of the common weeds which have been hoed at by a million farmers all spring & summer & yet have prevailed, and just now come out triumphant over all lands, lanes, pastures, fields, & gardens, such is their pluck & vigor. We have insulted them with low names too, pig-weed, smart-weed, red-root, lousewort, chickweed. *He* says that they have fine names: amaranth, ambrosia.

July 1852
Why did all manly gifts in Webster fail?
He wrote on Nature's grandest brow, For Sale.

Aug. 1852
I waked at night, & bemoaned myself, because I had not thrown myself into this deplorable question of Slavery, which seems to want nothing so much as a few assured voices. But then, in hours of sanity, I recover myself, & say, God must govern his own world, & knows his way out of this pit, without my desertion of my post which has none to guard it but me. I have quite other slaves to free than those negroes, to wit, imprisoned spirits, imprisoned thoughts, far back in the brain of man—far retired in the heaven of invention, &, which, important to the republic of Man, have no watchman, or lover, or defender, but I.

Aug. 18? 1852
Greenough* called my contemplations, &c. "the masturbation of the brain."

---

*Horatio Greenough (1805–1852) was a noted sculptor and proponent of "organic form" in the arts.

Aug.–Sept. 1852

H. D. T. read me a letter from Blake to himself, yesterday, by which it appears that Blake writes to ask his husband for leave to marry a wife.

Oct. 1852

"Pantheism," to be sure! Do you suppose the pale scholar who says, you do not know causes, or the cause of causes, any better for often repeating your stupid noun, deceives himself about his own powers? Does not he live in care, & suffer by trifles? Does not he shake with cold, & lose days by indigestion? Does not his shirt-button come off when he is dressing in haste? Does not his chimney smoke, & his wife scold? Has he not notes to pay?—and is he likely to overestimate his powers of getting johnny cake for his breakfast, because he perceives that you use words without meaning?

A Mr Schaad who printed an orthodox pamphlet lately at Pittsburg, Pa. says that "Mr Emerson is a pantheist by intuition, rather than by argument." So it seems our *intuitions* are mistaken. Who then can set us right?

The shoemakers & fishermen say in their shops, "Damn learning! it spoils the boy: as soon as he gets a little, he won't work." "Yes," answers Lemuel, "But there is learning somewhere, & somebody will have it and who has it will have the power, & will rule you: knowledge is power. Why not, then, let your son get it, as well as another?"

The prohibitions of society make perhaps the sexual appetite morbid, & the abortive generation, or, the death of a large fraction of the population before 3 years, proves it. The way to reach the healthy limits of the census is to have wise chastity & not forced, to have affection & not embargoed routine.

In the Elgin marbles, by representing a procession of horsemen, in which, though each part is fixed, yet all the attitudes of the horse are given, the one figure supplies the defects of the other, & you have seen a horse, put through all his motions, so that motion is enjoyed & you can almost see the dust.

The church is there for check of trade. But on examination all the deacons, ministers, & saints of this church are steering with all their sermons & prayers in the direction of the Trade. If the city says, "Freedom & no tax," they say so, & hunt up plenty of texts. But if the city says, "Freedom is a humbug. We prefer a strong government," the pulpit says the same, & finds a new set of applicable texts. But presently Trade says, "Slavery too has been misunderstood: it is not so bad; nay, it is good; on the whole, it is the best possible thing." The dear pulpit & deacons must turn over a new leaf, & find a new string of texts, which they are forward to do.

Last Sunday I was at Plymouth on the beach, & looked across the hazy water—whose spray was blowing on to the hills & orchards—to Marshfield. I supposed, Webster must have passed, as indeed he had died at 3 in the morning. The sea, the rocks, the woods, gave no sign that America & the world had lost the completest man. Nature had not in our days, or, not since Napoleon, cut out such a masterpiece. He brought the strength of a savage into the height of culture. He was a man in equilibrio. A man within & without, the strong & perfect body of the first ages, with the civility & thought of the last. *"Os, oculosque Jovi par."** And, what he brought, he kept. Cities had not hurt him, he held undiminished the power & terror of his strength, the majesty of his demeanour.

He had a counsel in his breast. He was a statesman, & not the semblance of one. Most of our statesmen are in their places by luck & vulpine skill, not by any fitness. Webster was there for cause: the reality; the final person, who had to answer the questions of all the faineants, & who had an answer.

But alas! he was the victim of his ambition; to please the South betrayed the North, and was thrown out by both.

Oct.? 1852

The worst of charity, is, that the lives you are asked to preserve are not worth preserving. The calamity is the masses. I do not wish any mass at all, but honest men only, facultied men only, lovely & sweet & accomplished women only; and no shovel-handed Irish, & no Five-Points, or Saint Gileses, or drunken crew, or mob, or stockingers, or 2 millions of paupers receiving relief, miserable factory population, or lazzaroni, at all.

If Government knew how, I should like to see it check, not multiply, the population. When it reaches the true law of its action, every man that is born will be hailed as essential.

---

*"A mouth and eyes equal to Jove." [*JMN*]

* * *

The argument of the slaveholder is one & simple: he pleads Fate. Here is an inferior race requiring wardship—it is sentimentality to deny it. The argument of the abolitionist is, It is inhuman to treat a man thus.

Then, for the Fugitive Slave Bill, we say—I do not wish to hold slaves, nor to help you to hold them. If you cannot keep them without my help, let them go.

Such provisions as you find in the Constitution for your behoof make the most of. You could not recover a load of hay, a barrel of potatoes by such law. The Constitution has expressly guaranteed your barrel of potatoes. No, the Courts would say, it has not named them. If it especially & signally wished by compromise to protect your potato crop, it would have said so. Laws are to be strictly interpreted, & laws of all things are understood to say exactly what they mean. But how then can you maintain such an incredible & damnable pretension as to steal a man on these loose inuendoes of the law that would not allow you to steal his shoes? How, but that all our northern Judges have made a cowardly interpretation of the law, in favor of the crime, & not of the right? The leaning should be, should it not? to the right against the crime. The leaning has been invariably against the slave for the master. But Thoreau remarks that the cause of Freedom advances, for all the able debaters now are freesoilers.

To write a history of Massachusetts, I confess, is not inviting to an expansive thinker. For, he must shut himself out from three quarters of his mind, & confine himself to one fourth. Since, from 1790 to 1820, there was not a book, a speech, a conversation, or a thought, in the State. About 1820, the Channing, Webster, & Everett aera began, & we have been bookish & poetical & cogitative since.

Edwards on the Will was printed in 1754.

I do not think the fame of Pitt very honorable to English mind; neither Pitt nor Peel. Pitt is a mediocre man, is only explained by the commanding superiority which a good debater in a town meeting has, & there is not a quotable phrase or word from him, or measure. Nothing for man. Mere parliamentary plausibility & dexterity, & the right external conditions, namely, of name, birth, breeding, & relation to persons & parties. Pitt is nothing without his victory. Burke, on the other side, who had no victory, & nothing but defeat & disparagement, is an ornament of the human race; & Fox had essential manliness. His speeches show a man, brave, generous, & sufficient. Always on the right side.

Nov.? 1852

The Democrats carry the country, because they have more virility: just as certain of my neighbors rule our little town, quite legitimately, by having more courage & animal force than those whom they overbear. It is a kind of victory like that of gravitation over all upraised bodies, sure, though it lie in wait for ages for them. I saw in the cars a broad featured unctuous man, fat & plenteous as some successful politician, & pretty soon divined it must be the foreign Professor, who has had so marked a success in all our scientific & social circles, having established unquestionable leadership in them all—and it was Agassiz.

England never stands for the cause of freedom on the continent, but always for her trade. She did not stand for the freedom of Schleswig Holstein, but for the King of Denmark. She did not stand for the Hungarian, but for Austria. It was strange that with Palmerston's reputation for liberalism, he went out because he favoured Louis Napoleon's usurpation. England, meantime, is liberal, but the power is with the Aristocracy, who never go for liberty, unless England itself is threatened. Few & poor chances for European Emancipation: the disarming; the army; & the army of office-holders, are the triple wall of monarchy. Then consider that the people don't want liberty—they want bread; &, though republicanism would give them more bread after a year or two, it would not until then, & they want bread every day. Louis Napoleon says, I will give you work—& they believed him. In America, we hold out the same bribe, "Roast Beef, & two dollars a day." And our people will not go for liberty of other people, no, nor for their own, but for annexation of territory, or a tariff, or whatever promises new chances for young men, more money to men of business.

In either country, they want great men, & the cause of right can only succeed against all this gravitation or materialism by means of immense personalities. But Webster, Calhoun, Clay, Benton, are not found to be philanthropists, but attorneys of great & gross interests.

Winter? 1852-53

'Tis said that the age ends with the poet or successful man, who knots up into himself the genius or idea of his nation; and, that, when the Jews have at last flowered perfectly into Jesus, there is the end of the nation. When Greece is complete in Plato, Phidias, Pericles, the race is spent & rapidly takes itself away. When Rome has arrived at Caesar & Cicero, it has no more that it can do & retreats. When Italy has got out Dante, all the rest will be rubbish. So that we ought rather to be thankful that our hero or poet does not hasten to be born in America, but still allows us others to live a little, & warm ourselves at the fire of the sun, for, when he comes, we others must pack our petty trunks, & begone. But I say that Saxondom is tough & manyheaded, & does not so readily admit of absorption & being sucked & vampyrized by a Representative as fluider races. For have not the English stood Chaucer? stood Shakspeare? & Milton, & Newton? & survived unto this day with more diffusion of ability, with a larger number of able gentlemen in all departments of work than any nation ever had?

It is the distinction of "Uncle Tom's Cabin," that, it is read equally in the parlour & the kitchen & the nursery of every house. What the lady read in the drawing-room in a few hours, is retailed to her in her kitchen by the cook & the chambermaid, as, week by week, they master one scene & character after another.

1852–53?
Henry Thoreau's idea of the men he meets, is, that they are his old thoughts walking. It is all affectation to make much of them, as if he did not long since know them thoroughly.

Jan. 1853
At Alton, we took the train for Springfield, 72 miles. Senator Breese & Mr Young of U. S. Congress, Gov. Edwards, & other railroad men were in the train, & made an agreeable party *in the baggage car*, where they had a box of brandy, a box of buffalo tongues, & a box of soda biscuit. They showed me eight or ten deer flying across the prairie, with their white tails erect, disturbed by the train; then, presently, one who stood & looked at us; then a fire on the prairie. The corn was not yet gathered, & a farmer told us, that they had not yet been able to get upon the land to gather it—too much mud for horse & wagon. It does not usually get all gathered until March. Gov. Edwards had been at St Louis in 1815 or 1816 when there was but one brick house in the place. And until lately any man arriving there & seeing the dilapidated old French houses, their posts all rotted away at bottom & swinging from the piazza above, would have been more struck with the air of decay than of growth.

At Springfield, found the mud of the deluge. Mr B. had said of a bread & butter pudding at the hotel, "It was a fraud upon Lazarus;" & told the story of the London milk-man, who, being indicted for adulterating milk, got off by proving that there was no particle of milk in the composition. A man brought patent churns here, & somebody there said, "You take Peters's milk, & if you can make a particle of butter out of that, you shall have not only a patent, but a deed of the State of Illinois!" Meanness of politics, low fillibusterism, dog-men, that have not shed their canine teeth; well, don't be disgusted; 'tis the work of this River, this Missisippi River that warps the men, warps the nations, they must all obey it, chop down its woods, kill the alligator, eat the deer, shoot the wolf, "follow the river," mind the boat, plant the Missouri-corn, cure, & save, & send down stream the wild foison harvest tilth & wealth of this huge mud trough of the 2000 miles or 10000 miles of river. How can they be high? How can they have a day's leisure for anything but the work of the river? Every one has the mud up to his knees, & the coal of the country dinges his shirt collar. How can he be literary or grammatical? The people are all kings: out on the prairie the sceptre is the driving-whip. And I notice an extraordinary firmness in the face of many a drover, an air of independence & inevitable lips, which are worth a hundred thousand dollars: No holding a hat for opinions. But the politicians in their statehouses are truckling & adulatory.

Jan.–March? 1853
Dr Kirkland & Professor Brazer mutually resolved one day to break off smoking for six months. Soon after, they met at a dinner party at Col. P.'s, where all the appointments were excellent. Segars were offered, & Brazer declined them. Dr Kirkland lighted one, & after smoking with much content for a time, he said to nobody in particular, as he puffed away the smoke—It is doubtful, whether we show more want of self control in breaking good resolutions, or self-conceit in keeping them.

Fate. "The classes & the races too weak to master the new conditions of life must give way." Correspondent of the Tribune—Karl Marx.

Walk with Ellery to Lincoln. Benzoin laurus, rich beautiful shrub in this dried up country. Particolored warbler. E. laughed at Nuttall's description of birds: "on the top of a high tree the bird pours all day the lays of affection," &c. Affection! Why what is it? a few feathers, with a hole at one end, & a point at the other, & a pair of wings: affection! Why just as much affection as there is in that lump of peat.

Thoreau is at home; why he has got to maximize the minimum; that will take him some days.

We went to Bear Hill & had a fine outlook. Descending E. got sight of some labourers in the field below. Look at them, he said, those four! four daemoniacs scratching in their cell of pain! Live for the hour. Just as much as any man has done, or laid up, in any way, unfits him for conversation. He has done something, makes him good for boys, but spoils him for the hour. That's the good of Thoreau, that he puts his whole sublunary capital into the last quarter of an hour; carries his whole stock under his arm.

William Ellery Channing (1818–1901): "There are men whose
opinion of a book is final. If Ellery C. tells me, here is a good
book, I know I have a day longer to live."

At home, I found H. T. himself who complained of Clough or somebody that he or they recited to every one at table the paragraph just read
by him & by them in the last newspaper & studiously avoided every
thing private. I should think he was complaining of one H. D. T.

Spring? 1853

It is a bitter satire on our social order, just at present, the number of
bad cases. Margaret Fuller having attained the highest & broadest culture that any American woman has possessed, came home with an Italian gentleman whom she had married, & their infant son, & perished by
shipwreck on the rocks of Fire Island, off New York; and her friends
said, 'Well, on the whole, it was not so lamentable, & perhaps it was the
best thing that could happen to her. For, had she lived, what could she
have done? How could she have supported herself, her husband, &
child?' And, most persons, hearing this, acquiesced in this view that,
after the education has gone far, such is the expensiveness of America,
that the best use to put a fine woman to, is to drown her to save her
board.

Well, the like or the stronger plight is that of Mr Alcott, the most refined & the most advanced soul we have had in New England, who makes all other souls appear slow & cheap & mechanical; a man of such a courtesy & greatness, that (in conversation) all others, even the intellectual, seem sharp & fighting for victory, & angry—he has the unalterable sweetness of a muse—yet because he cannot earn money by his pen or his talk, or by schoolkeeping or bookkeeping or editing or any kind of meanness—nay, for this very cause, that he is ahead of his contemporaries—is higher than they, & keeps himself out of the shop-condescensions & smug arts which they stoop to, or, unhappily, need not stoop to, but find themselves, as it were, born to—therefore, it is the unanimous opinion of New England judges that this man must die; we shall all hear of his death with pleasure, & feel relieved that his board & clothes also are saved! We do not adjudge him to hemlock, or to garrotting—we are much too hypocritical & cowardly for that; but we not less surely doom him, by refusing to protest against this doom, or combine to save him, & to set him on employments fit for him & salutary to the state, or to the Senate of fine Souls, which is the heart of the state.

In Boston, is no company for a fine wit. There is a certain *poor-smell* in all the streets, in Beacon street & Park & Mt Vernon, as well as in the lawyers' offices, & the wharves, the same meanness & sterility, & *leave-all-hope-behind*, as one finds in a boot manufacturer's premises, or a bonnet-factory; vamps, pasteboard, millinette, and an eye to profit. The want of elevation, the absence of ideas, the sovereignty of the abdomen, reduces all to the same poorness. One fancies that in the houses of the rich, as the temptation to servility is removed, there may chance to be generosity & elevation; but no; we send them to Congress, & they originate nothing and on whatever question they instantly exhibit the vulgarity of the lowest populace. An absence of all perception & natural equity. They have no opinions, & cringe to their own attorney, when he tells the opinion of the Insurance Offices.

But you can never have high aristocracy, without real elevation of ideas somewhere; otherwise, as in Boston, it turns out punk & cheat at last.

Certainly I go for culture, & not for multitudes. I suppose that a cultivated laborer is worth many untaught laborers, that a scientific engineer with instruments & steamengine, is worthy many hundred men, many thousands; that Napoleon or Archimedes is worth for labor a thousand thousands; and, that, in every wise & genial soul, I have already England, Greece, Italy walking, & can well dispense with populations of paddies.

* * *

'Tis very costly, this thinking for the market in books or lectures: As soon as any one turns the conversation on my "Representative men," for instance, I am instantly sensible that there is nothing there for conversation, that the argument is all pinched & illiberal & popular.

Only what is private, & yours, & essential, should ever be printed or spoken. I will buy the suppressed part of the author's mind; you are welcome to all he published.

June 10? 1853

Yesterday a ride to Bedford with Ellery, along the "Bedford Levels" & walked all over the premises of the Old Mill—King Philip's Mill—on the Shawsheen River; old mill, with sundry nondescript wooden antiquities—Boys with bare legs were fishing on the little islet in the stream; . . . as we rode, one thing was clear, as oft before, that it is favorable to sanity—the occasional change of landscape. If a girl is mad to marry, let her take a ride of ten miles, & see meadows & mountains she never saw before; two villages, & an old mansion house; & the odds are, it will change all her resolutions. World is full of fools who get a-going & never stop: set them off on another tack, & they are half-cured. From Shawsheen we went to Burlington; & E. reiterated his conviction, that the only art in the world is landscape-painting. The boys held up their fish to us from far; a broad new placard on the walls announced to us that the Shawsheen-mill was for sale; but we bought neither the fish nor the mill.

June–July 1853

H. seemed stubborn & implacable; always manly & wise, but rarely sweet. One would say that as Webster could never speak without an antagonist, so H. does not feel himself except in opposition. He wants a fallacy to expose, a blunder to pillory, requires a little sense of victory, a roll of the drums, to call his powers into full exercise.

Sylvan [Thoreau] could go wherever woods & waters were & no man was asked for leave. Once or twice the farmer withstood, but it was to no purpose—he could as easily prevent the sparrows or tortoises. It was their land before it was his, & their title was precedent. S. knew what was on their land, & they did not; & he sometimes brought them ostentatiously gifts of flowers or fruits or shrubs which they would gladly have paid great prices for, & did not tell them that he took them from their own woods.

Moreover the very time at which he used their land & water (for his boat glided like a trout everywhere unseen) was in hours when they were sound asleep. Long before they were awake he went up & down to survey like a sovereign his possessions, & he passed onward, & left them before the farmer came out of doors. Indeed it was the common opinion of the boys that Mr T. made Concord.

The sons of clergymen are lawyers & merchants, & the keenest hunters in all the pack, as if a certain violence had been done them in their abstinence in the last generation, & this was the violence of the recoil.

I admire answers to which no answer can be made.

July–Aug. 1853
'Tis curious that Christianity, which is idealism, is sturdily defended by the brokers, & steadily attacked by the idealists.

Aug. 3? 1853
These New Yorkers & Lenox people think much of N.Y.; little of Boston. The Bostonians are stiff, dress badly, never can speak French with good accent; the New Yorkers have exquisite millinery, tournure, great expense, &, on being presented, the men look at you, & instantly see whether your dress & style is up to their mark; if not (and expense is great part of the thing) they never notice you. . . .

The Boston women spend a great deal of money on rich & rare dresses, and have no milliner of taste who can say, 'this stuff, this color, this trimming, this ensemble does not suit you.' In N.Y. the milliners have this skill. Mrs Perkins, at the Opera, heard a dressmaker say, "how dowdy all the Boston ladies are! Mrs Perkins is dowdy."

Aug.? 1853
H. T. sturdily pushes his economy into houses & thinks it the false mark of the gentleman that he is to pay much for his food. He ought to pay little for his food. Ice—he must have ice! And it is true, that, for each artificial want that can be invented & added to the ponderous expense, there is new clapping of hands of newspaper editors, & the donkey public. To put one more rock to be lifted betwixt a man & his true ends. If Socrates were here, we could go & talk with him; but Longfellow, we cannot go & talk with; there is a palace, & servants, & a row of bottles of different coloured wines, & wine glasses, & fine coats.

Aug.–Sept. 1853
The Americans have the underdose. I find them not spiced with a quality. What poor *mots*, what poor speeches, they make! 'Tis all like

Miss Joanna's stories, wherein all the meaning has to be imputed. "O if you could only have heard him say it!"—"Say what?"—"Why he said '*Yes,*' but with so much intelligence!" Well, John Adams said "Independence forever!" and Sam Adams said, "O what a glorious morning is this!" and Daniel Webster said "I still live," & Edward Everett will say, when he comes to die, "O dear!" & General Cushing will say, "O my!" And Genl Butler will say, "Damn!" & however brilliant in the first & second telling these speeches may be, they somehow lack the Plutarch virility.

Sept. 5, 1853   Cape Cod
    Went to Yarmouth Sunday 5; to Orleans Monday, 6th; to Nauset Light on the back side of Cape Cod. Collins, the keeper, told us he found obstinate resistance on Cape Cod to the project of building a light house on this coast, as it would injure the wrecking business. He had to go to Boston, & obtain the strong recommendation of the Port Society. From the high hill in the rear of Higgins's, in Orleans, I had a good view of the whole cape & the sea on both sides. The Cape looks like one of the Newfoundland Banks just emerged, a huge tract of sand half-covered with poverty grass, & beach grass & for trees abele & locust & plantations of pitchpine. Some good oak, & in Dennis & Brewster were lately good trees for shiptimber & still are well wooded on the east side. But the view I speak of looked like emaciated orkneys—Mull, Islay, & so forth, made of salt dust, gravel, & fishbones. They say the Wind makes the roads, &, as at Nantucket, a large part of the real estate was freely moving back & forth in the air. I heard much of the coming railroad which is about to reach Yarmouth & Hyannis, &, they hope, will come to Provincetown. I fancied the people were only waiting for the railroad to reach them in order to evacuate the country. For the starknakedness of the country could not be exaggerated. But no, nothing was less true. They are all attached to what they call *the soil.* Mr Collins had been as far as Indiana; but, he said, hill on hill—he felt stifled, & longed for the Cape, "where he could see out." And whilst I was fancying that they would gladly give away land to anybody that would come & live there, & be a neighbor: no, they said, all real estate had risen, all over the Cape, & you could not buy land at less than 50 dollars per acre. And, in Provincetown, a lot on the Front street of forty feet square would cost 5 or 600 dollars.
    Still I saw at the Cape, as at Nantucket, they are a little tender about your good opinion: for if a gentleman at breakfast, says, he don't like Yarmouth, all real estate seems to them at once depreciated 2 or 3 per cent.

Fall? *1853*

Elizabeth Hoar said, 'Tis necessary, when you strike a discord, to let down the ear by an intermediate note or two to the accord again, & that Bloomer dress is very good & reconcilable to men's taste, if only it be not offensively sudden; so a woman may speak, & vote, & legislate, & drive coach, if only it comes by degrees.

Alcott tells me that Mr Hedge is to write an Essay on the importance of a liturgy. I propose to add an Essay on the importance of a rattle in the throat.

Dec. 1853

Wendell Holmes when I offered to go to his lecture on Wordsworth, said, "I entreat you not to go. I am forced to study effects. You & others may be able to combine popular effect with the exhibition of truths. I cannot. I am compelled to study effects." The other day, Henry Thoreau was speaking to me about my lecture on the Anglo American, & regretting that whatever was written for a lecture, or whatever succeeded with the audience was bad, &c. I said, I am ambitious to write something which all can read, like Robinson Crusoe. And when I have written a paper or a book, I see with regret that it is not solid, with a right materialistic treatment, which delights everybody. Henry objected, of course, & vaunted the better lectures which only reached a few persons. Well, yesterday, he came here, &, at supper, Edith, understanding that he was to lecture at the Lyceum, sharply asked him, "Whether his lecture would be a nice interesting story, such as she wanted to hear, or whether it was one of those old philosophical things that she did not care about?" Henry instantly turned to her, & bethought himself, & I saw was trying to believe that he had matter that might fit Edith & Edward, who were to sit up & go to the lecture, if it was a good one for them.

When some one offered Agassiz a glass of water, he said that he did not know whether he had ever drank a glass of that liquid, before he came to this country.

1853-54?

What is the reason we do not learn history of Greece, Babylon, Sweden, Turkey? not for want of interest: No indeed. Why not learn arts, useful & fine? Why not geology? why not anatomy? why not algebra? not for want of attraction or aptitude: But simply because of shortness of life: we decline prudently some, in order to master those few facts nearest to us. 'Twere ridiculous for us to think of embracing the whole circle when we know we can live only while 50, 60, or 70 whirls are spun around the sun by this nimble apple we are perched upon. Can the gnat swallow the elephant? 'Tis the cogent argument for immortality, this appetency we own to.

Saadi complained, that, old as he was, he could never get used to women, but every beauty caused him the most violent emotions.

Motherwit. Dr Johnson, Milton, Chaucer, & Burns had it.
Unless we had Boswell, we should hardly know how to account for Johnson's fame, his wit is so muffled & choked in his scholastic style. Yet it animates that, and makes his opinions real.
Aunt Mary M. E. has it, & can write scrap letters. Who has it, need never write anything but scraps.
H. D. Thoreau has it.

I often need the device of ascribing my sentence to another in order to give it weight. Carlyle does so with Teufelsdrock, &c.

I have been told by women, that, whatever work they perform by dint of resolution & without spontaneous flow of spirits, they invariably expiate by a fit of sickness.

The poet sprains or strains himself by attempting too much; he tries to reach the people, instead of contenting himself with the temperate expression of what he knows. Sing he must & should, but not ballads; sing, but for gods or demigods. He need not transform himself into Punch & Judy. A man must not be a proletary or breeder, but only by mere superfluity of his strength, he begets Messias. He relieves himself, & makes a world.

In Art, we value the ideal, that is to say, nothing is interesting which is fixed, bounded, dead; but only that which streams with life, which is in act or endeavor to proceed, to reach somewhat beyond, &, all the better, if that be somewhat vast & divine. A Daguerre from a bronze statuette or table figure, as, a suit of armour, a crusader, or the like, is prosaic & tiresome, however correct in details. A daguerre from a living head, man or animal, is of lasting interest.

We can do nothing without the shadow. The sun were insipid if the universe was not opaque. Art lives & thrills in ever new use & combining of contrasts, & is digging into the dark ever more for blacker Pits of night. What would painter do, or what would hero & saint, but for crucifixions & hells? and evermore in the world is this marvellous balance of beauty & disgust, magnificence & rats. Then let the ghost sit at my side, closer, closer, dear ghost! if glory & bliss only so can press to the other cheek.

Excellent S., if I could write a comedy, should be the hero. He came with German enthusiasm sparkling out of his black eyes, & Miss Somewhat at Georgia, wrote, that, if ever angel spoke in man, it was he. He came upcountry & Mrs S & Miss W were at his feet. J. was so affected by his eloquence that she could not speak to him. He complained & scolded to Mrs S. that J. would not be acquainted with him, that he could not be acquainted with her. Well, at last they got acquainted, & he told J. that she was his ideal of woman, & came daily there. She made him cakes & dinners & warmed his feet, & sat up nights, & stayed at home Sundays to make his shirts, & make him fine. One day he came home to C., delighted with the notice of his lecture in the Transcript, showing it to all; fancied that Mr R. or Miss P. or even L. might have done it. Could J. have any possible idea who had written it? "Why yes," said the happy J., "I have some idea—for I wrote it myself." S. was aghast. "Never breathe that you wrote it," he gasped out with passionate solemnity, being infinitely mortified that no distinguished townbody had been found to trumpet his fame.

Of Phillips, Garrison, & others I have always the feeling that they may wake up some morning & find that they have made a capital mistake, & are not the persons they took themselves for. Very dangerous is this thoroughly social & related life, whether antagonistic or co-operative. In a lonely world, or a world with half a dozen inhabitants, these would find nothing to do. The first discovery I made of Phillips, was, that while I admired his eloquence, I had not the faintest wish to meet the man. He had only a *platform*-existence, & no personality. Mere mouthpieces of a party, take away the party & they shrivel & vanish.

They are inestimable for workers on audiences; but for a private conversation, one to one, I much prefer to take my chance with that boy in the corner.

Feb.? 1854

At Jackson, Michigan, Mr *Davis*, I believe, a lawyer of Detroit, said to me, on coming out of the lecture room, "Mr E., I see that you never learned to write from any book."

*   *   *

Metres. I amuse myself often, as I walk, with humming the rhythm of the decasyllabic quatrain, or of the octosyllabic with alternate sexsyllabic or other rhythms, & believe these metres to be organic, or derived from our human pulse, and to be therefore not proper to one nation, but to mankind. But I find a wonderful charm, heroic, & especially deeply pathetic or plaintive in the cadence, & say to myself, Ah happy! if one could fill these small measures with words approaching to the power of these beats.

The man thinks he can know this or that, by words & writing. It can only be known or done organically. He must plunge into the universe, & live in its forms—sink to rise. None any work can frame unless himself become the same.

The first men saw heavens & earths, saw noble instruments of noble souls; we see railroads, banks, & mills. And we pity their poverty. There was as much creative force then as now, but it made globes instead of waterclosets. Each sees what he makes.

Realism. We shall pass for what we are. Do not fear to die, because you have not done your task. Whenever a noble soul comes, the audience awaits. And he is not judged by his performance, but by the spirit of his performance. We shall pass for what we are. The world is a masked ball & every one hides his real character, & reveals it by hiding. . . . People have the devil's-mark stamped on their faces, & do not know it, & join the church & talk virtue, and we are seeing the goat's foot all the time.

When you hide something we see that you hide something & usually see what you hide.

The Unitarians, you say, are a poor skeptical egotistic shopping sect. The Calvinists serious, still darkened over by their Hebraistic dream. The Saxon race has never flowered into its own religion, but has been fain to borrow this old Hebraism of the dark race. The Latin races are at last come to a stand, & are declining. Merry England & saucy America striding far ahead. The dark man, the black man declines. The black man is courageous, but the white men are the children of God, said Plato. It will happen by & by, that the black man will only be destined for museums like the Dodo. Alcott compassionately thought that if necessary to bring them sooner to an end, polygamy might be introduced & these made the eunuchs, polygamy, I suppose, to increase the white births.

* * *

Realism in literature. I have no fear but that the reality I love will yet exist in literature. I do not go to any pope or president for my list of books. I read what I like. I learn what I do not already know. Only those above me can give me this. They also do as I—read only such as know more than they: Thus we all depend at last on the few heads or the one head that is nearest to the stars, nearest to the fountain of all science, & knowledge runs steadily down from class to class down to the lowest people, from the highest, as water does.

Would you know a man's thoughts—look at the circle of his friends, and you know all he likes to think of. Well, is the life of the Boston patrician so desireable, when you see the graceful fools who make all his company?

I believe, the races, as Celtic, Norman, Saxon, must be used hypothetically or temporarily, as we do by the Linnaean classification, for convenience simply, & not as true & ultimate. For, otherwise, we are perpetually confounded by finding the best settled traits of one race, claimed by some more acute or ingenious partisan as precisely characteristic of the other & antagonistic. It is with national traits as with virus of cholera or plague in the atmosphere, it eludes the chemical analysis, and the air of the plague hospital is not to be discriminated by any known test from the air of Mont Blanc.

March? 1854

It occurred in the crowd of beauties on the pavé of Broadway that we grow so experienced that we are dreadfully quicksighted, & in the youngest face detect the wrinkles that shall be, & the grey that hastens to discolour these meteor tresses. We cannot afford then to live long, or nature, which lives by illusions, will have disenchanted us too far for happiness.

H. D. T. charged Blake, if he could not do hard tasks, to take the soft ones, & when he liked anything, if it was only a picture or a tune, to stay by it, find out what he liked, & draw that sense or meaning out of it, & do *that:* harden it, somehow, & make it his own. Blake thought & thought on this, & wrote afterwards to Henry, that he had got his first glimpse of heaven.

Henry was a good physician.

Strychnine, prussic acid, tobacco, coffee, alcohol, are weak dilutions; the surest poison is time.

* * *

The lesson of these days is the vulgarity of wealth. We know that wealth will vote for the same thing which the worst & meanest of the people vote for. Wealth will vote for rum, will vote for tyranny, will vote for slavery, will vote against the ballot, will vote against international copyright, will vote against schools, colleges, or any high direction of public money.

Plainly Boston does not wish liberty, & can only be pushed & tricked into a rescue of a slave. Its attitude as loving liberty is affected & theatrical. Do not then force it to assume a false position which it will not maintain. Rather let the facts appear, & leave it to the natural aggressions & familiarities of the beast it loves, until it gets well bitten & torn by the dear wolf, perchance it may not be too late to turn & to kill its deceiver.

May 1854

If Minerva offered me a gift & an option, I would say give me continuity. I am tired of scraps. I do not wish to be a literary or intellectual chiffonier. Away with this jew's rag-bag of ends & tufts of brocade, velvet, & cloth of gold; let me spin some yards or miles of helpful twine, a clew to lead to one kingly truth, a cord to bind wholesome & belonging facts.

May–Aug.? 1854

England does not wish revolution or to befriend radicals. Therefore you say, England must fall, because its moderate mixed aristocratico-liberal or finality politics will put it in antagonism with the republicanism when that comes in. Yes, but England has many moods, a war-class as well as nobles & merchants. It begun with poverty & piracy & trade, & has always those elements latent, as well as gold coaches & heraldry. It has only to let its fops & bankers succumb for a time, & its sailors, ploughmen, & bullies fall to the front. It will prove a stout buccaneer again, & weather the storm.

Thoreau thinks 'tis immoral to dig gold in California; immoral to leave creating value, & go to augmenting the representative of value, & so altering & diminishing real value, &, that, of course, the fraud will appear.

I conceive that work to be as innocent as any other speculating. Every man should do what he can; & he was created to augment some real value, & not for a speculator. When he leaves or postpones (as most men do) his proper work, & adopts some short or cunning method, as of watching markets, or farming in any manner the ignorance of people, as, in buying by the acre to sell by the foot, he is fraudulent, he is malefactor, so far; & is bringing society to bankruptcy. But nature watches over all this, too, & turns this malfaisance to some good. For, California gets peopled, subdued, civilised, in this fictitious way, & on this fiction a real prosperity is rooted & grown.

I am here to represent humanity: it is by no means necessary that I should live, but it is by all means necessary that I should act rightly. If there is danger, I must face it. I tremble. What of that? So did he who said, "It is my body trembles, out of knowing into what dangers my spirit will carry it."

The fathers made the blunder in the convention in the Ordinance of 10 July, 1787, to adopt population as basis of representation, & count only three fifths of the slaves, and to concede the reclamation of fugitive slaves for the consideration of the prohibition that "there shall be neither slavery nor involuntary servitude in the said (Northwest) Territory, unless in punishment of crimes." The bed of the Ohio river was the line agreed on east of the Missisippi.

In 1820 when New territory west of the Missisippi was to be dealt with, no such natural line offered and a parallel of latitude was adopted, & 36.30 n. was agreed on as equitable.

The Fathers made the fatal blunder in agreeing to this false basis of representation, & to this criminal complicity of restoring fugitive slaves: and the splendor of the bribe, namely, the magnificent prosperity of America from 1787, is their excuse before God & men, for the crime. They ought never to have passed the Ordinance. They ought to have refused it at the risk of making no Union; &, if no solution could be had, it would have been better that two nations, one free & one slaveholding, should have started into existence at once. The bribe, if they foresaw the prosperity we have seen, was one to dazzle common men. And I do not wonder that most men now excuse & applaud it. But crime brings punishment, always so much crime, so much ruin. A little crime a minor penalty; a great crime, a great ruin; and now, after 60 years, the poison has crept into every vein & every artery of the State.

Our senator was of that stuff that our best hope lay in his drunkenness, as that sometimes incapacitated him from doing mischief.

Modern Manners. Why count stamens, when you can study the science of men? The clergy are as like as peas. I can not tell them apart. It was said, they have bronchitis, because of reading from their paper sermon with a near voice, & then, looking at the audience, they try to speak with their far voice, & the shock is noxious. I think they do the same, or the reverse, with their thought. They look into Plato or into the mind, & then try to make parish & unitarian mince-meat of the amplitudes & eternities; & the shock is noxious.

Friends do not shake hands. I talk with you, & we have marvellous intimacies, & take all manner of beautiful liberties. After an hour, it is time to go, & straightway I take hold of your hand, & find you a coarse stranger, instead of that musical & permeable angel with whom I have been entertained.

Heaven takes care to show us that war is a part of our education, as much as milk or love, & is not to be escaped. We affect to put it all back in history, as the Trojan War, the War of the Roses, the Revolutionary War. Not so; it is *Your* War. Has that been declared? has that been fought out? & where did the Victory perch? The wars of other people & of history growl at a distance, but your war comes near, looks into your eyes, in Politics, in professional pursuit, in choices in the street, in daily habit, in all the questions of the times, in the keeping or surrendering the controul of your day, & your house, & your opinion, in the terrors of the night, in the frauds & skepticism of the day. The American independence! that is a legend. *Your Independence!* that is the question of all the Present. Have you fought out that? & settled it once & again, & once for all in the minds of all persons with whom you have to do, that you & your sense of right, & fit & fair, are an invincible indestructible somewhat, which is not to be bought or cajoled or frighted away? That done, & victory inscribed on your eyes & brow & voice, the other American Freedom begins instantly to have some meaning & support.

Aug.?–Sept. 1854
A man can only write one book. That is the reason why everybody begs readings & extracts of the young poet until 35. When he is 50, they still think they value him, & they tell him so; but they scatter like partridges, if he offer to read his paper. They think, it is because they have some job to do. But they never allowed a job to stand in the way, when he was 25.

I suppose, every one has favorite topics, which make a sort of Museum or privileged closet of whimsies in his mind, & which he thinks it a kind of aristocracy to know about. Thus, I like to know about lions, diamonds, wine, and Beauty . . .

Sept.–Oct. 1854

If I reckon up my debts by particulars to English books, how fast they reduce themselves to a few authors, & how conspicuous Shakspeare, Bacon, & Milton become. Locke is a cipher. I put the duty of being read, invariably on the author. If he is not read, whose fault is it? If he is very learned, & yet heavy, it is a double-shot which fells both himself & his authors.

All the thoughts of a turtle are turtles.

Last night talking with W. E. C. it appeared still more clear—the two nations in England—one in all time fierce only for mincepie— the old granniest beef-eating solemn trifler, a Cheap-side prentice, & growing to be a Cheapside lord; the other a fine, thoughtful, religious, poetical believer—fit for hero, fit for martyr, deriving in his flights only the solidity, & square elbows, & method, from his Cheapside brother, & rewarding him with puritanism, with drama, with letters & liberty.

Oct. 11, 1854

Never was a more brilliant show of coloured landscape than yesterday afternoon—incredibly excellent topaz & ruby at 4 o'clock, cold & shabby at 6.

Fall–Winter 1854

We live by our imaginations, by our admirations, by our words. A man pays a debt quicker to a rich man than to a poor one; wishes the bow & compliment of a rich man, weighs what he says; he never comes nearer him for all that. But dies at last better contented for this amusement of his eyes & his imagination.

I can never say often enough that science is not chronological, but according to the health of the inquirer. In a million men will be an Archimedes, if not in one million then in ten, and so often amid myriads of invalids, fops, dunces, & all kinds of damaged individuals, one sound healthy brain will be turned out, in symmetry & relation to the system of the world—eyes that can see, ears that can hear, soul that can feel, mind that can receive the resultant truth. Then you have the Copernicus without regard to his antecedents, or to his geography. This person sees the simple & vast conditions which every law of nature must fulfil, & is prepared to admit the circulation of the blood, the genesis of the planets, universal gravity, the analogy running through all parts of nature, & the correspondence of physics & metaphysics.

Feb. 1855

Some thoughts have paternity & some are bachelors. I am too celibate.

Feb. 18, 1855   Rome, N.Y.

What occurred this morng touching the imagination? In meeting a new student, I incline to ask him, Do you know any deep man? Has any one furnished you with a new image? for to see the world representatively, implies high gifts.

Feb.? 1855

Natural history builds us up from oyster & tadpole. Mythology gives us down from the heavens.

Greeks. 'Tis strange what immortality is in their very rags; so much mentality about the race has made every shred durable.

We run very fast, but here is this horrible Plato, at the end of the course, still abreast of us. Our novelties we can find all in his book. He has anticipated our latest neology.

Rhyme & Rhetoric. As boys write verses from delight in the music or rhyme, before they learn to delight in the sense, so, when grown older, they write from love of the rhetoric, sooner than for the argument.

And, in most instances, a sprightly genius chooses the topic & treatment that gives him room to say fine things, before the sad heroic truth.

I trust a good deal to common fame, as we all must. If a man has good corn, or wood, or boards, or pigs, to sell, or can make better chairs or knives or crucibles or church-organs than any body else, you will find a broad hard beaten road to his house, though it be in the woods. And if a man knows the law, people find it out, though he live in a pine shanty, & resort to him. And if a man can pipe or sing, so as to wrap the prisoned soul in an elysium; or can paint landscape, & convey into oils & ochres all the enchantments of spring or autumn; or can liberate or intoxicate all people who hear him with delicious songs & verses; 'tis certain that the secret cannot be kept: the first witness tells it to a second, and men go by fives & tens & fifties to his door.

Well, it is still so with a thinker. If he proposes to show me any high secret, if he profess to have found the profoundly secret pass that leads from Fate to Freedom, all good heads & all mankind aspiringly & religiously wish to know it, and, though it sorely & unusually taxes their poor brain, they find out at last whether they have made the transit, or no. If they have, they will know it; and his fame will surely be bruited abroad. If they come away unsatisfied, though it be easy to impute it (even in their belief) to their dulness in not being able to keep step with his snow-shoes on the icy mountain paths—I suspect it is because the transit has not been made. 'Tis like that crooked hollow log through which the farmer's pig found access to the field; the farmer moved the log so that the pig in returning to the hole, & passing through, found himself to his astonishment still on the outside of the field: he tried it again, & was still outside; then he fled away, & would never go near it again.

Whatever transcendant abilities Fichte, Kant, Schelling, & Hegel have shown, I think they lack the confirmation of having given piggy a transit to the field. The log is very crooked, but still leaves Grumphy on the same side the fence he was before. If they had made the transit, common fame would have found it out. So I abide by my rule of not reading the book, until I hear of it through the newspapers.

Our Concord mechanics & farmers are very doubtful on the subject of Culture, & will vote against you: but I notice they will all send their children to the dancing-school.

Philip Randolph was surprised to find me speaking to the politics of Antislavery, in Philadelphia. I suppose, because he thought me a believer in general laws, and that it was a kind of distrust of my own general teachings to appear in active sympathy with these temporary heats.

He is right so far as that it is becoming in the scholar to insist on central soundness, rather than on superficial applications. I am to give a wise & just ballot, though no man else in the republic doth. I am not to compromise or mix or accommodate. I am to demand the absolute right, affirm that, & do that; but not push Boston into a false, showy, & theatrical attitude, endeavoring to persuade her she is more virtuous than she is. Thereby I am robbing myself, more than I am enriching the public. After twenty, fifty, a hundred years, it will be quite easy to discriminate who stood for the right, & who for the expedient. The vulgar, comprising ranks on ranks of fine gentlemen, clergymen, college presidents & professors, & great democratic statesmen bellowing for liberty, will of course go for safe degrees of liberty—that is, will side with property against the Spirit, subtle & absolute, which keeps no terms.

Spring–Summer 1855

Munroe seriously asked what I believed of Jesus & prophets. I said, as so often, that it seemed to me an impiety to be listening to one & another, when the pure Heaven was pouring itself into each of us, on the simple condition of obedience. To listen to any second hand gospel is perdition of the First Gospel. Jesus was Jesus because he refused to listen to another, & listened at home.

For flowing is the secret of things & no wonder the children love masks, & to trick themselves in endless costumes, & be a horse, a soldier, a parson, or a bear; and, older, delight in theatricals; as, in nature, the egg is passing to a grub, the grub to a fly, and the vegetable eye to a bud, the bud to a leaf, a stem, a flower, a fruit; the children have only the instinct of their race, the instinct of the Universe, in which, *Becoming somewhat else* is the whole game of nature, & death the penalty of standing still.

'Tis not less in thought. I cannot conceive of any good in a thought which confines & stagnates. Liberty means the power to flow. To continue is to flow. Life is unceasing parturition.

It is on the completeness with which metrical forms have covered the whole circle of routinary experience, that improvisation is possible to a rhymer familiar with this cyclus of forms, & quick & dexterous in combining them. Most poetry, stock poetry we call it, that we see in the magazines, is nothing but this mosaic-work done slowly. . . .

Ellery Channing's poetry has the merit of being genuine, & not the metrical commonplaces of the Magazine, but it is painfully incomplete. He has not kept faith with the reader, 'tis shamefully indolent & slovenly. He should have lain awake all night to find the true rhyme for a verse, & he has availed himself of the first one that came; so that it is all a babyish incompleteness.

Nothing but thought is precious. And we must respect in ourselves this possibility, & abide its time. Jones Very, who thought it an honor to wash his own face, seems to me less insane than men who hold themselves cheap.

Let us not be such that our thoughts should disdain us.

If I could find that a perfect song could form itself in my brain, I should indulge it & pamper it as bees their queen.

If you would know what the dogs know, you must lap up the puddles.

The English are stupid because they reserve their strength. The Lowells ripen slowly. Hurrying America makes out of little vanities its great men, as now, the three leading men in America are of a small sort, who never saw a grander arch than their own eyebrow; never saw the sky of a principle which made them modest & contemners of themselves. Yet Washington, Adams, Quincy, Franklin, I would willingly adorn my hall with, & I will have daguerres of Alcott, Channing, Thoreau.

Foreigners to be sure! I had foreigners enough at home in my own town, streets full of people who used the same nouns & articles & pronunciation, that I do, but Turkish or Feejee in their ideas.

When I talk with a genealogist, I seem to sit up with a corpse.

I dread autobiography which usurps the largest part, sometimes the whole of the discourse of very worthy persons whom I know.

All America seems on the point of embarking for Europe. Every post brings me a letter from some worthy person who has just arrived at the execution, as he tells me, of a long-cherished design of sailing for Europe. . . .

Lues Americana, or the "European Complaint."*

Just as man is conscious of the law of vegetable & animal nature so he is aware of an Intellect which overhangs his consciousness like a sky; of degree above degree; & heaven within heaven. Number is lost in it. Millions of observers could not suffice to write its first law.

Yet it seemed to him as if gladly he would dedicate himself to such a god, be a fakeer of the intellect, fast & pray, spend & be spent, wear its colors, wear the infirmities, were it pallor, sterility, celibacy, poverty, insignificance, were these the livery of its troop, as the smith wears his apron & the collier his smutted face, honest infirmities, honorable scars, so that he be rewarded by conquest of principles; or by being purified & admitted into the immortalities, mount & ride on the backs of these thoughts, steeds which course forever the ethereal plains. Time was nothing. He had no hurry. Time was well lavished, were it centuries & cycles, in these surveys. It seemed as if the very sentences he wrote, a few sentences after summers of contemplation, shone again with all the suns which had gone to contribute to his knowing. Few, few were the lords he could reckon: Memory, & Imagination, & Perception: he did not know more for living long. Abandon yourself, he said, to the leading, when the Leader comes, this was the sum of wisdom & duty. Shake off from your shoes the dust of Europe & Asia, the rotten religions & per-

---

* *Lues* is the medical term for syphilis.

sonalities of nations. Act from your heart where the wise temperate guidance is instantly born.

M.M.E., if you praised a lady warmly, would stop you short, "Is it a colored woman of whom you were speaking?" When Mrs B. ran into any enthusiasms on Italian patriots, &c,—"Mrs Brown how's your cat?" When she had once bowed to Goodnow & his wife at the Lyceum, not quite knowing who they were (G. had offended her when she boarded with them), she afterwards went up to Goodnow, & said, "I did not know who you were, or should never have bowed to you."

The Mormons & AntiMarriage men have not thought or observed far enough. They do not like the privation. No, but Malthus establishes his fact of geometrical increase of mouths, & then we have a reason in figures for this perdurable shame in man & woman for unauthorised cohabitation. No more children than you will give your equal & entire protection & aid unto.
And this other; a man will work for his children no longer than he is sure they are his.

Abuse is a proof that you are felt. If they praise you, you will work no revolution.

The new professions
    The phrenologist
    the railroad man
    the landscape gardener
    the lecturer
    the sorcerer, rapper, mesmeriser, medium
    the daguerrotypist

July? 1855
A Scholar is a man with this inconvenience, that, when you ask him his opinion of any matter, he must go home & look up his manuscripts to know.

Aug. 27, 1855
Edward says, Father, today I have done three things for the first time; I have swum across the river; I have beat Walter Lewis at the bowling alley; and I have jumped over a stick two feet high.

Aug. 1855

The melioration in pears, or in sheep, & horses, is the only hint we have that suggests the creation of man. Every thing has a family likeness to him. All natural history from the first fossil points at him. The resemblances approach very near in the satyr to the negro or lowest man, & food, climate, & concurrence of happy stars, a guided fortune, will have at last piloted the poor quadrumanous over the awful bar that separates the fixed beast from the versatile man. In no other direction, have we any hint of the *modus* in which the infant man could be preserved. The fixity or unpassableness or inconvertibility of races, as we see them, is a feeble argument, since all the historical period is but a point to the duration in which nature has wrought. Any the least & solitariest fact in our natural history has the worth of a *power* in the opportunity of geologic periods. All our apples came from the little crab.

The Universities are wearisome old fogies, & very stupid with their aorists and alcaics & digammas, but they do teach what they pretend to teach, and whether by private tutor, or by lecturer, or by Examiner, with prizes & Scholarships, and they learn to read better & to write better than we do.

They make excellent readers & unexceptionable writers.

July–Oct. 1855

Woman. I think it impossible to separate their education & interests.

The policy of defending their property is good; and if the women demand votes, offices, & political equality as an Elder & Eldress are of equal power in the Shaker Families, refuse it not. 'Tis very cheap wit that finds it so funny. Certainly all my points would be sooner carried in the state if women voted.

The blazing evidence of immortality is our dissatisfaction with any other solution.

All great natures love stability.

Dec. 31, 1855 Davenport, Iowa

I have crossed the Missisippi on foot three times.

Jan. 1856

In Rock Island I am advertised as "the celebrated Metaphysician"; in Davenport as "the Essayist & Poet."

In Dixon I talked with Mr Dixon the pioneer founder of the city. His full length portrait was hanging in the town-hall where we were. He is

80 years old & a great favorite with the people, his family have all died, but some grand-children remain. He who has made so many rich is a poor man, which, it seems, is a common fortune here; Sutter the Californian discoverer of gold, is poor. It looks as if one must have a talent for misfortune to miss so many opportunities as these men who have owned the whole township & not saved a competence. He is a correct quiet man, was first a tailor, then a stage owner, & mail agent, &c. I went down the Galena river, once Bean river, Fève, then Fever, now Galena River, four or five miles in a sleigh, with Mr McMasters to the Marsden Lead, so called, a valuable lead mine, & went into it. Marsden, it seems, was a poor farmer here; & sold out his place, & went to California; found no gold, & came back, & bought his land again, &, in digging to clear out a spring of water, stumbled on this most valuable lead (leed), as they call it, of lead-ore. They can get up 7000 lb. of the ore in a day (by a couple of laborers), and the smelters will come to the spot, & buy the ore at 3 cents a pound; so that he found California here. He at once called in his brothers, & divided the mine with them. One of them sold out his share, one sixth, ("foolishly") for 12,000 dollars; the others retain theirs.

Mr Shetland said, 75 or 100,000 dollars had already been derived from this mine, & perhaps as much more remains. Hon. Mr Turner of Freeport said to me, that it is not usually the first settlers, who become rich, but the second comers: the first, he said, are often visionary men, the second are practical. The first two settlers of Rockford died insolvent, & he named similar cases in other towns, I think Beloit. I read at the bottom of a map of Wisconsin, that the motto of the State-seal of Wisconsin, is, *"Civilitas successit Barbarum."*

An idealist, if he have the sensibilities & habits of those whom I know, is very ungrateful. He craves & enjoys every chemical property, and every elemental force, loves pure air, water, light, caloric, wheat, flesh, salt, & sugar, the blood coursing in his own veins, and the grasp of friendly hands; & uses the meat he eats to preach against matter as malignant, & to praise mind, which he very hollowly & treacherously serves. Beware of hypocrisy.

Jan. 9, 1856   Beloit
I fancied in this fierce cold weather, mercury varying from 20 to 30 degrees below zero, for the last week, that Illinois lands would be at a discount, and the agent who at Dixon was selling great tracts, would be better advised to keep them for milder days, since a hundred miles of prairie in such days as these are not worth the poorest shed or cellar in the towns. But my easy landlord assured me "we had no cold weather in

Illinois, only now & then Indian Summers & cool nights." He looked merrily at his windowpanes, opaque with a stratum of frost, & said, that his was a fashionable first class hotel, with window-lights of ground glass.

This climate & people are a new test for the wares of a man of letters. All his thin watery matter freezes; 'tis only the smallest portion of alcohol that remains good. At the lyceum, the stout Illinoian, after a short trial, walks out of the hall. The Committee tell you that the people want a hearty laugh, & Stark, & Saxe, & Park Benjamin, who give them that, are heard with joy. Well I think with Gov. Reynolds, the people are always right (in a sense) & that the man of letters is to say, these are the new conditions to which I must conform. The architect who is asked to build a house to go upon the sea, must not build a parthenon or a square house, but a ship. And Shakspeare or Franklin or Aesop coming to Illinois, would say, I must give my wisdom a comic form, instead of tragics or elegiacs, & well I know to do it, and he is no master who cannot vary his forms, & carry his own end triumphantly through the most difficult.

Winter? 1856

Wm Little came to church & heard my sermon against minding trifles. He told me, had he preached he should have taken the other side. Probably not one hearer besides thought so far on the subject.

A writer in the Boston Transcript says, that "just in proportion to the morality of a people, will be the expansion of the credit system." Which sounds to me like better political economy than I often hear.

If I knew only Thoreau, I should think cooperation of good men impossible. Must we always talk for victory, & never once for truth, for comfort, & joy? Centrality he has, & penetration, strong understanding, & the higher gifts—the insight of the real or from the real, & the moral rectitude that belongs to it; but all this & all his resources of wit & invention are lost to me in every experiment, year after year, that I make, to hold intercourse with his mind. Always some weary captious paradox to fight you with, & the time & temper wasted.

Alcott thinks Conventions, the Newspaper, the Lecture, & Conversation, to be our American achievements; which he ascribes to Garrison, Greeley, RWE, & himself!

We have seen art coming back to veracity. . . . Wagner, in Music. The old musicians said, "the worse text the better score." Wagner said, "the text must be fixed to the score, & from the first invention."

* * *

A. B. A. saw the *Midsummers Night's dream* played, & said, it was a phallus to which fathers could carry their daughters, & each had their own thoughts, without suspecting that the other had the same.

Qu'est ce qu'un classique? The classic art was the art of necessity: modern romantic art bears the stamp of caprice & chance. This is the most general distinction we can give between classic & romantic art.

Eugene Sue, Dumas, &c., when they begin a story, do not know how it will end; but Walter Scott when he began the Bride of Lammermoor had no choice, nor Shakspeare in Macbeth. But Mme George Sand, though she writes fast & miscellaneously, is yet fundamentally classic & necessitated: and I, who tack things strangely enough together, & consult my ease rather than my strength, & often write *on the other side,* am yet an adorer of the *One.*

To be classic, then, *de rigueur,* is the prerogative of a vigorous mind who is able to execute what he conceives.

April 5, 1856

Walden fired a cannonade yesterday of a hundred guns, but not in honor of the birth of Napoleon.

April? 1856

Monochord. Mary Moody Emerson cannot sympathize with children. I know several persons whose world is only large enough for one person, and each of them, though he were to be the last man, would, like the executioner in Hood's poem, guillotine the last but one. 'Tis A's misfortune, & T's.

Elizabeth Hoar said of M. M. E., she thinks much more of her bonnet & of other peoples' bonnets than they do, & sends Elizabeth from Dan to Beersheba to find a bonnet that does not conform; while Mrs. Hoar, whom she severely taxes with conforming, is satisfied with anything she finds in the shops. She tramples on the common humanities all day, & they rise as ghosts & torment her at night.

What a barren witted pate am I, says the scholar; I will go see whether I have lost my reason. He seeks companions, he seeks intelligent persons, whether more wise or less wise than he, who give him provocation, and, at once, & very easily, the old motion begins in his brain, thoughts, fancies, humors, flow, the horizon broadens, the cloud lifts, & the infinite opulence of things is again shown him. But the right conditions must be observed. Principally he must have leave to be himself. We go to dine with M. & N. & O. & P. And, to be sure, they begin to be something else than they were, they play tricks, they dance jigs, they pun, they tell stories, they try many fantastic tricks, under some superstition that there must be excitement & elevation, and they kill conversation at once. It is only on natural ground that they can be rich. Keep the ground, feel the roots, domesticate yourself.

April 26, 1856
Whipple said of the author of "Leaves of Grass," that he had every leaf but the fig leaf.

The audience that assembled to hear my lectures in these six weeks was called, "the *effete* of Boston."

April–May? 1856
It is curious that Thoreau goes to a house to say with little preface what he has just read or observed, delivers it in lump, is quite inattentive to any comment or thought which any of the company offer on the matter, nay, is merely interrupted by it, &, when he has finished his report, departs with precipitation.

My son is coming to get his Latin lesson without me. My son is coming to do without me. And I am coming to do without Plato, or Goethe, or Alcott.

Education. Don't let them eat their seed-corn; don't let them anticipate, or ante-date, & be young men, before they have finished their boyhood. Let them have the fields & woods, & learn their secret & the base & foot-ball, & wrestling, & brickbats, & suck all the strength & courage that lies for them in these games; let them ride bareback, & catch their horse in his pasture, let them hook & spear their fish, & shin a post and a tall tree, & shoot their partridge & trap the woodchuck, before they begin to dress like collegians, & sing in serenades, & make polite calls.

I have but one military recollection in all my life. In 1813 or 1814, all Boston, young & old, turned out to build the fortifications on Noddle's Island; and, the Schoolmaster at the Latin School announced to the boys, that, if we wished, we might all go on a certain day to work on the Island. I went with the rest in the ferry boat, & spent a summer day; but I cannot remember that I did any kind of work. I remember only the pains we took to get water in our tin pails, to relieve our intolerable thirst. I am afraid no valuable effect of my labor remains in the existing defences.

Amos Bronson Alcott (1799–1888): "The Boston Post expressed
the feeling of most readers in its rude joke when it said of his
Orphic Sayings that they 'resembled a train of 15 railroad
cars with one passenger.' "

May 21, 1856

Yesterday to the Sawmill Brook with Henry. He was in search of
yellow violet (pubescens) and menyanthes which he waded into the
water for. & which he concluded, on examination, had been out five
days. Having found his flowers, he drew out of his breast pocket his
diary & read the names of all the plants that should bloom on this day,
20 May; whereof he keeps account as a banker when his notes fall due. . . .
he heard a note which he calls that of the nightwarbler, a bird he has
never identified, has been in search of for twelve years; which, always,
when he sees, is in the act of diving down into a tree or bush, & which
'tis vain to seek; the only bird that sings indifferently by night & by day.
I told him, he must beware of finding & booking him, lest life should
have nothing more to show him. He said, "What you seek in vain for
half your life, one day you come full upon all the family at dinner. You
seek him like a dream, and as soon as you find him, you become his

prey." He thinks he could tell by the flowers what day of the month it is, within two days.

June 1856
I go for those who have received a retaining fee to this party of freedom, before they came into this world. I would trust Garrison, I would trust Henry Thoreau, that they would make no compromises. I would trust Horace Greeley, I would trust my venerable friend Mr Hoar, that they would be staunch for freedom to the death; but both of these would have a benevolent credulity in the honesty of the other party, that I think unsafe.

I see the courtesy of the Carolinians, but I know meanwhile that the only reason why they do not plant a cannon before Faneuil Hall, & blow Bunker Hill monument to fragments, as a nuisance, is because they have not the power. They are fast acquiring the power, & if they get it, they will do it.

June 14, 1856
12 June, at our Kansas relief meeting, in Concord, $962. were subscribed on the spot. Yesterday, the subscription had amounted to $1130.00 and it will probably reach 1200. or one per cent on the valuation of the town.
$1360. I believe was the final amount.

June–July 1856
Professor Poikilus had one advantage over the rest of the University, that when the class gaped or began to diminish, he would with great celerity throw his heels into the air, & stand upon his head, & continue his lecture in that posture, a turn which seemed to invigorate his audience, who would listen with marked cheerfulness as long as he would speak to them in that attitude.

I think the *Ode on the Immortality* the high-water mark which the intellect has reached in this age. A new step has been taken, new means have been employed. No courage has surpassed that, & a way made through the void by this finer Columbus.

July 23, 1856
Returned from Pigeon Cove, where we have made acquaintance with the sea, for seven days. 'Tis a noble friendly power, and seemed to say to me, "Why so late & slow to come to me? Am I not here always,

thy proper summer home? Is not my voice thy needful music; my breath, thy healthful climate in the heats; my touch, thy cure? Was ever building like my terraces? Was ever couch so magnificent as mine? Lie down on my warm ledges and learn that a very little hut is all you need. I have made thy architecture superfluous, and it is paltry beside mine. Here are twenty Romes & Ninevehs & Karnacs in ruins together, obelisk & pyramid and Giants' Causeway, here they all are prostrate or half piled."

And behold the sea, the opaline, plentiful & strong, yet beautiful as the rose or the rainbow, full of food, nourisher of men, purger of the world, creating a sweet climate, and, in its unchangeable ebb & flow, and in its beauty at a few furlongs, giving a hint of that which changes not, & is perfect.

Dec. 1856

One would say that such a dinner party as L. desires, could only be arranged on the Resurrection Day—Zeus of Crete, Pericles of Athens, Rabelais of Paris, Shakspeare of Stratford, Lord Bacon, Dr Franklin, Montaigne, Columbus, Mr Alcott, & Tom Appleton, &c. &c.

Issues and Campaigns
1857-1865

" **I** TOO AM FIGHTING my campaign," Emerson notes in 1864. The dominant issue in his journals of these years is the Civil War—its inevitability, its prosecution, its aftermath. All other chronologies now seemed less important than this one: *Before the War, and Since.* The Transcendentalist had come to see that "it is impossible to extricate oneself from the questions in which your age is involved. You can no more keep out of politics than you can keep out of the frost." Indeed, he conceived of the War as a "frosty October, which shall restore intellectual & moral power to these languid & dissipated populations." The roar of the cannon made other sounds difficult to hear, and the vocabulary of war seeped steadily into his journal. He thought of most people as "raw recruits" so far as immortal life was concerned—"three-months' men, not to enlist for the war"; Henry Thoreau was a general "without a command"; righteous men were "pickets" in the eternal war of principles; the human mind itself "cannot be burned, nor bayonetted, nor wounded, nor missing." The War was bringing out the genius of men, testing the veracity of their speech and attitudes as well as their courage and determination.

Emerson's private campaign in this part of his life, in his mid-fifties and early sixties, concerned his struggle against the loss of physical and mental vigor. Old age was his major complaint, and he proposed to hold an "indignation meeting" against it, as Concord had protested the attack on Charles Sumner in May 1856. He had felt himself threatened by the "ebbtide" as early as 1849, though even before then he complained of a lack of stamina. By 1859 we hear him regretting that he is neglecting his

journal, seeing "few intellectual persons, & even those to no purpose," and generally coming to feel that his brain was pumped
dry and his life "quite at an end." But just as the unnamed visitor
on this day managed to magnetize Emerson's mind and spark new
thoughts, so the vital issues of these years drew him out of his
supposed apathy and gave him new life as a writer and speaker.

Emerson had been denouncing American slavery for two
decades, and he continued to do so during these agitated years.
He also delivered an address at the Woman's Rights Convention
in Boston in September 1855 and argued for "equal rights" and
an "equal share in public affairs." In the journal he noted that his
own "points would be sooner carried in the state if women
voted," and in the summer of 1862 he observed that if "some
strong-minded president of the Woman's Rights Convention
should . . . offer to lead the Army of the Potomac" she would not
"do worse than General Maclellan." Emerson strongly supported
John Brown and composed a letter to the governor of Virginia in
1859 to plead for Brown's life; he also spoke in Salem at a meeting
held to raise funds for Brown's family. He courted unpopularity
in speaking out on these issues and lost some lecture engagements, although one correspondent in Chicago assured him that
the West was "in insurrection to hear Ralph Waldo Emerson."
He knew that audiences wanted to be entertained, but he agreed
with Alcott that the Lyceum was the "University of the people"
and therefore had a serious responsibility.

"As we live longer," Emerson noted in 1862, "we live on in a
lessening minority." Now he was threatened by the loss of Henry
Thoreau, whose long battle with tuberculosis was coming to an
end. Once before, in the summer of 1850, Emerson's circle had
been diminished by the death of Margaret Fuller. "I have lost in
her my audience," he had lamented. "I hurry now to my work
admonished that I have few days left." That was a characteristically dour but unreliable prediction, for now it was the younger
man who was dying. As with Margaret, Emerson's relationship
with Henry had been as difficult as it was rewarding. After the
initial decade or so when their friendship was in its first flush,
Henry's increasing need for independence and Waldo's growing
distaste for his friend's paradoxes and prickly nature produced a
coolness between them. In view of Thoreau's manifest failure as
an author, it was hard for Emerson to take his literary pretensions

much more seriously than he did those of Ellery Channing (the witty poetaster who had married Margaret Fuller's sister and later wrote one of the first biographies of Thoreau). Ellery was equally devoted to both his friends, but Emerson seems to have come to prefer the easy manner and amusing repartee of Channing to the crooked genius of the man who loved to live in a swamp. In the spring of 1862, however, just after Thoreau's death, Emerson had the opportunity to read in his journals and was struck by the "erect, calm, self-subsistent" quality of his nature. But Thoreau was pathfinder for a society he could never abide. His principled aversion to taking an active part in politics and public affairs seemed a tragic waste—perhaps all the more so because he might have fulfilled Emerson's own dream of being a scholar able to legislate for all America. Emerson could not know that Thoreau's writings would help to further the aims of the War by inspiring civil-rights campaigns of a later day.

As an abolitionist "of the most absolute abolition," Emerson hailed the news of Lincoln's election in 1860 as "sublime." The following spring he pronounced the country "cheerful & jocund in the belief that it has a government at last." When he met Lincoln in January 1862 he found him frank and intelligent, "not vulgar, as described." Later he argued that the country was better off with the unrefined taste and simple probity of a Lincoln than with the polished manners of a "malignant selfseeker." He undoubtedly thought of the great leader as the enlargement on a national scale of those upright Concord farmers he had wanted to portray in *Representative Men*—and, in fact, Emerson eulogized him at funeral services in Concord as "the true representative of this continent." That was the highest praise he could offer, for Lincoln's spirit had been absorbed into the common righteousness of his countrymen, and Emerson could conceive of no greater achievement than to "represent humanity."

Jan. 1857 Chicago, Tremont House
   "In 1838," said Dr Boynton, "I came here to Waukegan & there were not so many houses as there are towns now." He got in to the train at Evansville, a town a year & a half old, where are now 600 inhabitants, a Biblical Institute, or Divinity School of the Methodists, to which

a Mrs Garrett lately gave some land in Chicago appraised at $125,000, but which, when they came to sell it, the worser half brought $160,000, & the value of the whole donation, 'tis thought, will be half a million. They had in the same town a College—a thriving institution, which unfortunately blew down one night—but I believe they raised it again the next day, or built another, & no doubt in a few weeks it will eclipse Cambridge & Yale! 'Tis very droll to hear the comic stories of the rising values here, which, ludicrous though they seem, are justified by facts presently. Mr Corwin's story of land offered for 50,000, and an hour given to consider of it. The buyer made up his mind to take it, but he could not have it; it was five minutes past the hour, & it was now worth $60,000. After dinner, he resolved to give the price, but he had overstayed the time again, & it was already 70,000; & it became 80,000, before night, when he bought it. I believe it was Mr Corwin's joke, but the solemn citizen who stood by, heard it approvingly, & said, "Yes, that is about the fair growth of Chicago *per* hour."

March 1857

Captain John Brown of Kansas gave a good account of himself in the Town Hall, last night, to a meeting of Citizens. One of his good points was, the folly of the peace party in Kansas, who believed, that their strength lay in the greatness of their wrongs, & so discountenanced resistance. He wished to know if their wrong was greater than the negro's, & what kind of strength that gave to the negro?

March–May 1857

Men's conscience, I once wrote, is local in spots & veins, here & there, & not in healthy circulation through their system, so that they are unexpectedly good in some passage, & when you infer that they may be depended on in some other case, they heavily disappoint you. . . . I learn from the photograph & daguerre men, that almost all faces & forms which come to their shops to be copied, are irregular & unsymmetrical, have one eye blue & one grey, the nose is not straight, & one shoulder is higher than the other. The man is physically as well as metaphysically a thing of shreds & patches, borrowed unequally from his good & bad ancestors—a misfit from the start.

I once knew of a man who drew a poor girl into his chamber. The girl quickly came to her penitence, & said she was bitterly ashamed. "Ashamed" said the man, "What is there to be ashamed of?" The speeches of our statesmen at Washington are much in the same clear key of correct sentiment, or like Talleyrand's reply to Bonaparte when he asked, "what is all this about non-intervention?"—"Sire, it means about the same as intervention."

Skeptic. I find no more flagrant proof of skepticism than the toleration of slavery. Another is, this running of the girls into popery. They know nothing of religions, & the grounds of the sects; they know that they do like music, & Mozart's masses; & Bach's, & run into the Catholic Church, where these are.

Another is, this mummery of rapping & pseudo spiritualism.

You cannot make a cheap palace.

Because our education is defective, because we are superficial & ill-read, we were forced to make the most of that position, of ignorance; to idealize ignorance. Hence America is a vast Know-Nothing Party, & we disparage books, & cry up intuition. With a few clever men we have made a reputable thing of that, & denouncing libraries & severe culture, & magnifying the motherwit swagger of bright boys from the country colleges, we have even come so far as to deceive every body, except ourselves, into an admiration of un-learning and inspiration forsooth.

We are called a very patient people. Our assemblies are much more passive in the hands of their orators than the English. We do not cough down or roar down the heaviest proser, nor smother by dissent the most unpalatable & injurious. 'Tis a pity that our decorum should make us such lambs & rabbits in the claws of these wolves & foxes of the caucus. We encourage them to tear us by our tameness. They drop their hypocrisy quite too early, & are not at the pains to hide their claw under velvet, from the dear innocents that we are.

The hater of property & of government takes care to have his warranty-deed recorded, and the book written against Fame & learning has the author's name on the title-page.

May 2, 1857
Walk yesterday first day of May with Henry T. . . . Saw a stump of a canoe-birch-tree newly cut down, which had bled a barrel. From a white birch, H. cut a strip of bark to show how a naturalist would make the best box to carry a plant or other specimen requiring care. & thought the woodman would make a better hat of birch-bark than of felt, yes, & pantaloons too—hat, with cockade of lichens, thrown in. . . .

We will make a book on walking, 'tis certain, & have easy lessons for beginners. "Walking in ten Lessons." . . . H. had found, he said, lately a fungus which was a perfect Phallus; & in the books one is noted *Ob-scoenum.*

May 1857

A man signing himself Geo. Ross (of Madison, Wis.) & who seems to be drunk, writes me, that "the secret of drunkenness, is, that it insulates us in thought, whilst it unites us in feeling."

May 25, 1857

At home, Daniel Ricketson expressed some sad views of life & religion. A thunderstorm is a terror to him, and his theism was judaical. Henry thought a new pear-tree was more to purpose, &c. but said better, that an ecstasy was never interrupted. A theology of this kind is as good a meter or yardstick as any other. If I can be scared by a highwayman or a thunderclap, I should say, my performances were not very high, & should at once be mended.

May–June 1857

I do not count the hours I spend in the woods, though I forget my affairs there & my books. And, when there, I wander hither & thither; any bird, any plant, any spring, detains me. I do not hurry homewards for I think all affairs may be postponed to this walking. And it is for this idleness that all my businesses exist.

July 8, 1857

This morning I had the remains of my mother & of my son Waldo removed from the tomb of Mrs Ripley to my lot in "Sleepy Hollow." The sun shone brightly on the coffins, of which Waldo's was well preserved—now fifteen years. I ventured to look into the coffin. I gave a few white-oak leaves to each coffin, after they were put in the new vault, & the vault was then covered with two slabs of granite.

July 1857

There is certainly a convenience in the money scale in the absence of finer metres. In the South a slave is bluntly but accurately valued at 500 to 1000 dollars, if a good working field hand; if a mechanic, as carpenter or smith, at 12, 15, or 20 hundred. A Mulatto girl, if beautiful, rises at once very naturally to high estimation. If beautiful & sprightly-witted, one who is a joy when present, a perpetual entertainment to the eye, &, when absent, a happy remembrance, $2500 & upwards of our money.

In the East, they buy their wives at stipulated prices. Well, shall I not estimate, when the finer anthropometer is wanting, my social properties so? In our club, no man shall be admitted who is not worth in his skin 500,000. One of them, I hold worth a million; for he bows to facts, has no impertinent will, & nobody has come to the bottom of his wit, to the end of his resources. So, in my house, I shall not deign to count myself by my poor taxable estate 20 or 30 thousand, but each of my children is worth, on leaving school, a hundred thousand, as being able to think, speak, feel & act correctly—able to fill the vacant hours, & keep life up to a high point.

July 19, 1857

A visit to Josiah Quincy, Jr., on his old place at Quincy, which has been in the family for seven generations since 1635. . . . There lives the old President, now 85 years old, in the house built by his father in 1770; & Josiah Jr. in a new house built by Billings, 7 years ago. They hold 500 acres, & the land runs down to the sea. From the piazza in the rear of the house of J.Q. Jr. you may see every ship that comes in or goes out of Boston, and most of the islands in the harbor. 'Tis the best placed house I know. The old man I visited on Saturday evening, & on Sunday he came & spent the evening with us at his son's house. He is the most fortunate of men. Old John Adams said that of him; & his good fortune has followed to this hour. His son said to me, "My father has thrown ten times, & every time got doublets." Yet he was engaged to a lady whose existence he did not know of, 7 days before, & she proved the best of wives. I made a very pleasant acquaintance with young Josiah 3d, the poet of "Lyteria." And I like him better than his poem. Charles Francis Adams also was there in the Sunday Evening. Old Quincy still reads & writes with vigor & steadiness 2 or 3 hours every night after tea till ten. He has just finished his "Life of J. Q. Adams."

July 1857

Peirce at Cambridge Observatory told me, that what we call a fine night is often no good night for the telescope; that the sky is not clear for astronomical observation, perhaps more than one night in a month. Of course, they hate to be annoyed by visiters at such times & I can well believe it. My days & hours for observation & record are as few: not every undisturbed day is good for the Muse. The day comes once in a month, & 'tis likely on that day the idle visiter drops in, thinking his coming no intrusion.

July 28, 1857

Yesterday the best day of the year we spent in the afternoon on the river. A sky of Calcutta, light, air, clouds, water, banks, birds, grass, pads, lilies, were in perfection, and it was delicious to live. Ellery

& I went up the South Branch, & took a bath from the bank behind Cyrus Hubbard, where the river makes a bend. Blackbirds in hundreds; swallows in tens sitting on the telegraph lines; & one heron (ardea minor) assisted. In these perfect pictures, one thinks what weary nonsense is all this painful collection of rubbish—pictures of rubbish masters—in the total neglect of this & every lovely river valley, where the multitudinous life & beauty makes these pictures ridiculous cold chalk & ochre.

July 28–Aug. 1, 1857
I can no more manage these thoughts that come into my head than thunderbolts. But once get them written down, I come & look at them every day, & get wonted to their faces, & by & by, am so far used to them, that I see their family likeness, & can pair them & range them better, & if I once see where they belong, & join them in that order they will stay so.

Oct.? 1857
October 14th, the New York & Boston Banks suspended specie payment. And, as usual in hard times, there are all sorts of petty & local reasons given for the pressure, but none that explain it to me. I suppose the reasons are not of yesterday or today; that the same danger has often approached & been avoided or postponed. . . .
I take it as an inevitable incident to this money of civilization. Paper-money is a wonderful convenience, which builds up cities & nations, but it has this danger in it, like a camphene lamp, or a steam-boiler, it will sometimes explode. So excellent a tool we cannot spare, but must take it with its risks. We know the dangers of the railroad but we prefer it with its dangers to the old coach. & we must not forego the high civility of paper & credit, though once in twenty years it breaks the banks, & puts all exchange & traffic at a stand.

Fall–Winter? 1857
Surfaces. Good writing sips the foam of the cup. There are infinite degrees of delicacy in the use of the hands; and good workmen are so distinguished from laborers; & good horsemen, from rude riders; & people of elegant manners, from the vulgar. In writing, it is not less. Montaigne dwells always at the surface, & can chip off a scale, where a coarser hand & eye finds only solid wall.

Henry avoids commonplace, & talks birch bark to all comers, & reduces them all to the same insignificance.

* * *

Alcott makes his large demand on the *Lecture*, that it is the University of the people, & 'tis time they should know at the end of the season what their professors have taught this winter: & it should be gathered by a good reporter in a book what Beecher, Whipple, Parker, Bellows, King, Solger, & Emerson, have taught. But the Lecturer was not allowed to be quite simple, as if he were on his conscience to unfold himself to a college class. But he knew his audience, & used the "adulatory" & "confectionary" arts (according to Plato) to keep them in their seats. He treats them as children; and Mercantile Libraries & Lyceums will all vote, if the question be virtually put to them—we prefer to be entertained, nay, we must be entertained.

I owe real knowledge & even alarming hints to dreams, & wonder to see people extracting emptiness from mahogany tables, when there is vaticination in their dreams. For the soul in dreams has a subtle synthetic power which it will not exert under the sharp eyes of day. It does not like to be watched or looked upon, & flies to real twilights, as the rappers do in their wretched mummeries. If in dreams you see loose & luxurious pictures, an inevitable tie drags in the sequel of cruelty & malignity.

When I higgled for my dime & half dime in the dream, & lost—the parrots on the chimney tops & church pinnacles scoffed at me, Ho! ho!

The shooting complexion, like the cobra capello & scorpion, grows in the South. It has no wisdom, no capacity of improvement: it looks, in every landscape, only for partridges, in every society, for duels. And, as it threatens life, all wise men brave or peaceable run away from the spider-man, as they run away from a black spider: for life to them is real & rich, & not to be risked on any curiosity as to whether spider or spider-man can bite mortally, or only make a poisonous wound. With such a nation or a nation with a predominance of this complexion, war is the safest terms. That marks them, &, if they cross the lines, they can be dealt with as all fanged animals must be.

Is there no check to this class of privileged thieves that infest our politics? We mark & lock up the petty thief or we raise the hue & cry in the street, and do not hesitate to draw our revolvers out of the box, when one is in the house. But here are certain well dressed well-bred fellows, infinitely more mischievous, who get into the government & rob without stint, & without disgrace. They do it with a high hand, & by the device of having a party to whitewash them, to abet the act, & lie, & vote for them. And often each of the larger rogues has his newspaper, called "his organ," to say that it was not stealing, this which he did; that if there was stealing, it was you who stole, & not he. . . . There is no abominable act which these men will not do, & they are not abominated. No meanness below their stooping; yet is there no loathsomeness which their party & the "organ" will not strain its elastic larynx to swallow, & then to crow for it.

I took such pains not to keep my money in the house, but to put it out of the reach of burglars by buying stock, & had no guess that I was putting it into the hands of these very burglars now grown wiser & standing dressed as Railway Directors.

The girl deserts the parlor to hear the delightful naiveté of the Milesians in the kitchen. The boy runs as gladly from the tutors & parents to the uproarious life he finds in the market & the wharf. The college is not so wise as the shop, nor the quarterdeck as the forecastle. Note the inexhaustible interest of the white man about the Indian, & the trapper, & hunter, & sailor. Then how awful are the hints of wit we detect in the horse & dog, & still more in the animals we have not demoralized, like the tiger & the eagle. By what compass the geese steer, & the herrings migrate, we would so gladly know. What the house dog knows, & how he knows it, piques us more than all we heard today from the chair of metaphysics.

My philosophy holds to a few laws. 1. *Identity,* whence comes the fact that *metaphysical faculties & facts are the transcendency of physical.* 2. Flowing, or transition, or shooting the gulf, the perpetual striving to ascend to a higher platform, the same thing in new & higher forms.

If men should take off their clothes, I think the aristocracy would not be less, but more pronounced than now.

Jan. 1858
I found Henry T. yesterday in my woods. He thought nothing to be hoped from you, if this bit of mould under your feet was not sweeter to you to eat, than any other in this world, or in any world. We talked of the willows. He says, 'tis impossible to tell when they push the bud (which so marks the arrival of spring) out of its dark scales. It is done & doing all winter. It is begun in the previous autumn. It seems one steady push from autumn to spring. I say, How divine these studies! Here there is no taint of mortality.

Jan.? 1858

Why do we not say, We are abolitionists of the most absolute abolition, as every man that is a man must be? Only the Hottentots, only the
barbarous or semibarbarous societies are not. We do not try to alter your
laws in Alabama, nor yours in Japan, or the Fee Jee Islands; but we do
not admit them or permit a trace of them here. Nor shall we suffer you
to carry your Thuggism north, south, east, or west into a single rod of
territory which we control. We intend to set & keep a *cordon sanitaire*
all around the infected district, & by no means suffer the pestilence to
spread.

Minds of low & surface power pounce on some fault of expression, of
rhetoric, or petty mis-statement of fact, and quite lose sight of the main
purpose. I knew a lady who thought she knew she had heard my discourse before, because the word *"Arena"* was in both of the two discourses.

Jan.–May 1858

1858
1776
___
82   years count the age of the Union, and yet they say the nation
is as old & infirm as a man is with those years. Now a building is not in
its prime till after 500 years. Nor should a nation be; and we aged at 80!

All the children born in the last three years or 8 years should be
charged with love of liberty, for their parents have been filled with Kansas & antislavery.

You are too historical by half. I show you a grievance, & you proceed to inquire, not if it is mischievous, but if it is old. I point the redress, & you inquire about a constitutional precedent for the redress.
That which only requires perception, mischiefs that are rank & intolerable, which only need to be seen, to be hated & attacked, with you are
ground for argument, & you are already preparing to defend them. The
reliance on simple perception constitutes genius & heroism; and that is
the religion before us.

May 11, 1858

Yesterday with Henry T. at the pond ... I hear the account of the
man who lives in the wilderness of Maine with respect, but with despair.... Henry's hermit, 45 miles from the nearest house, [is not] important, until we know what he is now, what he thinks of it on his re-

turn, & after a year. Perhaps he has found it foolish & wasteful to spend a tenth or a twentieth of his active life with a muskrat & fried fishes.

My dear Henry,
   A frog was made to live in a swamp, but a man was not made to live in a swamp. Yours ever,
                                 R.

May–June 1858
   We are all better in attack than in defence. It is very easy to make acute objections to any style of life, but the objector is quite as vulnerable. Greenough wittily called my speculations *masturbation;* but the artist life seems to me intolerably thin & superficial. I feel the reasonableness of what the lawyer or merchant or laborer has to allege against readers & thinkers, until I look at each of their wretched industries, and find them without end or aim.

   Nature overloads the bias, overshoots the mark, to hit the mark. Her end of reproduction & care of young is so dear to her, that she demoralizes the universe of men with this immense superfluity of attraction in all directions to woman: & see what carnage in relations results! Nothing is so hypocritical as the abuse in all journals—& at the South, especially—of Mormonism & Free-Love Socialism. These men who write the paragraphs in the "Herald" & "Observer," have just come from their brothel, or, in Carolina, from their Mulattoes. How then can you say, that, in nature is always a minimum of force to effect a change? It is a maximum.

Feb.? 1859
   My sheriff ought not to be forgotten down in Maine, who had once tasted a cordial, but did not know the name of it, at some hotel in New York, many years before, & had been tasting liquors at all places in all the United States ever since in the faint hope that he might yet cry *Eureka*, it is the same.

Spring? 1859
   'Tis very important in writing that you do not lose your presence of mind. Despair is no muse, & he who finds himself hurried, & gives up carrying his point this time, writes in vain. Goethe had the *"urkraftige behagen,"* the stout comfortableness, the stomach for the fight, and you must.

* * *

I am a natural reader, & only a writer in the absence of natural writers. In a true time, I should never have written.

The village of Amherst is eagerly discussing the authorship of a paper signed Bifid which appeared in the College Magazine. 'Tis said, if the Faculty knew his name, the author would be expelled from the college. Ten miles off, nobody ever heard of the magazine, or ever will hear of it. In London 'tis of equal interest today whether Lord Palmerston wrote the leader in Wednesday's Times.

I have now for more than a year, I believe, ceased to write in my Journal, in which I formerly wrote almost daily. I see few intellectual persons, & even those to no purpose, & sometimes believe that I have no new thoughts, and that my life is quite at an end. But the magnet that lies in my drawer for years, may believe it has no magnetism, and, on touching it with steel, it shows the old virtue; and, this morning, came by a man with knowledge & interests like mine, in his head, and suddenly I had thoughts again.

Why do I hide in a library, read books, or write them, & skulk in the woods, & not dictate to these fellows, who, you say, dictate to me, as they should not? Why? but because in my bones is none of the magnetism which flows in theirs. They inundate all men with their streams. I have a reception & a perception, which they have not, but it is rare & casual, and yet drives me forth to watch these workers, if so be I may derive from their performance a new insight for mine. But there are no equal terms for me & them. They all unwittingly perform for me the part of the gymnotus on the fish.

The number of conceited people is so great, that it must subserve great uses in nature, like sexual passion.

1. You shall be somebody.
2. You shall have catholicity.
3. You shall know the power of the imagination.

————

You shall come from the Azure.

————

You shall be intellectual.

I delight in persons who clearly perceive the transcendant superiority of Shakspeare to all other writers. I delight in the votaries of the genius of Plato. Because this clear love does not consist with self-conceit.

Not so, when I see youths coming to me with their books & poems. I soon discover that they are egotists & wish my homage.

I have been writing & speaking what were once called novelties, for twenty five or thirty years, & have not now one disciple. Why? Not that what I said was not true; not that it has not found intelligent receivers but because it did not go from any wish in me to bring men to me, but to themselves. I delight in driving them from me. What could I do, if they came to me? they would interrupt & encumber me. This is my boast that I have no school & no follower. I should account it a measure of the impurity of insight, if it did not create independence.

A man finds out that there is somewhat in him that knows more than he does.

Then he comes presently to the curious question, who's who? which of these two is really me? the one that knows more, or the one that knows less? the little fellow, or the big fellow?

No man's egotism covers his personality.

What a Critic is the Age! Calvinism how coherent! how sufficing! how poetic! It stood well every test but the telescope. When that showed the Copernican system to be true, it was too ridiculous to pretend that our little spec of an earth was the central point of nature, &c.

When India was explored, & the wonderful riches of Indian theologic literature found, that dispelled once for all the dream about Christianity being the sole revelation—for, here in India—there in China, were the same principles, the same grandeurs, the like depths moral & intellectual.

Well, we still maintained that we were the true men—we were believers—the rest were heathen. Now comes this doctrine of the pseudo-spiritists to explain to us that we are not Christians, are not believers, but totally unbelieving.

Now & then, rarely comes a stout man like Luther, Montaigne, Pascal, Herbert, who utters a thought or feeling in a virile manner, and it is unforgettable. Then follow any number of spiritual eunuchs and women who talk about that thought, imply it, in pages & volumes. . . .

Great bands of female souls who only receive the spermatic aura & brood on the same but add nothing.

People live like these boys who watch for a sleigh-ride & mount on the first that passes, & when they meet another that they know, swing themselves on to that, & ride in another direction, until a third passes, & they change again; 'tis no matter where they go, as long as there is snow & company.

Shall I blame my mother, whitest of women, because she was not a gipsy, & gave me no swarthy ferocity? or my father, because he came of a lettered race, & had no porter's shoulders?

May 25, 1859
The warblers at this season make much of the beauty & interest of the woods. They are so elegant in form & coat, and many of them here but for a short time; the Blackburnian warbler rarely seen by H. D. T.; the trees still allowing you to see far. Their small leaflets do not vie with the spaces of the sky—but let in the vision high—and (yesterday) Concord was all Sicily.

May? 1859
'Tis pity to see egotism for its poverty. All must talk about themselves, for 'tis all they know, but genius never needs to allude to his personality, as every person & creature he has seen serves him as an exponent of his private experience. So he communicates all his secrets, and endless autobiography, & never lets on that he means himself.

Dante cannot utter a few lines but I am informed what transcendent eyes he had, as, for example,

> "un foco
> Ch' emisperio di tenebre vincia."

How many millions would have looked at candles, lamps, & fires, & planets, all their days, & never noticed this measure of their illuminating force, "of conquering a hemisphere of the darkness." Yet he says nothing about his own eyes.

What marks right mental action is always newness, ignoring of the past; & the elasticity of the present object—which makes all the magnitudes & magnates quite unnecessary. This is what we mean when we say your subject is absolutely indifferent. You need not write the History of the World, nor the Fall of Man, nor King Arthur, nor Iliad, nor Christianity; but write of hay, or of cattleshows, or trade sales, or of a ship, or of Ellen, or Alcott, or of a couple of school-boys, if only you can be the fanatic of your subject, & find a fibre reaching from it to the core of your heart, so that all your affection & all your thought can freely play.

May–Aug.? 1859

T. Appleton says, that he thinks that all Bostonians, when they die, if they are good, go to Paris.

Aug. 16–19, 1859

Am I not, one of these days, to write consecutively of the beatitude of intellect? It is too great for feeble souls, and they are overexcited. The wineglass shakes, & the wine is spilled. What then? The joy which will not let me sit in my chair, which brings me bolt upright to my feet, & sends me striding around my room, like a tiger in his cage, and I cannot have composure & concentration enough even to set down in English words the thought which thrills me—is not that joy a certificate of the elevation? What if I never write a book or a line? For a moment, the eyes of my eyes were opened, the affirmative experience remains, & consoles through all suffering.

On Wachusett, I sprained my foot. It was slow to heal, & I went to the doctors. Dr H. Bigelow said, "a splint, & absolute rest;" Dr Russell said, "rest yes; but a splint, no." Dr Bartlett said, "neither splint nor rest, but go & walk." Dr Russell said, "Pour water on the foot, but it must be warm." Dr Jackson said, "stand in a trout brook all day."

Aug. 20, 1859

Home is a good place in August. We have plenty of sopsavines, & Moscow Transparents, & the sweet apple we call Early Bough . . .

Aug.–Sept. 1859

Mr Crump. The unfortunate days of August & September, when the two cows were due from the Temple Pasture, & did not arrive, & we learn that they strayed on the way, & are lost. When the Muster approached bringing alarms to all housekeepers & orchard-owners. When the foot was lame, & the hand was palsied, & the foot mending was lame again. When a strong southwest wind blew in vicious gusts, all day, stripping every loaded pear-tree of its fruit, just six weeks too early. The beggars arrive every day, some on foot, the Sardinians & Sicilians, who cannot argue the question of labor & mendicity with you, since they do not speak a word of English; then the Monumentals, who come in landaus or barouches, & wish your large aid to Mt Vernon; Plymouth; Ball's Webster; or President Quincy in marble; then the chipping lady from the Cape who has three blind sisters, & I know not how many dumb ones, & she had been advised to put them in the Poor House. No, not she. As long as she had health, she would go about & sell these books

Nathaniel Hawthorne (1804–1864): "I thought him a greater man than any of his works betray."

for them, which I am to buy, and she tosses her head, & expects my praise & tears for her heroic resolution; though I had a puzzled feeling, that, if there was sacrifice anywhere it was in me, if I should buy them; & I am sure I was very little inclined to toss my head on the occasion.

Mr Crump remarked that he hated lame folks: there was no telling how hypocritical they were. They are dreadful lame when you see them, but the lamest of them, if he wants something, & there's nobody will help him to it, will manage to get it himself, though it were a mile off; *if you are not by.*

I think wealth has lost much of its value, if it have not wine. I abstain from wine only on account of the expense. When I heard that Mr Sturgis had given up wine, I had the same regret that I had lately in hearing that Mr Bowditch had broken his hip; a millionaire without wine, & a millionaire that must lie on his bed.

* * *

Dr Johnson is a good example of the force of temperament. 'Tis surprising how often I am reminded of my Aunt Mary E. in reading Boswell lately. Johnson impresses his company as she does, not only by the point of the remark, but also when the point fails, because he makes it. Like hers, his obvious religion or superstition, his deep wish that they should think so or so, weighs with them, so rare is depth of feeling, or a constitutional value for a thought or opinion, among the lightminded men & women who make up society. And this, though in both cases, their companions know that there is a degree of shortcoming, & of insincerity, & of talking for victory. Yet the existence of character and habitual reverence of principles over talent or learning is felt by the frivolous.

Fall? 1859

The resistance to slavery—it is the old mistake of the slaveholder to impute the resistance to Clarkson or Pitt, to Channing or Garrison, or to some John Brown whom he has just captured, & to make a personal affair of it; & he believes, whilst he chains & chops him, that he is getting rid of his tormentors; and does not see that the air which this man breathed is liberty, & is breathed by thousands & millions; that men of the same complexion as he, will look at slaveholders as felons who have disentitled themselves to the protection of law, as the burglar has, whom I see breaking into my neighbor's house; and therefore no matter how many Browns he can catch & kill, he does not make the number less, for the air breeds them, every school, every church, every domestic circle, every home of courtesy, genius, & conscience is educating haters of him & his misdeeds.

We talk of Sparta & Rome, we dilettanti of liberty.

But the last thing a brave man thinks of is Sparta or Scythia or the Gauls: he is up to the top of his boots in his own meadow, & can't be bothered with histories. That will do for a winter evening with schoolboys. As soon as a man talks Washington & Putnam & General Jackson to me, I detect the coxcomb & charlatan. He is a frivolous nobody who has no duties of his own.

Anna Ward was at a loss in talking with me, because I had no church whose weakness she could show up, in return for my charges upon hers. I said to her, Do you not see that though I have no eloquence & no flow of thought, yet that I do not stoop to accept any thing less than truth? that I sit here contented with my poverty, mendicity, & deaf & dumb estate, from year to year, from youth to age, rather than adorn myself with any red rag of false church or false association? My low & lonely

sitting here by the wayside, is my homage to truth, which I see is sufficient without me; which is honored by my abstaining, not by superser-
viceableness. I see how grand & selfsufficing it is; how it burns up, &
will none of your shifty patchwork of additions & ingenuities.

Brown shows us, said H. D. T., another school to send our boys
to—that the best lesson of oratory is to speak the truth. A lesson rarely
learned—To stand by the truth. We stand by our party, our trade,
our reputation, our talent, but these each lead away from the truth.
That is so volatile & vital, evanescing instantly from all but dedication to
it.

And yet inspiration is that, to be so quick as truth; to drop the load of
Memory & of Futurity, Memory & Care, & let the moment suffice us:
then one discovers that the first thought is related to all thought & carries power & fate in its womb.

Mattie Griffith says, if Brown is hung, the gallows will be sacred as
the cross.

April–May 1860

The teaching of politics is that the Government which was set for
protection & comfort of all good citizens, becomes the principal obstruction & nuisance, with which we have to contend. Wherever we
look, whether to Kansas, to Utah, to the frontier—as Mexico & Cuba, or
to laws & contracts for internal improvement, the capital enemy in the
way is always this ugly government.

We could manage very well by private enterprise, for carrying the
mails, associations for emigration, & emigrant aid, for local police & defence, & for prevention of crime; but the cheat & bully & malefactor we
meet everywhere is the Government.

This can only be counteracted by magnifying the local powers at its
cost. Take from the U.S. the appointment of postmasters & let the
towns elect them, and you deprive the Federal Government of half a
million defenders.

Death. When our friends die, we not only lose them, but we lose a
great deal of life which in the survivors was related to them.

Advantages of old age. I reached the other day the end of my fifty
seventh year, and am easier in my mind than hitherto. I could never give
much reality to evil & pain. But now when my wife says, perhaps this
tumor on your shoulder is a cancer, I say, what if it is? It would not
make the gentleman on his way in a cart to the gallows very unhappy, to
tell him that the pain in his knee threatened a white swelling.

Oct. 1860   Earthquake 17 Oct. at 6 a.m.

Queenie's private earthquake. We had disputed about the duration of the vibrations, which I thought lasted 12 seconds, and she insisted returned at intervals of two minutes. Of course our accounts could not agree; but, yesterday, it chanced to turn out, that her earthquake was *in the afternoon,* & that of the rest of the world at 6 in the morning.

Nov. 15, 1860

The news of last Wednesday morning (7th) was sublime, the pronunciation of the masses of America against Slavery.* And now on Tuesday 14th I attended the dedication of the Zoological Museum at Cambridge, an auspicious & happy event, most honorable to Agassiz & to the State. On Wednesday 7th, we had Charles Sumner here at Concord & my house. Yesterday eve I attended at the Lyceum in the Town Hall the Exhibition of Stereoscopic views magnified on the wall, which seems to me the last & most important application of this wonderful art: for here was London, Paris, Switzerland, Spain, &, at last, Egypt, brought visibly & accurately to Concord, for authentic examination by women & children, who had never left their state. Cornelius Agrippa was fairly outdone. And the lovely manner in which one picture was changed for another beat the faculty of dreaming. Edward thought that "the thanks of the town should be presented to Mr Munroe, for carrying us to Europe, & bringing us home, without expense." An odd incident of yesterday was that I received a letter or envelope mailed from Frazer, Pennsylvania enclosing no letter but a blank envelope containing a Ten dollar bank note.

Jan. 4, 1861

I hear this morning, whilst it is snowing fast, the chicadee singing.

Jan.? 1861

We can easily come up to the average culture & performance; not easily go beyond it. I often think of the poor caterpillar, who, when he gets to the end of a straw or a twig in his climbing, throws his head uneasily about in all directions; he is sure he has legs & muscle & head enough to go further indefinitely—but what to do? he is at the end of his twig.

Jan. 1861

We have no guess what we are doing, even then when we do our best; perhaps it will not appear for an age or two yet: then, the dim out-

---

*Emerson is referring to the election of Lincoln.

line of the reef & new continent we madrepores were making, will sketch itself to the eyes of the dullest sailer. Luther would cut his hand off sooner than write theses against the Pope, if he suspected that he was bringing on with all his might the pale negations of Boston Unitarianism.

The furious slaveholder does not see that the one thing he is doing, by night & by day, is, to destroy slavery. They who help & they who hinder are all equally diligent in hastening its downfall. Blessed be the inevitabilities.

The best thing I heard yesterday was Henry James's statement, that, in the spiritual world, the very lowest function was Governing. In heaven, as soon as one wishes to rule, or despises others he is thrust out at the door.

Another fine spiritual statement which he made, was, to the effect, that all which men value themselves for as religious progress—going alone, renouncing, & self-mortifying, to attain a certain religious superiority—was the way *from*, not the way *to* what they seek; for, it is only as our existence is shared, not as it is self-hood, that it is divine.

Jan.–Feb. 1861

I know no more irreconcileable persons ever brought to annoy & confound each other in one room than are sometimes actually lodged by nature in one man's skin. Thus I knew a saint of a woman who lived in ecstasies of devotion, "a pensive nun devout & pure," and who, moved by pity for a poor schoolmistress, undertook one day to give her a little vacation which she sorely needed, & took her place in the school: but, when the children whispered, or did not mind their book, she stuck a pin into their arms, & never seemed to suspect the cruelty. I knew a gentle imaginative soul, all poetry & sympathy, who hated every inmate of his house, & drove away his dog, by starving him. Rousseau left his children at the Foundling Hospital. Mrs Ripley at Brook Farm, said the hard selfishness of the socialists ruined the Community. Hawthorne, I believe, sued the members for their debt to him. Howard the great philanthropist was harsh to his children, & Sterne the sentimentalist had a bad name for hardness to his mother.

Overture of the Quintette Club last evening.

Tuttle tuttle lira
tuttle tuttle liro
tuttle tuttle polywog po
tuttle tuttle up the stairs

tuttle tuttle out the window
tuttle tuttle all the world over
tuttle tuttle arms akimbo
tuttle tuttle all go smash.

Because I have no ear for music, at the concert it looked to me as if the performers were crazy, and all the audience were making-believe crazy, in order to soothe the lunatics, & keep them amused.

Edward's gameparty verse

The Kangaroo goes hop, hop, hop,
Until the hunter does her pop,
But when she fears partickler fits,
She ups & pockets all her kits.

Feb. 1861
Gurowski asked "Where is this bog? I wish to earn some money: I wish to dig peat."—"O no, indeed, sir, you cannot do this kind of degrading work."—"I cannot be degraded. I am Gurowski."

I often say to young writers & speakers, that their best masters are their faultfinding brothers & sisters at home, who will not spare them, but be sure to pick & cavil, & tell the odious truth. It is smooth mediocrity, weary elegance, surface finish of our voluminous stock-writers, or respectable artists, which easy times & a dull public call out, without any salient genius, with an indigence of all grand design, of all direct power. A hundred statesmen, historians, painters, & small poets, are thus made: but Burns, & Carlyle, & Bettine, and Michel Angelo, & Thoreau were pupils in a rougher school.

It is very hard to go beyond your public. If they are satisfied with your poor performance, you will not easily make better. But if they know what is good & delight in it, you will aspire, & burn, & toil, till you achieve it.

Do the duty of the day. Just now, the supreme public duty of all thinking men is to assert freedom. Go where it is threatened, & say, 'I am for it, & do not wish to live in the world a moment longer than it exists.'

Phillips has the supreme merit in this time, that he & he alone stands in the gap & breach against the assailants. Hold up his hands. He did me the honor to ask me to come to the meeting at Tremont Temple, &, esteeming such invitation a command, though sorely against my inclination & habit, I went, and, though I had nothing to say, showed myself. If I were dumb, yet I would have gone & mowed & muttered or made signs. The mob roared whenever I attempted to speak, and after several beginnings, I withdrew.

I read many friendly & many hostile paragraphs in the journals about my new book, but seldom or never a just criticism. As long as I do not wince, it cannot be that the fault is touched. When the adept applies his galvanic battery now to this part, then to that, on the patient's head, the patient makes no sign, for lungs are sound, & liver, & heart: but, at last, he touches another point, & the patient screams, for it seems there is bronchitis, or is hip disease.

And when the critics hit you, I suppose you will know it. I often think I could write a criticism on Emerson that would hit the white.

Feb.–March 1861

I like dry light, & hard clouds, hard expressions, & hard manners.

What came over me with delight as I sat on the ledge in the warm light of last Sunday, was the memory of young days at College, the delicious sensibility of youth, how the air rings to it! how all light is festal to it! how it at any moment extemporizes a holiday! I remember how boys riding out together on a fine day looked to me! ah there was a romance! How sufficing was mere melody! The thought, the meaning was insignificant; the whole joy was in the melody. For that I read poetry, & wrote it; and in the light of that memory I ought to understand the doctrine of Musicians, that the words are nothing, the air is all.

What a joy I found, & still find, in the Aeolian harp! What a youth find I still in Collins's "Ode to Evening", & in Gray's "Eton College"! What delight I owed to Moore's insignificant but melodious poetry! That is the merit of Clough's "Bothie", that the joy of youth is in it. Ah the power of the spring! and, ah the voice of the bluebird! And the witchcraft of the Mount Auburn dell, in those days! I shall be a Squire Slender for a week.*

March 16, 1861

I have seldom paid money with so much pleasure as today to Dr Barrett, fifty cents, for taking with a probe a little cinder out of my left eye, which had annoyed me for a week.

---

*Slender is a country lout in Shakespeare's *Merry Wives of Windsor*.

April 1861

When somebody said to Rev. Dr Payson "how much you must enjoy religion, since you live always in administering it," he replied, that nobody enjoyed religion less than ministers, as none enjoyed food so little as cooks.

Bishop Clark of Rhode Island told of a dispute in a vestry at Providence between two hot church-members. One said at last, "I should like to know who *you* are."—"Who I am!" cried the other, "Who I am! I am a humble Christian, you damned old heathen, you!"

One capital advantage of old age is the absolute insignificance of a success more or less. I went to town & read a lecture yesterday. Thirty years ago it had really been a matter of importance to me whether it was good & effective. Now it is of none in relation to me. It is long already fixed what I can & what I cannot do, & the reputation of the man does not gain or suffer from one or a dozen new performances. If I should in a new performance rise quite beyond my mark, & do somewhat extraordinary & great, that, to be sure, would instantly tell; but I may go below my mark with impunity. 'O, he had a headache, or lost his sleep for two nights.' Great are the benefits of old age!

May 1861

The country is cheerful & jocund in the belief that it has a government at last. The men in search of a party, parties in search of a principle, interests & dispositions that could not fuse for want of some base— all joyfully unite in this great Northern party, on the basis of Freedom. What a healthy tone exists! I suppose when we come to fighting, & many of our people are killed, it will yet be found that the bills of mortality in the country will show a better result of this year than the last, on account of the general health; no dyspepsia, no consumption, no fevers, where there is so much electricity, & conquering heart & mind.

So in finance, the rise of wheat paid the cost of the Mexican War; & the check on fraud & jobbing & the new prosperity of the West will pay the new debt.

May–June 1861

Our horizon is not far—say, one generation, or 30 years—we all see so much. The older see two generations, or 60 years; but what has been running on through three horizons, or 90 years, looks to all the world like a law of nature, & 'tis an impiety to doubt. Thus, 'tis incredible to us if we look into the sermons & religious books of our grand-fathers, how they held themselves in such a pinfold. But why not? as far as they could see, through two or three horizons, nothing but ministers, ministers, ministers. In other countries or districts, 'tis all soldiering, or sheep farms, or shoe-making, or Vermont cattle-driving.

Aug.–Sept. 1861
It occurs that I should like to have the statistics of bold experimenting on the husbandry of mental power. In England, men of letters drink wine; in Scotland whiskey; in France wine; in Germany beer. In England, everybody rides in the saddle. In France, the theatre & the ball occupy the night. In this country, we have not learned how to repair the exhaustions of our climate. Is the sea necessary in summer? Is amusement, is fishing, is bowling, hunting, jumping, dancing, one or all needful?

I am at a loss to understand why people hold Miss Austen's novels at so high a rate, which seem to me vulgar in tone, sterile in invention, imprisoned in the wretched conventions of English society, without genius, wit, or knowledge of the world. Never was life so pinched & narrow. The one problem in the mind of the writer in both the stories I have read, "Persuasion", and "Pride & Prejudice", is marriageableness; all that interests in any character introduced is still this one, Has he or she money to marry with, & conditions conforming? 'Tis "the nympholepsy of a fond despair", say rather, of an English boarding-house. Suicide is more respectable.

Sept. 9, 1861
Last night a pictorial dream fit for Dante. I read a discourse somewhere to an assembly, & rallied in the course of it to find that I had nearly or quite fallen asleep. Then presently I went into what seemed a new house, the inside wall of which had many shelves let into the wall, on which great & costly Vases of Etruscan & other richly adorned pottery stood. The wall itself was unfinished, & I presently noticed great clefts, intended to be filled with mortar or brickwork, but not yet filled, & the wall which held all these costly vases, threatening to fall. Then I noticed in the centre shelf or alcove of the wall a man asleep, whom I understood to be the architect of the house. I called to my brother William who was near me, & pointed to this sleeper as the architect, when the man turned, & partly arose, & muttered something about a plot to expose him.
When I fairly woke, & considered the picture, & the connection of the two dreams—what could I think of the purpose of Jove who sends the dream?

Sept. 1861

The war searches character, & acquits those whom I acquit, whom life acquits, those whose reality & spontaneous honesty & singleness appear. Force it requires. 'Tis not so much that you are moral, as that you are genuine, sincere, frank, & bold. I do not approve those who give money, or give their voices for liberty, from long habit, & the feminine predominance of sentiment; but the rough democrat who hates Garrison, but detests these southern traitors. The first class will go in the right way, but they are devoured by sentiments, like premature fruit ripened by the worm.

The "logic of events" has become a household word.

Dec. 1861

Good writing how rare! . . . the old Psalms & Gospels are mighty as ever: showing that what people call religion is literature; that is to say—here was one who knew how to put his statement, & it stands forever, & people feel its truth, as he did, & say, *Thus said the Lord,* whilst it is only that he had the true literary genius, which they fancy they despise.

Jan. 9, 1862

We should so gladly find the law of thought unmechanical: but 'tis a linked chain—drop one link, & there is no recovery. When newly awaked from lively dreams, we are so near them, still agitated by them, still in their sphere—give us one syllable, one feature, one hint, & we should re-possess the whole—hours of this strange entertainment & conversation would come trooping back to us; but we cannot get our hand on the first link or fibre, and the whole is forever lost. There is a strange wilfulness in the speed with which it disperses, & baffles your grasp.

I ought to have preserved the Medical Journal's notice of R. W. E. in Philadelphia, that, of all the persons on the platform, Mr E. was the least remarkable looking, &c.—which I could very often match with experiences in hotels, & in private circles.

Jan. 1862

Sources of inspiration.

1. sleep is one, mainly by the sound health it produces; incidentally also, & rarely, by dreams, into whose farrago a divine lesson is sometimes slipped.

2. solitary converse with nature is a second (or perhaps the first) and there are ejaculated sweet & dreadful words never uttered in libraries. Ah the spring days, summer dawns, & October woods.

3. New poetry; what is new to me, whether in recent manuscript or in Caxton black letter.

4. Conversation . . .

Mr Crump thinks, that, if there is one thing more disagreeable than another, it is getting up in the morning. Especially (adds Mr C., on second thought) as people are getting older; for, as long as you lie warm in your bed, one seems to be as good as another; but when you get up, & have to put yourself together, & find your wig, & your teeth, & your spectacles, & cane, you had better been asleep, or not been at all.

Jan. 17, 1862

We will not again disparage America, now that we have seen what men it will bear. What a certificate of good elements in the soil, climate, & institutions is Lowell, whose admirable verses I have just read! Such a creature more accredits the land than all the fops of Carolina discredit it.

Long ago I wrote of "Gifts," & neglected a capital example. John Thoreau, Jr. one day put up a bluebird's box on my barn fifteen years ago, it must be—and there it is still with every summer a melodious family in it, adorning the place, & singing his praises. There's a gift for you which cost the giver no money, but nothing he could have bought would be so good. I think of another quite inestimable. John Thoreau, Junior, knew how much I should value a head of little Waldo, then five years old. He came to me, & offered to carry him to a daguerrotypist who was then in town, & he, Thoreau, would see it well done. He did it, & brought me the daguerre which I thankfully paid for. In a few months after, my boy died, and I have ever since had deeply to thank John Thoreau for that wise & gentle piece of friendship.

To a perfect foot no place is slippery.

Old Age

As we live longer, it looks as if our company were picked out to die first, & we live on in a lessening minority. . . . I am ever threatened by the decays of Henry T.

Jan. 1862

It is impossible to extricate oneself from the questions in which your age is involved. You can no more keep out of politics than you can keep out of the frost.

Jan. 31, 1862   Visit to Washington

At Washington, 31 January, 1 Feb, 2d, & 3d, saw Sumner, who on the 2d, carried me to Mr Chase, Mr Bates, Mr Stanton, Mr Welles, Mr Seward, Lord Lyons, and President Lincoln. The President impressed me more favorably than I had hoped. A frank, sincere, well-meaning man, with a lawyer's habit of mind, good clear statement of his fact, correct enough, not vulgar, as described; but with a sort of boyish cheerfulness, or that kind of sincerity & jolly good meaning that our class meetings on Commencement Days show, in telling our old stories over. When he has made his remark, he looks up at you with great satisfaction, & shows all his white teeth, & laughs. He argued to Sumner the whole case of Gordon, the slave-trader, point by point, and added that he was not quite satisfied yet, & meant to refresh his memory by looking again at the evidence.

All this showed a fidelity & conscientiousness very honorable to him.

When I was introduced to him, he said, "O Mr Emerson, I once heard you say in a lecture, that a Kentuckian seems to say by his air & manners, *'Here am I; if you don't like me, the worse for you.'*"

Mr Seward received us in his dingy State Department.... He began, "Yes I know Mr Emerson. The President said yesterday, when I was going to tell him a story, 'Well, Seward, don't let it be smutty.' And I remember when a witness was asked in court, 'Do you know this man?' 'Yes, I know him.'—'How do you know him?' 'Why I know him. I can't say I have carnal knowledge of him, &c.'"

The next morning, at 10¼, I visited Mr Seward, in his library, who was writing, surrounded by his secretary & some stock brokers....

We went to Church. I told him "I hoped he would not demoralize me; I was not much accustomed to churches, but trusted he would carry me to a safe place." He said, he attended Rev. Dr Pyne's Church. On the way, we met Gov. Fish, who was also to go with him. Miss Seward, to whom I had been presented, accompanied us. I was a little aukward in finding my place in the Common Prayer Book, & Mr Seward was obliging in guiding me, from time to time. But I had the old wonder come over me at the Egyptian stationariness of the English church. The hopeless blind antiquity of life & thought—indicated alike by prayers & creed & sermon—was wonderful to see, & amid worshippers & in times like these. There was something exceptional too in the Doctor's sermon. His church was all made up of secessionists; he had remained loyal, they had all left him, & abused him in the papers: And in the sermon he represented his griefs, & preached Jacobitish passive obedience to powers that be, as his defence. In going out, Mr S. praised the sermon. I said that the Doctor did not seem to have read the Gospel according to San Francisco, or the Epistle to the Californians; he had not got quite down into these noisy times.

Mr S. said, "Will you go & call on the President? I usually call on him at this hour." Of course, I was glad to go.

We found in the President's chamber his two little sons—boys of 7 & 8 years perhaps—whom the barber was dressing & "whiskeying their hair," as he said, not much to the apparent contentment of the boys, when the cologne got into their eyes. The eldest boy immediately told Mr Seward, "he could not guess what they had got." Mr Seward "bet a quarter of a dollar that he could.—Was it a rabbit? was it a bird? was it a pig?" he guessed always wrong, & *paid his quarter* to the youngest, before the eldest declared it was a rabbit. But he sent away the mulatto to find the President, & the boys disappeared. The President came, and Mr Seward said, "You have not been to Church today." "No," he said, "and, if he must make a frank confession, he had been reading for the first time Mr Sumner's speech (on the Trent affair)." . . .

Mr Seward told the President somewhat of Dr Pyne's sermon, & the President said, he intended to show his respect for him some time by going to hear him.

In the Congressional Library I found Spofford Assistant Librarian. He told me, that, for the last twelve (?) years, it had been under Southern domination, & as under dead men. Thus the Medical department was very large, and the Theological very large, whilst of modern literature very imperfect.

There was no copy of the "Atlantic Monthly," or of the "Knickerbocker," none of the "Tribune," or "Times," or any N.Y. Journal. There was no copy of the "London Saturday Review" taken, or any other live journal, but the "London Court Journal," in a hundred volumes, duly bound. Nor was it possible now to mend matters, because no money could they get from Congress, though an appropriation had been voted.

Feb. 1862

H D T . . .

Perhaps his fancy for Walt Whitman grew out of his taste for wild nature, for an otter, a wood-chuck, or a loon.

He loved sufficiency, hated a sum that would not prove: loved Walt & hated Alcott.

* * *

Therien came to see Thoreau on business, but Thoreau at once perceived that he had been drinking; and advised him to go home & cut his throat, and that speedily. Therien did not well know what to make of it, but went away, & Thoreau said, he learned that he had been repeating it about town, which he was glad to hear, & hoped that by this time he had begun to understand what it meant.

The old school of Boston citizens whom I remember in my childhood had great vigor, great noisy bodies or I think certain sternutatory vigor, the like whereof I have not heard again. When Major B, or old Mr T. H. took out their pocket handkerchiefs at church, it was plain they meant business; they would snort & roar through their noses, like the lowing of an ox, & make all ring again. Ah, it takes a Northender to do that!

Holmes came out late in life with a strong sustained growth for two or three years, like old pear trees which have done nothing for ten years, & at last begin & grow great. The Lowells come forward slowly, & H. T. remarks, that men may have two growths like pears.

March 3, 1862
The snow still lies even with the tops of the walls across the Walden road, and, this afternoon, I waded through the woods to my grove. A chicadee came out to greet me, flew about within reach of my hands, perched on the nearest bough, flew down into the snow, rested there two seconds, then up again, just over my head, & busied himself on the dead bark. I whistled to him through my teeth, and (I think, in response) he began at once to whistle. I promised him crumbs, & must not go again to these woods without them. I suppose the best food to carry would be the meat of shagbarks or castille nuts. Thoreau tells me that they are very sociable with wood-choppers, & will take crumbs from their hands.

March 1862
Montgomery Blair rightly thinks, that, Salmon P. Chase, because he was always a Whig, will not have nerve. The Unitarians, born unitarians, have a pale shallow religion; but the Calvinist born & reared under his rigorous, ascetic, scowling creed, & then ripened into a Unitarian, becomes powerful, as Dr Channing, Dewey, Horace Mann, Wasson, Garrison, & others. So is it in politics. A man must have had the broad audacious Democratic party for his nursingmother, and be ripened into a Free soiler, to be efficient . . .

* * *

Latimer's story, that his father taught him not to shoot with his arms, but to lay his body to the bow, should be remembered by writers. The labial speech instead of the stomachic, afflicts me in all the poetry I read, even though on a gay or trifling subject. Why has never the poorest country college offered me a professorship of rhetoric? I think I could have taught an orator, though I am none.

March 24, 1862

Samuel Staples yesterday had been to see Henry Thoreau. Never spent an hour with more satisfaction. Never saw a man dying with so much pleasure & peace. Thinks that very few men in Concord know Mr Thoreau; finds him serene & happy.

Henry praised to me lately the manners of an old, established, calm, well-behaved river, as perfectly distinguished from those of a new river. A new river is a torrent; an old one slow & steadily supplied. What happens in any part of the old river relates to what befals in every other part of it. 'Tis full of compensations, resources, & reserved funds.

April 1862

Spring. Why complain of the cold slow spring? the bluebirds don't complain, the blackbirds make the maples ring with social cheer & jubilee, the robins know the snow must go & sparrows with prophetic eye that these bare osiers yet will hide their future nests in the pride of their foliage. And you alone with all your six feet of experience are the fool of the cold of the present moment, & cannot see the southing of the sun. Besides the snowflake is freedom's star.

April–May 1862

The first care of a man settling in the country should be to open the face of the earth to himself by a little knowledge of nature, or a great deal of knowledge, if he can, of birds, plants, & astronomy, in short, the art of taking a walk. This will draw the sting out of frost, dreariness out of November & March, & drowsiness out of August. To know the trees is, as Spenser says of the ash, "for nothing ill." Shells, too—how hungry I found myself the other day at Agassiz's Museum, for their names.

But the uses of the woods are many, & some of them for the scholar high & peremptory. When his task requires the wiping out from memory "all trivial fond records that youth & observation copied there," requires self-communion & insights: he must leave the house, the streets, & the club, & go to wooded uplands, to the clearing, & the brook. Well for him if he can say with the old Minstrel, 'I know where to find a new song.'

* * *

Resources or feats. I like people who can do things. When Edward &
I struggled in vain to drag our big calf into the barn, the Irish girl put
her finger into the calf's mouth, & led her in directly. When you find
your boat full of water at the shore of the pond & strive to drag it ashore
to empty it, Tom puts a round stick underneath, & 'tis on wheels
directly.

June–July 1862

Henry T. remains erect, calm, self-subsistent, before me, and I read
him not only truly in his Journal, but he is not long out of mind when I
walk, and, as today, row upon the pond. He chose wisely no doubt for
himself to be the bachelor of thought & nature that he was—how near to
the old monks in their ascetic religion! He had no talent for wealth, &
knew how to be poor without the least hint of squalor or inelegance.

Perhaps he fell, all of us do, into his way of living, without forecast-
ing it much, but approved & confirmed it with later wisdom.

I am so sensible to cold, that one of the abatements of the displeasure
of dying is the pleasure of escaping the east winds & north winds of
Massachusetts.

1862?

Thoreau's page reminds me of Farley, who went early into the wilderness in Illinois, lived alone, & hewed down trees, & tilled the land,
but retired again into newer country when the population came up with
him. Yet, on being asked, what he was doing? said, he pleased himself
that he was preparing the land for civilization.

June–July 1862

If there is a little strut in the style, it is only from a vigor in excess of
the size of his body. His determination on natural history is organic: he
sometimes felt like a hound or a panther &, if born among Indians,
would have been a fell hunter: restrained, modified by his Massachusetts
culture he played out the game in this mild form of botany & ichthyol-
ogy.

I see many generals without a command, besides Henry.

The points that glowed a little in yesterday's conversation, were,
that the North must succeed. That is sure, was sure for 30 or 60 years
back, was in the education, culture, & climate of our people—they are

bound to put through their undertakings. The exasperations of our people by the treacheries & savageness of the Southern warfare are most wholesome disinfectants from the potent influence of Southern manners on our imagination. It was certain also that the Southerner would misbehave; that he will not keep his word; that he will be overbearing, rapacious. Slavery corrupts & denaturalizes people. . . . There is no more probity in a slaveholder than truth in a drunken Irishman. Our success is sure. Its roots are in our poverty, our Calvinism, our schools, our thrifty habitual industry, in our snow, & east wind, & farm-life, & sealife. These able & generous merchants are the sons & grandsons of farmers, & mechanics & sailors.

If we should ever print Henry's journals, you may look for a plentiful crop of naturalists. Young men of sensibility must fall an easy prey to the charming of Pan's pipe.

July–Aug. 1862
I read with entire complacency that part of the history of art when the new spiritualism set the painters on painting the saints as ugly & inferior men, to hint the indifference of all circumstance to the divine exuberance. And I remember this with great satisfaction at the photographist's shop.

Goethe said, that we are in hell: and I find this Civil War abominably in my way, and, if peace comes again, I can still find blackbears enough in bad neighbors, failing resources, & ah & alas! the pathos of the house.

Aug. 13, 1862
W. E. C. remarked today, that, as the rebels burned their cotton & their towns, it would not be strange if they should Emancipate their slaves.

This day took up the bridge which crosses the brook in my pasture, in order to put a stop to the travel of the neighborhood through my yard. [*Nov. 7, 1862.* This day had the bridge replaced again by Francis Buttrick.]

Aug. 26, 1862
Little Waldo, when I carried him to the circus, & showed him the clown & his antics, said, "It makes me want to go home," and I am forced to quote my boy's speech often & often since. I can do so few things, I can see so few companies, that do not remind me of it! Of course, if I had the faculty to meet the occasion, I should enjoy it. Not

having it, & noting how many occasions I cannot meet, life loses value
every month, & I shall be quite ready to give place to whoso waits for
my chair.

Aug. 30, 1862

Several urgent motives point to the Emancipation.

1. The eternal right of it.

2. The military necessity of creating an army in the rear of the
Enemy, & throughout his country, & in every plantation, compelling
him to disband his army, & rush home to protect his family & estate.

3. The danger of the adoption by the South of the policy of Emancipation. France & England may peaceably recognize the Southern Con-
federacy, on the condition of Emancipation. Instantly, we are thrown
into falsest position. All Europe will back France & England in the act,
because the cause of the South will then be the cause of Freedom, the
cause of the North will be that of Slavery. . . .

Emancipation makes all this impossible. European govts. dare not
interfere for Slavery, as soon as the Union is pronounced for Liberty.

Aug.? 1862

Strange that some strong-minded president of the Woman's Rights
Convention should not offer to lead the Army of the Potomac. She could
not do worse than General Maclellan.

Aug.–Oct. 1862

I believe in the perseverance of the saints. I believe in effectual calling. I believe in life Everlasting.

How shallow seemed to me yesterday in the woods the speech one
often hears from tired citizens who have spent their brief enthusiasm for
the country, that nature is tedious, & they have had enough of green
leaves. Nature & the green leaves are a million fathoms deep, & it is
these eyes that are superficial. . . .

Henry said, "I wish so to live as to derive my satisfactions & inspirations from the commonest events, so that what my senses hourly
perceive, my daily walk, the conversation of my neighbors may inspire
me, & I may dream of no heaven but that which lies about me."

If we were truly to take account of stock before the Last Court of
Appeals—that were an inventory. What are my resources? A few moral
maxims, confirmed by much experience, would stand high on the list,
constituting a supreme prudence. Then the knowledge, unutterable, of
my strength, of where it lies, of its accesses, & facilitations, & of its obstructions; my conviction of principles—that is great part of my possession. Having them, 'tis easy to devise or use means of illustrating

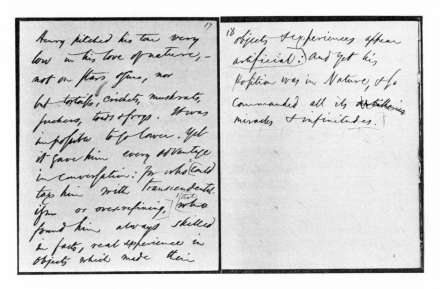

Entry on Thoreau made after his death, probably in 1864.

them—I need not take thought for that. Certain thoughts, certain observations, long familiar to me in night-watches & daylights, would be my capital, if I remove to Spain, or China, or, by stranger translation, to the planet Jupiter or Mars, or to new spiritual societies.

How remarkable the principle of iteration in rhetoric! We are delighted with it in rhyme, in poetic prose, in song, above all, allowing a line to be not only a burden to the whole song, but, as in Negro melodies, to be steadily repeated 3 or 4 times in immediate succession. Well, what shall we say of a liturgy? what of a litany? What of a Lord's Prayer, the burial service which is echoed & reechoed from one end of man's life to the other?

There is satire too in Nature, as when she goes over the ground of her nobler works again on a low & even base series, & makes the phallus which grew in the yard yesterday.

When I bought my farm, I did not know what a bargain I had in the bluebirds, bobolinks, & thrushes. As little did I know what sublime mornings & sunsets I was buying.

Great is the virtue of the Proclamation. It works when men are sleeping, when the Army goes into winter quarters, when generals are treacherous or imbecile.

Nov. 1862

In art, they have got that far, the rage for Saints & crucifixions & pietàs is past, and landscape & portrait, & history, & *genres* have come in. It is significant enough of the like advance in religion.

There never was a nation great except through trial. A religious revolution cuts sharpest, & tests the faith & endurance. A civil war sweeps away all the false issues on which it begun, & arrives presently at real & lasting questions.

When we build, our first care is to find good foundation. If the surface be loose, or sandy, or springy, we clear it away, & dig down to the hard pan, or, better, to the living rock, & bed our courses in that. So will we do with the state. The War is serving many good purposes. It is no respecter of respectable persons or of worn out party platforms. War is a realist, shatters everything flimsy & shifty, sets aside all false issues, & breaks through all that is not real as itself, comes to organise opinions & parties, resting on the necessities of man, like its own cannonade comes crushing in through party walls that have stood fifty or sixty years as if they were solid. The screaming of leaders, the votes by acclamation of conventions, are all idle wind. They cry for mercy but they cry to one who never knew the word. He is the Arm of the Fates and as has been said "nothing prevails against God but God." Everything must perish except that which must live.

Well, this is the task before us, to accept the benefit of the War: it has not created our false relations, they have created it. It simply demonstrates the rottenness it found. We watch its course as we did the cholera, which goes where predisposition already existed, took only the susceptible, set its seal on every putrid spot, & on none other, followed the limestone, & left the granite. So the War. Anxious Statesmen try to rule it, to slacken it here & let it rage there, to not exasperate, to keep the black man out of it; to keep it well in hand, nor let it ride over old party lines, nor much molest trade, and to confine it to the frontier of the 2 sections. Why need Cape Cod, why need Casco Bay, why need Lake Superior, know any thing of it? But the Indians have been bought, & they come down on Lake Superior; Boston & Portland are threatened by the pirate; more than that, Secession unexpectedly shows teeth in Boston; our parties have just shown you that the war is already in Massachusetts, as in Richmond.

Let it search, let it grind, let it overturn, &, like the fire when it finds no more fuel, it burns out. The war will show, as all wars do, what wrong is intolerable, what wrong makes & breeds all this bad blood. I suppose that it shows two incompatible states of society, freedom &

slavery. If a part of this country is civilized up to a clear insight of freedom, & of its necessity, and another part is not so far civilized, then I
suppose that the same difficulties will continue; the war will not be extinguished; no treaties, no peace, no Constitutions can paper over the
lips of that red crater.

Only when, at last, so many parts of the country as can combine on
an equal & moral contract—not to protect each other in polygamy, or in
kidnapping, or in eating men, but in humane & just activities—only so
many can combine firmly & durably.

I speak the speech of an idealist. I say let the rule be right. If the theory is right, it is not so much matter about the facts. If the plan of your
fort is right it is not so much matter that you have got a rotten beam or a
cracked gun somewhere, they can by & by be replaced by better without tearing your fort to pieces. But if the plan is wrong, then all is rotten,
& every step adds to the ruin. Then every screw is loose, and all the
machine crazy. The question stands thus, reconstruction is no longer
matter of doubt. All our action now is new & unconstitutional, & necessarily so. To bargain or treat at all with the rebels, to make arrangements
with them about exchange of prisoners or hospitals, or truces to bury
the dead, all unconstitutional & enough to drive a strict constructionist
out of his wits. Much more in our future action touching peace, any &
every arrangement short of forcible subjugation of the rebel country,
will be flat disloyalty, on our part.

Then how to reconstruct. I say, this time, go to work right. Go down
to the pan, see that your works turn on a jewel. Do not make an impossible mixture.

Do not lay your cornerstone on a shaking morass that will let down
the superstructure into a bottomless pit again.

Leave slavery out. Since (unfortunately as some may think) God is
God, & nothing satisfies all men but justice, let us have that, & let us
stifle our prejudices against commonsense & humanity, & agree that
every man shall have what he honestly earns, and, if he is a sane & innocent man, have an equal vote in the state, and a fair chance in society.

And I, speaking in the interest of no man & no party, but simply as a
geometer of his forces, say that the smallest beginning, so that it is just,
is better & stronger than the largest that is not quite just.

This time, no compromises, no concealments, no crimes that cannot
be called by name, shall be tucked in under another name, like, "persons
held to labor," meaning persons stolen, & "held", meaning held by
hand-cuffs, when they are not under whips.

Now the smallest state so formed will & must be strong, the interest
& the affection of every man will make it strong by his entire strength,
and it will mightily persuade every other man, & every neighboring ter-

ritory to make it larger, and it will not reach its limits until it comes to people who think that they are a little cunninger than the maker of this world & of the consciences of men.

Nov.–Dec. 1862

Isaac Hecker, the Catholic priest, came to see me, & desired to read lectures on the Catholic Church, in Concord. I told him that nobody would come to hear him, such was the aversation of people, at present, to theological questions; & not only so, but the drifting of the human mind was now quite in another direction than to any churches. Nor could I possibly affect the smallest interest in anything that regarded his church. We are used to this whim of a man's choosing to put on & wear a painted petticoat, as we are to whims of artists who wear a mediaeval cap or beard, & attach importance to it; but, of course, they must say nothing about it to us, & we will never notice it to them, but will carry on general conversation, with utter reticence as to each other's whimsies: but if once they speak of it, they are not the men we took them for, & we do not talk with them twice. But I doubt if any impression can be made on Father Isaac. He converted Mrs Ward, &, like the lion that has eaten a man, he wants to be at it again, & convert somebody.

We used, forty years ago, religious rites in every house, which have disappeared. There is no longer, in the houses of my acquaintances, morning or evening family prayer, or grace said at table, or any exact observance of the Sunday, except in the houses of clergymen. I have long ceased to regret this disuse. It is quite impossible to put the dial-hand back. The religion is now where it should be. Persons are discriminated as honest, as veracious, as generous & helpful, as conscientious, or having public & universal regards; are discriminated according to their aims, & not by these ritualities.

Feb.–March? 1863

I am a bard least of bards.

I cannot, like them, make lofty arguments in stately continuous verse, constraining the rocks, trees, animals, & the periodic stars to say my thoughts—for that is the gift of great poets; but I am a bard, because I stand near them, & apprehend all they utter, & with pure joy hear that which I also would say, &, moreover, I speak interruptedly words & half stanzas which have the like scope & aim.

March 1863

I like to see our young Irish people, who arrived here in their shabby old country rags, after a few months labor drest so well & gaily. When a young Irishman after a summer's labor puts on for the first time his new coat, he puts on much much more. His good & becoming clothes set him on thinking that he must behave like people who are so drest. And silently & steadily his behavior mends.

March–April 1863

The human mind cannot be burned, nor bayonetted, nor wounded, nor missing.

Who would live in the stone age, or in the bronze or the iron age, or in the lacustrine? I prefer the cotton, the calico, the paper, & the steam of today.

Machinery is good, but motherwit is better. Telegraph, steam & balloon & newspapers are like spectacles on the nose of age, but we will give them all gladly to have back again our young eyes.

April 1863

This running into the Catholic Church is disgusting, just when one is looking amiably round at the culture & performance of the young people, & fancying that the new generation is an advance on the last. Sam. Ward says, the misfortune is that when the young people have this desire, there is nothing on the other side to offer them instead. And it is true that stoicism, always attractive to the intellectual & cultivated, has now no temples, no Academy, no commanding Zeno or Antoninus. It accuses us that it has none—that pure Ethics is not now formulated & concreted into a *cultus*, a fraternity with assemblings & holy days, with song & book, with brick & stone.

Why have not those who believe in it, & love it, left all for this, & dedicated themselves to write out its scientific scripture to become its Vulgate for millions? I answer for one, that the inspirations we catch of this law are not continuous & technical, but joyful sparkles & flashes, and are recorded for their beauty—for the delight they give—not for their obligation; and that is their priceless good to men that they charm & uplift, not that they are imposed. These words out of heaven are imparted to happy uncontrollable Pindars, Hafizes, Shakspeares, & not to Westminster Assemblies of divines.

April–May 1863

I have never recorded a fact which perhaps ought to have gone into my sketch of "Thoreau," that, on the 1 August, 1844, when I read my Discourse on Emancipation, in the Town Hall, in Concord, and the selectmen would not direct the sexton to ring the meeting-house bell, Henry went himself, & rung the bell at the appointed hour.

Saladin caused his shroud to be made & carried it to battle as his standard. Aunt Mary has done the like all her life, making up her shroud, & then thinking it pity to let it lie idle, wears it as night-gown or day-gown until it is worn out (for death, when asked, will not come); then she has another made up, &, I believe, has worn out a great many. And now that her release seems to be really at hand, the event of her death has really something so comic in the eyes of everybody that her friends fear they shall laugh at the funeral.

June 1863
West Point Academy makes a very agreeable impression on me. The innocence of the cadets, the air of probity, of veracity, & of loyalty to each other struck me, & the anecdotes told us confirmed this impression. I think it excellent that such tender youths should be made so manly & masterly in rough exercises of horse & gun & cannon & mortar, so accurate in French, in Mathematics, geology, and engineering, should learn to draw, to dance, & to swim.

I think their ambition should be concentrated on their superiority in Science—being taught, that, whoever knows the most must command *of right*, & must command *in fact*, if just to himself. Let them have no fears, then, of prejudices against West Point. "West Point a hot bed of aristocracy," is a word of some political hack, which seems to rankle in their memories. Rather let them accept it, and make West Point a true aristocracy, or "the power of the Best," best scholars, best soldiers, best engineers, best commanders, best men—and they will be indispensable to their government & their country; will be, as they ought, the nucleus of the army, though it be three fourths or nine tenths volunteers—they will be the shop of power, the source of instruction, the organization of Victory.

At West Point, I entered some of the chambers of the cadets in the barracks, & found two cadets in each, standing as if on guard. Each chamber was perfectly clean, & every article orderly disposed. The mattrass on the camp iron bed was rolled up into a scroll. "Who makes your bed?" "I do." "Who brings your water?" "I do." "Who blacks your shoes?" "I do." In the battery drill, I saw each handsome dainty boy whom I had noticed in the Examination, flying over the field in the caissons, or loading or working the gun, all begrimed with powder. In the mortar practice, in the siege battery drill, each was promptly performing his part in the perfect exercise.

* * *

In reading Henry Thoreau's Journal, I am very sensible of the vigor of his constitution. That oaken strength which I noted whenever he walked or worked or surveyed wood lots, the same unhesitating hand with which a field-laborer accosts a piece of work which I should shun as a waste of strength, Henry shows in his literary task. He has muscle, & ventures on & performs feats which I am forced to decline. In reading him, I find the same thought, the same spirit that is in me, but he takes a step beyond, & illustrates by excellent images that which I should have conveyed in a sleepy generality. 'Tis as if I went into a gymnasium, & saw youths leap, climb, & swing with a force unapproachable—though their feats are only continuations of my initial grapplings & jumps.

June 29, 1863

'Tis a rule of manners that we keep cool, & avoid tension. A lady loses her charm, as soon as she admires too easily & too much. In man or woman, the face & the person lose all power, when they are on the strain to express approbation.

June? 1863

Lincoln. We must accept the results of universal suffrage, & not try to make it appear that we can elect fine gentlemen. We shall have coarse men, with a fair chance of worth & of manly ability, but not polite men, not men to please the English or French.

You cannot refine Mr Lincoln's taste, or extend his horizon; he will not walk dignifiedly through the traditional part of the President of America, but will pop out his head at each railroad station & make a little speech, & get into an argument with Squire A. & Judge B.; he will write letters to Horace Greeley, and any Editor or Reporter or saucy Party committee that writes to him, & cheapen himself. But this we must be ready for, and let the clown appear, & hug ourselves that we are well off, if we have got good nature, honest meaning, & fidelity to public interest, with bad manners, instead of an elegant roué & malignant self-seeker.

July 16, 1863

Rode this p.m. with Channing in wagon to White Pond. 'Tis perhaps ten years ago since I was there with him before, and in the reflections of the larger grown trees in the lake noticed the same peculiarities. The trees were all done in minute squares, as in the crochet work of girls; the colors of the foliage, russet & ruddy, added to the beauty. Pines on the distant shore, of which we saw only the short stem veiled above by the branches, in the water showed the stem of the tree to the top! We were on the farther side of the pond at the "Cove," & talked with a party, a young man & three young women from Sudbury 3½ miles distant. They left the shore in a boat. C. & I agreed that a picnic is like a "revival", it changes a man in an instant, & he forgets his home & habits, & thinks he will come & live with Nature. But he returns to his village to put up his horse, stops at the Post Office, takes tea with his family, and does not for ten years get a glance at the Paradise again. After a bath in the Pond came home by the beautiful road through Nine-Acre-Corner, where the farms were in richest array. An old hemlock tree in one field should teach every body to plant and guard a hemlock, that it may some day be old.

July–Aug. 1863

I went to Dartmouth College, and found the same old Granny system which I met there 25 years ago. President Lord has an aversion to emulation, as injurious to the character of the pupils. He therefore forbids the election of members into the two literary societies by merit, but arranges that the first scholar alphabetically on the list shall be assigned to the Adelphi, & the second to the Mathesians, the third to the Adelphi, & the fourth to the Mathesians; and so on, every student belonging to the one or the other.—"Well, but there is a first scholar in the class, is there not, & he has the first oration at Commencement?" "O no, the parts are assigned by lot."—The amiable student who explained it, added, that it tended to remove disagreeable excitement from the societies. I answered, Certainly and it would remove more if there were no college at all. I recommended morphine in liberal dose, at the College Commons. I learn, since my return, that the President has resigned—the first good trait I have heard of in the man.

Oct. 1863

Good out of evil.

One must thank the genius of Brigham Young for the creation of Salt Lake City—an inestimable hospitality to the Overland Emigrants, and an efficient example to all men in the vast desart, teaching how to subdue & turn it to a habitable garden. And one must thank Walt Whitman for service to American literature in the Apalachian enlargement of his outline & treatment.

My interest in my Country is not primary, but professional. I wish that war as peace shall bring out the genius of the men. In every company, in every town, I seek intellect & character; & so in every circumstance. War, I know, is not an unmitigated evil: it is a potent alterative, tonic, magnetiser, reinforces manly power a hundred & a thousand times. I see it come as a frosty October, which shall restore intellectual & moral power to these languid & dissipated populations.

*   *   *

We can let the year go round, if we know that October brings thoughts, & March lustres, & May love, and the tenth year honor for the insults & ribaldry of the nine foregoing winters.

It was an excellent custom of the Quakers (if only for a school of manners) the silent prayer before meals. When the table is ready, & the family have taken their places, they compose themselves, & sit for the space of a minute quite still, then open their napkins, & begin to eat. It has the effect to stop mirth & idle talking, & introduce a moment of reflection. After this pause, all begin again their usual intercourse from a vantage-ground. It would rebuke those violent manners which many people bring to the table, of wrath, & whining, & heat in trifles.

Nov. 1863

I remember reading a gay paper of N. P. Willis, seriously advising the New York youth not to follow anxiously the fashion in hats, but to see to it what kind of hat became him, & to buy that, for that every becoming hat was in fashion. That was good sense. I should say of dress in general, that some people need it, & others need it not. Thus a king or a general does not need a fine coat. And a commanding person may save himself all solicitude on that point. Longworth at Cincinnati received me to dine in the muddiest boots & trowsers, all his family being in gala. And Montaigne says, in his chateau, his servants & equipages can answer for him. This also is the rule in society. Some persons do not need this care. There are always slovens in state street who are not less considered. But some persons do. If a man have manners & talent, he may dress roughly & carelessly. If however a man has not aplomb, has sensibility—as certain youths whom I know—it is a grand economy to go to a good tailor at the beginning of the season, & dress himself irreproachably. He can then dismiss all care from his mind, & may easily find that slight confidence a fortification, that turns the scale in social encounters, & allows him to go gaily & without second thought into conversations where else he had been dry & embarrassed. It has the effect of that double glass of wine which my lawyer said he took with advantage when he was about to address the jury.

I will tell you why I value Boston, because, when I go to enumerate its excellent names, I do not take down the Boston Directory, but the National History to find them.

Dec.? 1863

Renan writes "*Vie de Jesus.*" Many of his contemporaries have no doubt projected the same theme. When I wrote "Representative Men,"

I felt that Jesus was the "Rep. Man" whom I ought to sketch: but the task required great gifts—steadiest insight & perfect temper; else, the consciousness of want of sympathy in the audience would make one petulant or sore, in spite of himself. Theodore Parker, of course, wished to write this book; so did Maria Child in her Book of Religions, and Miss Cobb, and Alcott, and I know not how many more.

Feb.–March? 1864

Elliot Cabot's paper on "Art" has given emphasis to one point among others, that people only see what they are prepared to see. Thus who sees birds, except the hunter? or the ornithologist? How difficult it is to me to see certain particulars in the dress of people with whom I sit for hours, and after I had wished to know what sort of waistcoat, or coat, or shirt-collar, or neckcloth they wore.

I have gone to many dinners & parties with instructions from home & with my own wish to see the dress of the *men*, & can never remember to look for it.

March 13, 1864

Last night talked with Alcott who returns much lately to the comparison between English & American genius. I gratified him by saying, that our intellectual performance, taken with our sentiment, is perhaps better worth than their performance taken with their limitation or downward tendency. For certainly we cannot count or weigh living writers with theirs.

But how to meet the demand for a religion. A few clergymen here, like Hedge & Clarke, retain the traditions, but they never mention them to me, and, if they travelled in France, England, or Italy, would leave them locked up in the same closet with their sermons at home, &, if they did not return, would never think to send for them. Beecher, Manning, Bushnell, hold a little firmer, & more easily to theirs, as Calvinism has a more tenacious vitality—but that is doomed also, & will only die last: for Calvinism rushes to be Unitarianism as Unitarianism rushes to be Naturalism.

How then is the new generation to be edified? How should it not? The life of these once omnipotent traditions was really not in the legend, but in the moral sentiment & the metaphysical fact which the legends enclosed—and these survive. A new Socrates, or Zeno, or Swedenborg, or Pascal, or a new crop of geniuses, like those of the Elizabethan age, may be born in this age, &, with happy heat & a bias for theism, bring asceticism & duty & magnanimity into vogue again.

Spring? 1864

School. First, see that the expense be for teaching, or that school be kept the greatest number of days & for the greatest number of scholars. Then that the best teachers & the best apparatus, namely, building, furniture, books, &c be provided.

School—because it is the *cultus* of our time & place, fit for the republic, fit for the times, which no longer can be reached & commanded by the Church. What an education in the public spirit of Massachusetts has been the war songs, speeches, & readings of the Schools! Every district School has been an antislavery convention for two or three years last past.

This town has no seaport, no cotton, no shoe-trade, no water power, no gold, lead, coal, or rock oil, nor marble, nothing but wood & grass, not even ice & granite, our New England staples; for the granite is better in Acton, Fitchburg, & our ice, Mr Tudor said, had bubbles in it. We are reduced then to manufacture school teachers, which we do, for the southern & western market. I advise the town to stick to that staple, & make it the best in the world. It is your lot in the urn. And it is one of the commanding lots.

Get the best apparatus, the best overseer, and turn out the best possible article. Mr Agassiz says "I mean to make the Harvard Museum such that no European naturalist can afford to stay away from it." Let the Town of Concord say as much for its school. We will make our schools such that no family which has a new home to choose can fail to be attracted hither as to the one town in which the best education can be secured. This is one of those long prospective economies which are sure & remunerative.

Bons mots. I am always struck with the speed with which every new interest, party, or way of thinking gets its bon mot & name, & so adds a new word to language. Thus Higginson, & Livermore, Hosmer, & the fighting chaplains give necessity & vogue to "muscular Christianity": The language of the day readily suggested to some theological wit to call hell "a military necessity"; and when some copperhead orator called Slavery a divine institution, a voice from the crowd cried out, "So is Hell." Which word became a compendium of antislavery argument henceforward.

I too am fighting my campaign.

Within, I do not find wrinkles & used heart, but unspent youth.

* * *

I have found my advantage in going to a hotel with a task which could not prosper at home. I secured so a more absolute solitude, for it is almost impossible for a housekeeper who, in the country, is also a small farmer, & who has guests in the house, to exclude interruptions & even necessary orders, though I bar out by system all I can, & resolutely omit to my constant loss all that can be omitted. In the hotel, I have no hours to keep, no visits, & can command an astronomic leisure. At home the day is cut up into short strips. In the hotel, I forget rain, wind, & cold, heat. At home, I remember in my library the wants of the farm, & have all too much sympathy. I envy the abstraction of some scholars I have known, who might sit on a curb-stone in state street & solve their problem. I have more womanly eyes. All the conditions must be right for my success, slight as that is. What untunes is as bad as what cripples or stuns me. Therefore I extol the prudence of Carlyle, who, for years, projected a library at the top of his house, high above the orbit of all housemaids, and out of earshot of doorbells. Could that be once secured—a whole floor—room for books, & a good bolt—he could hope for six years of history. And he kept it in view till it was done. And I remember that Henry Thoreau, with his cynic will, yet found certain trifles disturbing the delicacy of that health which composition exacted—namely, the slightest irregularity or the drinking too much water on the preceding day. And George Sand's love of heat agrees with mine. Even the steel pen is a nuisance.

A capital prudence, too, I learned from old President Quincy, who told me that he never goes to bed at night, until he has laid out the studies for the next morning.

Shall I add to my list of electrics, after Sleep, Conversation, New Poetry, Fact-books, &c., certain localities, as, mountaintops, the shores of large bodies of water, or of rapid brooks, as excitants of the muse? And yet the experience of some good artists would prefer the smallest & plainest chamber with one chair & one table to these picturesque liberties.

The grief of old age is, that now, only in rare moments, & by happiest combinations or consent of the elements can we attain those enlargements & that intellectual *élan*, which were once a daily gift.

Old age brings along with its uglinesses the comfort that you will soon be out of it—which ought to be a substantial relief to such discontented pendulums as we are. To be out of the war, out of debt, out of the drouth, out of the blues, out of the dentist's hands, out of the second thoughts, mortifications & remorses that inflict such twinges & shooting pains—out of the next winter, & the high prices, & company below your ambition—surely these are soothing hints. And, harbinger of this, what an alleviator is sleep, which muzzles all these dogs for me every day! Old Age. 'Tis proposed to call an indignation meeting.

Use of towns I considered in an old Journal in many points. But we are far from having the best aesthetics out of them. The French & Italians have made a nearer approach to it. A town in Europe is a place where you can go into a café at a certain hour of every day, buy *eau sucrée*, or a cup of coffee, for six sous, &, at that price, have the company of the wits, scholars & gentlemen fond of conversation. That is a cheap & excellent club, which finds & leaves all parties on a good mutual footing. That is the fame of the "Café Procope," the "Cafe Grec" of Rome, the "Cafe de Trinità" of Florence, & the principle of it exists in every town in France & Italy. But we do not manage it so well in America. Our clubbing is much more costly & cumbersome.

The test of civilization is the power of drawing the most benefit out of cities.

April 1864

Lowell told me, that, when Mrs Stowe was invited to dine with the Atlantic Club, she refused to drink wine, & it was banished for that day. But Lowell said, "Mrs Stowe, you took wine with the Duke of Argyle, when you visited him?" She acknowledged that she did. "And now do you mean to treat us as if we were not as good as he?" "No," she said. "Bring some Champagne," cried Lowell, & Mrs Stowe & the company drank. "And how did you know," I asked, "that she did take wine at the Duke's?"—"O, I divined that," he said, "Of course she did."

The single word *Madame* in French poetry, makes it instantly prose.

I heard Bandmann read Hamlet's soliloquy, the other day, at Bartol's. In conversation, he was polite & expansive enough, but plainly enjoyed the new expansion that the reading gave him. He stood up, & by musing distanced himself, then silences all the company, & gets out of doors, as it were, by a cheerful cry of a verse or two, & acquires a right to be the hero, & abounds in his own sense, & puts it despotically upon us, in look, manner, & elocution. He brought out the broad meaning of the soliloquy truly enough, but, as all actors will, with an *overmuch*, with emphasis & mouthing. They cannot let well alone: but must have

"Old age is a good advertisement. Your name has been seen so
often that your book must be worth buying."

the merit of all the refinements & second senses they have found or devised, & so drive it too finely. It is essential to reach this freedom, or gay self-possession, but temperance is essential too.

April 24, 1864

Yesterday the Saturday Club met to keep the birthnight of Shakspeare, at the end of the third Century.

April–May 1864

The only safe topic for an American meeting an Englishman with whom he is unacquainted, is, France & Frenchmen, whom they can both abuse at pleasure——and Shakspeare.

How to say it, I know not, but I know that the point of praise of Shakspeare, is, the pure poetic power: he is the chosen closet companion, who can, at any moment, by incessant surprises, work the miracle of mythologising every fact of the common life; as snow, or moonlight, or the level rays of sunrise—lend a momentary glory to every pump & woodpile.

When I read Shakspeare, as lately, I think the criticism & study of him to be in their infancy. The wonder grows of his long obscurity— how could you hide the only man that ever wrote, from all men who delight in reading?—then, the courage with which, in each play, he accosts the main issue, the highest problem, never dodging the difficult or impossible, but addressing himself instantly to that, so conscious of his secret competence; and, at once, like an aeronaut fills his balloon with a whole atmosphere of hydrogen that will carry him over Andes, if Andes be in his path.

We said, that ours was the recuperative age. Pascal is one of its recoveries, not only the Essay on Love, but the pure text of the *Pensées*.

Shakspeare should be the study of the University. In Florence Boccacio was appointed to lecture on Dante. But in English Oxford, or in Harvard College, I have never heard of a Shakspeare Professorship. Yet the students should be educated not only in the intelligence of but in the sympathy with the thought of great poets.

I must say that in reading the plays, I am a little shy where I begin; for the interest of the story is sadly in the way of poetry. It is safer therefore to read the play backwards.

I am inquisitive of all possible knowledge concerning Shakspeare, & of all opinions: yet how few valuable criticisms, how few opinions I treasure!—How few besides my own! And each thoughtful reader, doubtless, has the like experience.

Physiology of Taste were a good subject for a lecture. My epicure should sow marjoram in his beds, if it were only to see with eyes the buds: and his windows should look into great gardens.

My physiology, too, would in every point put the real against the showy; as, to live in the country, & not in town; to wear shoddy & old shoes; to have not a fine horse, but an old dobbin with only life enough to drag a Jersey wagon to Conantum, or Estabrook, & there stand contented for half a day at a tree, whilst I forget him in the woods & pastures; (as, in England the point is not to make strong beer, but beer weak enough to permit a great deal to be drunk in hot weather; as Mr Flower explained to me at Stratford.)

The intellect is alike old in the father & in his child. We old fellows affect a great deal of reticence with the young people, but their wit cannot wait for us. Mrs G explained to me that her children (one was 14 years) did not know what beef was: she had never allowed them to know that sheep & oxen were killed for our food. But my children knew that her children knew as much as they. Plutarch would use great precautions in young people's reading of the poets; & Plato also. But when young & old see "Faust" on the stage, or "Midsummer Night's Dream," or read them in the closet, they come silently to the same conclusions.
No age to intellect.

The Cannon will not suffer any other sound to be heard for miles & for years around it. Our chronology has lost all old distinctions in one date—*Before the War, and Since.*

It is hard to remember in glancing over our sumptuous library-editions & excellent pocket-editions of Chaucer, that for 100 years these works existed only in manuscripts, accumulating errors & false readings in every individual copy of every new transcriber. 'Tis alarming to reckon the risks, & judge of the damage done.

It is, I own, difficult not to be intemperate in speaking of Shakspeare; and most difficult, I should say, to the best readers. Few, I think none, arrive at any intelligence of his methods. His intellect does not emit jets of light, at intervals, but is incessant, always equal to the occasion, & addressing with equal readiness a comic, an ingenious, or a sublime problem. I find him an exceptional genius. If the world were on trial, it is the perfect success of this one man that might justify such expenditure of geology, chemistry, fauna, & flora, as the world was. And, I suppose, if Intellect perceives & converses "in climes beyond the solar road," they probably call this planet, not Earth, but *"Shakspeare."* In teleology, they will come to say, that the final cause of the creation of the Earth was Shakspeare.

In the experience of colleges, it is found, that whilst good mathematicians are rare, good teachers of mathematics are much more rare. It has happened that two or three female teachers in our schools have had great success & that in the college, *men* geometers & analysts of unquestionable ability utterly fail in the power to impart their methods to the willing student. All the aid the student gets is from some chum who has a little more knowledge than he, & knows where the difficulty he has just surmounted lay. I have just seen four of these skeleton sufferers, to whom all the studies in the University are sufficiently attractive, *excepting the mathematics*, & who find this (which they do not wish to acquire) thrust into absurd eminence—absorbing nominally one third of the academic time in the two first years, &, practically, often two thirds, a dead weight on the mind & heart of the pupil, to be utterly renounced & forgotten the moment he is left to the election of his studies, & a painful memory of wasted years & injured constitution, as long as he lives. Languages, Rhetoric, Logic, Ethics, Intellectual Philosophy, Poetry, Natural History, Civil History, Political Economy, Technology, Chemistry, Agriculture, Literary History, as, the genius of Homer, Dante, Shakspeare, & Goethe; Music & Drawing, even—all these may rightly enter into the curriculum, as well as Mathematics. But it were to hurt the University, if any one of these should absorb a disproportionate share of time. The European Universities gave a like supreme emphasis to the subtleties of logic in the days of Ockham, to Theology, when the priesthood controlled education.

Until recently, Natural Science was almost excluded, and it is inevitable that a man of genius with a good deal of general power will for a long period give a bias in his direction to a University. And that is a public mischief which the guardians of a college are there to watch & counterpoise. In the election of a President, it is not only the students who are to be controlled, but the Professors, each of which in proportion to his talent is a usurper who needs to be resisted.

May 24, 1864

Yesterday, 23 May, we buried Hawthorne in Sleepy Hollow, in a pomp of sunshine & verdure, & gentle winds. James F. Clarke read the service in the Church & at the grave. Longfellow, Lowell, Holmes, Agassiz, Hoar, Dwight, Whipple, Norton, Alcott, Hillard, Fields, Judge

Thomas, & I, attended the hearse as pall bearers. Franklin Pierce was with the family. The church was copiously decorated with white flowers delicately arranged. The corpse was unwillingly shown—only a few moments to this company of his friends. But it was noble & serene in its aspect—nothing amiss—a calm & powerful head. A large company filled the church, & the grounds of the cemetery. All was so bright & quiet, that pain or mourning was hardly suggested, & Holmes said to me, that it looked like a happy meeting.

Clarke in the church said, that Hawthorne had done more justice than any other to the shades of life, shown a sympathy with the crime in our nature, &, like Jesus, was the friend of sinners.

I thought there was a tragic element in the event, that might be more fully rendered—in the painful solitude of the man—which, I suppose, could not longer be endured, & he died of it.

I have found in his death a surprise & disappointment. I thought him a greater man than any of his works betray, that there was still a great deal of work in him, & that he might one day show a purer power.

Moreover I have felt sure of him in his neighborhood, & in his necessities of sympathy & intelligence, that I could well wait his time—his unwillingness & caprice—and might one day conquer a friendship. It would have been a happiness, doubtless to both of us, to have come into habits of unreserved intercourse. It was easy to talk with him—there were no barriers—only, he said so little, that I talked too much, & stopped only because—as he gave no indications—I feared to exceed. He showed no egotism or self-assertion, rather a humility, &, at one time, a fear that he had written himself out. One day, when I found him on the top of his hill, in the woods, he paced back the path to his house, & said, *"this path is the only remembrance of me that will remain."* Now it appears that I waited too long.

Lately, he had removed himself the more by the indignation his perverse politics & unfortunate friendship for that paltry Franklin Pierce awaked—though it rather moved pity for Hawthorne, & the assured belief that he would outlive it, & come right at last.

I have forgotten in what year (Sept. 27, 1842), but it was whilst he lived in the Manse, soon after his marriage, that I said to him, "I shall never see you in this hazardous way; we must take a long walk together. Will you go to Harvard & visit the Shakers?" He agreed, & we took a June day, & walked the twelve miles, got our dinner from the Brethren, slept at the Harvard Inn, & returned home by another road the next day. It was a satisfactory tramp; we had good talk on the way, of which I set down some record in my journal.*

---

* See pp. 288–290.

May? 1864

Reginald Taylor, a child of six years, was carried to see his moth kinsman, President Day. On his return home, he said, "Mother, I think that old man loves God too much. You know I say my prayers when I go to bed: well he talks just so all the time."

July 1864?

Henry pitched his tone very low in his love of nature—not on stars & suns ... but tortoises, crickets, muskrats, suckers, toads & frogs. It was impossible to go lower. Yet it gave him every advantage in conversation: For who that found him always skilled in facts, real experience in objects which made their objects & experiences appear artificial, could tax him with transcendentalism or over-refining: And yet his position was in Nature, & so commanded all its miracles & infinitudes.

In Journal, 1852, August 6, he writes, "Hearing that one with whom I was acquainted had committed suicide, I said, 'I did not know, when I planted the seed of that fact, that I should hear of it.' "

I see the Thoreau poison working today in many valuable lives, in some for good, in some for harm.

Mrs Cynthia Thoreau, Henry's mother, was a woman of a sharp & malicious wit, and a very entertaining story-teller, I have been told. But my wife repeats two or three passages of her wit. When I first bought a horse in Concord I looked about for a cheap carriage of some kind. Samuel Staples offered to sell me one called a rockaway which would carry four persons, & was decent & convenient. My wife had occasion to speak of it at Mrs Thoreau's, and she replied, "O yes, I know it very well. 'Tis the old one in which Sam Staples always carries his prisoners to jail: they sat right in front of him so they could not get away." A speech quite new to my wife, & which Mrs Thoreau hoped would not recommend her new carriage much to her imagination.

When Henry was at Staten Island, he wrote two or three letters to my wife. She spoke of them to his family, who eagerly wished to see them. She consented, but said, "She was almost ashamed to show them, because Henry had exalted her by very undeserved praise."—"O yes," said his mother, "Henry is very tolerant."

Mrs Brown who boarded with the Thoreaus, was one day talking with Mrs T. of the remarks made by many persons on the resemblances between Mr Emerson & Henry in manners, looks, voice, & thought. Henry spoke like Mr E. & walked like him, &c. "O yes," said his mother, "Mr Emerson had been a good deal with David Henry, and it was very natural should catch his ways."

Sept. 24, 1864

Yesterday with Ellery walked through "Becky Stow's Hole," dry-shod, hitherto a feat for a muskrat alone.

The sky & air & autumn woods in their early best. This year, the river meadows all dry & permeable to the walker. But why should nature always be on the gallop? Look now & instantly, or you shall never see it: Not ten minutes' repose allowed. Incessant whirl. And 'tis the same with my companion's genius. You must carry a stenographic press in your pocket to save his commentaries on things & men, or they are irrecoverable. I tormented my memory just now in vain to restore a witty criticism of his, yesterday, on a book.

Sept.–Oct. 1864

Napoleon's word, that, in 25 years, the United States would dictate the politics of the world, was a little early; but the sense was just, with a Jewish interpretation of the "forty days" & "seventy weeks." It is true, that, if we escape bravely from the present war, America will be the controlling power.

Criticism. I read with delight a casual notice of Wordsworth in the "London Reader," in which, with perfect aplomb, his highest merits were affirmed, & his unquestionable superiority to all English poets since Milton, & thought how long I travelled & talked in England, & found no person, or none but one, & that one, Clough, sympathetic with him, & admiring him aright in face of Tennyson's culminating talent & genius in melodious verse. What struck me now was the certainty with which the best opinion comes to be the established opinion. This rugged rough countryman walks & sits alone, assured of his sanity & his inspiration, & writes to no public—sneered at by Jeffrey & Brougham, branded by Byron, blackened by the gossip of Barry Cornwall & De-Quincey, down to Bowring—for they all had disparaging tales of him, yet himself no more doubting the fine oracles that visited him than if Apollo had brought them visibly in his hand: and here & there a solitary reader in country places had felt & owned them, & now, so few years after, it is lawful in that obese material England, whose vast strata of population are nowise converted or altered, yet to affirm unblamed, unresisted, that this is the genuine, & the rest the impure metal.

Dr Holmes, one day, said to me, that he disliked scientific matter introduced into (literary) lectures, "it was meretricious."

Oct. 9, 1864

Right-minded men would very easily bring order out of our American chaos, if working with courage, & without by-ends. These Tennesee slaveholders in the land of Midian are far in advance of our New-England politicians. They see & front the real questions. The two points would seem to be absolute Emancipation—establishing the fact that the United States henceforward knows no color, no race, in its law, but legislates for all alike—one law for all men: *that* first; and, secondly, make the confiscation of rebel property final, as you did with the tories in the Revolution.

Thereby you at once open the whole South to the enterprise & genius of new men of all nations, & extend New England from Canada to the Gulf, & to the Pacific. You redeem your wicked Indian policy, & leave no murderous complications to sow the sure seed of future wars.

Oct. 19, 1864

Bryant has learned where to hang his titles, namely, by tying his mind to autumn woods, winter mornings, rain, brooks, mountains, Evening winds, & wood-birds. Who speaks of these is forced to remember Bryant.

American. Never dispaired of the Republic. Dared name a jay & a gentian, crows.

His poetry is sincere. I think of the young poets that they have seen pictures of mountains & seashores but his that he has seen mountains & has the staff in his hand.

Feb. 13, 1865

Home from Chicago & Milwaukee. Chicago grows so fast that one ceases to respect civic growth: as if all these solid & stately squares, which we are wont to see as the slow work of a century, had come to be done by machinery, as cloth & hardware is made, & was therefore shoddy architecture, without honor.

'Twas tedious the obstructions & squalor of travel. The advantage of their offers at Chicago made it needful to go. It was in short this dragging a decorous old gentleman out of home, & out of position, to this juvenile career tantamount to this; "I'll bet you fifty dollars a day for three weeks, that you will not leave your library & wade & freeze & ride & run, & suffer all manner of indignities, & stand up for an hour each night reading in a hall:" and I answer, "I'll bet I will," I do it, & win the $900.

April 10, 1865

Like some of my trees, I am a "shy bearer."

April 1865

'Tis far the best that the rebels have been pounded instead of nego-
ciated into a peace. They must remember it, & their inveterate brag will
be humbled, if not cured. George Minott used to tell me over the wall,
when I urged him to go to town meeting & vote, that "votes did no good,
what was done so wouldn't last, but what was done by bullets would
stay put." General Grant's terms certainly look a little too easy, as fore-
closing any action hereafter to convict Lee of treason, and I fear that the
high tragic historic justice which the nation with severest consideration
should execute, will be softened & dissipated & toasted away at dinner-
tables. But the problems that now remain to be solved are very intricate
& perplexing, & men are very much at a loss as to the right action. If we
let the southern States in to Congress, the Northern democrats will join
them in thwarting the will of the government. And the obvious remedy
is to give the negro his vote. And then the difficult question comes—
what shall be the qualification of voters? We wish to raise the mean
white to his right position, that he may withstand the planter. But the
negro will learn to write & read (which should be a required qualification) before the white will.

President Lincoln. Why talk of President Lincoln's equality of manners to the elegant or titled men with whom Everett or others saw him?
A sincerely upright & intelligent man as he was, placed in the Chair, has
no need to think of his manners or appearance. His work day by day
educates him rapidly & to the best. He exerts the enormous power of
this continent in every hour, in every conversation, in every act—thinks
& decides under this pressure, forced to see the vast & various bearings
of the measures he adopts: *he* cannot palter, he cannot but carry a grace
beyond his own, a dignity, by means of what he drops, e.g. all pretension & trick, and arrives, of course, at a simplicity, which is the perfection of manners.

May 6, 1865

We are such vain peacocks that we read in an English journal with
joy, that no house in London or in Paris can compare with the comfort &
splendor of Delmonico's in New York.

But I was never in Delmonico's.

May 1865

It is becoming to the Americans to dare in religion to be simple, as
they have been in government, in trade, in social life.

They are to break down prisons, capital punishment, slavery, tariff,
disfranchisement, caste; and they have rightly pronounced Tolera-

tion—that no religious test shall be put. They are to abolish laws against atheism.

They are not to allow immorality, they are to be strict in laws of marriage; they are to be just to women, in property, in votes, in personal rights.

And they are to establish the pure religion, Justice, Asceticism, self-devotion, Bounty.

They will lead their language round the globe, & they will lead religion & freedom with them.

Assert forever that morals is the test, then these miserable religions that we have known will be exposed. There is no vice that has not skulked behind them. It has been shown the bad morals of the Southern population. It cries to heaven. Yet these poisoning, starving, town burning, ever-planting people arrogate to themselves all the Christianity of the nation, charge us with plot to kill their Christian President, accuse us of libertinism, reading & writing, slave stealing &c.

And it is only very lately that our own Churches, formerly silent on this crime & notoriously hostile to Abolitionists, wheeled into line for Emancipation. . . .

It was as all know, the experience of all abolitionists, that the Church was their chief Enemy.

The Pope that old impostor—what a history is that of the Catholic Church.

Now this is the mischief of suffering any doctrine of miracles, the immorality of miracles.

Put back the emphasis sternly & forever & ever on pure morals, always the same, not subject to doubtful interpretation, with no sale of indulgences—truth-speakers, just dealers, humble & useful.

It was his tender conviction of this power & presence that made Jesus a light in the world, & the spirit that animated him is as swift and puissant today.

The only incorruptible thing is morals. All the religions soon go to ruin. They get incrusted with miracles, & divert attention from the rule, the Eternal Presence, to the legend. It is no matter what Christ did or suffered, or Moses, or John, but of great import how you stand to your tribunal.

But morals must be fresh & perfect every day, they have no memory.

I am an old writer, & yet I often meet good English words which I never used once. Thus I met just now the word *wainscot.*

* * *

It should be easy to say what I have always felt, that Stanley's "Lives of the Philosophers" or Marcus Antoninus are agreeable & suggestive books to me, whilst St Paul or Saint John are not, & I should never think of taking up these to start me on my task, as I often have used Plato or Plutarch. It is because the bible wears black cloth. It comes with a certain official claim against which the mind revolts. The book has its own nobilities—might well be charming, if it was left simply on its merits, as the others; but this "you must"—"it is your duty"—repels. 'Tis like the introduction of martial law into Concord. If you should dot our farms with picket lines, & I could not go or come across lots without a pass, I should resist, or else emigrate. If Concord were as beautiful as Paradise, it would be detestable at once.

May 28, 1865

In the acceptance that my papers find among my thoughtful countrymen, in these days, I cannot help feeling how limited is their reading. If they read only the books that I do, they would not exaggerate so wildly.

Summer 1865

We see the dawn of a new era, worth to mankind all the treasure & all the lives it has cost, yes, worth to the world the lives of all this generation of American men, if they had been demanded.

It is commonly said of the War of 1812, that it made the nation honorably known: it enlarged our politics, extinguished narrow sectional parties.

But the States were young & unpeopled. The present war, on a prodigiously enlarged scale, has cost us how many valuable lives; but it has made many lives valuable that were not so before, through the start & expansion it has given. It has fired selfish old men to an incredible liberality, & young men to the last devotion. The journals say, it has demoralized many rebel regiments, but also it has *moralized* many of our regiments, & not only so, but *moralized* cities & states. It added to every house & heart a vast enlargement. In every house & shop, an American map has been unrolled, & daily studied—& now that peace has come, every citizen finds himself a skilled student of the condition, means, & future, of this continent.

Aug. 1865

In the Revue des Deux Mondes found a paper on the Future Life, which suggested the thought, that one abstains—I abstain, for example—from printing a chapter on the Immortality of the Soul, because, when I have come to the end of my statement, the hungry eyes that run through it will close disappointed; *That is not here which we desire:* & I shall be as much wronged by their hasty conclusion, as they feel themselves by my short-comings. I mean, that I am a better believer, & all serious souls are better believers in the Immortality, than we give grounds for. The real evidence is too subtle, or is higher, than we can write down in propositions, & therefore Wordsworth's Ode is the best modern Essay on the subject.

It is curious to see how fast old history is the counterpart of our own, as soon as we are intimately let into knowledge of it. Thus I am just now surprised by finding Michel Angelo, Vittoria Colonna, Savonarola, Contarini, Pole, Occhino, & the superior souls near them to be the religious of that day, drawn to each other, & under some cloud with the rest of the world, as the Transcendentalists of 20 years ago in Boston. They were the reformers, the Abolitionists, the radicals of the hour, separated, to be sure, by their intellectual activity & culture, from the masses who followed Luther & Savonarola, yet on their side in sympathy against the corruptions of Rome.

People have been burned or stoned for saying things which are commonplaces of conversation today.

Sept.? 1865

Nature is very rich in patterns, but cunningly, not so rich as she seems, & so repeats herself. Cousins of fourth & fifth degree have sometimes striking resemblance, & are therefore both repetitions of the common ancestor. Robert Winthrop, when young, strongly resembled the portrait in the Historical Society's Rooms, of Governor Winthrop. Indeed I suppose the Cunning Artist does not quite repeat her type until after four or five generations when all the rememberers are gone, & she can just duplicate every face of the fifth back generation, without risk of confusion or discovery. But I don't think even this interval will be safe now, art having circumvented her with the photograph, which will force her to invent new varieties or lose her reputation for fertility.

Sept.–Nov. 1865

Mr B. P. Hunt said, that a young man of good position in Philadelphia went to the war, & accepted the colonelcy of a colored regiment. On his return lately to Phila., all his acquaintances cut him. Judge Hoar said to me, that he had long ago made up his mind that the cutting was to be from the other side: that this country belonged to the men of the most liberal persuasion. . . .

Now in the time of the Fugitive Slave-law, when the best young men who had ranged themselves around Mr Webster were already all of them in the interest of freedom, & threw themselves at once into opposition, Mr Webster could no longer see one of them in the street; he glared on them but knew them not; his resentments were implacable. What did they do? Did they sit down & bewail themselves? No; Sumner & his valiant young contemporaries set themselves to the task of making their views not only clear but prevailing. They proclaimed & defended them & inoculated with them the whole population, & drove Mr Webster out of the world. All his mighty genius, which none had been so forward to acknowledge & magnify as they, availed him nothing: for they knew that the spirit of God & of humanity was with them, and he withered & died as by suicide. Calhoun had already gone, as Webster, by breaking his own head against the nature of things.

Nov. 5, 1865

We hoped that in the Peace, after such a war, a great expansion would follow in the mind of the country: grand views in every direction—true freedom in politics, in religion, in social science, in thought. But the energy of the nation seems to have expended itself in the war, and every interest is found as sectional & timorous as before. The Episcopal church is baser than ever—perfect Yahoo; the Southerner just the same Gambia negro chief—addicted to crowing, garotting, & stealing, as ever: the Democrat as false & truckling; the Union party as timid & compromising, the scholars pale & expectant, never affirmative . . .

Nov. 14, 1865

Williamstown. I saw tonight in the Observatory, through Alvan Clark's telescope, the Dumb-Bell nebula in the Fox & Goose constellation;
> the four double stars in Lyra;
> the double stars of Castor;
> the 200 stars of the Pleiades;
> the nebula in (Perseus?) . . .

I have rarely been so much gratified.

Early in the afternoon Prof. Bascom carried me in a gig to the top of the West Mountain, & showed me the admirable view down the Valley in which this town & Adams lie, with Greylock & his attendant ranges towering in front: then we rose to the crest, & looked down into Rensellaer County, New York, & the multitude of low hills that compose it. . . . & beyond, in the horizon, the mountain range to the West.

Of all tools, an observatory is the most sublime. And these mountains give an inestimable worth to Williamstown & Massachusetts. But for the mountains, I don't quite like the proximity of a college & its noisy students. To enjoy the hills as poet, I prefer simple farmers as neighbors. . . .

What is so good in a college as an observatory? The sublime attaches to the door & to the first stair you ascend, that this is the road to the stars. Every fixture & instrument in the building, every nail & pin has a direct reference to the Milky-Way, the fixed stars, & the nebulae. & we leave Massachusetts & the Americas & history outside at the door, when we came in.

Dec.? 1865

When I was a senior in College, I think, Samuel Barrett whom I had known in Concord was about to be ordained in the Chamber-street Church and I called upon him in his room in College. I think he must have been a proctor. We talked about the vices & calamities of the time—I don't recall what the grim shadows were, or how we came on them—but when I rose to go, & asked him what was the relief & cure of all this? he replied with cheerful ardor, "Nothing but Unitarianism." From my remembrance of how this answer struck me, I am sure that this antidote must have looked as thin & poor & pale to me then, as now. I was never for a moment the victim of "Enlightenment," or "Progress of the Species," or the "Diffusion-of-Knowledge-Society."

Carlyle. I have neglected badly Carlyle, who is so steadily good to me. Like a Catholic in Boston, he has put himself by his violent anti-Americanism in false position, & it is not quite easy to deal with him. But his merits are overpowering, & when I read "Friedrich", I forget all else. His treatment of his subject is ever so masterly, so original, so self-respecting, so defiant, allowing himself all manner of liberties & confidences with his hero, as if he were his hero's father or benefactor, that he is proud of him, & yet checks & chides & sometimes puts him in the corner, when he is not a good boy, that, amid all his sneering & contempt for all other historians, & biographers, & princes, & peoples, the reader yet feels himself complimented by the confidences with which he is honored by this free-tongued, dangerous companion, who discloses to him all his secret opinions, all his variety of moods, & varying estimates of his hero & everybody else. He is as dangerous as a madman. Nobody knows what he will say next, or whom he will strike. Prudent people keep out of his way. If Genius were cheap, we should do without Carlyle; but, in the existing population, he cannot be spared.

Taking in Sail
1866-1874

EMERSON WOULD NOT REACH his terminus until he was almost seventy-nine years old, but he knew by the mid-1860s that his important work was done. After *The Conduct of Life* (1860) and *May-Day and Other Pieces* (1867), he published nothing that substantially added to his reputation, though the reader of his journal notices that his pen had lost none of its sharpness. Within himself, as he had noted in 1864, he would continue to find not "wrinkles & used heart, but unspent youth." Thus we see him, early in 1866, coming upon a "good book" and wishing for an infinite expanse of time in which to explore new questions. The sciences especially, in this age of rapidly expanding knowledge, administered a dose of iron to Emerson's mind and made him feel immortal. (He wryly observed in 1868 that the "mechanical improvements" of his time—spectacles, false teeth, trusses, and the like—gave him a leg up over his ancestors, though he also noted that Dr. Ripley and Aunt Mary lived to be nonagenarians supported by little but the staunch bands of religious orthodoxy.)

Emerson may have thought it was "time to be old," but he was still physically vigorous enough in his sixties to continue lecturing throughout the country—on one occasion crossing the Mississippi by skiff in bitter cold weather, on another riding through an Iowa snowstorm in an open sleigh. We see him spending a "forbiddingly cold night" on Mt. Monadnock as well as enjoying a "rough & grand walk" on Mt. Mansfield. He also traveled by railroad to California in the spring of 1871 and rode

on horseback through Yosemite Valley in 100 degree weather.
"How *can* Mr. Emerson," asked one of the younger members of
the party, "be so agreeable, all the time, without getting tired!" It
is reported that Emerson maintained his serenity no less when
faced with "stupefied Mongolians" in a San Francisco opium den
than when he received a stolid reception from Brigham Young in
Salt Lake City. It is likely that Emerson, who was still making
lecture tours in 1872, could have continued doing so into his
eighth decade had it not been for the shock administered by the
burning of his house in July of that year. Thereafter, a decline in
his general health and mental alertness was noticeable. Still he
was able to muster sufficient energy and enthusiasm for a third
and final trip abroad in the fall. Accompanied by his daughter
Ellen, he not only renewed acquaintances in England, France,
and Italy, but also traveled up the Nile. He set down after his return the observation of Senator Choate's daughter Helen that he
and the Sphinx probably confronted each other on equal terms.
At least it is clear from the journals of these last years that Emerson never tired of posing difficult questions.

Agreeing with a text from Montesquieu in 1870, Emerson
believed it to be one of the pleasures of old age that new learning
was less imperative than releasing the storehouse of memory. He
found the dead living not only in his dreams but also in his conscious recollections. He thought often of his Aunt Mary, especially as he read her diaries, and—celebrating the grim grandeur
of her old-time religion—deemed her one of America's "great
men" along with Franklin and Edwards and Washington and
Adams. He reflected, too, on the history of the so-called Transcendental movement and in particular called to mind Margaret
Fuller, "with her radiant genius & fiery heart"; he also lamented
the "dismal mask" Hawthorne had used to sketch her portrait in
The Blithedale Romance. And reacting, presumably, to a harsh
criticism by Lowell, he reaffirmed his faith in Thoreau's genius,
observing poignantly that Henry "was well aware of his stubborn
contradictory attitude" and predicted his friends would find
the words "swamp oak" engraved on his heart. Perhaps Emerson
also wondered what the ultimate verdict would be on *his* character. By 1872 his own assessment was typically severe and not unlike the portrait of Thoreau: "I have no social talent, no wealth of

nature, nothing but a sullen will, & a steady appetite for insights in any or all directions, to balance my manifold imbecilities."

Emerson continued especially to record his insights into literary figures, for he had to admit finally (and sometimes with consternation) that his was essentially a life of reading and writing and books did not fail to turn him both "inside out" and "outside in." Looking over a new translation of Dante's *Inferno*, he admired, as always, the poet's skill but shuddered at the grotesqueness of his visions. Perhaps because he was himself dreaming a good deal, he no longer relished the "somnambulic genius" of this once close friend. He also felt the urge to "abuse" Wordsworth, as he had done in some of his earliest college notebooks, but now—with the terse wit of his later years—he summed up his objections by saying that Wordsworth suffered from "asthma of the mind." Yet this was clearly a love-hate relationship, and we see Emerson five years later reviewing and correcting his own criticisms. He would not, after all, reject his verdict that Wordsworth was "the manliest poet of his age." He set down, in addition, shrewd observations about such figures as George Eliot, William Collins, Shakespeare, Lowell, and Whitman. The question of America's achievement in poetry was a lively one for him, especially as he gathered selections for his anthology *Parnassus* (1874). Twentieth-century readers of Emerson's journal can only be touched by his wishing, in 1870, that Julia Ward Howe was a native of Massachusetts because "we have had no such poetess in New England." Emily Dickinson's cupboard was already filled with most of her best work, but Emerson could of course know nothing of that. Had he known her poems, one feels sure he would have greeted her as enthusiastically as he had hailed Whitman at the beginning of a "great career."

These pages are haunted by Emerson's awareness that his firmament was rapidly contracting. He would try hard to court the muse, but the times of inspiration were fewer and farther between. He was content to harp on the old strings but had to warn himself not to repeat his favorite sentences. His memory was flagging, and sometimes at a lecture he would reread a page without being conscious of it. The ever-vigilant Ellen asked her father to rehearse with her beforehand, but he thought it not important. "Things that go wrong about these lectures don't disturb me, because I know that everyone knows that I am worn out and passed by, and that it is only my old friends come for friendship's sake to have one last season with me." That last season prolonged itself, for Emerson declined very gently into senility, sailing over a period of years—as Auden would write of Melville—"into an extraordinary mildness."

Though death did not come until April 27, 1882, Emerson's journal effectively ends in the mid-seventies. His attitude remained hopeful, for he believed that his primary strength lay in affirmation. A decade before his death he noted that, if he lived another year, he would cite the last stanza of his own poem "The World-Soul":

> Spring still makes spring in the mind
>   When sixty years are told;
> Love wakes anew this throbbing heart,
>   And we are never old.

That perpetual expectation of the season of renewal represented Emerson's true faith, which he maintained always in the face of an honest doubt. Placed inside the front cover of his last regular journal is a statement, attributed to Longfellow, that seems to epitomize the wry humor with which this ultimate Yankee confronted the great verities: "Last night I dreamed of Emerson. He said 'The Spring will come again, but shall we live to see it, or only the eternal Spring up there?', lifting both his hands on high."

Feb. 1866

Martha Bartlett told me, that a lady said to Miss Andrews, "that the sense of being perfectly drest gave a feeling of peace which religion could never give."

Quick people touch & go, whilst heavy people insist on pounding. 'Tis in vain to try to choke them off, & change the conversation to avoid the slaughter-house details. Straightway they begin at the beginning, & thrice they slay the slain. Society shall be distressing, & there's an end of it.

March? 1866

When I read a good book, say, one which opens a literary question, I wish that life were 3000 years long. Who would not launch into this

Egyptian history, as opened by Wilkinson, Champollion, Bunsen, but for the *memento mori* which he reads on all sides. Who is not provoked by the temptation of the Sanscrit literature? And, as I wrote above, the Chaldaic oracles tempt me. But so also does Algebra, and astronomy, & chemistry, & geology, & botany. Perhaps, then, we must increase the appropriation, & write 30,000 years. And, if these years have correspondent effect with the 60 years we have experienced, some earnest scholar will move to amend by striking out the word "years," & inserting "centuries."

Reality. How rarely we live, with all our reading & writing! and are coming not to deal with virtue at all, but only with its literature!

It is plain that the War has made many things public that were·once quite too private. A man searches his mind for thoughts, & finds only the old commonplaces; but, at some moment, on the old topic of the day's politics, he makes a distinction he had not made; he discerns a little inlet not seen before. Where was a wall, is now a door. The mind goes in & out, and variously states in prose or poetry its new experience. It points it out to one & another, who, of course, deny the alleged discovery. But repeated experiments & affirmations make it visible soon to others. The point of interest is here, that these gates once opened never swing back. The observers may come at their leisure, & do at last satisfy themselves of the fact. The thought, the doctrine, the right, hitherto not affirmed, is published in set propositions, in conversation of scholars & at last in the very choruses of songs.

March–June 1866
   American Politics. I have the belief that of all things the work of America is to make the advanced intelligence of mankind in the sufficiency of morals practical; that, since there is on every side a breaking up of the faith in the old traditions of religion, &, of necessity, a return to the omnipotence of the moral sentiment, that in America this conviction is to be embodied in the laws, in the jurisprudence, in international law, in political economy. The lawyers have always some glaring exceptions to their statements of public equity, some reserves of sovereignty, tantamount to the Rob Roy rule that might makes right. America should affirm & establish that in no instance should the guns go in advance of the perfect right. You shall not make coups d'etat, & afterwards explain & pay, but shall proceed like William Penn, or whatever other Christian or humane person who treats with the Indian or foreigner on principles of honest trade & mutual advantage. Let us wait a thousand years for the Sandwich islands before we seize them by violence.

* * *

It is peremptory for good living in houses in a cultivated age, that the beautiful should never be out of thought. It is not more important that you should provide bread for the table, than that it should be put there & used in a comely manner. You have often a right to be angry with servants, but you must carry your anger & chide without offence to beauty. Else, you have quarreled with yourself, as well as with them.

June–July 1866

Bias. Seven men went through a field, one after another. One was a farmer, he saw only the grass; the next was an astronomer, he saw the horizon & the stars; the physician noticed the standing water & suspected miasma; he was followed by a soldier, who glanced over the ground, found it easy to hold, & saw in a moment how the troops could be disposed; then came the geologist, who noticed the boulders & the sandy loam; after him came the real estate broker, who bethought him how the line of the house-lots should run, where would be the driveway, & the stables. The poet admired the shadows cast by some trees, & still more the music of some thrushes & a meadow lark.

I suspect Walt Whitman had been reading these Welsh remains when he wrote his "Leaves of Grass." Thus Taliesin sings,

"I am water, I am a wren;
I am a workman, I am a star;
I am a serpent;
I am a cell, I am a chink;
I am a depositary of song, I am a learned person."

Read M. M. E.'s mss. yesterday—many pages. They keep for me the old attraction; though, when I sometimes have tried passages on a stranger, I find something of fairy gold—they need too much commentary, & are not as incisive as on me. They make the best example I have known of the power of the religion of the Puritans in full energy, until fifty years ago, in New England. The central theme of these endless diaries is her relation to the Divine Being; the absolute submission of her will, with the sole proviso, that she may know it is the direct agency of God (& not of cold laws of contingency &c) which bereaves & humiliates her. But the religion of the diary, as of the class it represented, is biographical; it is the culture, the poetry, the mythology, in which they personally believed themselves dignified, inspired, judged, & dealt with, in the present & in the future. And [it] certainly gives to life an earnestness, & to nature a sentiment, which lacking, our later generation appears frivolous.

July 2, 1866

I went with Annie Keyes & Mr Channing on Wednesday, 27th June, to Troy, thence to the Mountain House in wagon, &, with Edward & Tom Ward who had come down to meet us, climbed the mountain. The party already encamped were Story, Ward, & Edward, for the men; & Una Hawthorne, Lizzie Simmons, & Ellen E. for the maidens. They lived on the plateau just below the summit, & were just constructing their one tent by spreading & tying India-Rubber blankets over a frame of spruce poles large enough to hold the four ladies with sleeping space, & to cover the baggage. The men must find shelter, if need is, under the rocks. The mountain at once justified the party & their enthusiasm. It was romance enough to be there, & behold the panorama, & learn one by one all the beautiful novelties. The country below is a vast champaign—half cleared, half forest—with forty ponds in sight, studded with villages & farmhouses, &, all around the horizon, closed with mountain ranges. The eye easily traces the valley followed by the Cheshire railroad, & just beyond it the valley of the Connecticut river, then the Green Mountain chain: in the north, the White Hills can be seen; &, on the East, the low mountains of Watâtic & Wachusett. We had hardly wonted our eyes to the new Olympus, when the signs of a near storm set all the scattered party on the alert. The tent was to be finished & covered, & the knap-sacks piled in it. The Wanderers began to appear on the heights, & to descend, & much work in camp was done in brief time. I looked about for a shelter in the rocks, & not till the rain began to fall, crept into it. I called to Channing, & afterwards to Tom Ward, who came, & we sat substantially dry, if the seat was a little cold, & the wall a little dripping, &, pretty soon, a large brook roared between the rocks, a little lower than our feet hung. Meantime, the thunder shook the mountain, & much of the time was continuous cannonade. The storm refused to break up. One & another adventurer rushed out to see the signs, & especially the sudden torrents, little Niagaras, that were pouring over the upper ledges, & descending upon our plateau. But everybody was getting uncomfortably wet, the prospect was not good for the night, &, in spite of all remonstrance on the part of the young ladies, I insisted that they must go down with me to the "Mountain-House," for the night. All the four girls at last were ready, & descended with Storey & me—thus leaving the tent free to be occupied by Mr Channing, Tom W., & Edward. The storm held on most of the night, but we were slowly drying & warming in the comfortable inn. Next day, the weather slowly changed, & we climbed again the hill, and were repaid for all mishaps by the glory of the afternoon & evening. Edward went up with me to the summit, up all sorts of giant stairs, & showed the long spur with many descending peaks on the Dublin side. The rock-work is interesting & grand—the clean cleavage, the wonderful slabs, the quartz dikes, the rock torrents in some parts, the uniform presence on the upper surface of the glacial lines or scratches, all in one self-same direction. Then every glance below apprises you how you are projected out into stellar space, as a sailor on a ship's bowsprit out into the sea. We look down here on a hundred farms & farmhouses, but never see horse or man. For our eyes the country is depopulated, around us the arctic sparrow, *fringilla nivalis*, flies & *peeps*, the ground-robin also; but you can hear the distant song of the wood-thrushes ascending from the green belts below. I found the picture charming, & more than remunerative. Later, from the plateau, at sunset, I saw the great shadow of Monadnoc lengthen over the vast plain, until it touched the horizon. The earth & sky filled themselves with all ornaments—haloes, rainbows, and little pendulums of cloud would hang down till they touched the top of a hill, giving it the appearance of a smoking volcano. The wind was north, the evening cold, but the camp fire kept the party comfortable, whilst Story, with Edward for chorus, sang a multitude of songs, to their great delectation. The night was forbiddingly cold; the tent kept the girls in vital heat, but the youths could hardly keep their blood in circulation, the rather, that they had spared too many of their blankets to the girls & to the old men. Themselves had nothing for it but to rise & cut wood, & bring it to the fire, which Mr Channing watched & fed. & this service of fetching wood was done by Tom Ward once to his great peril during the night. In pitching a formless stump over into the ravine, he fell, &, in trying to clear himself from the stump now behind him, flying & falling, got a bad contusion.

July 1866

I see with joy the Irish emigrants landing at Boston, at New York, & say to myself, There they go—to school.

There is this to be said in favor of drinking, that it takes the drunkard first out of society, then out of the world.

'Tis certain that any consideration of botany, of geology, of astronomy, administers a certain iron to the mind, adds a feeling of permanency, suggests immortality; whilst dinners, dances, & Washington-Street, have a contrary effect.

Dr Channing took counsel, in 1840?, with George Ripley & Mrs Ripley, to find whether it were possible to bring cultivated thoughtful people socially together. He had already talked with Dr Warren on the same design, who made, I have heard, a party, which had its fatal termination in an oyster supper. Mrs Ripley invited a large party, but I do not remember that Dr Channing came. Perhaps he did, but it is significant enough of the very moderate success, that I do not recall the fact of his presence, or indeed any particulars but of some absurd toilettes.

I think there was the mistake of a general belief at that time, that there was some concert of doctrinaires to establish certain opinions, & inaugurate some movement in literature, philosophy, & religion, of which the supposed conspirators were quite innocent; for there was no concert, & only here & there, two or three men or women who read & wrote, each alone, with unusual vivacity. Perhaps they only agreed in having fallen upon Coleridge, Wordsworth, Goethe, & then upon Carlyle, with pleasure & sympathy. Otherwise, their education & reading were not marked, but had the American superficialness, & their studies were solitary. I suppose all of them were surprised at this rumor of a school or sect, & certainly at the name of Transcendentalism, which nobody knows who gave, or when it was first applied. As these persons became, in the common chances of society, acquainted with each other, there resulted certainly strong friendships, which, of course, were exclusive in proportion to their heat, & perhaps those persons who were mutually the best friends were the most private, & had no ambition of publishing their letters, diaries or conversation. Such were Charles Newcomb, Sam G. Ward, & Caroline Sturgis—all intimate with Margaret Fuller. Margaret with her radiant genius & fiery heart was perhaps the real centre that drew so many & so various individuals to a seeming union. Hedge, Clarke, W. H. Channing, W. E. Channing, jr., George Ripley, James Clarke & many more then or since known as writers, or otherwise distinguished, were only held together as her friends. Mr A Bronson Alcott became known to all these as the pure idealist, not at all a man of letters, nor of any practical talent, & quite too cold & contemplative for the alliances of friendship, but purely intellectual, with rare simplicity & grandeur of perception, who read Plato as an equal, & inspired his companions only in proportion as they were intellectual, whilst the men of talent, of course, complained of the want of point & precision in this abstract & religious thinker. Elizabeth Hoar & Sarah Clarke, though certainly never summoned to any of the meetings which were held at George Ripley's, or Dr Francis's, or Stetson's, or Bartol's or my house, were prized & sympathetic friends of Margaret & of others whom I have named, in the circle. The "Dial" was the only public or quotable result of this temporary society & fermentation: and yet the Community at Brook Farm, founded by the readers of Fourier, drew also inspirations from this circle. . . .

In a warmer & more fruitful climate Alcott & his friends would soon have been Buddhists.

An important fact in the sequel was the plantation of Mr Lane & Mr Alcott at Stillriver, "Fruitlands." The labor on the place was all done by the volunteers; they used no animal food; they even for a time dressed themselves only in linen; but there were inherent difficulties: the members of the community were unused to labor, & were soon very impatient of it: the hard work fell on a few, & mainly on women. The recruits whom they drew were some of them partly, some of them quite insane. And the individuals could not divest themselves of the infirmity of holding property. When the winter came, & they had burned all the dry wood they could find, & began to burn green wood, they could not keep themselves warm, & fled to the Shakers for their warm fires.

Humanity always equal to itself. The religious understand each other under all mythologies, & say the same thing. Homer & Aeschylus in all the rubbish of fables speak out clearly ever & anon the noble sentiments of all ages.

Calvinism was as injurious to the justice, as Greek myths were to the purity of the gods. Yet noble souls carried themselves nobly, & drew what treasures of character from that grim system.

I find it a great & fatal difference whether I court the Muse, or the Muse courts me: That is the ugly disparity between age & youth.

July 30, 1866
This morn came again the exhilarating news of the landing of the Atlantic telegraph cable at Heart's Content, Newfoundland. . . . We have grown more skilful, it seems, in electric machinery, & may confide better in a lasting success. Our political condition is better, &, though dashed by the treachery of our American President, can hardly go backward to slavery & civil war. Besides, the suggestion of an event so exceptional & astounding in the history of human arts, is, that this instant & pitiless publicity now to be given to every public act must force on the actors a new sensibility to the opinion of mankind, & restrain folly & meanness.

Aug.–Sept. 1866
On 31 August visited Agassiz by invitation with Lidian & Ellen, & spent the day at his house & on the Nahant rocks. He is a man to be thankful for, always cordial, full of facts, with unsleeping observation, & perfectly communicative. In Brazil he saw on a half mile square 117 different kinds of excellent timber—& not a saw mill in Brazil. A country thirsting for Yankees to open & use its wealth. . . . Agassiz says, the whole population is wretchedly immoral, the color & features of the

people showing the entire intermixing of all the races. Mrs Agassiz found the women ignorant, depressed, with no employment but needle-work, with no future, negligent of their persons, shabby & sluttish at home, with their hair about their ears, only gay in the ball room: The men well dressed.

I don't remember how long the "Brook Farm" existed, I think about six or seven years—the society then broke up, & the Farm was sold, &, I believe all the partners came out with loss. Some of them had spent on it the accumulations of years. I suppose they all at the moment regarded it as a failure. I do not think they can so regard it at this time, but probably as an important chapter in their experience, which has been of life-long value. What knowledge of themselves & of each other, what various practical wisdom, what personal power, what studies of character, what accumulated culture many of the members must have owed to it!

I hate nerves, they make such hedge hogs of people.

A patient under the dentist's hands thinks his mouth must have grown to a square foot.

I confess there is sometimes a caprice in fame, like the unnecessary eternity given to these minute shells & antediluvian fishes, leaves, ferns, yea, ripples & rain-drops, which have come safe down through a vast antiquity, with all its shocks, upheavals, deluges, & volcanoes, wherein everything noble in art & humanity had perished, yet these snails, peri-winkles, & worthless dead leaves, come staring & perfect into our day-light. What is Fame, if every snail or ripple or raindrop shares it?

I think the habit of writing by telegraph will have a happy effect on all writing by teaching condensation.

It is with a book as it is with a man. We are more struck with the merits of a man who is well-mannered, well-drest, & well-mounted, than with those of my neighbor in shoddy; and I am a little ashamed to find how much this gay book in red & gold with a leaf like vellum & a palatial page, has opened my eyes to the merits of the poet whose verses I long since coldly looked over in newspapers or monthlies or in small cloth-bound volumes.

The progress of invention is really a threat. Whenever I see a rail-road I look for a republic.

Oct. 24, 1866

Dreams. I have often experienced, & again last night, in my dreams, the surprise & curiosity of a stranger or indifferent observer to the trait or the motive & information communicated. Thus some refractory youth, over whom I had some guidance or authority, expressed very frankly his dissent & dislike, disliked my way of laughing. I was curious to understand the objection, & endeavored to penetrate & appreciate it, &, of course, with the usual misfortune, that, when I woke & attempted to recover the specification, which was remarkable, it was utterly forgotten. But the fact that I, who must be the author of both parts of the dialogue, am thus remote & inquisitive in regard to one part, is ever wonderful.

Oct.–Nov. 1866

Cunning egotism. If I cannot brag of knowing something, then I brag of not knowing it. At any rate, Brag.

At the grave of a poor devil about whom no one could think of a single merit to mention, an old Dutchman said, "Vell, he vas a goot schmoker."
Of him did not Wordsworth say, "Enjoys the air he breathes."

The negro, thanks to his temperament, appears to make the greatest amount of happiness out of the smallest capital.

Dec. 1866–April 1867

The treatises that are written on university reform may be acute or not, but their chief value to the observer is the showing that a cleavage is occurring in the hitherto firm granite of the past, and a new era is nearly arrived.

The advantage of the old fashioned folio, was, that it was safe from the borrowers.

Fences: a paling, a ditch, an arbor-vitae hedge, a pair of small eyes, a pair of large eyes, & at need a whip, at more need a pistol.

If a man happens to have a good father, he needs less history: he quotes his father on each occasion—his habits, manners, rules. If his father is dull & unmentionable, then his own reading becomes more important.

* * *

The word *miracle*, as it is used, only indicates the savage ignorance of the devotee, staring with wonder to see water turned into wine, & heedless of the stupendous fact of himself being there present. If the water became wine, became fire, became a chorus of angels, it would not compare with the familiar fact of his own perception. Here he stands, a lonely thought, harmoniously organized into correspondence with the Universe of mind & matter.

April 10, 1867

Yesterday at the funeral of George L. Stearns. Rode to Mount Auburn in a carriage with Mr Alcott & Mr Theophilus Parsons, & had long conversation on Swedenborg. Mr P., intelligent & well-versed on Swedenborg; but his intelligence stops, as usual, at the Hebrew symbolism. Philosopher up to that limit, but there accepts the village-church as part of the sky. In a day not far off this English obstinacy of patching the ecliptic of the Universe with a small bit of tin, will come to an end.

April 1867

You complain that the negroes are a base class. Who makes & keeps the jew or the negro base, who but you, who exclude them from the rights which others enjoy?

I thought as the train carried me so fast down the east bank of the Hudson River, that Nature had marked the site of New York with such rare combination of advantages, as she now & then finishes a man or woman to a perfection in all parts, & in all details, as if to show the luxuriant type of the race—finishing in one what is attempted or only begun in a thousand individuals. The length & volume of the river; the gentle beauty of the banks, the country rising immediately behind the bank on either side; the noble outlines of the Katskills; the breadth of the bays at Croton? & Tarrytown? then West Point; then, as you approach N. York, the sculptured Palisades; then, at the city itself, the meeting of the waters; the river-like Sound; & the ocean at once—instead of the weary Chesapeake & Delaware Bays.

Alcott told me, that he found a dictionary fascinating: he looked out a word, & the morning was gone; for he was led on to another word, & so on & on. It required abandonment.

May–July 1867

Aristocracy is always timid. After I had read my lecture on "Natural Aristocracy", in London, and had said, after describing the "man with-

out duties," "who can blame the peasant if he fires his barns?" &c.—
Lord Morpeth came to see me at Chapman's, & hoped I would leave out
that passage, if I repeated the lecture.

Why is Collins's Ode to Evening so charming? It proves nothing, it
affirms nothing, it has no thought, no fable, no moral. I find it pleases
only as music. It is as if one's head which was full of the sights & sounds
of a summer evening—should listen to a few strains of an Aeolian Harp,
& find it restoring to him those sights & sounds. 'Tis good whistling.

July–Aug. 1867
    I suppose every old scholar has had the experience of reading some-
thing in a book which was significant to him, but which he could never
find again. Sure he is that he read it there; but no one else ever read it,
nor can he find it again, though he buy the book, & ransack every page.

Next to the originator of a good sentence is the first quoter of it.
Many will read the book before one thinks of quoting a passage. As soon
as he has done this, that line will be quoted east & west.

Read Parson's Dante. The translation appears excellent, most faithful, yet flowing & elegant, with remarkable felicities, as when *Per tutti i
cerchi dello inferno scuri* is rendered "Through all the dingy circles
down in hell."
    But Dante still appears to me, as ever, an exceptional mind, a prod-
igy of imaginative function, executive rather than contemplative or
wise. . . . not like Shakspeare, or Socrates, or Goethe, a beneficent humanity. His fame & infamies are so capriciously distributed—What odd
reasons for putting his men in inferno! The somnambulic genius of
Dante is dream strengthened to the tenth power—dream so fierce that it
grasps all the details of the phantom spectacle, &, in spite of itself,
clutches & conveys them into the waking memory, & can recite what
every other would forget. What pitiless minuteness of horrible details!
He is a curiosity like the mastodon, but one would not desire such for
friends & contemporaries. Abnormal throughout like Swedenborg. But
at a frightful cost these obtain their fame. A man to put in a museum,
but not in your house. Indeed I never read him, nor regret that I do not.

Sept. 1, 1867
    Struggled hard last night in a dream to repeat & save a thought or
sentence spoken in the dream; but it eluded me at last: only came out of
the pulling, with this rag—"his the deeper problem, But mine the better
ciphered."

Sept. 1867

At the present day, thoughtful people must be struck with the fact, that the old religious forms are outgrown; as shown by the fact, that every intellectual man is out of the old Church: All the young men of intelligence are on what is called the radical side. How long will the people continue to exclude these, & invite the dull men? Beecher told me, that he did not hold one of the five points of Calvinism in a way to satisfy his father.

The good Heaven is sending every hour good minds into the world, & all of them on opening at maturity, discover the same expansion, the impatience of the old cramps, and a bias to the new interpretation. If you hold them in the old used-up air, they suffocate. Would you in new Massachusetts have an old Spain?

Oct.–Nov. 1867

O. W. Holmes looked last night at an Englishman in the company & said, "strange that these old families, after ages of strength, can't produce any thing better than that! Why, one of us could do better at an hour's warning." Agassiz was vastly amused.

I rarely take down Horace or Martial at home, but when reading in the Athenaeum, or Union Club, if I come upon a quotation from either, I resolve on the instant to read them every day. But—at home again, homely thoughts.

Quotation—yes, but how differently persons quote! I am as much informed of your genius by what you select, as by what you originate. I read the quotation with your eyes, & find a new & fervent sense: as my reading of Shakspeare's Richard II. has always borrowed much of its interest from Edmund Kean's rendering: though I had that play only at second hand from him, through William Emerson, who heard him in London. When I saw Kean in Boston, he played nothing so high. The reading of books is, as I daily say, according to the sensibility of the scholar, & the profoundest thought or passion sleeps as in a mine, until an equal mind or heart finds & publishes it.

In this old matter of Originality & Quotation, a few points to be made distinctly.

The apparently immense amount of debt to the old. By necessity & by proclivity, & by delight, we all quote. We quote books, & arts & science, & religion, & customs, & laws, Yes, & houses, tables & chairs. At first view, 'tis all quotation—all we have. But presently we make distinction. 1. By wise quotation. Vast difference in the mode of quotation.

One quotes so well, that the person quoted is a gainer. The quoter's selection honors & celebrates the author. The quoter gives more fame than he receives aid. Thus Coleridge.

Quoting is often merely of a suggestion which the quoter drew but of which the author is quite innocent.

For good quoting, then, there must be originality in the quoter—bent, bias, delight in the truth, & only valuing the author in the measure of his agreement with the truth which we see, & which he had the luck to see first.

And originality, what is that? It is being; being somebody, being yourself, & reporting accurately what you see & are. If another's words describe your fact, use them as freely as you use the language & the alphabet, whose use does not impair your originality. Neither will another's sentiment or distinction impugn your sufficiency. Yet in proportion to your reality of life & perception, will be your difficulty of finding yourself expressed in others' words or deeds.

And yet—and yet—I hesitate to denounce reading, as aught inferior or mean. When visions of my books come over me, as I sit writing, when the remembrance of some poet comes, I accept it with pure joy, & quit my thinking, as sad lumbering work; & hasten to my little heaven, if it is then accessible, as angels might. For these social affections also are part of Nature & being, and the delight in another's superiority is, as M. M. E. said, "my best gift from God." For here the moral nature is involved, which is higher than the intellectual.

Dec.? 1867

Sometimes you must speak, if only as Aunt Mary told me, when I was a boy, & quarreled with Elisha Jones & Frank Barrett. Dr Ripley sent for them one evening to come to the house, & there made us shake hands: Aunt Mary asked me, "Well, what did you say to them"? "I did not say anything."—"Fie on you! You should have talked about your thumbs, or your toes, only to say something."

Jan.–Feb. 1868

I have no knowledge of trade & there is not the sciolist who cannot shut my mouth & my understanding by strings of facts that seem to prove the wisdom of tariffs. But my faith in freedom of trade, as the rule, returns always. If the Creator has made oranges, coffee, & pineapples in Cuba, & refused them to Massachusetts, I cannot see why we should put a fine on the Cubans for bringing these to us—a fine so heavy as to enable Massachusetts men to build costly palm-houses & glass conservatories, under which to coax these poor plants to ripen under our hard skies, & thus discourage the poor planter from sending them to gladden the very cottages here. We punish the planter there & punish the consumer here for adding these benefits to life.

Tax opium, tax poisons, tax brandy, gin, wine, hasheesh, tobacco, & whatever articles of pure luxury, but not healthy & delicious food.

An advantage of the mechanical improvements, is, that it has made old age more possible, more tolerable, & more respectable. What with spectacles, artificial teeth, preservation of the hair, trusses, overshoes, drop-lights & sleeping-cars, we can hold this dissolving body staunch & fit for use ten or twenty years longer than our ancestors could.

What could Norton mean in saying that the only great men of the American past were Franklin & Edwards? We have had Adams, & Channing, Washington, & the prophetic authors of the Federalist, Madison & Hamilton, and, if he had known it, Aunt Mary.

March 1868

Can any one doubt that if the noblest saint among the Buddhists, the noblest Mahometan, the highest Stoic of Athens, the purest & wisest Christian, Menu in India, Confucius in China, Spinoza in Holland, could somewhere meet & converse together, they would all find themselves of one religion, & all would find themselves denounced by their own sects, & sustained by these believed adversaries of their sects. Jeremy Taylor, George Herbert, Pascal even, Pythagoras, if these could all converse intimately, two & two, how childish their country traditions would appear!

In an earlier page in this book I wrote some notes touching the so called Transcendentalists of Boston in 1837. Hawthorne drew some sketches in his Blithedale Romance, but not happily, as I think: rather, I should say quite unworthy of his genius. To be sure I do not think any of his books worthy of his genius. I admired the man, who was simple, amiable, truth loving, & frank in conversation: but I never read his books with pleasure—they are too young.

In & around Brook Farm, whether as members, boarders, or visiters, were many remarkable persons, whether for character, or intellect, or accomplishments. There was Newcomb, one of the subtlest minds—I believe I must say—the subtlest observer & diviner of character I ever met—living, reading, writing, talking there, as long, I believe, as the colony held together: Margaret Fuller, whose rich & brilliant genius no friend who really knew her could recognize under the dismal mask which, it is said, is meant for her in Hawthorne's story.

* * *

Mary Moody Emerson (1774–1863): "My aunt had an eye that went through & through you like a needle. 'She was endowed,' she said, 'with the *fatal* gift of penetration.' She disgusted every body because she knew them too well."

Revolutions. In my youth, Spinoza was a hobgoblin: now he is a saint. And Milton's "Paradise Lost" was in his day styled "a profane & lascivious poem."

April 1868
Greatness. The appearance of a great man draws a new circle outside of our largest orbit, & surprises & commands us. It is as if to the girl fully occupied with her paper dolls, a youth approaches & says, 'I love you with all my heart, come to me.' Instantly she leaves all—dolls, dances, maids, & youths, & dedicates herself to him. Or, as California in 1849, or the war in 1861, electrified the young men, & abolished all their little plans & projects with a magnificent hope or terror requiring a whole new system of hopes & fears & means. Our little circles absorb & occupy us as fully as the heavens: we can minimise as infinitely as maximise & the only way out of it is (to use a country phrase) to kick the pail

over, & accept the horizon instead of the pail, with celestial attractions & influences, instead of worms & mud pies. Coleridge, Goethe, the new Naturalists in astronomy, geology, zoology, the correlations, the Social Science, the new readings of history through Niebuhr, Mommsen, Max Muller, Champollion, Lepsius, astonish the mind, & detach it effectually from a hopeless routine. 'Come out of that,' they say, 'you lie sick & doting, only shifting from bed to bed.' And they dip the patient in this Russian bath, & he is at least well awake, & capable of sane activity. The perceptions which metaphysical & natural science cast upon the religious traditions, are every day forcing people in conversation to take new & advanced position. We have been building on the ice, & lo! the ice has floated. And the man is reconciled to his losses, when he sees the grandeur of his gains.

April–May 1868

It takes twenty years to get a good book read. For each reader is struck with a new passage & at first only with the shining & superficial ones, & by this very attention to these the rest are slighted. But with time the graver & deeper thoughts are observed & pondered. New readers come from time to time—their attention whetted by frequent & varied allusions to the book—until at last every passage has found its reader & commentator.

Spring–Summer 1868

It chanced that a dead pine-tree blown down by the wind fell against another dead pine, & by the friction kindled the dry leaves on the ground. The wind blew the flame, & the whole forest perished by suicide.

We had a story one day of a meeting of the Atlantic Club, when the copies of the new number of the Atlantic being brought in, every one rose eagerly to get a copy, & then each sat down & *read his own article.*

In the Board of Overseers of the College, the committee on honorary degrees reported unfavorably on all but the commanding names, and instantly the President Hill, & an Ex-President pressed the action of the Corporation, acknowledging that these men proposed for honors were not very able or distinguished persons, but it was the custom to give these degrees without insisting on eminent merit. I remember that Dr Follen, in his disgust at the Reverend & Honorable Doctors he saw in America, wished to drop the title & be called *Mister.*

* * *

There are inner chambers of poetry, which only poets enter. Thus loosely we might say, Shakspeare's sonnets are readable only by poets, and it is a test of poetic apprehension—the value which a reader attaches to them.

July 13, 1868

Mrs Hunt wished me to admire *George Eliot*'s "Spanish Gypsy", but on superficial trial by hearing passages, I refused. It was manufactured, not natural poetry. Any elegant & cultivated mind can write as well, but she has not insight into nature nor a poetic ear. Such poetry satisfies readers & scholars too at first sight—does not offend—conciliates respect, & it is not easy to show the fault. But let it lie awhile, & nobody will return to it. Indeed time, as I so often feel, is an indispensable element of criticism. You cannot judge of Nahant, or Newport, or of a gallery, or a poem, until you have outlived the dismay or overpowering of a new impression.

I took a volume of Wordsworth in my valise, & read for the first time, I believe, carefully "The White Doe of Rylstone"; a poem on a singularly simple & temperate key, without ornament or sparkle, but tender, wise, & religious, such as only a true poet could write, honoring the poet & the reader.

Aug. 16, 1868

Came home last night from Vermont with Ellen. Stopped at Middlebury on the 11th, Tuesday, & read my discourse on *Greatness, & the good work & influence of heroic scholars*. On Wednesday, spent the day at Essex Junction, & traversed the banks & much of the bed of the Winooski River, much admiring the falls, & the noble mountain peaks of Mansfield, & Camel's Hump (which there appears to be the highest) & the view of the Adirondacs across the Lake. In the evening, took the stage to Underhill Centre. And, the next morning, in unpromising weather, strolled away with Ellen towards the Mansfield mountain, 4 miles off; &, the clouds gradually rising & passing from the summit, we decided to proceed toward the top, which we reached (with many rests at the Half-way House, & at broad stones on the path) a little before 2 o'clock, & found George Bradford at the Mountain House. We were cold & a little wet, but found the house warm with stoves. After dinner, Ellen was thoroughly warmed & recruited lying on a settee by the stove, & meanwhile I went up with Mr Bradford & a party to the top of "the Chin," which is the highest land in the State—4400 feet. I have, later, heard it stated 4389 ft. Lake Champlain lay below us, but was a perpetual illusion, as it would appear a piece of yellow sky, until careful examination of the islands in it, & the Adirondac summits beyond brought it to the earth for a moment; but, if we looked away an instant, & then returned, it was in the sky again. When we reached the summit, we looked down upon the "Lake of the Clouds," & the party which reached the height a few minutes before us, had a tame cloud which floated by a little below them. This summer, bears & a panther have been seen on the mountain, & we peeped into some rocky caves which might house them. We came, on the way, to the edge of a crag, which we approached carefully, & lying on our bellies; & it was easy to see how dangerous a walk this might be at night, or in a snowstorm. The White Mountains—it was too misty to see; but "Owl's Head," near Lake Memphremagog, was pointed out. Perhaps it was a half mile only from the House to the top of "the Chin," but it was a rough & grand walk. On such occasions, I always return to my fancy that the best use of wealth would be to carry a good professor of Geology, & another of Botany, with you.

In the House were perhaps twenty visiters besides ourselves, a Mr Taylor of Cincinnati—a very intelligent gentleman—with excellent political views, republican & free-trader: George Bartlett was there with a gay company of his friends, who had come up from Stowe, where he had given a theatrical entertainment of amateurs, the night before. In the evening, they amused us mightily with charades of violent fun. The next morning a man went through the house ringing a large bell, & shouting "Sunrise," & every body dressed in haste, & went down to the piazza. Mount Washington & the Franconia mountains were clearly visible, & Ellen & I climbed now the *Nose*, to which the ascent is made easy by means of a stout rope firmly attached near the top, & reaching down to the bottom of the hill, near the House. Twenty people are using it at once at different heights. After many sharp looks at the heavens & the earth, we descended to breakfast. . . .

At 9.30 A.M. Ellen & I, accompanied for some distance by George Bradford, set forth on our descent, in the loveliest of mornings, &, parting from Mr B., at one of the galleries, arrived safely at the "Half-Way House"—there to find a troop of our fellow boarders of the "Underhill House," just mounting their horses to climb the Mountain. They advised us to take a little forest path to the "Mossy Glen," before we continued our journey from this point, which we did, & found a pretty fall. Returning to the Half-Way House, which is empty, & only affords at this time a resting place for travellers, & a barn for horses, we resumed our walk, & arrived (without other event than a little delay among the raspberries) at Mr Prouty's Hotel at Underhill, say at 1.30; dined, repacked our trunk, & took a wagon to Stowe, thence the Stage Coach to

Essex Junction, & thence the train, which brought us to Burlington, where we spent the night; &, the next morning, the Rutland & Burlington train, which brought us safely to Westminster, Massachusetts, where Ellen took a wagon for Princeton, & I continued my railroad ride to Concord, arriving at 6.30 P.M.

Summer–Fall 1868

The only place where I feel the joy of eminent domain is in my wood lot. My spirits rise whenever I enter it. I can spend the entire day there with hatchet or pruning-shears making paths, without a remorse of wasting time. I fancy the birds know me, & even the trees make little speeches or hint them. Then Allah does not count the time which the Arab spends in the chase.

Library. In the perplexity in which the literary public now stands with regard to University education, whether studies shall be compulsory or elective; whether by lectures of professors, or whether by private tutors; whether the stress shall be on Latin & Greek, or on modern Sciences—the one safe investment which all can agree to increase is the Library. A good book can wait for a reader hundreds of years. Once lodged in the Library, it is unexpensive & harmless while it waits. Then it is a good of the most generous kind, not only serving the undergraduates of the college, but much more the Alumni, & probably much more still, the scattered community of scholars.

A man never gets acquainted with himself, but is always a surprise. We get news daily of the world within, as well as of the world out side, & not less of the central than of the surface facts. A new thought is awaiting him every morning.

Dec. 9, 1868

In poetry, tone. I have been reading some of Lowell's new poems, in which he shows unexpected advance on himself, but perhaps most in technical skill & courage. It is in talent rather than in poetic tone, & rather expresses his wish, his ambition, than the uncontrollable interior impulse which is the authentic mark of a new poem, & which is unanalysable, & makes the merit of an ode of Collins, or Gray, or Wordsworth, or Herbert, or Byron—& which is felt in the pervading tone, rather than in brilliant parts or lines; as if the sound of a bell, or a certain cadence expressed in a low whistle or booming, or humming, to which the poet first timed his step, as he looked at the sunset, or thought, was the incipient form of the piece, & was regnant through the whole.

*   *   *

Wordsworth is manly, the manliest poet of his age. His poems record the thoughts & emotions which have occupied his mind, & which he reports because of their reality. He has great skill in rendering them into simple & sometimes happiest poetic speech. Tennyson has incomparable felicity in all poetic forms, & is a brave thoughtful Englishman, exceeds Wordsworth a hundredfold in rhythmic power & variety, but far less manly compass; and Tennyson's main purpose is the rendering, whilst Wordsworth's is just value of the dignity of the thought.

Winter 1868–69

An Englishman has firm manners. He rests secure on the reputation of his country, on his family, his education, & his expectations at home. There is in his manners a suspicion of insolence. If his belief in the Thirty nine Articles does not bind him much, his belief in the fortieth does—namely, that he shall not find his superiors elsewhere. Hence a complaint you shall often find made against him here, that, whilst at his house he would resent as unpermissible that a guest should come to a seven o'clock dinner in undress, he bursts into yours in a shooting-jacket. Well, it is for the company to put him in the wrong by their perfect politeness.

When I find in people narrow religion, I find also narrow reading.

In the matter of Religion, men eagerly fasten their eyes on the differences between their own creed & yours; whilst the charm of the study is in finding the agreements & identities in all the religions of men.

Of immortality, I should say, that it is at least equally & perhaps better seen in little than in large angles: I mean, that, in a calm & clear state of mind, we have no fears, no prayers, even, that we feel all is well; we have arrived at an enjoyment so pure, as to imply & affirm its perfect accord with the Nature of things, so that it alone appears durable, & all mixed or inferior states accidental & temporary.

March 29, 1869

Alcott came, & talked Plato & Socrates, extolling them with gravity. I bore it long, & then said, that was a song for others, not for him. He should find what was the equivalent for these masters in our times: for surely the world was always equal to itself, & it was for him to detect what was the counter-weight & compensation to us. Was it natural science? Was it the immense dilution of the same amount of thought into nations?

I told him to shut his eyes, & let his thoughts run into reverie or whithersoever—& then take an observation. He would find that the current went outward from man, not to man. Consciousness was up stream.

July–Aug. 1869

I am interested not only in my advantages, but in my disadvantages, that is, in my fortunes proper; that is, in watching my fate, to notice, after each act of mine, what result? is it prosperous? is it adverse? & thus I find a pure entertainment of the intellect, alike in what is called good or bad.

Sept.–Oct. 1869

I recall today Col. Shattuck's remark to me after Dr Jackson's (?) lecture on the central heat of the globe—he said "it must be sloppy there."

Oct. 19–20, 1869

I read a good deal of experimental poetry in the new books. The author has said to himself, '*Who knows but this may please, & become famous? Did not Goethe experiment? Does not this read like the ancients?*' But good poetry was not written thus, but it delighted the poet first; he said & wrote it for joy, & it pleases the reader for the same reason.

Oct. 21, 1869

I wish I could recall my singular dream of last night with its physics, metaphysics, & rapid transformations—all impressive at the moment, that on waking at midnight I tried to rehearse them, that I might keep them till morn. I fear 'tis all vanished. . . . I passed into a room where were ladies & gentlemen, some of whom I knew. I did not wish to be recognised because of some disagreeable task, I cannot remember what. One of the ladies was beautiful, and I, it seemed, had already seen her, & was her lover. She looked up from her painting, & saw, but did not recognize me—which I thought wrong—unpardonable. Later, I reflected that it was not so criminal in her, since I had never *proposed*. Presently the scene changed, & I saw a common street-boy, without any personal advantages, walking with an air of determination, and I perceived that beauty of features signified nothing—only this clearness & strength of purpose made any form respectable & attractive. 'Tis all vain—I cannot restore the dream.

Oct. 22, 1869

This morning at 5 h. 25 m. I perceived that the house was shaken by an earthquake. I think the motion was prolonged for a minute. I got out of bed, lit a match, & looked at the clock. I heard no other noise than the wave-like shaking of the house would make. At breakfast, I found that Mrs Small had also observed it, & thought it an earthquake.

Oct.–Nov. 1869

General Wayne was the Commissioner of the Government who first saw the importance of the nook of land at the foot of Lake Michigan round which the road to the Northwest must run, & managed to run the boundary line of Illinois in such manner as to include this swamp, called Chicago, within it.

Tides in men & children. A wave of sanity & perception comes in, & they are on a level instantly with adults—perfectly reasonable & right; out goes the wave, & they are silly intolerable miscreants. 'Tis all the difference between the bright water with the ships & the sun thereon, & the empty bay with its mud.

Good Writing. All writing should be selection in order to drop every dead word. Why do you not save out of your speech or thinking only the vital things—the spirited *mot* which amused or warmed you when you spoke it—because of its luck & newness. I have just been reading, in this careful book of a most intelligent & learned man, any number of flat conventional words & sentences. If a man would learn to read his own manuscript severely—becoming really a third person, & search only for what interested him, he would blot to purpose—& how every page would gain! Then all the words will be sprightly, & every sentence a surprise.

Dr Hedge tells us, that the Indian asked John Eliot, "why God did not kill the devil?" One would like to know what was Eliot's answer.

In the heavy storm I heard the cathedral bells squeaking like pigs through the snout.

Dec.? 1869

Calvinism. There is a certain weakness in solemnly threatening the human being with the revelations of the Judgment Day, as Mrs Stowe winds up her appeal to the executors of Lady Byron. An honest man would say, why refer it? All that is true & weighty with me has all its force now.

*   *   *

We meet people who seem to overlook & read us with a smile, but they do not tell us what they read.

I find myself always harping on a few strings which sound tedious to others, but, like some old tunes to common people, have an inexhaustible charm to me. We are easily tired of a popular modish tune, but never of the voice of the wind in the woods.

A member of the Senior Class in College asked me on Saturday, "whether, when I was in Europe, I had met with Spinosa?" I told him that I did not; that Spinoza must now be pretty old, since he was born in 1632.

Whipple made us laugh with his story of the worthy man who, when Shakspeare was named, said, "Pooh! Nobody would ever have thought anything of that fellow if he hadn't written those twenty three plays."

I asked Theodore Lyman on Saturday how it was exactly with Agassiz's health. He said, "that no further paralysis had appeared, & that he seemed not threatened. It was not apoplexy but a peculiarity of his constitution, these turns of insensibility which had occurred. It was *hysteria.*" I replied, that I had often said that Agassiz appeared to have two or three men rolled up into his personality, but I had never suspected there was any woman also in his make. Lyman insisted that he had himself seen hysteria oftener in men than in women.

Feb. 1870

Mr Charles Ware tells Edward, that the night before the Cambridge Commemoration Day, he spent the night at Mr Hudson's room, in Cambridge, & woke from a dream which he could not remember, repeating these words—

And what they dare to dream of, dare to die for.

He went to the Pavilion Dinner, & there heard Mr Lowell read his Poem, and when he came to the lines

"Those love her best who to themselves are true
And what— —"

Ware said, now I know what's coming—but it won't rhyme, & Mr Lowell proceeded—

"And what they dare to dream of, dare to do."

Feb. 24, 1870

A prudent author should never reprint his occasional pieces, which, of course, must usually be based on such momentary events & feelings as certainly to conflict with his cooler habitual mundane judgments.

The dead live in our dreams.

Feb.-March 1870

How dangerous is criticism. My brilliant friend cannot see any healthy power in Thoreau's thoughts. At first I suspect of course that he oversees me who admire Thoreau's power. But when I meet again fine perceptions in Thoreau's papers, I see that there is defect in his critic that he should under-value them. Thoreau writes, in his *Field Notes,* "I look back for the era of this creation not into the night, but to a dawn for which no man ever rose early enough"—a fine example of his affirmative genius.

March 15, 1870

My new book sells faster, it appears, than either of its foregoers. This is not for its merit, but only shows that old age is a good advertisement. Your name has been seen so often that your book must be worth buying.

March 16, 1870

After the Social Circle had broken up, last night, & only two remained with me, one said that a cigar had uses. If you found yourself in a hotel with writing to do—fire just kindled in a cold room—it was hard to begin; but light a cigar, & you were presently comfortable, & in condition to work. Mr Simon Brown then said, that he had never smoked, but as an editor (of the New England Farmer) he had much writing, & he often found himself taking up a little stick & whittling away on it, and, in a short time, brought into tune & temper by that Yankee method.

March 1870

Dream. The waking from an impressive dream is a curious example of the jealousy of the gods. There is an air as if the sender of the illusion had been heedless for a moment that the Reason had returned to its seat, & was startled into attention. Instantly, there is a rush from some quarter to break up the drama into a chaos of parts, then of particles, then of ether, like smoke dissolving in a wind: it cannot be disintegrated fast enough or fine enough. If you could give the waked watchman the smallest fragment, he could reconstruct the whole; for the moment he is sure he can & will; but his attention is so divided on the disappearing parts, that he cannot grasp the least atomy, & the last fragment or film disappears before he could say, I have it.

Steffens relates that he went into Schelling's lecture-room at (Jena?). Schelling said, "Gentlemen, think of the wall." All the class at once took attitudes of thought; some stiffened themselves up; some shut their eyes; all concentrated themselves. After a time, he said, "Gentlemen, think of that which thought the wall." Then there was trouble in all the camp.

April–June 1870
Henry Thoreau was well aware of his stubborn contradictory attitude into which almost any conversation threw him, & said in the woods, "When I die, you will find swamp oak written on my heart." I got his words from Ellery Channing today.

Churches are good for nothing except when they are poor. When the New Jerusalem Church was new in Boston they wrote an admirable magazine. Since they have grown rich, not a thought has come from them. Churches are best in their beginnings.

I wish we might adopt in Massachusetts, & in America, the rule of Sparta to *disfranchise a Citizen* who should be convicted of habitual drunkenness or other gross immorality. As, for instance, failing to educate his children.

July 14, 1870
Here at Nantasket Beach, with Ellen, I wonder that so few men do penetrate what seems the secret of the inn-keeper. He runs along the coast, & perceives that by buying a few acres well-chosen of sea-shore, which cost no more or not so much as good land elsewhere, & building a good house, he shifts upon nature the whole duty of filling it with guests, the sun, the moon, the stars, the rainbow, the sea, the islands, the whole horizon—not elsewhere seen—ships of all nations. All of these (& all unpaid) take on themselves the whole charge of entertaining his guests, & filling & delighting their senses with shows; and it were long to tell in detail the attractions which these furnish. Every thing here is picturesque—the long beach is every day renewed with pleasing & magical shows, with variety of color, with the varied music of the rising & falling water, with the multitudes of fishes & the birds & men that prey on them; with the strange forms of the radiates sprawling on the beach;

with shells; with the beautiful variety of sea-rolled pebbles—quartz, porphyry, sienite, mica, & limestone. The man buys a few acres, but he has all the good & all the glory of a hundred square miles, by the cunning choice of the place; for the storm is one of the grand entertainers of his company; so is the sun, & the moon, & all the stars of heaven, since they who see them here, in all their beauty, & in the grand arca or amphitheatre which they need for their right exhibition, feel that they have never rightly seen them before. The men and women who come to the house, & swarm or scatter in groups along the spacious beach, or in yachts, or boats, or in carriages, or as bathers, never appeared before so gracious & inoffensive. In these wide stretches, the largest company do not jostle one another. Then to help him, even the poor Indians from Maine & Canada creep on to the outskirts of the hotel to pitch their tents, & make baskets & bows & arrows to add a picturesque feature. Multitudes of children decorate the piazza, & the grounds in front, with their babble & games; and in this broad area every individual from least to largest is inoffensive & an entertaining variety. To make the day complete, I saw from the deck of our boat this morning, coming out of the bay the English steamer which lately made the perilous jump on Minot's Ledge, & this afternoon saw the turret monitor, *Miantonomok*, sailing into Boston.

The parlors, chambers, & the table of the Rockland House were all good, but the supreme relish of these conveniences was this superb panorama which the wise choice of the place, on which the house was built, afforded. This selection of the site gives this house the like advantage over other houses that an astronomical observatory has over other towers—namely, that this particular tower leads you to the heavens, & searches depths of space before inconceivable.

July 21, 1870

I am filling my house with books which I am bound to read, & wondering whether the new heavens which await the soul (after the fatal hour) will allow the consultation of these?

July–Aug. 1870

I honor the author of the "Battle Hymn," and of "The Flag." She was born in the city of New-York. I could well wish she were a native of Massachusetts. We have had no such poetess in New England.

Sept. 1870

Very much afflicted in these days with stupor—acute attacks whenever a visit is proposed or made.

Oct. 2, 1870

La portée, the range of a thought, of a fact observed, & thence of the word by which we denote it, makes its value. Only whilst it has new values, does it warm & invite & enable to write. And this range or ulterior out-look appears to be rare in men—a slight primitive difference, but essential to the work. For this possesser has the necessity to write—'tis easy & delightful to him—the other, finding no continuity, must begin again up-hill at every step. Now Plutarch is not a deep man, & might well not be personally impressive to his contemporaries; but, having this facile association in his thought—a wide horizon to every fact or maxim or character which engaged him—every new topic re-animated all his experience or memory, & he was impelled with joy to begin a new chapter. . . . The writer is an explorer. Every step is an advance into new land.

Oct. 6, 1870

Last night heard Mrs Dallas Glyn read or act Antony & Cleopatra. A woman of great personal advantages & talent— great variety of style, & perfect self possession: in dialogue between Antony & Cleopatra, the manly voice & the woman adequately rendered: and the dialogue between the queen & the boy with the asp was perfect. The great passages in which I have always delighted were not duely felt by her, & had therefore no eminence: Some of them quite omitted. She ought to go on to the stage, where the interruption by the other actors would give her the proper relief, & enhance her own part. Her cries & violence were all right—never vulgar. Her audience was not worthy of her reading, impertinently read newspapers & had a trick of going out. I am afraid they would have done the like to Siddons herself, until they had been told it was Siddons, & so had been afraid of being found out.

Today at the laying of the cornerstone of the "Memorial Hall," at Cambridge. All was well & wisely done. The storm ceased for us, the company was large—the best men & the best women all there, or all but a few; the arrangements simple & excellent, and every speaker successful. . . . Every part in all these performances was in such true feeling, that people praised them with broken voices, & we all proudly wept. Our Harvard soldiers of the war were in their uniforms, & heard their own praises, & the tender allusions to their dead comrades.

Oct.–Nov. 1870

I, as every one, keep many stories of which the etiquette of contemporariness forbids the airing, & which burn uncomfortably being untold. I positively resolve not to kill A. nor C. nor N.—but I could a tale unfold like Hamlet's father. Now a private class gives just this liberty which in book or public lecture were unparliamentary, & of course because here at least one is safe from the unamiable presence of reporters.

How right is Couture's rule of looking three times at the object, for one at your drawing—of looking at nature, & not at your whim. & Wm. Hunt's emphasis, after him, on the mass, instead of the details! & how perfectly (as I wrote upon Couture long ago) the same rule applies in rhetoric or writing! Wendell Holmes hits right in every affectionate poem he scribbles, by his instinct at obeying a just perception of what *is* important, instead of feeling about how he shall write some verses touching the subject; and eminently this is true in Rockwood Hoar's mind—his tendency to the integrity of the thing!

The progress of religion is steadily to its identity with morals. The ancient & the modern religions were immoral—full of selfishness. God belonged only to the *gentes*, & in no wise to the *plebs*. These were out of relation to the altar, *the foyer*, & therefore had no marriage, no rights, might be killed with impunity. It was so in India, Athens, & Rome; and the "heathen", in the middle ages, had no more rights than the brute. The Catholic & the English Episcopal Church & the Calvinistic Church are still deeply tainted with this barbarism. The fathers of New England shared it still.

When there was question about the Marchese & Marchesa d'Ossoli* coming to America (alas that day!), a young lawyer, G. R., remarked, "I suppose that title is about equivalent to *Selectman* here." Well it appears that the *Kings* of Homer & later Greeks did not really possess more authority, they were simply the heads of the families, *gentes*.

We get rid in this republic of a great deal of nonsense which disgusts us in European biography. There a superior mind, a Hegel, sincerely & scientifically exploring the laws of thought, is suddenly called by a necessity of pleasing some King, or conciliating some Catholics, to give a twist to his universal propositions to fit these absurd people, & not satisfying them even by these sacrifices of truth & manhood, another great genius, Schelling, is called in, when Hegel dies, to come to Berlin, & bend truth to the crotchets of the king & rabble. Not so here. The paucity of population, the vast extent of territory, the solitude of each family & each man, allow some approximation to the result that every citi-

---

*Margaret Fuller and her husband.

zen has a religion of his own—is a church by himself—& worships & speculates in a new quite independent fashion.

It really appears that the Latin & Greek continue to be forced in Education just as chignons must be worn, in spite of the disgust against both, for fashion.

Peter Oliver, in the "Puritan Commonwealth," insists like a lawyer on the duty the Pilgrims owed to their Charter, & the presumed spirit & intent in which it was given. He overlooks the irresistible instruction which the actual arrival in the new continent gave. That was a greater King than Charles, & insisted on making the law for those who would live in it. They could not shut their eyes on the terms on which alone they could live in it. The savages, the sands, the snow, the mutineers, & the French were antagonists who must be dealt with on the instant, and there was no clause in the Charter that could deal with these. No lawyer could help them to read the pitiless alternative which Plymouth rock offered them—Self help or ruin. Come up to the real conditions, or die.

Nov.–Dec. 1870

Mr Weeden told me, that his old Aunt said of the people whom she knew in her youth, that, "they had to hold on hard to the huckleberry bushes to hinder themselves from being translated."

I delight ever in having to do with the drastic class, the men who can do things, as Dr. Charles T. Jackson; & Jim Bartlett; & Boynton. Such was Thoreau. Once out of doors, the poets paled like ghosts before them. I met Boynton in Rochester, N.Y. & was cold enough to a popular unscientific lecturer on Geology. But I talked to him of the notice I had read of repulsion of incandescent bodies, & new experiments. "O," he said, "nothing is plainer: I have tried it;" &, on my way to Mr Ward's, he led me into a forge, where a stream of melted iron was running out of a furnace, & he passed his finger through the streamlet again & again, & invited me to do the same. I said, Do you not wet your finger? "No," he said, "the hand sweats a little & that suffices."

Dec. 25? 1870

Samuel Gray Ward said, nothing is so mean as the man that has a million, unless it be the man who has two.

Feb. 10, 1871

I do not know that I should feel threatened or insulted if a chemist should take his protoplasm or mix his hydrogen, oxygen & carbon, &

make an animalcule incontestably swimming & jumping before my eyes. I should only feel that it indicated that the day had arrived when the human race might be trusted with a new degree of power, & its immense responsibility; for these steps are not solitary or local, but only a hint of an advanced frontier supported by an advancing race behind it.

What at first scares the Spiritualist in the experiments of natural Science—as if thought were only finer chyle, fine to aroma—now redounds to the credit of matter, which, it appears, is impregnated with thought & heaven, & is really of God, & not of the Devil, as he had too hastily believed.

April 1871

Golden Gate: named of old from its flowers.
Asia at your doors & S. America.
Inflamed expectation haunting men.

The attraction & superiority of California are in its days. It has better days, & more of them, than any other country.

In Yosemite, Grandeur of these mountains perhaps unmatched on the Globe; for here they strip themselves like Athletes for exhibition, & stand perpendicular granite walls, showing their entire height, & wearing a liberty cap of snow on their head.

May–Sept. 1871

What was the name of the nymph "whom young Apollo courted for her hair"? That fable renews itself every day in the street, & in the drawing-room. Nothing in nature is more ideal than the hair. Analyse it by taking a single hair, & it is characterless & worthless; but in its mass it is recipient of such variety of form, & momentary change from form to form, that it vies in expression with the eye & the countenance. The wind & the sun play with it & inhance it, & its coils & its mass are a perpetual mystery & attraction to the young poet. But the doleful imposture of buying it at the shops is suicidal, & disgusts.

The splendors of this age outshine all other recorded ages. In my lifetime, have been wrought five miracles, namely, 1. the Steamboat; 2. the railroad; 3. the Electric telegraph; 4. the application of the Spectroscope to astronomy; 5. the photograph; five miracles which have altered the relations of nations to each other.

Add cheap Postage; and the Sewing machine; & in agriculture, the Mowing machine & the horse-rake. A corresponding power has been given to manufactures by the machine for pegging shoes, & the power-loom; & the power-press of the printers. And in dentistry & in surgery Dr Jackson's discovery of Anaesthesis. It only needs to add the power which up to this hour eludes all human ingenuity, namely a rudder to the balloon, to give us the dominion of the air, as well as of the sea & the land. But the account is not complete until we add the discovery of Oersted, of the identity of Electricity & Magnetism, & the generalization of that conversion by its application to light, heat, & gravitation. The geologist has found the correspondence of the age of stratified remains to the ascending scale of structure in animal life.

Add now, the daily predictions of the weather for the next 24 hours for North America, by the Observatory at Washington.

'Tis one of the mysteries of our condition, that the poet seems sometimes to have a mere talent—a chamber in his brain into which an angel flies with divine messages, but the man, apart from this privilege, common-place. Wordsworth is an example; (& Channing's poetry is apart from the man.) Those who know & meet him day by day cannot reconcile the verses with their man.

The vice of Wordsworth is that he is a lame poet: he can rarely finish worthily a stanza begun well. He suffers from asthma of the mind.

[*Dec. 20, 1876.* In reading the above lines on Wordsworth, which were probably written five years ago, I must add that in my new 8vo. Edition of his works, I find great improvement of the Sonnets which he must have made in his later days.]

Oct. 18, 1871   Bret Harte's visit

Bret Harte referred to my Essay on Civilization, that the piano comes so quickly into the shanty, &c. & said, "do you know that on the contrary it is vice that brings them in. It is the gamblers who bring in the music to California. It is the prostitute who brings in the New York fashions of dress there, & so throughout." I told him that I spoke from Pilgrim experience, & knew on good grounds the resistless culture that religion effects.

Oct. 1871

Names should be of good omen, of agreeable sound, commending the person in advance, &, if possible, keeping the old belief of the Greeks, "that the name borne by each man & woman has some connection with their part in the drama of life." The name then should look before & after.

Oct.–Nov. 1871

Algernon Coolidge, aged (6 or 7) years, was shown a picture of a Centaur. He looked at it a good while, & then asked, "Aunt Nina, when that Centaur goes to sleep, does he go to a bed, or to a stable?"—which speech I think an unanswerable criticism on Greek art.

How vain to praise our literature, when its really superior minds are quite omitted, & utterly unknown to the public. . . . Thoreau quite unappreciated, though his books have been opened & superficially read.

The father cannot control the child from defect of sympathy. The man with a longer scale of sympathy, the man who feels the boy's sense & piety & imagination, and also his rough play & impatience & revolt, who knows the whole gamut in himself—knows also a way out of the one into the other, & can play on the boy as on a harp, & easily lead him up from the scamp to the angel.

Dec. 1871–March 1872

When a boy I used to go to the wharves, & pick up shells out of the sand which vessels had brought as ballast, & also plenty of stones, gypsum, which, I discovered would be luminous when I rubbed two bits together in a dark closet, to my great wonder—& I do not know why luminous, to this day. That, & the magnetising my penknife, till it would hold a needle; & the fact that blue & gambooge would make green in my pictures of mountains; & the charm of drawing vases by scrawling with ink heavy random lines, & then doubling the paper, so as to make another side symmetrical—what was chaos, becoming symmetrical; then hallooing to an echo at the pond, & getting wonderful replies.

Still earlier, what silent wonder is waked in the boy by blowing bubbles from soap & water with a pipe.

March–April 1872

Parallax, as you know, is the apparent displacement of an object from two points of view—less & less of the heavenly bodies, because of their remoteness—& of the fixed stars, none at all. Well, it is thus that we have found Shakspeare to be a fixed star. Because all sorts of men have in three centuries found him still unapproachable. Our first view is only a guess: We feel that here is somewhat that we had not seen before; our attention is won, & presently riveted, so that we carry away a deeper impression than ordinary. Still it is a wild guess—wide of the mark. But the impression of somewhat superior remains, & works in the memory, so that when we meet the man or his work again, we give the greater heed.

May 26, 1872

Yesterday, my sixty ninth birthday, I found myself on my round of errands in Summer street, &, though close on the spot where I was born, was looking into a street with some bewilderment and read on the sign *Kingston street*, with surprise, finding in the granite blocks no hint of Nathaniel Goddard's pasture & long wooden fence, & so of my nearness to my native corner of Chauncy Place. It occurred to me that few living persons ought to know so much of the families of this fast growing city, for the reason, that Aunt Mary, whose MSS. I had been reading to Hedge & Bartol, on Friday Evening, had such a keen perception of character, & taste for aristocracy, & I heard in my youth & manhood every name she knew. It is now nearly a hundred years since she was born, & the founders of the oldest families that are still notable were known to her as retail-merchants, milliners, tailors, distillers, as well as the ministers, lawyers, & doctors, of the time. She was a realist, & knew a great man or "a whale hearted woman"—as she called one of her pets—from a successful money maker.

Walk in the city for an hour, and you shall see the whole history of female beauty. Here are the school girls in the first profusion of their hair covering them to the waist, & now & then one maiden of 18 or 19 years, in the moment of her perfect beauty. Look quick & sharply—this is her one meridian day. To find the like again, you must meet, on your next visit, one who is a month younger today. Then troops of pleasing well dressed ladies, sufficiently good looking & graceful, but without claims to the prize of the goddess of Discord.

June 12, 1872

We would all be public men if we could afford it. I am wholly private: such is the poverty of my constitution. Heaven "betrayed me to a book, & wrapt me in a gown". I have no social talent, no wealth of nature, nothing but a sullen will, & a steady appetite for insights in any or all directions, to balance my manifold imbecilities.

July 24, 1872

House burned.

Aug. 20, 1872   Norway, Maine

Forgot, in leaving home, twenty necessities—forgot to put Horace, or Martial, or Cicero's Letters, "Le Cité Antique," or Taine's England, in my wallet: forgot even the sacred chocolate Satchel itself, to hold them or their like. Well, at the dear Vale, 11 miles off yet, I may recall or invoke things as good.

Aug. 31, 1872   Naushon

I thought today, in these rare seaside woods, that if absolute leisure
were offered me, I should run to the College or the Scientific school
which offered best lectures on Geology, chemistry, Minerals, Botany, &
seek to make the alphabets of those sciences clear to me. How could leisure or labor be better employed. 'Tis never late to learn them, and
every secret opened goes to authorize our aesthetics. Cato learned Greek
at eighty years, but these are older bibles & oracles than Greek.

Dec. 30, 1872   Shepard's Hotel, Cairo Egypt

Nothing has struck me more in the streets here than the erect carriage & walking of the Copts (I suppose them), better & nobler in figure
& movement than any passengers in our cities at home. . . .

Egypt very poor in trees: We have seen hardly an orange tree. Palms
are the chief tree along the banks of the river, from Cairo to Assuan.
Acacias, the fig.

In Cairo, we had a banian with its boughs planting themselves
around it under my window, at Shepard's Hotel.

Egypt is the Nile & its shores. The cultivated land is a mere green
ribbon on either shore of the river. You can see, as you sail, its quick
boundary in rocky mountains or desert sands. Day after day & week
after week of unbroken sunshine & though you may see clouds in the
sky, they are merely for ornament, & never rain.

Jan.–Feb. 1873

All this journey is a perpetual humiliation, satirizing & whipping
our ignorance. The people despise us because we are helpless babies
who cannot speak or understand a word they say; the Sphinxes scorn
dunces; the obelisks, the temple-walls defy us with their histories which
we cannot spell. Every new object only makes new questions which
each traveller asks of the other, & none of us can answer, & each sinks
lower in the opinion of his companion. The people whether in the boat,
or out of it, are a perpetual study for the excellence & grace of their
forms & motion. No people walk so well, so upright as they are, &
strong & flexible; and for studying the nude, our artists should come
here & not to Paris. Every group of the country people on the shores as
seen from our dearbeah, look like the ancient philosophers going to the
School of Athens. The women too are as straight as arrows from their
habit of carrying every thing on their heads. In swimming, the Arabs
show great strength & speed, all using what at Cambridge we used to
call the "southern stroke," alternating the right arm & the left.

All the boys & all the babes have flies roosting about their eyes,
which they do not disturb, nor seem to know their presence. 'Tis said

that the ophthalmia, which is so common here, is thus conveyed from
one to another. 'Tis said that it is rare to find sound eyes among them.
Blind beggars appear at every landing led about by their children.

From the time of our arrival at Cairo to our return thither, six weeks,
we have had no rain—unclouded summer on the Nile to Assuan & back,
& have required the awning to be spread over us on the deck from 10
A.M. till late in the afternoon.

March–April 1873

The enjoyment of travel is in the arrival at a new city, as Paris, or
Florence, or Rome—the feeling of free adventure, you have no duties—
nobody knows you, nobody has claims, you are like a boy on his first
visit to the Common on Election Day. Old Civilization offers to you
alone this huge city, all its wonders, architecture, gardens, ornaments,
Galleries, which had never cost you so much as a thought. For the first
time for many years you wake master of the bright day, in a bright
world without a claim on you—only leave to enjoy. This dropping for
the first time the doleful bundle of Duty creates, day after day, a health
as of new youth. Then the cities know the value of travellers as purchas-
ers in their factories & shops, & receive them gladly.

In Paris, your mere passport admits you to the vast & costly public
galleries on days on which the natives of the city can not pass the doors.
Household cares you have none: You take your dinner, lunch, or supper
where & when you will: cheap cabs wait for you at every corner—
guides at every door, magazines of sumptuous goods & attractive fair-
ings, unknown hitherto, solicit your eyes. Your health mends every day.
Every word spoken to you is a wonderful & agreeable riddle which it is
a pleasure to solve—a pleasure & a pride. Every experience of the day is
important, & furnishes conversation to you who were so silent at home.

July? 1873

Egypt. Mrs Helen Bell, it seems, was asked "What do you think the
Sphinx said to Mr Emerson?" "Why," replied Mrs Bell, "the Sphinx
probably said to him, 'You're another.'"

For the writers on Religion—none should speak on this matter po-
lemically: it is the *Gai Science* & only to be chanted by troubadours.

Be a little careful about your Library. Do you foresee what you will
do with it? Very little to be sure. But the real question is, What it will do
with you? You will come here & get books that will open your eyes, &
your ears, & your curiosity, & turn you inside out or outside in.

Nov. 1874?

The secret of poetry is never explained—is always new. We have not got farther than mere wonder at the delicacy of the touch, & the eternity it inherits. In every house a child that in mere play utters oracles, & knows not that they are such, 'Tis as easy as breath. 'Tis like this gravity, which holds the Universe together, & none knows what it is.

Date uncertain (probably from the 1870s)

But of one thing I am well aware, that it is comparatively of little importance that I praise books to you. You will not read them the more that I should, nor the less if I held my peace. A better orator than I pleads for them with some of you, & to some of you a stronger dissuasion than I or any man could attempt, debars you from their use. I mean that some men are born to read, & must & will read at whatever cost, & others are born to work & executive skills, that take tyrannical possession of the man, & so absorb him that he has no ears or eyes for those pursuits which constitute the chief happiness of other souls. Books only put him to sleep. I surrender such willingly to the Fates—I hope, in each case, noble ones—that wait for them at the door.

But of one thing I am well aware,[87] that it is comparatively of little importance that I praise books to you. You will not read them the more that I should, nor the less if I held my peace. A better orator than I pleads for them with some of you, & to some of you a stronger dissuasion than I or any man could attempt, debars you from their use. I mean that some men are born to read, & must & will read at whatever cost, & others are born to work & executive skills, that take tyrannical possession of the man, & so absorb

[68] him that he has no ears or eyes for those pursuits which constitute the chief happiness of other souls. Books only put him to sleep. I surrender such willingly to the Fates,— I hope in each case, noble ones,— that wait for them at the door.

— English judges in the old time used to recommend prisoners to mercy, because they could read and write. Franks translation of Poetry. FOR 220

Acknowledgments

MY PRIMARY DEBT is to those scholars who have labored long and hard to complete the publication of Emerson's *Journals and Miscellaneous Notebooks:* William H. Gilman, Alfred R. Ferguson, George P. Clark, Merrell R. Davis, Merton M. Sealts, Jr., Harrison Hayford, Ralph H. Orth, J. E. Parsons, A. W. Plumstead, Linda Allardt, Susan Sutton Smith, Ruth H. Bennett, David W. Hill, Glen M. Johnson, and Ronald A. Bosco. I am grateful to William H. Bond, the Houghton Library, and the Ralph Waldo Emerson Memorial Association for many courtesies; to Edith W. Gregg, Constance Fuller Threinen, Anne McGrath, and Joseph Slater for helping with the illustrations; to Victoria Macy for her careful work in preparing copy for the press; and to Paula Spencer for making the index. Joyce Backman, my editor at the Harvard University Press, has collaborated at every step of the way, providing not only meticulous attention to detail but her own considerable literary sensitivity. I hope she will forgive me for not including more of her favorite passages. Finally, I must thank Helene and Susanna for patiently submitting to my endless litany, "as Emerson says . . ." (though they managed to counter quite well with their own cherished lines from Sigmund Freud and Garfield the Cat). Now, perhaps, we can return to our own thoughts. As Emerson says, "I hate quotation. Tell me what you know."

Sources of Illustrations

Essex Institute, Salem, Mass.: 487. Houghton Library, Harvard University: 4, 7, 8, 23, 42, 278, 505, 571. *Journals of Ralph Waldo Emerson,* ed. Edward Waldo Emerson and Waldo Emerson Forbes (Boston: Houghton Mifflin Co., 1909–1914): 64, 131, 174, 272, 468, 549. Ralph Waldo Emerson Memorial Association: 146, 193, 343, 392, 518. Thoreau Lyceum, Concord, Mass.: 208. Constance Fuller Threinen: 247. *Works of Ralph Waldo Emerson* (Boston: Houghton Mifflin Co., 1883): 228.

Index

Numbers in italics refer to the editor's introductions.

577